James Gregory was educated at the Universities of Oxford, Cambridge and Southampton. A Fellow of the Royal Historical Society, he has taught at the Universities of Southampton and Durham, and is a Lecturer in Modern British History at the University of Bradford. His first book, *Of Victorians and Vegetarians: The Vegetarian Movement in Nineteenth-century Britain*, was published in 2007. He has also published essays on 'eccentricity' in British culture *c*.1760–1901.

LIBRARY OF VICTORIAN STUDIES

Series ISBN 978 1 84885 247 1

See www.ibtauris.com/LVS for a full list of titles

1. *Aristocracy, Temperance and Social Reform:*
   The Life of Lady Henry Somerset

   Olwen Claire Niessen

   978 1 84511 484 8

2. *Sir Robert Peel: The Life and Legacy*

   Richard A. Gaunt

   978 1 84885 035 4

3. *Reformers, Patrons and Philanthropists:*
   The Cowper-Temples and High Politics
   in Victorian England

   James Gregory

   978 1 84885 111 5

REFORMERS, PATRONS AND PHILANTHROPISTS

The Cowper-Temples and
High Politics in Victorian Britain

JAMES GREGORY

TAURIS ACADEMIC STUDIES
an imprint of
I.B.Tauris Publishers
LONDON • NEW YORK

Published in 2010 by Tauris Academic Studies,
an imprint of I.B.Tauris & Co Ltd
6 Salem Road, London W2 4BU
175 Fifth Avenue, New York NY 10010
www.ibtauris.com

Distributed in the United States and Canada exclusively by Palgrave Macmillan
175 Fifth Avenue, New York, NY 10010

Library of Victorian Studies 3

ISBN: 978 1 84885 111 5

A full CIP record for this book is available from the British Library
A full CIP record for this book is available from the Library of Congress

Library of Congress catalog: available

Printed and bound in India by Thomson Press (India) Limited
Camera-ready copy edited and supplied by the author

Für Jens und Margaret

CONTENTS

LIST OF ILLUSTRATIONS

ABBREVIATIONS

British Library	BL
Broadlands Records, Broadlands Archive, University of Southampton Special Collections	BR
Houghton Papers, Wren Library, Trinity College, Cambridge	Houghton Papers
F.W.H. Myers Papers, Wren Library, Trinity College, Cambridge	Myers Papers
National Library of Scotland	NLS
Lady Mount Temple, *Mount Temple Memorials* (London: privately printed, 1890), version in the British Library, 010825.ff.7	*MTM*
Oxford Dictionary of National Biography	*ODNB*
Hansard's Parliamentary Debates. Third Series.	*PD*

ACKNOWLEDGEMENTS

This is the result of that stumbling upon a subject that is one of the joys of academia. My first book examined Victorian vegetarians and I have an ongoing interest in 'eccentricity' in modern British culture. Both topics find their conjuncture in the Cowper-Temples' espousal of vegetarianism and various eccentric causes and individuals.

Over the years I have benefited from research by many scholars. These include Michael J. D. Roberts, whose work on the Cowper-Temple circle was brought to my attention several years into my research: we have been in amicable and fruitful contact, our studies being, I believe, complementary. I am grateful to him for giving me access to essays on such aspects as the Medical Act, the Broadlands conferences, and Lord Palmerston's deathbed, before they were published. He also, very kindly, gave me transcriptions of notes from a number of archives that it improved impossible for me to visit. For assistance in other ways, I thank Barbara Amell, Barbara Burbridge, Jane Cowan, Tom Gillmor, Philip Hoare, Allan Macpherson-Fletcher, Alan Pert, D.C. Rose, William Serjeant, Miles Taylor and Ian Theaker.

It is a pleasure to record other debts. My fellow historians at Bradford supported my research through research grants and a lighter teaching load as I prepared the manuscript. I thank Chris Woolgar, Karen Robson and other staff at the University of Southampton Special Collections who made study there a delight. I am indebted to staff at the Royal Archives, National Library of Scotland, British Library, Hertfordshire Archives and Local Studies, Norfolk Records Office, Lilly Library (University of Indiana), B.L. Fisher Library (Asbury Seminary), Romsey Heritage and Visitor Centre, and Pat Lee at the Church Army Archives, for their assistance with my inquiries or for providing me with material. The Librarian of the Hartley Library,

University of Southampton, kindly gave permission for the use of the engraved portrait of Lord Mount Temple appearing in the *Illustrated London News*. The Duke of Devonshire's archivist at Chatsworth, Mr Andrew Peppitt, was most helpful.

I am grateful to the Trustees of the Broadlands Archives for granting me permission to quote from material and reproduce images from the archive. The quotations from material in the Royal Archives at Windsor Castle appear by gracious permission of Her Majesty the Queen. I thank Lord Tollemache of Helmingham Hall for a copy of Thorburn's miniature of Georgina Cowper and for his permission to reproduce it and quote from a letter in his family papers. I am grateful to the following copyright holders for permission to quote or cite material: Merlin Holland, for letters by Constance Wilde and her son Cyril Holland; the Duke of Devonshire, for material relating to the sixth Duke of Devonshire at Chatsworth; Lord Ashburton, for material in the Asburton Papers in the National Library of Scotland; Dr Hugh Cecil, for material in Lady Palmerston's diary at Hatfield; Mr C.A. Gladstone, for material in the Gladstone Papers in the British Library; Lord Cobbold and Henry Lytton Cobbold for material in the Bulwer Lytton Papers at Hertfordshire Archives and Local Studies; Larry J. Schaaf, for permission to quote from the *Correspondence of William Henry Fox Talbot* Project (the Fox Talbot Papers are now in the British Library); and Camphill Village Trust for Hannah Whitall Smith material previously in the possession of Barbara Strachey Halpern.

I thank the following for permission to cite or quote from material in their collections: the British Library, the Trustees of the National Library of Scotland, the Women's Library at London Metropolitan University, University College London, Lambeth Palace Library, Trinity College Cambridge, Durham University Library, the Manuscripts and Special Collections at the University of Nottingham, the Lilly Library at Indiana University, B.L. Fisher Library (Asbury Seminary), Beinecke Rare Book and Manuscript Library (Yale University), Norfolk Records Office, and the Royal College of Surgeons of Edinburgh.

I thank Rasna Dhillon and Jenna Steventon at I.B.Tauris for their support and encouragement. Jackie Latham's reading of a very rough first draft raised crucial questions and spared me numberless slips; the helpful advice of Kathryn Gleadle and David Brown stimulated me to pursue a number of significant areas that I had neglected, and in general to clarify the argument. Audrey Daly's meticulous proofreading and copyediting have again saved me from the blemishes that would otherwise have marred the final version. The errors that remain, are, of course, my own. Without the support of my family this book would not have been possible.

James Gregory

INTRODUCTION

This is the first full-length study of two prominent Victorians, William Francis Cowper-Temple and his second wife Georgina.* If one could choose an alternative title for this book it would be 'Two Blesseds' (a description applied to them in their lifetime), to convey their privileged circumstances – blessed with intelligence, good looks, powerful family connections and talented associates and the gift of amiability – and the aura of sanctity which pervaded their lives. Perhaps also, they were *too* blessed, for their devotion to religious inquiry led them into strange company.

William Cowper was the second son of the fifth Earl Cowper and stepson of Lord Palmerston. He became 'Cowper-Temple' when he inherited the Broadlands estate at Hampshire under the terms of his stepfather's will after his mother's death in 1869. In 1880 he was made Baron Mount Temple. Both Evelyn Ashley, his nephew and heir, and Georgina's nephew Lionel Tollemache thought William's posthumous fame lay in his amendment to the important Education Act of 1870, whereby 'no catechism, or religious formulary, which is distinctive of any particular denomination' was to be taught in Board schools.[1] But he and his wife merit detailed study on numerous grounds. They were prominent in religious revivalism from the mid-1870s, and in temperance, animal protection and spiritualism. Their friends included such eminences as John Ruskin, Lord Shaftesbury, Octavia Hill, Frances Power Cobbe and Josephine Butler, and they were treated as members of a leading group of

---

* In general, I refer to them by their first names, as it seems the easiest way to prevent the confusion of chronologically appropriate nomenclature. Georgina's first name was sometimes spelt at the time as 'Georgiana' and some later writers employ this version, but I follow the spelling she used and which appears on her gravestone.

reformers.[2] As a newspaper reported at William's death in 1888, the Cowper-Temples 'made Broadlands the centre of a social movement the influences of which will hardly be estimated in our day'.[3]

The Cowper-Temples have attracted only partial study. There are the memoirs Georgina wrote for private circulation, which drew on William's journals and manuscript notes. She presented William as a scion of the Whig aristocracy who in his youth was divided between the claims of Society and an Evangelical religion; her *Memorials* charted his political career, recorded their partnership in religious investigation and chronicled the trials and tragedies of their family circle. Georgina emphasised her life-long spiritual doubt and hunger but revealed little about her infancy and upbringing.[4] As she had noted in 1850, 'a journal is sure to omit the most interesting parts of one's life,' and the memoirs were reticent about a number of important episodes in their lives.[5]

Apart from this, there are biographical sketches of the couple or William by relations or friends such as Georgina's brother William Augustus Tollemache, her nephew Lionel, the American Quaker Hannah Whitall Smith, and George Russell, the Liberal politician and writer. William figures in Justin McCarthy's *Portraits of the Sixties*.[6] Contemporary and early twentieth-century collective biographies and encyclopedias testified to William's importance.[7] More recently, there was an essay on William by Penelope Wellington, and entries on the Cowper-Temples in the *Oxford Dictionary of National Biography*.[8] But the comment by Brian Harrison, a leading scholar of Victorian philanthropy and moral reform, that there was 'no adequate biography' of William, remained valid.[9] For a man described by Frances Power Cobbe as one of the most eminent philanthropists of his generation, alongside Shaftesbury and Cardinal Manning, his philanthropic career is neglected.[10]

This is not to claim that he is ignored by historiography. William's place in the 'paternalism' of early Victorian England was recognized by David Roberts, who noted that this social ideal concerning the duties of the wealthy and powerful involved in his case support for central administration.[11] Jonathan Parry named him among the 'whig-liberals' but noting his 'liberal evangelical' status, classed him with other ministers who contributed to an image of the Liberals in their years of dominance as social administrators responsive to administrative, educational and financial problems, to be contrasted in the political struggle with an incompetent or irresponsible Conservative landed rump.[12] Boyd Hilton's history of late-eighteenth and early-nineteenth century Britain classifies him as a social interventionist Whig who was, unusually, Evangelical, a combination made possible by his pre-millenarian belief in perpetual special providence allowing paternalistic interventionism (this earns him the sole company of Viscount Ebrington in Hilton's 'taxonomy of politics 1830–1846').[13] He appears as a Broad Church Whig in Michael J. D. Roberts' *Making English Morals*.[14]

The Cowper-Temples 'belonged to a society of pious people who, while living useful lives, were largely occupied in mystical contemplation'.[15] Their mystical, spiritualist and utopian connections have had some scholarly attention. Van Akin Burd's meticulous research on their spiritualism has, until recently, provided the most extended examination of their friendship with Ruskin, a friendship which was a well-known aspect of Ruskin's life as recorded by early biographers such as W.G. Collingwood.[16] Burd depicted Broadlands as a 'haven for Utopian experiments and new religions', whose 'saintly master and mistress abstained from field-sports and wine, and thought of vegetarianism as one of the courses to the Kingdom of Heaven'.[17] The couple's relationship with the spiritually unorthodox – with people such as the New Forest Shakers – is one aspect of Philip Hoare's *England's Lost Eden*.[18] Hoare does not exaggerate the transatlantic nature of their spiritual connections: as members of the aristocracy they were attractive clients for leading American spiritualists such as Daniel Home and Charles H. Foster. Marlene Tromp's *Altered States* includes a fine essay on spiritualism in the Victorian family, which explores the Cowper-Temples.[19] They appear in other works, such as Anne Taylor's brilliant biography of their close friend the writer, diplomatist and mystic Laurence Oliphant.[20] For Taylor, Georgina was 'large, warm, impulsive, and dangerously naïve. In spiritual matters it was she who chased after phantoms, drawing William irresistibly in her wake'. Georgina did what she wanted and her enthusiasm caused Society to laugh while enjoying her hospitality.[21]

William was 'born in the purple of the directing classes', more specifically graduating 'in the select school of Whiggery' or 'sacred circle of the Great-Grand-motherhood', those aristocrats who even pronounced words differently from their rival Tories, and who, as one of their descendants wrote, were, like the poet, born, not made.[22] He was nephew and private secretary to one Whig premier and stepson – perhaps natural son – of another, and his career as a junior minister in Whig-Liberal governments spanned two decades. Grenville Fletcher's *Parliamentary Portraits* provides one view of William, after two decades in parliament:

> Although strictly brought up in the Whig school of politics, his views are carried out with reasonable moderation, without any professions as to the extreme principles of the more advanced Liberal; and closely allied as the honourable member is to the 'family party,' which claims his immediate consideration, he is not

so united towards his political kindred; but if, in the course of its action, its policy becomes questionable, or at least unpalatable – if measures be agitated that admit of the slightest bias, or encroachment upon the happiness and pursuits of the people, his sense of duty impels him at once to repel their innovations.[23]

Cowper-Temple was made a peer by Gladstone, who had known him at Eton. Their relationship was affected by the great man's policies over Irish Home Rule, but, as William wrote to Catherine Gladstone shortly before his death, her husband was a man whom 'I have admired and loved since we were together at Eton'.[24] His association with Melbourne and Palmerston, and career as a reform-minded Liberal statesman, provide justifications for this study.

It was a political life which spanned the transition from the *ancien régime* 'Old Corruption' of William's childhood and youth in the Regency (when radicals struggled to alter the 'unreformed' polity and workers tried to improve living or working conditions through actions as varied as Luddism, trade unionism and the Cato Street conspiracy) to the Victorian liberal state forged in the aftermath of the Great Reform Act and the measures enacted during the Whig and Peel administrations of the 1830s-40s. By the time he died in the 'Late Victorian' era, William had witnessed and reacted to popular or parliamentary agitation for two further parliamentary reforms acts extending the franchise and raising the spectre of Demos dominant. Yet these years saw the continuing cultural and political significance of his aristocratic order, whose economic and political decline has tended to be located after the 'troubled decade' of the 1880s.[25] Politics was understood by William and his class as their natural terrain – the 'sublime cañons of the high political world' were to be crossed by the aristocracy. 'High politics' – the phrase appearing in this study's subtitle – acquired this altitude because it dealt with important or urgent matters of state and national interest rather than parochial or merely sectional interests. And one can detect in William's reformism, an effort to divert the labouring classes from political activity.[26]

William's career and outlook can be identified as part of that mode of government, political and cultural, which was seen as the responsibility of a leisured class whose members were connected by kinship, shared education and shared roles. 'To lead, to guide, and to enlighten,' had been Disraeli's summary of this duty and William's career (and his wife's) should be seen in this light.[27] The Cowper-Temples joined a select group of aristocrats keen to demonstrate their right to lead through their moral worth. Concern about the materialism of the new urban democracy, and the aristocratic 'fast set', was one aspect to the Cowper-Temples' public activity.[28] Perhaps symbolic of the desire to maintain an authentic aristocracy and despite William's record of supporting the most improbable individuals, he did not support the Tichbourne Claimant's release in 1876.[29]

We can also chart the century's spiritual developments through the journeys taken by the Cowper-Temples, which encompassed William's transition from youthful Protestant fervour in the Evangelical Alliance of the early 1840s, to mid-Victorian Christian Socialism, and into 'higher life' transcendentalism in the 1880s. At Georgina's instigation, and in common with many eminent and obscure Victorians who sought balm at a time when old religious verities were being questioned, the Cowper-Temples became keen investigators of spiritualist phenomena.

Her class meant that opportunities for Georgina's separate public action were in some respects more open than for non-aristocratic women. As Kim Reynolds argues, aristocratic women do not conform easily to the public/private roles of 'separate spheres' ideology which historiography once suggested dominated nineteenth-century gender relations. The lives of aristocratic women 'were not lived in accordance with any model yet advanced.'[30] As a friend wrote after William's death, 'it is almost impossible in contemplating his career, to do so apart from her who seemed so essentially one with him in all his life and work.'[31] But marriage did not involve her subordination, for she created a separate role in – and more than merely figurehead for – philanthropic activity. This was important in an era before the welfare state and harmonised with prevailing ideas about self-help, Christian benevolence and feminine virtues; but Georgina's philanthropy was not narrowly conventional, though it encompassed, when the Cowper-Temples inherited estates in Hampshire and Sligo, the duties that accompanied landed status.[32]

Georgina had many worshippers, as we shall see, due to a generous and sympathetic nature and striking looks: statuesque and angelic according to many, bringing the attention of royalty in her youth and admirers even in old age. Her diaries and letters reveal a complicated character: humorous and intelligent, but highly strung and sometimes fiery, given to self-dramatising statements about fatigue and anguish at earthly sufferings. Ruskin spoke of the 'grave-roguishness in the eyes' when remembering the 'old flame' of his youth. But the cynical comment from Arthur Benson that her smile was the sort 'which comes of having been told daily for many years that your smile is like a sunset or a strain of music', has a grain of truth.[33] William was the calm force in the marriage. She insisted she was 'dark – selfy – restless, rebellious'; while he was bright and joyous.[34]

Their marriage may be seen as an instance of the 'incorporated marriages' identified by Reynolds in her study of aristocratic women[35], for

Georgina supported her husband's political career (a career, after all still regarded as aristocratic), and if she did not live solely or even primarily for his public success there is evidence of her close interest in his political fortunes, and involvement in such reforms as the transformation of London parks which he undertook as a junior minister. But there is no indication that she wielded significant influence in his political career, and she certainly shied away from being a political hostess in the mould of her mother-in-law. Nor is there evidence of her role in political patronage, though posts were found for a favourite brother.

Yet patronage, the private nomination of relatives, friends and supporters to public office, as this study's title implies, was an important aspect of nineteenth-century society.[36] The Cowper-Temples' patronage of artistic genius – a major element of aristocratic identity – is an aspect studied here. Apart from Ruskin, acquaintances included George MacDonald, Dante Gabriel Rossetti, William Morris and Edward Burne-Jones, and lesser figures in the Pre-Raphaelite world such as Frederic Shields and Edward Clifford. They lacked the fortune for extravagant patronage but the Cowper-Temples' relationship with the cultural elite was important to them. And as members of the Whig aristocracy the Cowper-Temples had continental connections and tastes. Interested in European affairs, religious and otherwise, their associations also traversed the Atlantic to include American evangelicals, utopianists, and poets. Through their utopian links they even had Japanese acquaintances.

A dual biography covering almost ninety years presents the writer (and reader) with challenges. Firstly there is the need to acknowledge context in an era of bewildering social, political and cultural change. Their century has, historiographically, fissured into a number of eras, such as 'Regency', 'Reform crisis', 'early Victorian', 'mid-Victorian' or 'Age of Equipoise', 'high Victorian', and 'fin de siècle'. Without wishing to essentialise such labels, it is important to grasp the prevailing or emerging moods and sensibilities. Recent historiography has debated an aristocratic and Anglican 'long eighteenth century' ending in the 1830s following repeal of the Test and Corporation Acts in 1828, Catholic emancipation in 1829 and the Reform Act of 1832. For Boyd Hilton, the period from the 1780s to the mid-nineteenth century saw the transformation of a 'mad, bad and dangerous' people into 'respectable' Victorians; he also identifies it as the 'age of Atonement' when the dominant theology stressed human depravity and eternal punishment.[37] Historians have identified the mid-Victorian era as one of comparative stability, of anxious attentiveness by elites because of the 'coming of democracy' and as 'the period of highest refinement of Victorian moral sensibility'.[38] Their spiritualism and ecumenical work in this period links the Cowper-Temples to that wider response in the 1860s-

1870s to the onward march and growing pretensions of science, a reaction to the perception of materialism which stimulated an 'occult revival'. Such a reaction, in fact, stemmed from the strength of the prevailing earnestness and concern for religion.[39]

Secondly, there is the problem of structure when dealing with two people, one of whom had a public political career which ought to be a distinct theme. After chapters on their early years, including William's brief marriage to Harriet Gurney, I treat the Cowper-Temples as a couple where possible. Two chapters explore William as politician and statesman, but it must not be thought that the Cowper-Temples' lives, any more than other aristocrats, neatly divided between private and public realms, the idea of 'social politics' – the social aspect to elite politics in which women played important roles – is relevant, so chapters on their lives outside William's official or parliamentary duties relate activity of public significance rather than adopt an unhelpfully watertight demarcation.[40] William saw no split between public and private labours and he was described as 'one of those men, who engaged in business or official life, are entirely dominated by an inner sense of religion.'[41]

We live chronologically, but interests are diachronous and themes emerge retrospectively. A chapter describes and assesses the Cowper-Temples' varied reform activities. Georgina, rightly, privileged the religious dimension in her memoirs, and the following chapter considers their religious journey and their most important act of religious networking, the 'Broadlands Conferences for the Higher Life'. Georgina was no mere pendant to William, and her roles as saintly inspiration and maternal figure continued after William's death in 1888; a chapter explores the thirteen years until her death.

Lytton Strachey's generation reacted against the Victorian mausolea of *Lives and Letters* which idealised through respectful prose and judiciously pruned letters. William had the insider's knowledge of statesmen's lives and knew about the politics of posthumous reputation from involvement in the creation of Palmerston's official life.[42] Though given to self-reflection in his journals (as Georgina was), there is no evidence that he believed himself worthy of autobiography or posthumous life. Phillip Guedalla's view on the ideal biography as a single volume remains apposite still. He noted the oddity of biographies that, driven by chance existence or destruction of records, jolted from in-depth to impressionistic, and which, in a welter of general information, could not see the wood for trees. I am mindful of these comments, when encountering the years of relative archival silence or the significant episodes in the Cowper-Temples' lives which are now obscure. But I offer their lives in detail, believing that they merit this as major figures of the period.

1

THE CHILDHOOD AND YOUTH OF BILLY COWPER

William Francis Cowper was born, somewhat unexpectedly, at Lord Melbourne's house, Brocket Hall, in Hertfordshire on 13 December 1811.[1] He was the second son of Peter Leopold Francis Cowper the fifth Earl Cowper and his wife Emily, whose family home Brocket was. The paternity was, however, queried in his lifetime, for physical similarity gave credence to rumours that he was the natural son of his mother's lover and second husband, Henry John Temple, third Viscount Palmerston.[2] He was named apparently after his relation the poet William Cowper; though his poetic idol, at least in an adolescence in which poetry played an important part, was William Wordsworth.[3]

Emily's brother William Lamb, Lord Melbourne, reputedly said in old age, 'who the devil can tell who's anybody's father?'[4] Perhaps this was stimulated by gossip that Emily and his brother Frederick were really the children of the shy connoisseur George O'Brien Wyndham, the third Earl of Egremont.[5] Their brother George was commonly believed to be the Prince Regent's son. A comparison of photographs of Palmerston and William Cowper supports the contemporary view of a physical likeness. Another similarity distinguishing William Cowper and Palmerston from Earl Cowper and William's brothers was their lives of strenuous public activity. If pre-Victorian aristocratic morality, which brought uncertainty to parentage, did not embarrass Palmerston's generation, when William's sister Fanny went through family papers in the early 1870s her sister-in-law the dowager Countess Cowper told her son ironically, 'My love you are come of a virtuous stock!'[6]

William's childhood was spent happily at Brocket, a red-brick mansion built early in George III's reign and decorated by the Adam brothers.[7] Situated by the river Lea, it had a famous ancient oak in its beautiful parkland. Emily, his eldest sister, was his companion. Her parents' favourite, the beautiful Minny, as she was known, was highly eligible. She turned down an offer of marriage from the leading Whig politician Lord John Russell and married the philanthropist Anthony Ashley Cooper, subsequently Lord Shaftesbury.

William's brother George, Lord Fordwich, was his senior by five years. Clever but shy, he married Anne, the eldest daughter of the Earl de Grey.[8] William's younger sister was Frances, known as Fanny; she married Robert Viscount Jocelyn and became the favourite Cowper at Court as one of Queen Victoria's ladies-in-waiting. His younger brother, Charles Spencer earned the sobriquet 'Expensive' Cowper. As an attaché he had been patron of the dramatic art, 'or artistes rather; the votaries of Terpsichore were especially indebted to his liberality', and when he was left a fortune he acquired a reputation for extravagant dining in Paris.[9]

FIGURE 1. Panshanger, the Cowper seat in Hertford, engraving from *Jones' views of the seats, mansions, castles, etc., of noblemen and gentlemen, in England, Wales, Scotland and Ireland* (1820-1831).

The Cowpers lacked ancient noble lineage but traced themselves back to Edward IV's reign. One forebear was a baronet imprisoned for loyalty to Charles I, but the earldom was bestowed on the lawyer Sir William Cowper by George I, following his role as High Steward in the trial of Jacobite peers in 1716 and appointments as Lord Keeper of the Great Seal and Lord Chancellor. The third Earl, William's grandfather, was 'an Englishman who had never seen his earldom, who takes root and bears fruit in Florence, and is proud of a pinchbeck principality in a third country'.[10] He became a leader of the English community in Florence, supporting artists, scientists and musicians. He patronised Zoffany, whose *Tribuna of the Uffizi* depicts him admiring a Raphael, which he wanted as a sweetener to secure the Order of the Garter. His collection included another of Raphael's 'Virgin and Child' paintings, and works by Fra Bartolommeo, Pontormo, Andrea del Sarto, Titian, Claude Lorraine, Rembrandt and Van Dyck. It was described as perhaps the 'choicest private collection in this country … small but admirable'.[11] The collection adorned the Cowper seat at Panshanger, in Hertford. This was rebuilt by William's father to designs partly by Samuel Wyatt, in the gothic style. He built a picture gallery and added Turner's 'Harlech Castle'.[12] The estate, on the brow of a hill above the river Meriman, had beautiful gardens and fine woodland. William's father added a lake and enclosed the park. When the young Queen Victoria visited, she thought it 'so pretty and *wohnlich*'.[13]

The fifth Earl was educated at Christ Church and succeeded his unmarried brother who died in 1799 at an untimely age. Peter Cowper was a follower of Charles James Fox and his friends included the Foxite politician Thomas Creevey and Sackville Tufton, the ninth Earl Thanet.[14] Expected to play a prominent part in Whig politics, he proved a nonentity. He moved the amendment to the King's speech in 1806 at the time of William Pitt the younger's demise, shared in the disappointment when the Prince Regent betrayed his old Whig friends in 1812 and kept his Tory ministers, attended the trial of Queen Caroline in 1820, and visited the wronged and sinning royal consort at Brandenburgh House.[15] A few years later, he engaged in controversy against the radical William Cobbett over the resumption of convertibility of banknotes into gold.[16] John Wade's critique of corruption, *The Extraordinary Black Book*, included a mild entry on Cowper as a recipient of a state pension, as a man of 'high liberalism, and the most perfect independence', and Cowper supported parliamentary reform in 1832. After his death in 1837 one of the Hertford papers memorialised him as 'much respected as he was beloved as a kind and liberal landlord'.[17] A protégé identified 'too much delicacy of sentiment to take a leading part in public life, but to the most exquisitely pleasing manners he joined a manly understanding and a playful wit', and recalled 'his benevolent and exhilarating smile'.[18]

In July 1805 he married Emily Lamb, eldest daughter of the first Viscount Melbourne.[19] The union was planned by Lady Melbourne, for he seemed a catch for the *arriviste* Lambs, as a 'Whig nobleman of great influence'.[20] He was a Prince of the Holy Roman Empire as his grandfather had been raised to this dignity by Joseph II (though this empire was shortly to be abolished by Napoleon), handsome and wealthy (at the time of his death his brother had some £20,000 per annum).[21] At first the marriage was happy, but most people thought Cowper was not a playful wit but a bore.[22] Henry Fox, later fourth Lord Holland, described him as having a 'painfully correct memory and a dreadful voice. His stories are sometimes witty, but so heavily told that it is impossible to attend'.[23]

Emily soon tired of his ponderous personality, inattentiveness and the 'moping way he is in when nothing forces him to rouze himself'.[24] She turned to the attractions of Henry John Temple, Lord Palmerston, then in the War Office; on her deathbed her mother is said to have exhorted her to be true not to Cowper but to her lover.[25] Cowper suffered headaches and acute rheumatism and sought alleviation in German spas; despite Emily's infidelity she accompanied him and nursed him in his illness.[26] And her infidelity to her husband did not prevent her from creating an affectionate family circle. William was always close to her and she said that she 'always felt as if he was a contemporary' and some time before his first marriage described him as 'a great dear … it is a great pleasure to repose one's thoughts on any body so thoroughly good – and so amiable'.[27] William's relationship with his father was distant. Minny was doted on but he was found fault with, which pained his mother.[28] Unsurprisingly, William had little to say about his father in his private writings as an adult.

William was an amiable brother. In 1843 his sister Frances said 'Billy has been such a dear kind brother to me, all my life.'[29] Minny described him as 'so kind hearted & so good, so unselfish & with such a sweet temper & disposition, that I have never seen him out of humour in my whole life'.[30] This endured, though critical observers saw in this something weaker and effeminate. Lady Cowper once supplemented his infant locks by cutting some of Minny's curls to add to his cap; and Minny called him a 'girlish boy' in 1817.[31] He survived the usual infant illnesses. In late 1819 Emily wrote: 'Wm is getting well and looks himself again, but I think hardly stout enough yet to go to School' and, worried about his delicacy, she sought medical advice.[32]

The Cowpers cultivated no Evangelical house of faith in the Victorian (or Regency) mould, William's environment lacking the fervour which became central to his adulthood. Of course, Emily was not to be thought of as a paragon of homely virtue. Mrs Arbuthnot, the Tory diarist and friend of the Duke of Wellington, called the family 'one of the most profligate families in the kingdom', such was the reputation Lady Cowper had acquired through her social brilliance and affairs.[33] Although Emily ensured her daughters participated in the charitable activity expected of the aristocracy, and, unlike her husband, attended church with her children, hers was not a religious circle. Despite the Whig diarist Greville's description of the Cowpers as a 'real fountain of benevolence' and 'examples of the religion of the fashionable world, and the charity of natural benevolence, which the world has not spoiled', religious instruction was left to governesses and the head nurse, Mrs Hawk.[34] She would tell William to say 'God bless Papa and Mamma,' and jump into bed. But he would not be so summary and often said, 'Oh no Hawkey let me say my prayers,' and she would reply, 'very well Master William do as you please,' and though his siblings jumped into bed, he would kneel for the Lord's Prayer. As Hawkey could not explain the formularies, the children had only vague ideas of their meaning and Minny did not understand them until she married.[35]

William went to a school in Wimbledon, 'a very comfortable one and kept by nice people', as Emily wrote, in May 1820: 'I cannot tell you how sorry I am to part with him he is such an amiable boy – and improves every day.'[36] His friends included Lord Ossulton, the son of a family friend (the Countess of Tankerville), and Eugene Money, son of an East Indian merchant, and recalled by William as 'a very very good person … Almost one too good for the world'.[37] When his headmaster, Dr Joshua Ruddock, died of apoplexy in May 1821, William went to the Reverend Dr Thomas Hooker's preparatory school at Rottingdean. There was sport with chickens, ducks, rabbits, fights with hoops, seats in a mulberry tree, flowers to dry in his prayer book before Sunday service and 'I spy'.[38] The pupils drank cowslip wine, relished bread and butter in bed, and enjoyed pranks. William's lantern, called 'Jemmy Sneak', was hidden under the bedclothes when the candles were removed. The boys, he was shocked to recall later, played cards and sang until two in the morning.[39] As Hooker was apparently a smuggler, perhaps this laxity was unsurprising, yet the school had a reputation for 'great respectability'.[40]

On holidays at Panshanger he enjoyed riding and took to hunting and other 'manly exercises', so that the keeper praised his shooting excessively.[41] He attended a children's ball held by the new king, who said he was a remarkably pretty boy.[42] At this time the Cowpers were in favour with George IV, who made his godson Fordwich a page of honour, and invited the Cowpers to the Pavilion.[43] On other occasions there were holidays at the Brighton house of Lord Egremont, patron of J.M.W. Turner, a socially responsible aristocrat, and, it will be recalled, reputedly the father of Frederick Lamb and Emily Cowper.[44]

William was sent to Eton, the Lamb brothers' school, where he had the normal perfunctory education of the college's unreformed era.[45] Of the classical poets and philosophers, 'all I brought away was the power of reading & understanding them in after life. In the course of my tuition no serious thought was ever, I think, presented to my mind.'[46] But he said that the circulating library at Windsor 'contains every book an Eton schoolboy may wish for I never got near its limits'.[47] If he 'did not give into any vicious practices, tho' I was near it', he experienced schoolboy scrapes and liberties: having a pet dog and squirrel, being flogged for carving his initials in a pew and going out of bounds.[48] He was 'popular and happy'.[49] William's tutor was Edward Hawtrey who had been tutor to George and would become the headmaster of the college.[50]

He recalled many years later, a close friendship with another boy who went with him to a secluded spot in the playing-fields to discuss spiritual mysteries. William Gladstone, who entered Eton in 1821, recalled that 'from the very first he left very marked and clear recollections even from Eton days, the stamp of purity, modesty, gentleness was upon him in a peculiar degree.'[51] Gladstone thought him the most promising speaker in the pupil-run Eton Society founded in 1811, a school for orators and club membership of which was 'one of the chief glittering prizes' of the Eton experience.[52] Given his weakness (according to critics) in the Commons this is a surprising verdict. An extract from William's diary for 1827 (now missing) records debates on the deposition of Richard II and the Peerage Bill of 1719; after Gladstone's skilful speech on the latter, William thought he would be a great loss to the Society when he left.[53]

A letter from Emily in October 1826 gives another glimpse, chiding William for allowing another to do his lessons rather than profit from Eton as much as possible: 'you might as well be at home. Papa who saw your letter was rather shocked.'[54] A letter from Fordwich in Madrid, visiting his uncle the ambassador Frederick Lamb, chaffs William about the new governess, who 'seems to be the favourite of yours', though Lady Cowper thought her a 'little chattering French Woman'.[55] Fordwich also told him that his uncles exhorted him 'to pull in the boats and say you are a lazy fellow and unpardonable if you do not'.[56]

William went next to the Evangelical Reverend James Anderson, of St George's Chapel in Brighton, to study history, English, logic, mathematics and moral philosophy. Religious instruction was not neglected, and he attended church twice daily, enjoyed taking the sacrament for the first time, and listened to sermons from leading preachers. But he felt oppressed by the dangers and emptiness of the world. Several years later he recalled: 'I had frequent thoughts of taking the church as a profession.'[57] Over twenty years later, after revisiting St George's Chapel he recalled his 'struggle of feeling … as to whether I should one day ascend the pulpit stair close by in a surplice or not and the worldly spirit prevailed'.[58] Despite this, he had no intimate talks with Anderson or anyone except a fellow pupil, Chisholm.[59]

Before he left Anderson's he wrote to his father, fortified with pious quotations from divines such as the Jesuit Louis Bourdalue, about his eagerness to combat the world as a clergyman. He later learnt this gesture had 'put them in a dreadful pass, & they were disconcerted at it'.[60] It was left to his mother to dissuade him through discussing the matter 'rationally'.[61] Although he later condemned himself for dropping a half-hearted idea in the face of family indifference, family and relations actively diverted him to an army career and fashionable society.[62] His mother had sought a commission for Fordwich, anxious that languor, idleness, childishness and isolation from his peers were being prolonged, and with her friend the Duke of Wellington's advice, selected the Blues. Cowper had left things to her, though expressing a dislike for an army career for his heir. Fordwich, much to Emily's pride, came to enjoy the camaraderie and social life of the army, and this no doubt encouraged her to think that this career, which in Fordwich's case could be left whenever he got tired of it and turned to Parliament, would also suit her second son. For the next few years, William endeavoured to combine soldiering with piety: in later years he struck people by his saintliness and not martial spirit.

From 1829, through the surviving journals beginning this year, we can get more of a sense of the young William in his own words. When he was seventeen, William went on his first continental tour, with his friend Percy Burrell, son of Sir Charles Merrick Burrell of Knepp Castle, Sussex, married to an old friend of Emily Cowper, who as a staunchly conservative MP died the 'father of the Commons' in 1862.[63] Crossing the Channel by the recently developed steam packet, they visited the Netherlands and Germany, taking in Aix-la-Chapelle, Bonn, Cologne, travelling along the Rhine, and reaching Zurich.[64] The journey was slow but avoided the discomfort of public coaches as they took in royal art collections, opera and ballet, a guided tour of Waterloo where William paid respects to the Marquess of Anglesey's leg, assessed the beauty of Flemish women, viewed Rhenish castles and landscapes under Byronic influence, and saw the Prussian minister in Frankfurt. In light of his later attitudes, it is interesting that at Antwerp cathedral, which 'somehow escaped those modern Goths the revolutionists', William felt that the mass 'would have done some honour to a heathen temple, but appeared at first to have very little to do with Christianity'.[65]

Back in England he was examined by James De Ville, a leading phrenologist, who advised rising and going to bed earlier, identified a 'great deal of caution and diffidence', love of approbation and a strong sense of justice, but lack of perseverance and skill in words, writing and oratory. William was remarkably fond of travelling, his 'organ of constructiveness' was strong and he should be 'sent abroad with very little means'.[66] But preparation for soldiering instead involved almost six months' instruction in mathematics, natural history, fortifications and phrenology at Edinburgh in late 1829.[67] Perhaps Palmerston, who had spent three years at Edinburgh University and as a student and lodger of the political economist Dugald Stewart, advised Emily about this course. He arrived by mail coach in early October. He was a pupil of the Whig professor of natural philosophy John Leslie, who was unimpressed by the young man's handwriting during their first meeting.[68] Leslie was called the Falstaff of Edinburgh and William described him as 'a huge mass of bloated flesh in an old patched dining gown'. He asked for acorns from Hertfordshire as he hoped to promote oaks in Scotland. William unkindly commented *apropos* of a lecture on the centre of gravity, 'his has more to sustain than that of most people'. He had more appreciation for the lectures given by James Pillans, professor of humanity and Roman law, his Whig snobbery revealed in the comment on Pillans: 'Quite the difference between a gentleman & a mechanic however clever – everything quiet and in good taste – none of Leslie's clap-traps or of his pupils' boisterousness.'

Other lecturers included Dr Hope (professor of chemistry), and the renowned Evangelical minister and social reformer Dr Thomas Chalmers ('not a speech but a *continuous crack*'), who was professor of moral philosophy. One day's itinerary included an hour each of chemistry, natural philosophy, military drawing, German, history, and a lecture from an eloquent and amusing Dr Chalmers, with an hour at midday reading Rousseau's *Nouvelle Héloïse*.[69] He met Sir John Sinclair, the writer on finance and agriculture who was 'very full of a new method of tinting wool with extracts from the flower of the Potatoe'. There was much socialising through dinners, balls, shooting, and the occasional visit to barracks. He was invited to join the freemasons, apparently by Charles Cathcart, later second earl Cathcart, then in Edinburgh for scientific study. He dined with the Lord Chief Commissioner, met *The Scotsman*'s editor and visited aristocrats like the Swintons and the Earl of Hopetoun ('Dressed like a Greenland fisherman lolling about in the most time-killing manner, and hardly speaking a word').

He became acquainted with Sir Walter Scott, whom he first saw in a purple dressing gown at a table covered with bills. William spent Christmas at Abbotsford, listening to Scott's anecdotes, inspecting military relics and shooting woodcocks; at Hogmanay the men were 'pretty considerably drunk'. It is unclear if William was an admirer of Scott's work, but William found him 'very amiable not at all formidable, less so than almost any man' but thought 'his face would not give the idea of genius.' But the romantic movement evoked William's interest and in his openness to romantic poetry he reflected both a shift in Whig mentality and a development in Evangelicalism.[70]

William's youthful appreciation of beauty is shown in frequent comments, perhaps made self-consciously or with a touch of bravado, on the prettiness or otherwise of women he encountered. He described Anne Scott as 'lovely' and 'very blooming'. The society beauty Fanny Brandling, a daughter of an old friend of his father's (Charles Brandling of Gosforth

Park), had 'made a considerable sensation in Auld Reekie'. 'Venus of the North,' he noted, it accounted for her living so near the sea, 'shld like to pass by while she's bathing but am afraid I should offend her divinity by taking her for a mere sea-nymph, besides, she tells me she's tired of bathing so it's not likely.' At the same time as such carnal thoughts, William remained conscious of religious duties and regularly attended church, overcoming hostility to the Presbyterian form at St Giles to admire the Kirk service, particularly the singing.[71] 'At this moment,' he wrote, 'if some one came to me with the alternative of choosing the church or the army I shd not hesitate, but accept the former. But then what folly not to do so of my own accord.'[72]

Extracts from philosophers, historians, poets and novelists indicates the range of his reading, including Gibbon, Shelley, Southey, Balzac, Aristotle, Seneca, Sir Philip Sidney, Madame de Stael, de Tocqueville, S.T. Coleridge, and William Ellery Channing.[73] He jotted down in English, French and Latin thoughts on such themes as friendship, the pursuit of knowledge, marriage and love. He noted Kant's aphorism that 'to develop in the individual all the perfection of which he is capable is the great object of education'. From Byron came material on Society's hollowness. He made notes on the Irish court at Dublin Castle, the punishment of nations, the character of philosophers and Baconian compared with Platonic philosophy. In addition to Leslie, supervision between 1828 and 1830 was provided by Thomas Sheepshanks, the young rector of the Edinburgh Academy, later rector and headmaster of Coventry grammar school in 1834 and the future George Eliot's Latin tutor. William found the Sheepys 'very vulgar perhaps more in thought than in manner'. Sheepshanks, in a long reply to his earnest question about harmonizing frequent sinning with a complete identification with Christ, cautioned 'Beware of Religious curiosity, nay beware of the Religiousness, nay beware of the Holiness of the flesh.'[74] The association with Sheepshanks gave further opportunities for flirting as he later recalled, 'my friendship with Miss Scott was very pure, & there was no harm in my romps with Sheepshank's sister-in-law.'[75]

Fordwich was educated at Cambridge with little effect, although Emily asked Palmerston, 'for want of better advice', about further study and even considered Thomas Malthus as a tutor.[76] William did not go to university, but perhaps was more inquiring than Fordwich, at any rate in 1832 he investigated having an Oxford tutor, though perhaps this was a means to escape his military career.[77]

For in the late 1829 he rapidly moved through purchase from being second lieutenant in the Ceylon Regiment to being cornet, the lowest commissioned officer rank in the cavalry, in the Royal Horse Guards, the Blues.[78] He was 'all for action', but philosophical, not accepting a soldier was necessarily vicious, or that religion could not live as well under a red coat as under a black one. He resolved to live 'not for the present only but for eternity, and not to mistake means for ends'. Money, honour, glory, power, pleasure, etc., 'were certain steps in the assent to happiness but can never without great folly be made the ultimate object of our aspirations'.[79] Earnest pursuit of knowledge and sexual interest was reflected in his desire 'to see the world, especially the third part of the British Empire ... I think also the company of the Paget ladies very agreeable'. These were daughters of the Marquess of Anglesey.

His regiment was in London in early 1830, and he assisted Fordwich during the general election in July and August, when his brother contested Canterbury, making speeches in alehouses, and shaking the hands of the unwashed, the hardest work, he told Miss Scott, he had ever gone through, harder than work with Sheepshanks.[80] Nothing was happening in London, despite the accession of the alarmingly eccentric William IV: 'our new King is grown so frisky, is always having some expedition to make or some new place to show his august face in, and he walks about the streets with little brass spurs strapped round his ankles, like post boys.' We only have a few suggestive remarks about his response to the parliamentary reform crisis which brought his party back into power (in November 1830) after decades in the wilderness.

A fragment of correspondence from a fellow officer in June 1831 shows he was liked. He invented 'bills of fare' to while away guard duty, sending gastronomic effusions and gossip about flirtations. And flirtation was crucial for a reputation as a gallant, especially a son of the acknowledged leader of fashionable society. 'If you do not persuade the Reporters to put your name down in the Almacks list you will quite lose your character here,' this friend wrote.[81] But in a later journal, confessing his struggle for purity, William poured out a cryptic recollection, hinting at a decision to avoid sowing wild oats. He declared 'disapprobation of the favourite vice of all young men', and argued the point and was quizzed by friends such as Jack Villiers, 'in helping a fowl, he used to offer me some capon,' and when the Duke of Cumberland dined with them and the toast to 'our old friend' was given, he was requested not to drink it. William bore this sort of thing with 'much firmness & got through the mental temptations to wh I was exposed'. But he confessed that his thoughts had been impure; he talked as loosely as anyone and profited more by the bad than by the good learned at Rottingdean. He revealed his system of conduct unintentionally to Villiers and 'having once declared myself I was bound to defend myself wh I did unreservedly quoting the Bible to Murray &[c]'.[82]

This abstinence, he recalled, lasted until the winter spent in Naples in 1831, when he persuaded himself, influenced by the 'low mentality of [William] Paley's Philosophy' that he need not be so very good. The indulgence did not infringe duty to God or neighbours and the virtue was impractical in existing society. He confessed to taking up the new practice 'with great eagerness' and continuing it in London to the delight of regimental friends and Allen, the librarian of his mentor the Whig Lord Holland 'and to the lesser I added the greater crime – but all this time under a wilful delusion and without a deliberate intended opposition to the divine law'.[83] But, so he recalled, he became corrupt and numb 'under the dominion of Lust', his behaviour so improper that a friend was asked to warn him. We know from a letter of about 1834 that 'Hug' – apparently Henry Grenville – spoke about a '*ton*' which you have of late adopted towards certain of our *Lady* friends and complaints of what have been of late made more than once to me by relations of parties and with a recommendation that I as your great friend should entreat you to be more cautious how you conduct yourself … I think you cannot be aware that the sorts of things which you are in the habit of doing *indiscriminately* (for that makes all the difference) by girls in particular will get you into serious scrapes'.[84] Given William's later saintliness, this reputation may seem odd. Yet even Ashley, his brother-in-law and exemplar, was described as a 'male coquet' as a youth.[85] William certainly made an impact. His mother told his sister Minny: 'I should have liked you to see Billy here in a large Society. He is so improved and so very agreeable. I really never saw so young a lad have so much agreeable conversation – Mde Lieven was charmed with him and Mde Dino quite smitten.'[86]

William became extra aide-de-camp to Lord Anglesey, the reform-minded new Lord Lieutenant of Ireland, serving in this capacity for several years from 1831. This was a way of learning in a 'good school' the duties of an officer and an opportunity to explore the 'third part of the British Empire', the post was unpaid and his presence in Dublin was not always required.[87] A letter from John Robert Townshend, third Viscount Sydney, gives insight into life at Dublin, with ugly ADCs at the Vice Regal Lodge, and dinners enlivened by Tyrolese minstrels and followed by negus and punch. His Excellency was polite beyond measure and Sydney could not see why people feared him, unless they were clumsy at carving or slow at whist. William (back in London) was assumed to have access to courtly gossip, for Sydney inquired about the Duchess of Kent and asked if her ambitious Comptroller of the Household, Sir John Conroy, was the humble lover, or assiduous courtier?[88]

In 1832 William spent four months in Paris, Naples and Rome. In Paris the wife of the British ambassador was visited by him in the company of

Lord Elphinstone (governor of Madras from 1837-42, and governor of Bombay, 1858): Harriet Granville described the two as 'delightful partners, real Englishmen'.[89] 'For people,' he wrote, 'one must come to England; but for climate and beauty never leave Italy.'[90] In Naples he met the diminutive diplomat Moritz Esterhazy, of the famous Hungarian family. Moritz was in love with a daughter of the French legitimist Comte de la Ferronays and proposed, having met her at the salon of the Anglo-Italian Actons. Esterhazy was 'such a nice fellow, and we suit so well. We shall be friends, I hope, for life'. Certainly, over the next few years Moritz corresponded, discussing the Reform crisis and mutual acquaintances such as the Duchess of Sutherland.[91] Sir Walter Scott, unsuccessfully recuperating in the Mediterranean, sent books back by William from Naples, when his young acquaintance's leave was over.[92]

Visits to the country estates of relations and acquaintances was an important activity in the aristocratic calendar, associating the youthful William with a 'country Whiggery' which existed alongside and overlapped with the salons of the Hollands and others in the metropolis where he was also a fixture; salons which were connected to an elite of European liberal aristocrats.[93] In 1832 William became a close friend of a leading Whig, William Cavendish, the bachelor sixth Duke of Devonshire and son of the Foxite Duchess, Georgiana. This friendship was natural for the Lambs had grown up with the Cavendishes and Emily's brother George Lamb married the illegitimate daughter of the fifth Duke.[94] The sixth Duke had made a spectacular representative of George IV at the coronation of Tsar Nicholas I in 1826. Having carried the orb at the King's coronation, he was Lord Chamberlain from 1827 to 1828, and again in William IV's court from 1830–1834. Devonshire used his wealth to transform one of his mansions, Chatsworth, into a palace of art, with sculpture by Canova, a fine collection of books and advanced horticulture. William was frequently there or at Chiswick House in London, the Palladian villa where both Charles James Fox and George Canning had died.[95] He was at Chatsworth when Princess Victoria visited in October 1832, and thought her pretty, and skilled in singing and drawing.[96]

The Duke, though supportive of the Whigs in the Lords, was not a political animal, but aided friends and relations, including William, through political patronage.[97] For his part, William played a role in persuading the Duke to abandon his mistress, Eliza Warwick. It has been argued that William and the Cavendishes used the popular Irish clergyman, Henry Hamilton Beamish, to convert the Duke to Evangelical Christianity.[98] Beamish was described by Devonshire as perfectly gentlemanlike though he said 'you know' too much. 'I wished you with me all the time, though you would have taken all the talk to yourself,' Devonshire told his young friend after one meeting with Beamish.[99] William's influence was condemned by Joseph Paxton, who knew him as a 'wild harum-scarum youth'.[100] But Devonshire's gratitude for opening his spiritual nature was heartfelt.[101] And William felt that, arrested in his own career of vice and sin, he had been an instrument for good on Devonshire, 'for unless my bad example had been exhibited 1st, the good example wld have produced no effect'.[102]

William toured Ireland, then a major problem for the government, with rural outrages and 'coercion' against the Irish dividing the Cabinet. In late 1833 William became aide-de-camp to the new Lord Lieutenant, Lord Wellesley, the Duke of Wellington's brother.[103] But in November 1833, when the Duke of Devonshire intended to recuperate in Italy, William travelled from Dublin to accompany him and the Duke's young cousin. The Duke wrote, 'We are three travellers come to Dover, bound for Naples, the oldest of us alas as old as the other two together, he in search of health, and they of pleasure.'[104] The journal kept by the Duke, William and another young friend, György Károlyi, a Byronic-looking Hungarian count who joined them, survives. Károlyi was a nationalist who helped create the Hungarian Academy and revive Magyar, his account was in Magyar and German.[105] William's own notebook also survives.[106]

He socialised with British aristocrats in Paris like Devonshire's sister Lady Granville. He regretted the flat-features and yellow complexion of the women of Aix, which robbed the songs of the troubadours of some of their romance.[107] Crossing snowy hills, they reached Rome on William's birthday. He had a midnight vigil in St Peter's to experience a new and stirring sensation and 'seemed to be shut out from the world & to be a ghost haunting deserted aisles'.[108] Later, he was critical of his behaviour in Italy's foreign society. At Rome, he recalled, he acted on worldly maxims and aspiring to be *un homme à bonnes fortunes* studied with whom he could form the most agreeable liaison: not Madame de Courval, who was too much a coquette, but at Naples he flirted with the Princess Schouvaloff and befriended Maria Potocka who impressed him 'with some of those feelings which contributed shortly after to turn my imagination from the fascinations & glare of evil towards the pure beauty of Good'![109] Yet she was 'astonishingly careless of her self', and though she ought to have someone always to care for her, her husband was too stupid for this. Her moods were kaleidoscopic, and there seemed to be poetry and romance to her.[110] Maria fascinated the Duke too, and he preserved her letters.[111]

Papal ceremonies stimulated typically Protestant comments about the focus of adoration being worldly rather than divine.[112] This was not an encounter which made him anxious about the schism in Christendom, unlike Gladstone during his visit to St Peter's in 1832. But looking back at his trip to Rome William believed that it brought his mind and soul into a better tone. By a Benedictine convent in Subiaco in the Apennines he sat in an ilex tree and holy resolutions and prayers came to him as it rained.[113]

William's youthful self-confidence comes across in comments on the English and French colonies in Rome. De Courval was 'like an English housemaid but her Duke was like Henri quatre in face [,] is much to the taste of me [,] Bison who rolls her fine large dark eyes all round and round about and but for her mouth would be handsome'. Schouvaloff ('Sugarloaf') had a 'civil talking barbers-shop face', and Lord Pembroke was 'like the wooden men in the tailor's shops stuck up to set off a coat'. They saw the usual sites: Pantheon, baths of Caracalla, the miraculous image of the Virgin at Agostino, Cecilia's tomb and the Appian Way. William thought Raphael's *Cesare Borgia* at the Borghese perfect, disliked his *Fornarina* at the Barberini, admired the luscious *Europa* by Veronese, and was bewildered by the mass of objects at the Vatican. Guercino's head of Christ was 'as fine as anything I have yet seen. Such expression of agony of resignation and dignity, the lip curved, the eye swimming – one sees the iron entering into the soul'.[114] He purchased a copy which many years later decorated a chapel he built at Ridge in Hampshire.

He gossiped about Harriet Baring, William Bingham Baring's wife, Sugars and others, in French, English and 'pig-pen' code. Harriet wished to 'astonish and make effect instead of to please [,] always says what is most disagreeable to people', and he sent her (who became a great figure in society as Lady Ashburton and the intimate of Thomas Carlyle) a paper knife, in 'hopes it may help to turn your *cutting* propensities to something less sensitive and less apprehensive of them than the donor'.[115]

The Duke worried that 'with family and a delightful society courting him', William would not want to come to him in Naples, and William's flippancy about the delay in returning angered him. But as William was full of appropriate feeling when he arrived, the Duke rejoiced.[116] When he heard that uncle George Lamb had died, Billy insisted they went to church. On another occasion they caroused in the Duke's apartment, 'not drunk but happy and overflowing in friendship and confidence'. William galanted with a beautiful Espagnole and was 'more popular and cut up than anybody I ever saw – great charm about him to all – behaves well towards me'. In Naples William socialised with the de la Ferronays, Augustus Craven (son of a courtier of Queen Caroline and soon to marry Pauline de la Ferronays), Lady Harriet d'Orsay, whom he called a 'duck', the Bulwer Lyttons, and Austrians. Eugenie de la Ferronays said people observed *la mode* had passed over him and he grew condescending and fat which some thought a change for the better, but she thought for the worse. He carried a lady through Sibyl's grotto, 'splendid buttocks excitante we came out black as sweeps', and flirted at a waltz.[117]

Crossing over to Sicily on the steamer *Il Real Ferdinando*, William visited Etna and Syracuse, and stayed at a Capuchin abbey in Lentini, a town whose inhabitants 'treated me as they would the Boa Constrictor in a cage' and viewed Devonshire as the brother of king 'Georgie'. The Duke read William's journal, 'more like himself and more clever and droll than anything I ever read', and they found Károlyi's efforts at English killingly funny. But William offended the Duke by travelling with Károlyi to Palermo in pursuit of a letter from his colonel.[118] They roughed it in bad inns and William read George Sand's *Lélia*, crediting this with developing a 'love of the Good & the Beautiful', but there was 'certainly no alteration in practice for with Karolyi I sought to mark by *peculiar remembrance* our arrival at every Town'.[119] With his leave extended, they travelled by ship, lying on sacks and having poetic thoughts about starry skies.

In Paris, the Duke told Lady Cowper 'all about Billy, she sees him put right, I said nothing of any blame'.[120] But Devonshire had not palled of William's company, inviting him in August to shoot grouse, and to Chatsworth. They travelled together; at George Harcourt's place at Nuneham Courtney the Duke noted Billy was 'much taken with Lavinia', his cousin.[121] Back in Dublin, William wrote of his confidence in placing before the Duke notes of 'sleepy and thoughtless moments', but hoped it was not rash, 'and that you will not for anything you may read or not read in my journal withdraw from me that affection which I prize and heartily reciprocate'. Although he gossiped in this letter about Constantine Phipps, earl Mulgrave ('the cavalier way he treats his nice little fat lisping wife') and others, his tours in Ireland had a serious consequence.[122] For in Killarney in November he realised, after reading the Bible and the seventeenth-century puritan John Owen's treatise on the mortification of sin, that his Enlightenment-derived belief that the 'different modes of observing the Divine Law might be suited to different states of society', was fallacious.[123]

2

THE POLITICAL AND COURTLY LIFE OF FASCINATING BILLY, 1834–1842

William's military life was hardly strenuous. From a letter written by his mother in November 1834 we learn that he debated whether to be in barracks in London or stay in Dublin, and occupied some of his time in hunting in a country which she thought bad for horses. Evidently worried about his idleness, she advised him to accumulate information and improve a careless and sprawling orthography.[1]

With the encouragement of friends such as Devonshire, William turned to politics – the other traditional employment for younger sons of aristocratic families – in late 1834. He later said that the switch from regimental to parliamentary and official life 'facilitated my progress, by removing me at once from frivolous & dangerous companionship & filling up most of my time with prescribed occupation', an indication of the undemanding nature of aristocratic military duties. It also suggests that the move was for his benefit rather than for the public good, though William came to see politics as a moral and Christian mission.[2] William already had the example of his brother Fordwich, who represented Canterbury from 1830 to 1834 and was briefly Under Secretary of State for Foreign Affairs.[3] In addition, his mother's role as a political hostess and his friendship with the Foxes of Holland House in Kensington familiarised him with the high political world. He also had the advantage that his uncle Lord Melbourne was prime minister from July to November 1834 and from April 1835 to August 1841.

It was an easy transition to politics, certainly his participation in the Eton Society suggested William's interest, and his widow was to recall he was 'always keen about politics', enjoying the world 'all the more because he enjoyed it in a quite natural and unworldly way'. As he entered political life he harboured no high regard for fellow politicians, doubted their calibre in the new, 'reformed' system: 'the most that can be said for them is that they might have done worse.'[4] His comments on the leading event of the day, the parliamentary reform agitation, with associated riots, revealed aristocratic prejudices about the Lords being more talented and manly than the Commons.[5] But he had no inflated sense of himself as budding politician, though typically he saw benefit in this, 'as I have not a genius nor great talent, I am free from the temptation to conceit and impetuosity that often accompany these.' Though someone about to debut as an orator, he felt dull in conversation, 'I cannot start subjects, I believe I should be happier, imbedded in books & speculation.'[6]

His fascination with politics is reflected by memoranda of conversations with Melbourne, Palmerston and others, on such events as the exit of the Canningites from Wellington's ministry, Peel's liberalism in the 1820s, the departure of James Graham and Lord Stanley from the Whig administration in the crisis of 1834, and Peel's relationship with his departments.[7] His activity in electoral management of the Whig and liberal cause in Hertford can be traced in local newspapers and correspondence such as the letters sent to his friend Bulwer Lytton during the Corn Laws crisis of the 1840s.[8]

That was ahead of him. The general election at the beginning of 1835 gave William the opportunity to enter politics. With funds from Devonshire, William was elected an MP for the borough of Hertford, following in the footsteps of the first and third Earls Cowper and an uncle, who had represented Hertford.[9] The defeat of the Conservative candidate by eight votes in what had been a Conservative borough delighted him but alarmed relatives with the prospect of his demagogic turn![10] William's mother cautioned against being carried away by eagerness.

Not that it was uninterrupted eagerness. He wrote to Devonshire at the end of November 1834, almost deciding to retreat because the electors seemed to prefer the two Tories Ingestre and Masson, but he persisted, and told the Duke it had 'been one of the most exciting contests ever known'.[11] In a telling sidelight on the venality of electors, William commented: 'I delight in electioneering particularly as I am the popular candidate – Many of my fellows have behaved most nobly refusing £10 and £15 and there are some that have no price.'[12] Of the enthusiastic 'chairing' ceremony he enjoyed as victor, he boasted, 'the people would have jumped out of their skins if they had been loose enough.' It was almost unheard of, he believed, but above a third had given him plumpers (i.e., they had given both their votes to him, instead of also voting for a second candidate), yet he came in unpledged, even on the ballot question which was a long-standing radical demand. Relaxing on a sofa, he dreamt 'of purple and orange favours, and flags and hurrahs'.[13]

Melbourne's first government was essentially Grey's ministry without the great man, who observed its decline with satisfaction. The death of Lord Spencer in November 1834 added to Melbourne's difficulties, as Emily told her son, and provided William IV with the pretext for dismissing a ministry which increasingly alarmed him.[14] Reform was a worn out flag, Emily Cowper said, but the Tories identified the Catholic nationalist Daniel O'Connell as the Whigs' weak point, and exploited anti-Catholicism and fears for the Protestant ascendancy.[15] Yet Peel's Tory government was short-lived because its increased strength after the general election in early 1835 was insufficient against the Whig-radical alliance. William's cousin Lavinia thought he would be glad to be an MP, to assist 'in turning out the present Ministers, who, however, are very confident, & will not easily be moved; the Language of the Court is very violent.' But she also advised him, for the sake of the Ashleys, not to be such a 'Rad'.[16]

In these early years of political life he corresponded with Henry Fox (the third Lord Holland was made Chancellor of the Duchy of Lancaster by Melbourne) and his wife, giving accounts of parliamentary debates, Whig fortunes during the election of 1837 and gossip.[17] In one letter (to an unidentified recipient) in early 1835, from Hyde Park barracks as William made the transition to Parliament, the world of Holland House slides neatly into a discussion of Whig electoral fortunes. He had returned from dinner 'having been made to laugh by Sydney Smith, been amused by Rogers, been instructed by Allen, lectured by an artist, corrupted by De Ros, entertained by Lord Holland and cross questioned by My lady and am as well after as can be expected'.[18] William's comment was not an unusual response to these uncomfortable and tense affairs, but entertainments at Holland House were central to Whiggery and memorable because of their hosts' desire to invite the talented.[19] William was a handsome, graceful and blue-eyed youth and the fourth Lady Holland called him 'Beautiful Billy' and 'Fascinating Billy'.[20] And if Holland House was notorious as a 'sceptical house' it welcomed 'many Clergymen, very sincere and orthodox' according to Charles Greville.[21]

William played no significant part in debates in the Commons (housed in the former House of Lords' chamber after the fire of 1834) until he became a junior minister required to present and defend policies. His first recorded speech was to support military flogging, though trusting to the 'dread of its terrors' and deploring its exercise, unsurprising given his recent career.[22] At the same time he became private secretary to his uncle, the premier, replacing Tom Young, a farmer's son from Nairn.[23]

He had been corresponding with his uncle for several years, sending entertaining or informative letters. Melbourne thought William wrote 'so ridiculously like your Mother' when he corresponded in November 1833.[24] Melbourne supported reform of the established (Protestant) church in Ireland, and was sympathetic towards the Catholics and in 1834 William sent him a pamphlet on the Irish Catholic priesthood.[25] The correspondence, mostly Melbourne's instructions, political advice, and invitations from the Queen to stay at Windsor (in Melbourne's increasingly illegible hand), reveals a close relationship. But the two men differed over religion, on the worth of public education, on free trade and policies towards the poor: the premier being a notorious cynic.[26]

William's secretarial position provided no salary (neither did being a MP) but aided his emergence as a public figure.[27] He lived with his uncle at Brocket and in South Street in Mayfair (Melbourne did not live in Downing Street, but William stayed there, enjoying evenings 'reading & writing & listening to the quacking of the Ducks in the Park').[28] According to Ziegler, Melbourne's biographer, William lacked the toughness and resilience of Melbourne's other secretary, George Edward Anson, but 'had a sensitivity which his predecessor lacked and which was of service to his master in negotiations with the Press'.[29] He had to insert paragraphs in the press, and research and send copies of speeches from reports in the *Mirror of Parliament*, which he seems not to have done with great accuracy.[30] But during the crisis over the resignation of John Lambton, first Lord Durham, from his post as governor-in-chief in Canada, in October 1838, after criticism of his ordinance against leaders of the recent rebellion in French Lower Canada, when William sought support from editors such as John Black of the *Morning Chronicle*, Melbourne was satisfied: 'It is exactly what I wished to have said,' he wrote on reading Black's article.[31]

One pressing early concern for Melbourne's secretary was the charge made by a former Tory MP George Norton, that the premier had committed adultery with his young wife Caroline, the talented granddaughter of the Whig politician and playwright Sheridan. Melbourne was acquitted, as many expected, in June 1836. As a consequence, William must have had no illusions about Society's double standards (and the affair with Mrs Norton represented the less outré of Melbourne's passions[32]). William got to know Caroline, a few years his senior, and he told Devonshire after taking her to the opera that having worked up 'all the shreds and patches of feelings', she had created a 'cobbled grande passion' for Melbourne. Old Holly (either Lady Holland or her husband) had lectured William about interfering with Melbourne's amusement, unnecessarily since no witchcraft could induce him, he wrote, to do such a thing. Caroline's character was 'singular[,] unique … a medley of coarseness of language and refinement of feeling, apparent looseness of conduct with a good deal of real morality'. There was affectation in her eyes, voice and phrases, but she was natural in everything else. She could scheme for any object, but was open, even indiscreet in what related to herself. The children were her first object and enabled her 'to endure her worse half the Yahoo'. William admitted he liked her, but in the most proper manner imaginable.[33] William took notes in court for the family and acted as go-between for Caroline and his uncle. He told Lady Holland in one dramatic note on 22 June 1836: 'verdict for the defendant | *hurrah!!!*' He gave the news of deliverance to Melbourne and reported that Conservatives in White's Club looked doleful.[34] William told Lady Holland: 'There is a story going about that when told that Ld M cld not (after an unfavourable verdict) be fit to be his minister replied, "Then I am not fit to be king."'[35]

Caroline was upset by William's speaking against her about the time of the trial.[36] His advice to be patient annoyed her, as no one 'began these weary years which close with the last day of this month, with more romantic determination to endure all things, than I did'. She was angry at being distanced from Melbourne and reminded William (about 1839) that she was Sheridan's granddaughter and would stand up to 'your jealous aristocracy' (Lady Cowper refused to receive her), threatening to reveal the hypocrisy and immorality of 'your "Great Society" – I will shew who is received & is not received at this virgin Court'.[37] In 1845 he sought to prevent her publishing correspondence with Melbourne.[38] Yet William helped draft and supported in the Commons, her bill to alleviate the position for separated and divorced women.[39]

William complained about the 'dusty desert of a London political life', but there was turmoil as the government floundered. 'If the aristocratical influence in our Constitution can not be saved we shall all soon go to the Devil,' Melbourne told his nephew, after a recent division on the secret ballot and the parliamentary Radical onslaught.[40] But the accession of Victoria gave the premier new opportunities. Thankfully, given that his father had just died, there was no opposition to William in Hertford in the general election that followed.[41] William told Lady Holland that the Whigs' small majority simplified the political game, less conciliation of the Radicals was needed, 'the House of Lords need not be threatened, or the Church attacked, but we may rest quietly within the limits of Moderation.'[42] This was the line taken by Melbourne, who had faced a House of Lords led by the Tory Lord Lyndhurst, intent on defeating government bills. Unpopular reform measures such as those involving the Church of Ireland and the New Poor Law, and an inevitable Tory revival, had reduced the government's strength. William believed that the next election must be fought with an improved electoral register, and that the

Whigs 'must get hold of a cry before another dissolution'.[43] Melbourne, by contrast, seemed to accept reliance on support from Sir Robert Peel and the Duke of Wellington, and disliked any reforming energy.

A greater challenge, to law and order within Britain, appeared with the emergence of Chartism in 1839. William contrasted the rousing of the religious world by the Puseyites (the 'Oxford Movement' identified with the Regius Professor of Hebrew at Oxford, Edward Pusey) with the Chartists in the political, describing these to the Duke of Devonshire as 'operative Jacobins'.[44] He had earlier, in a letter to Lady Holland, talked about 'the mob' agitating against the New Poor Law, so his prejudices seem clear; his uncle as Home Secretary showed no meekness in dealing with the Tolpuddle labourers (and William displayed no sympathy for them) or the Swing rioters in rural England during the parliamentary reform crisis.[45] In criticising opposition to Whig educational reforms, he spoke of thousands raised ignorant of their interests, duty and themselves, 'if such a population were led away by the stage-antics of a madman, or fall prey to the harangues of visionary revolutionists, and burn and pillage, and like demons practise mischief for its own sake, and become a curse instead of a blessing; upon whom should the blame fall[?]'[46]

William supported the proclamation against torch-lit Chartist meetings, in late 1839, believing 'they talk sad seditious stuff'.[47] When he wrote to Devonshire (travelling in the Mediterranean) in July, he sent a clipping from the *Northern Star* 'to show what the West Riding thinks of you and your love of insurgents, even Caucasian ones'.[48] Certainly Melbourne, who believed that the existing legislation merely had to be applied with vigour, was not sympathetic with the Home Secretary, Lord John Russell's approach. Melbourne's concern was for injured policemen, and damaged property and interests.[49] The one virtue he saw in the crisis was that Chartism also posed a threat to parliamentary Radicalism.[50]

Another public scandal during William's period as secretary was the affair of Flora Hastings in 1839. The Queen was concerned to sustain a new moral tone after decades when the royal court had been seen as a source of elite immorality.[51] Rumours that the Tory protégé of the Duchess of Kent was pregnant led to a humiliating examination by the queen's physician Sir James Clark, which proved her innocence, and an outraged family resorted to the press to defend their reputation and attack the Whigs. William told Devonshire the publicity was down to the girl and her relatives, she had 'behaved like an idiot, Sir J. Clark like a blundering apothecary's boy, and Lady Portman with the zeal of a dragon of virtue,'[52] and that he thought the affair would soon be over, and this proved true, as the poor woman died of a liver tumour. And scandal was produced by the estranged wife of William's friend the novelist Bulwer Lytton. Rosina's roman à clef *Cheveley; or, The Man of Honour* depicted Melbourne and Palmerston as Lords Melford and Protocol, and included the Duke of Devonshire, 'the only one of many people described who gets off well'. William told Devonshire women were in turmoil, the writer Harriet Martineau rousing her sex to crusade for further rights and privileges, and 'many female Radical associations are found in the country with groceresses for Presidents and staymakers for Secretaries – I daresay your housekeeper at Chatsworth is now haranguing the females of Bakewell'.[53]

By 1839 the government was deeply divided and in poor spirits. As William told Devonshire, the Whigs tottered 'and were it not for their constant luck, would soon be upset'. For the time being, they were sustained by the cowardice of the 'ultra-foolish Radicals', so 'the great Whig machine will hold together for some time longer but perhaps you will never see me a private Secretary again.'[54] Although Melbourne resigned, believing the ministry unsustainable, they returned in the ensuing 'Bedchamber Crisis'. This brought William to prominence, in circumstances which emphasised his place at the heart of Whiggery, and suggested willingness to misrepresent events to secure a seat. He exploited sentiments of loyalty to the Queen during a by-election brought on by his appointment (through another act of patronage, of course) as commissioner of Greenwich Hospital.[55] Since it was the only election in this period it was seen by William and the government's opponents as a test of public confidence. He told Hertford electors on 13 May that honour, loyalty and justice impelled him to support the Queen's noble resistance to the cruel attempt to remove her prerogative of appointing 'those Ladies of her Court whom, from their sympathy and devotion, and from long acquaintance, HER MAJESTY could look upon as friends'.

He withdrew this address when the canvass was nearly over, claiming to have written it when indignant and 'without the leisure to balance critically the words'. It served its purpose, however, and the election was fought over the Queen's right to act in the 'spirit of an Englishwoman', with the electors of Hertford called upon by William to be patriots. Graffiti proclaimed 'Vote for Cowper and support the Queen', and 'Cowper and the Queen of England'; his opponents claimed 'Places and Petticoats won't do here; no calico influence in England'.[56] *The Times*, hostile to the 'O'Connell Cabinet', condemned the campaign as dishonest, for Cowper surely knew that Peel's request for a change of Ladies to show royal confidence in him, was not improper or disloyal. William was advised by Melbourne to stick to generalities on further reforms in his campaign, merely showing the Whigs were anxious to do all that was 'really useful'.[57]

The Times suggested that his narrow victory at the poll against the local Tory landowner was due to secret service money. That he was

Melbourne's nephew, that he had been his private secretary, and that the office was in the Prime Minister's patronage, were facts alluded to in press coverage. As a result of insinuations, in addressing the electors as a successful candidate William stressed that he had no salary as secretary.[58] In fact, Melbourne was determined to avoid a defeat which would have been a crushing personal blow: 'You must not lose the election, if it can be possibly avoided – never mind a few hundred pounds, if necessary – I will stand up that, but take great care how it is employed.'[59]

He won, which gave the Queen 'great pleasure', but only by a majority of 19.[60] The incident had revealed William's questionable judgement and the role of corrupt electoral practices; and the press had not ignored the necessary intervention, at the last minute, of the Radical Thomas Duncombe (who had in fact just voted against the government).[61] His victory, uncomfortable as it was for Conservatives, could embarrass the government. The journal *Cupid* denied he knew anything about 'what took place in the Cabinet, of which he was not a member, and the deliberations of which are hermetically sealed against all but members', when he spoke to his constituents, but *The Times* thought this nonsense.[62] For *The Times*, though he was a 'personage of such small political calibre', he represented all that was wrong with the Whigs. *John Bull* harped on about William's boastfulness about twitting Peel. [63] While Hertford friends feted him, comments on Wellington in his constituency address required his mother to apologise to the Duke.[64] The outcome was more significant than electoral notoriety, however, since William's new work as commissioner of Greenwich Hospital involved visiting the school and marine asylum with the former physician, educationist and social scientist Dr James Phillips Kay (the future Sir James Phillips Kay-Shuttleworth), appointed assistant secretary to the Privy Council's committee on education in 1839.[65] This began William's long involvement in educational reform.

The Puseyite or Tractarian controversy in the Anglican Church, caused by the tracts by a number of clergymen in Oxford, alarmed the Evangelical William Cowper and his brother-in-law Lord Ashley. This was unsurprising, since Tractarians such as John Henry Newman had condemned Whiggish Erastianism, including the acts of episcopal preferment exercised by Grey and Melbourne. John Keble's sermon on 'National Apostasy' in July 1833, the conventional starting point of the Oxford Movement, was triggered by Whig reform of the Irish Church. When, in 1840, William articulated concerns about Pusey, Melbourne expressed indifference to Puseyite religious views on the Reformation, but concern about the interpretation of the Reformation's political implications in *The British Critic* (edited by Newman). William hoped his friend Richard Monckton Milnes would cease to write favourably about the Puseyites, as he was 'too much of a Puseyite for me and nearly as great a one as the *Times* – which is a little of everything'.[66] William had seen Tractarian and Evangelical opposition whipped up against the appointment of Renn Dickson Hampden, a liberal clergyman, to the Regius Professorship of Divinity at Oxford, in 1836. Melbourne insisted that Hampden take the post despite the extensive petitioning, protests and threats from opponents inside and outside Parliament.[67]

In June 1841 William became a lord commissioner of the Treasury, a junior post which went with being a whip in the Commons. He was to hold this only for three months. The Tory *Quarterly Review* cited this as one of a chain of promotions in the ministry's final days: 'Thus died, as it had lived, in mystification and corruption, the Melbourne ministry,' whose history was a 'Book of Job'.[68] Melbourne moderated William's address during the general election which the premier had reluctantly agreed to. Although accepting the shift towards reform of the Corn Laws as an issue on which to fight, he recoiled from William's talk of 'free competition' against Tory 'monopoly'.[69] William for his part defended his uncle from the charge of cooping up voters in Melbourne Hall and wished to use Court connections to get the Queen to accept an address from Hertfordshire, but she feared establishing a precedent for every place she happened to pass through.[70] Yet, desperate to keep her Whigs, she visited Panshanger, Brocket and other Whig houses to show support.

Despite this, in August the government was defeated. William wrote to Lady Holland, 'I do not feel duly sorrow yet, but I suppose I shall when the affair is consummated.'[71] He did not admire Sir Robert Peel, the Conservative leader. In 1837 he noted a snobbish comment on Peel's provincial dialect ('woonder') and resemblance to a footman in blue coat and metal buttons.[72] He described one of Peel's speeches as 'bolder and nobler than is usual with him', in August 1841 and later noted that Peel's wordiness and special pleading was due to preparation of questions as a counsel would for a brief, through departmental notes and blue books, a strategy which worked because the House was more ignorant.[73] But like Peel, William came to accept that the Corn Laws needed to be reformed, and supported a fixed duty by 1842 (in fact he had voted for William Clay's parliamentary motion, in March 1837), and characterised farmers as 'a thick-skinned set and nothing good is to be made of them'.[74]

William was without official employment for six years, until the return of the Whigs under Lord John Russell in 1846. But public duties remained and he chose, for instance, to support Peel over the controversial transformation of the annual grant to the Catholic seminary of Maynooth College in Kildare into a permanent charge, a triumph of Whig principles he said, but an affront to some Protestants. One critic responding to a letter William sent to a Hertford elector, condemned his distinction between 'the duty of men acting together for religious purposes and acting for political ones'. According to William, the 'nature of a Christian's work must vary according to the powers he is intrusted with and the charge he has to perform ... his task will alter according as he is acting in a State or in a Church'. As the critic pointed out, this meant rallying to the Protestant cause at Exeter Hall (where an Anti-Maynooth Conference was held in April), but voting in parliament for a measure because it was for the 'greatest practical good of the country'. How could a corrupt system of religion bring about good? Cowper was a 'double person, knowing truth when he is in Exeter Hall, but knowing nothing about truth when he is in the House of Commons'.[75] But for William, Protestantism concerned the private judgement of the individual conscience, and toleration of Catholic error in Ireland was similar to toleration of other religions across the Empire. He argued that the Reformation had never been vigorously prosecuted by the English in Ireland and that Protestantism had become merely an adjunct to the Ascendancy.[76]

The departure of the Whigs in 1841 meant William's distance from the Court. Never again would he be so close to the Queen. His movements had until this point been regularly reported in the newspapers' fashionable and court intelligence after he became groom-in-waiting in July 1837.[77] In this capacity William was in the fourth carriage after the Queen at her Coronation. He was a frequent dining companion before Victoria's marriage.[78] A friend observed: 'I have seen nothing in the newspapers but your royal attendance – Are you to be our King – There would not I think be a better selection and I should be very glad to kiss your hand on presentation.' William's amiable disposition and 'inclination to be satisfied with what is – and interested in what you undertake', meant, his correspondent suggested, that he would find courtly duties pleasant.[79]

He attended the Queen at Buckingham Palace, Brighton and Windsor.[80] Windsor, for an old Etonian, was of course familiar, as he told Lady Holland, he had 'spent a quarter of my life, (and a very pleasant quarter) near Windsor'.[81] Melbourne took the role of private secretary to the Queen, and as his private secretary, William's tasks included sounding out ladies for the Bedchamber or as maids of honour.[82] Tories might tittle-tattle about him as a prospective husband and Charles Greville might complain in his diary that he and other Whig 'favourites' lacked 'any superior qualities either natural or acquired'.[83] But as Leslie Mitchell notes, 'Victoria became an honorary member of the Lamb family.'[84]

William initially enjoyed Court life. In early August 1837 he told Lady Holland that he found dinner at the Palace 'very amusing', there were 'no scrubby people there – even Sir F. Watson no longer dines at the Royal

Table. The queen is very chatty and I half adore her already'.[85] Ten days later he noted that he was exceedingly fond of Court life, though he would have thought it one of the last things he should like. The Queen was fascinating, and the company – including maids of honour such as 'the butterfly Miss Cocks' – good.[86] He enjoyed the gossip, undercurrents and tiffs of the courtiers. 'What an odd account,' he reported, 'Baroness Lehzen has given tonight of her being nearly dead & returning to life, after that she says, one must be perfection.'[87] He told Lady Holland that the reporting of Baron Stockmar's status as confidential secretary 'should be contradicted if it were worth while, which it is not'.[88]

In November 1838, again at Windsor, he still found the 'country house sort of life' agreeable, with lounging breakfasts without the women, mornings riding or in the company of books and pictures, and conversation and chess in the evenings. Sat by the Queen at dinner, he found her talk 'very gay & agreeable'. They chatted about William Wilberforce and she told William that her half sister – a great admirer of Wilberforce – had written that politics and religion could not agree and that she had not answered that.[89] He found Victoria 'the most adorable little female of her dominions' and perfected the knack of entertaining the Duchess of Kent by simply inverting the word order of old jokes.[90]

As duties became boring, visitors brought variety to the *vie de chateau*, thus in October 1839 William recorded the Chancellor's gravity 'goes off in a merry twinkle', and noted Macaulay's delight at the removal, at last, of foreign quarterings – lilies and white horses – from the royal standard. William witnessed the 'Royal flirtation', which led to the Queen's proposal of marriage in mid-October. William thought Albert 'exceedingly pleasing' and Victoria's fond and gay manner pretty. She was 'in very high spirits & then takes such care of his health, recommends great coat & dry shoes with earnestness'.[91] But this 'incessant round of company gives me a wish to escape,' he wrote, 'to be alone to employ my time more profitably.'[92]

William's sister Fanny, a maid-in-waiting, also found Court life tedious, especially when Victoria became enamoured with Albert, who, though Fanny admitted his good looks, had awful ankles. She said Victoria was a 'little dissipated thing' for refusing to stay quietly at Windsor after Albert left but she became her bridesmaid in 1841 and one of her closest courtiers. William became an admirer of the Prince.[93] When he visited Hampton Court in August 1840 he thought the Prince displayed taste and feeling for art, and the Queen as much as could be expected.[94] They had already been in each other's company at dinners and the Italian Opera House, and later examined the royal collection of da Vinci's anatomical drawings together.[95]

The rest of this chapter considers William's life beyond the round of courtly duties, parliamentary tasks and work as private secretary to his uncle. He enjoyed – though not without Evangelical soul-searching – the pleasures of a young aristocratic bachelor in Society. Thus we glimpse him in the company of Mrs Norton, Edward Trelawny the friend of Shelley, and Mrs Leicester Stanhope, in the journals of the troubled artist Benjamin Haydon, who painted the young Whig – over 1835-1836 – in a tableau vivant of 'The Scotch Girl and Her Lover' (or 'Highland Lovers').[96] The artist later recalled William's Whiggish enthusiasm. The tableau presented a tartaned Mrs Leicester Stanhope modestly if slightly ridiculously posed, hand clasped by a man resembling a be-kilted Prince Albert.[97] Her husband, Colonel Leicester Stanhope, acted as intermediary between the Nortons. William played the part of husband in charades with Caroline and Mrs Leicester Stanhope, and the latter wrote to him flirtatiously.[98] Given the painting's theme, David Cecil's comment on William in his biography of Melbourne is apposite: 'an amiable youth who combined a fervent Victorian piety with a propensity to fall frequently and romantically in love.'[99] For flirtation was combined with qualms about the morality of fashionable life and off-putting public zeal.

One important relationship involving moral purpose was his increasing intimacy with the Duke of Devonshire. In early August 1836, writing from the Commons, William talked of sharing his journal with the Duke, who should 'certainly read whatever is in it, and when you please, for after your forebearance I feel I have no right to withhold it, even if there should be anything in it I should wish to conceal'.[100] Thus the Duke read of William's first encounter with mystical literature which stimulated a desire for *la vie intérieure*.[101] The Duke, with William's encouragement and an ear trumpet to amplify the service and sermons, was 'much more turned to religion', through visits to Beamish at Trinity Church.[102] Of Beamish, William wrote, 'he is the most spiritual as well as the most imaginative preacher I know.'[103]

There was also an increasing friendship with Harriet Leveson-Gower, second Duchess of Sutherland. When, late in 1836, William stayed at Chatsworth he found she 'excels in whatever it is that inspires esteem and awe, and is more agreeable I think, to converse with, than Lady H[arrie]t [Baring], although without the flashes which light up what Lady H says'.[104] The leading Whig lady, she became Mistress of the Robes in 1837. They discussed questions such as the future life; 'my admiration for her character,' he wrote, 'developed in a considerable degree my sense of moral beauty and continued to the enfranchisement of my soul.' To her conversation he attributed bringing out 'ideas which had before floated ineffectively in the brain without influence upon conduct'. But despite her tonic effect, he felt dull and thought he would be happier 'imbedded in books and speculation'. Perhaps it is of her that he said in May 1837: 'My regard for — is now undoubtedly pure & friendly, elevated, adoring & intense. She embodies to me some traits of the angelic character & her beauty is the beauty of goodness.'

Devonshire's relationship with Eliza Warwick reached a crisis in 1837 and he confided in William. Visiting Panshanger in mid-January, and finding Earl Cowper was 'in a very sad and weak state', the Duke went for a long walk with his young friend and then recorded that Billy had 'done me unspeakable good'.[105] Devonshire's diary is full of visits from William, the Duke seeing his 'grand official room' at Downing Street, William staying all day and reading, after services at Beamish's church, or dining and sleeping at Chiswick where 'we walked and read and he was pleasant as usual'. 'What a blessing that miraculous event is, come without a temporal cause, but the soil had been evidently been preparing for some time past,' William wrote, acknowledging his share in the Duke's moral reclamation. If it was 'above my merits, in sowing that seed,' he appreciated 'how fortunate to gain so sincere, so sympathetic, and so useful a friend'.[106] Under William's influence, the Duke went to church and received the sacrament.[107] The Duke commissioned Thomas Perronet Briggs to paint his friend ('picture vile', the Duke felt). And when Earl Cowper died in June, the Duke offered Chiswick to the grieving widow.

The sharing of diaries cemented their closeness but William's contradictions perplexed Devonshire, who confessed that he was in a 'strange conflict': 'I was exceedingly struck with your original view of things both in it and in our conversation out of doors – you have the best natural feelings and sense to know your difficulties, but I am tormented by the thoughts of your present danger.'[108] Devonshire worried about his spirit of justifying worldly intimacies and pursuits, and lack of method and constancy in prayer, 'it is as if you required excitement from new preachers and new theories to keep your devotion awake.' Given Panshanger's worldly milieu this was unsurprising.[109] However, Devonshire wrote, if balls and parties were not wrong, for someone whose religious inclinations were known in Society he was opening himself to attacks and lamentations. William did not avoid the 'impurities and unsuitable discourse' of one 'Lady S' and Devonshire was perplexed at the juxtaposition of fine and sublime thoughts with references to the charms of a dancer in 'Le Diable Boiteux' at the Philharmonic Concert. But perhaps, this was similar to William's profit from George Sand's work, the Duke thought.[110]

Just before Victoria's coronation, Devonshire wrote in a 'great fit of affection' having seen little of him, 'who constantly are dearer to me than anything in the world'.[111] When William spent some of September 1837 at Chatsworth, with Moritz Esterhazy ('clever dwarf', the Duke noted) he resolved not to abandon active life for contemplative solitude, and instead to educate himself, develop his resources and use his political advantages: 'Action is now my object. I have in the course of a few minutes become ambitious, not of new distinction, but of an advance towards perfection moral and intellectual.'[112] Such was his resolution but pleasant dinners with relations, Lady Mulgrave, and the Queen at the Pavilion followed.[113] Life there was 'agreeable and exciting. Every sort of success is pleasing and that at Court particularly so. I have the greatest enthusiasm and attachment toward my Sovereign'.[114] But regret about diversion from contemplation caused melancholy, and he reflected, 'I certainly have a distaste for ordinary fashionable society, and would much rather read or meditate – I am always happy when I'm alone.'[115] Yet in self-examination in 1837 he commented, 'a delightful and affectionate family, with many friends, as popular on the whole as I wish to be, for it is an odd thing, the knack I have hitherto found myself to possess of pleasing those I like'.[116]

One fashionable circle was the 'silver fork' novelist Marguerite Countess Blessington's, which William became associated with by 1836, dining with Benjamin Disraeli at her Kensington mansion, Gore House, and visiting with his friend Edward Lytton Bulwer – a close acquaintance of the Countess – in 1838.[117] William and his younger brother were sketched by the Countess's lover, the dandy Alfred Count d'Orsay, who was persuaded to marry Lady Harriet Gardiner, Blessington's only legitimate child.[118] Much scandal surrounded the ménage, but Harriet's future was to be intertwined, more happily, with the Cowpers.

FIGURE 2. William Cowper, lithograph by R.J. Lane after Alfred d' Orsay, 1842.
©National Portrait Gallery.

William's relationship with his father was distant (a diary in 1851 is unusual in recording the anniversary of his death) but dutiful. The Earl had been seriously ill for several years, and he was dying when William visited him in Putney in early June 1837. William walked with Scott in pocket over fields toward the pleasure ground at West Hill, reflecting on the 'Beauty of Matter independent of Mind' after seeing a gust-shaken horse chestnut tree.[119] What disturbed him, he told Devonshire, was his father's faith, 'Oh that his mind could have been enlightened as yours and mine have been to see the truth as it is in Christ Jesus and to know where and how to trust.'[120] The day after William IV's death, Cowper died 'without pain or struggle'.[121] William heard the bells tolling for the King and recorded the scene of a motionless Thames under grey and misty sky, with grief within and without, 'The load that weighs on our hearts in this cottage hangs upon the elements & over the force of nature.'[122]

Reading religious novels and studying Calvinism, William was in reflective mood, but he would shortly become immersed in more mundane political life, stimulated by the accession of a new monarch.[123] A month after his father had died, with Devonshire's backing, William completed an enjoyable three weeks canvass in fine weather at Hertford and found delightful repose to be 'at large in London again'.[124] 'When the whirlwind and the fever were over it was pleasant to ride and chat and sit with Maurice,' he noted, Esterhazy's 'spiritual career' resembling his.

In 1838 a fractured leg kept him inside for several weeks from early March and in crutches for several months. Lady Holland and Devonshire visited him, the Duke finding him in 'wonderful and in good spirits'.[125] He delighted in sparrows' song and opportunities for study, 'there are so many books I want to read, so many subjects I want to think and write upon.'[126] Wilberforce's *Life* was an alarming mirror in the great philanthropist's self-reproach about time wasting. When the leg refractured and swelled to a great size, his 'Patience and goodness beyond compare' impressed his ducal friend.[127] William recovered sufficiently to visit Chiswick in June, where he admired the tulips and female guests, and the next month chaperoned his sister Fanny at Almack's, the exclusive assembly rooms.[128]

With the parliamentary recess, William visited the Lake District and Scotland, travelling up to Birmingham by railway.[129] In the Lakes in that 'happy and favourite condition' of his, he felt close to God in contemplation of nature, rowing on Windermere and lying by its shore.[130] On a Scottish tour with his mother, he read work by the high churchman Alexander Knox and delighted in deer-stalking, telling Lady Holland that he thought he 'could creep about on the heather for a month'.[131]

When he visited Chatsworth in early November 1839 William imparted 'curious news': probably regarding his mother's impending marriage to

Palmerston. Melbourne was glad: 'It is the very best thing she could have done.'[132] But Harriet Granville reported her children's opposition; Fordwich declaring he'd rather be hung than attend the wedding, Fanny deeply hostile (such was her lack of respect for Palmerston that she had recently been amused at 'Cupid' being forced to dance with the Queen[133]), and William preparing to leave his mother's house.[134] Minny's response was probably different, for Palmerston was always affectionate; perhaps recognising she was his daughter. He sent 'Tokens of Recollection and Regard' from Paris in the new year of 1827 for instance, and was joyful to be able to 'gratify any wish' when it came to helping Minny.[135] Emily wrote of their 'liking and approving' her decision and that had they been hostile she would have abandoned it.[136] In fact Fanny was outraged at the pretence that they were favourable and the suggestion Palmerston was 'a very old friend of poor Papa's!'[137] She was converted however, partly by Palmerston's generosity when she needed financial aid. Palmerston told Minny in 1856, 'When I married Emily I considered myself as adopting all her Children as my own, and I have always felt for all of you the warm affection which belongs to our reciprocal Relations and which could not fail to be inspired by a Family so full of good and amiable Qualities and so united together.'[138]

'I am quite pleased with the Country and with everything, and feel much more inclined to be happy than I have now done for a great while, or indeed ever hoped to feel again in this world,' Lady Palmerston told William from her new home at Broadlands in Romsey, Hampshire.[139] She had thrown over all doubts and anxieties and looked forward to domestic comfort and consolation. William was apprehensive, perhaps even jealous, his 'wise and affectionate letter' sent with a ring, prompting the reply: 'I do certainly depend upon your affection, and it is one of my greatest comforts.'[140]

As Melbourne's secretary William had corresponded with Palmerston about political patronage, he came to admire Palmerston's policies and parliamentary performance, such as his 'brilliant and masterly speech' in April 1837 and vigorous policy in China and India in 1842: 'How universally events justify Lord Palmerston's policy – and how brilliantly all our transactions except those committed to Ld Ashburton have terminated.'[141] He noted that one did not 'hear so much fear of the war-like tone of the Whigs since it has been proved that war may be a profitable occupation and the only thing that leads to an extension of Commerce.'[142] In 1844, shortly after William had suffered a great personal sorrow, Palmerston told him he saw all Emily's children as his own, by adoption and affection, and that it was a great pleasure to find the same attachment reciprocated. It was a 'real Happiness to me [to] have as my Son a Person whom all who belong to him must be not only fond of, but proud of.'[143] William seems to have reciprocated and a close relationship developed, but nowhere is there a hint that William knew the rumours about his paternity. To do that, would be to acknowledge his mother's infidelities. In writing to his own adopted daughter, Juliet, many years later, he asserted that when Palmerston made him his heir and gave him his surname, this was 'without my being a relation of his by birth'.[144]

William's varied recreation is exemplified by his activities at the end of the parliamentary season in 1839. After seeing the 'adorable' Duchess of Sutherland at Stafford House, William headed for Cowes where he sailed.[145] At Blackgang Chine, natural grandeur, prayer and meditation made him resolve that Parliament should be used to 'bear witness to the truth ... and in some degree to reach my great object – utility'. He stayed at Castle Howard, studying the Canalettos and playing 'consequences, conglomeration and preferences'. At Chatsworth, where the Duke was practically alone, he took to the moor with a 'pocket full of Coleridge'. In Birmingham he studied the iron furnace at Lilleshall.[146] In December he was at the de Grey mansion of Wrest, 'a beautiful specimen of Louis 15th architecture ... without a fault', but he hoped, so he told Lady Holland, the neighbours would not think the decoration of the hall emblematic of the morals of the drawing room.[147]

At the same time, he made efforts to consecrate his life through the interdenominational London City Mission which sought to bring spiritual succour to the poor. In June 1840, he inspected one of his districts, depressed by the degradation in the heart of the metropolis: one poor fellow's wife had not touched food for a day and he could get no work, a room costing 1s 6d a week was unfurnished and 'throughout those streets, each room containing a family, many ragged, many sick, some dying, & the streets filled with thieves & bad women'.[148] But this visit to slums was followed by attendance at the Commons and the Queen's Ball where he waltzed with Lady Seymour (Caroline Norton's sister), 'gorgeous in a velvet tiara studded with diamonds'.[149] He had the melancholy pleasure of visiting the Duke at Chiswick in early July, where he read the poet Martin Tupper: 'he's for praying for the unknown who is to be one's bride – I prayed for her my heart pointed to – I wonder – and I trust – but why dive beforehand into futurity.' [150] Whitsuntide had been spent at Chatsworth, where he gladly kept the Duke company.[151] A centre for political society was the Palmerstons' mansion in Carlton House Terrace, and William was often present in the evenings, noting in his diary in 1840, for instance, that the French ambassador François Guizot looked at Princess Lieven (his mistress) like a 'cuffed old poodle', at one dinner.[152]

William indulged romantic sensibilities in the Lake District, travelling via Liverpool where he visited a mechanics' institute and a Unitarian chapel ('it's delightful to be able to join even here in prayer and praise').[153] Inevitably, he visited William Wordsworth at Rydal Mount, feeling as apprehensive as a dental patient beforehand. Wordsworth's monologue lasted three hours, William breaking in occasionally. The poet was a 'rugged, haggard man with eyes as deeply set into their sockets as a lobster's before they start from boiling, a skin tough & seasoned as Spanish leather, a scanty supply of greyish hair'. Wordsworth ranged over opposition to centralisation, stipendiary magistrates, church reform and New Poor Law ('here are 30, 000 men in Newcastle ready to rise in the first opportunity') and the link between mountains and great poetry. Wordsworth had seen all the lakes of Europe and 'classed them as completely as a conchologist his shells'.[154] William did not write extensively about Wordsworth's poetry, but one imagines that the poet's optimistic and irenic view of God and humanity was attractive.[155] Apart from this visit, William occupied himself with books and contemplation of Nature 'and Him of whom these and all creation speak'.[156]

William's subsequent journey into Northumberland struck him by the 'grandeur and solidity of our farm buildings many of them fit for a farming squire of property'. He thought the 'Bondages at work in the field' better off than southern freemen and recorded a luxurious middle-class lifestyle at one house he visited, 'dinner was as good & as well served by a tall footman as at any 2nd rank house in London.'[157] But how fond the women were of talking about the Queen! He visited Lord Grey at Howick, and was disappointed with the aged statesman. Grey was 'looking rather low in spirits & broken & droops his head & his voice is feeble'. He disliked innovation even though he led the race for reform all his life, even in farming he refused sub-soil ploughing and farrow draining and declared he would rather go to London by wagon than by railway.[158]

On William's return to the south he met various prominent Evangelical associates. On a 'useful and improving' visit to Sir Culling Eardley Smith at Bedwell, Hertfordshire, he met the Welsh Congregationalist Reverend Caleb Morris, and 'benefited immensely from his conversation, & learned as much in our drive in the pony chaise as in a month of study'.[159] Visiting Captain John Trotter of Dyrham Park, he saw the impact of teetotalism.[160] Trotter, an officer in the Second Life Guards, had become a Methodist, but supported the Church of England and paid for a church at Barnet whose first minister was a converted Jew, Alfred Myers. William was struck 'by his sedate, oriental manner, pausing before he speaks and rolling his eye-balls through half the compass'. This 'dancing young man about the Town' now led a district's reformation via teetotalism, which had improved the behaviour and material condition of labourers and directed them towards religion. William thought Trotter had taken Christianity 'into his nature without any other outward alteration, His phraseology is not altered, his manner is cheerful and simple, and the truths of religion are his household words. No forced gravity, no assumed decorum'.[161]

What a contrast, to spend a fortnight waiting on the Queen, the duty enlivened by the reappearance of the 'boy Jones', 'a cunning sharp good-looking little boy', who for a second time had slipped into Buckingham Palace and gone around the Royal Apartments 'from curiosity being anxious to see how things go on in a Palace', and who reminded William, when he saw him, of Oliver Twist's companions.[162] Christmas was spent at Broadlands, where the guests were 'ministers, foreign & domestic – my time not well spent'.[163] In January 1841 William visited the Ashleys at their house in St Giles, in Dorset. Given the sixth Earl's iciness towards his progeny the prospect must have been unpleasant but the earl proved to be 'particularly courteous, & his strange stories were amusing'. Despite his daughters' attractions, William thought, 'out damned spot, Minny is the most charming woman under the sun.'[164]

This visit was shortly followed by a meeting at Trotter's to convert the Jews. Then he attended the christening of the Queen's first child: 'The Babby behaved well & without a squall, the D of Cambridge much struck with the handsome wet nurse began some enquiries about the child: well, has she a good appetite.'[165] Attending parties at the Palace and Carlton Terrace led to a new resolution to avoid unbecoming and unprofitable social gatherings.[166] But it was impossible to keep, despite a fervour that led to unrestrained prayers in a carriage. His distraction provoked a guest at Panshanger to criticise his verbal tic of 'ah-yes', as well as his party spirit.[167]

The rest of the year passed in visits to the Sutherlands' remodelled Trentham House in Staffordshire, which William found exquisite, Evangelical projects, and visits to Chatsworth. Spending a Sunday in the rhododendron nursery after Easter, the Duke 'discoursed gravely', saying it was enough to get to feel ready to die, but William urged 'that you must daily overcome or succumb, that there is no time for cessation, & that you must beware of lying by'.[168] In the combat of a general election, Dyrham Park and Bedwell provided peace. If the subsequent loss of office meant no end to parliamentary duties, William also had duties to his uncle, whom he travelled with to Castle Howard in December.[169] Over the next few years William provided companionship, especially after Melbourne's stroke in October 1842 and a fall in April 1845, walking with him, reading him works such as Guizot's history of France ('curious though villainous,' William told Lady Holland), and writing correspondence.

In January 1842 William was again at Dyrham. His mother prayed for 'a strong sense and judgement to guard you against the excesses of enthusiasm and folly – into which so many of the best intentioned now unfortunately fall'.[170] But he continued to combine earnestness and frivolity. After a 'heart-stirring' meeting for Jews at Exeter Hall, William joined the 'Order of the German Quadrille', in the Queen's elaborate masque, designed to reproduce the costumes of the times of Edward II and so aid distressed Spitalfields weavers. One wonders how comfortable he was with fancy-dress philanthropy.[171] He joined the great and good (including Ashley) on the Committee of the anti-slavery African Civilization Society, seconding a resolution in honour of the 'illustrious Prince' [Albert] who had supported the society at its inception.[172] But that scurrilous paper, *The Satirist*, evidently picking up on gossip about his flirtations, asked in July if William, 'before he became a saint, ever read the story of Molière and Béjart? If not we recommend it to his perusal'.[173]

Trotter informed him of missionary efforts and in early August he embarked on his own during a tour of Germany, Italy, Switzerland, and France.[174] His companions and new acquaintances proved amusing and instructive, as he met religious people of all persuasions and was edified by conversations with Catholics, Greeks, Calvinists and Lutherans. He had no success with his 'Controversion' but 'they enlightened me a little with respect to the Romish faith.' This was noted in a book which served over the years to record the anti-Popish views of clergymen he heard.[175]

The Duchess of Sutherland had been the source of moral inspiration, as we have seen, and about this time, William received advice from a younger woman with an unhappy past. 'You ask me to tell you more about myself. There is little to say. I had a very retired life,' she told her 'truly attached friend'.[176] It was little wonder that she sought 'social oblivion', for this was Harriet d'Orsay, the notorious Lady Blessington's daughter, who had separated from her husband in 1831, only to find herself amid 'weary and complex litigation', after her Gardiner relations attacked her father's will and the court took over administration of the Blessington estate.[177] She became the mistress of the Duc d'Orléans (heir to the French throne), enjoying his protection until his death in July 1842. Then she turned Evangelical, looking after blind and elderly women, studying German with a Lutheran theologian, and dressing three hours earlier than formerly.

William's resolution to take a decided course, she warned, involved greater opposition than he imagined. She herself had been denied the status of Christian for wearing a feather in a bonnet.[178] She exhorted William, writing about the doctrine of assurance and a meeting at Trotter's.[179] From Harriet's letters (William's do not survive) it would seem that the correspondence dealt with spiritual matters, so that this does not seem to have been another of his flirtations. As it turned out, Harriet became his sister-in-law through marriage to Spencer in 1852, but in any case William was starting to give his attentions to another lady.[180] When he returned from the continent in early November he occupied his time partly in attending his invalid uncle Melbourne at Brocket (sending reports and gossip to Lady Holland) and partly amid the gaiety and religious services at the Noels' house at Exton in Rutland. But he was also becoming involved with the beautiful daughter of the wealthy banker Daniel Gurney. In December he was Gurney's guest at Runcton Hall, in New Lynn, Norfolk. What followed was the promise of marital happiness, but this was rapidly destroyed.

3

HUSBAND AND WIDOW, 1843–1848

At some point in 1842, probably before his continental tour, William met the beautiful nineteen year old Harriet Alicia, eldest child of Daniel Gurney of Norwich. Gurney was a brother of the prison reformer Elizabeth Fry and William knew their brother Samuel from work with the 'British and Foreign School Society' (which instructed children in reading the Bible through pupil monitors; Samuel was the treasurer). Daniel's family belonged to an elite of middle-class moral reformers rather than Whig aristocrats, but Harriet's maternal lineage – Daniel had married a daughter of the fifteenth Earl of Errol – meant she could be admitted into Society, especially as she had not been raised in the strict or plain Quakerism of Daniel's siblings.[1]

Harriet's first taste of the Season was in April–June 1842, when she went to balls and dinners given by leading members of the aristocracy, and delighted in balls at Buckingham Palace. William was at Court entertainments at the same time and appeared fleetingly as one of her many dancing partners, in her journal.[2] Harriet became acquainted with his circle after being introduced to Lady Jocelyn, the Pagets and Lord Melbourne.[3] Curiously, she even met a Miss Tollemache at an Ancient Music concert, destined to be her future husband's second wife.[4]

William could not avoid noticing the difference between Whig polish and the society at Gurney's house, when he stayed. He was horribly bored to begin with, ashamed of being so fastidious, like a white cat in a muddy road. But he appreciated Harriet's warm feelings and untouched heart. She liked reading, had a simple and unaffected temper, was charming, but knew her mind. She did not care for poetry and thought living in the clouds would be dreadful, 'but of course poetry cannot well be felt till the passions are awakened'. Though it was something of a touchstone for William, she was no devotee of John Keble's popular *Christian Year*, thinking it mostly unintelligent. Though parties amused her she made useful things such as babies' caps and was sensible about singing.[5]

William's Christmas was spent in Brocket with a visit from the 'Queenly Duchess', who was 'amiable as ever and fatter – with all her refinement and elevation of feeling she is a little in the world and I am getting confirmed in a thirst for spirituality to have my conversation in Heaven and alas in talk I am almost always led instead of leading – towards edification'.[6] At Chatsworth in January he claimed that 'the fine things give me no desires or regrets'.[7] Yet rumours circulated about his reputation and intentions toward women. William preserved a letter from one, 'Jenny', who felt she 'had taken *leave* of *you for ever*'.[8] William still enjoyed socialising, to Harriet d'Orsay's dismay, but he asked her advice about marrying, '& I presume,' she said, 'that "the charming devoted little girl" who converses "profitably" … is to be the individual who is only to go to balls for useful purposes'.[9]

With 'reports now so generally spread Respecting you & her', Daniel Gurney asked what William's intentions were and whether he could provide a comfortable marriage settlement.[10] An old family friend, the millionaire John Motteux, gave William £1000 when he heard about the engagement.[11] But William was not wealthy and his sister-in-law Anne tried to persuade Lord Melbourne to contribute to the sum William had fixed on. He thought it only a flirtation, especially as William had written about giving the 'thing up'. Scrawled letters cautioned his nephew to avoid flirtation if there was no intention to marry. Though he was glad that William was consoled by the epistles of St Paul to the Corinthians, Paul would disapprove of his letters being used in trifling with girls. Happiness was a calm, settled and satisfied state, unlike William's frequent change of objects, 'it lies in the knowledge of causes of things and in rejection by yourself of all vain and superstitious terrors.'[12] Melbourne thought 'as you *would* flirt you would be *caught.*' It did not help that Lady Palmerston had said William went to Runcton to see if he really liked Harriet.[13]

William thought that marital sympathy and union of feeling might lead to spiritual advancement and vigour and Gurney seems to have impressed upon him the fact that Harriet must marry a religious man to be happy.[14] Perhaps suspicions about William's commitment were justified. According to Anne Cowper, the marriage was promoted by Minny and Fanny, and William was 'comparatively a passive object in it for some time'. He felt that the marriage was God's will and that he had 'not sought it but it had come to him as it were'.[15] So there is no evidence that this was a love match on his part, as his second marriage was.

The engagement brought a happy response from Lady Palmerston, who declared Harriet was a 'very great accession to our family'.[16] Palmerston wished William as much happiness as his marriage had given him, 'for more it is impossible to say'.[17] Devonshire thought William had found 'somebody worthy of you, no easy matter in my opinion'.[18] Captain Trotter was suitably earnest against 'pay[ing] worldly visits "to shew her off" as it is called', and about her religious state.[19] Lady Palmerston passed on the Queen's good wishes.[20] William told Lady Holland that despite his bachelor habits he felt more light-hearted and joyous than fearful. Harriet had 'been very little out in the world' but she was a cousin of Jocelyn (Fanny's husband) and he was 'under the illusion that she is a piece of moral perfection & I am sure that she suits me perfectly'.[21] Melbourne, understandably, mourned the loss of constant and intimate companionship. 'No doubt it is a selfish view of the subject,' Lady Palmerston wrote, 'but we are all apt to be selfish in what concerns our own comfort.'[22] But Melbourne became reconciled to the marriage, and gave William money to buy his fiancée a gift.[23]

Harriet's voice is preserved in their correspondence during their engagement.[24] William wrote from the Commons where he was on a select committee on allotments and nursing a face swollen by toothache. He chatted about politics for she was 'willing to take [her] dose with a good grace', and told her about riding in Kensington Gardens, hearing the Life Guards Band and meeting her relations.[25] He joked about helping other people to marry.[26] He mentioned religious controversy such as Dr Pusey's suspension from university preaching and they discussed chapters from the Bible, William berating his careless, apathetic and theoretical response to sin.[27] It seems clear she loved William (she wrote of her happiness and that 'how much his being so really good, must add to that feeling'[28]), being terribly lonely when he was away and hoping she was 'worthy of all the very great kindness that all your family have shown'.[29] She was glad he did not take the general anti-Dissenter view on the education clauses to the Factory Bill introduced by the Home Secretary, Sir James Graham and cultivated an interest in politics, 'as I am to have the *good* fortune of being the wife of such a politician as yourself. I like looking at the bright side of things, which you say is your way.' If Lady Holland wished to see her, 'I shall be very glad to see any lady you like and wish her to see and like too.'[30] 'With rather a trembling hand and heart, I have written to Lord Melbourne, and hope I have said what I ought,' she told her Billy.[31]

William's friends and relations praised Harriet as charming, lovely and good.[32] Later Emily Palmerston told William that she had never doted before on any young thing that had not been her own child. Harriet 'was so Childlike, so loveable, so singleminded'.[33] Lady Holland wrote: 'They will not be rich, but in love, & good qualities.'[34] One of her good qualities was her piety: she talked often of heaven and seemed tuned to better things, a relation recalled, '& I have often been astonished to see with what *delight* she would leave the gay & cheerful party to converse on serious matters'.[35] Her mother had 'diffused her bright, loving and hopeful spirit through her husband's family' but had died in 1837. She often thought of her, but she was not maudlin; a relative described Harriet as 'that lovely, laughing, happy creature'.[36] Ashley was delighted in her, full of praise to God for her good principles and character.[37]

The marriage, predicted several weeks earlier in the *Morning Post*, took place in St James's Church in London on 24 June 1843. The *Age* had snidely reported the union with a wealthy banker's daughter, 'this noble family is always getting into one good thing or another.'[38] The honeymoon in Broadlands was intended by the Palmerstons to attach William to the place.[39] The Duke of Devonshire offered them one of his estates to use and William told him that honeymooning 'makes one feel quite young again and brings back boyish days in my old age'.[40]

But suddenly Harriet became seriously ill, despite port and quinine medication at Broadlands.[41] One of her relatives, the wife of the philanthropist and banker Samuel Gurney of Upton Manor, was shocked at her appearance in April. [42] She died surrounded by her family at Runcton, whence the Cowpers had journeyed a week before, on 28 August. Her relatives appreciated William's fervour, believing he had been instrumental in sustaining her faith, had displayed a generosity in sorrow and 'no ordinary character'.[43]

The Duke of Devonshire could not believe the news, which appeared in *The Globe*, *The Age*, *Standard* and other papers.[44] Harriet's death shocked Queen Victoria, who wrote almost immediately to Lady Palmerston from the Château d' Eu where she was visiting King Louis-Philippe, to express her sympathy 'for your poor bereaved son, whose grief must be heart rending, so young, so lovely, to be thus cut off in the midst of great happiness is very awful'. [45] Melbourne told the queen they were quite struck down, and that Harriet had 'promised to suit us all well, my sister particularly, and to be a great source of happiness and comfort'.[46]

The family rallied. William's elder brother and Anne invited him to Panshanger.[47] Anne and Lady Palmerston seem to have felt guilty that Harriet had not had sufficient medical attention.[48] Palmerston, Emily wrote, 'feels very deeply for you and we can think and talk of nothing but you'.[49] Palmerston offered reassurance that 'particular Calamities form but a Part of a great Scheme of good', trusting to William's strength of mind and character, and deeply rooted sense of religion, and speaking of his own grief when his sisters died. He invited William to Broadlands to be alone if he wished, though the place now had painful associations, 'that House is your Home, and there, you will, I hope, pass many Days in Time to come. I think there can be none with whom you would in present Circumstances feel more at ease, than with your Mother & myself.'[50]

William's calm resignation was punctuated by violent bursts of sorrow.[51] He thought of going to Cumberland alone, worrying his mother that he would unbalance his mind by contemplating the 'great objects of the Almighty'. She suggested he should have the company of a right-headed and religious person like William Wordsworth. Anne Cowper thought that as he always loved solitude it might help.[52] Georgina Cowper-Temple's bare record of her husband's first marriage said that he kept a 'holy and lovely memory' of Harriet.[53] Certainly he preserved mementoes and when he and his second wife tried to reach beyond the veil, through spiritualism, William was contacted by Harriet. But within a few months of the loss, his relish at the prospect of hunting at Broadlands, the very place of their honeymoon, disconcerted his brother-in-law, Ashley.[54]

William had briefly been in a world beyond the Grand Whiggery and he kept some ties with the Gurneys. [55] It may be that experience of Quakerism enhanced his spirituality, though he shortly characterized the determination to cut the world from their hearts as leading many Quakers to have 'severed only its pleasant amenities [,] its relaxing softness', leaving a 'hard incrustation of avarice & selfishness checking its pulsations & preventing its healthful action'.[56]

Devonshire offered Bolton Abbey as a refuge, but William left for Ireland, travelling via Belfast to the Jocelyns at the Roden mansion of Tullymore Park by the shores of the Irish Sea in Downshire.[57] Late in that year he was at Sheffield with William Wellesley, who 'was 10 years in obscurity and anxiety about his Soul'. They talked about religion and visited the Cistercian monastery designed by Pugin at Charnwood Forest in Leicestershire where he discussed mortifications of the flesh. Then he visited the aged prison reformer Elizabeth Fry, whom he admired, as well as being his former father-in-law's sister. She advised him to avoid being judgemental towards relations and others 'who are of the world'.[58]

William's private life in the five years following the death of Hannah Cowper is obscure. A few diary entries shed light on occupations and concerns. Without office from 1841-1846 he had time to assist schemes to alleviate material and spiritual poverty through allotments or 'self-supporting villages', his Evangelical friend Sir Culling Eardley Smith's Syrian Medical Aid Association [59] and church matters. He canvassed the Duke of Devonshire for a memorial in defence of the Church of England, looking to the laity to increase the supply of clergymen, and referring to the 'subtle Jesuitism of the Puseyite leaders and the silliness of their followers'.[60] After 1846 he returned to office in the junior capacity which suited his ambitions (see chapter 5). That he was not determined on remaining a widower is clear from hints of flirtations in his journal and correspondence. Within five years of bereavement he remarried; this time it would be a union of forty years.

In early 1844 William again visited Elizabeth Fry, who was in frail health.[61] Fry knew the Sutherlands and wished William to give her love to them when he visited, her message of love included 'dear lady Elizabeth': she was 'a nice young woman & I do believe serving the Lord ... I wish you to love Lady Elizabeth very much'. William evidently thought of Elizabeth as a possible wife, for he wrote 'I felt inclined to answer – I do love her perhaps more than I ought.'[62] But he was also in Caroline Norton's company over the summer, leading his brother-in-law to ponder the incongruity of a religious man enjoying expeditions with 'his uncle's real or suspected paramour', who despite her 'religious talk' had sent obscene letters to Melbourne and dallied with Sydney Herbert. Ashley grieved that William's weakness of head and heart meant he could never place the smallest confidence in him. Ashley had already been dismayed by William's volte-face over opposition to the Dissenters' Chapel Bill.[63]

In the autumn he toured the north of England with Ashley and Minny. From Worsley Hall in Manchester (seat of Lord Francis Egerton, MP) he wrote to his friend Richard Monckton Milnes, then addressing the Manchester Athenaeum, of Manchester as the 'Capital of young England and the scene of the Triumph of poetry over prose', with 'young England' having successfully introduced 'pitch and toss and other manly sports' into utilitarian Birmingham.[64] In early October he was with Kay-Shuttleworth at Gawthorpe conversing about the immoral and defective university training of clergy.[65]

In the following year, Florence Nightingale, whose family had an estate in the New Forest and were occasional guests at Broadlands, noted that William had 'an enormous quantity of interests and subjects'. She liked him 'excessively' and thought that though he had 'grown very serious', he was not at all gloomy. [66] He reflected over the summer about his mission to the working classes, 'I will now try to minister systematically to the spiritual needs of neglected Londoners,' and yet, 'I am not without ambitions or the desire to rise,' he noted.[67] However, earnest friends found his flitting between mission and fancy ball disturbing. At Dyrham Park in early August 1845, he heard their concerns, learning that whenever inconsistency was mentioned he was cited. Many of 'God's saints' were pained, with members of the London Missionary Society viewing his participation in the Queen's fancy ball on the day that he chaired their anniversary, as insulting the body of Christ. His picture in the *Illustrated London News* displayed a public professor of religion and supporter of Evangelical undertakings as a prominent mover in a frivolous *bal costumé*. He seemed to show that the religious could indulge in worldly amusement like other people, and if they had any object to secure. People lost patience with him: he should be one thing or the other.[68] The contrast was nicely expressed by the fact that a visit to Bedwell where he may have met Samuel Gobat, second Lutheran-Anglican bishop of Jerusalem, took place a week after attending the Disraelis' breakfast with Monckton Milnes and the Comte Louis de Noailles.[69]

His serious side was displayed during an autumn tour of Ireland. He made notes about the peasants and priests in his journal.[70] He was not merely an observer, for he tried to distribute Protestant Bibles to the peasants (at Cashel and at Lismore only Douai Bibles – Catholic translations – were accepted). He thought the Irish were 'chaste, honest, with a strong sense of responsibility for their daily conduct before God', as a result of the priests, but like the Pagans of antiquity their faith was at the stage of awe and reverence. The peasantry of Waterford 'might have been good looking if they had been decently clean', whilst those in Lismore reminded him of picturesque Italians. He learned about confession from a Catholic cabby who had been in the United States and was a good abolitionist. The people of Shannon were charming and 'intelligent with natural good-breeding, fond of the society of Gentlemen, never presuming in consequence of familiarity or in the least forgetting their proper place – very affectionate'. At Piltown in Bessborough he noted the fastidiousness of the occupants of the cabins about dirt, vying for a prize for the cleanest home. At Dingle he heard Father Matthew, the famous Catholic temperance lecturer. Having voted for the Maynooth bill in May 1845 – 'If I aim at practical good, I shall not find it it in leaving Maynooth in its present penury, degradation and discontent' [71] – he now found the college barrack-like as Peel had described it, with a filthy classroom, and 'sturdy, big calved students with gaiters hanging loosely about their ankles'.

The tour confirmed his prejudices. He thought the Irish were more concerned about land than the franchise ('Ireland for the Irish and our own again. What is that about your own. What do you mean. I mean my 10 acres 5 of which I already hould [sic]. Repeal is to give fixity of tenure – that is to say the land they hold and more besides'). He felt that the slovenliness he saw was by choice. The government could offer nothing to the priests who ruled the peasantry that they did not have, though ending the necessity for superstition on the part of their flock as a source of fees might be one policy: payment of Catholic priests would fortify the Protestant establishment. Agricultural societies would promote friendliness between landlords and tenants, remove politics and combine private or individual advantage with public benefit. Palmerston, he noted, thought the small farmers – those of 5 acres – were the most active and enterprising. In popery, he wrote, 'we see that natural religion which men have framed for themselves in the absence of knowledge of Revelation interwoven with those doctrines which have been revealed through our Blessed Lord and his Apostles.'

Tractarianism proved to be a stumbling block in his dalliance with another woman, possibly the Miss Isabella Talbot who was given the impression she was being courted.[72] When this relationship was over, Isabella thanked William for his religious conversations, and the 'sweet comfort of his prayers', but warned about trifling with hearts and the 'strange vanity in winning woman's love and then casting it aside that the world may see their triumph'.[73] The 'most unmixed happiness and deepest despair in my life have been caused by you', was her pathetic verdict.[74] But it seems William also paid attention to another lady in November 1846, meeting her at Bryansford Church (Tollymore), and visiting her at Chesham Place and in a drawing room at Carlton Terrace. Fresh topics and vistas appeared in conversation, though the acquaintance was slight. 'I am taken by an eyelid, I am borne away by smiles.'[75] He found she had a 'proper love of the arts, and decided and discriminating judgement upon pictures'. Who was this captivating individual? Was this a meeting with Miss Tollemache, living in Evangelical seclusion at Chesham Place? Perhaps it was another lady who was invited to meet William at Lady Mary Wood's.[76] Whoever it was, William was not entirely confident for several weeks later he thought 'it would be well to give up the occupations of domestic life and to employ the time so saved in teaching in schools or visiting the poor.' The romantic dream seemed to have passed, William believing he could never be anything to one who had the 'choice of wealth, lands, titles, social and intellectual notabilities'.[77]

William returned to public office following the destruction of Peel's administration in the aftermath of repeal of the Corn Laws, becoming a junior Lord of the Admiralty. William told Devonshire that he liked the Admiralty very much and admired Lord John Russell's statesmanlike pose, without the 'flummery' of Peel, who assumed a 'patronizing and reserved position, and supports the Government in a condescending tone'. There was also a dearth of parties and dinners, perhaps due to the Irish famine, and William felt a subscription of £120,000 'a good sum for the abused and hated Saxons to send to the proud and disdainful mendicants across the Channel'.[78] He had expounded to Devonshire on the Irish: they were so idle and confident of being able to bully that they made it a grievance to be obliged to work for the food that was given them and for low wages. They contrasted Peel's rash gifts of the previous year with the Whigs' more provident arrangements, saying Peel gave them grain, 'but now when we ask for food the Whigs give us the bayonet'. If William lacked the sympathy for the starving Irish that Ashley displayed at this time, and if his faith did not seem to be troubled by the scale of the disaster, his insensitivity was not uncommon. [79]

Trentham's charms in early February had an element of tantalization, perhaps due to an infatuation with Lady Elizabeth Leveson-Gower. After Admiralty duties and visits to Panshanger and Arundel, he was at Dyrham, where the Plymouth Brother Reverend Charles Hargrove was 'full of unction'. He was at Lady Olivia Sparrow's Evangelical dinner in early May with the Reverend James Haldane Stewart (an Irvingite), the Reverend Edward Bickersteth (a friend and important influence on Ashley) and Lady Sparrow's daughter the Duchess of Manchester, 'an interesting and sensible woman'.[80] Elections in July were 'very satisfactory barring a few disasters' – with some 'desperate republicans having come in'.[81] In the same month he was transported into prayer at Covent Garden Opera House and thought that despite the prejudices of the leading Evangelical paper, *The Record*, if he were troubled like Saul with a dark spirit he would find solace here, only it would appear inconsistent if he was seen.[82]

In August he went to Castle Howard, with Edward Ellice, Monckton Milnes, Frederick 'Poodle' Byng (the youngest son of Viscount Torrington and a Society fixture) and others. Then he toured Scotland and the Hebrides.[83] He spent an agreeable New Year with the Duke of Bedford at Woburn where guests included Lord John Russell and Milnes.[84] But his performance in private theatricals was reported in the press, again scandalizing Trotter and other Evangelicals, as worldliness in one brought to a full knowledge of Christ. It was, they said, damaging to the cause of believers, but though William was sorry and wished to avoid future offence, he denied this recreation was wrong.[85] Yet he turned to more serious pursuits, telling the Duke of Devonshire he was sick of girls now: 'I have foresworn petticoats as they say on the stage.'[86] He heard a 'very clever and amusing' lecture on eloquence by the American Ralph Waldo Emerson, who found him courteous when they talked together at Palmerston's mansion in 1848, and he studied the phrenology of Cornelius Donovan.[87] He met the reformer Dr Hodgkin, who was pleased about the recognition of the independence of Liberia, the state for freed slaves.[88] He breakfasted with the Disraelis and met Guizot.[89] In September he holidayed in Edinburgh before visiting Albury in Surrey (where Henry Drummond the banker, erstwhile Tory MP and founder member of the Catholic Apostolic Church in 1826, lived) and attending an agricultural dinner with Monckton Milnes and the journalist Albert Smith.

Then, in mid-October he was at Helmingham Hall in Suffolk, the ancient seat of the Tollemaches. He rode in rain and hail with the youngest sister of his host, Georgina, who in her ermine-bordered purple tunic and tawny wideawake seemed to William the 'equal to la belle

Isoude'. As they went helter skelter through the puddles they managed to talk pleasantly.[90] Georgina, at twenty six, was ten years the junior. He had, he told a friend, fallen 'over head and ears in love' with her.[91]

His delighted mother told William that Palmerston was pleased 'for he has the same affection for you & all my children as if they were his own'; Palmerston wrote 'if you bring us a daughter endowed with the same fine qualities of Head & Heart which we prize in our sons you will add to our Happiness as well as to your own.'[92] Lady Palmerston claimed her brother was 'very kind & amiable' because he had known Georgina's mother and admired her 'in her *beaux jours* as well as her Sisters & feels therefore as if he was acquainted with the family and that it was no news'.[93] But Melbourne, in declining health, was far from ecstatic in his response, telling William in a failing hand that 'If you had asked my choice beforehand, not knowing the Lady I could have given none, & now you tell me of the matter as a fait accompli make no observation.'[94]

4

THE CHILDHOOD OF GEORGINA
AND A NEW LIFE

The lady William chose as his second wife was a fascinating individual, fulfilling Palmerston's hopes for his stepson. She was born into a family with colourful antecedents and notoriety due to the behaviour of several of her sisters. This chapter explores Georgina Tollemache's background before providing a narrative of her early married life.

Georgina Elizabeth Tollemache was born in Englefield Green in Surrey in October 1822.[1] She was the 'admirable daughter of an admiral', for her father was Vice-Admiral John Halliday, later Tollemache. Her mother, Lady Elizabeth, daughter of the third Earl of Aldborough, was sixteen when she married and Georgina was one of nine daughters and three brothers born between 1797 and 1822. A Tory who stood as a radical candidate for parliament in 1833, in order to provoke his neighbours, John Tollemache was vigorous and virile and ruled his family with a whip. He was also an Evangelical. He died at the Tollemache mansion in Piccadilly a couple of months after the Earl Cowper in 1837 at the age of 65.[2]

The Tollemaches had become wealthy through estates in Suffolk, Cheshire, Northamptonshire and Antigua. John Tollemache was the sixth Earl of Dysart's nephew and inherited most of the Tollemache estates. Georgina's family could claim an ancient if not more distinguished lineage than the Cowpers and Lambs, in their pre-Conquest ancestry. A curse was said to have left the family undistinguished but unharmed through the centuries: though an inscription in Helmingham church stated the Tollemache name had 'been always unfortunate'.[3] By contrast, Georgina's grandmother, Elizabeth Stratford, Countess of Aldborough, had been distinguished for her eccentricities, outspoken language and a sense of humour characterized by Captain Rees Gronow in his reminiscences, as 'cynical naïveté'.[4] She was banned from court functions by William IV due to her coarseness. She had been the mistress of the Lord Lieutenant of

Ireland, Lord Westmorland, and was a friend of the Duke of Wellington and King Louis-Philippe. In Paris from 1814, her correspondence with Louis-Philippe about the threat of an Anglo-French war appeared in *Punch* in 1844. She died, probably a nonagenarian, in January 1846.

FIGURE 3. Helmingham Hall, a Baxter print from F.O. Morris, *A Series of Picturesque Views of Seats of the Noblemen and Gentlemen of Great Britain and Ireland* (1884), vol. 3, facing p.20.

Georgina's childhood was isolated, following her mother's withdrawal from Society. Lady Elizabeth had moved to 17, Chesham Place, a new mansion in select Belgrave Square. It was a quiet 'household of faith' in which Georgina had her beloved mother and a 'good many devoted friends' for company, but they were all female. Georgina's sister Charlotte and sister-in-law Georgina 'led me to pray', she later recalled. [5] The youngest of the children, Georgina was made to feel anxious about the propriety of going out in the world, by her mother and Evangelical sisters, while more worldly relations thought it unfair that she should be kept in.[6] On the few occasions when she was allowed out she was made to feel guilty or endangered and she attended no ball or theatre. As Lady Holland, who happened to be an old friend of Lady Aldborough, told her son, this upbringing 'in quiet very strictly' followed her mother's fright at the misdeeds of many of her elder sisters.[7]

Georgina's second sister, Emily, was one reason for her mother's fright. She eloped with Charles Tyrwhitt Jones of the Brigade of Guards. Emily's daughter was brought up with her aunt Georgina, who was almost two years her junior.[8] Another troublesome daughter was the fifth, Selina, who eloped at seventeen with the handsome William Locke, formerly in the Life Guards, whilst the family were at church, as Maria Fitzherbert told the Prince Regent.[9] The ensuing marriage was short-lived as Locke drowned in Lake Como. Their child married an Italian nobleman.[10] But it was Georgina's eldest sister who caused the greatest public scandal. In the early 1820s Elizabeth committed adultery with James Thomas Brudenell while married to Captain Frederick Johnstone, who charged Brudenell with debauching his wife. The legal proceedings were reported in *The Times* and the marriage was subsequently dissolved.[11] The 'most dammed bad tempered and extravagant bitch in the kingdom', according to Johnstone, she married Brudenell in 1826 and in the year that her father died he became Earl of Cardigan and as such gained 'Light Brigade' fame. The marriage was unhappy; Elizabeth had affairs, separated from her husband, and died in 1858.[12]

Two other sisters married deeply religious men. Jane married George Finch, the illegitimate son of the Earl of Nottingham, in 1826. He was, as Lionel his nephew by marriage recalled, an otherworldly religious character. Marcia married Admiral Frederick Vernon Harcourt of Nuneham in Oxford, who was the fourth of the sons of the Archbishop of York. Georgina recalled her as the 'dearest and most devoted of sisters'; her nephew Lionel described Frederick as his holiest uncle.[13] Frederick taught Georgina her first hymns.[14] The sixth daughter was Marianne, known as 'Mummy', who married Hubert de Burgh of West Drayton in Middlesex, and was a friend of Augusta, Duchess of Cambridge.[15]

Her eldest brother, John, first Baron Tollemache, was a puritan like his father. The heir to the last Earl of Dysart, John inherited Helmingham in Suffolk and the Cheshire estate of Peckforton, where he built a castle designed by Anthony Salvin. He fathered twenty-four children, represented Cheshire from 1841-1872 as a Tory MP, and acted as a paternalist on his large estate.[16] Georgina's other brothers were Wilbraham, of Dorfold Hall in Cheshire, who devoted himself to horses and played little part in Georgina's life, and William Augustus, known as Augustus, soldier, diplomat and then Treasurer of the County Courts through Georgina's influence with Palmerston, and who, her senior by five years, was always close. 'I *have* a feeling towards you,' he wrote in 1848, 'apart from the love I bear others'; in 1852 he told her 'I cannot look forward to anything in life beyond you.'[17] In a memoir published after Georgina's death, Augustus recalled that she had the family's 'effervescence of temper'. He, if phrenological examination is anything to go by, was also assertive, forceful and intrepid, with a 'talent for any kind of artistical invention, of a very extensive kind', but lacked 'any strong degree of love for children'.[18]

The phrenologist who examined Georgina in January 1845 said her mind was very large, indicating mental strength and energy, but that she could strengthen concentrativeness by reading whilst listening, her amicable feelings being very developed she would like old friendships and scenery. 'There is here a tendency to analyze well the state of the future, before giving the adhesion to any particular theory, or opinion. There will be clear perceptions of the nature, and applications, of the doctrines of

Ethics ... There is a very fertile and intuitive imagination.' Purportedly gleaned from cranial bumps, the snippets of information and perception about the young lady's intellectual tastes and forceful personality had produced an analysis not without insight.[19]

Her intimate female friends included Julia Tomkinson, sister-in-law of her brother Wilbraham. Julia married the Liberal politician Henry Rich, later baronet, of Sunning in Berkshire. When Georgina became engaged, Julia wrote, 'how we are to improve each other in the way of advice & contradiction as we have done I can't think.'[20] One glimpses through Julia's engaging letters, their intellectual curiosity and unorthodox piety: identifying with the controversial theologian F.D. Maurice, rather than accepting Calvinist belief in man's complete depravity, for instance. Another influence was John Tollemache's first wife, Georgina Louisa, who died in 1846.[21] John had adored her as the pattern of a Christian. As one son recalled, 'to have known her was a Christian education': he traced the Evangelicalism which 'overspread our family' to her. John and she made their home welcoming to Georgina.[22] Augustus' wife Marguerite (known as 'Magsie') was another important figure, in Georgina's adolescence and adulthood. Marguerite was a niece of the Countess of Blessington and stepdaughter to Charles Manners-Sutton, Speaker of the House of Commons. Intelligent and beautiful, Marguerite shared Georgina's mysticism, and was, according to Georgina, 'the ideal of womanhood' in the opinion of her future husband, William Cowper.[23] The pretty and gentle Marguerite became close to Georgina before she married, telling Georgina that she could 'never love as I have doted on you – never be with another as I have been with you'.[24]

In 1840 Georgina went to Rome with her mother: as this was the first occasion she had been out in society, she knew no one. Instead she looked round the galleries, antiquities, and churches. At the church of Santa Maria d'Aracoeli she was watched from afar by John Ruskin – then on a recuperative break from study at Oxford and romantic disappointment – who fell in love with her, 'a fair English girl, who was not only the admitted Queen of beauty in the English circle of that winter in Rome, but was so, in the kind of beauty which I had only hitherto dreamed of as possible' and he spent the winter in following her.[25] Augustus recalled that Georgina was not particularly beautiful as a child, but she blossomed into the 'loveliest of the Tollemache sisters'.[26] The Reverend Sydney Smith apparently called her the 'Evangelical Beauty'.[27] Certainly Lady Holland called her 'beautiful' in 1844 and her ethereal looks attracted Queen Victoria, who saw her at the opening of Parliament, and invited her to a Court Ball. She went to the Powder Ball in a costume based on one worn by her grandmother Lady Carteret.[28]

These rare forays into Society brought her no enjoyment because of her Evangelical sisters' disapproval and her own morbid sensitivity and shyness. But she could not accept unquestioningly the Evangelical horror of Society and became doubtful about the compatibility of a loving God with such fears. Evangelical desire to honour the Sabbath meant cold meals, and in reaction she determined never to have cold Sunday dinners when she married.[29] Her perplexities worried acquaintances. One, Leila Murray, stressed the blessings of a simple faith where reasoning was laid aside and hoped that she would become a 'happy *simple-minded* follower of the Lord Jesus'.[30] The vicar of Helmingham had 'many great searchings of heart' about her soul, too.[31]

It was unsurprising when Georgina, raised in a cocoon of female Evangelicalism, saw William Cowper's arrival as a form of liberation.[32] Appropriately, he fell in love with her when he saw her at church and their acquaintance developed in Sunday night walks from St Michael's in Belgravia.[33] They met at Bible readings, at the Noels' house at Exton, and at Brighton, where the Tollemaches had a house.[34] They may have met, indeed, years earlier, for a somewhat garbled account in a letter from Georgina's friend Portia Galindo referred to an encounter between the 'fair child just arisen from infancy and this youth just advancing into manhood who met at Brighton at his Tutors'.[35]

Four days after William's arrival in Helmingham, on 20 October, he proposed. What he thought of Georgina before his proposal is recorded in appraisals preserved with correspondence congratulating her on the engagement. There was as much charm and liveliness as he required, he wrote, and right feeling and good sense. She showed unselfishness and devotion to relations. The only thing wanting was more cleverness and power in talk. She was not a person with whom he could talk continuously, with whom fresh vistas and new openings would appear, whose talk would stimulate his mind. William was dull with most people, but with some it was not so. But here the dullness was mutually present. He heard no flutter of heart, no yearning or impatience for the presence, no void, no waking dreams of Elysium. But there was regard and gratification, and a pleasant laugh rang in his ears. Might one look there to a quiet and useful life, without much poetry or romance but with comforts and elegances? Here would possibly be a better sphere of action than a more imaginative existence might produce. She was singular in opinions but so was he. Fond of study, she had been left to follow this at her own discretion and was ready for, and attracted to, all new and striking theories. She was addicted to solitude and liked scenery. Her life of reflection and listening probably contributed to a modesty or inexperience that made her reluctant to deliver her views as if they mattered.

In another appraisal William noted Georgina's Tory attitudes towards monarchical legitimacy and sympathy with both the ideas of the Broad Church Thomas Arnold *and* Roman Catholicism. Seclusion had preserved the purity and winning charm of a child, but she had adult gravity and sense, and looked heavenly. If 'love, joy, peace, gentleness, elevation beam from her countenance', and views on spiritual matters were sound, she had a little of the usual indistinct apprehension of the undisciplined female mind. She liked and understood poetry (including Keble's *Christian Year*, that touchstone for William) and would be a charming and easy companion for a husband's leisure hours. Her superior mind, strong character, vivid imagination, ambition of usefulness and consciousness of mental power were noted. She was restless and energetic rather than calm and patient – how true this verdict was! Also true was the comment that she wanted to 'do good not only in the narrow circle of domestic life but in the wide arena of a Nation, to fix an impress of good for far & wide. To help in the reformation of society in the extension of the Kingdom of Christ'. On the other hand, her 'logical and disputatious faculty' was exercised more in conversation than in religious belief and William recorded 'submission to the claims of the church and a preparation even for Popery', though he thought this rather the 'strong grasp of a great principle, than the want of passive leaning upon an infallible Priest'.[36] The high church Duchess of Sutherland was unclear about this point when William told her, 'You think she is inclined to Roman Catholicism in our church but you do not mean that she has left it?'[37]

Writing to the Duke of Devonshire from Helmingham, William said that he had been 'rattling the dice Box of life and am just going to make another throw for domestic happiness'. His betrothed had 'kept aloof as you know, from Balls and parties, and this at least has had the advantage of preserving unsullied the most pure, angel-like nature I ever met'.[38] The marriage was welcomed by Georgina's friends and family. 'The *clouds have passed away from you dearest, & may they never return* for I know they have *often hung very* heavy over you & pressed you down,' wrote one friend.[39] Her Evangelical sisters approved of William. Her sister Lady Cardigan said she knew this event had been 'the long treasured secret wish' of Georgina's heart.[40]

Naturally, given the intimacy of the relationship, Augustus felt saddened: penning her a letter on the night of 20 November which was 'the last I can write, with the same feeling of entire and full affection' and telling her that if her marriage proved less than happy she could 'come back to one who has doted on you – & who will make his House yours & love you again, as he has done these many years, with all the fondness of his loving Nature'.[41] As he told his mother, they had been 'first in her affections' and the marriage represented a loss for him, and for Lady Elizabeth, 'the last of your children, and the one who has been as we must all feel, more to you than any of us'.[42] For Augustus, it was 'not *quite* the marriage I shd have *chosen* for the handsomest & the one I love the best of all my sisters'.[43] Several letters of congratulation also asked what Lady Elizabeth would do without her 'peculiar treasure'.[44] Georgina joked that they would not realise what a treasure she had been at home until she was gone (here was a hint of the self-regard which Georgina sometimes revealed in letters and diaries).[45]

John Tollemache, a Tory like his father, had doubts about William. William's religious journey took him away from his brother-in-law's stricter Evangelicalism and John perceived inconsistency and a lack of commonsense.[46] He was pleased when William agreed to Harcourt as a trustee for the marriage settlement, as he was a 'very proper person, and has always taken a great interest in Georgina', but needed to be persuaded by Marcia to attend the wedding when William's impatience led to an inconvenient date being selected.[47] Speedy marriage was made possible by Spencer Cowper's present of £20, 000.[48]

A miniature by the fashionable Scottish artist Robert Thorburn shows her beauty at this time: a determined chin and strong forehead, darkly intelligent eyes and light brown hair. If she seems a very mid-Victorian type – a slender version of Sir John Tenniel's Britannia – she was no insipid angel. There is an air of authority, hardly surprising for a member of an ancient family. Another portrait, a profile by Augustus, depicts sharper features and the Tollemaches' aquiline nose and forehead.[49] No description survives from this period of her voice – an aspect which in general we know too little about – although an American friend many decades later described a 'gentle patrician voice'.[50]

We cannot fully appreciate the early years of Georgina and William's marriage, from late 1848 to 1859, but fragments of diaries and letters allow glimpses of their private activities, interests and anxieties as well as their public lives. William believed that 'a wife should be wings to a man, to help him upwards'.[51] He had specified his perfect wife as 'something between Mrs Norton and Mrs Fry'.[52] Like the marriage of William's mother to Palmerston, this was a close and happy union, as numerous affectionate notes written by William, the letters of desire for her when they were parted, and Georgina's journals, demonstrate. They were rarely separated for long, except when family crises called Georgina away. Of course, William's duties as MP, junior minister and magistrate, meant absences. In one letter from the Commons in 1855 he said that he looked to her as spur and counsellor in redeeming lost time for 'acquaintances filch away a good deal and then if I try to keep it up late at night I fall asleep'.[53] Nor was Georgina confined to her new family, for life was partly organized around her circle of female friends, frequent visits to her mother, sisters and relations, and philanthropy. In a letter probably from 1854, enjoining his darling not to fatigue herself, William added, 'but keep yourself beautiful and strong as in duty according to Ruskin'.[54]

One extensive absence, as we shall see, which generated many letters from William, was when Georgina went to Edinburgh for medical treatment in the early 1850s. She worried about the trouble caused and asked if she was worth her board and lodging, he replied she was worth more than the mines of Golconda and pearl oyster banks of Demerera. She was a better Doctor of Divinity for him than Candlish or Baylee, he liked her histories better than Macaulay's and Alison's, her chat better than Lady Ashburton's or Thackeray's, and her own little self better than all the multitudes of individuals that he had seen.[55] He desired her soft cheek on his breast, her smooth silky hair between his fingers, her wise words and elevated thoughts breathing melodiously in his ears, longed to clasp her dear and slender waist and feel the palpitations of a fluttering heart.[56]

'I agree with Hahn Hahn,' William wrote about 1853, referring to their reading of works by the German Ida Gräfin Hahn Hahn, 'and I admit the great moral superiority of the fairer sex though that very perfection is sometimes inconvenient. If I were to compare my love to yours I should say it moved steadily along like a fish in the water while yours soars like the Lark and whirls like a swallow and pounces like a hawk charming and beautiful in all its variations'.[57] Georgina thought her husband an 'angel of kindness and comfort', in whose company she would 'never be anything but glad & thankful'.[58] Lionel Tollemache quoted Tennyson when recalling his aunt and uncle: 'As the husband is, the wife is.'[59] He thought his uncle was 'hen-led', though not hen-pecked.[60] Ruskin, in his *Praeterita*, said that Georgina always had her own way.[61]

An interesting sidelight is provided by analyses from the well-known phrenologist Cornelius Donovan. If they lack scientific value their perceived accuracy in delineating character and intellect was crucial to the pseudoscience's credibility and William's probity and philosophic cast, his want of spirit and ambition, were identified if one ignores the sham science and fawning.[62] Georgina's strength of character and religious doubt were also apparent. Donovan discerned a heroically developed head for a female, its upper regions lofty, perhaps too metaphysical and speculative and needing less frequent and lofty flights. Donovan reported '*Perhaps* Firmness is too strong – *perhaps* control, & denial are not well borne – Perhaps the desire of my Lady to be my Lord – is sometimes strong – perhaps – while at the Altar Lady blushed at "Love" but whispered "obey."' Georgina 'cannot be that pliable, patient, submissive, self denying

Saint of a wife, that we often read of – and sometimes see, in real life'. Nor was the pursuit of character finished as a graphologist identified 'generosity so elevated & at the same time so judicious'.[63]

FIGURE 4. Georgina Cowper, by Robert Thorburn.
By courtesy of Lord Tollemache, Helmingham Hall.

William married Georgina on a fine winter's day, 21 November 1848. The Tollemaches' clergyman and friend, the Reverend John Charles Ryle, officiated at St Peter's Church in Eaton Square. They breakfasted at Chesham Place, where the door bell broke because well-wishers received half a crown every time they rang it.[64] Lady Palmerston was absent, feeling that the transition from Melbourne's sick room to a wedding would be too painful.[65] Georgina's family was tearful, as the succeeding day brought rain and gloom and they felt their loss, especially her mother and Augustus, who penned a sad letter from his club where he fled to escape her absence.[66] Marguerite mourned a 'portion of my own happiness'.[67] Mummy warned: 'if ever we see a cloud in your face – he will have that formidable Sisterhood he saw today all arranged in hostility against him.'[68]

After the wedding they visited Panshanger, where William said that his father had been one of the few men he knew who had enjoyed his own art collection.[69] His stepfather advised on a suitable horse for Georgina, sending his mare O'Brien.[70] Despite such kindness, it was a traumatic introduction to the Palmerstons and Cowpers. Harold Nicolson aptly described the 'sharp gusto' of the Palmerston circle: it was an environment alien to the young woman.[71] She felt a caterpillar among butterflies: years later, she remembered how ashamed she was amid a family of such beauty.[72] She found comfort in Sophia Noel, the Vicar of Romsey's wife, and her step-daughter Caroline. Gradually she was endeared to Panshanger as shyness warmed into friendship with William's sister-in-law Anne and as nieces and nephews became, in her words, 'devoted worshippers'. Henry and Florence (known as Dolly) were especially close to the UBs (Uncle Billys).[73]

Lady Palmerston reassured Fanny Jocelyn that, though Georgina was 'most amiable and kind and makes me very happy to see her and William so loving, and both seeming so perfectly happy', Fanny was not supplanted in her affections. Georgina was not very handsome but good looking enough and with a very agreeable countenance 'and so the more or less is of very less importance, and then she's very good, as Hawkey says, and that's of more importance. She plays well on the piano and is very cheerful.'[74]

Shortly after the marriage Melbourne died. The title went to his brother Frederick Lord Beauvale, a diplomat who had married Countess Alexandrina Maltzahn, an Austrian forty years his junior. Until his death in 1853, Brocket Hall was a frequent home for the Cowpers. Their own residence was a 'delightful little house' at 130 Park Street, belonging to the Whig politician Edward Ellice, son of Uncle Frederick's friend 'Bear' Ellice.[75]

The first year of marriage, almost blank in the surviving family papers, presumably passed in marital bliss. They took gallops like those of the previous year, 'helter skelter through muddy leaves, splashing through floods & galloping wildly' in Helmingham in May.[76] In July William was at Henry Drummond's house at Albury, before an autumn of Admiralty inspections.[77] Georgina stayed with Augustus at a little place on the banks of the Dee. In September, William met her at Carbogie and they toured the area, visiting Kinnaird at Rossie, Inverness, and staying at Dunrobin with the Sutherlands and their relations.[78] At Dornoch Cathedral William was taken ill with cholera – a year after the cholera reappeared in Scotland (there had been a major outbreak in London over the summer).[79] But recovering, they photographed by the sea, and toured Sutherland – notoriously depopulated of crofters by the Leverson-Gowers since the time of the first Duke of Sutherland – with rests at the homes of the Duke's agents.

In February 1850 Georgina hosted a dinner for the Duke of Devonshire at which her relations the de Burghs and Selina Locke were present, probably for moral support if this was the first occasion she had hosted a dinner for William's ducal friend. William's visits to Chiswick were less frequent.[80] At Easter they stayed at a hotel in Tunbridge Wells which had been graced by Queen Victoria in her childhood and found it very bracing.[81] In mid-July Georgina joined the fête at Holland House, 'given I believe chiefly to bring the feeling of the Beau Monde towards poor Ly H'. She met Lord Brougham there, looking odd with 'twinkling nose and his hat full of holes for ventilation', and she danced with William on the Upper Terrace as the moon rose. This was the time for sentiment, enjoying a moonlit walk among the trees, but she wrote, 'sentiment must be over for you Mrs C mustn't it? With one exception I hope.' But then William had gone to the tiresome House and she was writing to beguile the tedious hours of his absence. Truly, she reflected, solitude showed us what we should be and Society what we were. She had been good sitting over her book and working, feeling indifferent to the world and above Man's opinion. But, 'great was my fall when only gentle gales beat against me – I yield to exaggeration of nerves – My feelings to begin with are exaggerated and then my manner does them. – I know it arises very much from myself but [it] is sinful as it arises from self-conscious[ness] and Vanity.'[82] What the problem was, is unclear, but she was 'rather tiresome with d[ear]r Wm. He spoils me so much & makes my life such a luxury & I complain of the crumpled rose leaf!' Anyway, a tête à tête followed, reading the politician Plumer Ward's life and sitting on their balcony.[83]

That unsettled state in religion which friends referred to at the time of her betrothal, still tormented her. Following advice from the Reverend Joseph Baylee she saw Douglas 'the Evangelist' (Herman Douglas, a clergyman who had converted from Judaism, and friend of Georgina's from before her marriage[84]) and found his conversation helpful, as she had been 'hunting in my wretched heart in Vain all my life and waiting almost hopelessly for conversion ... I want a little devotional exercise for I have perhaps been given too much to controversy of late – or perhaps have not continued with it sufficient'.[85] Baylee delighted Georgina with his hopeful talk about the Church of England's destiny, but when Douglas returned, William was antagonistic about his plans, whatever these were, and Georgina prayed earnestly for light, 'we must wait and watch – if a tabernacle ... by man it sh. fall before the first stone, if of God...'[86]

They had a party in late July where guests came from High and Low Church, 'German School' and Plymouth Brethren, with Baylee as the no-party man in the centre. But Georgina wanted more than 'outward expression and talk and controversy'. She copied William's habit of weekly self-examination. She thought she should believe in him, though she was 'quite atheistical'. She berated inattentiveness during family prayers, 'strange with my unbelief am constantly looking upward for help & guidance', and felt she should honour her mother more. She confessed love of popularity and envy ('rebellion against God because he has been pleased to withhold some gifts I covet f[ro]m me[.] Envy in consequence towards those who have them') but admitted little understanding of bodily intemperance.[87]

Whitsuntide was spent in Albury[88], before visiting friends and relations (the Beauvales, Chatsworth, Alton Towers, and then tripping the light fantastic to a village band at Melbourne) in August.[89] William contrasted the dim galleries, heraldry and grotesque ornaments like the 'creed of the dark ages' of the gothic Alton Towers with the 'clear bright joyousness' of classical Chatsworth.[90] After visiting Portsmouth docks, they journeyed on the Admiralty steam yacht *Black Eagle* to the Channel Islands where William continued official inspections. Georgina read Shelley in the moonlight as they sailed to Dieppe in late September. She recorded observations on inhabitants and visitors ranging from the sharp and superior to self-deprecatory. 'William as usual met acquaintances,' including a Pole, Count Zamouiski, who entertained them by describing the recent war in Hungary and analysing Lajos Kossuth's character. William met his friend Moritz Esterhazy's brother Paul, who it transpired had known Georgina in Rome in 1840; a hero in the Hungarian war, he was 'now obliged to travel'.[91] Georgina was impressed by the gorgeousness of the Catholic mass, struck by the contrast it made with working-class hovels, and reflecting that in this elevating effect, 'the superiority in the manners of the lower classes here and in Italy over ours may thus be sustained'. They travelled to Rouen, Bayeux ('Saw the Tapestry – Very amusing and full of movement and expression,' Georgina noted) and Cherbourg before returning to London.[92]

The major public event was the 'papal aggression' scare when the Pope assumed territorial titles in Britain, Georgina noting with displeasure the 'rascally mob' surrounding the 'high Anglican' church of St Barnabas. Lord John Russell's 'Durham letter' had stoked the fires of anti-Catholicism, though he had largely been anxious about Tractarians. Georgina thought the public had been thrown into a state 'bordering on madness' as 'Volcanoes of Protestantism … burst open with fury in all parts of England'. It included Fred Harcourt her brother-in-law, shaking the platform in public meetings, and even Billy threatened the demonic church at Hertford; a Protestant Alliance was established against popery in

1851 under Ashley. Though Georgina admitted to being as wild as anyone else in her own way she was inclined 'to welcome any Christian who have any share of God's love and light' to carry into the frightful darkness and crime of London.[93] Looking back in 1889, she wrote that the episode had had 'a good deal of the hue of the Fifth of November'.[94]

In December she wrote: 'We have had more public excitement. We have been on the verge of an European war if I am not boasting too soon even now, in speaking of it in the Past tense.' But, 'after all, the events of one's family and private life are so much more interesting to a woman and these public ones wd not I suppose excite one so much but for the electric chain wh binds us all together, so that the smallest quivers when the heart is touched.'[95] The events of her family life included Augustus' departure for a post in Berlin and her own enforced rest at home for six weeks. Then she became involved in the tragedy of young Ernest Fane, Lord Burghersh, son of the Earl of Westmorland, husband to Georgina's niece Augusta (known as Leila). On 18 December he visited Georgina, speaking as if the Millennium had come and repenting of his past. Diagnosed with paralysis of the brain, he was confined in a private asylum near Regent's Park, and restrained as he had symptoms of violence. William visited to soothe him by reading but his delusions returned to trouble him about Sin and the Voice of God. Georgina recorded the horror of his weakening state, '[t]hey say he did not suffer but who can tell – death is always fearful to witness.' He died in January. It was 'a dream of the night – quick, confused, and crowded with conflicting emotions,' she wrote, recalling Ernest's endlessly repeating of the child's hymn, 'And if from sleep to death I wake.' The last line, 'Pity my simplicity', had sounded so touching.[96]

In January 1851 the Cowpers entered their new home, at 17, Curzon Street in exclusive Mayfair.[97] Before the Cowpers spent a couple of months in Brighton, clearly for their health, William visited Henry Drummond at Albury in Surrey. The Cowpers were drawn to the Apostolic Church which Drummond and others developed out of Irvingism. In a letter about this year, William discussed the millenarian Albury doctrine: the Anglican Collect that Pentecost, requesting 'right judgement', he thought in its sobriety and moderation more useful 'than the special gifts which our friends have coveted and believed themselves to have attained, but which appear to me to lead too much to a contemplation of the future and so to divert from the present'. If he had to ask for a gift it would be 'something that would enable me to do a great thing in the present to draw men's Souls to Christ now, rather than something that would prepare the way for a glorious period to be established hereafter'.[98]

Georgina's interest in the theologian F.D. Maurice developed through attending his services at Lincoln's Inn chapel. In 1851, from the Arnoldian atmosphere of Rugby, her old friend Julia Rich wrote she was 'still fermenting with Maurician yeast'.[99] 'How,' she asked, 'can he swallow the Articles. Do ask him if you meet in the aisle'; in another letter Julia reiterated her rejection of some of the Thirty Nine Articles of the Anglican *via media* and her belief that Maurice would avoid them in his book on the Prayer Book.[100] Georgina sent her a copy of Maurice's sermons and enthused about the services. If this interest placed her in a small band, his posthumous reputation has led Maurice to be described, exaggeratedly, by one intellectual historian as a 'gigantic force during the Victorian period', nevertheless, at the time Georgina's admiration was shared by such important figures as Octavia Hill, Tennyson and Henry Sidgwick.[101]

When one of Georgina's brothers-in-law, Ralph Leycester, died in April, Herman Douglas sent Georgina his sympathy from Bavaria. He also asked if she knew the work of the theosophist and 'philosophe inconnu' Count Louis-Claude St Martin, *L'homme de desir* (1790), 'more evangelical and holy and more satisfactory' than the crystal ball (recently used to divine the fate of Franklin's Arctic expedition).[102] Georgina remained unwell, so the Cowpers stayed at Edward Lane's hydropathic establishment at Sudbrook Park in Surrey, hoping 'water cure' and rest would help.

In early August Georgina travelled with Augustus to Schwalbach.[103] Her health was one reason,[104] but the siblings stayed on because of the illness of Constance, daughter of Georgina's sister Marianne de Burgh, who had married the son of Baron Ward in April and had then separated, according to one account after being dismissed for adultery ('a fatality seems to have attended all our married nieces,' Augustus observed a few years later, after another disaster). But Constance's mother reported her son-in-law's affectionate care of his wife.[105] William completed an official tour of the docks, naval hospitals and barracks and then travelled to Georgina. They went to Schlafenbad, Wiesbaden, Frankfurt, and Wurzburg where they heard Franz Hoffman talk about Franz von Baader, the mystic or Romantic philosopher of love.[106] On 19 September, Georgina recorded 'My disappointment' – was this a miscarriage?[107] Then they returned to Schwalbach where Constance had herself miscarried. In mid-November came news that she had died of 'consumption'.

Palmerston was dismissed from the Foreign Office in December, following his support for Prince Louis Napoleon's coup d'état against the Second Republic. 'This home coup d'état,' Georgina wrote, 'has shaken us even more than the French one.' Palmerston was sacrificed, she believed, to Austria, the Queen, and little John's vanity and wish to manage the Foreign Office. Despite this, characteristically, William thought it a 'year of home joy and blessing without a peck of discomfort from within its happy hearth'.[108]

1852 began with William and Georgina at Broadlands (where fellow guests included relations like the Sulivans and Shaftesburys – Ashley had succeeded to the earldom in June 1851 – and friends like the Walewskis, Bulwers and Milneses), then William went off to Hertford for Quarter Sessions before visiting the new castle of Peckforton ('does great credit to Salvin') and being shown Jewish curiosities by a Jewish convert, the Reverend Joseph. Georgina met a young lawyer called Furnivall at Romsey. A Christian Socialist and an ardent friend of working men's associations, he 'came to plead the cause of the one just formed by 18 poor silk weavers of Bethnal Green. Poor fellows they have been working on quietly and perseveringly for the last 16 months, laying by about 6 a week to make a little fund to begin with'. So began a close friendship between the Cowper-Temples and Frederick James Furnivall.[109]

Russell's government resigned in February, the Tories forming the minority 'Who? Who?' Protectionist government under Derby. Out of office, William's regular religious retreat was unaffected by political vagaries; he was at Albury in April.[110] About this time, presumably referring to Furnivall, William told Georgina that *if* he were touchy and unconfiding, which happily for her he was not, he might complain of her little scrap of a note, 'I am glad that you should have been exercising your dear brain on such high subjects and instructing our handsome Socialist in the true theory of Church government.' Had she been at Devonshire House the evening before, he added, she might have resolved her doubts by appealing to the Bishop of London, although had she sat by the Duke of Argyll she would have got Maurician notions instead.[111]

The Cowpers travelled to the west of Ireland with the Palmerstons; this was Georgina's first visit to Ireland and she was 'much amused' and affected by the experience, which continued after the Palmerstons' return to England. 'I half laughed, half cried all day,' she wrote, of the drive from Sligo to Cliffony. Georgina approved of the improvements Palmerston had made at Mullaghmore for his tenantry, with school and harbour construction, and instruction in fishing and agriculture. But she wondered whether Palmerston's near neighbour was not wiser to economic realities in evicting tenants during the famine, for Ahamlish was like a rabbit warren.[112] William heard about priestly electoral interference, and learned from landlords of the cowardice of tenants who attempted to assassinate them. He was told about the violence towards 'Jumpers' who were converted from Catholicism during this new Protestant Reformation (which William supported). They experienced the anger for themselves as they were stoned by boys hidden in a priest's potato garden after visiting a 'Souper's School'.[113]

William was accosted by a beggar who said that Georgina was 'pour [sic] terrible ill looking'.[114] But it was Lady Palmerston who was ill, with cholera, and they hurried back, receiving reassuring bulletins from Palmerston, who praised Emily's constitution and angelic temperament.[115] With her recovery they visited Albury and stayed with the Grosvenors at Moor Park over Christmas. Then it was back to canvassing – again – after the Tories resigned following the defeat of Disraeli's budget. William's own health gave Georgina a worry when he collapsed from fatigue as they read together, at some point in 1852. She never forgot this terrible warning of the thread which held them together, 'it is awful I know and feel to have one's all staked on one life.'[116]

The new year saw William re-elected for Hertford. He was appointed five days later to the Admiralty. At the start of January William's younger brother, Spencer, married Harriet d'Orsay at the Embassy in Paris. Augustus Tollemache, who scarcely knew the couple, gave the bride away, it was 'a Sensible wedding – without sentiment', he said.[117] Spencer had inherited Sandringham from the 'little Huguenot' Motteux, which Greville the diarist described as 'a good house, ugly place in a dry soil' just when he was low in funds.[118] The inheritance dismayed sister Emily since Billy missed a slice; she found it hard to picture Spencer as a respectable Norfolk squire, 'feeding Deer and stuffing Turkeys'.[119]

Harriet had sought 'growth in grace and increase of faith and holiness'.[120] She lived in piety and charity in Sandringham and the Avenue Friedland with her almshouse for elderly women and French biblical commentaries. Harriet felt Georgina had been dutiful in going out, 'but though I have not the same temptations as in my young, and unprotected days', she herself shunned a worldly life and meant to re-educate herself to teach the Bantling, her baby Marie Henriette, 'that will be my recreation from more serious pursuits'.[121] Did her piety, directed after dabbling with Catholicism, toward Evangelical Protestantism, act as an inspiration to Georgina, who was often with the Spencer Cowpers at this time? Sartorially, with her quasi-religious clothing, seen by Mrs Craven (the Catholic Pauline de Ferronays whom William had first met in 1833) at Brocket in 1856, perhaps she was a model for Georgina's later years.[122]

Shortly after her birthday, Georgina said farewell to Augustus as he and his wife set sail for his post in the British Legation at Rio de Janeiro. The separation was painful and despondent letters and requests for reading material, india-rubber baths, and clothes, came back. Georgina sent sketches, family news, sermons by Pusey and Henry Manning, and an article on a candle factory. While Augustus worked Marguerite met no

Englishwoman capable, in her view, of intelligent conversation: a fruit of her boredom was a picture of Rio which was subsequently lithographed.[123] The comfort of family portraits (four of Georgina) was denied them too, as the climate compelled their return.[124]

Georgina, not in vigorous health or high spirits, according to William, stayed at Peckforton while he visited the Sutherlands at Trentham in early January 1854. He skated and sledged with guests including the Grosvenors and Cholmondeleys (Hugh Cholmondeley being dressed up as a woman for a prank), Stafford 'driving like a Russian' and Lady Constance like she came from a Norwegian fjord.[125] 'Dearest,' he wrote, the separation prolonged by the weather, 'I find that every time I leave you I can bear it less well and miss you more' and, 'the more I see of other women the more I feel that you were made to suit me more than any other person could have done ... an approach to that combination of high reflective thought and deep feeling and simplicity of nature which makes you so exquisitely dear to me.'[126]

In late March Britain embarked on war with Russia. In July William joined a large crowd of MPs who answered Lord John Russell's call to Downing Street, and he sent Georgina a long account of the exchanges there, about Lord Aberdeen's leadership and Palmerston: Dudley Stuart tediously advocating Palmerston as Secretary for War (it was a 'mistake to put him among the sewers and cemeteries').[127] The family suffered a loss even before troops were sent out to the Crimea, when William's brother-in-law, Jocelyn, caught cholera when quartered in the Tower of London. William was with his sister when he died at the Palmerstons' house.

As Olive Anderson has said, 'the Admiralty shone out like a good deed during the Crimean War,' perhaps undeservedly avoiding the odium heaped on the Army.[128] William supported the scheme suggested by Georgina's old friend Miney (Lady Maria) Forester – who as a girl had an 'intense romantic kind of devotion' for her[129] – for nurses to be sent to the naval hospitals. Georgina, unsurprisingly, was involved in these attempts.[130] Miney had contacted Florence Nightingale about nursing and William (at the Admiralty) thought that sailors could be similarly nursed. Nurses were led by a daughter of the Scottish divine Thomas Chalmers, and through William, they had free access to the hospitals at Scutari and Therapia in the Bosphorus.

But she felt the war was unchristian, despite the enthusiasm for the contest with tyrannical Russia which Augustus felt.[131] For Augustus told Georgina that he blushed at her joy at having none she cared for on service. 'I thought you had something of a Roman Spirit in you – and would rather wish that your husband and your brother were employed in the defence of the common weal.' Augustus also wished Georgina and Magsie were on Nightingale's staff 'ministering to the spiritual need of our wounded and sick'.[132] In truth, having very reluctantly gone to Brazil, the Tollemaches found the post did not meet their financial needs. Augustus frequently wrote about attaché-ships and secretary-ships (William endeavoured to get his brother-in-law's return via Clarendon at the Foreign Office).[133]

In September the Cowpers went to Bad Kreuznach, a resort for the rich and aristocratic, to restore Georgina. Their friend the Reverend John Llewellyn Davies, son of the prominent Evangelical clergyman John Davies (and brother of Emily Davies the promoter of female education), asked Georgina whether she learned German to read the *Deutsche Theologie* in the original.[134] In the same month, Spencer and Harriet lost their daughter to cholera (the epidemic made a most deadly visitation of Britain, Palmerston refusing a national fast day). As Marguerite said, Harriet had been 'so completely bound up in the life of her little darling'.[135] In her grief she created a shrine of furniture from the death chamber and founded an orphanage at Sandringham initially intended for the children of Crimean soldiers. But it was badly managed and may have contributed to Spencer's financial woes.

John Ruskin – seemingly the unperturbed centre of the 'most violent social storm of the mid-nineteenth century' as gossip about Millais' love for poor Effie was followed in July of 1854 by the decree of nullity dissolving the marriage – became reacquainted with Georgina after meeting her at an evening party where she was introduced as one 'beside whom it was evidently supposed I should hold it a privilege to stand for a minute or two, with leave to speak to her' and found her too pretty to look at directly, until a chance reference to Rome in 1840 recalled his brown-haired 'Egeria' – as he named her after the water nymph who symbolised wisdom – to him. So began the relationship with 'a tutelary power – of the brightest and happiest', as Ruskin vividly recalled in *Praeterita*.[136] The year also brought a new clerical friend, when William met Edward Monro of Harrow Weald, an Evangelical who had become a Tractarian, at Moor Park. Monro wrote *Parochial Work* (1850), pastoral theology praised by Edward Keble as a successor to Herbert's *Country Parson*; his St Andrew's College for poor boys was admired by Charles Kingsley.[137] Monro was concerned at parishioners' ignorance about the sacraments and Christian faith. William thought he led an ideal parish and for several years took a retreat there in Easter until Monro's move to Leeds.

In February 1855 the Aberdeen coalition resigned. William's stepfather was now premier and remained in this position, with the exception of a sixteen-month Conservative government, until his death a decade later. What the Cowpers felt about this elevation is difficult to know from surviving letters and journals. William's official duties (studied in the next chapter) changed, as he moved from the Admiralty to under-secretary in the Home Office. Shortly after, he was President of the Board of Health. At the same time, he experienced the trauma of extended separation as Georgina underwent 'manipulation' by an Edinburgh physician, John Beveridge, who diagnosed a spinal tumour or hiatus.[138] A friend told her that a little *real* quiet was the only medicine in a case like hers and that in her experience 'if I had not *given way* as it is called I should not have had a little living son to reward me now.'[139] Another declared that Georgina 'never could get well in London'.[140] And William was concerned that she should not stint on nourishment for she had lost weight: 'I firmly expect you to be as round & as fat as you were formerly – I look forward to the day when you will not be able to clasp yr Bracelets.'[141]

Georgina did not limit herself to medical treatment. According to a brief diary entry she cleaned a little Irvingite church in the afternoons.[142] She met a deaconess, William advising her, 'you will hold very wide language and explain how you acknowledge them to be a branch and a sprout but not exclusively the Trunk to improve all the rest of Christendom – Don't be too communicative, for small bodies are liable to gossip.' She heard sermons from the Reverend Thomas Guthrie, who had helped establish the breakaway Free Church of Scotland in 1843.[143] William hoped his 'Darling Doctor of Divinity' would find time to meditate on her reading. It was so important for her soul to have a *retraite*, to leave gossip and frivolity for a season and so have a long commune with her heart and be still. Though a good reader she had to practise being a good thinker, 'you know you have got to practise meditation – to view a Statement in all its bearings.'[144]

The distance ('my darling is 400 miles off & I can't get at her') and William's doubts about the diagnosis of a tumour and the motives of 'the wizard', as he called Beveridge, led him to seek the opinion of Dr Protheroe Smith, who thought the diagnosis 'contrary to received pathological knowledge'.[145] William, thinking of the exercise therapist Mathias Roth, suggested one of his 'little women' attend her in England and asked her to speak to the famous surgeon and obstetrician James Simpson.[146] Their correspondence was daily, although he had much official work, had the usual dinners with the Palmerstons, Sutherlands, Shaftesburys and Trevelyans (Macaulay was 'in great form – and argued strongly against the notion of Westward Ho … he thinks we have gained in humanity, virtue and everything else over any of the periods that preceded us'[147]). Invitations to Buckingham Palace concerts had to be declined in her absence, and Mrs Disraeli had invited them twice, so Georgina should explain, or it would seem like scorn now Disraeli was out of office.[148]

He told her when he relished a sermon from F.D. Maurice (and took Sir Robert Peel, son of the late prime minister, to one of Maurice's Bible Classes[149]), though he struggled to précis it: as it was characteristically 'difficult to condense and crystallize into positive form – though it is suggestive and interesting'.[150] He told her about the course of the war and prospects for peace, noting that a 'day of humiliation' was not for Palmerston, given the 'posse comitatus of several hundred, following & cheering the Premier', on 21 March. He reported the arrival of Napoleon III ('an ugly pig – with very short legs') and Eugénie ('has hoops & is obliged to have a cushion stuck into her back when she sits') in April, on a state visit to reinforce the coalition.[151]

He had the demands of parliament (where he approved Gladstone's speech on marriage to a wife's sister), plans with Francis Egerton, Lord Ellesmere, for a penny newspaper, requiring £70,000, and the criticism of the War department, to distract him.[152] 'Darling I can't bear anyone else in your absence – you may rest assured of that,' he wrote.[153] But it was unbearable, and he requested her return, telling her at the start of May that he could not allow her to be humbugged.[154] She came back in June.

Life apparently returned to its routine: with Georgina involved in the newly established Ladies' Sanitary Association, hospital visits and listening to sermons by Charles Kingsley, John Llewellyn Davies and F.D. Maurice, and attending the latter's Bible classes and lectures. One of Kingsley's lectures in June made Georgina realise that the clothing and coal clubs were a sign 'of the degeneracy of an age that needs such helps'. Wages should give everyone independent and comfortable subsistence, but this was beyond the sphere of women, who should do what they could to comfort and alleviate, beginning at home.[155] A monster meeting to resist Lord Robert Grosvenor's Sunday Anti-Trading bill delayed their seaside trip to St Leonards at the end of the month, William thinking it better for him to stay in the capital (the bill had stimulated the Hyde Park riots of June and July).

In August he stood for Hertford at a by-election after becoming President of the Board of Health: as it was not known there was to be a contest it was dull, but interest in Palmerston's stepson meant his utterances on Russia were extensively reported.[156] He assured his audience that being an MP meant considerable labour, and if the last session was the model, he would begin at noon and with little repose, 'would be occupied until one or two o'clock in the following morning, so that although they shortened the hours of labour in the factories, they certainly had not done so for themselves'.[157]

In September, as Sebastopol fell, the Cowpers visited Paris. William then joined the Luton, Dunstable and Welwyn Railway Company, Palmerston cautioning against being chairman or director if he could not attend, as this would make it a 'Dangerous Eminence'.[158] Yet he used the inaugural dinner to praise the navy and army, criticise the Peace Society's position, and identify public support as an indication that prosperity had not led to mere materialism; the speech appeared in *The Times* and other papers.[159] A speech about the Public Libraries Act, also reported, argued that municipal institutions should expand to educate the people and not remain merely for repression of crime, 'such institutions fell short of their real object while they were only institutions to repress'.[160]

Augustus and Marguerite returned from Rio in May 1855 on the pretext of a post in the British legation at The Hague. William sympathised with his brother-in-law's disinclination, an attaché's clerical work was unpalatable and the prospect hardly sufficient to justify it.[161] 'Diplomacy may well be at a discount,' Augustus had told his sister the previous year, 'if it were worth anything, it ought to have prevented this War.'[162] In fact the post was given up with the offer of a staff appointment in the Foreign Legion organised for the Crimea, and Augustus got to work briefly in the War Office before the peace.

The new year began at Broadlands amid diplomats and Shaftesbury (who was alarmed at the prospect of life peerages being introduced[163]), and the year unfolded in Board of Health work, sabbatarian schemes, residence at Windsor and Harrow Weald for Easter, and country house visits. In mid-February William noted a domestic fracas 'made G ill'. But Drummond and Lord Robert Grosvenor (a son of the Marquess of Westminster and an advanced Whig MP) dined with them.[164] Suddenly, in early April William's eldest brother, a 'kind, good, amiable Creature,' according to Shaftesbury, died of heart failure at Maidstone when attending court as Lord Lieutenant of the county; he was only fifty.[165] The new Earl Cowper stayed with them at St Leonards after a breakdown produced by his father's death and the consequent crushing of his hopes to sit in the Commons. In writing of his fondness for Uncle Billy and his wife, he said that if William's vague and fanciful ideas were tiresome at times and if his manner was perhaps foolish, yet 'there is really an immense deal of good sense in him, more than in most people; and what is worth much more, such kindness and real goodness of heart, it is impossible not to love him.' He thought Georgina 'quite perfect; quite in fact what the girls call her an angel without wings'.[166]

William appointed Augustus his private secretary after the war was ended by the Treaty of Paris in early 1856. Palmerston also made Augustus treasurer of the County Courts in December 1857, causing one reader to tell the *Daily News* that William's influence 'over the Premier in all questions of patronage is notoriously great'.[167] The Cowpers regularly visited the Tollemaches at Nutfield, Surrey, during the parliamentary session. Nutfield came to reflect the Cowpers' and Tollemaches' taste for pre-Raphaelitism, with 'large golden sunflower on highest gable', motto over doorway, windows of bottle-end glass, Morris jars and 'everything artistic'.[168] Though practically a cottage, it was a picturesque heap of old purple bricks, gables, eaves and lattice windows, with rustling poplars close by.

Georgina cultivated the Brownings, in the year that *Aurora Leigh* was published, when the Brownings were in London for the summer.[169] In early August they were invited to dinner, 'rather pleasantly', as Elizabeth told her sister, for Robert – if hostile to the performances of professional mediums – 'took an extraordinary fancy to her, THOUGH she believes in the spirits!' They were 'very sympathetical', and Georgina was 'like a swan for grace and refinement, and with such a sweet human smile'.[170] She asked to see work by their infant son.

After going to a Belgian sanitary congress with Georgina, William went to Edinburgh in October, and sought Dr James Simpson's advice on Georgina's illness, 'a chronic one of long standing' which had so far baffled medical experts (William noted he was 'penetrating as a gimlet and guessed all the symptoms at once explained and sent books to read and thinks that … the malady may be cured, though not to be as strong as some people'[171]), met Dr Candlish and Dr Guthrie and visited lodging houses and a lock-up house.[172]

In January 1857 William again stayed at Albury, before Parliament. His appointment as Vice President of the Committee on Education entailed re-election and when in March Palmerston's ministry fell after discontented Liberals united with the opposition over policy in China, William was re-elected in the ensuing general election. After Easter at Harrow Weald he went to Manchester to the opening of the Art Treasures of masterpieces in private collections and thought Scheffer's picture of Dante's Beatrice was dreamy like Georgina.[173]

The new Parliament assembled after the general election at the end of May. William's duties included chairing a Literary Fund dinner, and attending an education conference. In October he was at Birmingham for the inauguration of a National Association for the Promotion of Social Science, established to provide expert guidance for politicians and moral reformers in general, sharing the platform with Lord John Russell and Henry Brougham, the veteran popular educator (who patted William on the cheeks), and seconding Russell's motion to establish the association, 'to unite together as far as possible the various efforts now being made for the moral and social improvement of the people'.[174] Told he was heard the best, he said, 'if my voice was the loudest you can imagine how the others must have mumbled,' adding, 'I like all this bustle so much that I have no wish for it to be over and I'm learning much about my proper business.'[175]

At the start of 1858 Palmerston was defeated in the Commons through the efforts of Lord John Russell and other malcontents, using the Conspiracy to Murder Bill (drafted in response to British involvement with Felice Orsini's plot to kill the French Emperor outside the Paris Opéra), as the opportunity. The *Belfast News-Letter* reported the 'ministerial crisis' in the Commons: Palmerston's stepson walking up the centre of the House to sit behind him, his manner betraying excitement.[176]

The modernization of the French fleet worried press and public a great deal this year, and in August the Emperor invited the Queen to the opening of the 'Napoleon III' basin at Cherbourg to show the British had no cause for mistrust. After seeing the French steam-powered ships, which did nothing to alleviate Victoria's anxieties about her navy (1859 was a year of invasion scares), William and Georgina holidayed. They climbed in Switzerland with John Llewellyn Davies, ascending the Grimsel, Siedelhorn and Riffell above Zermatt, and met the poet Matthew Arnold.[177] Then, though William had left the Education Committee, when the National Association for the Promotion of Social Science met in Liverpool in October, he led the expert discussion on education with a 'rare assiduity and patience'.[178] Palmerston was in Compiègne in November, meeting Napoleon III, who intended to discuss Italian affairs. As a sign of William's place in his stepfather's affections and will (as successor to Broadlands) he presided over the Labourers' meeting in Romsey, winning 'Golden opinions from everybody', as Palmerston's representative, according to his mother.[179]

In January the Cowpers, like many aristocratic English, were in Rome. Nathaniel Hawthorne met William at the American sculptor Harriet Hosmer's studio.[180] At Easter William was with Monro at Harrow Weald.[181] After a general election in May strengthened the Tories, Derby's government was brought down by its Whig-Liberal opponents who had displayed unity at Willis's Rooms. Palmerston became premier and William was Vice President of the Board of Trade, the press identifying his step-parentage as sufficient reason.[182] When William told Georgina this news, she was at West Farm at Barnet in Hertfordshire, home of the Liberal MP and fervent Protestant, Arthur Kinnaird, enjoying a 'Revival' with Lady Dunsany, Baptist Noel and others. Across Britain, and through the pages of *The Revival*, an Evangelical reawakening was being attempted.[183] William Pennefather, rector of Christ Church at Barnet, organized a gathering of the great and humble, Anglican and dissenters, in 1858, and Georgina seems to have attended the next year.[184]

Georgina became involved with a Diocesan Association of 'ladies of rank and influence' who improved the London Season by visiting 'suffering and fallen fellow-creatures' in workhouses, hospitals and other places.[185] Such work offered participants the feeling of usefulness and connection with poor neighbours, as well as the satisfactions of self-denial and the appeal of alien environments.[186] It may have strengthened a friendship with Archibald Tait the Broad Church Bishop of that most populous of dioceses, London, who was to become a vigorous Archbishop of Canterbury, and his wife Catherine, cousin of Samuel Wilberforce. Tait had been translated to London by Palmerston (advised by Shaftesbury) in 1856 and Georgina must have been associated with his wife through diocesan work.[187] She also attended services for the poor given by Thomas Rowsell of St Peter's, Stepney, a supporter of the Ladies Sanitary Association who had established a school-church in his overcrowded and impoverished parish.[188]

Her desire to do good was reflected in support for the teaching of fine arts as a ladylike employment, with other 'ladies of high rank and character' including the Duchess of Argyle and Countess of Granville, in June 1857, a response to concerns about 'surplus' women.[189] For the late 1850s saw a number of debates and agitations about female rights, capacities and opportunities, which her surviving diary for 1859 and new philanthropic endeavours suggest she responded to. She was active, for instance, in the Ladies' Sanitary Association, attending lectures, studying its tracts and revising Susan Power's *Women's Work in Sanitary Reform*.[190] She entertained Dr William Farr and the pioneer female doctor Elizabeth Blackwell in April 1859, a 'thoroughly sensible right-minded little woman', free from the nonsense – so Georgina then thought – of the rights of women but 'only wishing to see her nature developed & turned to more general account'.[191]

Glimpses of her intellectual and religious explorations appear in her journal for 1859. She joined Maurice's Bible classes (where presumably she met the future social reformer Octavia Hill, another Maurician) and learned the true duties of women according to Charles Kingsley's lectures. As a consequence, she gathered that social reform entailed reform of employment, which was beyond the power of women, but 'they may do much to comfort and alleviate sufferings they cannot remove'. She enjoyed but struggled through the 'dark language' of the surgeon James Hinton's idiosyncratic work, *Man and His Dwelling Place*, which dealt with man's spiritual deadness.[192] Darwin's *Origin of Species* seems to have passed her by when it first appeared (it was published late in November 1859).

Georgina's intellectual pursuits and philanthropic work suggest a marriage in which she had considerable space for self-development and opportunity to engage with the wider world. In part this reflected her lack of children and William's political work which took him away from their home, and which are studied in the next chapter. We will see in a later chapter that Georgina's maternal desires, after what appears to have been at least one miscarriage, found fulfilment.[193] In the first decade of their marriage she had the duties of a wife of a politician at the heart of the Whig establishment but she did not relish political socialising. Since William was not simply a political animal, this did not create serious tensions and in religious and philanthropic interests they were united. There was apparently little discord: the separation occasioned by Georgina's illness showing her husband's affection as well as frustration at her determination to prolong the stay in Edinburgh. Her ability to ignore his pleas for some time might suggest her dominance but this renders the power relationship in the marriage too crudely. William could appreciate the intelligence and talents of married women from his own mother, who had been 'accustomed to considerable autonomy' and his was not a domineering or ungenerous nature.[194] Georgina's strong will, perhaps a Tollemache trait, had not been crushed by the despotism of her father, who had died when she was fifteen, and in the years since then she had lived amid gentle womenfolk and an adoring brother. Donovan the phrenologist had divined correctly that she could not be the 'pliable, patient, submissive, self denying Saint of a wife, that we often read of'.

5

JUNIOR MINISTER, 1846–1867

The fall of Sir Robert Peel's Conservative government after the repeal of the Corn Laws provided an opportunity for William to return to office after six years. In July 1846 Lord John Russell flattered the ailing Lord Melbourne by offering a place in his new government for his nephew. Melbourne knew William had little ambition: 'I do not think that he would mind being left out himself, but it would have been very unpalatable to his mother.'[1] William was appointed a Commissioner or 'Civil' Lord of the Admiralty, to the bemusement of *The Satirist*, which already characterized him as 'not over-gifted in the cerebral department' and now asked what experience he had of matters maritime.[2] Yet he held this junior post for most of the period from the summer of 1846 to early 1854. But his more substantial work came as President of the Board of Health from August 1855 to 1858, and as commissioner of the Board of Works from 1860 to 1867. In the latter post especially his achievements and reputation were partly assessed in terms of the association with Palmerston.

In becoming a Civil Lord of the Admiralty, William followed in the footsteps of Palmerston, a Lord of the Admiralty in 1808, and Ashley, who was offered the post by Peel during his short-lived ministry in 1834. William's duties never loomed large although the office occupied him for nine years (he never became a keen mariner).[3] The lay lords took an active part in framing the naval Estimates and were responsible for dockyards, slips, factories, smitheries, harbours of refuge and breakwaters – hence William's official inspections in the Channel Islands and along the south and west coast. They watched private bills and reports affecting navigable waters. They oversaw the Packet Service, Greenwich Hospital and its schools, the Dockyard and Royal Marine Schools, and education on board ship. They appointed schoolmasters and were referred to on all positions relating to chaplains and charitable institutions. The appointment of Dockyard

Artillery Brigades officers, and their drill times was their responsibility. They appointed naval cadets.

The First Lord of the Admiralty was not the most prized office. As Correlli Bartlett notes, 'The Admiralty during these years [1815–1853] attracted established politicians rather than ambitious and rising men of the future.' Professional knowledge of the navy was not required, competence and hard work was. The administration had been reorganized in the 1830s in line with Whig desire for improved efficiency and centralization, and greater Parliamentary control. For the lay lords, work was perhaps easier, Palmerston had claimed in 1808 that it was mainly signing documents.[4] Opportunities for patronage meant William could offer cadetships or midshipman's posts to the Duke of Devonshire's connections or as he himself desired, to the sons of clergymen and poor gentlemen.[5] William was interested in the calibre of naval chaplains, the First Lord, Lord Minto, writing of William's wildness about one clergyman's spiritual failings.[6] But few of his surviving papers relate to this office.[7] He was not in Sir John Briggs's memoirs of naval administrations, a sign perhaps of his unexceptional talents (though part of a successful team that managed the Navy during the Crimean war).[8] He did, of course, have a stepfather keenly interested in naval strength; Palmerston wrote in September 1846 to urge fortification of the dockyards, 'for what the French are doing in Spain is a pretty sure indication that they will take an early opportunity of paying their Respects to us at our own Home'.[9]

In early 1851 'Finality' Jack proposed further parliamentary reform as a government measure and resigned when his bill was defeated; the Conservatives' inability to form a government brought him back in March. Then came 'exciting times', as William recorded in his diary, when Russell forced Palmerston's resignation from the Foreign Office in December.[10] William was astonished by his stepfather's 'magnanimity, indulgence for others & cheerfulness' and found it impossible that the head of a weak and unpopular Cabinet could discard his most popular colleague for 'a punctilio[,] a fancied act of indiscipline'. The press was a chorus of eulogy and no Liberal or Conservative could be found to applaud Lord John.[11] William resigned from the Admiralty in early February, despite entreaties by the judge-advocate-general Sir David Dundas and a meeting with Russell.[12] Thanks to Conservative support for Palmerston's amendment to the Militia Bill, Russell's government was defeated on 16 February 1852 and resigned four days later, the Tories forming a minority government under Derby, so that in March William was out of office.

But the Tory ministry was short-lived, and following the defeat of Disraeli's budget, resigned. A general election was held in July 1852 and William was returned again. In Lord Aberdeen's Liberal-Peelite coalition,

Palmerston had the 'harmless' Home Office (the description is John Morley's) and a place was found for his stepson. Palmerston applied himself to mastering the Office and supported social and sanitary reforms, William returned to the Admiralty under Sir James Graham. His mother wrote: 'I should have been more satisfied if you could have had something better, but when two great parties coalesce there must be great difficulties in providing for so many claims – and it is a great thing under these circumstances to keep what one had.'[13]

When Gladstone presented his Budget in April 1853, William recorded his thoughts on this great parliamentary performance: a great credit to the speaker and the Cabinet. Gladstone spoke for nearly five hours 'without in the least tiring his audience, not a redundant word not a phrase for effect, nothing left in obscurity, but large and complicated as the scheme is he led us through its mazes with perfect ease and gave a sound reason for every part'. This delighted the Liberals and even pleased the Radicals. William thought Dizzy would be forced to oppose the plan and feared his ingenuity.[14] A threat closer to William was the possibility that Hertford would lose an MP in a new measure of parliamentary reform.[15]

In late March 1854 Britain declared war on Russia. The next February the Aberdeen coalition resigned and William's stepfather was summoned by the Queen to form a new government, at the age of seventy. William left the Admiralty to become under-secretary for home affairs under Sir George Grey. He told Georgina that he liked the prospect, there was more work than at the Admiralty, but it was more interesting: 'It is of a more parliamentary character than most other offices – I mean there are more bills to be framed & opposed – & more necessity for taking a part in the ordinary legislation of Parliament.'[16] Traces of work in this department in his private papers include preparation for the problem of Smithfield market on the Sabbath.[17] The attempt to form a new cabinet involved dealing with Sir Robert Peel, son of the prime minister, who was to have succeeded William at the Admiralty, with the Colonial Office mooted for William ('Johnny declines Sir Rob but said at the same time he wld like to have me, Sir R is irritated & indignant...'[18]) though he preferred 'sticking to domestic concerns'.[19] But on 13 August he became the President of the Board of Health, replacing Sir Benjamin Hall. He was sworn in as a Privy Councillor.

'The Honourable Mr. Cowper is a very proper man for the post of President,' wrote the author of an historical sketch of the progress of 'health of towns' movement, provided there was 'nothing more to be done than present an annual report to the House of Commons'. The new President was 'amiable, gentlemanly and the son of Lady Palmerston', and the country lost nothing by having minor sinecure posts in which to train the young aristocracy and keep them out of mischief, if the office was purely admonitory, statistical and advisory. The *Monthly Christian Spectator* was more disparaging of Whig patronage and nepotism: grapes would not come of thistles and one could hardly expect wise government when beardless and empty-headed coxcombs from the junior clubs, with enormous salaries, headed the most important and responsible departments of state.[20] In fact it suited him, for, as one historian has said, he was 'zealous, competent and knowledgeable' – perhaps the six years Shaftesbury had spent in the Board also gave him insight. His supervision at the Board's office in Richmond Terrace was close.[21] He told his friend Richard Monckton Milnes that he was 'very fond of my present office'.[22]

The Board advised local authorities, and though few took up the 1848 Public Health Act their plans were scrutinized by the Board. William's aim was to lead a Board involved in legislation and scientific research rather than a coordinating body during epidemics or source of routine authority.[23] The Board's unpopularity as a body deemed unnecessary, expensive and a dangerous example of centralization, hampered this. It was confronted by enemies of 'England's most Prussian minister', the sanitary reformer (and disciple of Jeremy Bentham), Edwin Chadwick, and received weak support from Palmerston's government in general. It was therefore a high-profile and controversial department, with press attention and contentious debates in the Commons over its activities and very existence. Indeed the survival of the Board was only possible through annual continuance Acts.

One of the most important decisions William made was to appoint John Simon, Medical Officer to the City of London, the Medical Officer to the Board, as Sir Benjamin Hall had intended (but Shaftesbury saw the appointment as 'coxcombical, self-sufficient, time-serving' in ignoring the claim of Dr Sutherland, aiding the army in the Crimea). Simon was a friend of John Ruskin and his sympathies were Christian Socialist.[24] The two men became friends and worked closely together in attempts to develop the Board. The staff also included as the Secretary, the playwright Tom Taylor.[25] In response to the requests of F.D. Maurice, F.J. Furnivall and Thomas Hughes, William made the former Chartist Thomas Cooper a copyist.[26]

William steered a commission on ventilation and warming of houses and barracks.[27] Simon issued reports, and inspectors tested metropolitan water. Legislation was prepared, including a Public Health Bill and Simon's Vaccination Bill in March 1856, but prorogation in late July saw all his bills postponed. William pleaded for the Board to be prolonged, to do some work (to laughter in the House).[28] *Punch*'s satire on the session's failed bills included the ghost of the Health Bill astride Cowper, 'Dr Jenner's outraged sprite | Shook a lancet at his side'.[29] The campaign against the Board had been successful and the bill was defeated by a mere twelve votes, chiefly, William noted in his diary, down to a speech by Tom Duncombe 'to whom I unfortunately gave offence about Vaccn'.[30]

In September 1856 William was in Brussels coping fairly well in French, as President of the Third Section of the Congrès Internationale de Bienfaisance, finding discussion interesting, but 'cannot say there was much result – many professions. Chadwick dined frequently'.[31] The next year was equally unlucky for the Public Health Bill. Opposition from radicals opposed to centralization and cost, and vested interests, again proved too strong. The Vaccination Bill was withdrawn after pressure from anti-vaccinationists and parliamentary opponents of the Board. William agreed to a select committee to investigate vaccination: it never sat because the Board's position was so weak.[32]

Indeed the one great achievement of William's tenure was the Medical Practitioners Act in 1858 which helped to regulate the profession: 'a united body with legal powers for protection, for the promotion of science, and for the advancement of the public good'.[33] *Punch*, punning on the work by his collateral relation, thought this merited the 'appellation of Cowper's *Task*'.[34] It was a collaboration with Simon, although the association of Irish general practitioners thanked William for his 'great talents and persevering exertions' which had largely led, in their view, to enactment. A General Medical Council now established a register and sought to distinguish orthodox professionals from quacks. William's speech outlining the Act appeared as a pamphlet. Unfortunately William was not to remain at the Board as the Bill passed through Parliament, for the Liberal ministry fell, and he sponsored it instead as a Private Member.[35]

From 9 February 1857, William was vice-president of the Education Committee of the Privy Council, which regulated and dispensed grants for education. The Sardinian Minister in London, Emanuele d'Azeglio, told Camillo Cavour that William, ambitious but unsuccessful in the Board of Health, was to have the post and salary of a couple of thousand pounds, after Palmerston's fear of the charge of nepotism had been overcome.[36] His master as Lord of the Council was the second Earl Granville, a contemporary of Spencer Cowper's at Eton.[37] William said 'he greatly desired to see effective aid given to the education of the more studious and intellectual of young men who were willing to pass their evenings, after working hours were over, in the cultivation of their minds and the acquisition of knowledge.'[38] He opposed dilution of doctrinal teaching by secularism, rejecting the idea that 'cardinal virtues' such as truthfulness and morality could be inculcated without doctrine, as Thomas Milner Gibson's bill proposed: an ironic statement given the reputed consequence of his amendment to the 1870 Education Act.[39] The vice-president also had responsibility for sanitary matters as Palmerston tried to protect the sanitary department from parliamentary critics. But William was condemned by the anti-centralizer Joshua Toulmin Smith as 'Jupiter Bifrons' for his watch over souls and sewers. He had approved a list of books for schools and Smith thought it odd to allow prayers to the Virgin (in the Sequel to *First Book of Reading Lessons*): 'unquestionably the Chairman earns his salary: only it ought to be paid by the Pope, instead of the People of England.' At the same time, he ordered 'that Manchester and Birmingham shall drain away their sewerage through a six-inch pipe'.[40]

Due to opposition from MPs to Palmerston's strategy the sanitary department was not transferred and endured a fitful existence with William from late September 1857 directing it from the Privy Council. Early in 1858 he introduced another Public Health Bill, but the Board's days were finally over. The government fell after the defeat of the Conspiracy to Murder Bill on 21 February, as discontented Liberals united with the opposition. William was out of office. His role in dispensing of patronage had made him unpopular, with one disgruntled 'Independent Liberal Member' identifying him in the *Morning Chronicle* as a leading figure among Palmerston's 'political minions and sycophants' who treated independent MPs with hauteur and employed 'politically swindling contrivances'. 'I can most solemnly declare,' this writer said, 'that no persons ever managed the distribution of the loaves and fishes in a more partial, ungrateful, and anti-Liberal manner than the Right Honourable Sir William Hayter, Baronet, and the Hon. William Cowper, the stepson of Lord Palmerston.'[41]

When Derby's government was brought down in June. William returned to junior office. Palmerston told Lord John Russell he would offer the Poor Law Board to his stepson.[42] But from August 1859 to February 1860, William was Vice President of the Board of Trade.[43] Palmerston was 'very glad to be able to put you back again into the Regiment'.[44] Gladstone also asked William to assist with the committee inquiring into the civil service.[45] Having earned his spurs in public health William was able to speak with authority about the State's role in public health at the National Association for the Promotion of Social Science annual meeting in 1859. He said that real improvement dealt with three inseparable parts of our nature: moral, intellectual, and physical. Schools and institutes would direct to loftier regions in vain if there were repulsive homes, where the atmosphere was so debilitating that even women sought alcohol for a stimulus that nature was unable to supply. If anyone still asserted that the government had no call to meddle in this matter, William asked what notion of government had they formed which ignored thousands of premature and preventable deaths, over a million serious preventable illnesses, and ensuing moral and physical degradation and misery? The state was directly interested in guarding against racial deterioration. The English workman was the best; the British soldier was unequalled; but crowding large towns without efficient sanitation or prudent regulations in many occupations enfeebled the people.

William made lasting improvements to London in his next public office. For on 9 February 1860, he became First Commissioner of the Board of Public Works, yet another exercise of Palmerston's patronage in his favour which had been the subject of press speculation.[46] The *Belfast News-Letter*'s correspondent claimed (in 1864) that whenever the political cards were shuffled, 'What is Cowper to have next?' was asked in Cambridge House, the Palmerston mansion in Piccadilly. 'For the last five-and-twenty years Mr Cowper may be said to have become fastened to the Treasury like a barnacle to a rock.'[47]

His relatively long tenure was of 'basic importance to the amelioration of London's image': he was one of a select band of ministers who became the 'acknowledged *aediles* of imperial London'.[48] The office was junior, but as the *Daily News* said, in a critical editorial on Cowper (and most of his predecessors), it had opportunities, removed from the 'heat and dust of political discussion', for achieving good by stealth. It offered the possibility of doing in a metropolis what a gentleman of taste did on his estate, 'a little ornamental gardening, model farming, fancy architecture, road making, and planting, and making his "people" comfortable and contented'.[49] The work provided plenty of opportunities, unfortunately, for difficulties with vested and competing interests which a partisan press was not slow to magnify. But even a critic, the *Belfast News-Letter*, acknowledged that despite these scrapes William was popular in the Commons.[50] And he enjoyed the office, as Georgina recalled.[51]

The Board had varied responsibilities for civil building: providing offices, residences and equipment for other government departments. Having its origins in the King's Works, it had responsibility for palaces (occupied and unoccupied) and work connected with ceremony, such as the temporary walkway for the Prince of Wales' wedding in 1863.[52] Efforts to restore the Tower of London, which involved Anthony Salvin, the architect for Tollemache's Peckforton Castle, also concerned the Board.[53] It had responsibility for the Houses of Parliament, for Royal Parks and roads, and metropolitan statues. Other buildings outside London and Windsor for which the Board had responsibility included Holyrood Palace, Linlithgow Palace, Glasgow cathedral and major Post Office buildings such as the one in Edinburgh whose stone was laid by the Prince Consort in October 1861. Overseas, property was held in the First Commissioner's name and in William's period embassies became the Board's responsibility.[54] The minister needed to work closely with the royal household and with other departments, above all the Treasury, whose instructions were paramount if in accord with legislation, and tended to view the Board as its own subordinate.[55]

The buildings initiated by William were a new National Gallery, new Law Courts, and the museums at South Kensington. He was involved with the question of sites for the University of London and various Learned Societies and plans to enlarge or construct buildings for civil servants.[56] He oversaw work on the New Palace of Westminster, supporting Edward Barry's restoration of St Stephen's crypt against the Commons' penny-pinching or anti-Puseyite prejudices, and in general endorsing efforts to make a magnificent and beautiful structure. The condition of the external masonry, commissions for artwork and decoration, for the Peers' and Queen's Robing Rooms for instance, concerned William, involving him with artists such as Daniel Maclise, William Dyce and John Rogers Herbert.[57] Barry said, when William left the Board, that he had shown consideration and kindness, and later described him as 'quite without official airs … considerate and accessible'.[58]

The Board was responsible for the Crown's annual requisition for restoration and improvements. Work on Henry VIII's Library or Queen Anne's Closet at Windsor, and the chapel at Buckingham Palace, involved dealing with the Prince Consort or Queen through the household staff. William followed certain principles in his role as restorer of royal and other structures, his view that restoration should preserve the 'evident witness of its antiquity' was just becoming more common.[59] On Holyrood Palace, he told Georgina, 'I shall make an immense improvement in these apartments & shall remove many of the modern additions that have been made.'[60] Unveiling a new window in Glasgow cathedral in 1864, he defended using German artists: the point was to promote native art through the best examples, rather than be narrowly patriotic. The object 'is to get high art, and the best art'.[61]

Getting the best art had a price, which involved Treasury, parliamentary and press scrutiny. In his dealings with the Treasury, generally, as he told his successor but one, the relationship was harmonious, 'I had thorough gentlemen to deal with as secretaries of the Treasury … though I was sometimes restricted in expenditure beyond my wishes.'[62] The Chancellor of the Exchequer was Gladstone, whose relationship with Palmerston was tense at times, Palmerston once accusing the Chancellor of acting without due regard to the First Lord of the Treasury; in 1861 a dispute over the financing of the new Law Courts arose from a scheme involving the Office of Works. In dealing with Gladstone, William's relationship with Palmerston, which indeed explains his appointment, helped.[63] The 'most cordial support and assistance from the head of Government' was something which his successor Austen Layard stressed and he told William he must have felt that even with this, the post was 'scarcely tenable'.[64]

In Prince Albert, William had to attend to a quasi-monarch keenly interested in the aesthetic and architectural improvement of the metropolis. Matters such as the embellishment of the Palace of Westminster with paintings and statuary involved the Board and Prince as the president of the Fine Arts Commission established in 1841. Other subjects bringing contact with the Prince included a statue to Robert Peel and an agricultural exhibition in Hyde Park, where the Prince's concern was also to mollify the Ranger, the Duke of Cambridge (on whom more, below).[65] The decoration of the Royal Parks interested the Prince, and he requested access to designs for embellishing Hyde Park, 'for anything more abominable than most of the drinking fountains that have been erected he never saw,' the prince's private secretary told William.[66]

When the Prince died, the Fine Arts Commission's existence was examined by the government, aware that the work had been considerably reduced by this period. The First Commissioner, concerned at the office expenses, and consulting with Gladstone, proposed that though it should continue to exist its expenses be stopped. Defenders of the secretary, the art historian Sir Charles Eastlake, mobilised the Queen. She had a 'special interest' in the Commission as the first British public body to which Albert belonged, and she therefore ensured the future of the Commission and Eastlake to her satisfaction.[67] As William was told, the Queen was even more anxious now that any work in which Prince Albert was interested should be executed.[68] The commemoration of the Prince involved the Board with plans for an 'Albert Hall' and buildings in South Kensington. Disputes about using gunmetal for the Mausoleum at Frogmore, between War Ministry and Treasury on the one hand and the Queen on the other, also reached William's department.

The Queen's first cousin, the Duke of Cambridge, as Ranger of the Royal Parks, also had to be handled tactfully, in negotiations with the Crown about temporary roads through the Parks, the use of the Parks for events such as agricultural shows, and the policing of such activity. The Office was supposed to manage the Parks but the Crown alone granted concessions and the Duke was jealous of his position.[69] He closely followed the cutting of new roads, infringements such as fishing in the Serpentine, and incidents such as a temporary shed sheltering people of the 'lowest description'.[70] The plan to pull down his Gloucester House, in widening Park Lane in 1866, did not endear William to HRH.[71]

It was in relation to roads that William proved to be most controversial. Much of the controversy was motivated by party politics as response to his decision to allow a new horse road and carriage drive in Kensington Gardens in 1860 exemplifies. It became a 'grievance' for opponents like Lord John Manners (once leader of 'Young England', and First Commissioner when the Conservatives returned to office).[72] The Palmerstonian *Times* sprang to defence, deriding the effort to make it an instance of Whiggish insensitivities to working-class recreation and selfishness about the 'horseback interest'.[73]

There was a curious development. When the radical *Reynolds's Newspaper* decided that there must be Palmerstonian blood in William's veins, it alluded to a 'general personal resemblance' redolent of father and son, but also to traits 'strongly suggestive of a common origin'. Apart from the Palmerstonian quality to William's racy snubbings, the paper thought there was a Palmerstonian touch to his conduct before a crowd in Hyde Park, revealing courage, impulsiveness and willingness to flout ministerial convention.[74] Harangued by a socialist while in the Park, William decided to rebut the charge that he and the aristocracy were selfish, and won the crowd's attention and applause. Though a critic of the Kensington Gardens scheme raised the episode in the Commons to ridicule him, William presented it as a manly address to the people, and *Reynolds's* acknowledged his English pluck, suggesting only he and Palmerston out of the Upper Ten Thousand would have been so bold.[75] The event amazed some of his graver colleagues, but impressed many: 'I had never before thought of Cowper-Temple as the possible orator of a platform in Hyde Park,' Justin McCarthy recalled, 'he had always seemed to me an extremely formal, methodical, and somewhat self-centred sort of person.'[76]

A key task William faced was the Thames embankment on the north side, from Westminster Bridge to Mansion House. A commission investigated the scheme (discussed since the time of Wren) and funds from the coal tax were set aside in 1861 for this project. But he had to persuade Gladstone to continue the coal tax. William argued that the tax was no undue burden on the poor; Gladstone queried what they got apart from expulsion.[77] The embankment sparked City opposition and required William to negotiate the claims of the Metropolitan Board of Works. Learning from Gladstone that £200,000 was apparently owed to taxpayers and London freemen through funds for the Irish Society and City Trades Union, he argued that if this was spent on improvements, the city might make as rapid advance in convenience and beauty as Paris, but the Corporation 'would probably prefer to spend it in turtle and venison or at least as a substitute for other Taxation'.[78] He had already deplored the cry for self-government, telling Gladstone he had seen enough neglect and abuse of power by local authorities to be convinced of the blessings of some central authority against jobbery and other abuses.[79]

Critics in the press enjoyed his troubles: the *Caledonian Mercury* describing him as a 'pert' gentleman receiving a seasonal rebuff for being 'very insolent, offensive and mischievous' in vandalizing Kensington Gardens.[80] The *Belfast News-Letter*, in the context of the Palace of Justice scheme (where he hoped to use a million and half pounds from the Suitors' Fund in Chancery), said he was always the 'square man in a round hole', always with a hobby, 'now for a great ditch, now for a great palace'.[81] A correspondent to the *Birmingham Daily Post* described his performance as 'so much weakness and indiscretion, not unmixed with obstinacy, not to say pig-headedness'.[82]

His near-relationship to the premier, and Palmerston's 'extreme susceptibility when he is attacked', could scarcely save him from his scrapes. 'He is the alter ego – the "counterfeit presentment" of our Premier – in everything but tact, ability, and discretion.'[83] At that moment (May 1862) William was accused of treating Sir Edwin Pearson shabbily over the Westminster Improvement Commission by offering him the chairmanship and then giving it to William Tite. Palmerston defended him, and though *The Times* supported him, the blunder brought further criticism. The radical MP Trelawney privately described him as a 'block head'. There were asides along the lines of 'tinkering, not coopering' as he made a long defence, but the House was disgusted, the moral was, 'let Ministers beware of putting a weak man in a high Public office.'[84] *Punch* ridiculed him as a drawling, incompetent aristocrat needing Palmerston's protection and called him 'Dundreary Cowper', claiming the nickname was given him by friends after the popular music-hall figure.[85] *Fun* presented him as a 'Pam-pered' mediocrity, a 'Babe in Woods and Forests', amiable but incapable, and more concerned with the comfort of his aristocratic order in Rotten Row than the starving denizens of park benches or middle-class children in pursuit of outdoor recreation.[86]

The Thames Embankment Bill involved another 'scrape' which Georgina recorded indignantly (as she recalled, she writhed under the abuse he experienced in his public career[87]). As chairman of the Embankment Committee he attempted to influence *The Times* through the journalist Matthew James Higgins (a friend of Thackeray who wrote as 'Jacob Omnium'), to put weight on fellow committee members in relation to the construction of a public road between the river and Montagu House. Unfortunately he sent his letter to the wrong Higgins, the son-in-law of Lord Chelmsford who had been denied a post as Master in Lunacy partly due to *The Times*. The Conservative Lord Robert Montagu exploited the gaffe, informing other Committee members and making it the basis of an attack as Georgina indignantly recorded. The Commons listened with incredulity to William's explanation.[88] The *Daily News*, cruelly, wrote that the period had now arrived when Cowper 'annually distinguishes himself', Lord Robert being the providential instrument this year.[89] The *Belfast News-Letter*'s correspondent called him 'a most unfortunate individual ... he is always in a mess of some kind or another'.[90] Georgina was satisfied when Montagu had to eat humble pie. 'People generally,' she wrote, 'think W's conduct irreproachable & that his attackers have only damaged themselves & helped on his bill.'[91]

FIGURE 5. Left: undated portrait of William Cowper outside Parliament. Right: *carte de visite* portrait by Frederick Richard Window, 1850s. By courtesy of the Trustees of the Broadlands Archives.

It was an era when national art institutions were the target of reform.[92] A Royal Commission studied the future of the Royal Academy, whose royal associations meant the Queen's close interest. William was responsible for the composition of the Commission with her advice (she made 'many enquiries')?[93] He told Sir Charles Grey, the Queen's secretary, that the involvement of painters would only exacerbate the difficulties, for 'the art feuds which hang round the Academy question are as bitter and unjust as theological hatreds are supposed to be'.[94] If the Academy were to move from Trafalgar Square, which had long been discussed by governments eager to return its rooms to the National Gallery, then it would require a building which Gladstone worried would be a charge on the public purse.[95] William was involved in the negotiations with Sir

Charles Eastlake and Sir Francis Grant, the successive Presidents of the Academy, for an accommodation for the Academy and constitutional changes in relation to the number of Academicians and the size and role of associates.[96] Before Grant had been elected President, William gave the Academy notice to quit, offering Burlington House on condition that the associates should be allowed to vote for RAs and associates.[97] The increase in the number of associates and the move to Burlington House were both achieved in 1867.

The Office of Works was responsible for control and management of public meetings in Trafalgar Square, with the commissioner of police. It also had authority for permitting lectures and demonstrations in the royal parks, and William was criticised in late 1862 when English Garibaldian oratory at Hyde Park stimulated riots involving thousands of incensed Irish Catholics.[98] In April 1864 William was involved with access to the parks for a meeting on the sudden and 'unsatisfactory' departure of the Italian hero Garibaldi from Britain. Radicals involved associated him with the despotism or interference of the Police Commissioner Sir Richard Mayne and Sir George Grey at the Home Office.

In the same year, William attended to the problem of casting the lions sculpted by Sir Edwin Landseer for Trafalgar Square, a task which threatened to make their creator mentally unstable again. If the government would not agree to pay Baron Marochetti for the casting, then 'the Column might remain in its baseness and poverty for the remainder of our lives,' he warned Gladstone.[99] He had already told Gladstone that given the location, the 'Country ought not to grudge the money necessary to make them first rate works of art – and I should be disposed to say either have excellent ones or none at all'.[100] Commissioned in 1858, the lions were finally unveiled in January 1867.

The problem of Landseer's lions, controversies over Burlington House and the National Gallery, War and Foreign Offices and Buckingham Palace, were presented as a 'tragedy of errors' in an attack in the Conservative periodical *Fraser's* in early 1864: it was a 'remarkable feature of the proceedings of the last session of Parliament, that the public works of the metropolis occupied an unusual amount of attention'.[101] The controversies were not due to the lack of important crises, but a sense of shame about public buildings in the metropolis. William's taste was rubbished: Alexander Munro's statue in Hyde Park became 'a boy with a small dolphin tucked under his arms, squeezing out a few drops of dirty water out of its snout', the monolith in Hyde Park blocked a spring and Kensington fountains created a smelly lake. Yet William's contribution to protection of the capital's green spaces was acknowledged by others. With advice from

William A. Nesfield (and Georgina), he improved the parks.[102] One obituary said this 'conduced to the pleasure of millions of his fellows'.[103]

As in garden design, William was conscious of superior continental models when it came to the design of manufactured goods such as carpets and tiles, and he supported the educative role of the South Kensington museum which also housed the Government Department of Science and Art. Matters of taste were not trivial, he argued, supporting the involvement of the state in the improvement of art education and design reform which had been greatly stimulated by the Great Exhibition, in the belief that British industry benefited.[104]

We have seen the press repeatedly associating William with the premier, with justifiable accusations of nepotism. In the 'style wars' over the building of the Foreign Office, William was seen as the mouthpiece of his anti-Gothic stepfather.[105] William was frequently reported in his stepfather's company, when for instance, Palmerston triumphantly visited Scotland in the spring of 1863, along with Lord Shaftesbury's son Evelyn Ashley, who had become Palmerston's private secretary.[106] In June 1863 Palmerston was visited by the wife of Timothy O' Kane, an Irish radical journalist who subsequently accused them of adultery, citing the prime minister as co-respondent in the divorce petition in October, but the case unravelled when it was revealed that O' Kane had not married his wife, who denied any adultery. Lady Palmerston treated it as ridiculous, Lady Shaftesbury reporting that her stepfather was 'in excellent spirits' and street balladeers joked[107]; how William reacted is impossible to know.[108] July 1865 saw a successful general election for the aged premier but he died in October. William had been closely informed of his health, receiving that famous letter from Lady Palmerston, for instance, reporting Palmerston's surprise that he had lived so long without finding out what a good breakfast mutton chops were.[109] His stepfather's death brought great change to his private life, but for now William stayed in office.

About 1867, a newspaper, surveying William's tenure, argued that though the Office required no great political qualities, there was ample room for energy and good taste and he had been 'most successful, and the public owe him a large debt of gratitude for the immense improvements he has introduced into the Parks'.[110] If he enjoyed the improvements to the parks, another satisfaction was ecclesiastical patronage as First Commissioner. But even this caused controversy, since his decision in 1860 to offer Maurice the incumbency of St Peter's Church, Vere Street, evoked a furore in the Evangelical *Record*, horrified at recognition of one doctrinally unorthodox. The Evangelicals' appeal to the Bishop of London was rejected: an address by his supporters, published in *The Times*, stressed Maurice's efforts among the working classes. The *Record* commented, 'The moral of this seems to be – True, we differ on the great cardinal doctrine of the Atonement on which the gospel rests; but what signify doctrinal diversities if we are all earnest men, desiring to promote peace on earth.'

Obviously some of the Office's projects were initiated by predecessors, and the Office worked with bodies such as the Fine Arts Commission. Nevertheless, William's role was active and important. But this office was no springboard to an enhanced political role, not that William aimed to be his stepfather's political heir, wisely given his baiting. If a fellow MP, John Trelawny, identified him as a 'worn out Whig placeman' and 'favoured incompetency', plenty in the press, as we have seen, similarly depicted him.[111]

Some of the criticism seemed to focus on his oratorical weaknesses, in an age in which public speaking was central to politics (in the Commons and outside) and in which a burgeoning press exhibited much interest in the utterances, eloquent or otherwise, of public men.[112] William's doubts stimulated letters from his mother passing on Palmerston's praise for his slow delivery: 'he came home quite pleased – so I thought you would like to have his unbias'd opinion.'[113] She admired his speech at Luton in 1855: 'It was so very *very* well put together, that I took and read it to Ld Palmerston who was equally delighted with me and thought it *quite excellent* and likely to be very useful – all about Peace was so true and so well worked out.'[114] Grenville Fletcher's portrait of 1862, referred to his industry and intelligence as a minister, and characterized his performance in the chamber as 'lucid and argumentative, unpretending in … manner, and without the least pretension to the display of oratory'. When he was deeply interested in the subject he impressed the audience with the 'conscientious feeling and sincerity of an attached and zealous labourer in the cause of which he is an advocate'.[115] The satirical paper *Fun* thought otherwise, writing about the confusion of his own ideas and expression: 'he is to say the least, amusing.' *Once a Week* in 1876 referred to his gentle purr.[116] Lionel Tollemache detected, among the 'odd tricks of manner' which William had picked up from his step-father, the habit of stroking his hat while making a speech. One admirer recollected that he was 'soft and beautifully modulated, and in power of public speaking … far above the average of public men, with a peculiar sweetness and winningness'.[117] But William partly rejected Gladstone's subsequent offer of office because 'he had not the power in debate, nor the eloquence in speech, that he thought necessary for that position (Cabinet); but he loved work.'[118] But if a position as junior minister was over after 1866, a role in political life continued. The study of that career is taken up in chapter 8.

6

THE PRIVATE LIFE OF THE
COWPERS, 1860–1867

When her beloved nephew Henry Cowper set off for Italy at the start of 1862, Georgina contrasted this delightful prospect with her own. She wanted no paradise but rest, 'I think sometimes how happy I shd be as a cottager sitting alone mending William's shirts & boiling my potatoes & working in my little Garden. Life in our class is a fever.'[1] Apart from the social round of the Palmerstons' gatherings and the Season, there were family calls in London, days at Nutfield with Augustus and Marguerite (with her beloved dog Tiff), church-going, work in the Ladies' Sanitary Association, district and workhouse visiting, while William fulfilled ministerial and parliamentary duties. In this Georgina's experience was that of many a wife of a public man whose political duties called him away from home. But they did not live separate lives, for when it was time to rest from work, they shared recreation such as reading John Ruskin, religious works and the latest novels, singing hymns to Georgina's piano accompaniment, visits to the National Gallery, concerts by Jenny Lind and readings by Charles Dickens. A new study, stimulated by Georgina's mother's death in 1861, was spiritualism, which brought the Cowpers into a circle of prominent spiritualists. With servants and no children of her own, Georgina could be intense about many things.

1860 brought long-lasting and close relationships with the middle-class Russell Gurneys (particularly a friendship between Emelia Gurney and Georgina) and the Anglo-American mystic Thomas Lake Harris. Close acquaintance with the Russell Gurneys followed a dinner at the Trevelyans. 'I cannot grasp the infinite stream that was discovered to me in the desert of that dinner party at the dear Trevelyans,' Emelia was later to recall to Georgina, 'the face that I then looked at past my neighbours contained it all, as Seed does the June rose – as the nightingale does its song!'[2] The 'absolutely uncommonplace' Emelia belonged to the Kensington society of female reformers and feminists; her social activism was one reason why Georgina should become close to her. Another was Emelia's self-confessed 'intense pleasure in being converted', for Georgina 'really longed to be converted'.[3] Emelia's husband, twenty years her senior, was already linked to the Cowpers through William's first marriage. He was to become the Recorder of London and a Conservative MP. The Ladies' Sanitary Association had been invited to hold a lecture on memory at the Gurney mansion at the end of February, which may have been a consequence of the meeting between the Cowpers and the Russell Gurneys, who first appear in Georgina's diary in 1859.[4] In June Georgina held a private conversazione for the Association, attended by her Cowper connections, Julia Rich and Ellen Ranyard, the promoter of those missionaries and proto-social workers, the 'Bible women'.[5]

The Cowpers and the Augustus Tollemaches were at Harrow Weald in Easter for the last time, as Monro moved to Leeds.[6] But perhaps they found a new source of inspiration, if they attended lectures by the 'eloquent spiritual preacher of America', the Reverend Thomas Lake Harris. He advertised these, apparently a second set (he had preached and conducted worship at the Marylebone Institute in May 1859), in *The Times*. The lectures took place in the Music-hall in Store Street in January. Many years later, an unsympathetic reader described the printed versions as 'floods of fustian verbiage' but noted the evident magnetism which Harris possessed: it was a magnetism which the Cowper-Temples proved susceptible to.[7]

The next year was pivotal in the Cowpers' lives. For in May 1861 Georgina's beloved mother died.[8] Georgina looked back at this year, despite great grief, as 'almost the happiest of my life because it seemed to me that a door was indeed opened to me into Heaven'.[9] This became possible through spiritualism, that study of supernatural phenomena stimulated by the rapping of spirits in the United States in the early 1850s, which formed a prominent feature of mid-Victorian culture as a movement attracting plebeian, middle-class and aristocratic investigators: drawn to it for many reasons, including, as in Georgina's case, its potential to demonstrate the existence of an afterlife and spiritual forces, where orthodox religion might no longer wholly convince.[10] If she had not been active in the first wave of spiritualism in the 1850s, now she became a serious investigator. Within a couple of months Georgina attended séances with her sister Mummy (Marianne) and William.[11] Georgina, in her misery, contacted the writer Mary Howitt, having heard that she was a follower of spiritualism. After a kind response she visited Mary and her husband William (also a well-known writer) in Highgate. The couple showed their artwork (and work by Annie Watts their daughter) undertaken through spiritualism: 'we both came away much impressed by what we had seen and heard.' Mary came to consider the couple 'amongst the angels of god now on earth, who celebrate the second coming of their Lord'.[12] Georgina was also stimulated by acquaintances such as Arethusa Milner Gibson (political hostess and wife of the Radical-Liberal MP) who said that her daughter had become betrothed through spirits.[13] Through the mesmeric practitioner and spiritualist Dr John Ashburner, Georgina and Mummy learned they could be mediums.

We have a detailed glimpse of this activity through the Cowpers' joint notes. From early July, through Mrs Howitt, they had séances with a famous medium, the American Daniel Dunglas Home (accompanied by his wealthy young Russian bride Alexandrina, known as 'Sacha').[14] Home was known throughout Europe, having had audiences with the monarchs of Russia, Bavaria, Holland and France, and having been expelled from Rome by papal instruction. The Cowpers' co-investigators included the publisher and anonymous author of the *Vestiges of Creation*, Robert Chambers, 'not a man one would suspect of a credulous or imaginative temperament,' Mummy noted (Chambers wrote the anonymous preface to Home's autobiography in 1862); the author Catherine Sinclair, and the Radical MP Joseph Hume. Beautiful-browed 'Purity' – the 'spirit name' for Georgina's mother – was seen by Home, appearing kind and gentle, but 'with such a clear sense of duty'.[15]

The séances introduced William and Georgina to spiritualist theatrics in the exciting but disturbing darkness, with verbena sprigs and feathers moved by unseen hands and unearthly accordion music. Home was possessed by a whole host of departed relations, from Robert Jocelyn and Ernest Fane, to the flashy Alfred d'Orsay. Mummy wrote that to suppose these communications lucky guesses on his part required more credulity than to believe them 'to proceed as they profess from Spiritual intelligence'. William had a message from his first wife, who through the medium, kissed and assured him that in the darkness of his bereavement she had been there.[16] Another early séance was a *tête à tête* with Home after William went to the House, with Daniel 'occasionally starting at the appearance of a Spirit' and Georgina begging him to say who it was. Home recreated Ernest Fane's shake of the hand and 'looked so much like him that it has brought back his face to me most vividly'. Alfred d'Orsay appeared, and longed to be with '*her* [i.e., Lady Blessington] not his wife'. Georgina had seen him when a child, and thought the accent quite unlike his; she also defended d'Orsay's talents despite the spirit's revelations that his art had not all been his. He left with a grandiose patronizing look, to be followed by her sister Louisa, Robert Jocelyn and Georgina's father, with admiral's epaulettes and Tollemache pose. The finale was 'the most wonderful thing I ever heard', he brought the accordion and held it over her head and she heard the mid-ocean, complete with wind. Probably after this séance, she wrote to Home that she had stayed up late thinking over and recording the wonders.[17] On another occasion she told him, 'I feel now no interest, except in the spirit world.'[18]

In mid-September, when reports resumed (after the Cowpers accompanied Palmerston, as Lord Warden of the Cinque Ports, to his official residence at Walmer Castle), there were visits to Lady Poulett's mediumistic maid, along with their friend the Reverend Herman Douglas, and interesting talk with Dr Ashburner on matter, magnetism and human will. Georgina's acceptance was furthered by the reaction of Ashburner's visitor, the German chemist Baron Karl von Reichenbach, propounder of an 'Odilic' vital force, who left utterly astonished after a table took small leaps and knocked him into a corner (the Cowpers apparently witnessed this).[19] Séances in early December – following a cultural tour of German cities – were held with the celebrated American Charles Foster, who they sought out soon after he arrived in England. Foster's approach was distinct, using ballot papers and his arms to receive spirit communications (his spirits misspelt 'Cowper'). He brought messages from Georgina's childhood friend, Jessy Ryle (wife of the Reverend Ryle), from Georgina's mother, and from Lord Melbourne and his brother Frederick. By the time Georgina visited Foster with Fanny she was noting 'the usual common place speeches ending with Robert Jocelyn quite correctly given'. Despite whirling candles and tilting furniture the sisters-in-law left dejected.[20] Georgina's grandparents the Aldboroughs joined the spiritual throng, but dissatisfaction remained. News of this activity leaked out through publications such as the *Spiritual Magazine* in 1862, and Epes' *Planchette* in 1869, reporting that von Reichenbach's attitude to spiritual phenomena had altered as a result of the incident.[21]

The Prince Consort died on 14 December, and William was shortly afterwards at Windsor. The Cowpers had an intimate view of royal grief as Fanny showed the Queen's reply to words which 'went to the poor utterly desolate broken widow's heart': 'Oh Fanny, can I bear it?' the Queen asked.[22] Later, Fanny said a speech by William alluding to the Prince's death had pleased the Queen.[23] Royal connections continued as Spencer arranged to sell Sandringham for £230, 000 in 1862, following Palmerston's advice to Prince Albert about an estate suitable for the heir to the throne's shooting. Improvements were soon made to the estate; the house itself was demolished.[24]

Georgina's diary for 1862 is extensive, with comments about staying at Broadlands in the company of Abraham Hayward (whose 'venom and slime' led her to reflect that the world would be very pleasant without people[25]), on the American Civil War and the fact that many were repelled by the North's bluster and insolence into supporting the South whilst she, who had read Harriet Beecher Stowe's *Uncle Tom's Cabin*, dreaded the result of a triumphant South.[26] Her letter against the use of arsenical green dye for artificial floral decorations appeared in *The Times* in February. Sanitary Association work (correcting or writing reports and inviting speakers), mothers' meetings, and district and workhouse visiting continued. About now, she formed a temperance society in Mayfair.

The year began with the Palmerstons at Cambridge House, the arrival of the King of the Belgians hanging over Georgina. But the Cowpers enjoyed seeing their nephew Henry, Georgina having a 'spiritual grope' with him over character and Divine Law, and discussing Socrates, Comte and the Book of Job. Georgina also saw John Ruskin, returned from Switzerland: 'charming and spoke so cleverly & interestingly & beautifully about all sorts of things' – including the 'advisability of bettering oneself & one's surroundings rather than attempting in vain to reform the world'. He spoke 'sadly of his loneliness but with a brave heart'.[27] Then at Panshanger, Georgina enjoyed the gallery, played Mendelssohn and recited Tennyson's 'Palace of Art' in the 'lordly pleasure house ... Life here *too* luxurious'. Her niece Dolly read from *Cornhill's Magazine*, Georgina perused Dolly's journal and Henry's essay about religion and advised him, Anne amused them with anecdotes, they botanised among primroses and Georgina sat up late talking spiritualism. Georgina was reading Bulwer Lytton's occult *Strange Story* (wherein Anne detected a fictionalized portrait of herself), Carlyle's *Characteristics*, and George Sand's *Consuelo*.[28]

Returning to town, Georgina bewailed a bill to allow plays during Passion week, when people should instead be finding 'fellowship with the sufferings of our Divine Lord', and fretted about William's legislative difficulties. But she also had family woes and domestic charities, as she looked after an infant, George Herbert, until his mother recovered and collected him in January. Concerned about an acquaintance, Maria Shaw, she interfered despite Mummy's indignation: 'I was sorry for it but think I was right to speak.'[29]

Georgina had visited Thomas Heaphy, author of a narrative about ghosts in *All the Year Round*, in January. He was 'most unsatisfactory & not believing his own story can hardly expect other people to do so'. She believed he fabricated ghost experiences after failing as a painter. Then she attended séances at Dr Ashburner's, with notables such as Joseph Hume MP and the former colonial secretary and traveller Sir James Emerson Tennent.[30] Georgina's spiritualist investigations with Mummy and William continued at Mrs Milner Gibson's, with Forster and Baroness Goldenstubbe ('a queer witch like woman with immense bumps of identity and distinctiveness,' she thought) who channelled Milton and Shakespeare while ignorant of English.[31] She went to séances with the tall and handsome Prince George von Solms-Graunfels, relation of the blind King of Hanover. The prince became a spiritualist after séances with Home and befriended the noted American spiritualist James Peebles.[32] To William came Harriet Cowper's spirit again, 'watching the united happiness and usefulness of your lives'. Further séances round the three-legged oak table in Curzon Street brought John the Evangelist, saying there was no harm from manifestations if preceded by prayer. The Evangelist came frequently to give Georgina and Em religious instructions, tell them to abandon doubt, pray more, and from the heart.[33]

Other mediums included 'the wonderful and *good* medium', Miss Annie Andrews at Greenwich, 'Love's Messenger', first visited by Georgina in May.[34] There were further illustrious spirits, from Christopher Columbus and Lord Byron, to Jack Cade who told the company that 'emoluments are too large' and warned them to 'cheat the people no longer'.[35] At Mrs Milner Gibson's the women were enjoined by a slave to support American abolitionism.[36] Queen Anne appeared at Lady Poulett's to say Gladstone was the minister of the future.[37] Spiritualism, clearly, provided no escape from worldly concerns. Sisters Mummy and Sell thought they were psychic and had séances with 'Fisco' the mesmerist (an unidentified figure named after Wilkie Collins' villain).[38] Through Andrews, Georgina became acquainted with the astronomer royal of Woolwich, Alfred Wilks Drayson, who was a writer on diverse subjects from the ice age to whist, who collaborated with Andrews on various books.[39] She thought Drayson's interpretation of comets as scavengers, '[v]ery simple but ideas suggested very great'. Drayson claimed his theories were prompted by spirits.[40]

During this spiritual excitement, Georgina suffered persistent headaches and resorted to chloroform. She appears to have had a prolapse.[41] Eventually, in early March, with much anxiety, she was operated on by Dr Isaac Baker Brown, of the London Surgical Home. This involved caustic chemicals and a month's convalescence in bed, and she viewed it so seriously that she arranged accounts and got her 'house in order', i.e., presumably arranged her will. Baker Brown specialised in female diseases and later became notorious for cliterodectomies to cure hysteria, irritability (and masturbation) in upper-class women. It is unclear what Georgina's illness was, but Dr Protheroe Smith told them later, in advice which was partially destroyed, that it was 'possible…miscarry without knowing it'.[42] Georgina was approaching forty and it must have seemed unlikely that the couple would ever have children.

Whatever the nature of the operation, it brought no restoration of health. As she later admitted, she did not take enough care, though she sought the advice of a Miss Julia who had claimed to restore Lord Llanover's eyesight, and who said she stood and walked too much after the operation.[43] She used Reichenbach's electric machine 'with no effect', though she later found chloroform loosened one from the earth, 'Looked down on things as from a height and felt a restful confidence in all being good and right.'[44] Chest pains and worry about her heart persisted and she turned to mesmerism, engaging the services of Thomas Capern.

In late April the International Exhibition at the 'Brompton Boilers' in South Kensington opened, Georgina's thoughts turning to the widowed Queen, and Albert's superior Great Exhibition. Taking her relation Edith on another visit, they regretted John Gibson's controversial 'tinted' Venus but Georgina thought the Boilers a brilliant sight. At Lady Louisa Goldsmid's concert there was scarcely anyone she knew and most appeared, so she wrote in her diary, Jewish or Scientific Socialists (Goldsmid was a promoter of higher female education). Dickens' reading of *Christmas Carol* and *Pickwick* was amusing but a week later Georgina was unable to enjoy poor Smike at Dotheboys Hall, or Mrs Gamp, leaving disturbed and doleful. Calling without invitation, she found the celebrated Swedish singer Jenny Lind irritably tired and 'so blunt and abrupt in manner that I might have thought her rude', but also sincere and an earnest Christian. Having got a house in Cumberland Street for Spencer and Harriet, Georgina found it was a 'bad bargain for everybody'.[45]

Friendship with the poet and novelist George MacDonald began about this year, with the earliest surviving letter from MacDonald a belated verdict on poetry (not hers) which Georgina had asked him to comment on; he feared seeming a dreadful Philistine, 'but you asked me to say what I judged'.[46] MacDonald's admiration for Maurice was one close bond between them; like the Cowpers' his religious tastes were mystical. About this time too, William became acquainted with the brilliant Laurence Oliphant, a young man whose varied career had already encompassed MP, spy, novelist and travel writer; shortly he became a disciple of the American utopian Thomas Lake Harris, with fateful consequences for the Cowpers. Oliphant came to Broadlands in December and impressed the diarist Henry Greville with his Japanese anecdotes and general talk.[47]

When civil war apparently impended in Italy, Georgina – whose niece Selina (known as Leila) had married the Duca di Sant' Arpino – anxiously followed events, getting news from an acquaintance who said, no doubt thinking of her stepfather-in-law, 'I know you will make only good use of this,' and offering assistance to Garibaldi's cause which she believed to be guided by God, though she felt he was being foolish and reckless.[48] She stifled indignation when the Piedmontese minister Count Corti, attending Palmerston at Dover, expressed a wish to shoot Garibaldi for his actions in Sicily, from where he intended to march on Rome.[49] The Cowpers planned an Italian holiday against the medium Madame Julie de Bonnevilliers' advice to Georgina.[50] Exhausted and depressed, she felt as if her brain were 'decompressing, so aching & heavy & muddled. Long to bore myself a quiet hole in the earth like the moles & be still'.[51]

But in the winter, the Cowpers in the company of Edward Monro, after feeling humbled by the Parisian public gardens, stayed briefly at Mentone where they met William's former colleague from the Board of Health, John Simon. Georgina joined the hundreds of English who offered medical assistance for the imprisoned Garibaldi.[52] In Milan they read newspapers sympathetic to Garibaldi and kept to their hotel to avoid the 'horrid' Abraham Hayward. In Venice they found their friends Mary Stanley and Thomas Hughes and with Ruskin's *Stones of Venice*, toured *duomo*, churches and galleries. 'Venice,' wrote Georgina, 'would have been but half what it has been to us without the aid of his "precious" Stones!'[53] She felt St Mark's 'bewildering in its glorious beauty,' and awoke, not to an English 'sweet Sunday,' but a 'glorious Sunday' and a 'Turner day'.[54] Characteristically, she found time to write to her workhouse and orphans.

William was deep in Ruskin as they left Italy on the eve of Georgina's fortieth birthday. Their return through Vienna allowed William to meet Moritz Esterhazy after twenty-five years: Esterhazy, Austrian minister in Rome until 1859, was now minister without portfolio in Austria (with great influence over the Emperor Franz Joseph, indeed, his hostility towards Prussia contributed to the Austro-Prussian war). The English papers were full of Hyde Park riots and blame for William allowing preaching in the park (*Fun*, for instance, thought this had been a calculated move by William to ingratiate himself with the fanatical followers of 'Stiggins'[55]): Georgina dreaded returning. She heard as they prepared to leave Harriet at Paris that F.D. Maurice (in a quandary over the controversial Biblical research by his friend Colenso, bishop of Natal) had resigned from St Peter's, although in the end he decided to stay on.[56]

They were at Wrest, Anne Cowper's ancestral mansion, in early November, where Georgina met the good looking and softly-voiced James Anthony Froude, the historian and critic. Henry Cowper intended to stand for the parliamentary representation of Hertfordshire, the diarist Henry Greville – an old friend of Lady Cowper's who came to Wrest – described him as 'clever' and hoped he would distinguish himself.[57] The Cowpers' London guests included an 'ill and sulky' Ruskin and the medium Daniel Home. A big event was meeting Maurice at Augustus Tollemache's house: 'So pleasant – he was quite cosy and I not shy. After tea he read the last chapter of St John's Gospel.'[58]

No detailed diary exists for 1863 or 1864, but glimpses of activity are found in their spiritual notes and in William's engagement diary for 1864 when official concerns included Landseer's Trafalgar Square lions and chairing the Shakespeare Tercentenary Committee. In early 1863 at a séance with Home at Lady Poulett's the spirit of Sacha Home (who had died the previous July) scribbled an autograph. Sacha had said she would return after death and pinch Georgina and obliged. Later in the year, spirits told William to support Henry's parliamentary candidacy. Henry's unsuccessful contest the following year was attributed to 'Billy's' unpopularity.[59] In February 1864 John Ruskin accompanied the Cowpers in one séance with the professional medium Mary Marshall, Captain Drayson, and the homeopathist Dr John Rutherford Russell. His mother Margaret Ruskin seemed to appear, and a table and piano played a jig. They met again and a large table danced to a country tune and a little table hung in the air. Ruskin attended a few days later when a guitar accompanied Georgina playing 'God save the Queen' on the piano. Georgina corresponded with Ruskin about Home and spiritual manifestations and in May the Cowpers met Ruskin with Drayson.[60]

There was public rumour in August, as in the previous year, that Lady Palmerston would receive a peerage in her own right, which would then go to William.[61] Throughout the same month the Cowpers attended séances with the Russells at Clarges Street. Through the spirit world, William was urged by Frederick Lamb on a number of occasions to find and publish Melbourne's letters and speeches, to help foreign affairs in this year of the Schleswig-Holstein crisis; uncle Frederick revealed Melbourne's gladness that Prussia and Austria took the lead. By November William learned that he should get Spencer to preface a collection of material making a life of Melbourne, for the public good, the spirits knowing that William 'has so much to do in his office'.[62] There were further séances with the Russells into December. They resumed in January and February. About this period, too, the Cowpers came across the spiritualistic Misses Orinna and Margaret Greenfield, of 4, Cranbury Terrace, Southampton. Their father was a non-practising barrister devoted to heraldry and genealogy and a friend of the theologian Rowland Williams. Margaret told Georgina a day with her was 'like breathing fresh air to be with people who find the key to the outer life in the inner'.[63]

In early April the Cowpers visited the Louvre and Palais des Beaux Arts.[64] When parliament was dissolved in early July, Palmerston won the election and William was re-elected. He supported his nephew's candidacy for Hertfordshire.[65] There followed séances with the Wattses and Prince George, and William Champernowne and his young son.[66] There were also meetings with Dante Gabriel Rossetti whose acquaintance the Cowpers had just made.

In late September the Cowpers visited Wales to promote the interests of Palmerston and other share-holders in the Welsh Slate Company at the Phiwbryfdir and Meolwyn Mawr quarries. Palmerston assigned William four shares by his will of 1864, with the remainder of twenty four shares to come when Lady Palmerston died.[67] Established as a company in 1825, leased from the Oakeleys, the business was profitless for shareholders for a quarter century, though it paid large royalties to the lessor. But by 1864 Palmerston's shares were worth £400 a year each and he believed the quarry would be very productive. William looked round the quarry, agreed with the decision to remove unnecessary walls to release more slate, assessed the virtues of gun cotton and improvements to the quarrymen's hovels, and advocated machinery.[68] A new lease was secured. Then they visited Ireland, where Palmerston believed that William could learn more about the Fenians than 'we on the other side of the water can tell you'. If there was any movement (and Ireland from the mid-1860s experienced a revival of political radicalism) Palmerston feared that Fenians fresh from the American Civil War would exacerbate the problem of crime.[69] 1865 was to be the first of the Cowpers' annual visits to Ireland. But after attending the Dublin Exhibition, they returned due to a telegram from Brocket Hall, informing them of Palmerston's ailing state.

On the morning of Wednesday 18 October, Palmerston died amid those who were dearest to him, with the exception of his wife who had to be removed from the room. With him were William and Georgina, Shaftesbury and his son Evelyn, Fanny and his physician Dr Protheroe Smith. William and his brother-in-law were keen that Palmerston's Anglican faith should be affirmed and prayed with him; William publicised this by a letter to the people of Romsey stating that 'he appeared to join in it'.[70] Georgina told Augustus that it was desperately dreary, but that Lady Palmerston bore up ('how unlike me!').[71] Spencer came from Paris, where Harriet tended to cholera, typhus and small-pox victims.

Palmerston's choice of heir had already been the subject of speculation, newspapers in August 1864 pointing out that Palmerston, without offspring and with the demise of his brother Sir William Temple, lacked collateral heirs. He always showed 'an extraordinary affection' for William, the *Inverness Courier* stated, and it was also assumed that most of the Melbourne estates would be his after his mother died. It was rumoured that Palmerston wished the title to go to William and that he shared this ambition.[72] In the funeral arrangements and condolences that followed William had a prominent part. After arranging for interment at Romsey, the family agreed to a public funeral and burial at Westminster, with

William, Lord Shaftesbury and the dead premier's Cabinet present. The Queen, following advice from the new premier, Lord John Russell, offered a peerage in her own right to Lady Palmerston with a remainder to William, but she refused. William encouraged a memorial to his stepfather, and his effort secured a statue in Romsey.[73] He helped search for papers for Henry Bulwer's biography. Both wanted to deal, in Bulwer's words, 'very justly & calmly & without spite of any kind – but to vindicate Lord Palmerston's policy and conduct' over the quarrel with Russell, and generally.[74]

Georgina saw the next couple of years as 'sad and grey' and 'covered with a pall': her sense of the sands of life slowly dribbling out perhaps a natural reaction to the abrupt loss of a place by the nation's centre-stage. She told Florence Nightingale of the 'great gulph it has made in which our poor little lives are swallowed up'.[75] William was in poor health. In late November 1865 he consulted Dr Weldon, who said he had red sand about the kidneys and a 'fore-brain so intensely full … you must pursue rest'.[76] At the same time, they found solace in spiritualism. As Georgina recalled: 'It happened that it was just at that time that our souls were being filled with visions of a far greater and more enduring inheritance which made our earthly one seem to us of little account.'[77]

The following year, 1866, saw the Overend and Gurney bank collapse, general economic crisis, and parliamentary reform riots in Hyde Park in July threatening mass disorder in London.[78] It was a dramatic year for the Cowpers too. It began at Panshanger where Anne Cowper recovered from apoplexy, they read J.R. Seeley's *Ecce Homo* (which Shaftesbury condemned as the most pestilential book vomited from Hell's jaws), and the life of F.W. Robertson.[79] In the same month came advice from Shaftesbury about the Irish estates and private papers of Lord Palmerston. He anticipated the usefulness especially of correspondence with Gladstone.[80]

There followed a party for poor people in the drawing room at Curzon Street which left Georgina 'dreadfully knocked up' after standing so long, and she was put to bed, with Protheroe Smith in attendance.[81] While she was soon able to enjoy reading (including William Blake) and attend séances, William was reported to be ill at Broadlands after the Easter recess.[82] His official role ended with the resignation of Russell's ministry in late June; if this gave him more time this was just as well since Georgina was ill, and received medical attention at Elizabeth Cottage (not the house established for Charles Dickens' mistress).[83] Despite this, foreign affairs drew her into the public arena, the Austro-Prussian war stimulating a 'Ladies' Association for the Relief of the Sick and Wounded of All Nations engaged in the Present War' to issue a circular signed by Georgina, Florence Nightingale, Mrs Salis Schwabe and other philanthropic lights.[84] From Annie Watts she learned how Prince George fared in his 'terrible time of anxiety' with Hanover's defeat.[85]

With Georgina's health still poor, their homeopathic and spiritual helper Mrs Wagstaff visited. Wagstaff, formerly Eliza Hetty Hall, had made a name as a clairvoyant healer before marriage to the surgeon Philip Wynter Wagstaff of Leighton Buzzard.[86] Their socialising did not stop. Laurence Oliphant visited, the Cowpers saw Dante Gabriel Rossetti at his studio in Cheyne Row, and held a party comprising Ruskin, Daniel Home, Mrs Marshall and Captain Drayton. The Cowpers also had the writer Arthur Helps (the Clerk of the Privy Council, he was keen to write Palmerston's official biography) and Rossetti to dinner, and saw the artist Burne-Jones.[87]

From mid-August and for two months, William and Georgina were away from Curzon Street. They went to Tan Y Bwlch for quarry business and to Sligo to meet tenants (Georgina recorded a 'dreary drive' round their houses). They were addressed by the mayor and dignitaries, attended school feasts and received petitioners and tenant deputations. More importantly, the Irish visit allowed them to see Rose La Touche, for they were closely involved in the tortuous and ultimately tragic relationship between Ruskin and the young daughter of the La Touches of Harristown, Kildare, who had been Ruskin's pupil and who was to succumb to the 'furnace of his love' (to quote Mary Gladstone's retelling of Georgina's recollection). [88] Ruskin proposed to Rose in 1866 when she was eighteen and he was almost thirty years her senior. In the summer the Cowper-Temples were asked – implored – to discover if Rose's love was childish or something he could trust 'against the absolute device of both her parents'. [89] At the start of September they visited the La Touches briefly and brought back the judgement that the marriage could not be.

Tim Hilton, one of Ruskin's most recent biographers, has noted that '[s]o little is known about Rose, her character and health'. Details of this significant visit come from Rose's fragmentary correspondence for the Cowper-Temple papers preserve little record of their involvement with the La Touches: any fuller account in their diaries was probably destroyed after William's death when Georgina went through their papers and her words survive only in the responses in Rose's letters. [90] They travelled to the Curragh with Mrs La Touche on 4 September and walked in the garden with Rose the next day. They talked about Ruskin certainly, but Rose also delighted in bringing Georgina flowers and visiting her drawing room. Their visit made a great impression on the troubled girl, but when they left Rose felt wretched: 'I don't know when I have missed *anybody* as much as you...You will let me belong to you both.'[91] In her letters to $\Phi \iota \lambda \eta$, 'Phile', as Rose named her, 'for that means dear and loving and you know you are that', Rose said Georgina had hallowed her room. 'I am in your old room', she wrote, 'it's a nice $\Phi \iota \lambda \eta$–like room.' She recalled visiting their back-drawing room, 'where we sat once and looked into each other, silently'.[92] As a memento she had Georgina's rose and picture. Georgina responded by pressing for Rose's reconciliation with her mother. She worried that her love 'takes away from home-love'; 'oh no, it helps so,' Rose protested, 'If you knew how I *want* to be just what you say "a child of light and sun" I wish I was!'[93] Georgina tried to impress upon the girl the fact that she had her life ahead of her, a 'beautiful young golden life', but Rose felt beleaguered at Harristown with her mother misunderstanding and extravagantly rejecting her.[94] In one striking image, she wished to be Georgina's beloved dog Tiff, 'to lick your hand and get stroked'.[95]

But she tried to make things up with her mother, 'now we will try and be what you would like us to be,' and repeatedly expressed her desire for 'unerring love', in reference to Georgina's own words (from Wordsworth's 'Ode to Duty' probably). That the visit was no rest for Georgina is clear: 'Childie you look so tired,' Rose's sister once told her, 'you look like Mrs Cowper tonight.'[96] Rose sent drawings, painted with Ruskin's ultramarine and gold, a story about a lonely woodland flower, and verse, and asked Georgina to 'think of me sometimes – I know you do for I am very unhappy, and would tell you all about it, only I think Mama might not like it – I constantly think of your letters and your verse'.[97] Having had her mother's permission, she wrote to Georgina 'your letters are so dear – and have helped me so, the little end bits particularly … It helps me very much, to think you care for me, and that you want me to do right.'[98]

Georgina's correspondence complicated the relationship between Rose and Ruskin in the years of 'poignant distress and difficulty' which followed Rose's decision to end the engagement [99] Misunderstandings were magnified, as Rose told her, she feared that 'St C' (Georgina's name for Ruskin) examined her 'minor feelings – or different ways of expressing my feelings – which were meant for you'.[100] There were more letters, but only those stimulated by Emily La Touche's death in 1868 are known; Rose contrasted her sorrow with Ruskin's suffering which she could not pity as he had 'broken with laws of honour', and all Dublin was roused and her name was in every one's mouth (Mrs La Touche had contacted Effie Millais to learn the basis for her annulment). 'I think of you so much and your loving heart seems to be woven up with mine in sorrow and in joy,' Rose wrote.[101]

After this emotionally taxing visit, the return to London was short-lived. Georgina rushed to Aix as Teresa, her niece Leila Carraciolo's daughter, was apparently dying. William, whom Mrs Wagstaff thought improving from 'derangement of the mucus lining',[102] set off with Stephen Pleasance his valet, while Georgina sat with Teresa or walked with her beautiful niece Edith de Burgh.[103] By late October, with Teresa improving, they could return. They found the new home selected at Princes Gate 'terribly behind hand'. Georgina noted, amid socialising and book arranging, meeting Rose La Touche and taking her to the station. In November they joined Lady Palmerston at a service at Romsey Abbey for the first time since her bereavement.[104]

Soon, at the start of December, there was spirit guidance from Palmerston about his papers at Brocket. Palmerston revealed his awareness of William's prayer in times of necessity, though he had not believed in prayer when alive, he found death pleasant![105] William had been seeing the medium 'Agape' who had been receiving letters from George de Solms, which had evidently stimulated her to make some geopolitical predictions which Georgina sceptically recorded. She foresaw an impending Franco-German war but proved inaccurate about the success of a future anti-Prussian combination and the severance of British India under an English prince. William also recorded messages from the famous clergyman Frederick Robertson (who had died in 1853), telling his 'dear friend' not to be 'over anxious to quit the body until you have worn out the last fine atom of that wonderful tissue that links your spirit with it'. William certainly agreed that he had prematurely died through over-exhaustion and earlier asceticism.[106]

When the Cowpers saw the parliamentary reform demonstration in Piccadilly in early December, Georgina described it as 'wonderfully quiet'. At Broadlands she enjoyed twilight walks but the idyll was broken by news that their friend Edward Monro had died; his mother was invited to Hampshire.[107]

Before the narrative of their marriage is resumed, something more should be said about their activity in Society and emergent role as substantial landowners (with William to inherit Broadlands on his mother's death). Their prominence came through birth, and through William's official positions, which came through nepotism. He joined those statesmen whose portraits were published, and figured in Henry Barraud's panorama of the Season in Rotten Row, exhibited in 1870.[108] They were fixtures, reluctantly in Georgina's case, in the Season's entertainments. Evenings often ended with dinner at 94, Cambridge House in Piccadilly in family gatherings or in Lady Palmerston's political dinners where they met diplomats and statesmen. They were also regularly at Anne Cowper's St James's Square mansion, with the Shaftesburys, Lady Jocelyn and Ripons, in a 'very happy and devoted' circle.[109]

The American John L. Motley described Georgina as 'a very pretty and agreeable person, disposed to please and to be pleased', when they met at one *salle à manger*.[110] William was agreeable too. Despite his anxieties as an orator and conversationalist, George Russell asserted William 'spoke far above the average of English public men, with a peculiar sweetness and winningness'.[111] His brother-in-law, John Tollemache, not 'over fond' of him, thought him the 'model of a high-bred gentleman'. Although Justin McCarthy thought him an 'extremely formal' person, Lionel Tollemache remembered his ability to refuse with charm and 'knack of repeating pleasantly and unostentatiously curious details about the many distinguished men whom he had known'.[112]

Through their connections they had an intimate glimpse of the widowed Queen's prostration, 'crushed but gentle & considerate for everyone'.[113] William attended royal garden parties, levées and balls, but Georgina had no relish for courtly duties, dreading a Drawing Room in 1876, when she wore a Marie Stuart cap and her niece Leila's jewellery. It was a poor event and she had to propitiate the Queen, probably for Leila's non-attendance.[114] Relatives and friends got her to present daughters.[115] Sadly, for their adopted daughter Juliet, who entered their lives in 1869, presentation was impossible, for William explained to her in the 1880s that as someone of unknown family she was ineligible, as the Queen ruled 'that she must know to what family a Lady belongs'. He consoled Juliet with the assurance that her adoption was itself a 'complete certificate to society of your right to occupy in it a distinguished part'.[116]

About 1867, on returning from an Irish visit, he made for Hampshire to show himself and learn what went on there. 'Latimore tells me,' his mother wrote, 'the Hertford people are quite in despair to lose you which is I daresay true on every account.'[117] For political, social and private life outside the parliamentary season had shifted. Hampshire life, immersed in the estate and philanthropic work expected of aristocrats in their locality as well as the country house entertaining that had punctuated their own lives as guests, was more to Georgina's tastes than the Court and London Society.[118] She led, as most aristocratic women did, her local mothers' meeting and made district visits. They socialized with Edward Lyon Berthon, vicar of Romsey and an inventor whose collapsible boat scheme was supported by William and other local notables.[119] Berthon was improving Romsey Abbey with gas lighting and coloured ceilings, thus providing Lady Palmerston with an unfailing topic particularly when he came for subscriptions. His brother Spencer thought William's sermon better than Berthon's.[120] William patronized agricultural prize giving, and social clubs, and continued his stepfather's horse breeding.[121]

7

THE PRIVATE LIFE OF THE COWPER-TEMPLES, 1867–1877

The Cowper-Temples' lives were enriched through Juliet, the adopted infant daughter of Harriet Cowper who died in 1869. Apart from devotion to the upbringing of a girl who often caused anxiety to someone of Georgina's sensitive nature, their lives followed the same course of political duties, religious exertion and investigation, philanthropic work, and close involvement in the joys or sorrows of relations (perhaps it was a family mission which occasioned the following outburst from William, about 1867: 'The lowest working man expects his wife to be with him on Sundays but I must not grumble – for it's of no use'[1]).

They relished their new position at Broadlands, and devoted themselves to local patronage in the market town of Romsey, in Southampton and the county of Hampshire. Keeping their house in London, they made frequent journeys by train between London and Broadlands and in both homes welcomed an eclectic range of the great and good. They loved Broadlands and enjoyed making architectural and artistic changes to the house, and improving the estate. The castle of Classiebawn in Mullaghmore, completed in 1874, was another haven, though their Irish tenants provided other problems and responsibilities. The small castle, built of Mountcharles stone shipped in from Donegal, in a sober Gothic style (perhaps reflecting Palmerston's own tastes), had a rectangular tower with turret, joined to a square building, and about twenty rooms. They apparently selected the dramatic site so that no land would be taken from their tenants. At the same time, the mid-1870s, their lives were transformed by the inauguration of what became both an annual pleasure and additional call on their time and energies: the Broadlands religious conferences which I examine in chapter 11.

Georgina's diary expressed her frustration after a long talk with a female relation in 1867: 'Alas! How our fellow creatures and those who love us best contrive to make life that should be so happy a constant martyrdom!'[2] This sentiment must have been frequently felt by Georgina as she continued to be involved in the complications and sorrows of Ruskin's doomed relationship with Rose. Her frustration must only have exacerbated her temper, for in March she deplored crossness towards the 'Beloved who is always so unspeakably good to me'.[3]

The year had started with enjoyable socializing with the Arthur Kinnairds, Tom Taylors, and Sir Henry James, of the Ordnance Office of Works, whose talk about polar variation from tropics to Arctic, and the deluge, Georgina thought: 'Very grand but one feels lost in such contemplations.'[4] Georgina liked their old acquaintance, the playwright Taylor, thinking him a devoted husband and father. He enjoyed his shooting, she noted, 'having fired oftener than any one but never having troubled anything! (of which he was quite unaware!!)'. A more perplexing encounter was with the sculptor Richard Lucas (a frequent guest at Broadlands in the 1860s) at nearby Chilworth. Unwashed, uncombed and wearing a velvet helmet and wonderful costume, Lucas was writing a study of William Blake and John Flaxman, and talked about spiritualism, claiming to often leave his body, 'or thinks he does but alas! Alcohol is the first and indispensable means of liberation!' She noted his declaration: 'We live in an imperfect state in a Carnivorous age but we are going on to something better.'[5]

She did not neglect her wider philanthropy, machine-sewing for the Ladies' Dressmaking Company and assisting with Ladies' Sanitary Association meetings and petitioning over vaccination. Georgina felt the mesmerist Spencer Hall's arguments against vaccination the 'weakest possible' but the physician (and homeopathist) James Garth Wilkinson spoke with the 'usual force' at another meeting. She also encouraged a feeding scheme for London children, telling Shaftesbury and others about it, and it occupied her on and off through the year.[6]

Amid this activity the Rose La Touche saga unfolded. 'Rosie' and her mother visited in early February; Georgina took Rosie to a German bazaar and endured a 'tiresome' dinner including the La Touches and Rossetti. There was a long talk with Rosie who was waiting for her in Curzon Street when she returned from Sunday visits, on 24 February. The next day her mother interrupted an afternoon reading the American Thomas Lake Harris's *Arcana of Christianity* and hymns and 'painful' talk until 'all at 6s and 7s' ensued.[7] Georgina wrote to Ruskin the next day, receiving an unsatisfactory letter in reply and then a touching, nice letter from 'St C' – who had not been invited to Curzon Street while the La Touches were there. She wrote to Rosie and 'St C' over the next few weeks and in mid-May the Cowper-Temples paid a pleasant visit to Ruskin.[8]

William attended the debates on further parliamentary reform as the Conservative government stumbled towards what became the Second Reform Act. Georgina followed events, filling her diary with press clippings, and viewing a reform procession from the Welsh Slate Company's office: 'It all looked scrubby in that large open space.'[9] A few days later she chatted with the political economist and follower of Thomas Arnold, Bonamy Price, about reform, the Reichsrath and the identification of Church and State.[10] In May she saw the reform meeting in the park from Lady Palmerston's house and thought the people behaved 'perfectly well', though William was concerned that a mob would ruin the park.[11]

FIGURE 6. Left: detail from *carte de visite* of Georgina Cowper, by Heath and Beau, undated. Right: portrait of William Cowper, undated, pasted in Georgina's diary for 1867. By courtesy of the Trustees of the Broadlands Archives.

It was discovered that Georgina's sister Mummy had developed a tumour, and they anxiously canvassed homeopaths, galvanists and physicians for a cure which avoided surgery. They tried the Berlin graduate Dr Julius Althaus's galvanism, which Georgina considered for her own complaints (she was afraid of cancer herself).[12] When this failed to work, they investigated mesmerism with Lizzie Nicholl, who tried to convince William that he had a dangerous heart problem which she could cure.[13] Georgina had doubts after visiting Nicholl at the Mesmeric Hospital: 'one might say "What a palpable Humbug!" but there is something so good and genuine about the girl one cannot distrust her, her honesty I mean for *clairvoyance* is too uncertain a gift for implicit trust.'[14] In her effort to convince the Cowpers she brought the spirit of William's father, 'a tall man with aquiline nose dark whiskers and hair very much off his forehead' (not too far off a description of Palmerston), followed by falling flowers, supposedly from Georgina's mother (an old lady with a Roman nose and tight cap): 'Hyacinths, Jonquils, Calmia, Pomegranates, Heartease, all wet as if just watered'.[15] Then Lizzie was whisked up on her chair. Lizzie stayed at Curzon Street to mesmerize William, and though he doubted some of her utterances, Mummy took her to Brighton to aid in her treatment. Perhaps it was during one of these séances that William received a message via the table, the letter 'P' being spelt out, 'he spoke of love and interest towards me – is occupied about Politics don't trust Gladstone to do what is right or best.'[16]

At the beginning of February, William had told Laurence Oliphant when they met at his London club that he would like to meet Thomas Lake Harris.[17] Oliphant informed them about 'spiritual breathing' and the conversion of some Japanese men to Harris's beliefs. The growing friendship between the Cowpers and Oliphant, who was also a friend of Evelyn Ashley, William's nephew, was developed during visits to Curzon Street. It was a fateful acquaintance, involving the Cowpers vicariously and directly with Oliphant's extraordinary career. Oliphant was to call them 'Motherling' and 'God Father', so close was the relationship.

With Oliphant, they met Harris and a wealthy follower, Jenny Lee Waring (eventually the third Mrs Harris), recording the conversations in William's spiritual book. Georgina thought he was 'wonderful and delightful'. They read Harris's sermons, hymns, and periodical, *Herald of Light*.[18] They were strongly attracted to his personality, likening it to 'being brought close to the Lord'.[19] But there were 'some things so beautiful others so strange and repelling', in what Oliphant told them.[20] 'Faithful' (as Harris was styled by the spirits) wanted to save Georgina from doubts and fetched her for a four-hour discussion which left her, already low due to the weather, dreary and disconsolate.[21] When Oliphant revealed Harris's plan for a colony, Georgina wondered what they were being drawn into, 'and yet how horrid to draw back in such a proposal. Sometimes I feel – Life is harder than I can bear. W so good'.[22] They offered support, only for Harris to reject it. It was a 'terrible blow', Georgina claimed, in her diary. William wrote to Harris in tears, saw him, and all seemed right. 'Such a strange attraction I never felt,' Georgina wrote, 'filled with the Spirit of Christ. One feels as if one cd follow him like the women in the Gospel to the world's end.'[23] But Harris wanted a considerable amount of money and the phrase 'narrow feeling' was applied to William when he wavered.[24] He offered £6000.

For Georgina, Oliphant's attraction was partly that he had escaped materialism through spiritualism, believing his deceased father had communicated with him.[25] Though she felt 'more sympathy with him then almost every one', Georgina still felt 'unsteady & bewildered & unsure of everything' when she talked with Oliphant.[26] Yet he had grown 'so tame with us', she wrote after another lunchtime chat in late March.[27] She was interested in two Japanese followers of Harris – Noda and Nagga – who stayed with Oliphant (Nagga was baron Kanaye Nagasawa, who came to England in 1865; photographs of him appearing in her diary are reproduced below).[28] The Cowpers entered the world of American utopianism aware of the vagaries and eccentricities involved, for having been told by Lady Airlie of the sects described by the writer William Hepworth Dixon (whom Georgina met in late April), they read his accounts of Shakers and others, Georgina concluding that the Shakers were a 'holy harmless stupid people' who stamped out natural instincts, whilst Perfectionists at Oneida, abominably, indulged in them.[29]

Yet they set off to visit Harris, Miss Waring, Oliphant and the Japanese in Abergavenny over Easter (Mrs Harris was also there, but so 'open that she cannot bear Society'). It was no doubt hoped this meeting would cement their support for Harris's scheme. On the morning of Good Friday, Faithful appeared in a semi-trance, and gazed through the open window at the lovely blue sky and hills, and the garden bright with spring flowers, and described how they appeared to him 'in Spirit'. Georgina was surrounded by spinning maidens but declaring she could not spin, 'but soon I set to work and did it – a good spirit omen he thought'. William was talking with ecclesiastics; 'all very strange to me,' Georgina wrote, 'and I thought wistfully of Church for which we were too late.'[30] Here was a note of caution, of nostalgia for the safer religion of Georgina's more orthodox Easters and their dear friend at Harrow Weald.

Whilst Olly and the Japanese gardened, Georgina was told of her faults by Harris, 'with great faithfulness and love and then he prayed for me with a yearning intensity that I can never forget. He is like a strong angel of God – a St Michael in constant battle … stern yet intensely loving'.[31] As they returned, William made notes of the visit while Georgina read Harris's *Millenial Age* (the *Twelve Discourses on the Spiritual and Social Aspects of the Times*, which had been delivered at the Marylebone Institute in 1860) and the mystic works of Emanuel Swedenborg, well regarded by the Howitts and their spiritualist circle, and a major influence on Harris.[32] She continued to read the mystic at Panshanger, studied James Froude's essay on free discussion of theological differences (published in 1863) in the Orangery with Dolly, and thought over Harris. Olly brought Noda to lunch in London and read works by Harris to them. The Cowpers were also stimulated to reread the eighteenth-century Behmenist William Law's *Spirit of Love*. In late July the 'Beloved Harris', who had visited Mullaghmore, stayed briefly in London with the Cowpers, who found him 'more than delightful'.

In their relationship with Harris the Cowpers were at their most credulous. He told them that Gladstone was under the influence of the secret Italian society of Carbonaros and perplexed Georgina by suggesting England's fate was somehow down to her.[33] She even mused on America being the 'only Earthly home below', as Carroll the architect talked of plans to complete Classiebawn on their Sligo estate.[34] Ultimately, William drew away from Harris, though he could still reverence Harris as a seer.[35]

FIGURE 7. *Cartes de visite* by Maull of London, in Georgina's diary, believed to be of Kanaye Nagasawa. By courtesy of the Trustees of the Broadlands Archives.

The new world opened up by Oliphant and Harris did not monopolize their time. The Cowpers' spiritualism continued, through séances with Dr Ashburner, the medium Mrs Annie Acworth ('Love's Messenger', described by the Russells of Amberley as 'unprepossessing' in appearance[36]) who stayed with them at Curzon Street, and the brothers de Solms at Park Lane. Prince George was to be an occasional guest of the Cowpers at Curzon Street during the remainder of 1867.[37]

A new clerical friend was Hugh Reginald Haweis, who played his Stradivarius to Georgina's accompaniment at Curzon Street. Haweis' letter to Georgina on the last of his bachelor days was full of enthusiasm for his bride's artistic genius (the marriage proved unhappy).[38] William had appointed Haweis to St James's, Marylebone, which was in the patronage of the Office of Works, and it became a fashionable church under Haweis, who dedicated his *Thoughts for the Times* to William in 1872. Another new acquaintance who blossomed into a friend was the feminist, philanthropist and journalist Frances Power Cobbe, with whom Georgina had an interesting talk in late March about the Brahmo Somaj or 'One God Church in India', and Mary Carpenter's missionary work. Cobbe had written a paper in support of the Ladies' Dressmaking Company: in the future the Cowper-Temples were to become important recruits to her anti-vivisection crusade, in which she appreciated the value of the titled and political elite. And there were still services at Vere Street where the Prophet received them so kindly. By contrast, the court was dull and 'scrubby' and Georgina made it clear in her diary how little she thought of her Court duties.[39]

Georgina was in Paris with Lizzie Nicholl in the summer, and returned in the winter, to nurse Mummy as her tumour was removed using a caustic substance by a Dr Michel.[40] 'I am getting an adept at nursing,' Georgina boasted, 'and shall be able to enlist as a nurse in the next war.'[41] She stayed with Harriet Cowper, enjoying 'codging' and hymn-singing. William came briefly and they deplored the new Madeleine church, toured the Exposition Universelle and were entertained by Lady Wallace, who told them about the frightful anti-Christian results of spiritualism in France. In late August Georgina's niece Edith de Burgh and Edith's cousin Rafe Leycester came, and Edith accepted his proposal of marriage.[42]

William feared Georgina would over exert herself, which was likely as Dr Michel, Harriet Cowper, and their companion Lady Poulett became ill. Harriet, Georgina wrote, 'thinks herself very ill and longs to depart and be with Christ – feeling as if she should no longer be able to work for Him here'.[43] She pleaded with William that she alone should provide her sister with comfort, that for once she felt of use in the world and that the cold would exacerbate his lumbago. She asked for the same 'liberty of judgement' he had. It was 1855 all over again: Georgina absent and obstinate.[44]

There was plenty to interest her in Paris from a religious perspective for it was a ferment of sectarians and spiritualists. She became fascinated by 'Jacob the Zouave', the North African healer whom she glimpsed surveying the crowds of patients and onlookers drawn by press accounts.[45] Lizzie, Rafe Leycester and Miss Blackwell (presumably Anne Blackwell, sister of the doctor Elizabeth Blackwell, and the translator of George Sand, who became the disciple and translator of the spiritualist Hippolyte Rivail, known as Allan Kardec) visited the Zouave. Miss Blackwell also attended several séances at their old spiritualist friend Lisett Gregory's lodgings. There were manifestations of grapes and flowers, but these had ceased to make any impression on Georgina, and she was disturbed at Mrs Gregory's irritable state and lapsed Christian faith.[46]

Georgina hoped to listen to the Catholic priest Père Hyacinthe.[47] The Protestant 'revival' led by the handsome if prematurely bald Granville

Waldegrave, Lord Radstock, an aristocrat influenced by the Plymouth Brethren, also drew her.[48] She thought him a good, simple-headed man, with no thought but to win souls for Christ.[49] Georgina met the Brethren, then the '*avant-garde* of keen Evangelicalism', and liked them.[50] Every Friday they had a prayer meeting and Plymouth Brethren stayed for tea and talks, and once three leading Brothers put Georgina through all her heresies, which she thought rather hard on her single handed and in French.[51] Spencer (and presumably Harriet) had met the Brethren at Geneva, Spencer telling William that J.N. Darby (Irish founder of the sect) was wonderfully active despite his years, having just returned from North America and Jamaica, and was a perfect gentleman, 'nothing of the Stiggins and Mawworm ways'. Georgina was eager for news about the Japanese and Harris's community: 'I want some communion with our Salemites very much. I trust you hold your slate,' she wrote. But Olly's news from 'Salem-on-Erie', or Brocton, by Lake Erie, was 'much beyond my reach'.[52]

When she returned to England she read Harris's 'wonderful breath book' (*The Breath of God with Man*) which she found 'very striking and in parts beautiful'. Through Prince George she made the acquaintance of the mediumistic Leaf family. After a brief stay with Lady Palmerston at Tunbridge Wells, and some shooting by William at Panshanger,[53] they set off for an Ireland in Fenian inspired unrest. Georgina read Harris's *Republic* on the way and liked it immensely. She mixed the reading of *Arcana* ('very difficult to take in and I feel terribly at sea without a Pilot or compass or star!'[54]) with shirt-making for the poor children, 'full of plans for people', but 'ready to scream at the sight of all the people all wanting help and feeling no Help in me. So difficult to know what to do for their real good'.[55] Georgina wrote to Rose and Mrs La Touche, and on 22 October reached Harristown, where she found 'Rosie very poorly all over for poor R'.

When they returned to London they found that Georgina's close friend, 'almost her Sister', Adelaide Noel, the Countess of Gainsborough, had died.[56] She found comfort in Edith de Burgh's wedding, the newlyweds looking like a 'pair of young angels', before they set off for their honeymoon in Alexandria. Then Georgina took Mummy to Mrs Gregory's to defend Lizzie Nicholl, whose integrity was questioned. Olly asked them to have two 'dear Japanese boys to spend Xmas with us' (Yūki Kōan and Ōba Genjobī, but Eukie and Uball to Georgina[57]). Having been sent to study Western society and knowledge they now desired to learn from Harris the 'Pure Life' with their compatriots.[58] Oliphant wanted the Cowpers to recruit others from this Japanese group to Harris's sect, and they were permitted to send copies of Harris's works anonymously, and discuss his ideas with select acquaintances.[59]

Georgina rushed to Paris when Mummy determined on another operation. Harriet Cowper's health worsened as she delayed treatment for ailments that included coughing up blood. Despite this, Harriet held religious gatherings to which Lord Radstock, 'just now one of the sights of Paris', according to the *Daily News*, came and delivered sermons on absolute election and grace before an audience of splendid Anglo-Parisian ladies.[60] William mourned a tenantless sofa in the sitting room which he was using as his dressing room, her dog Tiff sniffing 'at long black petticoats in hopes of finding you in them'.[61] 'How good and Self Denying you are,' he told her at the end of the year, 'and how unlike other people in your readiness to see duty in distasteful directions,' but asked her to return.

On New Year's Day Georgina asked for more money, for a friend in distress (one of the German kindergarten promoters the Misses Praetorius, who had supported the young dressmakers[62]), saying that if she had taken to dress and diamonds, or a second horse, there would be bigger holes in his purse: 'You can't think how true it is that I am at heart *a screw*! And how I run about to save my cabs!'[63] And referring to Harris's utopian regime, the 'Use', in response to a letter of concern from William, she said: 'You darling how *fine* you are! What airs you give yourself for me? How shall you like to see me Char-woman for the use carrying coals and emptying slops! This is a nice little preparation for you!' William had distractions in schemes to improve estate cottages at Broadlands and enlarge the vista by felling trees. He had spoken of his increasing delight in Harris's *Truth and Life*, 'when they speak of the Homeland my eyes gush out'.[64] Now he investigated how the Japanese fared in London.[65] But he asked if the divorce would ever end, and fetched Georgina in February when Mummy seemed better (in a fragment of a letter he insisted that she be at the station for collection, 'I see I am too matter of fact in taking in what you say about returning to me when you leave me'[66]).

She had been away over six weeks, and the letters in which she argued her right to remain in Paris are a good expression of her strong character and humour. When Lady Poulett was ill in bed without a voice, Georgina had her 'fixed without retreat' and proceeded to read Faithful's *Modern Spiritualism* (the year saw critical coverage of Harris in the *Spiritual Magazine*).[67] In another letter she told William she did not want him and that 'the constant *self-restraint* of my life must be a good discipline'.[68]

In the spring of 1868 they seem to have attended (or certainly followed) spiritualist lectures by Emma Hardinge and the American Davenport brothers.[69] But Georgina's diary for the rest of the year is destroyed and we rely on fragments, copied into another diary, which avoided her ongoing role as mediator in Ruskin's private agony over Rose.[70] Easter passing without a visit to Harrow Weald, they thought much of Monro and tried to follow his teachings, whilst staying at Broadlands. At the same time, Georgina backed a proposed college for the advanced education of women, attending a public meeting with John Llewellyn Davies, Louisa Twining, the Countess of Airlie and others. Lady Palmerston planned a new lodge at Broadlands and they inspected the site with the architect Nesfield. Georgina tried to buy 'Dr Michel's secret', so that sufferers like Mummy would not have to depend on the survival of a one-eyed and gout-ridden French physician.[71]

Life in Hampshire in July was turned to charitable work through bazaars, and to politics, for William's election address in South Hampshire was published, a memorial window to Palmerston was unveiled in Romsey Abbey, and a statue of the premier carved by Noble, which William thought better, at least, than Baron Marochetti's, was unveiled by Lord Granville.[72] Gladstone could not attend but came later to receive an address from the corporation and support William's intended electoral campaign.[73] Georgina dreaded the large party of Whig and Liberal grandees but found time to read Harris under the trees.

Oliphant tried to persuade William to follow his example and abandon the Commons for the New Life under Harris, in August. Georgina was eager, but William hesitated, summoning up Melbourne's caution in a letter to Oliphant ('whenever you don't see your way clearly stand still') in refusing to follow him, in early August.[74] The letter came from Kingstown, for they were on their now customary trip to Ireland, Georgina bringing MacDonald's novel *Robert Falconer* and getting 'rather depressed about the people' at Mullaghmore.

They returned to England in September, when Georgina heard of sister Marcia Harcourt's illness. Mrs Wagstaff's medicines alleviated William's neuralgia, which was just as well since electioneering was a time of 'much painfulness' according to Georgina, as William addressed meetings and attended poultry shows, and ploughing matches.[75] It seemed unsuccessful, with bribery and faithless voters. The Liberals appeared defeated, and all looked hopeless to Georgina, who developed one of her headaches. But Disraeli was defeated and in early December the government resigned; Gladstone was sent for by the Queen to form a government.

At Broadlands, at this moment, Ruskin was a guest with Edith and Rafe Leycester, entertaining them with photographs, woodcuts and lectures on architecture and botany.[76] But Georgina went back to London with Marcia who died in late December.[77] Georgina accompanied her to a burial in a dreary Helmingham on New Year's Eve.

On the spiritual plane, séances with Mrs Acworth and others continued in 1869, with the Reverend Douglas being advised, in his mission to restore the people of Israel to the Holy Land, to try to win the Emperor for the protection of the oppressed.[78] Georgina saw Annie Watts' spiritual pictures at Notting Hill and joined séances at Garth Wilkinson's house.[79] A new exotic acquaintance was François-Louis Bugnion, self-styled Bishop St Paul.[80] An 'uplifting and holy' Swedenborgian wearing a purple cap, Bugnion was a follower of Thomas Lake Harris, whom Oliphant had written about from Salem in Erie in May (his fairy name was 'Eaglewing', Oliphant said).[81] Several of his letters to William survive from a later date, when he was a missionary in Alexandria and Australia, with the financial support (partly through William) of the British government. His stationery bore mysterious emblems and the motto *Ta destine est aux Indes* (Bugnion had a coffee plantation in India). He corresponded about talks between American Episcopalians and the Greek church, the duality of male and female in God and Australian aborigines' fear of the white man due to alcohol and other European luxuries. At this time, Georgina found the contrast between his uplifting presence and breakfast at Buckingham Palace dreadful.[82] She needed the uplift of the bishop's presence when Mummy, back at Eccleston Square, endured another operation.

More conventional socializing included dining with Ruskin at Denmark Hill in January and receiving Emelia Gurney at Broadlands in mid-May; the blind Post-Master General, Henry Fawcett, also came to fish on the Test.[83] Philanthropic work ranged from the anniversary festival of the North Surrey District Schools to attendance with the Ladies' Sanitary Association and the Council of the Society of Arts at Edwin Chadwick's garden party, to discuss improved dwellings.[84] The Cowpers' interest in the subject of vaccination led to a meeting in Curzon Street in late July.

The Cowpers entertained Bugnion in the company of the Wattses, Garth Wilkinson and Prince George. Then they travelled, via their relations the Leycesters at Toft Hall, to Dublin and Mullaghmore, where they enjoyed the company of Bugnion. But they were summoned to Brocket Hall by a telegram from Fanny Jocelyn and were present at Lady Palmerston's death, at eighty three, in the morning of 10 September.[85]

As her old friend Abraham Hayward recalled, Lady Palmerston confined her domestic circle 'almost exclusively' to family and connections after Palmerston's death, and her children had frequently visited and corresponded.[86] Characteristically, whilst William saw a 'wonderful look of renewed youth and beauty' before his mother died, Georgina was distraught. Typically, for one who had the habit of dwelling on the suffering side of existence, she asked her friend Emelia Gurney, 'shall I ever again be able to think of the angel soaring and singing? – and to look at Mrs Watts's drawings and believe in them?' which was a strange response to an event which was hardly unexpected.[87] William's mother was buried as she requested, in Westminster Abbey, in a plain and small-scale ceremony marred only by a guest falling into the grave. Georgina's headache was too bad for her to accompany William, and instead she wrote praising him for having taught her and the servants to pray, and explaining how she could not be near the spirit world in crowds, but could when the world was shut out and she was alone with God and him.[88] The entailed Melbourne estates went to William's nephew, Earl Cowper. William inherited the Palmerston estates in Ireland and Hampshire. He assumed the additional name of 'Temple' by royal licence.[89]

Oliphant and Bugnion were their guests at Curzon Street a few days later, staying there until early October.[90] Georgina told Emelia Gurney that Bugnion, like the Saint and child he was, would not show off and that it was in being with him, one found out 'that Heaven is within and around him'.[91] Oliphant departed for America, leaving Georgina 'nearly at my short wit's end with agonizing bewilderment', although she was 'so happy – read aloud little angel story of [Frederick William] Faber's'.[92] She visited George MacDonald at his damp river-side home in Hammersmith (later to be William Morris's), finding him ill, she thought, but busy 'as usual writing Books he said to support his eleven children poor man'.[93] In late October the spirit of Lady Palmerston came to her most 'affectionate son'.[94] Palmerston appeared in Melbourne's company, giving his altered opinion on the Irish Church Bill and advising about farmers' leases, access to the park, and cottages.[95]

They entered Broadlands 'with no exhilarating sense of possession' according to Georgina, but she inspected the mansion, visited the new cottages, and made her will.[96] In this serious frame of mind she aimed to rise early and read lessons (and Faber) before her working day. Then, after William presided over an educational congress at Manchester, and after meetings of the Sanitary and Dressmaking societies, they planned a new lodge and cottages with Nesfield, finding him as charming as his brother had been tiresome.[97] They were intent on improvements with their agent William Kendle's advice.[98]

In the early morning of 17 December 1869 Harriet Cowper died. She was fifty seven. Though she had been reluctant to seek medical advice her death came after an apparent improvement. 'I feel poor Spencer must be very helpless,' Fanny Jocelyn wrote, 'with no one but the orphans, and this Baby "Juliette" for I suppose they have no one else.'[99] Spencer came to England shortly afterwards and Georgina told Emelia that she had been left by Harriet '– a Pug dog – and a little adopted girl! – an alarming responsibility!'[100] The 'poor little dear she is at present most ungainly and unattractive', Georgina told Emelia, who had herself taken responsibility for a large family of Gurney nephews and nieces.[101]

The surviving remnants of Georgina's diary barely mention Juliet's arrival (her name was anglicised). Born in 1867, she was the daughter of a labourer called Latour who, with his wife (befriended by Harriet), had died young. The Spencer Cowpers may have adopted her to come to terms with their own daughter's death. Fuller details of Juliet's parentage were not apparently revealed to Georgina. According to William, before Harriet died she had made no communication about Juliet, although elsewhere it is stated that Harriet had wished Georgina to adopt the infant whom she first saw in 1867.[102] Harriet had said that one fine morning Georgina would find a baby tied to her door knocker.[103] Unable to produce offspring which would fulfil Georgina's 'passion for children', now she and William experienced the delights and responsibilities of parentage through her 'wayward little feather', as she called Juliet.[104] Not that Juliet was raised to think of them in conventional terms as parents for she called Georgina 'Lily' and William 'Gellum'.[105] A remarkable photograph features Georgina sitting in profile against a backdrop of oriental rugs, in lace cap and silk dress, clasping Juliet to her. At Georgina's feet, gazing searchingly, is William.[106] It is an eloquent image of mutual devotion, love for 'the treasure of our hearts', and, in the recumbent pose adopted by William, of Georgina's power. Georgina said Juliet was warmly welcomed by William, who 'loved her with the most touching and devoted love'.[107]

FIGURE 8. The Cowper-Temples with Juliet, c.1876.
By courtesy of the Trustees of the Broadlands Archives.

Juliet did not know her origins until she was sixteen.[108] In August of 1874 Juliet had 'something important to ask her' at bedtime, was she really ever christened? 'Yes darling, certainly, by a very good man – Mr Darby,' Georgina replied, at which Juliet asked, 'Then who were my Godmothers and Godfathers?'[109] Georgina didn't know, but Darby was the Plymouth Brother, who seems to have baptised her for the Spencer Cowpers in Geneva, where he had established himself in the late 1830s, and from where he had attracted followers in Germany. But when Juliet came to marry, it was impossible to find evidence of this event, or any official record of her birth, because of the destruction during the Paris Commune.

Georgina's efforts to win Juliet's affections began unsuccessfully as she told Emelia Gurney, the baby screaming whenever she saw her, crying '"no, no," in a most valiant and resolute way resisting me as her impending fate!' As ever, Georgina dramatized the situation: she was denied a selfish joy which she confessed she had bounded at, the sensation of a 'dear soft loving thing' pressed to her heart, sometimes 'Life seems to play with me like a cat with a mouse – with refinement of cruelty!'[110]

The MacDonalds and four of their children were guests at Broadlands in the new year, followed by Georgina's brother-in-law Admiral Frederick Harcourt, his mind 'so far gone', came briefly and 'spiritualistic visitors' followed.[111] The Cowpers also saw their neighbour Louisa Lady Ashburton, second wife of William Bingham Baring, at Melchet; their association was to become closer through dramatic circumstances.[112] Georgina saw Ruskin and presented her relation Eva de Burgh at court. Band of Hope and sanitary meetings, bazaars, the Ladies' Dress-making Company and 'poor peopling' as she called it, otherwise filled up her days. With the outbreak of the Franco-Prussian war in July (the Cowpers followed events partly through Oliphant's reports in *The Times*[113]) Georgina became involved, through a Catholic priest she met at the Greenfields, in a Committee for Relief of Refugees in Southampton.[114] The war greatly disturbed her, stimulating a lengthy letter praising her correspondent (perhaps Emelia Gurney) for '*Peace* ordained sacrifice', despairing at the press's exultant treatment of the French casualties and hoping for another world instead of one with coarse, loud-voiced creatures.[115] But William described Gladstone's speech against 'Manchester School' isolationism as excellent.[116]

There was the usual journey to Ireland after visiting the Welsh quarry. They settled the site for Classiebawn with Carroll in early September. Laurence Oliphant, the Leycesters and Spencer Cowper joined them. They travelled to the Giant's Causeway, and seem to have met La Touche before returning to England.[117] William had recorded in his journal for 18 August that Ruskin '[h]as lost all pleasure in life', and the meeting in Ireland was probably related to Ruskin's anxieties about Effie Millais' account of their annulled marriage which she gave the La Touches: at any rate Georgina gave Rose Ruskin's statement on the marriage in 1870.[118]

Back in Broadlands after a busy time in London, Georgina wrote to Emelia Gurney of her longing for more unity, strength and depth, as she had whirled 'like a poor little used up Autumn leaf, leaving Mullaghmore – visiting Tollymore – arriving in London – saying goodbye to Neapolitans – arriving here'.[119] Emelia's mother died in 1870, and Georgina's sympathy encouraged increased closeness. She insisted Emelia drop formalities and treat her like a sister and was thankful that Emelia shared her 'love and sorrow'. She wanted Emelia to write as 'Theodora' and she would be 'Phile'. Emelia was at Broadlands with her husband in October.[120]

Guests at Broadlands in March 1871 included their friends Madame de Bunsen (presumably Frances, Baroness Bunsen), the singer and writer Adelaide Sartoris, Lord Houghton and Sir James Shuttleworth, William's acquaintance from Greenwich Hospital days. Oliphant came fleetingly on his way to America. Georgina had possession of Dante Gabriel Rossetti's *Beatrix* at the end of the month and relished the masterpiece's expression: 'closed eyelids ... most exquisitely beautiful and touching'.[121] Ruskin, his cousin Joan Agnew and her betrothed (Arthur Severn) came to Broadlands, along with a son of the Earl of Carnarvon, Auberon Herbert, courting Dolly Cowper, in early April. Ruskin persuaded William to be a Trustee of his utopian St George's Fund, announced in the August number of his newsletter *Fors Clavigera*, and which was designed to buy land for settlement.

Ruskin's private problems drew on their time and sympathies. They had rushed to Matlock Bath in July 1871 after a telegram about his serious illness which had been partly caused by the strain of his anxieties about Rose. Georgina bought an expensive notebook to act as scribe at his sickbed, only to receive a bizarre condemnation of Coleman's Mustard! The Cowper-Temples learned that Ruskin's legal adviser thought he was able to marry if Rose accepted his offer: she refused.[122]

In late May Thomas Lake Harris and Miss Waring, who had embarked on a European tour as an excuse to leave the Brocton community which was under severe strains, came to London. They visited Curzon Street and then stayed at Broadlands, where Ruskin came to join. Georgina told Emelia that Harris looked 'ill and strange and feeling weak and bewildered through the complete withdrawal of guidance for the first time for years. Still he thinks there is a wonderful change in England and a repression of evil – and a descent of good'.[123] Emelia was invited to hear his 'strange utterances of judgements', including his predictions about France.[124] From France, Oliphant discussed the complementarity of Prussians and French: the former were 'pitiless and inexorable, but just', French equality was based on envy.[125]

It was a year of marriages. William's brother remarried, at the British Embassy in Florence, Jessie Maclean, daughter of Colonel Clinton Maclean and granddaughter of General Maclean of Newburgh, New York.[126] Georgina felt 'very sad & like a night mare – hard to realize'.[127] But she became a friend of Jessie, who was, like her, a student of spiritualism and a music lover.[128] Auberon Herbert finally married William's niece. While sharing William's concern with preserving the New Forest, and with similar humanitarian and spiritualist interests to the 'Billies', he was a radical MP and the next year supported Sir Charles Dilke's motion for inquiring into the Crown's finances. The other bridegroom was Laurence Oliphant, whose marriage to the much younger Anne le Strange was resisted by Thomas Lake Harris, disapproved of by Alice's family but assisted by the Cowper-Temples who were witnesses at St George's, Hanover Square in June; the couple stayed at Curzon Street.[129]

At the end of July William almost suffered a fatal accident when Palmerston's white mare died under him: his legs took several weeks to heal but otherwise he was unharmed. Georgina went with her relation Amy Leycester to Ruskin, returning to house hunting as the Cowper-Temples had decided to leave Curzon Street, rejecting a place in Albertgate as 'too dreadfully in fashionable gang way for any chance of repose or retirement' (eventually they found a place at 15, Great Stanhope Street).[130] After a little yachting round the Isle of Wight William laid the stone of the new school at Romsey (William's beneficence in relation to a working men's club there was reported in the press: he dwelt on the advantages of co-operation, hoping the club would emulate this spirit of fraternity and self-reliance[131]). They said goodbye to the Russell Gurneys, bound for the United States, where Emelia's husband represented Britain in the commission on claims arising from the American Civil War.

They departed themselves, on family missions. They went to Paris to be with Lady Jocelyn's ailing son Eric. They sought Teresa, granddaughter of Selina Locke (probably to help her in her marital difficulties), missing her in Milan before finding her after sightseeing, in Rome in early November.[132] They had not been to Rome since 1863 and Georgina (looking at frescoes guided by a letter from Ruskin) listed those she had lost in the interval, from the Palmerstons to her beloved dogs Oman and Tiff. On the credit side, had she done this calculation, she might have added the friendship developing with Basil Wilberforce since the Church Congress at Southampton in 1870, when Basil had stayed at Broadlands as chaplain to his father Bishop Samuel Wilberforce of Oxford. In the future the Cowper-Temples championed his claims for advancement and the relationship with William stimulated Basil's ideas in the 'forward school' of theology.[133]

Hospitality on their return to London and Broadlands was, as ever, varied, mixing religion, the arts, and politics. In early 1872 guests at Broadlands included the sculptor Robert Jackson, a 'Japanese Gentleman', Bonham Carter (John, MP for Winchester, or his brother Henry), and a young painter whom they had been patronizing since 1869, Edward Clifford. Clifford was recalled by George Wyndham as a 'curious compound of sensitiveness and obtuseness, of the artist, the worldling and the saint, but with a largeness and constancy'.[134] The son of an Anglican controversialist, the Reverend John Clifford of St Matthew's, Kingsdown, Bristol, Edward's brother Alfred was a missionary in Bengal who later became Bishop of Lucknow and his sister Mary was prominent in Bristol, where she became a Poor Law Guardian.[135] The Cowper-Temples also became acquainted with George Eliot through the Tollemaches, and Georgina visited the novelist: a gesture no longer in defiance of Society's disapproval of Eliot's ménage with George Lewes as it might have been a decade previously.[136]

A fire at Lady Ashburton's new Elizabethan mansion brought out their neighbourly sympathies in August. William sent his estate fire engine, organized the salvaging of art works and effects, and gave Louisa Ashburton shelter.[137] Thereafter she often dropped in unannounced and perhaps tried their patience.[138] But they liked her, William writing at the end of the year, of her beautiful smile and rich, touching voice, and hoped that the event would 'lead to closer intimacy'; Georgina writing about this time, 'We have got to love you so much – we cannot spare you.'[139]

While Ruskin was in Italy, Rose was invited by the Cowper-Temples and by George MacDonald (who had been a close friend of Ruskin's for almost a decade) to visit. MacDonald believed that a meeting should be arranged between them. Georgina wondered whether she should try to heal the breach. Was it not sad, she asked George, 'those two should be thus tortured who might perhaps have been happy together?'[140] She invited Rose to Broadlands in late May; a month later Ruskin received MacDonald's note about meeting Rose.[141] In early August Ruskin came to Broadlands to see her and left hopeful, having been permitted to kiss her.[142]

William brought his nephew Evelyn Ashley with him when he visited the slate quarry to settle prices, in early October. His mother, William's sister Minny, died in the autumn, worn out by nursing her ailing children.[143] 'It is terrible to me,' William told Lady Ashburton, 'to lose so perfect a sister, the companion of my childhood and the admiration of my mature years, who was dearer to me than anyone but my wife.'[144] Another important figure in William's life died that year, Maurice the 'Prophet'.[145]

Georgina had surgery in late 1872, for what reason it is unclear.[146] She recovered sufficiently to impress a young visitor, Margaret Leicester Warren, in November with her stately and handsome appearance, 'such a strong face like a statue, with a low forehead & straight overhanging eye brows. I was frightened, but she was kind to me, and showed me all her lovely things and rooms'.[147] But something seems to have happened to one arm, which was 'quite useless' well into February. William looked after her tenderly and Georgina felt sad at leaving the 'dear solemn room – where we had passed such an intense time together of Love and Pain', when she came to Broadlands in late December.[148] But she herself looked after an invalid, Miss Shaw, getting her 'well through her illness'.[149]

In the spring they played host to the Oliphants, Orinna Greenfield and the Wattses at Broadlands. The Oliphants put off going to America, 'Faithful' having allowed 'Woodbine' to visit the Cowper-Temples before his return because it would 'do them good'. 'I do not advise Mr C because nothing was given to me to say to him but I have no doubt that had he been prepared, I should have had words given to me … I know God and the Angels dearly love that kind and upright man,' Harris wrote.[150] Other spiritual activity included attending an exhibition of 'Spiritual photography' where Georgina met the spiritualist Reverend Stainton Moses and séances with the spirit artist Robert Sutherland at Stanhope Street.[151]

Georgina made the acquaintance of Catherine Marsh, a friend of Shaftesbury famous for missionary work among navvies at Beckenham (recounted in *English Hearts and English Hands*) and her biography *Captain Hedley Vicars* ('the noble example of a CHRISTIAN SOLDIER').[152] Georgina also heard black singers at a concert, supported by Shaftesbury, for converting Africans, and noted their soft voices.[153] Attending Shaftesbury's London costermongers' parties made her reflect on the contrast between banquets and these feasts of bread and tea in broken pitchers.[154]

Ruskin hoped that the Cowpers would become intimates of his American friend Charles Eliot Norton, then in England.[155] In early August Rose La Touche visited Broadlands and Georgina invited Ruskin.[156] In mid-August they were in Lancashire for a couple of days at Brantwood, Ruskin's home overlooking Coniston. Ruskin anticipated a gypsying and caravanning adventure for Georgina. It was 'a lovely little house – by the grey lake and mountains – but very rainy,' Georgina noted.[157] But the La Touche crisis continued its course. Rose was ill – probably suffering from *anorexia nervosa* – at the beginning of 1874; she stayed at Broadlands until 9 February, Georgina telling Mrs MacDonald that it was thought best for Rose's health to separate her from her mother.[158] At the same time, there was a new member of the household, with a governess for Juliet in the form of Annie, sister of the Pre-Raphaelite sculptor Alexander Munro.[159] Annie kept her friends the MacDonalds informed about Rose as the crisis developed.[160]

1874 was a pivotal year for the Cowper-Temples, opening a new field of activity through association with the prominent American Evangelicals, the Smiths, Philadelphian Quakers who were eager to continue their evangelizing for the 'holiness movement' which preached immediate sanctification, across the Atlantic. The association came about through Catherine Marsh, who stayed at Broadlands giving addresses to the household, though Georgina seems to have met Robert Pearsall Smith already in July 1873. Georgina now read one of his wife's devotional books which Marsh gave her. Hannah was 'vetted' by leading Evangelical aristocrats at a gathering in which Georgina, as a 'queen of evangelical Christians', crucially supported her heretical rejection of eternal torment. Many years later Hannah's son pictured the incident: 'from the depths of that great drawing-room there floated forward, swathed in rich Victorian draperies and laces, a tall and stately lady, who kissed my mother, and said, "My dear, I don't believe it either."'[161] Georgina's 'enfant terrible' question felt fateful, for Hannah thought the truth would ruin her in the influential Miss Marsh's and others' eyes and hinder Robert's work of faith. But loyalty to God required the truth, and there was 'the unspeakable comfort of thy dear kiss and the approval it contained. From that moment to this my heart has been knit to thine as to a *sister in the Lord*'.[162]

A new chapter had opened in Georgina's emotional and religious life. She described in her diary 'a beautiful woman with a fine frank radiant face, delightful talk – never to be forgotten – with her'. Hannah could not help giving thanks, she noted, whenever she saw a funeral, to think 'there is another delivered from the bondage of Corruption'.[163] An enduring friendship began, becoming the third point in a triangle of females – Emelia, Georgina and Hannah – calling themselves the 'Trins'.

In April the Cowper-Temples attended a conference involving the Pearsall Smiths in Brighton. Here, or at the Smiths' 'Bible reading breakfasts' in Stoke Newington they met the theologian and erstwhile Plymouth Brother Andrew Jukes, who became a close friend of the Cowper-Temples and Emelia Gurney.[164] Jukes had become famous in 1867 for a work rejecting the doctrine of everlasting punishment.[165] Georgina welcomed the Smiths for Easter; the service with Georgina in Romsey Abbey would seem in retrospect an epoch in Hannah's life. Hannah urged Georgina to throw off the 'death trammels and claim the new life', convinced religious anxiety was simply a failure to recognize she had the 'new life' since birth.[166]

Yet Georgina and William continued their spiritualism, following Hannah's Hanover Square ordeal with dreadful mediumistic theatrics at Mrs Gregory's. Georgina met the octogenarian mesmerist Baron Du Potet at the Haweises: 'At one time he made experiment in magic. Some awful creatures came through and shook him and he wisely gave it up.'[167] More significantly, she met the Cambridge graduate and spiritualist Frederic Myers in early May, introducing him to the spiritualist Stainton Moses at a séance with Emelia and her nephew, Edmund Gurney, a man whose interests included music and aesthetics, and whose sensitivity to suffering was akin to Georgina's.[168] Several weeks later John Morley, the man of letters and a sceptic on the occult, skirmished with Myers at Broadlands. Colonel Drayson was there to show spirit photographs. A séance was held in 'Cinnamon' (a favourite sitting room at the top of the house, 'hung with lovely things' and text around the wall[169]) and there were discussions in the saloon and portico. Adelaide Sartoris and Auberon Herbert joined. Georgina thought Drayson's astronomical theories 'splendid'.[170]

Travelling to Ireland – with Georgina engrossed in *Silas Marner* on the way – the Cowpers reached Mullaghmore to inspect Classiebawn, hoping it would help the people by providing 'some civilised life among them'. From their agent, Kincaid, they learned of the poor potato crop and fish season; Georgina thought emigration the only solution. They returned in autumn to the 'dear little house', relishing their tower of the winds. Standing a hundred yards from the sea, with the black rock of Roskeragh Point below, it was exposed to the Atlantic, and desolate with the Mayo and Sligo mountains behind: Georgina recalled an 'Apocalyptic vision from every window'.[171]

Clifford brought his friends the ritualist clergymen George Body and George Wilkinson, along with Andrew Jukes, to lunch, and a religious meeting at Stanhope Street was opened by William. This was significant because it stimulated the Cowper-Temples to offer Broadlands for a gathering in 17 July in which the Smiths figured prominently. So began the 'Broadlands conferences' which continued until 1888. If great things were anticipated of the conference by Hannah – the outpouring of God's spirit – she also hoped for a successful resolution of Georgina's spiritual crisis by the defeat of the powers of darkness and release from doubt, but Georgina had to rush to Fanny Jocelyn, undergoing galvanic treatment.[172] But she met the Smiths in the autumn at a conference at Oxford for promotion of 'scriptural holiness', inspiring Hannah by her 'dear responsive face' at ladies' meetings.[173] William took the opportunity to see the oriental scholar Max Müller at All Souls' College.

At the end of the year they were involved with the New Forest Shakers, after learning about the sect which had acquired public notoriety not least for their belief in physical immortality, from Henry and Dolly in August. Georgina, as the press reported, offered to pay the rent for a house large enough to shelter them after they were evicted; and William appealed for help in *The Times*.[174] We lack a diary for the next year, so that glimpses of their lives are limited to political activities or public works of philanthropy, the lack of a diary is particularly frustrating given that this was the year that Rose la Touche died, after which event the Cowper-Temples provided valuable comfort to Ruskin.

Georgina followed the reforming efforts of Samuel Plimsoll, and in the Commons William supported Plimsoll's bill to end overloaded 'coffin-ships'. He also engaged in committee work for the Metropolitan Visitation and Relief Association, and joined a deputation to the RSPCA in January. In addition, he worked in the Charles Kingsley memorial campaign, and an Oral Instruction of Deaf and Dumb committee. He was prominently involved in the effort to preserve Epping Forest, which set him against Gladstone's administration as we shall see in another chapter, but in May, Gladstone, at that point retired from the leadership of the Liberals, met the Smiths at the Cowper-Temples'.[175]

Guests at Broadlands included the poet and writer Roden Noel whom William had invited without knowing anything about him, thinking he was a lawyer, so Anne Cowper told her son, a habit with Billy. Other guests included Frederic Myers and Edmund Gurney with their spirit photographs, and an Indian lady called Mrs Ramsden.[176] But the main event at Broadlands followed in July with the second religious conference. This was attended by the ritualist Reverend George Wilkinson and various nonconformist ministers. Charles Darwin's cousin Frances Julia Wedgwood (known as 'Snow', she was a daughter of the philologist Hensleigh Wedgwood and a friend of Emelia Gurney) came; she remembered Georgina 'from those far off years when I used to see you at Lincoln's Inn Chapel in the dim light of those afternoon services'.[177] The artistically-inclined Lady Waterford left the conference radiant.[178] A memento was a Gothic clock by the important designer Bruce J. Talbert, inscribed 'The Web thou Weavest Everyday I Meander Off & Fold Away. Jesus Christ The Fame Yesterday, Today & Forever'.

The Smiths did not attend the 'conference of heretics' (as Hannah called it), but Hannah urged Georgina to have courage to speak the Lord's words herself, and hoped the conferences would be a regular event.[179] Already controversial for teachings which were castigated as 'self wrought up Holiness', the Smiths were embroiled in a scandal which forced them to leave England. Robert was alleged to have behaved inappropriately towards a woman who had sought spiritual help. Though he maintained that he simply performed the 'Baptism of the Holy Spirit' (by which a person felt the physical manifestation of the Holy Spirit), the couple were shunned by English Evangelicals, but characteristically the Cowper-Temples remained friends and Hannah corresponded regularly with Georgina, who asked her to visit Harris in America, something that Hannah was not yet ready to do.[180] There was more personal disappointment, for in late 1874, William was forced to resign from a committee promoting Robert's work, due to his support for spiritualism. Hannah, no spiritualist herself, was outraged at the bigotry. She was increasingly broad-minded under Jukes' influence.[181]

Rose La Touche died in May. The Cowper-Temples invited Ruskin to Broadlands and Georgina offered to 'adopt' him like Juliet, an offer which indulged his wish to be mothered and stimulated him to call her 'Granny' (William became 'Grandpapa').[182] He stayed in his apartment and wrote for most of October, comforted by the company of Juliet, 'amusing, and not the least troublesome' he told his American friend Charles Eliot Norton, and a girl who was there to help Juliet's French.[183] With the Russell Gurneys, and Annie Munro, Ruskin collected faggots for the poor. Ruskin returned from his lectures (as Slade Professor of Fine Art in Oxford) to Broadlands in December where guests included George MacDonald.[184] Ruskin told his cousin Joan Severn that Georgina was a great mischief who delighted in 'setting William and me by the ears, and then somehow, getting the better of us both which she always does'.[185] As well as further manual work, painting and writing, Ruskin attempted to communicate with Rose in séances with Waggy and Mrs Acworth, a medium whom he had met before as Miss Andrews, who claimed to see a young woman's spirit.[186] Whether Georgina colluded with the mediums to comfort Ruskin and restore his faith will never be known, but she put Waggy into a trance to diagnose Ruskin's health and later, Rose's character. Joan and Norton were suspicious.

William supported the mission of the American evangelist Dwight L. Moody (who had arrived in England in 1873) in London, and attended the farewell metropolitan meeting in July.[187] He also helped fund Baron Karl Andreas's House of Faith, in Tower Street in Hackney, where prayers and holy oil were the sole means of healing the sick, boarders and out-patients, a therapy influenced by the Swiss Dorothea Trudel. In its emphasis on the power of belief, the House of Faith was very much in keeping with the spirit of the Broadlands conferences and with American practitioners like the homeopath and devout episcopalian Charles Cullis, whom the Cowper-Temples had been informed about by Hannah, though a correspondent in *The Times* claimed that the establishment was not against medical treatment, but merely for those 'who have faith enough to believe that they may be cured in answer to fervent prayer'.[188] Apparently William believed that Andreas had reset a boy's broken bones through prayer, and he and Georgina visited the House.[189]

Ruskin visited Broadlands again in late January 1876 where he met Edward Clifford, a recuperating Mrs Acworth, and Frederic Myers.[190] In what was to be his last visit to the house, Ruskin joined spiritualist discussion and heard contact with his hero Turner, who grieved that he had cast a shadow over Ruskin through pursuit of earthly brightness only.[191] Ruskin's loss of orthodox faith had been one of the ostensible stumbling blocks in his relationship with the pious Rose. Now, writing his latest *Fors Clavigera* letter, Ruskin found mention of Turner's religion wonderful, as he brought more Christianity into the series.[192] Georgina recorded his conversation about Turner's 'zoroastrianism'. Myers (whose poetry Ruskin praised) seemed, according to Georgina, to be 'much comforted altogether & is looking quite young & happy' after the talks.[193] She thought his work would be reanimated; the change was 'really life from the dead'.[194] Ruskin read letters from Charles Norton and bits from Scott and Dante to them. He left with renewed faith after communications with his mother and hoped to develop his ideas about the 'rich beautiful joyful Christian life'.[195] Georgina followed Ruskin's apparent recovery ('Oh[,] is looking very little boyish and radiant,' she noted on 16 February) when she attended his lecture on Precious Stones at the London Institute with Edith Leycester.[196] She also attended lectures by George MacDonald, for whom the Cowper-Temples and friends were collecting funds for the freehold of a house.[197] Other lectures included Frederick Furnivall's, though characteristically she found one on *Hamlet* too severe, 'not making allowance enough I think for the hard circumstances of his life'.[198]

In the spring, Georgina befriended Madeline Wyndham, amateur artist and patron of Pre-Raphaelites, and saw her 'beautiful things and beautiful dear self'.[199] Wife of Percy Wyndham, younger son of the Earl Leconfield (an illegitimate son of the Earl of Egremont who was supposedly related to the Lambs) and daughter of Sir Guy Campbell the soldier, she was just the sort of intelligent and talented woman – interested in psychical research and a member of the aristocratic Souls clique – who would attract Georgina.

The Cowper-Temples attended sermons from the Anglican priest George Congreve and other 'Cowley fathers' (in the celibate missionary Society of St John the Evangelist) at Rownhams in Southampton.[200] They hosted a 'conference' on missions with Alfred Gurney, George Body, Jukes, Basil Wilberforce and others. They met James Froude – who became a friend of Henry Cowper – at Anne Cowper's. In early April they visited Cambridge to meet Henry Sidgwick (professor of Moral Philosophy and a supporter of Emily Davies), his friend and colleague in spiritualism, Frederic Myers, and Ruskin, talking with them until midnight.[201] After further deep talk with Ruskin and Davies, and William's departure for the Quarter Sessions, Georgina read *Daniel Deronda* in bed 'in the most self-indulgent way'. The Cowper-Temples made a nostalgic visit to Brocket and found the old grounds in disorder. Anne Cowper was amazed at her seemingly evergreen brother-in-law's running to and from church and to breakfast.[202] They continued their séances; meeting the hydropath Dr James Gully (Daniel Home's physician) at Mrs Gregory's.

When they visited the Wattses and Sophia De Morgan (widow of the mathematician Augustus De Morgan) they enjoyed 'scraps of Infinite talk – opening new worlds and far off vistas. The unity of all religions'.[203]

In early May they were visited by 'Père Hyacinthe', a leading French Catholic preacher. Charles Loyson (whom Georgina had hoped to see in Paris in 1867) was a friend of John Henry Newman, but opposed the doctrine of papal infallibility and in 1871 established a Gallican church similar to the 'Old Catholics' in Utrecht. He had married an American, Emily Meriman and the couple stayed at Stanhope Street, Georgina finding Emily 'so simple and true'.[204] After their guest recovered from bronchitis the Cowper-Temples held a dinner in his honour to which Gladstone came. Gladstone favoured the conference planned in support of Hyacinthe, but the Cowper-Temples thought that the High Church was generally shy of him. They attended the Père's lectures in London, and William wrote to ask Archbishop Tait to endorse the Frenchman's work.[205] Georgina thought Hyacinthe's talk on Mrs Butler's subject – presumably abolition of government regulation of prostitution – splendid, 'I did not think Human speech could be so fine.'[206] Their support was not unusual for the Frenchman was feted by Protestants more widely.[207]

FIGURE 9. Georgina Cowper-Temple, c.1876, under the beeches at Broadlands, by Edward Clifford, photograph of the original.
By courtesy of the Trustees of the Broadlands Archives.

The Père later recalled the blue dining room at Great Stanhope Street, with its brilliant and perfumed flowers and gifted conversation, and commented that Georgina 'a besoin comme vous, et même plus que vous, de ce bon repos de l'âme et du corps. Elle ne sait se refuser à rien de ce qui est noble et généreuse, et elle se dépense, à Londres où les occasions abondant, un delà de ses forces.'[208] The allusion was to Georgina's animal welfare activity. She forced herself to publicly criticise a supine Animals' Friends committee on vivisection, and contacted every peer she knew to support the vivisection debate on Lord Carnarvon's bill in May. Evidently urged to consider vivisection, the Père asked William in September to tell his wife he thought of the 'frères inférieurs', as St Francis called them.[209]

The Cowper-Temples went down to Broadlands where the Loysons joined them and Clifford worked on a portrait of Georgina which she later described as 'outrageously' flattering and which William Rossetti thought not one of his best efforts when it was exhibited.[210] It depicted her, heavy browed and sharp-nosed, in a lace-fringed mob cap and apron over a black gown, with silver chain and crucifix of *putti*, and a snake-entwined purse about her waist, against a background of beeches. A female guest was besotted with Clifford, and talked religion to the painter, who preached in the Abbey. Their other guests included Anne Cowper, Miss Marsh, the Sartorises, Bishop Bugnion and the Spencer Cowpers.[211] 'This is the funniest house, but very pleasant,' Anne told her son.[212] Bugnion prepared a mission to South Russia, to take emigrants to Australia. When the Loysons left Hampshire at the end of June, their new friends contrasted this visit with the horrors of more superficial social gatherings.

Socializing took a Pre-Raphaelite turn in the following weeks. Georgina visited the 'Enchanted Ground', of Burne-Jones' home with Edward Clifford, seeing wonderful paintings and meeting Mrs Wyndham. She visited Rossetti at 16, Cheyne Walk to see the 'development of my Blessed Damozel' – a birthday present from William – 'Happy ones all in blue among green hedges. She still gazing for the beloved one who does not come.' She found Rossetti low, he was suffering from insomnia and physical pain, and taking high doses of chloral.[213] Then she left William in town for an Education Bill debate, to oversee a donkey show at Broadlands. During William's fleeting visit he read her *Omnipotence* by the mystic Lydia Brewster Macpherson, of Balavil in Inverness-shire, who acknowledged William's encouragement in the book's introduction and who became Georgina's 'wonderful Scotch seeress'.[214]

At the start of August Rossetti came for a brief visit but this was extended for almost a month.[215] He was accompanied by his friend George Hake and brought the *Blessed Damozel* to work on. The poet-artist read Wordsworth's and Christina's poems to his hostess, and she stayed while he painted, sitting in his room on several occasions.[216] He sketched her, transfiguring, according to Georgina, her 'commonplace old head'.[217] He sketched a baby which Annie Munro brought from the workhouse, but found the parson's son more suitable for the *Damozel*. Georgina's young friend Georgina Holme Sumner, whose presence wonderfully picked him up, was also sketched and came to figure in a number of studies of stately Roman matrons.[218] He gave the predella for the *Damozel*, depicting the earthly lover amid beeches, in gratitude for their hospitality.[219]

Rossetti avoided the religious conference which again took place out of doors in early August, having been accorded 'the utmost toleration ... as an entirely foreign substance'. He wanted his friend Watts-Dunton to see Georgina, describing her as 'my most womanly & most queenly hostess', praising her to another for 'ineffably womanly goodness' and telling his mother she was 'simply an angel on earth'. William, if less radiantly angelic on the surface, was 'no less so in fact'.[220] Rossetti left in late August with the 'two Georges,' his chloral intake not reduced, to Georgina's dismay; perhaps concern for his health made her visit him later at Cheyne Row, when she saw a splendid drawing of William Morris. In late September she offered to look after Christina Rossetti.[221] When she and Mrs Sumner visited a month later she thought him pretty well, but shy due to 'George'.[222]

FIGURE 10. In the entrance to Broadlands, undated photograph, *c.* 1876.
+: William Cowper-Temple, O: Henry Cowper, Φ: Georgina Cowper-Temple,
X: Augustus Tollemache, Juliet stands in the foreground, and Edith de Burgh sits to make lace.
D.G. Rossetti stands on the far right. By courtesy of the Trustees of the Broadlands Archives.

The religious conference had involved George MacDonald, the popular novelist Mrs Rundle Charles, Laurence Oliphant, Alfred Gurney and many others, with almost seventy house guests and twenty more to lunch in mid-August. William had returned from parliament where a 'very poor' Vivisection Bill – though as Georgina noted, better than nothing – had been passed. After the conference the Cowper-Temples had another guest in the form of the Parsee convert to Christianity, Manekji Mody, who interested them by comparing Zoroastrianism and Christianity. He returned to India with an English wife and preached the gospel.[223]

Juliet had alarmed Georgina by the intensity with which she read the poems 'Sister Helen' and the 'Blessed Damozel' while Rossetti stayed. Then, in early September when they visited Wales, William had to carry a screaming and kicking Juliet from the hotel.[224] Georgina found some distraction in Frances Power Cobbe's *Hopes for the Human Race* and *Daniel Deronda*. But Juliet shared in their holiday at Classiebawn with Evelyn Ashley and his wife. Augustus and Magsie brought their foster children, and Lord Houghton came with his daughters. They revelled in the fresh air, read Balzac's *Le Livre Mystique* on the beach, and admired the work of their housekeeper and gardener, who had cultivated a kitchen garden and planted geraniums, verbena and mignonettes. William decided to give the estate to Evelyn and Georgina agreed: 'quite right I think for them – for the place – & for us.'[225] William was confident that Evelyn would do 'all that is right' (later it was rumoured a codicil to Palmerston's will had led William to this, really it was his feeling that he could no longer visit Ireland frequently).[226]

Less happily for the family was the press attention given to the failed marriage of one of Georgina's nieces. William gave evidence about the marriage of Augusta Selina (Leila) Duchessa di San Teodoro, the daughter of Georgina's sister Selina Locke, who obtained a divorce from Luigi Caracciolo on the grounds of cruelty in late November.[227]

In the winter the Cowper-Temples toured Devon and Cornwall. They visited the aged Quaker geologist and natural philosopher Robert Were Fox and his daughter Anna Maria at Penjerrick ('a Quaker House simplicity … combined with a great deal of intellectual life, knowledge of and interest in all that is going on in the world. Politics, Missions, Charitable work, love of nature and a prevailing sense of goodness and loving kindness') and attended a Quaker service.[228] But their motive for the holiday was the search for a seaside home now Classiebawn was Evelyn's. Dismayed by cockney villas, they found a property at Babbacombe near Torquay, that haven to 'solvent valetudinarianism' which had developed into a sprawl of grand villas, and a few very smart hotels, over the decades. Statesmen, aristocrats, ecclesiastics and 'jaded beauties' came here for recuperation in the mild maritime climate.[229] The house had just gone on the market, the limited space available for building on the cliff helped ensure the romantic seclusion. Below were sandstone and marble cliffs and a bay pebbled with quartz, 'so small that a strong arm could easily whirl a stone across it,' one writer claimed. Though it was a 'squirmy little house' and unprepossessing in misty weather, too small even for their modest requirements, they liked the site and hoped that with the ingenuity of William Eden Nesfield, son of the artist and gardener who had advised on William's improvements to Regent's Park, this could be the place 'given to us in our extremity', as Georgina wrote dramatically. Indeed, it became a haven, and, as intended, after William's death, Georgina's refuge.[230]

Georgina received a 'quite exonerating letter' from Robert Pearsall Smith at the beginning of 1876, and Hannah wrote frequently and gratefully. She was eager for them to enjoy the 'simple American life'.[231] Her own trials had led her to realise that Georgina's 'inveterate doubts' were not as serious as she had thought. Hannah saw a similarity between her husband's misguided spiritual gropings and the 'Brocton experiment' which 'must be very much the same though explained in a different way'.[232] Wonderful, puzzling, and painful letters came from Faithful (Harris) and visits from Laurence Oliphant were bewildering, and unsatisfactory like everything, Georgina wrote.[233] Though she felt that the 'simple life of work & struggle for good' was attractive, a long visit from Olly did not answer her doubts.[234] She was 'much disturbed by the specimens we received of the forthcoming Brocton book'.[235] Emelia Gurney, returned from Egypt, was surprised by Laurence's unimaginativeness and found the talk too complicated, when they dined at Georgina's.[236] When Harris's new book finally arrived she found there was much good, 'much most strange [,] grievously bewildered'.[237]

Georgina's birthday self-analysis was harsh. 'Em and Augustus have both built Churches besides doing many good things. What good shall I leave behind me! ... failure and fruitlessness mark my life yet goodness and mercy have followed me.' This ignored her ongoing and varied philanthropy. Through Clifford, they became acquainted with Frederick Charrington, youthful heir to a brewery but now a missionary in the East End and a temperance activist.[238] Their support for Emma Cons, an associate of Octavia Hill and Christian Socialists, who trained as a restorer of stained glass and watch-maker, was inspired by temperance concerns. Cons had worked in Hill's housing project at Drury Lane and Marylebone and established the Central London Dwellings Company in 1870. Georgina became involved in mothers' meetings at Drury Lane, and supported the view that temperance improved working-class lives.

Religious activities of various sorts – spiritualist, mystical, and ecumenical – dominated the Cowper-Temples' lives in 1877. They met the American theologian and revivalist Asa Mahan, and William joined him at a holiness conference in Freemasons' Hall in early March, alongside the noted preacher Henry Varley and others.[239] Georgina became a vegetarian early in March, but her sympathies already caused her a sense of surprise when she became acquainted with Varley, for he was a butcher by trade, converted to Evangelicalism by Baptist Noel. Initially she found Varley's denunciation of 'loathsome unbelief' repellent and thought him a good man 'incapable of understanding natures unlike his own'.[240]

Pursuing their interest in the faith-healer Karl Andreas they took their protégé Emma Cons to him, and learned more about Hannah Smith's dabbling in faith healing.[241] Georgina regularly attended meetings at the home of the mediumistic Leaf family with the Americans Dr Thomas Low Nichols and Mary Gove Nichols, the Wattses, Sophia De Morgan and James Farquhar.[242] Farquhar, a friend of the Howittses, was 'a self-taught man of considerable gift and research', according to *The Christian* in 1879, whose books included *The Gospel of Divine Humanity*, which considered humanity as the body of God. He uttered, in his strong Scottish accent, a message of perfect patience, for 'nothing could be wrong, since nothing could happen out of the will of God'. The Cowper-Temples' séance with the celebrated medium William Eglinton was reported in *The Spiritualist.*[243] Visitors included the biographer of Swedenborg, William White, and the Spanish Marie Lady Caithness, whom Farquhar later described as one of the two most truly Catholic minds he knew and an illustration of the charity which 'believeth all things'.[244] She played a major role in financing the theosophical movement and leading French theosophy.[245]

Another of their religious conferences took place in the summer, with meetings in a tent and evangelizing services in the Orangery. Roden Noel the writer – with whom William had once conversed by chance on free will and religion on a train to Woking – could not attend, but said his views were now 'far more in harmony with religious people and their principles and views than I was before my darling child was taken. This I hope will appear in my future writings'.[246]

In August the Cowper-Temples became acquainted with the American theosophist Colonel Andrew Jackson Rogers and Victoria Woodhull, notorious exponent of free love. Rogers wrote of the 'Two in One' and a 'whole kingdom within'.[247] 'Are these vagaries?' Georgina asked. They met Victoria at 'a very ill smelling and untidy lodging' and Georgina thought her 'half fanatic half impostor'. Nevertheless Victoria and her sister Fanny Claflin stayed with them for a few days, surrounded, according to Rogers, by angels honouring 'two of the Lord's chosen Servants'.[248] 'Very strange,'

Georgina recorded, 'but interesting & seems very good.' Fanny pressed Georgina with mesmeric healing of her ailments. Victoria publicised the fact that she was their guest and it was reported that prior to a lecture in St James's Hall they had 'expressed grave concerns' for her life if she spoke on eugenics. In reality the Cowper-Temples were not won over.[249] Destitute, she left without saying goodbye, although William offered £50. William charged Rogers and Victoria with opposing marriage, though Rogers claimed to be revising lectures to avoid misleading and demoralizing the lower orders, and that 'Victoria will not promulgate anything here not evolved by the Holy Spirit of God. She will obey her inspiration, and will not go forth till she is inspired to do so.'[250] No more money came from William, who plainly but firmly refused to support her lectures on the 'Scientific Propagation of the Human Race' (which however brought her marriage to a wealthy Englishman six years later).[251] Rogers, convinced it was 'the beginning of the New Era – the Christ of God glorified in the flesh', sent a defence of his 'noble, and self sacrificing' compatriot's view on the body as essential to a modernized 'Christ of Humanity'.[252] He wanted to sustain the acquaintance with the Cowper-Temples before his return to America, 'for I always feel the better for being within your more immediate spirit-magnetic spirit'.[253]

If patronage of Woodhull was wisely rejected, they supported the 'blessed Cobbe' in anti-vivisectionism, a 'coffee tavern' movement and Emma Cons' temperance work.[254] In mid April Georgina's London home provided the venue for six health lectures from Frances Hoggan, the first Englishwoman to obtain a European MD but unable as yet to be registered as a medical practitioner in Britain (this was to change in that year), and prominent with her husband in Cobbe's anti-vivisection society. Georgina continued to give time to mothers' meetings at Drury Lane. Horror at the Eastern atrocities also led her to attend meetings in support of Bosnian victims of Turkish outrages.

The plight of friends and acquaintances also worried her. Shocked by what she saw of Rossetti at Cheyne Walk in July, she wrote, 'How art thou fallen Lucifer son of the morning.'[255] She was also involved with the former curate at Romsey, Erasmus Van Deerlin, a philanthropic object in 1874, when he required surgery and now guilty of a terrible sin (perhaps his conversion to Catholicism), as she confided in her diary. The Cowper-Temples tried to interest American friends in finding him a job, while helping to support his family.[256] They were also closely involved with George MacDonald. At the beginning of April he thanked them for money that friends had given him and stayed briefly at Broadlands.[257] Suffering from bronchitis, pleurisy and loneliness at Hammersmith while his wife took an ailing daughter to Italy, Georgina brought him to Great

Stanhope Street in mid-October after he said 'it would be like a fairy story to have you to take care of me ... It is so grasping to take you from William for days. But then he is as good as you, and I owe it to him not to be afraid of his grudging you.'[258] Then she took him to Broadlands to stay in Ruskin's room. 'Great heart's' conversation with his 'best of sisters' delighted her. He had cheering news of a Literary Fund grant, and William gave £200, charmingly described as 'a few of his slates'.[259] At Christmas MacDonald set off for Nervi leaving his friends to deal with his ponies. Georgina sent on handkerchiefs and shawls to Louisa MacDonald who irritatingly styled her 'God's Messenger'. Yet Louisa was peeved to find her husband pouring out family affairs to her, 'You see,' he told Georgina, 'I got in the way of talking to you about anything and everything, and I feel certain she will not mind it long.'[260]

Babbacombe was rebuilt and replanted through the year, with the Cowper-Temples paying brief visits to see Nesfield's plans develop. Georgina was surprised at a 'little bit of Peckforton attached to our Cardboard villa' in September.[261] When they returned to Broadlands guests included the scholar of pre-Christian and Eastern religions, John Newenham Hoare, who delighted them with talk of the Rig Veda and Buddha. But Herman Douglas regretted that Edith Leycester and Georgina dabbled in the unorthodox: 'O do let dead and infidelity alone, dear dear friends! – It will only chill, and contract your hearts. Dearest Mr Temple said more than a quarter of a century ago, that he had a witness in his own soul, better than philosophical synthesis and analysis.'[262]

This narrative, as in the previous chapters, conveys some sense of their participation in a high political and social culture where leading artists and intellectuals rubbed shoulders with aristocrats and in which women had central roles as hostesses and dining companions. As one historian has noted, 'Victorian political society was so intimately linked with the literary and cultural world, that historians, classicists, theologians, and even scientists, in writing and speaking as they did, were consciously making contributions to the political debate.'[263] Before his inheritance, William had belonged to various important circles: the Duke of Devonshire's, the Foxes, and of course, the Palmerstons, now the Cowper-Temples could employ enlarged resources for philanthropic patronage. Broadlands and their London home were meeting places for the good and great, and Georgina's role as hostess was important. They transformed the tone of life at Broadlands; as one newspaper reported in 1888, they 'made Broadlands the centre of a social movement the influences of which will hardly be estimated in our day'.[264]

The Cowper-Temples left their mark in bricks and mortar. A three-storey 'bachelor's wing' provided more accommodation at Broadlands.

The Orangery was extended for the religious conferences and made available for friendly societies and working men's institutions on application, with freedom to roam the grounds (tourists also came to Broadlands in their thousands). During one temperance gathering the grounds were 'gay with banners, decorated vehicles and crowds of people in summer dress'.[265] Such accessibility should also be seen in the light of William's involvement in efforts to save open spaces for public recreation.

William commissioned Nesfield to design a gate lodge for Lady Palmerston.[266] This and another lodge on the estate were pioneering essays in the 'vernacular' revival. Nesfield advised on an Italianate flower garden on the south front of the house, with agave, laurel and bays, ornamented by a sixty-foot fountain, and created a Pre-Raphaelite fireplace for the house. He designed a Boys' National School in Romsey, which became a memorial to William's mother in 1871. There was a chapel at Ridge, with a school, so that all who lived on the estate would have a place to worship. William paid for an estate curate.

FIGURE 11. Broadlands, a Baxter print from F.O. Morris, *A Series of Picturesque Views of Seats of the Noblemen and Gentlemen of Great Britain and Ireland* (1884), vol.1, facing p.69.

The beautiful white-brick Palladian mansion, with its compact grounds planned with Capability Brown's advice, and its fine collection of Italian paintings, was a haven. It was a home full of flowers; of large rooms smelling of orange blossom, presided over by a tall and stately Georgina. It had been 'handsome and convenient' rather than grand in Palmerston's time, when he performed the role of country gentleman, and under the Cowper-Temples the arrangements often seemed informal, as Margaret Leicester Warren noted in 1873: 'here people come and go just as they like. One has breakfast when one gets up, dinner when one comes home, and luncheon when one's hungry. One couple had salmon in their bedrooms at 11 am.'[267] And Andrew Jukes recalled Juliet, the 'bright little girl … running about with her bare little feet over the lawns'. Augustus Hare, that seasoned country house visitor, thought the place 'a pleasant liveable house' with lovely gardens.[268]

Their gatherings of socialites, savants, seers and theologians seem at first glance mismatched, but were an attempt at social and cultural brokering or networking, a harmonization of views through hospitality and charm, the smoothing over of ideological divisions through friendships, and the creation of communities of sympathy across apparent intellectual or religious gulfs. These motives were most apparent in the religious conferences examined in another chapter. For contemporaries, this experimentation seemed rather foolhardy or daring. Lionel Tollemache recalled one occasion with amusement, when his aunt and uncle planned the guests to meet their Evangelical brother-in-law Shaftesbury and a succeeding party involving the agnostic man of letters and liberal politician John Morley. Lionel thought they had the sense to keep apart hostile camps but Morley's visit, as we have seen, involved the spiritualists Stainton Moses, Myers and Gurney. The visit was a great event in Myers' life, leaving him with a lasting sense of a reposeful 'home of high thoughts'. What hours of spiritual nurture had he experienced in the long drawing-rooms, he wrote, beyond which broad lawns sloped in sunlight down to the crystal river Test. And the 'high souls' seemed immortal, 'they moved without shock or wandering upon a far-seen sacred goal'. Immemorial trees heightened a sense of changelessness, and if a fair girl-guest wandered though the deep-shadowed isles of lawn, 'her beauty took something of sabbatical from the slow-moving stately day'.[269]

Clifford recalled Georgina as a hostess, 'full of the kind of vivacity which stimulates talk in other people', and 'never hurried or in a fidget'.[270] In reality, Georgina's health was often strained: 'I get so utterly exhausted after a few days of company.' This seems an extravagant comment, but being mistress of a London mansion and country house hosting varied and ambitious gatherings would have taxed any chatelaine, despite an army of servants under efficient head servants. It was more so for a woman like Georgina with highly strung nerves, and in her memoirs she paid tribute to the servants who bore the chief stress of their assemblages.[271]

8

LORD MOUNT TEMPLE: THE LIBERAL STATESMAN

Although Palmerston died in 1865, William's position as a junior minister continued until the Liberal government's downfall in June 1866. So closed a career in public office which unkind commentators in the press, Tory or Radical, argued with some justice was the result of Whig nepotism rather than an aptitude sufficiently flexible for the varied expertises required. *Reynolds's Newspaper*, for instance, cited him as the example of a man thrust into widely different departments without regard to the silly democratic notion of merit. 'What Mr Cowper might next have become had Lord Palmerston been alive and Chief Lord of the Treasury, it is difficult for us to conjecture.' The *London Review* noted him as a person of 'considerable importance' in Palmerston's lifetime (and no more).[1] If, after 1866 he never took up public office again, he remained prominent in public life; in part this was due to his role in cultivating his stepfather's posthumous reputation.[2]

Derby's government proved short-lived despite the passing of the Second Reform Act in 1867, about which William's mother wrote: 'The Reform Bill is very candid, and very like Ld Derby's speech and Jump in the dark but what fools they shew themselves to be, and how unfit they are to Govern.'[3] William did not lead in the debates over the reform bill. A letter from him to Gladstone, in late March, suggests he wished, with 'what were called conservative members', to support a £5 franchise, 'provided that the guarantee of personal payment were prepared in some satisfactory form', but otherwise there is no extended record of his views.[4] With Shaftesbury, he advised the reformer Edmond Beales against a reform march on Good Friday.[5] He was no democrat (very few politicians were), and he looked at the extension of the franchise effected by the Act with some concern. Politicians needed to be statesmen, he asserted in 1868, and that for 'statesmanship, like every other profession, you must serve an apprenticeship, that men must give it time, thought, labour, and must exercise themselves in the art of government before they could be fit to lead their fellows'. [6] The Second Reform Act certainly interested Georgina, who stuck newspaper articles on the bill into her diary.[7]

The Second Reform Act deprived Hertford of one of its MPs. After 33 years, William no longer represented the town, having been chosen to represent South Hampshire – a natural choice as he was clearly to be master of Broadlands – at the election of November 1868, which saw the Tories defeated despite their promotion of Reform. William represented his new constituency for twelve years, and initially played a part in representing Southampton while they lacked a Liberal MP.[8] He turned down the chancellorship of the Duchy of Lancaster (with or without a peerage) from Gladstone, who became premier in December 1868 after Disraeli's resignation. Lady Palmerston, in congratulating Mrs Gladstone on her husband's good fortune, had said, 'I am very sorry that my son William Cowper was unable to join it.'[9] He refused because he felt it would be a sinecure since he lacked skill in debate and the office went to his bête noire, the Quaker radical John Bright.[10] Also, William 'desired to cling to the House of Commons as long as he could', probably appreciating the upper chamber's somnolence.[11] From the backbenches – on the fourth bench behind the Treasury during Gladstone's first ministry – he introduced or supported significant measures, in education (including female education) and preservation or access to common land.

When Gladstone came to Romsey in June 1868, he honoured Palmerston's memory and aided William's electoral fortune: both men thought it advantageous to stress their associations with the deceased premier. Gladstone spoke of long association: 'for we have been united, I am glad to think, for many years in cordial cooperation on every subject of public interest'. William praised Gladstone as the sharer of the counsels and right-hand man of Palmerston in the Commons. He felt grateful that the mantle of that statesman had fallen upon Gladstone.[12] But his response to Gladstone's first ministry was mixed. Promised retrenchment touched relations: abolition of County Courts meant Evelyn Ashley and Augustus Tollemache lost their posts, and Income Tax measures hurt.[13]

William remained as active in the Commons as ever. He chaired a select committee to study how far provisions of the Inclosure Act of 1845 related to the labouring poor, had been carried out in the annual inclosure bills; and to investigate whether an amendment to protect the interests of the public 'in respect to the provisions for places of public recreation and for allotments for the labouring poor' was required. The committee was unable to give any 'general opinion as to the sufficiency or insufficiency of the public allotments which have been made by the Commissioners since 1845' but suggested legal alterations and stated that 'constant attention' was necessary during the annual introduction of the Inclosure Bill.[14]

Outside the Commons, William used the Christmas stock show in Romsey to comment on the Irish land question (too much subdivision of land, no alternatives to agriculture for the peasantry) and education of children in the countryside.[15] When William received a testimonial from his former constituencies at Hertford, this stimulated a homily on the necessity of party in politics, the Reform and Conservative parties acting as a proper element of the constitution: 'I am a party man and respect partisans when they are actuated by a fair and honourable spirit.'[16]

In 1870 came the measure which brought him lasting statutory fame, the 'Cowper-Temple Clause', though the measure had been discussed by others, and William drew on the expertise of Canon David Melville of Worcester.[17] An elementary education act reforming the system for children between 5 and 13 had long been on the political agenda, when the Liberals returned to power. W.E. Forster, the vice-president of the Committee of Council on Education, created an Elementary Education Bill which, delayed by the disestablishment of the Church of Ireland, and other pressing claims on the Privy Council, was introduced to the Commons on 17 February 1870. It inevitably roused nonconformist ire because Gladstone insisted that the Bill either permit denominational religion in the new schools or have no religious instruction and thus be a secularist bill doomed to failure. The National Education League, with its centre in Birmingham under Joseph Chamberlain, was determined to defeat the Bill. William was chairman of the National Education Union defending voluntary schools from the threat of secularism, though he was a rare Liberal in this largely Conservative and Anglican organization. In early March he led a deputation from the Union (whose members included Shaftesbury, Salisbury, and Thomas Hughes) to Gladstone.

To secure the bill, various amendments were offered. William's amendment, clause 14, forbade the teaching in elementary Board schools of any 'catechism or formulary which is distinctive of any particular denomination'.[18] He wanted to avoid the inevitable sectarian flavour which instruction involving particular books or a distinctive formulary of words would suggest, but did not mean a teacher to be forbidden from explaining the Bible according to his own views or opinions (English denominations had long been opposed to the 'common Christianity' model of Irish education established by Whigs in 1831[19]). Jacob Bright's amendment to prevent Board schools using religious instruction 'in favour of or against the distinctive tenets of any religious denomination' was rejected. But in practice most rate-built schools excluded denominational forms of religious education, in line with Bright's amendment. This appalled the High Church Gladstone, who had been preoccupied with other matters such as the Irish land question, but he had to acquiesce.[20]

William believed that 'by excluding the catechism it silences the rallying cries of Controversy and limits the range for dispute'.[21] He advised the Church of England that it should try to lead the new system.[22] He presented the act as a whole, as a 'truly Liberal and wise policy', whereby local authorities were obliged to fund primary education, with the Government's responsibility to superintend and direct balanced by continued voluntary exertion: this 'dual system', whereby the voluntary schools continued alongside the first tentative acknowledgement of the state's direct role in elementary education, continued until 1902 when voluntary schools received rate-support. In the short term the Act contributed to Nonconformist discontent with Gladstone's government and its electoral defeat in 1874. William's name continued to figure prominently in relation to legislation on religious matters, when he supported a bill to admit non-Anglicans to parish pulpits in 1873, which excited, amused and outraged press comment (see chapter 11).

The Franco-Prussian war frightened many Britons about preparedness for modern warfare and William, while declaring a horror of war, felt that war was to be eradicated 'by being so strong that nobody dared to attack us'. As he told a Hampshire audience in February 1871, he took the following lessons from France's defeat: if a country was not ready for a war before it commenced, it had no time to get ready afterwards and war was now so varied and complex that old forms of organization would no longer do; nations which wished to keep pace in operations had to organize and put armies on a new footing. Army purchase was indefensible. He detected wholesome energy and active patriotism not seen in any previous period, things went fast now, and one reason was that electors had given a large majority to the Liberal party in Parliament.[23]

Like Gladstone and many others, William disliked the introduction of a secret ballot in 1872, seeing it as a shameful admission that 'rich men and men of influence in the country used their wealth and influence to intimidate poor voters from voting according to their consciences' and that the voters lacked energy and courage. He accepted the Radicals' measure as a necessary evil. But he objected to the abolition of nominations and declarations of polls which put candidates face to face in public. He also wished to see candidates who lacked the wealth which had until now been 'an indispensable preliminary to becoming a candidate'.

In April of 1871 the *Manchester Guardian* reported 'Mr Cowper-Temple on Public Affairs', implying his opinion was noteworthy. William generally approved George Goschen's bill on local tax, and Henry Bruce's Licensing Bill but had doubts about a permissive bill to deal with drink through prohibition. He endorsed a bill facilitating land transfer and Army reform. Somewhat surprisingly – given that he was generally regarded as a Whig – he said he was 'an advanced Liberal, but not advanced enough to vote for Mr Miall's motion, believing that the rural parishes could suffer considerably by the disestablishment of the English church'.[24]

William had joined the Commons Preservation Society at its inception in 1865, and a bill to protect metropolitan commons, by giving legal powers to preserve and manage to local authorities, was enacted in 1866. He chaired the Select Committee on the Enclosure Acts in 1869 and in February 1871 introduced a bill to improve, protect and manage commons and waste lands near English cities and towns. The commons protection effort enjoyed a notable success with the defeat of government plans to enclose Epping Forest in 1871 and so rob inhabitants of the East End of their 'natural playground'. Support for William's motion, presented, according to one MP, 'with much dexterity', considerably embarrassed the government in May (the Cabinet was defeated by a majority of 101).[25] It was a popular action even among country gentleman, but those who voted against enclosure did so partly to embarrass Gladstone, who had asked for the motion to be withdrawn.[26] Artificial gardens and parks were no substitute for the wild and open beauty of the forest, William argued. Gardens could be remade but primitive forests could not, he observed. *Punch* decided 'LORD PALMERSTON'S step-son … gave the Ministers a most tremendous beating. And, moreover, he was in the right, and they were in the wrong.' Not that William lacked sympathy for the government when, in 1871, the Chancellor of the Exchequer, Robert Lowe proposed a tax on matches in the budget and protests led to this highly unpopular and 'cruel infliction on the poor' being dropped.[27] William was glad that 'Lowe got a warning lesson' but felt it hard on the prime minister and Lowe that events had conspired to undermine their pacific and economical campaigns.[28]

In 1872 William was mentioned as a potential leader of a third party of moderate conservatives, according to the *Western Morning News*, alongside Sir George Grey, Charles Villiers, Edward Ellice and E.P. Bouverie, the correspondent thinking his chances slim given that he 'can with difficulty make himself heard' and looked as old at 61 as Palmerston did at 75.[29] The association between the two men was stressed when William played host to the Associated Chambers of Commerce, his speech in the library of Broadlands linked the memory of Palmerston with patriotic commerce and was reported, with a nostalgic editorial, by *The Times*.[30]

In late January 1874 there was a general election and William found his campaign threatened by another Liberal candidate; having pledged himself not to have a contest he was in difficulty.[31] Foreign affairs having become centre stage in politics, when the Central Liberal Association for the borough was established in Southampton in early 1876, William advised a close watch over foreign policy because of the threat to European peace from the Turkish question.[32] He committed himself to a Palmerstonian approach to the Ottoman and Russian empires. The policy of the Crimean war era should be enforced more fully and completely, their duty was to protect Turkey from misrule and Russian aggression and give the Christian provinces self-government.[33] He joined the National Conference on the Eastern Question at St James's Hall in December 1876, endorsing Gladstone's campaign against Disraelian policy and Turkish atrocities. Gladstone made a 'chivalrous and Christian protest' against Disraeli's desire to commit England to a course that would uphold the 'savage tyranny' of Turks over Christian subjects, William told him. England would be degraded in Europe by being represented 'by such a Bombastic untruthful Charlatan if he were not known to be more of a Jew than an Englishman,' he wrote. William accepted Gladstone's claim in the *Contemporary Review* that Palmerston would have joined Russia in the protection of Christians, and in general associated Palmerston with anti-Beaconsfieldism.[34]

William was never a strong enthusiast for imperial endeavour, deploring recent wars in Africa and Asia in 1879, in response to a deputation to Broadlands, though observing they at least provided a 'fair and satisfactory test' of naval and military strength and abilities.[35] He defended Gladstone and argued that Beaconsfield had in reality adopted the 'bag and baggage' approach to Turkey.[36] His comments on the Treaty of Berlin and Beaconsfield's acquisition of Cyprus (which he disapproved of) were reported. But in response to events in Afghanistan in 1878 he certainly wanted atonement for Shere Ali's affront: 'Englishmen must now all join heartily in the assertion of our supremacy in India, and in showing that no insult could be put upon the English nation by an Afghan chief without ample chastisement being imposed.' British rule 'properly managed, would be the benefit and civilization of the Asiatic subjects'.[37]

Land reform attracted no support from William, not surprisingly in an era when the landed interest was faced by a range of reformers intent on nationalizing land, or punitively taxing the landlord. Though he suggested in 1879 that the example of the Irish Encumbered Estates Court (established in 1849) ought to be followed in England, he saw no future for the idea of an English peasant proprietorship, which he saw as a 'wild speculation contrary to the spirit and genius of the country'.[38] He thought that the interests of Irish tenants were now on a level with landlords.

But a legislative measure which he supported was the University Degrees of Women Bill (1874-1876) which became part of a government bill in 1878. William and Russell Gurney wished to amend the medical act of 1858 in relation to women's medical degrees from foreign universities and wanted to enable women to study for medical qualifications at home. William defended the measure 'in his mild way' as the *Manchester Guardian* put it, by arguing for women's equal intellectual power (citing the literature produced by women), the possibilities for female doctors in the *zenanas* of the upper Indian provinces (and stressing, more generally, that the male medical profession would not be harmed), and the progressive position taken by other European universities.[39] His support for female education was also shown by chairing a public meeting at Great St James's Hall in Piccadilly in May 1871, for a Ladies' College in Cambridge, where 'solid information' would replace 'accomplishments'.[40]

He supported Gladstone's disestablishment of the Anglican Church in Ireland, by now recognizing a 'badge of conquest ... so galling to the great majority of the Irish people'.[41] Despite shared anti-Beaconsfieldism, there were points of difference: as an Irish landlord, unsurprisingly William did not support Gladstone's later policies in Ireland, and he joined the cry against 'grand maternal government' led by the former Radical Sir William Harcourt (a connection of the Cowper-Temples) after 1870, over access to parks and commons, the Thames Embankment and other issues. He told Harcourt it was necessary – in order to secure power – to sustain the moderate Liberal wing.[42] But Gladstone and he remained amicable. The Cowper-Temples were invited to Hawarden in late 1879 and in response William rejoiced for Gladstone's sake that there was rest between past and future labours dealing with Beaconsfield and Salisbury's 'presumptuous blunders', and in bringing before the public as only he could, 'the natural connection of the sorrowful disaster in Asia and Africa and the policy of the Government'.[43]

When he was again offered the Chancellorship of the Duchy of Lancaster by Gladstone, who apologised for offering no cabinet post, William asked for time to consider. He learned that there would be a contest for his seat if he vacated it on taking up office. If he had really wanted office he would have accepted the risk, as he told Evelyn. The truth was he did not, 'having had as much of it as I like, and am personally glad that it does not seem to be my duty to go into harness again – so that on the whole I am well pleased with what has happened'.[44]

On the forty-first anniversary of Victoria's accession the papers noted that of the MPs in 1837 only Cowper-Temple, Gladstone and six others were still in the Commons.[45] But within a couple of years, in March 1880, William announced his retirement because of 'diminution of strength and health'.[46] This was plausible as he approached seventy; if he had impressed Ruskin by doing parliamentary and estate work 'without ever seeming to be hurried or fatigued', his health was now failing.[47] Juliet's former governess was glad, Georgina would 'get more of his society, I hope, and he can always aid his country in many other ways outside the "House" & help young members with his matured advice on any great question'.[48] Divisions within the Liberal party in Hampshire encouraged his decision; the illness of sister Fanny also provided a pretext to leave with honour.[49] Though 'embers of dissatisfaction in the constituency' still smouldered when he asked for support for Evelyn Ashley's candidacy in 1881, William continued to work in Hampshire politics, as president of the South Hampshire General Liberal Association.[50]

FIGURE 12. Studio portrait of Lord Mount Temple, by Russell and Sons, *c*.1880–1888. By courtesy of the Trustees of the Broadlands Archives.

Gladstone returned as premier in April 1880, and in May William's inclusion among new peers was announced.[51] Gladstone had offered a peerage in 1874, and though he regretted William's departure from the Commons, said the elevation was a well earned honour.[52] William became Baron Mount Temple of Mount Temple, Sligo, a near revival of the title bestowed on Palmerston's great grandfather. At the same time, William sought Gladstone's support for the French Catholic Père Hyacinthe, who was invited with William to breakfast at the Gladstones': Gladstone had attended his lectures in 1876.[53] William also told Gladstone of his great admiration 'for the way in which you have become the friend and patron of the Farmer'.[54] He said it was a blessing to the nation that they had him to deal with Irish Home Rulers rather than Beaconsfield.[55]

William was less active now, speaking little in the Lords, though given the status of 'leader of the Broad Church' there according to the *Liverpool Mercury*.[56] Papers gleefully reported his gaffe in the Lords' gallery in the Commons, in wearing a hat, in April 1882.[57] Occasionally he showed interest in foreign affairs such as Portuguese pretensions to territory by the River Congo, Russian pogroms and persecution of German Jews.[58] He replied in print to Auberon Herbert's criticism of party politics in 1882.[59] He opposed a railway through the Lake District in 1883, fearing it would vulgarize the district and stood up for the rights of the poor over parochial burial ground against Euston railway station.[60] He was on select committees examining the Smoke Nuisance Abatement (Metropolis) Bill, and canine rabies, introducing a bill for compulsory registration of dogs in London in April 1887.[61] Lord Cranbrook noted a 'drawling and needless speech' and 'much foolish evidence' from him.[62] He also supported a cross-party parliamentary social reform committee in May 1888.[63]

'Social purity' and agitation against trafficking British girls for sexual purposes kept him before the public. He was appointed to the Lords' select committee in 1881 investigating the traffic (members of the committee included the Marquess of Salisbury and Lord Tollemache).[64] The horrors were strikingly revealed by W.T. Stead in the *Pall Mall Gazette* (the 'Maiden Tribute of Modern Babylon') from July 1885 and the Cowper-Temples gave public support to Stead on his release from prison, where he was sent for procuring a girl as part of the campaign, in January 1886.[65] William was at the inaugural meeting of the Church of England Social Purity Society at Lambeth Palace in 1883, with the Head Master of Harrow, the Bishop of Truro, George Russell and others. The Society combated impurity 'by direct action upon those of the stronger sex, without whom the weaker cannot be led astray or encouraged to pursue degraded lives'.[66] He stressed the duty to warn the young about immoral practices even if it meant touching pitch, to awaken consciences to 'the true nature of the animalism and devilry into which so many men have thoughtlessly fallen for want of a warning and appealing voice'.[67] He supported the Criminal Law Amendment Bill's attempt to raise the age of consent for girls in 1883.[68] Several bills (following the recommendations of the Lords' committee) tried to raise the age from thirteen to sixteen and amended legislation against prostitution; William's amendments to a bill of 1883 aimed to keep regulation of brothels under public control rather than absolutely under police control; a bill was eventually passed by the

Conservatives in 1885.[69] He opposed the presence of women and children at trials involving certain actions, to prevent their moral pollution. William had lived through parliamentary reforms in 1832 and 1867. He was to see a third reform act in 1884, and redistribution act in 1885. Salisbury in the *Quarterly*, William noted, was despondent about the prospects for his party and he anticipated that a franchise bill and Gladstone's popularity would floor the Tories.[70] William congratulated Gladstone on his 'marvellous success in saving the Lords from a dangerous Crusade against its power and independence' and at the same time securing his wants about redistribution.[71] The crusade was the agitation from the spring to autumn 1884, involving protest meetings, press onslaught, and a People's League for the Abolition of the Hereditary Legislature, in response to the peers' blocking of the Franchise Bill, for franchise extension which comprised part of the Third Reform Act.[72]

In 1885 William wrote to Gladstone 'rejoicing that you will have repose from the absorbing cares and anxieties of governing this Country until the General Election has relieved Salisbury from the office which requires for its taking so many excuses and misrepresentations'.[73] But he told Evelyn Ashley that Gladstone, eager for office on account of his majority, would try a 'milk and water Home Rule which will be only a temporary sop to the Nationalists and increase their appetite for more'.[74] He and Evelyn, with Irish estates, worried about Gladstone's support for repeal of the Union. William had other Irish associations at this time. His nephew Earl Cowper was Lord Lieutenant; his resignation in April 1882 was shortly followed by the shocking murders of Lord Frederick Cavendish and T.H. Burke in Phoenix Park.[75]

To Evelyn, William reflected in May 1886, one of the 'sad results of the too great old man is the opposition it will probably produce, if there is a dissolution, between the upper and the middle Classes on one side and the lower on the other'.[76] Evelyn thought it his duty to oppose 'separationists' but said Gladstone's manifesto was the 'most profligate attempt to raise class feelings that any man, much less a Minister of the Crown – has ever gone in for'. [77] William, who had publicly rejoiced in being one of Gladstone's followers in 1885, [78] joined 'dissentient Liberals' in Liberal Unionism in 1886, attending the Liberal Unionist conference the next year.

He viewed politics in a millenarian light. In February 1886 William told George MacDonald that politics were very difficult and the Irish problem impossible. Europe was being influenced by rising democracy and socialism, which he hoped was preparatory to 'the manifested dispensation of the Holy Ghost'. He thought he saw preparations for the Second Coming: 'Pentecostal blessing was poured on the whole multitude, and now the Banks of Privilege and Superiorities are being overwhelmed by the claims and the combined force of the masses.'[79] But an undated letter (probably at the time of Joseph Chamberlain of Birmingham's 'unauthorized' radical programme in September 1885) expressed anguish at the state of politics. He could not bear it, it was too detestable, were the English driven mad by the extravagance of that domineering demagogue who judged of the world by Brummagem?[80] His anxiety was shared more widely by an aristocracy feeling itself beleaguered by economic and political forces in the mid-1880s.[81]

William's reduced activity in the House of Lords was in keeping with its dignified silence, and noted by papers such as *British Illustrated Magazine* as shared with other new peers such as Lord Sherbrooke (Robert Lowe). He was preoccupied with religious and philanthropic efforts. The *Illustrated Magazine*, unsubtly hinting about his paternity, said he 'grows more than ever like the ghost of Lord Palmerston'.[82] Yet he was deemed worthy of inclusion in Andrew Reid's *Why I Am a Liberal: Being Definitions and Personal Confessions of Faith by the Best Minds of the Liberal Party* in 1885.[83]

William ended his long political career a Whig, but a liberal-minded one loyal to what he interpreted as Palmerstonian foreign policy. Like his stepfather, he was no radical. Indeed, the only occasion when Georgina's nephew Lionel, 'Gladstone's Boswell', heard him being acerbic, was in reference to Richard Cobden and John Bright. [84] Aristocratic disdain combined with insensitivity to nonconformist grievances – ironically given William's later efforts to reach out to nonconformists. After dining together once, when he was a Lord of the Admiralty, he wrote that 'Bright is a pleasant lively chap; fond of poking his face at people.'[85] But William detected the domination of 'self-affections'. Mill owners were 'accustomed to direct absolutely great work and large bodies of men and to turn aside for no obstacle. It is not a politic man, but a passionate, self-willed one'. Bright did not recognize that England had a history, looking at events, whether war or constitutional change, from the aspect of the present without associating it with the past or future. He was mortified that he lacked a social or political position he thought he deserved and resented the Church of England for ancestral sufferings.[86]In his attitude to these middle-class critics of Palmerstonian policy, imperialism and aristocracy, we see William's Whiggism (and perhaps an echo of Ashley's hostility after Bright opposed factory reform). Though he backed such radical concerns as repeal of the corn laws, state-supported education, and commons preservation, William had little in common with the leading mid-Victorian parliamentary radicals.

After his death the political reporter Henry Lucy was disparaging, stating that he never shone in debate during his long time in the Commons, with minor posts being found for him, before he was shelved in the Lords.[87] This was unfair, because it judged him on his performance in the chamber, and neglected his achievements in legislation. He had administrative ability, and worked. There might not have been a succession of brilliant acts, but despite his detractors' comments, he made few major mistakes despite the 'scrapes' gleefully reported by the press and noted in an earlier chapter, and was not the mediocrity that some parliamentarian critics suggested.

9

THE FINAL DECADE OF MARRIAGE, 1878–1888

Georgina's reposeful portrait by Clifford of 1876, sat under the beeches in Broadlands, belied a life at feverish pace. Physical decline was to force a slowing down at least on William's part, but from 1878 until their earthly marriage was ended, the Cowper-Temples pursued public tasks of religious, moral and social reform, and privately sought religious truth. At their London home, Hannah Smith wrote, 'one always meets interesting people on Sunday afternoon.' Broadlands continued to host meetings of diverse and like-minded groups, whether in the ecumenical conferences or smaller-scale gatherings, in a period characterized as one of 'ethical renaissance' and 'new moral rigorousness'.[1] The activity was recorded in detail in Georgina's diaries, William having largely abandoned the practice.

As ever, the activities and well-being of their friend John Ruskin brought interest and anxieties. William had resigned from the trusteeship of Ruskin's Guild of St George with Sir Thomas Acland in the previous year, possibly in response to Ruskin's indiscretions about his finances in *Fors* for April 1877.[2] Now, as Ruskin published further letters in *Fors Clavigera*, he was 'behaving very naughtily' towards Octavia Hill, so George MacDonald told Georgina in February 1878.[3] But *Fors* was suspended in the spring due to Ruskin's mental illness, and the Cowper-Temples asked for prayers for his recovery.[4] Shortly afterwards, Georgina had a long conversation with Mary Gladstone, daughter of W.E.G., about Ruskin's personal history, telling her the sad story of the marriage to Euphemia Gray. 'I remember being transported miles from this world's atmosphere,' Mary recalled, 'when with Lord and Lady Mount Temple.'[5]

In June, Great Stanhope Street hosted a controversial lecture in a series for the Ladies' Sanitary Association on obstetrical matters for women acting as nurses in cottage-hospitals, in the slums of the city, and intending to go to India as medical missionaries. An 'outraged matron' who wrote to the journal *Truth*, described the gorgeous décor, and aristocratic females in the audience, and then, in highly offended tones, alluded to the demoralizing nature of the lecture (on anatomy) by the former military nurse, Florence Lees. 'I can scarcely believe I am in a respectable private house,' the lady wrote, 'Is it possible that any circumstances in life can ever arise to justify in these boudoir ladies a knowledge of subjects hitherto held sacred to the consulting room and hospital?'[6] A letter in defence pointed out that the topic had been advertised, that Lees was devoted to her 'suffering kind', and that to bring along an unmarried girl (and pay for admission), and then characterize the subject as a 'dark and Haymarketty side of human life', was unfair and unreasonable.[7] Unfortunately the diary which might have revealed Georgina's response to this scandal no longer exists.

The Broadlands conference must have been, by contrast, blissful. It took place as usual, in early August,[8] with guests including the 'pale, refined, intellectual' French Protestant pastor Théodore Monod, the Scottish 'seeress' Lydia Brewster Macpherson, Andrew Jukes, and the mystic John Pulsford, who sent a joyful letter on his return to Edinburgh, about the mixture of the 'divine human, human-Divine'.[9] More publicly, during the Paris exhibition, they had joined Shaftesbury and others in the spring, in patronizing the 'Salle Évangélique' at the Place du Trocadero.[10]

Juliet's governess, Annie, sister of the sculptor Alexander Munro, was seriously ill at the end of this year. Georgina spoke of her as lost in a fog,[11] though the MacDonalds could not believe she was mentally ill.[12] F.J. Furnivall said, 'This then was at the back of that certain strangeness – repression & outbreak – that from some thirty years ago she has shown,' and Magsie wrote, 'how sad this loss of balance in the poor mind, so full of knowledge, so full of interest in all round her.'[13] Annie was looked after by Georgina and nurses, and received homeopathic treatment. Annie was well enough to be sent to her sister in Scotland, Juliet being told by Georgina that it was 'certainly a triumph of Homeopathy for during the 8 weeks of Dr Reynolds' treatment she made very little progress'.[14]

William had loaned £8000 to his brother Spencer, in June of 1878, but otherwise there seems to have been little contact between the brothers. Then in March 1879 Spencer died of malaria fever in Albano, where he had been sent for his health.[15] One reviewer thought it was William who had died, but the *Annual Register* rehearsed his brother's brief diplomatic career, and referred to the 'social charms and conversational talents' which had made him well-known in European capitals.[16]

About this time Georgina befriended Emily Ford. An artist in her early thirties, Emily's sister was the socialist and suffragist Isabella Ford. A student at the Slade with Evelyn De Morgan, Emily's studio at 44, Glebe Place, near to the Cowper-Temples when they moved to Chelsea, was a centre for 'people who did things'; at this point she worked on decorations for the famous slum priest Father Dolling's schools.[17] Like Georgina, she supported psychical research and anti-vivisection.[18] But during the next few years the young, beautiful companion, 'serviceable as well as adoring', made Emelia Gurney feel jealous.[19]

The medium Julia Leaf told the Cowper-Temples that the new life was coming but hindered by the 'magnetism of people about you'.[20] William's health was monitored and Georgina received electric treatment, their health journal noting: 'Jenny [William's affectionate name for her] is vitalized by intellectual life and exhausted by those who don't meet your ideal and intellectual needs.' [21] Despite their health problems, the Broadlands conference, by now an annual fixture, took place in early August. Guests included the African-American Amanda Smith, whose subsequent mission to India (advocated by the prominent American Congregationalist minister Asa Mahan and others) attracted William's interest. Also enjoying the 'angelic natures' was Roden Noel, who found Mrs Brewster Macpherson 'a very remarkable and pleasing person'.[22] From Keswick conference came the Swabian faith-healer Otto von Stockmayer.[23] The Reverend Rowland W. Corbet of Stoke Rectory in Hodnet, Shropshire, who had his own mystical conference, was thankful for 'coming of age in Christ' there.[24]

After this, a Baptist follower of Moody and Sankey, James Mountain (editor of *The Christian Era*, author of *Hymns of Consecration and Faith*, musical director at the Broadlands conference in 1878, and a 'British Israelite') and his wife rested at Broadlands, enjoying cricket and showing Sunday School children the grounds, whilst the Cowper-Temples recuperated at Babbacombe.[25] When the Cowper-Temples returned, they invited Myers who entranced Georgina by his essay on Oracles (published in 1880), 'such a lift into Wider Vision – and – being brought to know something of Porphyry and Plotinus with that beautiful letter – and most beautiful renderings of those lost oracles,' she wrote. 'It is altogether – *on the whole* very confirmatory and hope giving.'[26]

William's recuperation continued at Babbacombe without his wife, who travelled via a Parisian Lapland to the region of sun – Mentone – where Fanny Jocelyn and her son were ill.[27] William followed with Juliet, arriving in Mentone to be with 'dear beautiful loveable Bob' who died in early January. The Queen asked for an account and hoped that Georgina would stay a little longer with Fanny, 'to whom she feels you must be such a comfort'.[28] Myers' news that he was to marry Eveleen Tennant raised Georgina's spirits, such joy she believed, 'is our true element into which we shall all plunge some day', yet she hoping he would not be distracted from the 'great pursuit – even in the absorption of present happiness for joy most specially demands Immortality and the Garden of Eden would have no colour or brightness without the sky – but you don't want my prose just now'.[29]

William surprised himself, he told Georgina, by his goodness in allowing her to stay at Cannes with Fanny. He worried about the Hampshire Liberals, believing he should return to counsel and direct in their crisis.[30] Though there were no party fights and the Liberal spokesmen had fired their shot during the recess, he told Evelyn Ashley, they needed to be prepared for a dissolution, especially as the Home Rulers' obstructive tactics might persuade the Cabinet to appeal to the electorate.[31] When parliament was dissolved, he faced the problem of whether to stand again for South Hampshire when there was another Liberal candidate, a Tory paper surmising that he would avoid the hustings despite making no public declaration. 'The shell has exploded which is to blow the House and to terminate my Parliamentary Life,' he told Georgina.[32] As Liberals returned to power in such a way that pessimistic patricians feared the rule of Demos, William retired on family grounds. 'I long for you to turn your back on all the scramble and turmoil and come back and seek the Higher Life with me in this Paradise,' Georgina said, fearful he would waver.[33] He wanted to leave public life with honour, 'that we may together for the rest of our time here devote ourselves more exclusively to our Master's service'.[34] To Evelyn Ashley she insisted, 'he is quite satisfied about his retirement.' But to Juliet she advised: 'I am sure it will be a sharp pang … You must love him more than ever and coax him and cheer him.' 'I trust that I shall be more to you than I have ever been,' she wrote, 'now that we are likely to be more together and I must love you more – every hour of my life. Your dear beautiful nature compels it.'[35]

With a physician on hand to give advice, Georgina looked after Fanny, giving chloral and morphine to ease pain. William had various evangelistic meetings. He joined gatherings to hear 'true narratives of personal experience' arranged at Edward Clifford's which attracted fifty or so ladies of fashion (as well as addresses from Radstock and Miranda Hill, Octavia's sister[36]), and breakfasted with Max Müller, learning in a pleasant and lively way about the Buddhist Nirvana, 'he asserts that in England there are 1000s who find life so dreary and painful that they look forward to annihilation as better than what they know of life.'[37] Fanny declined, and on Good Friday William joined Georgina at her side as she died. She had outlived her children.[38] Georgina was asked by the Queen to write an account.

Georgina then looked after Sybella Ashley (Sissie) for her husband Evelyn, who worried about his electoral prospects.[39] Her own health was taxed, for William noted, 'Jenny has not got into bed for these three months.'[40] And there were visitors, including Jessie Cowper and the half-English wife of the Swedish minister, Countess Constance Wachtmeister (whom William already knew as he had told Georgina that she was 'very remarkable and kindly she said a good deal that will interest you greatly'[41]), a recent convert to spiritualism, and soon to be a leading figure in Blavatsky's theosophical society. William and Emelia Gurney then travelled to Bordighera in the Italian Riviera, where William laid a foundation stone to George MacDonald's house, Casa Coraggio, which had been built with financial support from admirers and friends.[42] George had dedicated *Paul Faber, Surgeon* – a book in his 'Wingfold' trilogy – to William in 1879, glad that he was not offended by this public act: 'your letter says of my books just what I try to go upon,' he said, '– to make them true to the real and not the spoilt humanity.'[43] Louisa MacDonald hoped that the 'Temple and Gurney given hall' would form the venue for family services.[44]

The Cowper-Temples rushed home at the news of Mummy's pleurisy but found her in better health when they arrived in London, where news trickled out about Gladstone's ministerial appointments (Georgina's diary adding an exclamation mark by the side of his name as Prime Minister). In late April Gladstone wrote to William ('So good of him!' Georgina wrote) to tell him he was to be offered a peerage.[45] When William was created 'Baron Mount Temple' his old friend Lord Houghton joked about the line in *Don Juan* on the alcoholic Lord Mount Coffee-House.[46] Georgina watched him take his place on the scarlet benches, proud of his 'refined beautiful face and quiet gentlemanlike movement' as he was introduced by Houghton and Lord Enfield.[47] The Corporation of Romsey said it was recognition of the 'benevolent desire displayed both by Lady Mount Temple and yourself for improvement and well being of the poorer section of its people'.[48] Georgina seems to have enjoyed her elevated status. Juliet was the first to write her name as Lady Temple, but 'poor Mrs CT' had not yet exited, as the Queen disapproved of announcements before her pleasure was expressed. So Juliet possessed a state secret and must not let it out. Georgina was unsure whether she should be allowed to keep her dear name, 'I may come out something else. And then I am so afraid nobody will know me *except the dogs*.'[49]

Mummy's recovery was short, and Georgina, 'having been endowed with the humble but blessed gift of nursing', stayed with her at Eccleston Square as much as possible, using mesmerism, with the advice of Annie Watts and Spencer Wells, and rubbing, to soothe her.[50] But she died in late July, her death following shortly on that of Anne dowager Countess Cowper. Georgina must have been exhausted, because she still played the hostess in London for the Loysons and others. She met Countess Wachtmeister, and Anna Kingsford. She had to attend to Juliet's first lessons in English, French and dancing. There were preparations for philanthropic and religious gatherings at Broadlands. They had an

Animals' Friends meeting to which Frances Power Cobbe came, and a large Liberal picnic and speeches in the park: William praised Gladstone for his Midlothian speeches.[51] Georgina planned her 'Quiet Days' of guests. Before this gathering, there was a brief stay at Babbacombe with little Juliet, who swam and listened to Georgina reading her MacDonald's *At the Back of the North Wind*. But even then, it was no holiday for Georgina, with a Band of Mercy branch formed, early morning study of Boehme, notes made on the ritualist Reverend Body's lectures and talks about Indian religion with the Cowley Brother, Father Rivington.[52]

Back at Broadlands they received Emelia Gurney, Andrew Jukes, James Farquhar, Rowland Corbet, Frederic Myers and others, for prayers, poetry and religious talk. A letter to Myers outlined William's idea of a party similar to that appearing in a well-received novel of ideas, William Mallock's *The New Republic, Or Culture, Faith and Philosophy in an English Country House* (featuring barely concealed sketches of such personalities as John Ruskin, Walter Pater, Benjamin Jowett and Matthew Arnold), only on the metaphysics of Christian life. The guests were to include a poet, a student of Buddhism and Asian culture, a spiritualist investigator, and various orthodox and unorthodox Christians. [53] The religious conference had shifted temporarily to the Deanery at Southampton, Georgina having asked for the conference to be postponed so that she could shake herself and turn herself round.[54]

In mid-November they set off for what proved to be a traumatic visit to Ireland, for William became seriously ill in Dublin. Visiting his nephew the seventh Earl Cowper, Gladstone's reluctant new Lord Lieutenant, a cold turned into a fever and Waggie, reported in the newspapers as 'a clairvoyant lady doctor', was summoned. They brought him back to London, and Georgina rushed backwards and forwards on anxious mid-winter journeys between him and Juliet, who had caught scarlet fever at Broadlands.[55]

In the new year Georgina became more closely acquainted with the charismatic and beautiful Anna Kingsford through conversations with the 'Seeress' and Edward Maitland ranging over materialism and vivisection, as they dined together. [56] She studied astrology, discussed with Kingsford planetary influences and the distinction between the physical and astral body, and noted Kingsford's vegetarian rationale. [57] She read Maitland's strange novel *The Soul and How it Found Me*. She was visited by the Countess Wachtmeister and went to the British National Association of Spiritualists' establishment at 38, Great Russell Street, for séances with her and the Reverend C.M. Davies, student of London's mystic and unorthodox religious milieux.

Their spiritual life was cultivated in other directions. At Babbacombe they supported George Body's spiritual mission, attending instructions on prayer, sacrament, self-examination, confession. And after visits from the Duchess of Sutherland (the third Duke's first wife, resident in a villa at Torquay), the vicar of Babbacombe, and the Quaker Hanburys,[58] they returned to Broadlands to receive Rowland Corbet, 'like one of those Burne Jones angels encircled with the Stream of Life', Corbet later wrote. He met John Pulsford but felt the occultists 'interesting but hardly inspired ... they were to me wanting in the sense of direct issue from the fount of life'. It was a treat to have 'St S' to stay at London for almost a week.[59] Georgina held spiritualist meetings with the mystic and philosopher Lady Victoria Welby (described by Corbet as 'one who had found the Centre and had learned the Child-like spirit'), the homeopath Dr George Wyld and C.C. Massey (both prominent figures in the early British Theosophical Society; Massey's father, sometime undersecretary for the Home Department, was known to William in his days at the Board of Health), the novelist Eliza Keary, and others.[60]

In April they returned to Broadlands, where Lady Ashburton and Georgina had 'much talk about Carlyle'. The railway provided rapid journeys to London to give addresses at Victoria Hall, attend Band of Hope meetings, visit the Grosvenor Gallery, see Ellen Terry in *Othello*, meet Maitland, Farquhar, Jukes and Wylde, join Edward Clifford's meetings and attend 'unsatisfactory' séances at Great Russell Street.[61] Shaftesbury, Lyonel Tennyson and George MacDonald came to Hampshire. The Cowper-Temples invited the teetotal Good Templars to Broadlands, and joined United Kingdom Alliance meetings at the Town Hall. The notable guest at the Broadlands conference in July was the African-American missionary Amanda Smith. Then they squeezed in further visits to Babbacombe, and a trip to the Welsh quarry before holding another Broadlands gathering with Jukes, Lady Welby, Hoare, Olive Seward and others. Olive talked with them about Brocton.

They were in Devon over November for a recuperation which encompassed sermons from George Body, reading Plato, Swedenborg, Jukes, and Abraham Hayward's *Essays*. Visitors included a duchess, Waggy and the Bishop of Exeter. Babbacombe also sheltered Oliphant, returned from America following his mother's death.[62] Georgina had given Alice Oliphant refuge in Broadlands while Laurence obtained control over land at Brocton and finally split with Harris. Alice's 'sad eyes' haunted Andrew Jukes and he worried for her under the bewitching power of Harris at the 'Fountain Grove' community established in Santa Rosa, Californa.[63] But she was 'so frank and so deeply interesting' about what had been a trying time for her at Brocton and Santa Rosa. Jukes had been discussing with William the writings of his physician Edward Berridge, a homeopath follower of Harris and later active in the 'Order of the Golden Dawn'.[64]

Company in the new year in 1882 included Augustus and Magsie, the latter busy on a work of devout extracts (published as *Many Voices*), the 'noble-blessed *Saint of God*' (Jukes) and the Oliphants. Georgina likened the beautiful and talented Alice to the biblical alabaster box of precious ointment 'the odour filling the house and blessing us all [,] pouring love into the heart of my precious Juliet'. Georgina was with Alice much, as she recovered from the strain of Santa Rosa.[65] When the Oliphants visited Broadlands later in January, Georgina recorded a 'Long too deep talk with them'.[66] Georgina also had discussions with Orinna Greenfield and meetings with a 'Rosicrucian'. She saw someone called the 'Mystic Child', perhaps identical with one of their visitors at Babbacombe in the winter, the adopted son of the Comtesse Borel, known as Prince Baptiste St John Borel or Mr Northlew.[67] The next year Georgina asked Jukes about him; he was said to be the 'man-child' who was to rule all nations with a rod of iron, the son of the woman clothed with twelve stars of Revelations. Northlew had been born in Wales about 1858, and was raised by Marie Borel, who came from Honfleur. In Torquay Borel had established a headquarters for an 'Order of the Temple'. Jukes was acquainted with the circumstances surrounding Madame Borel; her 'son' had been given to her by a spiritualist. Emelia Gurney was convinced she was mad.[68] But contact was sustained, with the youth bewildering Hannah Smith when Georgina presented him to her in 1888. When Juliet was in Paris about 1893, a card from Northlew ('fancy what Lacey at the Babbacombe Post Office must have thought') invited her to accompany him to Australia.[69] Georgina knew another religious oddity too, Father Ignatius Leycester Lyne, founder of an Anglo-Catholic Benedictine monastery.[70]

A new spiritual front opened with the Society for Psychical Research, intended to make an organized and systematic attempt to investigate psychical phenomena, formally established in February. Georgina's membership (with Myers, Basil Wilberforce, Lord Houghton and other friends) was publicized by the press.[71] The Cowper-Temples invited Myers at the time of the British Association meeting in Southampton, hoping that the Psychical Society could meet at Broadlands as the scientists William Crookes and William Barrett, who had made influential public interventions in the controversy over spiritualism, also visited.[72] Georgina, according to Hannah Smith, experienced 'trembling enjoyment at seeing the increasing heavenly mindedness' of William, in October.[73]

Alice and Laurence Oliphant set off to establish a Jewish settlement in the Holy Land. 'What serious souls they are,' Georgina told Juliet, 'leaving family friends and country to try and benefit the race. They dined at Marlborough House on Saturday and seem to have interested the Prince of Wales and the Duke of Edinburgh very much in their scheme.'[74] There was leave-taking of another kind when Dante Gabriel Rossetti died in April; Georgina noting it was 'Pouring for dear Rossetti's funeral'. She went with Edith Leycester to 'poor 16' to see the disconsolate Theodore Watts-Dunton and told Christina that Cheyne House had been a 'gate of heaven' and recalled her brother's 'rich cordial greeting'.[75]

Philanthropy was not neglected. For the temperance cause, Georgina presented the singer Eva Scorey at the Old Vic but found a 'horrid exhibition of low class manners' at the Women's Church Temperance meetings in London in early April.[76] When she held Band of Hope meetings with Lady Pembroke in May she heard 'odious speeches'.[77] At the beginning of the year Georgina had 'donned the blue' at a teetotal 'Blue Ribbon' meeting in Romsey and it was William's turn at Southampton in March.[78] The American Blue Ribbonite leader, Richard Booth, who had been befriended by Basil Wilberforce, came to Broadlands for rest and was shown Palmerston's room and family memorials in the Abbey by Georgina, who took him with her as she went on 'one of those errands to which novelists owe their most beautiful touches of country life'.[79] Georgina endorsed the Vegetarian Society, permitting a letter to be published in April in which she accepted the role of a vice-president, sought advice and attacked vivisection.[80] She had attended Kingsford's anti-vivisection lecture at the Quebec Institute with Alice Oliphant in February.[81] She continued to study Kingsford's ideas, reading her *Perfect Way*, but found talk with Anna 'troubling'.[82]

One of their London visitors was Mary Gladstone, who recorded a dinner at the Cowper-Temples' where guests had been shown into a room 'literally so dark that in the vague outlines you could not distinguish furniture from figures. It was so odd'. When they reached the dining room they were all in the act of discoveries.[83] In the beginning of August Mary met Ruskin there for a delightful tea. He was 'chaffed on his idiosyncrasies', and at dinner she met Lords Rosebery and Wolverton, and Andrew Carnegie, the 'Scotch American rolling in gold'.[84] To their London home also came the Loysons; there were meetings about the Gallican church this year. Georgina had Emily Ford's company and visited the devout artist Frederic Shields with her. Shields went to Babbacombe shortly after.

There were visits to Hampshire from Emma Cons, the Lycesters (Rafe read Montaigne to Georgina) and Madeline Wyndham. Socializing was devoted partly to the British Association meeting at Southampton in August. The scientists Lord Rayleigh and Professor Barrett, and Auberon Herbert, George Russell, George Sclater-Booth (Conservative MP), the anti-vivisectionist Lawson Tait and others, came to view Palmerstonian relics.[85] William had told Alfred Russel Wallace that he had a 'very great wish' for him to stay at Broadlands and hoped to entice him to Babbacombe later to discuss a book Wallace had sent on 'one of the most pressing subjects of the day' (his book on land nationalization).[86] Broadlands hosted a donkey show in mid-September to promote kindness through inspections and prizes.[87]

Santa Rosa had not faded from view. Hannah Smith met Harris and initially took his side in the dispute which had developed with Laurence Oliphant. Harris feared the Cowper-Temples had been turned against him by Oliphant and Hannah relayed a rumour that Oliphant was boasting he had developed William as a medium.[88] William and Georgina believed Laurence and Alice were the wronged party, and supported their efforts to win over Arthur Cuthbert, a follower of Harris, who was invited to Broadlands so that his wife Violet could get him back.[89] Laurence said there would be a spiritual battle there, as Alice and Harris both had influence over the place.[90] But the Oliphants became occupied with their Palestine project, with Alice Oliphant writing to her 'Beloved Motherling' from Constantinople, where the Oliphants settled temporarily, in September.[91]

Jukes provided another perspective on Santa Rose. The Cowper-Temples let him read Hannah's letters at Broadlands and he felt disquietened about the sect's treatment of scripture and marriage.[92] 'St Andrew' was being looked after by the Cowper-Temples, as Hannah had alerted them to his financial straits.[93] At the end of the year Jukes enjoyed the 'shelter of the gables' at Babbacombe, enjoying the play of light on cliff and seascape and appreciating Georgina's feathered friends, though he said they wanted more than the vegetarian diet she provided.[94]

The Cowper-Temples were back at Broadlands at the end of the year, William endeavouring to recover from a fever.[95] With them were James Farquhar and Emelia Gurney. William blamed his illness on the damp Test valley, and though Georgina wondered if Cannes would be better he sought refuge and healthier daily walks at Babbacombe.[96] They were visited by Henry Cowper and his sister Dolly, William's old friend Lord Houghton and neighbours such as little Emma Keyse whose house 'The Glen' was by the beach, and the Duke of Somerset who lived at nearby Stover Lodge. The distinguished musician William Rockstro, a neighbour, gave Juliet lessons.

Georgina also began a friendship with Olive Seward, the adopted daughter of President Lincoln's secretary of state. The young lady, briefly a follower of Thomas Lake Harris, stayed at Babbacombe where Georgina enjoyed interesting talks about her 'miraculous experiences', the 'last chapters of Brocton', and other matters. Olive left rapturous about Georgina, Rowland Corbet and the teachings of James Hinton.[97] Then Myers informed them about psychical research when he visited Broadlands, and read his poetry to the party in the portico. Georgina helped Lady Welby to index her theological *Links and Clues*, which had first appeared anonymously in 1881, before staying with her at Grantham.[98]

Georgina used contacts to advance anti-vivisection, chatting about vivisection with Shaftesbury when he visited Broadlands in Easter, and she found another guest, Lord Lymington, was now 'quite on our side'. She worked through a list of MPs and prepared letters for the campaign.[99] William's efforts to reform sexual behaviour took the form of attendance at 'social purity' meetings and he presided over the annual meeting at Exeter Hall in June. In the Lords he participated in that controversy – so alien to the modern eye but a source of much anxiety at the time – about marriage to 'deceased wives' sisters'. Lord Dalhousie and the Pre-Raphaelite William Holman Hunt made efforts to secure the support of the Cowper-Temples to the private member's bill repealing prohibition of these marriages (the law was amended in 1907).[100]

The Cowper-Temples also furthered aristocratic temperance, despite Georgina's anxiety about a Blue Ribbon meeting at the Evangelical Anne Duchess of Sutherland's Stafford House; 'all did well not many worldlings[.] Lady Borthwick took the blue.' William was active in the Band of Hope and gave an eloquent address for the Blue Ribbon movement in Stafford House, to encourage support from the 'Upper Ten Thousand', exhorting the aristocracy to be in the vanguard in social progress as in politics. Several signed the pledge.[101] This event demonstrated the fashionable and aristocratic brought into contact with the philanthropic. Similarly, when the Liberal politician Sir William Harcourt had visited Broadlands he joined Shaftesbury at the Romsey Labourers' dinner. Georgina lent her social talents to the popular ritualist Canon Wilkinson when she chaired his last Sunday tea at St Peter's Church.

A street accident damaged Georgina's spine in early May and there was 'long lingering pain and helplessness' at Great Stanhope Street.[102] She was whisked to Babbacombe to recuperate, where she read one of Ruskin's Oxford lectures, Lilias Trotter's books, something on the Brahmo Somaj and Wagner's recently completed *Parsifal* with the German governess Clara 'Alfkins'. The Leycesters, Augustus and Magsie, and Mrs Sumner came. Her mobility returned but she did not recover fully despite or because of a variety of treatments including rubbing by a spiritualist and an 'electric machine', which was 'too stimulating and exhausting'.[103]

When they returned to London, amid visits to relations and temperance work, they met Ruskin, who was cultivating the drawings of the American Esther Frances Alexander, which appeared in her *Roadside Songs of Tuscany*. She found him 'so gentle and kind' in early June. Emelia Gurney came to Broadlands in July, joining a little company which included Emily Ford and Wilfrid Ashley (Evelyn's son). The guests following Waggie's medical consultations included Lady Sandhurst, the Wyndhams, Mrs Sartoris and the 'dear Macs'. Frederic Shields joined in the reading of uplifting literature by reciting from William Blake and George Fox's life. He painted 'The Good Shepherd', as a birthday gift to Georgina from William. Emelia's gift was a set of grand religious visions by Shields.[104]

William, having sent money the year before, again assisted Andrew Jukes while Georgina tried to promote his son for a curacy in Hull, where Jukes had once been curate. Jukes sponsored ecumenical work in the spirit of Broadlands with his 'Clerical Friends in Council', George Wilkinson and Boyd Carpenter.[105] Jukes then came to stay at Babbacombe after the MacDonalds had relieved his mind about William's health. But William decided to take Georgina to Bordighera to convalesce and they set off in late October.[106]

FIGURE 13. *Looking for the Prodigal's return*, by Edward Clifford, featuring Andrew Jukes and Georgina Cowper-Temple. By courtesy of the Church Army.

They travelled with Juliet and Clara Alfchen (a governess), reading Dante and other uplifting works *en route*. They sent to Emelia Gurney news of their delight in peaceful olive groves.[107] The party met George MacDonald at Casa Coraggio. Their niece Florence Herbert and her brother Henry came. George Wilkinson, now Bishop of Truro, was brought to Casa Coraggio. Georgina met the Irish poet and writer Emily Lawless and the novelist Kathleen O'Meara appeared, to tell ghost stories and speak of cures at Lourdes.[108] Augustus and Magsie came, followed later by Emily Ford, and Emelia. They supported the MacDonalds and O'Meara in raising money for a Catholic church, a local paper observing their 'très rare tolérance religieuse'.[109] MacDonald suffered from asthma and felt less able to work, but to Georgina he was 'beautiful and Christlike

... It is a gift – to know him'.[110] As they enjoyed their idyll, thoughts of General Charles Gordon, her other unorthodox Christian hero, occupied Georgina's mind. Gordon had returned to the Sudan, and eagerly she read W.T. Stead's interview in the *Pall Mall Gazette* and followed rumours of his capture with anxiety. With Emelia, who had corresponded with Gordon, the Cowper-Temples followed unfolding events.[111]

It was back to parliamentary work for William when they returned in early April, though Georgina feared for his health with late sessions in the Lords: Waggie staying in early May to attend him.[112] While Georgina joined a meeting at the Victoria Hall, he was 'protecting girls' in the Lords until 9 o'clock, she noted. Georgina's contribution to moral reform, at the same time, reflected concern by earnest aristocratic women that moral standards amongst younger members of society seemed to take their cue from the 'Marlborough House set'. She joined a delegation to the Archbishop of Canterbury seeking to establish devotional gatherings in Lambeth to which the Princess of Wales was invited.[113] She attended Benson's Lambeth Palace chapel Bible readings for ladies with Lady Muncaster, Lady Welby, Lady Aberdeen and others.

The Cowper-Temples were employed as ever in a host of philanthropic and religious activities, including public meetings on anti-vivisection and social purity, preaching at Victoria Hall, attendance at the Mildmay Park conference of Christians, visits from the ritualist Reverend George Body, and mystic investigation in the new Hermetic Society.[114] One bizarre event was William's role in an American's thought-reading exhibition at Westminster Hotel: Washington Irving Bishop (responding to the MP and journalist Henry Labouchère's challenge) found a pin hidden on his coat, and *The Graphic* illustrated the incident.[115] In a more serious vein, Georgina attended the Lords as the third Reform Act progressed through the House and noted the 'most orderly' reform demonstration in the Park on 21 July.

'Everywhere there was Theosophy; the tide was rising,' recalled the co-founder of the Theosophical Society, Colonel Olcott, of this period. Georgina was, unsurprisingly, drawn. Her guests in London included Kingsford and Maitland, and the Hindu mystic Mohini Chatterji, associated with Olcott and the Russian Madame Blavatsky, now settled in England.[116] Georgina's young friend Laura Tennant, whose entry with her sister into the Season signified for many the ending of select Society (the Tennants were daughters of a wealthy Glasgow manufacturer[117]), joined her in the Hermetic Society established after a schism from the London Lodge of the Theosophical Society.[118] Though Georgina met Blavatsky on several occasions she seems to have preferred her rival for the queenship of the esoterics. Kingsford's mysticism was based on Judaeo-Christian tradition and she shared Georgina's zoophilia.

In August, with the religious conference relocated to the Deanery at Southampton, they sought continental recuperation since Georgina's treatment by rubbing and electricity had not alleviated her pain. They journeyed to Wildbad spa in Württemberg in August, staying initially at the unprepossessing Klumpf's Hotel, where Lady Maidstone suffered from typhoid and William developed an 'ugly feverish tongue'.[119] At Davos they met the writer John Addington Symonds and his wife, whom Georgina later invited to Broadlands and corresponded with (Edward Clifford's sister Mary was a friend of Catherine Symonds). Catherine's admiration for Georgina's beauty was expressed in the display of her portrait. [120]

They returned to the usual social round and philanthropic meetings. Georgina went with Edith to Manchester, hearing Henry Stanley talk about the Congo. There were visits from Lady Caithness and the bereaved Alfred Alaric Watts, for Annie Watts had died in July. Suddenly horror burst in with news that Emma Keyse had been murdered at Babbacombe on 14 November. The failure to hang the culprit, her servant John Lee, despite three attempts, made the case notorious. Georgina was haunted by the event, despite comfort from Lady Margaret Sandhurst. Another friend hoped that though she took it so much to heart it would not spoil her little paradise as the house was 'not so *very* near'.[121]

The Cowper-Temples did return to Babbacombe in December, holding religious gatherings with Basil Wilberforce and supporting temperance meetings and prayers with Karl Andreas. Hannah sent news from America about the mind cure which was causing a great stir.[122] Edward Clifford was with the Smiths and wrote that after Robert's errors Hannah regarded men 'with a pity which is too near to contempt! I can see she thinks we are a poor lot, and it is only when we get middle-aged or old that we can be allowed to be even tolerable adjuncts'.[123]

The next year featured scandals of sexual immorality in the Cowper-Temples' private circle and in the national arena. A crisis involving their friend Georgina Sumner became the subject of public interest when she appeared in court in March.[124] Her daughter Beatrice had been a ward of court to protect her from the married banker Charles Hoare's attentions which began when she was hardly out of the nursery. When she was twenty one she became pregnant by him: a fall 'which no woman could live to recover from', *The Times* reported. Georgina, attending the court, found it 'all very dreadful quite hideous!'[125] The affair was sordid for Mrs Sumner had hoped despite the injunction on Hoare communicating with her daughter, for a loan from the banker to save her husband from ruin. Major Fitzhardinge Kingscote had also used his niece Beatrice to attempt to get money from Hoare. When she fled to Geneva for privacy and cheaper living, Mrs Sumner denied having sold her daughter.[126]

If the Cowper-Temples had an intimate view of the sexual peccadilloes of the wealthy haute bourgeoisie and impecunious members of their class; they were also associated with a greater scandal, for 1885 was also the year of the 'Maiden Tribute of Modern Babylon', the journalist W.T. Stead's theatrical revelations (in July) about child prostitution. Georgina's diary has no mention of the events which led to Stead's imprisonment in early November, but she signed a letter of thanks to Stead, published in early August and William made his sympathies known to Stead by letter, and through participating alongside George Russell and others at a large meeting of the Church of England Social Purity Society in the Prince's Hall in Piccadilly.[127] Georgina also met Miss Ellice Hopkins, active in the Ladies' Associations for the Care of Friendless Girls and a leading purity agitator.[128]

At the start of the year, William was involved with Basil Wilberforce's mission meetings and services (with the Earl of Aberdeen and others) to the upper classes, at rooms provided by the Duke of Westminster at Grosvenor House. Members of the clubs – Brooks, Guards, St James and others – were invited.[129] Now Wilberforce became the focus of Georgina's sympathies when he required abdominal surgery. When he stayed at 15, Stanhope Street for operation in April, he was tended by William and they lent Babbacombe to the dean for his recovery. 'He is such an Heroic self-forgetting spiritual Servant of our Lord and likely to be so effectual an instrument if he completely recovers,' William told Lady Ashburton.[130]

Other friends who figure at this time included the charismatic Josephine Butler, with whom they stayed during a diocesan conference in Winchester, talking about the Salvation Army and conversion. From characterizing William as a 'poor lisping aristocratic fool', lacking the intellect to be a wolf in sheep's clothing, during the heat of the agitation to repeal the Contagious Diseases Act, Josephine came to appreciate the power to help which derived from the 'real humility' of the Cowper-Temples, partly through their mutual friend Emily Ford and also because of William's inspiring visit to her ailing husband, Canon George Butler, in 1886.[131] Catherine Symonds came to Broadlands in April. There was a terrible talk between William and Mrs Sumner about her plan to settle in Romsey alone. At Babbacombe Edward Clifford painted Georgina while she enjoyed reading an elevating mixture of Max Müller, Shelley and the Indian religious reformer Keshub Chunder Sen. London visitors included Phillips Brooks the American Episcopalian (taught about Pre-Raphaelitism by Clifford), Alice Oliphant's mother, Anna Kingsford and Maitland.[132] Hannah Smith came in July and gave readings. Georgina also attended meetings of the Hermetic and Psychical Societies.

William joined a conference of foreign and English faith healers in Islington. 'Miraculous cures in abundance have been certified,' he told Lady

Ashburton, after appearing beside the American Presbyterian William Edwin Boardman, author of *The Higher Christian Life* (1858) which had helped to inspire the holiness movement, who anointed blind and lame participants.[133] Mind cure was discussed at the Broadlands conference in mid-July and Clifford worked on Georgina's portrait. She then sought relief in the brine baths in Droitwich. William had travelled with Juliet to Ireland to make what proved to be his last visit. They joined Georgina and William held a chapel meeting.[134]

In October came Lord Shaftesbury's death. The funeral at St Giles took place on Georgina's birthday.[135] The friendship with Shaftesbury had been momentarily strained after William's surprising decision to support a motion for Sunday opening of the Natural History Museum in March, having voted with Shaftesbury against this in 1883.[136] The anguish William felt at the thought that he had lost the good opinion of one he valued so highly and which he was 'not conscious of having deserved to lose', is reflected in drafts of a letter meant to show his brother-in-law that this was a 'conviction of duty' and would not be the thin end of the wedge.[137]

William offered comfort to Evelyn, with whom he was also much involved over the Welsh quarries.[138] Late in the following year, William enjoyed Evelyn's work on his father's diary, finding the insight on his 'heroic' brother-in-law invigorating and instructive; did he see the originals with their occasionally acerbic references to him?[139] Not that he was without criticism of Shaftesbury's lack of the 'give and take habit that helps people to be coadjutors in the same work and towards the same object'. In 1878 William's appeals for assistance had been replied by the following: 'How is it that as you grow older, you do not grow wiser? How can you think that I have left in me any means of doing good, or harm, to any one?[140] But William said Evelyn's father was 'the personification of the Philanthropy of the titled Classes in this and the previous generation'.[141] He hoped that the work on the diary would have an important influence over public opinion.

When that other Christian hero, General Gordon, died at Khartoum, Georgina was comforted by the Oliphants, who had known him.[142] Alice chided her 'darling little Mother' that wrangling with God was very naughty, very silly and not fair on Him, and tried to make her see 'anguish of spirit' was proof that she had ministered.[143] The Oliphants had published a strange book, *Sympneumata. Evolutionary Forces now Active in Man*, on the present 'Messianic epoch', informing the Cowper-Temples of the work in progress which Laurence had left to Alice. William told Oliphant it was a comfort and encouragement.[144] It came as a shock to Georgina when news came of Alice's death from malaria in January.

William had loaned George MacDonald £200 for a book; when MacDonald worried that the loan would be recalled in September 1885, it was a response to the Cowper-Temples' catastrophic finances.[145] The 1870s had been a period of depression for agriculture, with a decline in income which forced members of the landed elite to sell or let land and property, but the Cowper-Temples' problem was due to litigation after a legal ruling gave William Oakeley the vast award of £97, 000 in damages for breach of the covenants of the lease on the Welsh slate quarry. In early 1886 the Cowper-Temples decided to leave Stanhope Street. Georgina said later, 'it had become a problem how we were to live at all' and recalled he often said 'I am a ruined man.'[146] Their nephew Henry offered assistance, saying it was like 'giving a small trifle back to parents who have given of their abundance of love to me'.[147] But servants were dismissed and work and wages reduced on the estates.

William suffered a recurrent fever, reported in the papers as inflammation of the lungs, from February. In desperation about William, Georgina fancied Alice Oliphant's spirit came to comfort her 'foolish little motherling'.[148] William came to Broadlands in an invalid carriage with Waggie.[149] Death was pronounced likely by Sir Andrew Clark (Gladstone's doctor) and Dr Collins. 'Well then I may do as I like,' Waggie said, and vigorous rubbing and brandy rescued him. Recuperation entailed sitting outside in a 'sentry box' in Broadlands, which was visited by Pulsford, Basil Wilberforce and the Ashleys. Broadlands was also a rendezvous for Arthur Cuthbert to discuss Brocton affairs with Oliphant as William hobbled round the kitchen garden. Oliphant had just published *Masollam*, a novel depicting Thomas Lake Harris, which intrigued Andrew Jukes, who asked the Cowper-Temples what the novel aimed at. Georgina read *Sympneumata*, with its Harris-derived doctrine of 'counterparts' and its discussion of a force, a divine love called 'the sympneuma', under the portico. [150] But as discussions proved unsatisfactory, Olly and the Cuthberts left at the end of the month.

Their 'loving child' Dolly Herbert's death in late April was a further blow. The bereavement worried Emelia Gurney who had thought that Dolly, like Alice Oliphant, refreshed Georgina's spirit, and that Dolly was the only one in the younger generation capable of receiving all the wideness of her blessings.[151] There might have been another, in the form of Laura Tennant, who had married Alfred Lyttelton, but she died in childbirth in the same month. When Georgina saw her at Portman Square, Dolly had said that Bordighera had been a turning point in her life.[152] When they returned to Broadlands, Georgina had séances where dear Doll gave messages to Auberon Herbert. For William, now approaching his seventy-fifth year, the loss was faced with hope, for he said that what was called death was going out of death's reach. He was at the stage, he told Evelyn, where he felt more at home with the many he loved in heaven.[153]

With William's recovery slowly continuing, in late April they brought him to Babbacombe, where Georgina immersed herself in the Bacon-Shakespeare controversy. Muscular strength seemed to return but he felt his nervous strength too scanty. The spirits channelled through Lady Sandhurst – who had hosted a séance for Gladstone – (and was later famous for her feminist attempt to be elected to the London County Council), claimed he must conserve his voice.[154]

Georgina attended the Women's Jubilee Meeting with Hannah Smith, who was busy organizing a women's union of the world for temperance and social purity.[155] Hannah was apprehensive, several months later, when Oliphant stayed with the Cowper-Temples and attempted to embrace Georgina to impart Alice's love, following the practice of 'sympneuma' of Brocton. Georgina resisted it at first, but relented.[156] But Hannah warned her that the 'bridegroom experience' which Emelia Gurney shared, was dangerous. Hannah's posthumously published account of Harris and Oliphant's sexual theology would reveal how far Oliphant was prepared to go in imparting this experience, through the request to join him in bed, which he made when Georgina accompanied Hannah to hear Oliphant's exposition at a private house in Dorking.[157]

They had horse and donkey shows in July, and bipedal guests included the Percy Wyndhams.[158] Georgina visited the Wyndhams' grand new country house in Wiltshire, 'Clouds'. Then it was back to prepare for their conference, a sign, for Hannah, of William's recovery. She urged them to have 'some of the most advanced souls we can get hold of '.[159] In that category, certainly, was Anna Kingsford, at the 'retreat' with Edward Maitland.[160] Georgina had delightful mystic talk; she examined Kingsford's *Esoteric Christianity* and *Perfect Way* at this time.[161] Shortly after, General Booth of the Salvation Army stayed.

There was a sad parting from Evelyn's ailing wife Sybella, sent to South Cliff House in Eastbourne. She shared her terror of death with Georgina, and asked her to look after Evelyn. She died in August and Georgina stayed in the same rooms in Eastbourne afterwards in an attempt to improve her health, hopeful that she might feel Sissie's presence.[162] 'The fact is,' Georgina's niece Edith Ashley wrote, 'you never rest as you ought to do, and you are always over-fatigued.'[163] Despite the sadness they enjoyed the bracing air and avoided society apart from the poet Algernon Swinburne and the man who had taken custody of him, Theodore Watts-Dunton.[164] They went for a few nostalgic days in Helmingham, where William recalled the time almost thirty eight years before, when he had gained the blessing of his life.[165] Juliet, after a holiday in Schwalbach with Madeline Wyndham at the close of the Season, had been there a week already and was 'off her head' with excitement.

Over the winter Georgina joined the Ladies' Sanitary Association's campaign for ladies' and children's public lavatories, seeking the support of the 'father of Sanitation', Edwin Chadwick.[166] Georgina, who invited him to Broadlands and asked his advice on Romsey sanitation, championed his pursuit of a peerage for his work in reform; William was pessimistic about the likelihood.[167] Mind cure continued to be studied, with Hannah and other 'noble ladies'. In addition to her role in a Plumage League against the cruel fashion for bird-derived ornamentation, she endorsed a campaign to prevent a laboratory commemorating the surgeon Sir Erasmus Wilson. She also supported the Queen's Bounty and Church House schemes for the Queen's jubilee, and Elizabeth Wordsworth, the High Church principal of Lady Margaret Hall, thought her the 'person who was worth going all that way to see', at the jubilee reception at Buckingham Palace in June. She had the *ancien régime* look of old portraits, with fine regular features, lovely complexion, beautiful small mouth, and as upright as she might have been fifty years ago. 'She is said to be as good as she is beautiful,' she wrote, and most other people 'looked common beside her'.[168]

To economise, the Cowper-Temples moved to Shelley House, Chelsea Embankment, in July 1887, having sold the lease on 15 Stanhope Street and sought sanitary advice about the Embankment from Edwin Chadwick.[169] A religious service dedicated the house, which was decorated in William Morris.[170] Georgina loved the area: the river was a 'constant delight' and there were romantic associations due to Rossetti.[171] William would endure no inferior place in Mayfair.

At Broadlands they hosted readings and parties of temperance workers. Then Georgina ordered and prepared for another religious conference in early August. The guests included Hannah Smith, Emelia Gurney, Alfred Gurney, Basil Wilberforce, Norman Forbes-Robertson the actor (son of a friend of George MacDonald), Sir Baldwyn Leighton Bt., MP for South Shropshire (married to a Leicester Warren of Tabley, a Tollemache connection, and active in the East End teaching factory girls hymns) and the American singer Antoinette Stirling, who shared Georgina's interest in the esoteric and occult. Then they opened the Orangery for a Band of Mercy meeting and entertained Frances Power Cobbe. William was intent on making Broadlands a second home for his nephew Evelyn, inviting him to shoot partridges and pheasants whenever he liked, with his son Wilfrid and friends.

William and Georgina were present when their nephew Henry Cowper died, in a chilly Panshanger in November, having been almost constantly with him for over two months as he weakened.[172] Henry had written before that his aunt was the one in the family 'who was sent for by any and every member of it who was ill. I always wondered if I had been laid up if I wd have had the moral courage to spare her, and refrain from sending the normal summons'.[173] The melancholy accentuated William's sense of transience. Walks in the park made him think about the spirit body's perception of earthly events and places, but he could rejoice in having outgrown his terrestrial existence. He only wished for the 'zeal and discernment and power' of his blessed brother-in-law Shaftesbury to do some effective work before death.[174] Henry and Dolly had been the closest of the Cowpers to the Billys, and the death of Henry following Dolly's was a blow from which William never recovered.[175] But for the moment, it was Georgina's health that was a worry, for the strains of London society compounded the trial of attendance at Henry's deathbed, and she had not recovered from her falls.[176] 'Electric baths' and mind cure had not helped.

Heeding their doctor's advice, to seek a 'dry salubrious locality abroad', they travelled to Cimiez near Nice in December.[177] They intended to make as few acquaintances as possible and instead studied holy and truly spiritual ideas, William hoping his 'drooping lily' would revive.[178] In fact they continued to socialize. They met an Arab physician whom they called 'Karshish' after a poem by Browning, who belonged to a sect that did not pray but adored, and had curious beliefs about human evolution from animals and vegetables.[179] Georgina saw Josephine Butler and visited the mystic Lady Caithness and an Irish group including Sir Charles Gavan Duffy, ex-premier of the State of Victoria, and Miss Sharman Craufurd. This stimulated study of Irish history and she had 'much talk about Ireland'.[180] Her reading mixed Spinoza, Max O'Rell's Scottish anecdotes, Marie Corelli's *Romance of Two Worlds*, biographies of Bismarck and the Prince Consort ('strange story') and Cobbe's essays in the *Contemporary*. Their return took in Paris where they visited the O' Mearas, dined with the theosophist Madame Leila Canrobert, an acquaintance of the Oliphants, Théodore Monod and Père Hyacinthe. William held a meeting of the City Mission.[181] Before their return William invited Evelyn to join the Romsey Bench, underlining his succession to the Broadlands estate.[182]

Juliet had gone with the Wilberforces to Homburg for her health; her hypersensitive skin, nervous irritation and cramps worrying her parents. The Swede Jonas Kellgren treated her, although William worried about 'torturing massage' and the patients who left with incomplete treatment ('Kill-*green patients*,' he punned[183]). But Kellgren remained in attendance and Juliet went to Sweden with him after Georgina was assured it was necessary, Kellgren having diagnosed morbid products on the brain.[184] A day after this departure, Edmund Gurney died at Brighton. He had gone on a psychic quest but died, perhaps intentionally, of an overdose of chloroform.[185] Initially shocked, Georgina noted in her diary that he had 'slept and awoke!' and after a séance with Emelia Gurney, learned he 'was rescued from Sin, misery and despair'. Gurney's spirit implored Kate's forgiveness and begged Myers 'to repent or he will be sorry as I am now'.[186]

The Cowper-Temples patronized the Christian Scientist Frances Lord and Georgina wrote to Walt Whitman; Juliet had received an autographed photo via Hannah Smith and prepared a gift for him.[187] Georgina enjoyed the Wyndhams' company, going to Madeleine's birthday party and accompanying her to talks on *Parsifal* from the Swedish Dr Carl von Bergen.[188] Her study of Dante continued with Emily Ford, Juliet listening to Wagner in Bayreuth as Georgina missed 'our Master of languages'.[189] Then in July there were preparations for the conference. Some forty guests were expected and more came to participate.[190] In 'over fatigue and wet atmosphere', Georgina's health was as troublesome as ever. But the Swedish theosophist Hulda Beamish pointed out how appropriate Juliet's name for Georgina -- Lily -- was, as queen among flowers.[191] William told Juliet that it was the best of the conferences, and that 'the influx of the divine Holy Spirit was manifestly felt'.

At the end of the month William spoke in the Lords against indecent publications and the press reported his intervention.[192] Georgina was fatigued and when they returned to Broadlands she took to a couch to read Olly's *Ellen Searle*, before her friend the American contralto singer Antoinette Stirling and her son arrived, followed by Emelia, who tried to heal her mesmerically. But a vegetarian lecture, mothers' meetings, and Band of Hope and Bible Society activity drew on her energies. Georgina later thought that her friends had gathered 'as if they felt the time was short'.[193] Hannah felt the Cowper-Temples looked too saintly: 'I began to be afraid,' she told Georgina, 'that the harvest was getting nearly ripe. The world cannot spare you yet.'[194] But William -- who had confided to Basil during his severe illness in 1886 that he did not want to recover -- now told a local benevolent society that death was 'only a promotion, and when it comes, I hope all my friends will rejoice with me that I have gained my real home at last'.[195]

Juliet returned looking well, if bloodless, in Swedish costume. But if she appeared better, within a week William was seriously ill after catching a chill at Malcolm Stirling's baptism in the Abbey.[196] Medical attention could not shake off the fever and Georgina sent for Emelia Gurney to come for one last look. Emelia detected heavenly smiles and supernatural light on his face and told Hannah that he looked 'so peaceful and lovely', while Georgina was strong, calm and uplifted, never taking her eyes from him, anxious not to keep him from the 'crown of Life -- yet now & then feeling things of faith nothing & present possession everything'.[197] He was moved onto a couch in 'Cinnamon' and died there on the morning of 17 October with Georgina, Waggy and Stephen Pleasance present.[198] During his funeral at Romsey the mayor ordered business to be suspended.[199]

William's failing health had been reported from early 1886.[200] In that year a biography in *The Christian* recounted his 'quiet, unostentatious work' and important place in the Church. His death now brought condolences from the philanthropic bodies he supported and eulogies in the provincial, national and Christian press. 'He attracted around him and in his household many well-known philanthropists,' one paper said, 'by whose help he has striven to solve some of the social problems of the Age.'[201]

William felt Edwin Arnold's *After Death in Arabia* expressed his idea of the afterlife, 'for death, | Now I know, is that first breath | Which our souls draw when we enter | Life, which is of all life centre'.[202] Hannah Smith quoted the poem in an obituary she wrote, and said that William was 'one of those who went in and out before men, bearing about in his body so unmistakeably the marks of immortality, that all who knew him could not but be convinced of the truth of those words of our Lord, "Whomsoever liveth … shall never die" '.[203]

FIGURE 14. Lord Mount Temple, steel engraving in the obituary notice, *Illustrated London News*, 27 October 1888, p.481.
By courtesy of the Hartley Library, University of Southampton.

10

WILLIAM AND GEORGINA AS REFORMERS

This chapter, the first of three with a more thematic approach, explores the Cowper-Temples as 'reformers', who identified themselves, and were identified by others, as promoters of improvements or restorations in society. What were their motives? Did they spring from religion, *noblesse oblige*, a Liberal political creed, or the need for self-affirmation? To answer these questions, their roles in a number of reform projects or causes, such as education, temperance, zoophilia and social purity, are studied.[1]

It is instructive to start with a statement by William in 1839, setting out his desire to be a reformer, devoted to 'the propagating of some new beneficial truth, advocating with all my powers the interests of some suffering class!' The 'scorn of the frivolous, the hatred of the selfish, the hostility of the worldly', would be welcome, as they 'should prove to me that I was performing my duty!'[2] Here, explicitly, are several interesting themes such as the role of reform as an affirmation of self-worth, and as a distinction between oneself and the worldly and frivolous. William sought action which would identify him with a new cause or truth. An early but undated statement sees the political realm as a place where principled activity was possible and where legislation, especially in relation to Ireland, could cause good. He wanted 'to obtain good government for Ireland and to put the people of both countries into such circumstances as may assist the practice of morality and the development of good English feeling'.[3] Agonizing, as a youth, over worldliness, and trying to find a vocation, William reflected that his position in parliament and similar circumstances led him to take the amelioration of the working classes as his duty, since their 'poverty & heathenism seems to be the crying evil of the day', and efforts in this direction were most appropriate now. If the evil was enormous, its removal was possible as the public mind was turning towards it and receptive to schemes of remedy. But while political and public measures for social and moral improvement occupied him, 'may I not also find time for more direct attempts for their spiritual instruction. I rejoice at having had a part in the establishment of the Scripture Readers Society and Visiting ditto, but I might find time for some personal work.' He resolved to 'labour uninterruptedly amidst some abandoned portion of this Babylon', when he came up to London.[4] Here is expressed a need for a personal and arduous role, an identification of the working classes as materially and spiritually bereft, and the context of a movement in public opinion. The distinction between moral improvement and religious education is important. William saw himself particularly ministering to the 'spiritual needs of neglected Londoners'.

The springs of philanthropy in William's case were a strong sense of Christian brotherhood and the need to lose 'self' in helping others. He saw life as a trust; God had given us our powers, opportunities and time and we would have to render an account. It would not be a satisfactory account to say 'I've been an agreeable companion, I've told good stories – I've cultivated knowledge both of nature & men,' if there was work to do in helping out the Divine purpose and benefiting and instructing fellow creatures. All had a function in the body politic, some as handicraftsmen, some as brain workers, some as heart or spiritual workers and it was a comfort to think that 'we are under rule, & that obedience not self assertion is our Duty.'[5] His papers contain many such passages, prayers and quotations concerned with the problem of egocentricity, the distinction between the self-centred natural man and the spiritual man who was given a glimpse of the divine: 'What I want,' he jotted down in one note, 'is recollection of divine presence and obedience to Divine will.'[6]

Like Shaftesbury, William was influenced by an aristocratic sense of obligation and Christian paternalism. The role of the aristocracy was to act as public servants and William believed, as he told an audience in 1867, that work in the community was a duty which followed Christ's words: 'I am among you as he that serveth' (Luke 22:7) and 'I came not to be ministered unto, but to minister' (Matthew 20: 28). Public service gave peace of mind through cultivating self-respect.[7] Undoubtedly, with this due modesty, the role of public servant also reflected a confidence that the values of the enlightened and Christian aristocrat were correct. The aristocrat offered himself as untainted by exploitation of the workers in factories and at least competed with the middle class for moral leadership.

If it was not merely a party creed that motivated William, politics played a part. Parliament was seen as the source of national reform. William's Liberal identity is important in this regard: the recognition of a positive role for the state is apparent from his activity in the Board of Health.

Many years later, William's political creed was summed up by him as the belief that 'God has sent me into the world to do my best to improve it.' He was a Liberal because he could not rest satisfied with the defects and deficiencies of the political and social conditions of the country. His disposition was to 'hope and trust that legislative remedies may be found for much of the suffering and error that now afflict the people', and he contrasted this with the Conservatives' distrust of the benefits of change, and their fear of failure in attempts at improvements.[8]

What motivated Georgina in philanthropy was a desire to *prove* to herself her goodness, a sort of justification by works; she was 'perplexed in faith but pure in deeds' (to quote Tennyson).[9] There was also a powerful sympathy for suffering of any sort, as the Reverend Hugh Reginald Haweis said at the time of her husband's death, she was 'ever zealous in the amelioration of human suffering', and possessed an 'extraordinary "grace of ministration" in her – and a heart which embraced the woes of the animal creation in its tender comprehensiveness'.[10] The problem of pain, George Russell wrote, was one of the 'unsearchable mysteries of God' for her.[11]

Of course, many Victorians, eminent or otherwise, tried to come to terms with the compatibility of suffering and pain, with a loving God.[12] The Cowper-Temples' lives bridged a transition from an 'age of Atonement' in which the punishments of Hell were believed to be eternal and human salvation came only through Christ's vicarious punishment, to one which placed faith in this-worldly melioration and the doctrine of the Incarnation.[13] She knew several – F.D. Maurice, John Llewellyn Davies and Andrew Jukes – who assisted the dissolution of the old punitive theology. But her response to the behaviour of fallen humanity was unconventional. Logan Pearsall Smith said her one flaw was that she had no sense of moral distinctions and could not see the difference between right and wrong, when no cruelty was involved, hence her willingness to support individuals, such as Oscar Wilde, in their disgrace.[14]

Arguably, for many years, until the appearance of Juliet in her life, charitable work fulfilled some of her maternal longings. But she was also typical of earnest women of her class, in her good works in Hampshire and on the Cowper-Temple estates in Ireland. But her 'unfathomable and extraordinarily wide sympathy' made her a patron of social and moral reform nationally.[15] Her charities in the 1880s included the Band of Mercy, Vegetarian Society, a Bible Society, Psychical Society, Women's Hospital, Dublin Cats' Home, Torquay Animals, Ladies' Sanitary Association, and charities for cabmen and governesses. Nor was her involvement purely decorative. Although she did not quite have the prominence of an unmarried reforming women such as her acquaintances Frances Cobbe,

Octavia Hill or Florence Nightingale (and William claimed Georgina 'would have done as much in similar circumstances' in comparing her with the latter), Georgina played a part in creating a public role for women and became well known in the sphere of philanthropy.[16]

In her political sympathies, perhaps not surprisingly, she moved from her family's Toryism towards her husband's Liberalism. Although Georgina chose to dwell on religious and family matters in her memoirs she had more than a passing interest in politics. She followed the events of the high political world as a spectator in the Commons (accompanying Lady Palmerston or on her own) and also played her part in political socializing, though she found balls, even those hosted by Lady Palmerston, 'glare, bad air, & vapid small talk!'[17] Her sympathies became Liberal, but like William she was no fan of 'rough vulgar middle class' John Bright or democracy in the 1850s, disliking Bright's campaign against the aristocracy: would he like mill workers to apply their sentiments about the aristocratic 'order' to their masters, she asked? Yet she recognized a greatness about Bright, 'Oh that he wd use his great gifts for good & never for mischief.'[18] She followed the debates on the Reform Bill of 1859 and witnessed the agitation around the Second Reform Act. She admired Gladstone as the Liberal party's best man, but knew that he was considered an oddity: 'He was of course as usual laughed at & depreciated,' she wrote in 1859, '& his beautiful book [perhaps the recent *Studies on Homer and the Homeric Age*] ridiculed & yet in the political world he is out & out our greatest man.'[19]

Having indicated the religious motivations, the sense of aristocratic obligation, the elements of egocentricity in the search for purpose or meaning, the 'gendered' aspects and the political dimensions to their philanthropy; it is important to establish some form of map to navigate the Cowper-Temples' extensive and varied philanthropy. The philanthropic causes are examined below in the following sequence: the efforts to create harmonious and thriving rural and urban communities that avoided class antagonisms by addressing problems of poverty and alienation (via the mechanism of allotments or the Reverend John Minter Morgan's Oweniteinfluenced idea of 'self-supporting villages'); specific 'environmental reforms' in the sanitary sphere and in aesthetic enhancement of the urban environment; which included Georgina's activity in the Ladies' Sanitary Association (tackling the vast amount of disease and death which sanitary experts had revealed to be preventable); temperance and social purity; reformation of the aristocracy in the specific area of duelling; support for extending state education and opening up education to women; animal welfare and medical unorthodoxy; and philanthropy beyond Britain.

The starting point for understanding the Cowper-Temples as social reformers might be William's early association with Christian Socialists like

Thomas Hughes and Charles Kingsley, and the impact that the latter's novels apparently made on the couple. Georgina stated that *Yeast* and *Alton Locke* – which many found shockingly explicit about carnal matters – 'made an era in our life', and if the phrase 'Christian Socialist' appears almost nowhere in his papers, Georgina claimed William joined the movement. Hughes recalled an 'avowed and liberal supporter' who from his social and public position, risked more than all the rest of us put together'.[20] As there was no agreement among its leaders about what Christian Socialism meant, it is difficult to be certain what William was drawn to, beyond the social reformism which many outside the movement were in any case supporting. Perhaps it was the Maurician stress on brotherhood in Christ, the call to re-knit society through aristocratic paternalism and co-operation; certainly it was not the democratic or socialist reading which someone like J.M. Ludlow followed. William's social views might also be inferred from his later support for Ruskin's Guild of St George, but he was not in fact enthusiastic about the scheme of peasant proprietors, trade guilds and hierarchy. [21] The essential point is that, though the Cowper-Temples did not deny or underplay their 'caste' (and accent and appearance marked William off, making it easy to caricature him as a drawling Whig), they tried to bring people together across classes, in their religious activities (studied in the next chapter) and social reforms. Basil Wilberforce recalled William's absence of 'condescension' toward inferiors. Indeed they were sought out: Clifford learnt that his patrons had hoped he was a *workingman* painter in inviting him to Broadlands.

We have seen William's support for allotments in the 1840s, when he supported legislative remedies for the plight of the agricultural labourer. The historian of this movement identifies the stimulus to the Labourer's Friend Society (created in 1832) and Parliamentary bills, in the agricultural riots of 1830-1, but Parliamentary interest had to be renewed by the early 1840s. The promoters of allotments saw them as sources of manly independence (from the Poor Law), self-help and self-respect, rather than as an attempt to revive feudal relations and sustain dependency.[22] Indeed, William felt that an allotment allowed the rural labourer to see himself as a landowner, thus enhancing his sense of status, and gave him a better life than the urban artisan.[23] Where land was enclosed by Parliamentary act, allotments would relieve poor rates but not 'make him [the labouring man] independent of his work'. [24] William subscribed to the Society, which attracted many Whig and Reform MPs. It is probably important that his brother-in-law Ashley was also a promoter of allotments.

In April 1842 William's motion for a select committee on allotments was supported in a Commons which had already in that year heard several MPs propose schemes to respond to rural poverty (such as home colonization, and compulsory cultivation of waste lands). William chaired the committee of allotment supporters, including Ashley and Lord Robert Grosvenor. In early 1844 he introduced a bill following Ashley's failed allotment bill in 1843. The bill did not succeed then or in 1845, being opposed by John Arthur Roebuck, Bright and Milner Gibson and failing in the Lords, though supported by Peel and Sir James Graham (and indeed, landowners came to see supporting allotments as one of their normal social responsibilities[25]). But it influenced the Conservative's General Enclosure Act of 1845 which enacted that the enclosure of any waste entailed provision of allotments.[26] When he returned to office in 1846 William was unable to sponsor a new bill, but his bill was later seen as the precursor to Jesse Collings' bill of 1885.

Like other members of the movement, the allotments formed part of his opposition (no doubt reflecting opposition to a Malthusian analysis of population and resources) to emigration. Through enabling labourers to raise their own livestock and ensuring all cultivable land was used, food output would match population growth.[27] Undoubtedly there was a political thrust to the allotment movement too, for they would secure property by making labourers more contented, and, as William said in 1844, 'turn their attention from politics to subjects which would benefit themselves and society at large'. Later, William backed an Agricultural and Horticultural Co-operative Association which successfully provided seeds and nursery equipment for working men, with the Christian Socialists Tom Hughes, Edward V. Neale and others.[28]

William's views on the ideal relationship between farmers and agricultural labourers, and the duties owed by landowners to their communities, were expressed as president of Romsey Labourers' Encouragement Association, continuing Palmerston's role. In his seventieth year a correspondent in the *Hampshire Independent* eulogized his work for the Hampshire Hodge.[29] The association was patriotic and Anglican; its leaders presented the work of the clergy as in harmony with theirs. The Association meant to show that better-placed classes respected and sympathized with labourers, the agency of prizes and sociability was meant to stimulate inter-class amity and give the upper-classes knowledge of labourers' lives. The progress of the working classes in intelligence, good conduct, and influence made it increasingly the duty and interest of other classes to bring the best influences to bear upon them, William said in 1867. He was not alone in fearing that labourers would start to act as a class and see their interests as opposed to other classes.[30] In 1877 he said no employment in which a working man could engage was more comfortable and happy than that of the agricultural labourer.[31] In accordance with resistance to the creation of class antagonisms, he resented attempts by 'agitators' – infiltrators from outside the locality – to disturb the relationship between employers and workers, for 'the interests of the farmer and his men were much more identical than was commonly supposed'.[32]

He was patron of the Romsey Social Club and took adult Bible classes, inviting celebrities such as Shaftesbury and the Liberal politician and social reformer A.J. Mundella to participate.[33] As Georgina recalled, William relished his role of improving landowner; she also took to the role of the paternalist 'lady bountiful', being praised as an 'angel of light' for ever-ready local charity.[34] At Romsey she visited the poor and organized workhouse treats to alleviate their inmates' wretchedly Spartan lives, but she did not conceal her repulsion in her diary, thus in 1876 she noted that the treat was 'dismal as usual – all the poor men looking like caricatures'.[35] The Romsey mothers' meeting – where religion combined with the production of cheap clothing – gave her a print of 'Dorcas giving clothes to the poor' in the same year.[36]

Though he could never live there for any extended period, William attempted to be a model landlord on his Sligo estate (over 12, 000 acres) and visited Ireland annually for a month to six weeks, from 1865 to 1874. Georgina established a school for crewel work which provided a living to a number of young women. The drawing room of a shooting lodge at Mullaghmore was decorated by blind people as part of Georgina's philanthropic mission, leading one newspaper to report her as 'one of those rarely gifted workers'.[37] But Georgina was uncomfortable with her Irish 'people'. She appreciated their warm-heartedness, was amused by their flattery and proud of their 'affectionate remembrance': like other English aristocrats she had a patronizing view of the Irish. The suspicion created by their Protestant religion frustrated two attempts to establish a lending library for the peasantry and hampered their dissemination of sanitary tracts.[38]

The mix of paternalism and self-help apparent in the Cowper-Temples' rural philanthropy clearly motivated their 'urban' reforms too. Allotments were presented by William and others as assisting the 'manufacturing labourer' by employing waste lands around Yorkshire and Lancashire, for instance. In the 1840s he aided John Minter Morgan's scheme of self-supporting villages to promote the 'religious, moral and general improvement of the working classes'.[39] William also championed factory reform, following his brother-in-law Ashley. Though one of his interventions Ashley described as 'very shallow and rather foolish' in 1844, two years later he spoke effectively in the Commons against 'theoretical objections to interference by the State'.[40] Attending the celebration for the Ten Hours' Bill at the Free Trade Hall in Manchester, he said the reform was especially a women's question, echoing the appeals to a 'domestic ideology' made by many other reformers. He saw it as an expression of State paternalism: 'to protect those who, from weakness, their position, or age, were unable to defend themselves'. If the workers would make use of the time granted to them, 'to elevate themselves as rational, moral, and religious beings', then it would be as futile to attempt to repeal the measure as it was to roll back the Mersey to its source.[41] He also supported model housing schemes, joining Palmerston at a meeting in Romsey in 1861 to discuss improving working-class housing as 'a perfectly safe method' of assistance, unlike charity, which might reduce the impulse to self-exertion. Only the capitalist could afford to build model housing and since poor housing led to poor health and intemperance, William detailed the scheme of a cottage improvement association.[42]

The maritime equivalent of appalling factory or housing conditions was the overloading of vessels. Georgina espoused the campaign led by the MP for Derby, Samuel Plimsoll, and supported by Shaftesbury, for marking on the side of ships to prevent overloading: a bill was introduced at the same time as William's commons preservation bill in February 1871. Georgina was on a 'Ladies Committee of the Plimsoll and Seamen's Fund' as the honorary treasurer.[43] Though his efforts were defeated in 1875, Plimsoll persisted and Georgina found him, in early 1876, 'made quite ill by all the terrible cases brought under his notice of cruelty & carelessness in Ship owners & suffering & loss of crews'.[44] William supported Plimsoll's amendment in late April, and the Merchant Shipping Act was passed.

William stressed the primary importance of self-help through temperance and efforts such as Post Office Saving Banks and friendly societies. Georgina's comparison between the Palmerston and neighbouring estates in the aftermath of the Irish famine (noted earlier) suggests that her ideas on economics were conventional: the ultimate determination of labour was the law of supply and demand.[45] But amelioration of the system designed to provide aid to the deserving poor and repel the undeserving, attracted them. William was the first president of the Workhouse Visiting Society, established by the daughter of a tea merchant, Louisa Twining, with the support of the Social Science Association in June 1858, and Georgina joined it with a host of prominent social and moral reformers.[46] The Society's volunteers aimed to comfort the sick and elderly enduring the reformed poor law system, and rehabilitate and support those who would be released. Georgina visited workhouses in London to read stories, attend the sick and dying, and bring Christmas gifts. If she came to feel a useless member of this Society, which came to an end in 1861, she gave her support to Louisa's St Luke's Home for epileptic women, opened in April 1866.[47]

Georgina was active in other metropolitan endeavours from Anglican district visiting to the London Dress-making Company established to improve the working condition of women and encourage a maximum working day of ten hours.[48] Patronized by Shaftesbury and the bishops of London and Oxford, the Company was managed by Fanny Rudkin, with offices off Bond Street. *Punch* promoted it and the *Journal of the Society of Arts* reported its ambition to be a model business, where dressmaking would not be a 'detriment to the minds and bodies of the workers'. Georgina herself acquired a sewing machine to make, among other items, 'a little striped pink garibaldi ... for "Katie" at Ridge School'.[49]

That cluster of 'environmental' concerns – William's health reforms and improvement of the urban environment; Georgina's activity in the Ladies' Sanitary Association and support for Samuel Plimsoll's maritime reforms – were expressive of anxiety about letting the forces of urbanization, industrialization and commercial enterprise operate untrammelled. William was a member of a Select Committee on the health of towns in 1840, and joined the Health of Towns Association's central committee with Ashley, when it was established in 1844, after the revelations of social statistics and Chadwick's *Report on the Sanitary Condition of the Labouring Population of Great Britain* of 1842. In his official capacity, of course, he tried to promote public health from the Boards of Health and Public Works.[50]

William saw being Commissioner as an opportunity to 'minister to the good and happiness of the people' and improve metropolitan parks, 'to produce as much enjoyment as possible to all classes of the community'. He was 'anxious that every public space in London which could afford a pleasant view or promote or provide for the recreation of the public, should be turned to the best account'.[51] His innovative scheme to distribute flowers from the parks to the poor at the close of the season was highlighted by obituarists. With Georgina he studied 'French methods' of planting flower beds to improve the parks and develop them as splendid gardens for those lacking their own.[52] A newspaper publicized Georgina's role in transforming flower beds in Rotten Row, reporting a rumour she had 'planned and arranged most of them from designs obtained from various celebrated foreign gardens and pleasure grounds'.[53] She was certainly 'very much humbled by the superior taste of their gardening & arrangements over ours', when they visited Paris in 1862.[54]

One of the last to habitually ride a horse about London, William attended to horse-riders' needs at Hyde Park and therefore faced charges of 'class' (i.e., elite) interest from the press and other critics, as noted earlier.[55] But in his promotion of the metropolitan parks William's general 'class' concern, like other social reformers – temperance advocates and others – was to reshape working-class leisure on rational and gentler lines. Towns across Britain lacked open space for the public to enjoy.

William's activity in the Commons Preservation Society from 1865 expressed these concerns about recreational spaces for the inhabitants of the 'crowded centres of civilization', and he became its president; one might view his involvement as an effort to combat more radical and plebeian battles to prevent enclosure and assert customary rights.[56] As chairman of the select committee on the enclosure acts (1869) he helped preserve many rural commons. When in 1871 he led a backbench Liberal defence of public access to Epping Forest (threatened by the Treasury), he became a public figurehead for a movement which assumed a party-political tinge, for safeguarding access to commons and parks has been seen as a 'Palmerstonian' resistance by Whig-Liberals to Gladstonian 'grand maternal Government'.[57] But the cause was close to home as the New Forest was also imperilled; in the New Forest Bill's committee stage William introduced the clause preventing any further enclosure of waste land for plantation.[58] For William, the forest represented a rare vestige of wild scenery, with magnificent beeches and ancient oaks, and the natural (and national) equivalent of one of the pictorial masterpieces hanging in the National Gallery, rather than simply a source of timber for the Office of Woods and Forests: 'The British public delighted in the picturesque, and surely it was impolitic to drive them abroad in search of it?'[59]

Georgina helped create and was variously the president, honorary secretary and patroness of the Ladies' National Association for the Diffusion of Sanitary Knowledge among the Poor (also known as the Ladies' Sanitary Association), which was created in 1857 and formally established in July 1859. This lectured and published tracts to spread sanitary knowledge, organized outings for poor children and dinners and nurseries for the destitute or motherless.[60] The stimulus came from the Hungarian homeopath and promoter of exercise therapy, Dr Mathias Roth, who pointed out that British philanthropy created institutions to deal with British sanitary carelessness: Roth and others stressed the amount of misery which was entirely *preventable*. Georgina paid her modest female tribute to the male supporters of their 'feeble' efforts, Shaftesbury and medical men such as the 'Physician of Mankind', Thomas Southwood Smith (Jeremy Bentham's physician and a friend of Shaftesbury). The Association was linked to the National Association for the Promotion of Social Science, which supplied a public platform for female social reformers, and Georgina was listed as the Sanitary Association's president in the NAPSS's *Transactions*. William became honorary auditor and in her memoirs she presented her own role in the Society as being 'enabled' by William.[61]

Georgina's role was not honorific, as she frequently attended lectures, visited the office, applied for lectures, and edited reports, speeches and tracts.[62] This was unusual for few aristocratic women were involved closely in middle-class charities at this time.[63] She asked the art historian Anna Jameson, who had lectured on nursing sisterhoods, to join, and in 1865 invited William White to work with the Association and Garth Wilkinson to lecture (both men were Swedenborgians and spiritualists).[64] She expressed views in her diary, thus Mrs Baines' tract on wet nursing in 1862 was 'odious'. [65] When an artificial-flower maker was killed by arsenical dye, Georgina, with William's help, wrote a letter (signed with her fellow Sanitary Association secretary) to *The Times*, published 1 February 1862, as 'The Dance of Death'. [66] It accompanied a letter from Professor Augustus Hofman as an introduction to his analysis of Emerald Green ball wreaths they had sent him, 'His facts are astounding. A wreath of 50 leaves contains 40 grains of arsenic, a tartaline gown of 200 yards 8900 grains & it is calculated that a lady shakes off her at least 60 grains in the course of an evening.'[67] William and Georgina were concerned, as many were, about the poisoning of women workers and children. As a result, John Simon, the Medical Officer of the Privy Council, commissioned an investigation.[68]

The controversy in *The Lancet* and elsewhere, stimulated by Miss Lees' sanitary lectures in May 1878, because parts of the syllabus were considered inappropriate for single ladies, shows how controversial *LSA* work could be, although the journal had encouraged the Association in its early days.[69] Sanitary work was one activity which linked Georgina to her brother-in-law Shaftesbury (as did anti-vivisection), though the Lees episode showed his qualms about female instruction outside medical schools.[70] Georgina also became acquainted with Elizabeth Garrett, the first British woman doctor, possibly through the *LSA* or Garrett's presence in Maurice's Bible classes. Georgina's involvement endured.[71] In 1881, for instance, she invited Edwin Chadwick to talk over the 'street question' with her, for the *LSA*, and Chadwick gave the prizes in connection with Dr B.W. Richardson's lectures.[72]

William liked his wine and so was a latecomer to temperance, but became vice president of the prohibitionist United Kingdom Alliance, joined the Church of England Temperance Society, chaired the executive committee of the Coffee Taverns Association, and patronized temperance work at Romsey (at one time giving lectures under Palmerston's statue in the Market Square) and Torquay.[73] He was led in this field by Georgina, who formed a temperance society in fashionable Mayfair in 1868.[74] She preceded William as a 'Blue Ribbonite' in the temperance cause. Receiving the ribbon at Southampton's skating rink, William was reputedly the first peer to wear it in the Lords. [75] At his funeral a wreath from the Torquay Blue Ribbon Committee honoured a 'valuable president and friend'. [76] If they were aristocratic pioneers, the Cowper-Temples' involvement also reflected the prominence of Anglicans in temperance from the 1860s, as the established Church competed with Nonconformity in publicizing social and moral credentials.[77]

Connected to this was the Cowper-Temples' support for counter-attractive recreation for the working classes and lower middle-classes which would not degrade or harm husbands, wives and children, as improper songs at existing music halls did. A meeting to establish 'Coffee Music Halls for the People' was held at their Stanhope Street home in 1879 and their involvement was recognized in *Punch*.[78] In 1880 William and Georgina helped guarantee Emma Cons' Coffee Palace Association at the Royal Victoria Hall, the future 'Old Vic', and Cons recalled them as the 'most stalwart reporters at the start', largely financing and aiding in every other way an unpromising venture.[79] William preached there. He also supported, with Shaftesbury, work in the East End by the teetotaller Frederick Charrington (a brewer's son), backing his music-hall Sunday services and addressing the Foresters' Music Hall in Bethnal Green.[80] He was involved, too, in the working men's clubs movement.[81]

Temperance dealt with one source of carnal and social pollution but the Cowper-Temples also joined philanthropic endeavours to tackle another – sexuality or 'social purity' – when it emerged as a prominent cause in the 1870s-80s. William supported longstanding efforts to suppress obscene literature (a Pure Literature Society was established in 1854), which had made London 'smut capital of Europe' and discussed the problem with Josephine Butler.[82] In 1888 he tabled a notice in the Lords and wrote to *The Times* on the subject.[83] He was associated with the Contagious Diseases Acts controversies in which feminists and nonconformists opposed the extension of inspection of women as 'reputed prostitutes' outside garrison towns to the rest of the country in 1866 and 1869 on moral and constitutional grounds. He served on the Royal Commission studying the Act in 1870, and recommended repeal.[84] He joined the Church of England Social Purity Society and the men-only White Cross Army and was a member of the Lords' Select Committee on Law Relating to Protection of Young Girls (triggered by revelations of a traffic in girls to the continent), set up in 1881.[85] He belonged, too, to the Central Vigilance Committee for the Repression of Immorality established in 1883. One friend praised his ability to lighten 'foul caverns of corruption' without contamination.[86]

Her sister Marianne's paean to Georgina in 1858 had said: 'whatso'er their failings be, | None are beneath her sympathy; | And when the sin she can't defend, | She still remains the sinner's friend.'[87] George Russell spoke of her 'sympathy with suffering so keen that she could never be so happy in a world where others were miserable' and recalled the 'dominant note ... was her passionate indignation against cruelty and injustice. She had a genuine love of the outcast and down-trodden, a chivalry of spirit which always instinctively allied her with the weaker side'.[88] At Torquay, late in life, she supported a refuge for reclaimed women.[89] Her support for social purity reflected hatred of suffering.[90] And immorality involved her class, as she combated the behaviour of the 'Marlborough House set', alongside the Duchess of Leeds, the Countess of Aberdeen, Lady Muncaster and others.[91]

Clearly a matter of sexual morality and religion was one of the final reforms that the couple supported, William Holman Hunt's campaign to legalize marriage to one's deceased wife's sister. William had not initially favoured this as he thought it might lead to other changes in the law of marriage. He thought it unfair to create 'this irregularity of sex', but though the law was not recognized by many of the lower classes, 'for the wealthier classes to whom the legitimacy of their offspring is of importance ... they have choice enough for wives without coveting their sisters in law'. He feared the legislation would give a pretext for conservative clergy to call for disestablishment.[92] Holman Hunt was gratified by their change of heart: 'the facts of your sympathy with us will soon be known throughout all ranks of the divided army' and 'would have a wonderful effect in aiding us'.[93]

Opponents thought the issue of marriage to one's deceased wife's sister represented the selfish interests of the rich. Another reform concerned the aristocracy as a military caste. Duelling, the formalized mechanism for maintaining individual character and honour in response to insults in aristocratic society was increasingly criticized in the early decades of the nineteenth century. In 1843 William joined efforts to render it illegal.[94] His role is revealed by correspondence with another former private secretary of Lord Melbourne, George Anson, now Prince Albert's private secretary, and drafts for a petition and rules of arbitration to replace duelling.[95] The petition asserted that duelling – 'the monstrous fiction of a man deriving satisfaction for an insult by exposing himself to the risk of death or murder' – was a barbaric survival outraging Christianity and common sense. William's activity is unsurprising, given Evangelical opposition to duelling and his concern about the immorality of Society.[96] It took place at a time of personal upheaval – his marriage to Harriet – and he was at Runcton when he notified Anson of progress in the cause and asked for support from Prince Albert, whom he was, of course, acquainted with.[97] He joined other 'noblemen and gentlemen' of military and naval background at a meeting to consider memorializing the Queen.[98] As opponents hoped, military duelling ended with the Prince's intervention.[99] Despite opposition from the Admiralty and Master of Ordnance, the Articles of War were altered to allow insults to be redressed by apology and explanation.

Education provides a conjunction of the Cowper-Temples' religious, intellectual and class concerns. The Church's position, the relative roles of state and family, and social and individual progress were involved. The demoralisation of the masses which so frightened Victorian statesmen and reformers could be addressed, William once declared, by an education that offered the 'superior attractions of imagination and knowledge' and promoted self-control and forethought. [100] Such sentiments were unexceptional but William shared the autodidact's enthusiasm about the power of knowledge, being 'vehemently stirred up' by Capel Lofft's autobiographical *Self Formation* in 1841, for instance, and persuaded that 'intellectual greatness' could be reached by all.[101]

Critical awareness of the shortcomings of his formal education was a stimulus to what proved to be an enduring interest in pedagogy. The educational efforts of his brother-in-law, Ashley, must also have played a part. In the 1840s William supported the British and Foreign School Society's undenominational instruction, often linked with non-Anglican places of worship. His early role, as Commissioner to Greenwich Hospital, also developed this interest and brought association with James Kay-Shuttleworth the educationalist. He became involved with ragged schools, visiting the 'excellent but singular establishments' with Kay-Shuttleworth.[102] He established one at Whitechapel and earned praise for 'unostentatious liberality and charity' towards poor and needy children. [103] Though the problem of how the lowest classes were to be made happy, prosperous, and good, might be answered by cooperative action or some other scheme, William told an audience in 1869, at present the best way was the time-honoured method of exercising Christian sympathy and kindness via ragged schools.[104] These would inculcate duty, so that the poor should not 'continue to extend and transmit the evil habits and ways which they may have learnt in their childhood'![105] Recognising one serious obstacle to this led William and Georgina to support schemes for dinners, which would enable otherwise malnourished children to concentrate on lessons and demonstrate their teachers' kindness and sympathy.[106]

With practical support for voluntarism went acceptance that the state had a crucial role. Although publicly William implied a positive association between voluntary, Church and individual effort and the absence of passports, conscription and ministry of police in England, he recognised, as in health matters, the necessity for intervention. Privately, he observed: 'all experience[,] all reasoning proves we can't have an educated people without the intervention of the State'.[107] Kay-Shuttleworth believed in the state's superiority to voluntary effort in schooling and public health and William joined the educationalist's discussions with Milner, Ebrington and Cobden in April 1846, when Cobden said Corn Law repeal was easy compared with organizing educational reform in such a way that religious scruples were accommodated, and that secular education was the only plan now![108] But William's association with Kay-Shuttleworth and his awareness of alternative approaches on the Continent[109] did not lead him to spurn efforts by the Church and others. It was a question of the state as an auxiliary, hence William's support for the education clauses of the Factory Bill of 1843.[110] The lack of a national system of state education did not prevent a vitality – driven by 'compassion, sympathy, and religious zeal' – in provision, though William admitted defects in upper-class and commercial education, and major inadequacies in working-class schooling. Education *should* train in a way that suited people for their likely careers, thus botany for pupils in agricultural districts, but he told an audience of 'social scientists' in 1858 that there was insufficient data to generalise from the limited research in pedagogy. Typically, as a nineteenth-century Liberal, he prized individual and voluntary exertion. He stressed the family's role in forming character and habits. 'Habit,' he said, was a highly important thing to study, for beginning in a small degree, 'it grew upon a man until it held him in chains of iron.' Parents played a crucial part, and they should not be able to deprive children of an education (as he told labourers at Romsey in the 1860s)![111]

Such views mattered, especially when William oversaw educational policy, and at a time when nonconformists and secularists were so exercised about the state's or established Church's roles. Given his ministerial experience and famous intervention through the 'Cowper-Temple clause', his views remained newsworthy. Thus the *Daily News* reported his commitment to a 'free trade' in middle-class education, as the state should not interfere where parents could pay, nor hamper 'spontaneous action' characteristic of the country.[112]

In the Cowper-Temples' promotion of female higher education we can perhaps trace the influence of Maurice, Llewellyn Davies and the Russell Gurneys. In 1874 William supported a bill to allow women to graduate, but was disappointed by hostility from the MPs for Oxford and Cambridge and hampered by university charters.[113] He said the day was 'fast passing away in which the old fashioned prejudice prevailed that girls should not receive as good training as boys' and told the Commons that deficient mental capacity stemmed largely from deficient education, and that evidence from Girton suggested women could excel equally at examinations.[114] The Cowper-Temples supported female doctors, and William attempted to open the medical profession to women. He argued for this widening of the 'narrow routine' of female employment on the basis of fairness, women's desire to alleviate suffering, their need to earn a livelihood, their aspirations for an honourable profession and the contrast with the liberal approach to female doctors abroad, even in Russia. The medical establishment was reviving the 'old barbarous usages' in blocking female rivals from their profession.[115] Georgina visited Girton College at the same time as these efforts in 1874, shown round by John Llewellyn Davies' sister Emily; she recorded her impression of Alfred Waterhouse's new building and the students' achievements in mathematics and classics.[116] She also had shares and an interest, as patron, in Harrage Hall Ladies' College in Romsey, and became president of the council of the Romsey High School for Girls.[117]

Given this desire to promote female education, it was not surprising, though by no means automatic, that Georgina should be a supporter of the extension of the franchise to women, signing, with upwards of two thousand women, a declaration calling for this, in 1889, which was reprinted, with her name selected as one of those representative of her section of society, in the *Fortnightly Review*.[118] Thirty years before she had described the call for female rights as 'nonsense'. Perhaps it was significant that her gesture now, took place after William's death.

The Cowper-Temples were also active in animal welfare, as members of the RSPCA, supporters of the Metropolitan Drinking Fountain and Cattle Trough Association[119] and founder members of the 'Universal Band of Mercy', which promoted kindness to animals amongst children (rather than simply prevent cruelty). William also gave support to legislation. In 1887 he criticized measures to deal with rabies, viewing muzzling as ineffective and harmful to the animals, and introduced a bill to require compulsory registration of dogs in London as a measure against rabies.[120] When he died the *Zoophilist* memorialized his 'ever-ready hand to help, and heart to sympathize'.[121] Georgina's obituary also appeared in the *Zoophilist*. The animal welfare reformer John Frewen Moor wrote privately of her 'vast service' for the 'lower animals'.[122]

The Cowper-Temples helped establish a Romsey auxiliary of the RSPCA in 1876, presided over by William and including Florence Horatia Suckling who asked permission to dedicate her *Humane Educator and Reciter* to Georgina in 1891.[123] The British branch of the Band of Mercy was established at Broadlands in 1885, with the Unitarian Reverend Thomas Timmins. William found, as he told Lord Carnarvon, who had introduced a Vivisection bill, 'numbers of persons in all parts of the Country ready to encourage the training of school children in habits of sympathy and consideration for their pets and other creatures within their power, and I expect that Bands of Mercy will become more popular than Bands of Hope as interest is more easily excited about animals than about Pots of Beers and glasses of gin'.[124] The chief warden of the society was to be Shaftesbury with William as the warden and Lord Ashley as treasurer.[125] The executive committee included Georgina.[126] By 1886 there were some 87,000 members in the English division of the Band. The 'Fellowship of Animals' Friends', as it was first styled, was initiated at the Cowper-

Temples' house with Shaftesbury.[127] There were yearly gatherings of the local branches of the Band of Mercy at Broadlands.

Georgina was one of a pioneering band alarmed at the slaughter of wildlife, and in her keenness to protect wild birds she helped establish the Plumage League in late 1885, which was widely reported, the *Leeds Mercury* describing her as 'always to the front in movements of a humane character'.[128] The League opposed the grotesque fashion for bird corpses as ornaments in headwear and dresses: a milliner informed Georgina that one dress was decorated by twelve bodies, and another told her of a ball gown enriched with canaries. At the end of her life, Georgina joined the new Society for the Protection of Birds (the future RSPB).

Anti-vivisection – a crusade against scientific materialist infliction of pain – experienced a 'massive upwelling' in the 1870s; and as Turner argues, expressed anxieties about the sentimental and compassionate side of humanity becoming imperilled by amoral rationalism. [129] The Cowper-Temples' sympathies brought the friendship of Frances Power Cobbe, who they encouraged to seek Shaftesbury's assistance in 1875 (overcoming Cobbe's prejudices against his narrow-minded Calvinism). Georgina sympathized with her scorn of half-measures: in March 1876 at an Animal Friends' Society meeting, Georgina took courage and like a timid hare (she said in her diary) fought for her young and reproached the Society for supineness on vivisection: 'Oh the inertia of selfish humanity'. This outrage explained her letter-writing frenzy in support of Carnarvon's bill in May 1876.[130] It was not surprising, then, that the Cowper-Temples should join Cobbe's Victoria Street Society and later reject the 'lesser measures' of the National Anti-Vivisection Society.[131] Religious inquiry also provided a link between them and Cobbe, who visited Broadlands and gave Georgina advice on religious literature.[132] Their interest in the pursuit of religious and spiritual truths was also shared by Anna Kingsford, who involved Georgina in a campaign when the police killed a dog in Baker Street in 1886 (she mentioned the Cowper-Temples in writing to the Queen about this).[133]

We have seen how Georgina adored her pet dogs, and probably she led in their zoophilism, though she said William encouraged her to form the Plumage League. [134] Hunting seems to have been forbidden in the Broadlands estate – quite a dramatic impact on the social life of a country house, although fishing was permitted. Georgina had a cattle trough installed in Romsey marketplace.[135]

When Georgina read the *Westminster Review* on vegetarianism in 1874 she hoped 'we are going to it'.[136] Taking zoophilism to its logical conclusion, she became vegetarian in 1876.[137] The decision became public knowledge when she accepted the office of vice-president of the Vegetarian Society in 1884, providing one of the few titled members at the time. She gave money to pay for vegetarian badges and in aid of the London vegetarian society and special mission fund.[138] Her letter to the president, Francis Newman (brother of the cardinal, and a noted freethinker), seeking clarification about the implications of vegetarianism, was widely reported by the press in 1882.[139] Interviewed by *The Vegetarian* in 1893, she modestly claimed to have 'done nothing, dear, worth telling', and made clear her moral objection, her 'shrinking from pain' in diet and scientific inquiry.[140] A vegetarian dish which she served appeared as 'Lady Mount Temple soup' in the *Refreshment News*. William's sympathies were influenced by spiritualism, possibly through advice from the spiritualist-vegetarian Chandos Leigh Hunt Wallace, or perhaps through reading Swedenborg.[141] Vegetarianism, he noted, was 'one of the signs of the coming of the kingdom of Heaven ... The development of spiritual life frees from the necessity of meat'.[142] William played no active role in vegetarianism,[143] but diet reform and cheap food supply attracted his support. He backed propaganda to encourage working people to eat colonial meats and endorsed a National Training School of Cookery.[144] He was a chairman of a bread reforming 'Golden Bread and Milling Association', announced in the *Homeopathic World* and the *Vegetarian Messenger*, with Edward Clifford as treasurer.[145]

Illnesses led them into mesmerism, electrotherapy, homeopathy and other novel curative approaches, as their health diaries reveal. William helped secure protection for medical examinees from anti-homeopathic prejudices, when the 1858 Medical Act was passed.[146] However, William White's history of the anti-vaccination movement was less complimentary, describing him as an agent in the Commons for the Epidemiological Society, and characterizing him as 'simple-minded' and extremely docile; when, as a minister, he had introduced a vaccination bill in 1856, William believed in compulsory vaccination for infants.[147] Georgina believed that though mesmerism had remarkable successes, 'the process demands so much time & patience it is not I wd think likely to become an ordinary method of treatment'.[148] But they were prepared to allow Frederic Myers and the French physiologist and mesmerist Charles Richet to experiment on Juliet when they visited in October 1886. Through one of her spiritualist acquaintances, Dr Ashburner, Georgina knew the spiritualist inquirers Baron von Reichenbach and Dr Daniel Hornung of Berlin.[149] She received cranky religious letters from Dr William Washington Evans who combined an 'antiseptic' system of cure with predictions of the Second Coming and thoughts on the purity of aristocratic blood. Like many Protestants in this era they investigated faith healing.[150] Faith and medical unorthodoxy later combined in their patronage of American 'New Thought' in the form of Christian Science. Georgina studied Baker Eddy's *Christian Science* in 1886.[151]

They backed Frances Lord, feminist editor of *Woman's World* and a pioneer translator of Ibsen, lending her Shelley House to attract a fashionable crowd for Christian Science lectures during the London season in 1888.[152]

National boundaries did not circumscribe the Cowper-Temples, as their dabbling with the American Christian Science movement suggests, and as the religious work studied in the next chapter indicates. William became vice-president of a French anti-slavery organization in 1860 in response to a letter he sent full of generous and humane sentiments.[153] Foreign affairs interested Georgina as they did the public in general in the 'mid-Victorian' period. If William's Italian sympathies are not clear, Georgina's were strong: she admired Italian 'patriots' in 1859 and met them at Stafford House. With her sister-in-law Minny she helped organize a Ladies' Garibaldi Association for the Relief of the Sick and Wounded, and she followed the war between the Franco-Piedmontese forces and the Austrians closely.[154] There was 'Garibaldi fever' when the great man visited Britain in 1864, when he stayed with the Duke of Sutherland and was feted by 'foolish ladies of fashion'.[155] The Cowpers met him at the dowager Duchess of Sutherland's luncheon at Chiswick and at the Palmerstons' with the two Duchesses of Sutherland, the Duchess of Argyll and various ministers.[156] Then Georgina supported aristocratic aid to female refugees and orphans from France in October 1870.[157] The Cowper-Temples had news via Spencer of martial events in Paris, Napoleon III 'employing his time in examining and comparing all kinds of guns which is not promising for peace'; so the outbreak of war must have been no surprise.

They were drawn into the 'Bulgarian agitation', one of those 'great semi-religious, semi-political agitations which aimed … at bringing the force of organised moral indignation to bear on the conduct of public affairs', stimulated by Turkish atrocities against Bulgarian nationalists in May, the agitation was at its height from July to December 1877.[158] Friends and relations prominent in the agitation included Ruskin (and via William Morris, many Pre-Raphaelites), Henry Fawcett, Auberon Herbert, Earl Cowper, Shaftesbury and Evelyn Ashley, who was suitably Palmerstonian about foreign barbarism after completing his *Life of Palmerston*.[159]

The Cowper-Temples were recognized as leading reformers beside Shaftesbury and Josephine Butler, their support valued not simply because of rank or political connections but because of their reputations for virtue and piety. Some of the Cowper-Temples' causes were widely supported, others, such as vegetarianism or aristocratic teetotalism, were not. William's reputation is nicely summarized in doggerel linking him with factory reform, corn laws repeal, Hodge's welfare, Thames Embankment ('noblest Boulevard in all the world'), commons preservation and the wondrous conscience clause:

'Full justice – thus his glorious programme ran – | For Jew, Dissenter, Sceptic, woman, man, | Afghan and Zulu, white, black, yellow, brown, | Dwellers in savage wilds or populous town; | For fellow creatures with four feet or wings, | 'Gainst cruel science's base torturings; | In days of clouds and storms, | He championed sound reforms.'[160]

In assessing his reputation, contemporaries contrasted William's political mediocrity ('not a politician of the first brilliance. He did not shine out among his fellows') with his good work and contribution to the 'sum of benevolence'. Of course, William had the resources for such activity. One obituary denied William 'made a trade of charity'. The Cowper-Temples' openness to philanthropic requests was widely-known; they 'acted upon the idea that wealth was a trust intended to be used in the diffusion of happiness'.[161] A religious journal, purporting to be offended by the comfort of the 'Broadlands Retreats', was 'informed that the noble host's income is not less than £30, 000 a year'.[162] We have seen that the quarry lawsuit strained finances and brought (in their view) 'comparative poverty'.[163] Their charity was liable to abuse, acquaintances complained. They took risks: their hospitality was described as 'adventurous'. Ruskin's name for Georgina, 'Isola Bella', conveyed both her general unapproachability (in his view) with openness 'on all sides to waifs of the waves, claiming haven and rest in her sympathy'.[164] If this attracted parasites and bores it also made them foci for 'the best and strongest' in philanthropy.[165]

One might see this philanthropy as part of the aristocratic effort to sustain moral authority when the middle-class sought to lead organized philanthropy (and it would be quite wrong to convey the impression that the targets of this philanthropic endeavour, the poor, were inactive in organizing their own efforts at social and moral reforms).[166] If there was an element of aristocratic obligation behind this the Cowper-Temples did not limit themselves to the benevolent patronage, purely honorific roles, or personal charity conventional for the upper class.[167] The range and depth of their philanthropy stemmed from a religiosity which scorned frivolity and eschewed bigotry, though for analytical reasons I have separated religion and philanthropy. The next chapter examines religious activities, including their spiritualism and interest in the esoteric. If William exercised ecclesiastical patronage and influenced Palmerston's appointments, Shaftesbury, keen to see the elevation of their mutual friend the Reverend J.C. Ryle, anticipated Georgina's influence on the Lord Chancellor in 1860.[168] Her interest in ecumenicalism is represented in her centrality to the Broadlands conferences.

11

THE COWPER-TEMPLES AND RELIGION

William's abiding interest was religion, talk on mundane matters was likely to end in religious conversation and he devoted only as much time as he thought necessary to business matters before turning to sacred concerns.[1] 'Oh, nothing of course compares in interest with communion with my Master, and work for him,' he said.[2] Georgina's piety was a major factor in William's selection of her as wife, and religion – or desire for faith – remained her preoccupation.

They lived through major developments in British, and western Christianity: the working out of the influences of Evangelicalism in the established Church and Protestant dissent, the flourishing of the Nonconformist conscience, the Oxford Movement and its challenge to a Protestant nation hostile to popery, the conflict between liberal and ultramontanist Catholicism, the threat from Enlightenment-inspired infidelity and the emergence of High Victorian agnosticism. It was an era of new religions stimulated by crises in orthodox faith; and spiritualism and esoteric religion became serious concerns to the Cowper-Temples. At times it seemed as if 'charity believeth in all things'. [3]

This was a culture in which religion mattered, a 'religious society in a deeper and completer sense than any western country since the Reformation', not since the seventeenth century had society 'been so much preoccupied with problems of doctrine and Church order'.[4] The new biblical criticism and scientific developments stimulated debate, particularly in the 'High Victorian' periodicals of the quality press.[5] Jonathan Parry has noted the 'incestuous relationship at this time, between the literary, social and political worlds' which allowed the widespread acceptance of liberal religious views by the social elite.[6]

As a prominent politician, William was involved in major religious issues, concerning religious liberties, Sabbatarianism, disestablishment of the Church of Ireland and the future of the Anglican establishment. Famously, he considered elementary education's relationship to religion. He participated in controversies surrounding ritualism in the Church of England and Catholic ultramontanism. The electorate saw politics as important because of the relationship to religious concerns and because politics had a moral purpose which Cowper-Temple exemplified – as a 'disciplinary, educative and uplifting activity'.[7]

This chapter begins with William's developing religious identity, before surveying his intervention in the church through patronage, support for societies and movements and friendships. A similar study of Georgina's beliefs and interests follows. I then consider their spiritualism and exploration of forms of religious utopianism and mysticism. The second part studies their most important contribution to nineteenth-century Christianity, the annual conferences which were held with 'but one or two breaks' from Broadlands, between 1874 and 1888, and which expressed William's pursuit of Christian unity and the 'wide catholicity of his spiritual life'.[8]

A brief description of William's religious identity would be to say that he journeyed from the coolness of Regency Whiggery (which 'embraced a good deal of Voltairean scepticism and hedonism, and perhaps some materialistic utilitarianism' but also manifested a 'rational' and simple Protestantism[9]), into the fervent heat of Evangelicals, with their desire for conversion of the Jews and opposition to 'Puseyism', but thereafter, rather than narrow-minded Low Churchism, he became increasingly non-denominational. One sympathetic with his later work asked, 'Was Lord Mount Temple not right when he said, "we have had the High, the Low, and Broad Church, we now want the Deep Church"?'[10]

Late in life, William identified the components of his experience and identity.[11] These were: infant assurance of God, an upbringing without doctrinal bigotry (a polite gloss!), the influence of Henry Drummond's 'intensely spiritual High Churchism', F.D. Maurice's 'broad instruction in unconventional real Christian facts' and 'deep Churchism' at his Broadlands conferences.[12] Religion underlay his ambition to be a 'reformer', by which he meant amelioration of 'the people' and politics subordinated to God.[13] 'Because I believe that God has sent me into the world to do my best to improve it,' William said, in his later apologia for being Liberal.[14] This was not unusual, for though William's journey took peculiar directions, the political world he inhabited was animated by religion and his generation of Whigs was earnest. The piety, humility and 'philanthropy on a massive scale', characteristic of peers such as Devonshire, Jonathan Parry has suggested, makes it 'in some senses irrelevant to treat them as culturally distinct from the mass of the Liberal party'.[15]

Georgina's memoirs refer to the 'low ebb' of religion in William's infancy, and the neglect of 'maternal duty'. As with Shaftesbury, it was left to a maid to teach William about his religion, but instruction really began at Brighton following his desultory time at Eton. We have seen that William considered ordination to escape the 'imminent dominion of sin'.[16] He was repelled, though, by the 'quiet and monotony of a parson's life'.[17] In November 1829 he wrote that the 'grand object of my thoughts, & my actions' was to be the pursuit of heaven, but that he lacked a 'hearty sense of my own unworthiness, I have not a complete devotion to Christ my saviour, I still love the world, its pleasures, its vanities, its idols'.[18]

Fragmentary writings on the Christian's relationship with the world from this period survive in William's papers. About 1829 he planned a treatise, though hesitant because his ideas differed from those 'most prevalent among those who are seeking to take up their Cross'. Examining the definition of the 'world', he tried to show that the separation required of a Christian was not physical (flight from the ungodly), but separation from ungodly thoughts, acts and principles, 'the latter alone is required of the Christian in a country where his religion is universally professed and the law of the Land'.[19] 'Will the Person who has been in the habit of opening his house to the fashionable of London,' he queried, 'be most beneficial to the religious interests if he continues or if he ceases to give parties and balls,' answering with the reflection that the latter encouraged the worldly to think Christianity a 'gloomy, sad, unsocial, thing'.[20]

The calamity of William's first marriage did not, as Philip Mandler believes, trigger his religiosity.[21] He already associated with 'extreme' or pre-millenarian Evangelicals and attended their services and city missions. If his religion was not dour like Shaftesbury's, there was youthful extremism. Lady Palmerston worried about his 'great zeal on those Subjects and that it should not be always kept within the bounds of reason'. With her generation's fear of enthusiasm, she deplored new-fangled ideas, could not bear that religion 'instead of being a comfort and a consolation should be made a terror and a torment' and said his expressions and feeling were occasionally exaggerated.[22] He said she had not been blessed 'with that conviction of the inspiration of Scripture, and with that knowledge of God and communion with Him in prayer, which has been given under the providence of God to others less good by nature than yourself, & apparently far more unworthy of such a blessing'.[23] But even at his narrowest – before the 1850s, when a sister-in-law noted his charity toward High, Low and Broad and interest in other religions – his outlook prevented bigotry.[24] He appreciated Harriet Martineau's novel

Deerbrook for instance, regardless of her Unitarianism and in 1836 enjoyed services held by Catholics, Unitarians, Wesleyans, Baptists, Quakers and Plymouth Brethren.[25]

By the late 1830s William was closely associated with Evangelicals, finding the popular Henry Beamish of Conduit Street Chapel a 'most imaginative & fervent preacher' in 1836.[26] Other associates included Captain John Trotter of Dyrham Park, Sir Culling Eardley Smith, Caleb Morris and the pre-millenarian Edward Bickersteth.[27] Evangelical causes were organized through societies, missions and agitations. William first joined the London City Mission, in which his brother-in-law Ashley took a lead, an interdenominational effort to bring the gospel to the poor through ragged school classes, tracts, prayer meetings and home visits. William paid for and superintended a district missionary and at one point frequently accompanied him.[28] He belonged to the Parker Society (Ashley was president), which republished the fathers and early writers of the English church from Edward VI's reign to Elizabeth's death. He supported Eardley Smith's Evangelical Alliance.

George Russell, the chronicler of Evangelicalism, included him among its aristocratic leaders, but his Evangelicalism was never orthodox.[29] Georgina plausibly described his position as from the first, the 'opinions of the Broad Church with the fervour and warmth of the Evangelical', and Russell noted that he was 'deemed by sterner theologians too tolerant of errors, and so rather lost his position in the movement'.[30] It helps to understand Evangelicalism in William's context (and other Whig-Liberals'), as 'not a rigid doctrinal Calvinism, but rather a sense of devout Protestant piety and duty, overlying entrenched Whig latitudinarianism', though many Anglican Evangelicals came to see *Whig* Evangelicalism as impossible.[31]

According to Georgina's memoirs, they embarked on a search for religious truth after their marriage.[32] They studied the Bible, attended church services and got to know people of all denominations, and limited attendance at political and social parties. First they investigated the millenarian Evangelicalism of the banker Henry Drummond.[33] They visited him at Albury, attended services by the apostle Nicholas Armstrong and hung on Drummond's words for hours, finding the whole atmosphere of Albury stimulating.[34] It was hoped that they would join the Catholic Apostolic Church which Edward Irving had established in the 1830s and which appealed to aristocrats (including the Duke of Northumberland) as well as professionals; the denominational title for what was in actuality an effort to be ecumenical was an error produced by the 1851 Census.[35] Georgina recalled the experience as one of hope, which 'quickened our religious life'.[36] William took from Albury a sense of Christian unity where each sect had its truths. Drummond's correspondence with Georgina suggests that she found his anti-Catholicism and criticisms of monasticism problematic. [37] Georgina's acquaintance Joseph Baylee of St Aidan's Theological College in Birkenhead advised her to avoid Irvingism, as a system 'of man, and unscriptural. You need no humanly invented comforts'. Baylee criticized Drummond's stress on *heteroglossia* and prophecy and came to see it as a snare.[38] But Georgina saw the episode as an education in a wider view of the Church and in the meaning of symbolism and ritual.[39]

Given their interest in the millenarian group, it is worthwhile considering their attitude to the Lord's Second Coming. Boyd Hilton includes William as a 'pre-millenarian evangelical Whig', who thought Christ would return *before* the commencement of the millennium and not wait until the Church was in prosperity. The Second Coming, in this belief, was not in the distant future. William was in contact with a scholar of scriptural prophecy in the early 1880s, but for most of his life he seems not to have been impressed by 'signs of the times' indicative of the impending advent of the millennium, in fact, as his letter from Albury about 1851 suggested, he thought concentration on Christ's future return stopped work in the present.[40]

In considering interpretation of scripture, it is interesting to regard William's words to the Hertford Auxiliary Bible Society in 1864. He thought understanding of the Bible had grown as knowledge (of ancient civilizations, geography, languages) increased, 'as science advances and knowledge increases, more and more light is thrown upon those pages, and we are enabled to understand more fully and to bring home more satisfactorily to our minds the lessons they teach.'[41] He accepted that some saw German 'higher criticism' of the Bible as an unmixed evil but thought it would reveal the Bible's 'full meaning, its great beauty, and its applicability to human nature and human affairs'. Bishop John Colenso of Natal was a vain man, William said, whose controversial thoughts on the Pentateuch were premature, but errors stimulated able men to produce better interpretations. It was not enough now to read the Bible as good little children did, 'straight on to the end, gathering from it only what the first impressions may be'. Their duty was 'really and truly to study the Bible – that is to try and ascertain its fullest meanings and their bearings on our daily life'. [42] For William believed the Bible was a source of instruction.

Evangelical philosemites like Ashley hoped pressure on Turkey would allow the Jews to return to the Holy Land and lead to the Lord's Second Coming. William's attitude to the Jews was partly a Whiggish desire for liberty, hence support for the Jewish Disabilities bill as the 'last stone on that temple of religious freedom which they had been rearing the last twenty years'.[43] But he thought it presumptive 'to act with a view to the accomplishment of prophecy'.[44] Yet William told Palmerston in 1849 that he might help them by obtaining from the Turks 'such rights or privileges ... as are necessary for their becoming cultivators of the Soil. You would be doing a good work for the civilization of that country besides gaining the gratitude of a people who have somehow continued to have great influence in the world in the midst of their ill-treatment'.[45] The fate of the Jews was also brought before the Cowper-Temples through Herman Douglas, who acted as an emissary between various crowned and ex-crowned heads when recuperating on the Continent in 1867. Georgina thought it strange this 'little obscure odd looking German Jew English clergyman should have gained admission to these Courts[,] Ministers[,] Empress, Ex-King of Hanover ... Emperor of Austria, Metternich, Emperor of the French and found them all ready to listen to him'.[46] William thought his 'amateur diplomacy' a satanic temptation but wrote a letter of introduction to the ambassador at St Petersburg.[47]

The next influence was that grouping of Christian Socialists concerned with cooperation and anti-Chartist paternalism, with which William became acquainted through F.D. Maurice, then at Lincoln's Inn chapel, in the late 1840s.[48] The timing was important: like Ashley, William probably saw social reform as a way to combat Chartism and revolution. But the attraction was also theological. Movement from Evangelicalism to Christian Socialism was not so unusual, for these were overlapping groups, even if many Evangelicals opposed Maurice.[49] The Cowper-Temples joined others in calling Maurice 'the Prophet', like many, they were attracted to a theology denying the literal existence of Hell and eternal punishment (which Maurice notoriously did in 1853) or a God who punished in anger. Though critics found Maurice obscure and nebulous, his ideas, inspired by Neo-Platonism, were an important bond between many of the Cowper-Temples' acquaintances.[50] William's public activity was shaped by a Broad Churchmanship influenced by Maurice and Christian Socialism.

The only letter from Maurice in the Broadlands papers thanked William for what turned out to be a controversial appointment in 1860: 'If I only may do any good in Vere St I know you will forgive all the trouble and reproach I have caused you.'[51] They deplored his apparent resignation from St Peter's, in late 1862, partly in consequence of 'a book coming out on Old Testament that he thinks *detestable* by Colenso whom he wants to answer unshackled by the feeling that he is benefiting pecuniarily by the Church'.[52] His motives were the noblest and highest, Georgina wrote, 'beyond common appreciation – so he will be misunderstood & read backwards'.[53] Another time, when Lord Houghton sought a place for

Maurice, though William wished Maurice could have anything that became vacant, he was 'not prepared to take the responsibility of urging him'.[54] While the Cowpers were not intimates of the Prophet, though the absence of extensive letters by Maurice hampers the attempt to gauge their relationship, they prized contact.[55] When Georgina dined with him in December 1862 she recorded this with an exclamation mark.[56] Maurice asked her to help with female education in 1855 (Maurice was a proponent of female suffrage, though no democrat).[57] Georgina became close to his second wife, and after Maurice died, reminisced about 'our beloved Prophet' with her.[58]

Through Maurice they got to know Thomas Hughes and Charles Kingsley, and also Frederick Robertson at Brighton (the latter was a liberal theologian and social reformer but not a Christian Socialist) whom they would hear occasionally on Sundays when they went for the sea air.[59] Hughes, known affectionately by them as 'Tom Brown', remembered William as 'an avowed and liberal supporter'.[60] Maurice's disciple John Llewellyn Davies, brother of the suffragist Emily Davies, was also a close friend, and one of the Queen's favourite clergymen for his Broad Church beliefs.[61] In 1868 he contributed to liberal *Essays in Church Reform*, and joined William and the theologian William Henry Fremantle in establishing the National Church Reform Union in 1870. Another clerical associate of Maurice was George D'Oyly Snow of Blandford, who shared William's interest in a more widely based established Church and his efforts to aid the New Forest Shakers.

Although he surprised the Quaker John Bright by 'remarks on the subject of Church Establishment: he thought the time for them and for the need of them was passing',[62] William hoped – in this time of Irish diestablishment – to reform, not abolish, the Anglican establishment, by reforming Church rates, dropping the Athanasian creed and enhancing lay activity in parochial government or preaching. The Church could be made 'more efficient and better adapted to the wants and spirits of the present day'.[63] His efforts were controversial. Thus the *Morning Post* speculated in July 1871 about his amendment relating to the Act of Uniformity binding the Prayer Book to the Church of England, which 'has quite taken the Church's breath away', since it threatened (or encouraged) competing ecclesiastical parties.[64]

He introduced in 1872 and 1873 a bill to allow bishops to license laymen – and non-Anglicans – to preach in churches. He saw this removal of exclusiveness as in harmony with a liberal age, and the source of new insights and conscience-awakening eloquence from speakers outside the episcopally ordained. But critics pointed out the bill – a Church Reform Union measure – was fraught with difficulties, was not demonstrably demanded by worshippers, and hardly addressed dissenters' hostility to the established Church.[65] The *Hampshire Telegraph* described the bill as one of those measures 'elaborated in the closet, and which are submitted to the House of Commons for the purpose of remedying grievances of which no one complains'.[66] 'Mr Cowper-Temple appears to think that you can teach religion upon the same principles that you mix a seidlitz powder,' another paper commented, pointing out that it was impractical to have a situation where Newman Hall and Monsignor Capel (the 'dissenter's bishop' and Catholic apostle to the genteel[67]) could speak from the pulpit, to an audience which would thus be placed at the mercy of rectors of eccentric liberality. People went to church to have their opinions confirmed and to dissenters this 'good-natured liberality' was merely a mop against a comet.[68] Unsurprisingly critics saw him as a threat: 'When Mr Gladstone has disestablished the church, or when Mr Cowper-Temple has arranged that we may find a costermonger in the pulpit one Sunday,' one critic wrote in the journal *London Society* in 1873, 'and a "rescued woman" the next, it will be time to cast about for a suitable sect.'[69]

With the Conservative Evangelical Lord Sandon and the help of Thomas Hughes William introduced a Parishioners Rights' Bill and a Parochial Councils Bill (1870–1871); the latter was defeated by High Church opponents led by Beresford Hope.[70] These efforts, also represented in the National Church Reform Union, expressed Whig-Liberal concern with the laity's growing disassociation from the Church, partly due to High Church revival. By cooperating in parish councils clergymen would be obliged to regard parishioners' feelings and mutual help, and 'vital action' would follow.[71] Fear of the clergy's isolation from the laity was also reflected in his support for Archbishop Benson's House of Laymen (established in 1886), to balance the growth of Convocation.[72] William attended church congresses, established in 1861 partly in emulation of the Social Science Association.[73]

William's opposition to the Athanasian Creed was not unusual, since many rejected damnatory clauses as inauthentic to the early church (they had been revived, indeed, by the Tractarians). He joined Shaftesbury's campaign to see the Creed removed from a prayer book which needed to be modernized to attract nonconformists and perpetuate the establishment.[74]

In Church-State relations he is above all remembered for the 'inspired' amendment to the Education Bill of 1870 which removed denominational instruction in order to preserve teaching of the Bible in rate-paid schools from secularist or atheist attacks; though the High Church was offended.[75] William considered the clause permitted the Creed or Lord's Prayer, seeing these as a common bond between Board and denominational Schools.[76] He joined the Anglican-dominated National Educational Union, formed in 1869 to defend religious instruction and voluntary schools in the education system. He resisted the disestablishment pressed by the Liberation Society in the general election of 1885.[77]

One way to shape the established Church was by patronage. Shaftesbury was paranoid that his brother-in-law's 'liberal' or 'neological' influence would determine Palmerston's ecclesiastical appointments and in his diary bewailed the unholy influence of 'W.C.' who had 'neither talent, nor knowledge, nor political position'.[78] Though the Hammonds believed Shaftesbury was the only friend of Palmerston with theological expertise, William did indeed have some influence from the 'very antipodes of doctrine, opinion, and feeling'.[79] Palmerston evidently felt enough trust in his stepson's judgement in 1856 to ask for religious reading for his ailing younger brother, 'a rational work in the English & not in the German Sense of the word, that is reasonable; for all exaggerated works produce the opposite effect from that which they are intended to produce', and to recommend a sensible clergyman.[80] William favoured 'unexceptionable broad Churchmen', he told a friend in 1856, when he sought information on a candidate for the bishopric of Ripon.[81] He influenced the appointment of Richard Trench as Archbishop of Dublin, whose advancement was pressed by Samuel Wilberforce,[82] and secured livings for John Llewellyn Davies in 1856 and Maurice in 1860.[83] But William failed to persuade Palmerston to appoint the prominent Evangelical John Charles Ryle, a friend of Georgina who occupied a Tollemache living at Helmingham.[84] Indeed, conversation with his friend Baylee – grown very liberal-minded after reading Maurice – made William feel that Ryle's appointment would encourage 'bumptious & combative partizanship'.[85]

Despite the episodes of rivalry in patronage, William supported many of Shaftesbury's reforms. His views on sabbatarianism, however, became different. Those who could not go to church, he quoted approvingly in the early 1880s, would find the works of the creator in museums, and exercise their intellect rather than risk demoralizing amusements.[86] 'I can't make him out,' his brother-in-law John Tollemache said, perplexed at his religious talk when, 'would you believe it, he goes into the same lobby as the infidels in the House of Commons to vote for the opening of the British Museum and the Picture Galleries on Sunday.'[87] Shaftesbury, chairman of the Lord's Day Observance Society, opposed Sunday opening or music in the Parks.

William's attitude to working-class religion is clear in his missionary work, support of the Americans Dwight Moody and Ira Sankey's revival campaign in England and Scotland in 1873–1875[88], in his response to the Salvation Army, and encouragement of the Church Army at the end of his life. He attended Moody's services at the Royal Opera House and Agricultural Hall and, as we saw, tried to interest Gladstone in the American. He admired Moody's simple graphic language, 'earnestness and self-forgetfulness', and told an audience of nonconformists that with Moody, there was no attempt to address difficulties 'that many learned men have put forward; but he appeals to the hearts of men, he appeals to the moral force, he tells them they have a Father in Heaven'.[89] *The Christian* noted in 1886, 'many remember him during Moody's visits as an earnest helper.'[90] Moody and Sankey's hymns were sung at the first Broadlands conference and William worked to get the Albert Hall available for Moody.[91]

'A thunderstorm is good to clear the air, but it is not good to live always in a thunderstorm,' so William commented on the Salvation Army.[92] He thought the Army was 'good for awaking and breaking up the ground, but can't carry on the education – they should let the Church do that. They are not dogmatic and think little of the Sacraments'. He was concerned about sensationalism, emphasis on actions rather than holiness, and the irreverence of the 'wage earning class'. The uneducated generally lacked will power and were apt to be swayed by comrades, having not thought out principles of individual action.[93] The Prayer Book's Latin or archaic vocabulary was incomprehensible without education, and phraseology such as 'dearly Beloved Brethren' was unattractive. Catherine Booth knew little of the Bible, he noted, evidently after meeting her. Yet the Army suited the tastes of the lower classes, and stimulated self-sacrifice.[94] If his reaction reflects his patrician mindset – the Army presumed to act outside aristocratic guidance – at least William did not reject the Army as Shaftesbury did.[95] He also deplored the assaults on Salvationists for their teetotalism. The Salvationists aimed to make working-class people 'lead pure, honest, sober, and religious lives' and violence towards them represented a struggle between moral and physical force, he told peers in May 1882.[96]

Nevertheless General Booth was welcomed to Broadlands, and William proposed at one Anglican gathering, 'That the action of the Salvation Army deserves the kind and careful consideration of Churchmen,' and welcomed members to his own religious conferences.[97] The Church Army founded in 1882, which diverted Edward Clifford's energies away from art, by contrast brought converts to the established Church, where they took the sacraments, and so William became an early and keen supporter. Its first annual meeting was held at Broadlands.[98] The missionary work that William undertook included preaching at the Victoria Theatre (the Old Vic) and sermons from carts or cottage windows in the New Forest.[99]

Although William later supported efforts, examined below in the context of Broadlands conferences, to cultivate a European Christian community, his initial concern was to combat Catholic *errors*. His hostility to Puseyism and membership of Sir Culling Eardley Smith's Evangelical Alliance reflected this. Samuel Phillips Day, an ex-monk from Youghal who was briefly an anti-Catholic lecturer, dedicated *Life in a Convent* – which deplored the incarceration of 'the blooming maiden and the promising youth' – to William 'with deep respect and as a testimony for numerous favours' in 1848.[100] William was in touch with Johann Czerski of Posen, who had rejected orthodoxy over mixed marriages and clerical celibacy, and established a 'Christian Catholic' church in Germany after excommunication in 1844.[101] The Prussian Lutheran Chevalier Hans Christian von Bunsen asked William to use his influence with Palmerston to gain the release of the anti-Catholic lecturer Giacinto Achilli, arrested in Rome in 1849.[102] When Achilli returned to London he was received by Palmerston and feted by the Evangelical Alliance. William also apparently supported the London Society for the Religious Improvement of Italy and the Italians, after revelations of barbarities committed in Rome were published by Raffaele Cioci.[103] But if these associations and activities indicate a typical English Protestant prejudice, it is worthwhile to note that Shaftesbury in 1856, surveying his brother-in-law's bewildering religious oscillations, wrote 'I have known him within a hair's breadth of dissent, then of Popery.'[104]

The Vatican council ordered by Pius IX declared the doctrine of papal infallibility in 1870, as had been widely anticipated, at the time that the Liberal government was struggling over the Education Bill. It can be imagined that William, like the Tractarian Gladstone, who wrote a best-selling pamphlet, *The Vatican decrees in their bearing on civil allegiance* in November 1874, was appalled at this doctrine. If he supported Sir William Harcourt's speech calling for toleration of Catholics, in December 1874,[105] he also contacted critics of the pope's temporal power. The Cowper-Temples, as we have seen, supported the 'reformed Catholic' movement in France, providing hospitality to the former Carmelite Père Hyacinthe (Charles Loyson) and an entrée into British society during Loyson's London lectures. William introduced Loyson to Gladstone.[106] In 1879 he hoped, so he told Gladstone, that a few strong-minded French Catholics might appear, devout and zealous enough to spurn the 'powerful self-asserting mystical Babylon of Ultramontanism', and go into the wilderness to listen to the solitary voice that was seeking an echo in the conscience of a worldly Church.[107] He hoped that Gladstone, interested in the 'Reunion' conferences between members of the 'Old Catholic' church, Eastern Orthodox and Anglicans in Bonn in 1874 and 1875,[108] would support fund-raising for a church and headquarters for the Gallican church, to make it permanent.[109] He also had contact with 'Old Catholics' in Italy.[110]

In 1874 the Liberal statesman and Christian Socialist Lord Ripon (formerly Lord Goderich) converted to Catholicism. William told him 'how much I admire and respect you for the self sacrificing spirit in which you are striving to follow the call of the Master and to do what appears to you to be his Work.' He sympathized with Ripon's determination but not his decision, because like other Whigs William supported the removal of Catholic civil disabilities but saw the Catholic Church as a barrier to religious progress. He rejected an intermediatory agency in the form of church and priests, seeing the role of the priesthood as 'witnesses to lead us to Christ and not exclusive Channels through which we are to receive grace indirectly'. This was written when he was convinced that Jesus was 'coming closer and closer to the hearts and souls of those who surrender themselves to him in entire consecration'.[111]

Though he had been aware of Catholic Apostolic ritual, William was no supporter of the independently developed (and Tractarian-inspired) ritualism in Anglicanism. The 1860s–1870s saw a number of prominent controversies where the ecclesiastical Court of Arches was opposed by the Judicial Committee of the Privy Council (containing laymen and bishops), already offending many by overturning judgements about heresy, angering others in condemning rituals as alien to the Anglican reformed Church.[112] William was perhaps influenced by Shaftesbury, a staunch anti-ritualist; at any rate he supported the 'putting down of Ritualism' in the Public Worship Regulation bill which Archbishop Tait had intended to use against ritualist extremists threatening the Protestantism of the established Church in 1874, and supported Tait by introducing a bill with Russell Gurney to provide for a salary for Lord Penzance as judge under the Public Worship Regulation Act.[113] But Georgina befriended the ritualist George Wilkinson, later Bishop of Truro.

Georgina's religiosity was manifested early. She was 'much addicted to hospitals' and her broad views, expressed in such actions as giving rosaries to Catholic patients, agitated her elders.[114] Shaftesbury disapproved of her 'heretical views' and feared her influence on William. Palmerston diagnosed her as a likely convert to Catholicism (she would have been a notable addition to the converts, as the premier's daughter-in-law, from the mid-1850s); she thought Newman's *Grammar of Assent* a 'wonderful book', in 1871, and there was an attempt to convert her in her dotage, as we shall see.[115] Kim Reynolds cited her 'highly coloured religious correspondence' with Adine Beauvale in examining generational trends in religiosity. The contrast of Georgina and her sister-in-law Emily with Lady Palmerston's response to enthusiasm is clear.[116] Tending sick acquaintances was a recurrent activity, when Emelia Gurney contracted smallpox in 1877 Georgina immediately offered to nurse her. If this 'tender sympathy for all who are in trouble' had morbid elements she was also inspired by the faith-sustained deaths of relations that figure prominently in her *Memorials*, a volume for private and family readership.[117]

Unfairly, John Bradley, the editor of the Ruskin/Cowper-Temple correspondence distinguishes between what he called her sanctimony and William's 'more genuine kind' of Christianity.[118] There are more just contrasts to make: her brother contrasted William's placidity and her 'effervescence of temper', her 'vehement indignation' against cruelty and dislike of ill-natured gossip.[119] She made her own distinction when she described herself as 'only a seeker after truth, without the confidence and clear vision' of her husband.[120]

She shared an interest in the theology of F.D. Maurice and German rationalism with her friend Julia Tomkinson of Dorfold Hall in the 1850s, as we have seen.[121] Since the Broadlands papers have left no discussion by Georgina of Maurice's influence on her, it is impossible to be certain what she drew from Maurice's sermons and other publications but these proved influential for a number of prominent female reformers from Octavia Hill to Mrs Nassau Senior. The philanthropic endeavours which preoccupied Georgina, within her wider family and in public, were certainly not discouraged by Maurice's stress on Christian self-sacrifice and sympathy for fellow humanity.[122]

Through Emelia Gurney, Georgina knew Thomas Erskine of Linlathen, an influence on both Maurice and George MacDonald. Erskine, a Scottish Episcopalian, believed in a divine love available for propitiating the sins of all mankind.[123] She surprised Thomas Carlyle with this acquaintance when she met him in 1862: 'there is not I believe a better & truer man left upon earth than Thos Erskine,' he said, 'Faith has well nigh died out of Scotland. In my youth there were some fit to be named with Cromwell who read their bibles & believed them. Now you find nothing but a set of dogmatical tyrannical hypocrites.'[124]

Georgina received comfort during religious anxieties in the 1850s, from the Irish Protestant Joseph Baylee, introduced to the Cowpers by the Duke of Marlborough. He tried to alleviate her sense of guilt. 'I often think over our conversations,' he wrote in April 1850, 'and do not forget to pray for what I know you need. I am greatly indebted to them for having led me to reflect more fully than ever upon the nature of evidence.'[125] He told her that it was a pleasure to find her mind 'so accordant with mine upon so many subjects which belong to our highest & holiest nature in its best refinement': religious perplexities allowed middle-class clergymen to develop intimacies (epistolary or otherwise) with aristocratic women.[126]

If childhood friends expressed concerns at her religious doubts before marriage [127] and Baylee combated anxieties in the 1850s, these never dissipated. But mystical interests and willingness to explore spiritualism and esoteric religions provided absorbing ways of truth-seeking and also accorded with William's disposition. Georgina's interest in mysticism was enduring: in the early years of marriage, if not before, she read the mystic Jacob Boehme, for Julia Tomkinson referred to 'your Behmen' in correspondence.[128] Later she studied the 'sacred socialist' and vegetarian, James Pierrepoint Greaves, who had a following of moral and social reformers in the 1830s. A fellow student discussed Greaves' philosophy relating the fall of man to marriage, by which Greaves had meant sex, and feared misapprehension when teaching this philosophy to a mixed audience, as it seemed like 'giving gunpowder to little children'.[129] Anne Judith Penny, a scholar of mysticism, also promoted Greaves and Boehme with Georgina. The Cowper-Temples had the opportunity of supporting publication of a manuscript completed by a disciple, William Oldham, once 'Pater' of the Greavesian community near the Tollemache mansion of Ham House in Richmond. Oldham, a friend of Anna Maria Watts, was encouraged by William's offer of financial assistance. Though William was released from the commitment when he did not sympathize with the philosophy, the encouragement had stimulated Oldham, his wife and the Wattses, to work on the proofs of *Triune-life: divine and human*, which Georgina read when it appeared in 1880.[130]

Georgina's interest in mysticism explains her friendship with Lydia Brewster Macpherson, who published (without family support) works influenced by Erskine, Macleod Campbell and theists, her *Gifts for Men* exciting discussion 'among profounder thinkers in religious circles'. 'My long Home is in the Scriptures. They are the first and the last of my life,' she declared in *The Son of the Blessed*. Brewster Macpherson gave 'wonderful Spiritual inspirations (we think) from the Bible – thro' which she has received all her teachings', Georgina told Frederic Myers, who did not take to the woman.[131] Another interested in Boehme and Greaves was James Farquhar, the 'Philosophe Inconnu', a Scotsman who spent most of his life in England, collecting a loyal following of the 'brightest and most intellectual'. For Georgina he was 'our constant friend and teacher'.[132] His works included *Hamartia*, on the nature of evil, *The Gospel of Divine Humanity* – lauded by Roden Noel in 1884 – and an essay in the Christo-Theosophical Society's *Things to Come* (1892) alongside other essays 'towards a fuller apprehension of the Christian Idea' by the Cowper-Temples' acquaintances Rowland Corbet, C.C. Massey and Elizabeth Blackwell.[133] Another close mystical friend was John Pulsford, based in the 1870s-1880s in Edinburgh, author of the well-regarded devotional *Quiet Hours*, and more opaquely metaphysical, Swedenborgian-influenced works, who shared their admiration for Thomas Lake Harris and perceived the Second Coming.[134] He came to the religious conferences at Broadlands, and was once touched to find William appear with dressing gown, shirt, slippers and hairbrush to lend him.[135] Though like Farquhar he was hardly a well-known name for contemporaries he had his admirers, one classing him with George MacDonald as *the* nineteenth-century 'Seers' for restoring a religion of naturalness and simplicity. Basil Wilberforce treated Pulsford as part of his 'theological forwards' school of thought, and as with the Cowper-Temples' intimate friendship with Basil, their support for Pulsford, Farquhar, Macpherson and Corbet expressed their desire to simultaneously broaden and deepen faith.[136]

The Cowper-Temples were interested in theosophy, but acquaintance with Madame Blavatsky of the Theosophical Society did not lead them to accept her oriental-garbed occultism.[137] Georgina was drawn instead to Anna Kingsford, perhaps because of her zoophilia, but also because of the Christian nature of her Hermetic Society (founded in 1884). Many had been diverted from the 'splendid wealth and Light of Christianity to follow strange teachers whom we do not know and can never identify', Anna wrote, seeking the Cowper-Temples' financial support for the publication of translations of Judaeo-Christian mysticism including kabbalist texts. She invited them to Hermetic Society meetings.[138] Georgina studied Kingsford's *Perfect Way*, and *Woman Clothed with the Sun*.[139] A rare letter survives in the Broadlands papers from Kingsford's collaborator Edward Maitland on the 'Adonai' and future visions.[140]

Georgina's quest for religious comfort was reinforced by her mother's death, which stimulated her spiritualism. We have seen how extensive this activity became and how it was sustained for the rest of her life. Georgina was not alone in seeing it as offering support for the idea of life after death and the belief in the connection of earthly life to the spiritual, as a confirmation of scripture (and supported by scripture).[141] Spiritualism did not furnish insights of a 'higher kind' but showed there was 'something' and thus saved her from 'absolute infidelity'.[142] Not all acquaintances thought that spiritualism was wholesome: her sister-in-law Fanny Jocelyn heard it was evil and abandoned it and Maurice sermonized them on falling into superstition, but Georgina argued that the strange phenomena, low as they were, helped much to 'confirm our feeble Faith in the Divine Spiritualism of the Bible'.[143] Other female relations still dabbled in spiritualism too; Mummy de Burgh received messages from sister Elizabeth, and Marguerite Tollemache sent excited reports.[144] Friends such as the preacher Newman Hall provided anecdotes endorsing spiritualism.[145] Georgina's sister-in-law Jessie patronized leading mediums in London with their mutual acquaintance Lady Caithness. Van Akin Burd ably recounts Georgina's attempt to interest John Ruskin in spiritualism.

The Cowper-Temples came to know leading British, American and European spiritualists. Georgina knew that table moving, automatic writing and other manifestations might be fraudulent rather than 'some unknown natural phenomenon' or 'external Spiritual agency'. The Cowper-Temples knew that spiritualism sometimes involved people of dubious morality, such as Daniel Home, whose attempt to marry a wealthy woman created scandal, and who tried to cultivate the Cowper-Temples again after this controversy.[146] Often Georgina was bewildered and her memoirs are notably defensive about experiences which were 'so utterly disappointing'.[147] These included a 'dreadful performance, horrible if imposture – almost still more horrible if reality' at a séance at Mrs Gregory's, in February 1874.[148] Mrs Gregory admitted she was inclined 'sometimes to give up séances. Spirits often of such a low character but for the sake of convincing Materialists perseveres'.[149] 'Still,' as Georgina had earlier written, '*Truth* at any price!'[150]

Her husband, for her sake, became involved. William's notes on lectures and séances reveal spiritual and secular anxieties as refracted by mediums. His concern with the efficacy of prayer, for himself and the departed, is clear. Spirits exhorted rest and adjustments of diet or work habits and brought advice on legislation and estate management.[151] For William, spiritualism was a Christian activity involving guardian angels and God's continuing revelation to man during a materialistic age, and reinforced a sense of duty. Spiritualism encouraged his sense that the world was merely a phase leading to a 'higher life'. As Georgina affirmed, he had no difficulty believing in a spiritual 'great cloud of witness encircling the world'.[152] Séances with the young and sickly Julia Leaf seemed to indicate a significant role for William, perhaps in lieu of a major political career?[153] In February 1877, a spirit in white robes revealed William was chosen 'for the work of bringing together the persons who are scattered about and who might join together', the Messenger being sent from an angelic society with which William was connected, which was working in preparation for the Lord's coming.[154]

William's spiritualism did not wane but was not publicized in most of his obituaries.[155] Yet the Cowper-Temples' spiritualism was well known in Anglo-American spiritualist circles, and through open discussion acquaintances knew about these interests, thus the Liberal man of letters John Morley, a guest at Broadlands, sent them Alfred Russel Wallace's essay on spiritualism in 1874.[156] Georgina gave public support for later organized psychical research and befriended the poet and psychical researcher Frederic Myers, whose daughter Silvia was named in her honour, as she lived 'amidst her stately trees and on the edge of the great forest'.[157] The Cowper-Temples introduced Myers to Edmund Gurney, and one acquaintance even thought the Psychical Research Society was conceived in their home.[158]

The Cowper-Temples were further associated with the religious unorthodox through their links with utopian sectarianism. The American 'theosocialist' Thomas Lake Harris was the most significant in this respect, exerting a powerful force on William to 'enter into the New Earthly Life', which would, however, necessitate putting aside all the ties of the old earthly life. 'You must choose between our world,' Harris told him in the mid-1870s, 'where all is being made new, or the one where all is old.'[159] Harris, born in Buckinghamshire but raised in New York, had returned to lecture in England in 1859 and though Georgina recalled making his acquaintance in 1867 it is possible the Cowper-Temples knew about this charismatic and complex man from a lecture in 1860. They studied his writings, corresponded with him and disciples such as Laurence Oliphant, and preserved their conversations with Harris whom they met on his English visits.[160] They gave funds to him in the 1870s.

A community to embody Harris's ideas was formed in New York at Brocton, by Lake Erie. It attracted wealthy American ladies, and, as we have seen, Japanese recruits via Laurence Oliphant. Though one of Georgina's friends told her of the lack of perfection there, after staying there,[161] Harris hoped the couple would join the community. The hope seemed likely to be fulfilled, for no one attracted William more than Harris, according to Georgina's memoirs. Harris wooed them during a European tour at the time of the Franco-Prussian war. He wrote directly rather than use a follower, to persuade them that Truth and the final days unfolded in the community established at Santa Rosa in California.[162] Purporting to be concerned at the exhaustion he saw in William, which he linked to the 'dead magnetisms and … chilly atmosphere of the old world', he offered to build a cottage for them with ponies and woodland for Lowly (Georgina: her name derived from 'the little fay Lowly – little lowly to remind her to be tender and gentle – at her place at the Master's feet').[163] Lowly asked Harris if the Lord was a reality; as real as the swans on the Test and their drawing-room pictures, came Harris's reply, with the invitation to write whenever it would do her good.[164]

Georgina later recalled Harris 'particularly interested us by his belief that the kingdom of Christ was soon to be set upon the earth and that we might all help in its unfolding'.[165] William told Georgina that Harris expected the Coming of the Lord would be in the hearts of men as self-sacrifice, even if that was not obviously religious but as patriotism or political reformation.[166] If they learned later of the community's bizarre, cruel and sexually-dissident habits, 'conjugial relations' *were* discussed by followers of the New Life with them: 'sex is eternal. Angels live as 2 in one – They delight in conjugial unions – The Devils delight in Polygamy.'[167] The Cowper-Temples were perplexed by letters from Brocton, received accounts from Emelia Gurney who visited Harris in 1872, and further insight from Hannah Smith when she visited.[168]

In 1881, writing to Harris's follower Edward Berridge, William set out his differences. He revered and loved Harris and learnt much from him. Harris was a marvellous seer but his visions concerned the natural sphere. William was called towards the celestial sphere and was convinced the risen Lord was 'drawing us into direct personal relationship with His precious glorious Being and does not require us to look out for intermediate agencies whether of Pivotal men and women who are undergoing a transformation, in lieu of the death, of the material body'. So his duty was to devote his very limited faculties and time to 'the Conscious assimilation of what has been given to us in the New Testament – and then to prepare in Spirit rather than in body for the new second advent'.[169]

We have seen the friendship which they developed with the English supporter of Harris, the brilliant writer Laurence Oliphant who had described the Cowper-Temples to his American associates as 'so true and loving and faithful'. Georgina defended Alice le Strange, Oliphant's wife-to-be, against Harris's accusations, in 1882.[170] When the Oliphants abandoned Harris they turned to a utopian project in the Holy Land, where Laurence died shortly after visiting Broadlands.[171] Through the disillusioned Oliphants and critiques produced by such acquaintances as Jukes and Hannah Smith, the Cowper-Temples lost their enthusiasm for Harris.[172] Not surprising then, that in her memoirs Georgina included the qualification that Harris when they had first met was '*at that time* a devoted servant of Christ'.[173]

Another sect with which William and Georgina became involved was the New Forest Shakers. Georgina was entranced by one Shaker, Isaac Batho, who told them Mother Girling's beliefs at Christmas in 1874 and struck Georgina as 'very simple, humble & heavenly minded' with a 'beautiful heavenly face'.[174] But the Cowper-Temples were motivated by sympathy for the sect's predicament rather than their beliefs, which they thought wrong or extravagant.[175] When they learned of Girling's death despite her belief in immortality, Georgina wrote 'alas! For vain hope no answer to her passionate language.'[176]

Given the Cowper-Temples' illustrious companions in séances it would be wrong to see their aristocratic spiritualism as unusual. But what should one make of their support for religious 'eccentrics'? Lionel Tollemache suggested this was 'excessive credulity', with spiritualism followed by 'crystal-reading, palmistry, the Great Pyramid and other follies'.[177] He implied William's credulity was a feminine aspect shared with 'all very charming men and nearly all saints'.[178] It is true that William had investigated crystal gazing and the famous Zadkiel (the astrologer Captain R.J. Morrison RN) sent him the report of the use of a crystal to divine the fate of the missing explorer Sir John Franklin in October 1850, though he was told Zadkiel's predictions were 'One of the least creditable exhibitions of the present day'.[179] But there is no sign that the Cowper-Temples entertained Pyramid or flat-earth delusions. And Georgina seemed to have limits, in scepticism about the Baconian theory of Shakespeare, 'Of course impossible but it shows how much proof there may be of a falsehood,' adding later, 'it is almost horrible to see how easy it is to prove a lie.'[180]

Eulogists called William a 'saint' but as the epithet was used to mean a sanctimonious Evangelical (inquiring of acquaintances if they were saved), Grenville Fletcher explained in 1862 that he was 'nothing of the sort; those who intimately know him will testify that he *is* utterly free from sanctimonious notions of intolerance, and that his Christianity is as pure as the light of truth itself, which is his constant guide'.[181] Purity and an angelic temperament seemed to be Georgina's attributes according to so many people who met her.

FIGURE 15. South front of Broadlands, with orangery. From *Mount Temple Memorials*. By courtesy of the Trustees of the Broadlands Archives.

The major expression of the Cowper-Temples' saintliness and of their 'notions of tolerance, and pursuit of the light of the truth', was the conferences held almost yearly from 1874-1888.[182] They became famous as a 'type of the times'.[183] If little reported in the mainstream press, they were noted in Evangelical and other religious journals and recorded in privately printed accounts for participants.[184] The printed suggestions for the 1875 conference are evocative:

    1. Come in a prayerful receptive spirit, waiting on the Lord Himself, for teaching and blessing.

2. Heartily renounce all evil, and consecrate yourself afresh to the service of the Divine Master.
3. Lay aside for the time, as far as possible, all worldly thoughts and occupations.
4. Avoid all conversation that may divert your mind from the object of the meeting. Avoid particularly all controversy. If any differ with you, pray with them.
5. Take time for private prayer and meditation, live and dress simply, and retire to rest early.[185]

A grateful participant, Théodore Monod praised 'days of beauty and of balm! | Green pastures – quiet waters – table spread – | Goodness and mercy – all that David said | Stood forth, a living Psalm.'[186] And one key figure in their creation, Robert Pearsall Smith, said in 1874 that it was sweet to think that Broadlands, 'whence once the history of the *world* was partly made, may again, be the place where the history of Christ's *church* may be modified to a higher and purer course'.[187]

They represented the quickening or deepening of British religion in the 1870s, reflecting the new spirituality of the 'holiness' or 'higher life' movement influenced by American developments.[188] Its British promoters believed the holiness revival, a 'more definite, all-embracing consecration to the Lord', could be non-denominational, though it was principally Protestant. In the words of the prospectus to one of its periodicals, it would 'rather vitalize to Christians in the various Churches their own highest standard of faith and service'. But the 'Higher Life' term confused onlookers. For believers, a remarkable time opened up with 'deep longings for entire consecration of life and unbroken trust for victory over sin', and a 'hunger and thirst for practical holiness', rather than carnal or legal religion. By faith rather than by mere works, they could be holier. Critics, however, rejected the 'assertion of the possibility of an unsinning life and of absolute perfection'.[189]

There had been religious conferences before. The undenominational Mildmay Park conferences which William attended had been established in north London by Canon William Pennefather, one-time assistant curate at Captain Trotter's church at Barnet, in June 1856, and carried on after his death by Stevenson Arthur Blackwood with Lord Radstock and others. But the Broadlands conference followed on more directly from the holiness revival across the Atlantic and the close relationship which developed between the Cowper-Temples and Smiths. The immediate origins are unclear, or rather accounts differ. One account suggests they began in conversation between the Cowper-Temples and Smiths, when William (or perhaps Georgina, the record is not consistent), suggested that Broadlands could host the meetings she had enthused about.[190] For

Hannah had told them of the American 'holiness meetings' where Christians of various denominations camped out in the forests. Another account suggests the meetings also met the wishes of a group of young university men, who had found blessing in some meetings for consecration, at Cambridge, for a few days of 'prayer and meditation on Christian life, its communion with God and its victory over sin'.[191] William said: 'My place is at your service if you will accept it.'

'To some,' wrote the holiness organ *The Christian's Pathway of Power*, 'have been given wonderful ingatherings such as have been rarely known since apostolic times.'[192] These wonders were manifested in six days in July 1874 by the first Broadlands conference, designed to deepen the work of sanctification through the reading of scripture, short addresses, prayer and discussion of personal experience of grace.[193] The hundred guests included the Smiths, George MacDonald, Andrew Jukes, Edward Clifford and his sisters, Catherine Marsh, the Cowper-Temples' old friend Lady Gainsborough, and the young Lilias Trotter, amateur artist and future missionary.[194] Jukes was 'overcome by the intensity of his realization of the Christian love through the hearts of all present' at the final meeting.[195] The high churchman George Wilkinson, 'lodestar of devout Belgravia', and notable for lambasting sinful Society (from the church where the Cowper-Temples had been married; he became Bishop of Truro and then Primus of the Scottish Episcopal Church), attended. Apprehensive of the 'devotional assembly', he found it 'very blessed' and thought 'every one in the house seemed to live in the same spiritual atmosphere. The servants spoke quite simply to us of the service the night before.'[196]

Other participants included Stevenson Blackwood – friend of Shaftesbury, John Trotter and Catherine Marsh – who confessed to having a narrower platform than William and disputed William's view about the compatibility of spiritualism with Christianity.[197] We shall see that this was an unbridgeable difference, but at the time Blackwood said the place was such a 'happy Christian atmosphere ... all easy, happy, and quiet ... love reigning, and I trust real good out of it all'.[198] A group of French pastors invited by the Smiths included Théodore Monod of the Église Reformée de Paris and Professor St Hilaire of the Sorbonne; at Broadlands they met in Christian amity with 'German brethren' despite the recent war.[199]

Many guests stayed at Broadlands, others were boarded in Romsey. Services were held under the beeches, in the Orangery (which could accommodate two hundred and fifty) and dining room. The meeting was commemorated by Clifford's painting, with a weak-looking William beside Hannah while Georgina stood modestly off centre in the background clasping a book. 'It was only earth,' Clifford recalled, 'however at its very best. Green trees, a flowing river, soft grass & God's saints walking about there talking of Him & dwelling in love.'[200] William told Lady Ashburton, who had left before it had ended, that the chief feature of the conference was that the Smiths and others 'appeared before our eyes as having in them a power of the spiritual life and a sense of the presence of the Divine Master – It was a fact not merely a belief or a theory or an opinion, but a reality – and the phrase – the realization of the higher Christian Life conveys as well as any other the purpose and result of the meetings'.[201] He sent her Jukes' comment about 'something of Pentecost' there.[202]

After such giddy spiritual heights, there was to come, almost inevitably, a crash. But for the moment, the hopes raised in Hampshire were expressed elsewhere. Conferences followed at Oxford, at Sir Thomas Beauchamp's house in Norfolk, and elsewhere. Various annual religious conventions had already developed in the wake of Mildmay in the 1860s and though it was not anticipated that Broadlands meetings would be annual, 'so many circumstances of interest arose', this happened.[203]

FIGURE 16. *The Broadlands Conference, July 1874*, by Edward Clifford.
By courtesy of the Church Army.

The holiness movement allowed Anglo-American reformers to missionize continental Europe with a sense of their special gift or privilege of vitalized faith, in contrast to what they detected as the 'present discouraged, low condition, of evangelical faith over a large portion of the Continent'. The land of Luther was infected by rationalism, Switzerland lacked 'free-hearted, joyous faith' and Holland lacked 'vital piety'.[204]

Distribution of literature was one response. William gave his support to a continental fund designed to support the spread of Evangelicalism, which aimed to raise the £4000 deemed essential for producing periodicals, tracts and books. Funds were to be collected to support Basle in Berlin, and Monod in Paris (who reported 'Paris has been a small Broadlands', in late 1874[205]), and William was announced in the *Christian's Pathway of Power* as the honorary treasurer of the committee of arrangements for Robert Pearsall Smith's meetings in September 1874.[206]

Blackwood's colleague, the retired Admiral Edmund Gardiner Fishbourne (friend of Pennefather and Shaftesbury), arranged the funding of copies of Hannah Smith's *Frank. The Record of a Happy Life* (a memoir of her dead son).[207] William received letters from Evangelicals such as Paul Gobat of Bale, son of the Protestant bishop of Jerusalem and a publisher of religious books who planned a version of *Pathway* entitled *Des Christes Glaubensweg*.[208] This was translated by Carl Rappard, Gobat's brother-in-law, who had attended the Oxford meeting in 1874.[209] But in late 1874 William was asked to resign from the committee by Fishbourne and Blackwood because of his spiritualism and deviation from strict Evangelicalism.[210] Georgina was outraged and wanted to tell them she was 'Spiritualist, an universalist & compendium of all the heresies,' but William – as ever – was calm.[211]

Despite this, the next year was a propitious time for the conference to be repeated. The American Evangelist Moody was in Britain, and William hoped Gladstone would attend Moody's meetings and meet his 'great friend' Pearsall Smith, whose 'simplicity and spiritual insight', he felt sure Gladstone would find interesting.[212] Pearsall Smith had become 'the instrument of a religious movement among the Lutheran clergy and laity in Berlin and some other German towns parallel in many respects to Moody in London'. 'It seems,' William went on, 'as if he had a special mission to impart life into the dry doctrinal Evangelicals and to point to the way in which they make progress.'[213]

In early June William wrote to Gladstone from a large conference in Brighton where Hannah Smith led daily meetings of ladies and evening meetings were addressed by the Earls of Cavan and Kintore, Lord Radstock, Arthur Stevenson Blackwood (who thought it 'very like a Mildmay Conference from faces one sees'[214]) and Henry Varley. Present were some seventy German and Swiss pastors, 'deeply impressed with the reality of this higher spiritual life'. William said he intended to invite German and Dutch Pietists interested in Pearsall Smith's teachings on 'Sanctification of Faith and a life of Trust in Divine Guidance' to Broadlands for a Protestant retreat, including Bülow the Undersecretary of State for Foreign Affairs at Berlin, some professors at Bonn and leading men at the Hague.[215] France had been defeated by Prussia and her allies in 1870 and as *Evangelical Christendom* reported, German pastors made symbolic peace with their French brethren by removing military badges and embracing them after Communion. Missionary funds were raised.[216] The Smiths planned a tour of northern towns and organized an itinerary as far as Kendal.

But in late 1875 scandal touched the movement when a young lady told Blackwood that Robert Pearsall Smith had molested her at Brighton under the guise of offering a spiritual experience, the possession of the whole being (physical and spiritual) by Christ. The idea of the 'Baptism of the Holy Spirit' was to stir emotions in an innocent way through the pressure of the hand or an arm about the waist. Robert claimed to be actuated by feelings 'like a father, utterly removed from any possibility of wrong thoughts or feelings'. According to Hannah, he had imbibed the doctrine partly through Emelia Gurney and the practice of the Fellowship of the New Life at Brocton. Hannah came to see it as a satanic delusion but held that her husband had not consciously sinned.[217]

The Smiths left England and advertisements for their works were dropped from the papers where they had previously appeared. Rumours spread into the mainstream national and provincial press. The *Banner of Holiness*'s assertion that Robert had not been guilty of 'real immorality', was not accepted, one allusion being made to 'the morality of Utah and its prophets' being practised under the guise of Moody and Sankey. The affair outraged many of the Smiths' associates, and Blackwood made a damaging statement in *The Record* in January.[218] But the Cowper-Temples remained in friendly contact with them (a note in March 1876 recorded William's 'utter desolation', but 'I've taken my refuge in the fortress of the will of God'[219]). Hannah identified 'divine sympathy' resulting from her friends' 'own inward difficulties'.[220] Robert came to appreciate William's 'Catholic spiritual life' and recognize how restricted were his own views.[221]

Edward Clifford explained Robert's absence from the second conference as a consequence of a breakdown and Miss Marsh, already antagonistic after Hannah's treatment of notes made at the Oxford meeting of 1874, used illness as a pretext to stay away but her forswearing of 'Perfectionism' reached the press.[222] Clifford said people lacked confidence in the things they had believed in those 'celestial days last July'. The conference began unpromisingly in the rain and Emelia Gurney thought that even Juliet, who had flitted about in 1874, 'had lost a little of the early morning song, and its dance of joy'.[223] There was no longer the Smiths' triumphalism, which critics such as Charles Spurgeon had, in the aftermath of the scandal, condemned as boastful holiness. Clifford presented this second gathering as an advance on the dream that the 'new man' would be attained immediately, a 'graver and even a sadder tune' came from George Body (who led the instruction), Andrew Jukes and Théodore Monod. Clifford learnt the 'depth of corruption and sin that God is saving us from and something of how patiently and lovingly He does it'.[224]

The third conference was notable for George MacDonald's address, 'such an outburst of heart in glowing thrilling utterance' and 'the sort of inspiration that is manifested in dramatic Poets,' William thought.[225] Lord Radstock, the prominent Evangelical encountered during Georgina's stay in Paris in 1867, who had lost 'caste' by such actions as distribution of religious tracts in Rotten Row, flirtation with Plymouth Brethrenism and healing by prayer, attended the fourth conference.[226] A turning point, it led him toward William's espousal of the 'essential unity underlying all the divergencies of other branches of the Church Catholic'. Radstock gave an address on Ephesians iv.4, 'There is one body, and one Spirit.'[227] He told William, 'I feel there is much in yourself wh I seek to imitate but I fear not very successfully.'[228]

Eli and Mary C. Johnson of Brooklyn, connections of the Russell Gurneys, came to the fifth conference and enthused about the grandeur combined with Christlike simplicity, the world shut out to allow thoughts entirely on God, 'We had to take no thought about *anything*,' Mary said.[229] The German Protestants Gerhard von Niebuhr and Pastor Strube were invited.[230] The Evangelical temperance worker Frederick Charrington made notes and his intimate friend the missionary Ion Keith-Falconer, son of the Earl of Kintore, sent George Body's addresses to the printers.[231] The most striking guest in 1879 was the African-American missionary Amanda Smith, a protégé of the Johnsons who had impressed Evan Hopkins at Keswick in the Lake District (where holiness conventions had recently begun) the year before. She 'kept up the fire, and the hallowed influence was so great, that one appeared to feel like Paul, "whether in the body, or out of the body. I cannot tell".'[232] McDougall of Winchester hoped to attend to 'shew how true Churchmen may lead the way'.[233]

In 1882 the conference shifted to Southampton, a move repeated in 1883 and also 1884 because of Georgina's illness.[234] In 1886 Anna Kingsford attended and recorded 'spiritual things' as the sole topic whether 'wandering through the garden, or sitting on the sunlit lawns, or pacing the terraces under the beautiful stars at night'.[235] Guests at the penultimate conference – on 'love, faith and life' – included the actor Norman Forbes-Robertson (son of a friend of George MacDonald) and the Cowper-Temples' friend, the American singer Antoinette Stirling. Clifford thought the conference 'very, very good'.[236] The holiness movement's aristocratic supporters were still represented at the final conference in 1888, with titled friends or relations joining old participants such as Basil Wilberforce, Rowland Corbet, Andrew

Jukes, the MacDonalds and Radstock, and the newcomers Father Stanton (an Anglican ritualist), Newman Hall, and Professor Von Bergen and Hulda Beamish from Sweden.[237] The meetings considered, 'How are Christians to open themselves to the reception of the inflowing of the powers of the holy Ghost?'; 'How are individual Christians to manifest their union with Christ' and 'How is the Church to manifest in its representations as the Temple of God the mystical body of which Christ is the Head and as his Bride the Lamb's Wife?' Hannah wrote after William's death that he 'seemed to soar right above all earthly limitations into the heavenly places in Christ Jesus, where all differing things are harmonized in the vision of the love of God'. Clifford said Georgina was revitalized when MacDonald spoke, 'every line went out of her face, she had a heavenly smile and looked ideal in grace and strength and youth'.[238]

The paperwork generated by preparations for the conference and by thankful participants keen to send their testimonies, survives in a scattered mass of material in the Broadlands Archives.[239] The Cowper-Temples 'invited a large number of friends and acquaintances, male and female, who had this much in common – that they were interested in religious enquiry – and nothing more'.[240] Participants spanned the Anglican spectrum, old and new Nonconformity, native Catholics and continental clergymen. Guests were selected by consultation, thus Edward Clifford suggested young men in metropolitan mission work such as Tom Varley.[241] A few weeks before the conference, a syllabus of subjects for consideration circulated. Broadlands might fill to the attics, with other conference guests lodged in the Old White Horse and other hotels in Romsey. There was early morning celebration in Romsey Abbey but those who preferred non-sacramental religion could make domestic devotions. Family prayers and expositions followed breakfast. At one conference in fine weather, the company assembled at eleven in the beech grove where a rostrum and seats were arranged. William presided 'with infinite grace and devoutness'. The debate was 'animated, amiable and desultory ... we went on debating till teatime'. In the evening there was a mission-service in the park, and the day ended with family prayers and more expositions.[242]

Théodore Monod described their hostess as 'the queenly, gentle-hearted dame'; H.B. Macartney described her as throwing 'the charm of high culture and exceeding kindliness around the circle which her husband summons'.[243] But other women played public roles, as speakers from the start, following a practice developed at Mildmay from 1862, where there were ladies' meetings. Hannah Smith was followed by other women at later conferences. Fittingly the *Christian's Pathway of Power* had reviewed Margaret Gordon's *Chief Women; or Higher Life in High Places*, which asserted the duty of rich women to engage in Christian work.[244] In 1878

Gordon's sister-in-law Lydia Brewster Macpherson spoke incomprehensibly about Psalm 24 for two hours according to one account, and the Quaker Evangelical Sarah Smiley, who had stimulated controversy as a female preacher in Brooklyn in 1872, spoke in the Prayer Room on 'the types in the Tabernacle'.[245] In 1879 there were addresses from Elizabeth Baxter and Amanda Smith. Amanda, William told Gladstone, 'helped me to understand how primitive races are led to the worship of the Elements'.[246] The novelist Charlotte Yonge was invited. The American Amelia Quinton, behind the Woman's National Indian Association, attended in 1888.[247] Not everyone approved of female speakers, for as a woman participant said, 'one of those Germans felt offence in a woman speaking.'[248]

FIGURE 17. Lady Mount Temple clasps a book beside Edward Clifford while Emily Ford gazes at Lord Mount Temple, from an original print held by the Moody Museum within Romsey Heritage Centre, by courtesy of King John's House and Tudor Cottage Trust Ltd.

Although they did not monopolize arrangements, the Cowper-Temples' role in creating a 'delightful home feeling' regardless of class, sect, or race (the Cowper-Temples embraced and escorted to dinner Amanda Smith in 1879) was crucial. Some saw it as 'adventurous hospitality' given this diversity.[249] The beautiful setting, like the similar Keswick conferences, created a 'foretaste of heaven'. Quarto volumes on the hall table recorded participants, printed reports, testimonies and poems, including Monod's famous 'The Altered Motto'.[250] The Cowper-Temples were immersed in prayers, meetings and lectures. William delivered 'intensely real' and 'trustful, reverent, soul-lifting prayers' and he helped maintain cordiality between the various groups. His still graceful figure appeared in the crowd of guests more like a servant than lord of the manor, so one writer reported; his eyes were often half-closed 'in a fashion,' George Russell recalled, 'which gave an expression of quaint fun to his face.'[251] In his 'natural element', the 'mainspring, their very heart', he planned the programme, counselled participants and in writing about them, spoke of '*My* Conference'.[252]

Friends bestowed the epithet of 'Uniter' on William, in recognition of a commitment to Christian brotherly love across denominations, which he had manifested since he had joined the London City Mission in the late 1830s. For him, the early Broadlands conferences aimed at a 'union of all sorts of Denominations who concurred in Evangelical opinions'.[253] This became a desire 'to try if the same blessed feeling of loving harmony could not be found in an union of Evangelical with others who are not included under the Denomination of Evangelical'. This had been Robert Pearsall Smith's suggestion, and William saw similar desire for union in the Moody and Sankey meetings. Anyone who saw the signs of the times, he said, must perceive that if the Church of Christ earnestly sought it, a Baptism of the Holy Spirit might be received. A barrier was jealousy between bodies that 'really intensely loved Christ', but felt unable to love other bands of His disciples. That atmosphere of holy and unselfish love which allowed God's blessings might emerge if 'we could join together men of different schools of thought and of different theological training, provided only that they were all filled with the same desire for entire consecration and in a life of Trust and of faith and of full salvation'.[254]

William thought – as he told an audience of nonconformists at Portsmouth in 1875 – that at a time when science led its votaries into great difficulties in receiving the old truths of revelation; when, terribly, universities produced materialistic atheists; when philosophers or patriots tried, unsuccessfully, to find ways to live good lives without religion; just at the time when the country's intellect concentrated on assaulting the Bible and religion, God stirred up a power of spiritual life and brought moral forces, in gatherings such as those led by Moody and Sankey, to conquer the intellectual forces.[255] The conferences expressed hope that believers of all denominations could meet and demonstrate the validity of their belief through Christian love and 'faith in that great and blessed truth that God loves the creatures He has made', rather than in doctrine. As he told Robert Pearsall Smith, he worried about the spread of materialistic atheism among the highly educated under the influence of scientific research on natural laws (Darwinism).[256] If William conceded the battle against infidelity was to be fought on the spiritual plane rather than the intellectual, Georgina supported pedagogic efforts to show that knowledge of biblical criticism and modern science was not antagonistic to religion, 'but rather purifies and increases it'.[257]

At one level, the conferences were private gatherings hosted by a wealthy aristocrat in gracious surroundings. Anna Kingsford commented that though a convent life, it was 'with all the beautiful surroundings of wealthy circumstances and the refined and cultured accessories which wealth procures'.[258] This was echoed by critics in religious journals: 'the luxurious appliances of the "Broadlands Retreat" made capital fun for people accustomed to the more austere regimen of Cowley or Keble.'[259] This ignored the effort to invite people across sectarian and social divisions – unlettered workmen and duchesses, Anglican ritualists and Low Churchmen, and actors and army officers. Did they have influence beyond the many hundreds who attended over the years? Some critics thought the conferences amiable but ridiculous.[260] Others reacted against the expression there of beliefs (such as perfectionism or efficacy of prayers for the dead) which they saw as pernicious or heretical. But many participants were grateful and saw much to imitate, such as the clergyman from Ireland who hoped in 1876 that people there would emulate Broadlands, 'we are so terribly sectish ... we need so very much the spirit of Christian fellowship, which a "Broadlands" has such a wonderful power of developing.'[261] *The Christian*, in 1879, argued that it was good for God's children, 'who may be wide as the poles asunder, to make a journey now and then from their Arctic and Antarctic Circles to the equator, to look each other in the face, to hear each other's voice, to grasp each other's hand'. Broadlands had enabled men to hear 'in other tongues beside their own the wonderful works of God.'[262]

An account of the conferences in reminiscences by the Cowper-Temples' acquaintance Pauline Craven, contrasted the Palmerstonian and new dispensation in Broadlands, which 'substituted prayers for politics, and religion for worldly amusements'. Because of the fame of her sentimental *Le recit d'une soeur*, this work was reviewed in Britain and America, so that the conference attracted public attention.[263] Before Georgina's death the conferences became visible through other published memoirs. George Russell felt it 'almost impossible to avoid transcendentalism' in thinking of the company which gathered; for participants the transcendental mood in which they were experienced was heightened by nostalgia.[264] They seemed like some perfect prospect by Claude Lorraine.[265]

12

THE CULTURAL PATRONAGE OF THE COWPER-TEMPLES

The preceding chapters have conveyed a sense of the cultural world which the Cowper-Temples inhabited; this chapter examines more closely their cultural patronage, networks and interests. William's inheritance in the late 1860s allowed the Cowper-Temples to indulge architectural and other tastes, and support favoured artists and writers. Their relationships with a number of eminent cultural figures – Ruskin, Rossetti and George MacDonald – became intimate from this point.

Their refinement was a matter of class and perhaps also of heredity. William's father the fifth Earl Cowper was a cultured man, with a superb collection of inherited paintings, who was said to have been a student of Dante who could spend hours in front of his Correggio.[1] Although William's education was considered by him to have been rudimentary, the cultured environment of his upbringing, friendship with the Duke of Devonshire and foreign tours in his youth, stimulated an appreciation of art and literature which survived the hostility of a 'Recordite' Evangelicalism also fearful of such entertainments as the opera or theatre. A child of the Romantic era, he vividly appreciated nature, delighting in sunsets, spring flowers and autumn tints, as Georgina recalled.[2] Georgina's upbringing is more obscure, so that the only glimpse of her education in high culture is her Roman holiday of 1840, but that William sought a cultivated spouse is clear.

It would be surprising, given their moral earnestness, if their cultural activity had no public dimension, and indeed, William was keen to make his art collection available. The *Glasgow Herald*'s London correspondent stressed that one of William's most noteworthy characteristics was 'his intense love of art, and his efforts to diffuse a similar taste among all with whom he came in contact'. The Cowper-Temples' London home was open to visitors at all ordinary times, whether strangers or acquaintances, who wished to see the paintings and other art treasures.[3]

Walter Bagehot in 1864 declared that a 'highly developed moral nature joined to an undeveloped intellectual nature, an undeveloped artistic nature, is of necessity repulsive'.[4] William could not be condemned on this score. Despite self-deprecation the young William's erudition allowed him to amuse the Queen by clever talk on poetry and writers.[5] Some of these he had met, such as Scott and Wordsworth. Others no doubt contacted him, or were referred to him, as potential patron or conduit for pensions, thus the Duke of Devonshire who described William to Mary Russell Mitford, author of *Our Village*, as 'a very great friend of mine', had hoped William would use his connection with Melbourne on her behalf.[6] William befriended Bulwer Lytton, dining with him in the company of d'Orsay and Countess Blessington. He thought Bulwer 'extremely agreeable, he was vivacious as well as profound', recorded his criticism of Landor's novel *Aspasia and Pericles* and noted his idea that the 'habits of concentration of thought of a writer are the opposite of what is required in a talker'.[7]

William feared contamination by idle society and told his first wife that he liked 'talking to literary men, there is generally a thoughtfulness & an abstraction from the passing gossip that is pleasant to me'.[8] Given William's convictions, literature and art had to be moral purposive, though he did not abandon novels as some other Evangelicals did. His most explicit views on literature appeared in a letter which apologized for an over-hasty verdict on Bulwer's *Lucretia, Or Children of the Night* of 1846, a work which had been heavily criticized when it appeared but which William now perceived as a 'grand epic'. He explained that to the thoughtful reader, reflecting on the story and characters, it would do good, 'it must illustrate and enforce deep moral truths,' but his first impression had been that for the chief users of circulating libraries, for whom novels provided ideas and images to their passive and vacant minds, *Lucretia* suggested the way to wealth was to poison relatives and that clever people could evade discovery.[9] He explained his ambivalence: he had partly accepted the view 'in this age of refinement' that sin was avoided by not mentioning it, but now saw that sin was made hateful by being 'dragged out into the light in its natural colours'.

As a prominent social figure, William met many literary and artistic lions at dinners in London. Socially important, culturally inquisitive and wealthy enough to reciprocate by entertaining in London and Hampshire, the Cowper-Temples knew many leading cultural figures, such as the artist Millais and the poets Robert and Elizabeth Barrett Browning, on fairly superficial terms.[10] But other friendships were closer, including their associations with the MacDonalds, Rossettis and Ruskin.

If we turn first to the visual arts, they both showed a keen appreciation of painting. William gained experience of artists through the portraiture which he, relatives, and friends, could afford to commission. As a young man he was painted by the ill-fated Benjamin Haydon, who was briefly taken up by Melbourne.[11] William had his views on portraiture perpetrated on relations, describing the Palmerston portrayed by John Lucas as a horror on canvas and thinking his claim to paint by spirits no compliment to them.[12] His own collection after he inherited Broadlands was to be shared: thus he loaned a Giorgione, depicting a Venetian house with dames and gallants, to an exhibition in 1871.[13] The collection was apparently concentrated in their town house simply because they preferred London as the centre for philanthropy for most of the year.[14]

William's tastes encompassed a conventional admiration for the Old Masters, and he bought, for example, a painting of Vittoria Colonna by Cornaro in 1874.[15] In their gallery visits abroad in 1862 William deplored the over-restoration of works such as Titian's Magdalene at the Palazzo Barbi and paintings in the Belvedere in Vienna which German artists had 'coloured highly after their taste, & varnished all in the tea-tray style. One can see how great they were tho' even through their modern costume'.[16] At the Munich Hofkirche Georgina thought the new religious art (by members of the Nazarene circle) had harmonious and pleasing colouring, and that the drawing was correct and graceful, 'but one misses the serious earnestness & reality of feeling of the old frescoes'.[17] They regularly attended the exhibitions which formed a fixture of the London Season, and Georgina's diaries record her responses to Old Masters and modern artists' works. In 1876 she thought, for instance, William Blake's art 'nightmarish in great part but in much beautiful also & full of interest', and Luke Fildes' *Widower* 'made my dry Eyes fill' and Millais's landscapes were wonderful.[18] The Cowper-Temples did not share Fanny Jocelyn's interest in photography, though Elisabeth Fielding once told her son, the pioneering photographer Fox Talbot that William 'is so charmed with the art he wants to learn it'.[19]

To this mix of Society art appreciation, private patronage and connoisseurship, was added the influence which William had on public taste in the Office of the Public Works. Here as a 'Minister of Beauty' the aristocratic *aedile* could compete in that patronage of the fine arts which increasingly the rich middle-class indulged in. As Georgina recalled, his position gave contact with the leading architects and artists of the period and he was determined to harness their talents to improve the metropolis.[20] Through Rossetti, he turned to William Morris's firm to redecorate the Armoury and Tapestry rooms in St James's Palace and create the Green Dining-Room in the Victoria and Albert, which proved to be a highly influential commission for the future of interior decoration.[21] He commissioned two drinking-fountains from the firm, and Alexander Munro, a protégé of the Duke of Sutherland and Pre-Raphaelite associate, produced a 'Boy and Dolphin' sculpture for Hyde Park in 1863. William commissioned the architect William Eden Nesfield at Kew and Regent's Park, and drew on his father's skills as a garden designer. Responsible for the continued work on building and ornamenting the Palace of Westminster, when he himself preferred a 'severer, grander, and broader' decor, William defended Edward Barry's reputation as architect in 1870 and attended Sir Gilbert Scott's funeral in 1878.[22] But William was attuned to Palmerston's classicism, having seen Augustus Pugin's home at Ramsgate, he thought it as open to satire as those in Pugin's book, *Contrasts*, in its 'incongruously joined' sections.[23]

This was the age of the 'commonplace' book, and those which William and Georgina kept and shared contained poems and extracts from novels or theological works. Some of these were for public viewing on the drawing room table, as 'thoughts which could bear to be laid (for all to judge and to criticize)…' and others, their 'little imperfect thoughts', for private use.[24] Georgina's diaries also record her reading. We have information on their library at Babbacombe at the time of Georgina's death: though without studying the volumes for possible annotations and lacking sustained written responses to this reading in their papers, it is impossible to know what they thought about some of these works.[25] Not surprisingly, much of Georgina's reading involved theology, mysticism and philosophy, from the published sermons of F.D. Maurice, to the works of Spinoza, Swedenborg, Emerson, and Thomas Lake Harris. She had Chevalier Bunsen's works, essays by Mazzini, and the lives of Blanco White, Ernest Renan, Benjamin Jowett, and Anna Kingsford. There were copies of works by acquaintances such as Garth Wilkinson's *The New Jerusalem and the Old Jerusalem* and Andrew Jukes' *Types of Genesis*. Georgina had copies of Aubrey de Vere's *Religious Problems of the Nineteenth Century*, Charles Voysey's *The Mystery of Pain*, Ralph Waldo Trine's *In Tune with the Infinite* and Hugh Chapman's *Steps to the Higher Life*. There was the Swedenborgian William White's *Other-world order*, Horace Hastings' *Primitive and Modern Spiritualism*, and William Crookes' *Researches in the Phenomena of Spiritualism*. There were copies of the *Psychological Review* and Annie Oppenheim's *Phreno-Physiognomy*. Titles such as *Animals' Rights*, *Animal Torture* and *Our Canine Companions* reflected her zoophilia.

Georgina enjoyed the novels of Victor Hugo and George Eliot (*Romola* she thought 'very clever') and had work by Leo Tolstoy, Henrik Ibsen and Henry James in her library, though she found *Washington Square* 'very uninteresting'. Emelia Gurney actually identified Georgina with the character Princess Casamassima in James's novel of 1886, 'let me say I don't know how she is to turn out – *not* very well I think – I'm only in 2nd vol. – but so far I seem to see the *stock* of your nature.'[26] As these titles suggest, Georgina's reading was modern. The Cowper-Temples read Olive Schreiner's *African Farm*, Georgina describing it as 'wonderful'.[27] She enjoyed *King Solomon's Mines* and found *Jekyll and Mr Hyde* 'awful'.[28] She read bestsellers such as Bulwer Lytton's *Zanoni* and *Strange Story* and Mrs Braddon's sensational *Lady Audley's Secret* in 1862. Other works included Sergius Stepniak's *Career of a Nihilist* and Emile Erckmann's historical novel *Year One of the Republic*.

Georgina met George Eliot in 1871 and heard her recite the poem 'Boudicea' at a party. The Cowper-Temples dined with Eliot and her partner George Lewes at the Augustus Tollemaches' and Georgina visited her. Magsie had sent Eliot a copy of her work on Spanish saints and developed an acquaintance which led to an offer of Nutfield in May 1872, but conversation with Georgina about the location decided Eliot against it.[29] Georgina read her novels as they appeared. Her commonplace book of 1866 included lengthy quotations from Eliot and she told Lewes there were excerpts from *Romola* in her New Testament.[30] She had thought *Adam Bede* the 'most beautiful novel I ever read' in 1859, and was discerning about *Felix Holt*, praising it for being 'so full of thought – serious & deeper than ever – with a vein of wonderful humour running through the whole – like sunshine dancing along a fathomless deep lake – rich and deep enough to suggest unseen treasure – too far down to be visible to any but real Divers for truth'.[31] She liked it less when reread in 1886.

The narrative of Georgina's life in the 1870s–1880s has indicated her interest in Dante, whom she studied in the Italian. Indeed, Dante became something of a cult in her circle; for Emelia Gurney the poet was a 'fount of continual interest, and also of consolation'.[32] Georgina's taste in poetry also included an interest in Robert Browning: she was probably attracted by his intellectual depth, seriousness and commitment to religious faith.[33] Perhaps like F.D. Maurice's theology, there was the appeal of obscurity and truths to puzzle over. The Cowper-Temples appear to have been acquainted with the Brownings from 1856, when *Men and Women* was but newly published [34] and Georgina was one of the founding vice-presidents of the Browning Society in 1881, though her role was purely nominal.[35] Robert was invited to Broadlands but always declined.[36] Georgina's close friend Julia Wedgwood had been an intimate of Browning's, and Countess Cowper knew him and invited him to Wrest Park.

It was essential for men and women in their class to be up-to-date in their conversation in London and country house society. Georgina and her husband kept abreast of periodical literature, reading Walter Bagehot's essays on Clough and Molière in *The Cornhill* in 1880 for instance.[37] Her library contained the *Fortnightly*, *Contemporary Review*, and *Fraser's Magazine*, but she also read *Good Words*, *Lady's Realm*, *Monthly Musical Record*, *Woman at Home*, and W.T. Stead's bestselling earnest digest of journalism *Review of Reviews* and his spiritualist journal *Borderland*.

Concerts were part of the entertainment of aristocratic London, but Georgina's love of music extended beyond these, and playing hymns on the organ at home, to an appreciation of Wagner. When Wagner was on a conducting tour of England in 1877, she took friends to the performances, this at a time when a taste for Wagner was described by British critics as the gospel of a little band.[38] Georgina made sure that Juliet received musical lessons, given by the noted educator (and pupil of Mendelssohn), William Smith Rockstro, a frequent visitor to Babbacombe Cliff in the mid-1880s, whom she promoted with Louisa Ashburton. Rockstro, a Catholic convert, was at one point a beneficiary in her will. Sending his study of Handel, he told her, 'I know well that you will sympathize with me, in this, though the outer world would treat the idea with scorn.' There were so few to whom he could speak unreservedly about the dearest and most sacred of subjects, 'you would read, between the lines, a great many things which I could not express in words, and which I did not care to convey to the unsympathizing intelligence of the "general reader",' he said.[39]

Georgina enjoyed visiting the theatre with relations – William's religion did not forbid the theatre – witnessing Sir Henry Irving's performance as Handel in 1874, believing the play brought out his real powers 'without the exaggeration that marred his other performances'.[40] She liked his later performance as Othello, 'much better than I expected'.[41] She thought Tennyson's *Mary Tudor*, which she had read, poor when she saw it on stage in 1876: 'at its best it must be utterly dreary – nothing to admire or love or care about through out. Of course being Tennyson in reading it there are lines that are beautiful but there are some left out & others scarcely observed in the representation.' Strangely, given an adulthood of 'honest doubt', Tennyson does not appear to have loomed large in her cultural life.[42]

The Cowper-Temples' intimacy with Ruskin has been documented by scholars. It was well known in their lifetimes through Ruskin's autobiography, *Praeterita*. After their deaths, W.G. Collingwood characterized her as confidante and sympathetic adviser.[43] She could write no recollection to counterbalance Ruskin's account of his captivation by her in Rome in the winter of 1840, since he had admired her statuesque severity, 'the purest standards of breathing womanhood', from a distance.[44] One of his names for her, 'Isola', derived from her unapproachability. They met again in 1853 and grew closer through Georgina's involvement in the Rose La Touche tragedy, spiritualism which she and others encouraged Ruskin to investigate, and their support for the Guild of St George, which William had no faith in as a scheme but which he assisted for friendship's sake.[45] William had been instrumental in introducing Ruskin to Palmerston and no doubt, as Collingwood wrote, helped channel Ruskin's views on the National Gallery and public art.[46]

Georgina's memoirs included no account of the friendship, merely noting, 'We became great friends, I was fond of his Cousin Joan, and also of the "Rosie" of whom he writes in "Preterita", and she was a strong link between us.'[47] During and after the La Touche episode, Georgina gave maternal support, and Ruskin wrote in 1871 that without the help of $\phi l\lambda\eta$ 'the day would probably have come before now, when I should have written and thought no more.'[48] Other friends of Ruskin recognized her importance: Edward Burne-Jones asked Georgina, when Ruskin left the Severns at Coniston in a temper, to invite him to Broadlands.[49] The second edition of Ruskin's best-selling hymn to female moral and spiritual power, *Sesame and Lilies*, was dedicated to her in 1871. What she thought of the work is unclear, though possibly she is referred to in the Preface to the 1871 edition as the 'wise and lovely English lady', who told him 'that in the *Lilies* I had been writing of what I knew nothing about'; she read it with Juliet in 1886.[50] Ruskin was certainly a cultural influence. Like many English visitors she viewed Venice partly through his *Stones of Venice*, and was personally tutored to appreciate Turner by him at the National Gallery ('The Temeraire by far my favourite').[51] But the Cowper-Temples had their own opinions about what they saw in galleries, failing, for instance, to see the religion Ruskin detected in the Louvre's Murillos in 1862.

Another friendship with a cultural eminence was with the novelist, poet, preacher and lecturer, George MacDonald. MacDonald was a friend of the Russell Gurneys and F.D. Maurice in the early 1860s, and the acquaintance came about through John Llewellyn Davies.[52] Friendship was cemented through correspondence and the MacDonalds' visits to Broadlands as ordinary guests and participants in the conferences.[53] William gave money to George and contributed to the scheme to give the MacDonalds a freehold house, so that it was natural he should lay the foundation stone to Casa Coraggio.[54] George came to address them as 'brother William' and 'dear sister', and once called Georgina his 'great great princess grandmother', alluding to his magical or divine character in *The Princess and the Goblin*. [55] The Cowper-Temples, after the MacDonalds began performing *Pilgrim's Progress*, called him 'Greatheart', promoted the 'Pilgrims' to friends such as Lady Ashburton, attended his lectures and even hosted some in Mayfair.[56] We have seen that in 1879 *Paul Faber* was dedicated to William, MacDonald also sent poetic gifts. Georgina read his children's tales to Juliet and used her copy of the privately published *Diary of an Old Soul*, to mark the deaths of friends and relations. She had most of MacDonald's works, including presentation copies and the proofs of *Weighed and Wanting*.[57]

Their friendship with Dante Gabriel Rossetti stemmed from their early interest in purchasing his artwork, though their acquaintance developed in 1865 after he arranged an inspection of Morris furniture for them. William's role as Chief Commissioner involved him with Morris and Company's stained glass and other items, and though Rossetti then referred to him as 'fool Cowper' to Ford Madox Brown, friendship developed. Georgina sent sunflowers and pomegranate blossom for him to paint and in August 1866 William bought a replica of the haunting *Beata Beatrix*, depicting Elizabeth Siddal as Beatrice transported in a trance to Heaven. Rossetti's price was modest because William was not so rich and because their liking for his art was not based on its commercial value: 'he & his wife particularly,' he wrote, 'are very appreciative people & it is pleasanter sending a poetic work where it will be seen by cultivated folks than to a cotton spinner or a dealer.'[58] Rossetti later admitted the *Beatrix* was his masterpiece and cost him, as a portrait of his dead wife, the most suffering.[59] In 1867 Georgina recorded visiting Rossetti, loving more than ever 'our dear Beatrice', and admiring a 'jewel' of a painting showing Francesca de Rimini reading in a window.[60] Georgina allowed the *Beatrix* to be copied by the artist in 1871. In a letter to Juliet she writes with admiration, 'The sun is shining Radiantly on our Beata Beatrix as I write and she looks so lovely.'[61] Her decision to donate it to the Tate Gallery in William's memory reflected his own intention to leave the work to the nation.[62] In 1874 he brought a version of the *Blessed Damozel* for Georgina's birthday: 'such a golden remembrance of golden times'.[63] Her other Rossettis included studies of a baby and Jane Morris as the lady pitying Dante after Beatrice's death, with a quotation from the *Vita Nuova*, 'Color d'amor'.[64]

Through Georgina, Rossetti hoped to use William's influence to secure the Slade Professorship of Art for Ford Madox Brown in late 1872, and they secured testimonials for the candidacy. Later, Rossetti obtained their help for the mentally afflicted artist James Smetham.[65] As was her wont, Georgina's nurturing sympathies were also directed towards the Rossettis. She offered to look after his sister Maria and sent heartfelt condolences when she died.[66] The relationship was sufficiently close for Georgina to mark the death of Rossetti's mother among the deaths of friends and family, noting it left 'Christiana [sic] very desolate'.[67] It will be recalled that Rossetti stayed at Broadlands during a conference, partly to evade the workmen at his studio, and there he met 'George III' – Georgina Sumner – who subsequently sat for a number of his works and became a friend. Rossetti's treatment by the mesmerist Chandos Leigh Hunt Wallace, to prevent a return to chloral, was possibly through the Cowper-Temples, who had tried to arrange Waggie's assistance in 1876.

Georgina by this period was frequently in Rossetti's studio and noted that only his close friend the solicitor and critic Watts-Dunton could alleviate his depression. Later, friendship with Watts-Dunton apparently brought them 'affectionate intimacy' (odd, given the poet's personality and the sadomasochistic content of works such as his *Poems and Ballads*) with Swinburne for many years, especially as the Cowper-Temples were nearby during their time in Eastbourne in 1886.[68] When Rossetti's friend William Morris died, one of Georgina's nieces wrote, 'how I envy you having known him and all that wonderful brotherhood.'[69] If the Broadlands papers indicate no intimacy, they were sufficiently acquainted for Eleanor Vere Boyle, asked by Morris to support a scheme, to query if he did not think Lady Mount Temple 'would have far more influence with the public'.[70] Another Rossetti connection was his only pupil, Walter Knewstub. William purchased a tempera portrait by Knewstub when the artist became ill, in order that the artist's family could be supported, and the Cowper-Temples endorsed Rossetti's efforts to raise funds.[71] Mrs Knewstub was said to have been drawn towards Catholicism by Georgina, though there is no evidence for this.[72] Georgina also knew Rossetti's publisher F.S. Ellis, treating him to tickets to hear Paderewski in 1899; Ellis wanted to visit Babbacombe in return to read her a lecture on Burne-Jones.[73]

The Cowper-Temples patronized other artists. Probably through Rossetti, they knew Edward Burne-Jones, visiting his studio and inviting his wife to dinner.[74] Virginia Woolf's privately performed Bloomsbury joke about eminent Victorians, *Freshwater*, includes a reference to a 'Lady Raven Mount Temple', who bestows the ring of Petrarch's Laura on the artist George Frederic Watts, perhaps a conscious echo of the real Lady Mount Temple's associations with the artist. They met in 1862 at Panshanger and chatted about Tennyson, 'so simple & so open – quite transparent'. Shortly afterwards she saw Watts' portraits at Little Holland House, and thought his Tennyson 'quite Shakespearian against bright leaves'.[75] Later William bought a copy of Watts' bust of the nymph Clytie tilted back as if for a kiss.[76] His study of Georgina in 1894, capturing her 'spiritual beauty', was highly regarded and published.[77]

Having been guardian angels in his artistic infancy they remained close to Edward Clifford, who painted several portraits of his patrons.[78] A friend of Burne-Jones and the writer J.A. Symonds, Clifford depicted inspirational characters like Walt Whitman, Charles Gordon, Octavia Hill and the missionary to lepers in Hawaii, Father Damien. His studio over a shop in Wigmore Street displayed the 'ultra-refined faces of thoughtful, high-bred women', sitters included Mrs Gibbs of Tyntesfield, Countess Cowper, and the future wife of Edwin Lutyens.[79] He preached to the East End poor with Frederick Charrington until unsoundness about future punishment led one of the mission's financial backers to press for his departure.[80] Georgina later befriended the devout Frederic Shields and through inflaming Emelia Gurney with her admiration he carried out his great if short-lived painting in Gurney's Chapel of Rest.[81] Shields told Georgina 'what I owe you is past words to express, but often & often your image rises up before me, as when you once came to the old studio, & turned it with your being and incited me by more generous appreciations.'[82]

Other friendships reflected shared interests in spiritualism, social reform and religion. There was the vegetarian, socialist and literary scholar F.J. Furnivall, for instance.[83] Furnivall hoped in 1867 that William would help get him the post of Librarian of the House of Commons.[84] The Cowper-Temples supported the various literary societies that he established. The New Shakspere Society, 'to promote the intelligent study of him', was established in 1873 (the year William endorsed Furnivall's application for the Royal Academy Secretaryship), the Browning Society in 1881, the Shelley Society in 1886. Spiritualism and mysticism was one link with the novelist Annie Keary, and certainly led the Cowper-Temples to the pre-Raphaelite Anna Mary Watts and her husband, the writer Alfred Alaric Watts. Efforts to assist through patronage, as with Furnivall, also figured. William helped secure Anna Mary's father, the writer William Howitt, a pension.[85] Georgina befriended Elizabeth Rundle Charles, author of *Chronicles of the Schonberg-Cotta Family* and other Christian tales, and a noted hymnologist. Georgina illumined her place at Combe Edge 'with her singular charm and exquisite beauty'.[86]

Surprisingly, given mutual friends, they were only slight acquaintances of Thomas Carlyle, though Georgina had an insight into the Carlyles through Lady Ashburton. After the fire at Melchet, and perhaps eager to know the celebrity, William invited Carlyle to Broadlands in 1873, since he had 'the good habit of going into Hampshire' and Lady Ashburton's house was not yet rebuilt.[87] Lady Ashburton did bring Carlyle, perhaps at this time, and he made 'a long and indignant Jeremiad on the sins and shams of this base time; all going to squash as fast as it can, and we crying "Hurrah" over it'.[88] Other acquaintances will be apparent from the previous chapters. Georgina corresponded with the American poet Walt Whitman, for instance.[89] Her acquaintance with Oscar Wilde was through Constance, and was not close.[90]

In their patronage of the Pre-Raphaelites, the Cowper-Temples turned to an explicitly moral and religious movement, which cast itself in the vanguard. Oddly, Ford Madox Ford included Georgina alongside Wilde, O' Shaugnessy and Theo Marzials, as figures in an 'English Aesthetic Circle' interested in Flaubert, Turgenev and the European mainstream, but though she read Henry James, it would be wrong to present her as an intense patroness of the 'new' *à la* Gerald du Maurier's *Punch* cartoons of Mrs Cimabue Brown (just as it would be unfair to interpret her patronage as mere pursuit of celebrity *à la* Mrs Ponsonby de Tomkyns).[91] For Georgina had no sympathy with the posing of the Aesthetes, quoting Gilbert and Sullivan's *Patience* to Juliet after an exhibition at Grosvenor Gallery: 'Oh! The funny people we saw! Greenry Yalleries in abundance – some very pretty and many "too too" and daffodilly in excelsis,' finding the painting a mixture of the lovely and absurd. Art and the cult of the artist was not, as it was for many Grosvenor Gallery devotees, a substitute for a fading faith in conventional religion.[92]

But some of the defining decorative aspects to the Aesthetic movement were taken up by them after they remodelled their house in Curzon Street following Rossetti's advice and when they employed Nesfield.[93] Glazed chintzes were ditched for the designs of Morris and others, though Georgina's memoir confided that 'between you and me I still think it was very pretty', of the banished fabric.[94] William might have seen this personal reform in the context of progress in public taste which he detected as Commissioner of the Public Works; supporting an art school for Hertford, he claimed that 'we have of late years seen a vast improvement in the ordinary decoration of houses. The paper upon our walls, all our articles of furniture, have been greatly improved, and all this is, I believe attributable to these schools.'[95] Interior décor testified to improved 'art feeling'.

A description of their home in 1872 was penned by Margaret Leicester Warren, overawed by an 'enchanted house'. The boudoir was decorated in emerald green satin, with 'the most lovely pictures' copied from Italian works, 'beautiful sketches and painted allegories' and the *Beatrix*.[96] Smaller pictures rested on a golden dado and *objets d'art* cluttered tables. The dining room was panelled in the Morris style in green with squares of gold, sunflowers and other plants, a recess had Morris stained-glass.[97] Mary Gladstone described Stanhope Street as 'very beautiful and different to everything else'.[98] Babbacombe Cliff had Burne-Jones stained glass and Morris wallpaper which gave the rooms their names, drawings by Rossetti and (according to Oscar Wilde) 'many lovely things'.[99] Of Babbacombe Cliff, Robert Pearsall Smith said: 'I know not who but yourself could have created so fascinating a house pitched in so fascinating a scene ... It were easy to be good here! No "Conferences" & "Conventions" needed – nor preaching or exhorting – Nature in her most fascinating displays would win the soul for Good which is God.'[100]

Perhaps she dressed the part too. Her costume was idiosyncratic in Clifford's portrait of the 1870s, in which she wore a silver necklace of cherubs climbing a ladder, and a habit-like garment of black and white that made her appear like a 'Sister of Mercy'. She eschewed the fashions of Paris and also the costumes of the aesthetes, for plain black merino gowns and white mob caps.[101] At Babbacombe in the widowhood to which I now turn, Emelia imagined her as some figure from a Pre-Raphaelite painting, the Lady of Shalott, her weaving only interrupted by the 'white wings flapping and the pattering of the coral feet[,] to crumble them bread and butter with answering little love coos to theirs'.[102]

13

AFTER WILLIAM, 1888–1901

Georgina was nearly seventy when William died. Her health had not been robust and old age was to reduce her mobility until she was confined to Babbacombe. Life meant enduring the loss of old friends and relations, and tragedy in her immediate family, without her Beloved's calming presence, but Georgina did not surrender to despairing inactivity. She attracted a new host of admirers such as the young composer Clement Harris, or Constance Wilde, who thought her a mixture of saint and mother. Georgina cultivated William's memory through her private memoirs. Her intellectual curiosity and religious inquiry (or gullibility) continued: Emelia Gurney agreeing with her that 'the intellectual region is one in which the old may find much to distract from miseries'.[1] Vyvyan, son of Oscar Wilde, who spent holidays from preparatory school visiting Georgina, recalled her 'shrewdness, wit and prodigious memory'.[2] Physically, she could still captivate: Maud Ashley, daughter of the eighth Earl of Shaftesbury, remembered her as 'one of the most beautiful old ladies I have ever seen'.[3]

In the immediate aftermath of William's death, there were practical matters to arrange: financial security for Georgina and a home and income for Juliet. The executors of her husband's will were Georgina, Augustus and Basil Wilberforce. William left a personal estate of £76, 123. Georgina inherited the leasehold on Babbacombe, his Irish estates, residuary personal estate and the London leasehold property at Great Stanhope Street and Shelley House for her life.[4] Juliet had £12, 000 secured on the Broadlands estates. Broadlands and the Yorkshire estates were inherited by Evelyn, with £8,000 secured on the Blessington estate which had come to William on Spencer's death.

William wished his nephew should take 'Temple' as his principal name, a touch of step-filial piety to Palmerston. Evelyn did not, which

Jessie Cowper at any rate deplored; she felt, indeed, that he had taken the 'lion's share'.[5] Georgina was characteristically generous; knowing he had insufficient money to keep up Broadlands she offered £12, 000, though as one newspaper put it, 'she is not particularly well off.' She also gave carriages, horses and pictures, and 'would probably have made him a present of the plate if it had not been entailed'.[6] She hoped he would not have to sell off the furniture or artwork such as Watts's *Clytie*.[7] Evelyn and Augustus quarrelled as executors: Evelyn complained that Augustus had the most disagreeable manner he had encountered, but Georgina asked him to excuse her brother's warm temper and edginess: 'Certainly Vile Mammon shall not separate us!'[8]

Augustus inherited a share in the slate company, William's old valet Stephen Pleasance received *GNR* shares. Jessie Cowper got £7000 secured on the Blessington estates, but she had large mortgages to pay for her husband's debts after 1881, with no return from Irish property inherited from Spencer because of falling land values, and she lived, as the press was to report after a moneylender took her to court in 1894, on handouts from her friends.[9] Georgina was not so wealthy now, due to the slate company disaster and Evelyn's inheritance. George MacDonald, on a lecturing tour in England, returned a gift of money with touching words for his dearest 'sister': 'I have to take care of you as well as of me.'[10] Her nephew the seventh Earl Cowper, shocked when she contemplated selling Babbacombe and her London home, about 1894, offered assistance.[11]

'It is no winter night comes down | Upon our hearts, dear friends of old; | But a May evening, softly brown, | Whose wind is rather cold': thus did George MacDonald write to Georgina in 1889.[12] He had offered her such consolation as he could in the immediate desolation of her bereavement, 'you will have, I think, to consent to be miserable, so far as loneliness makes you miserable, and look to him and him only for comfort.'[13] But Georgina's temperament – her sensitivity to the world's suffering – made it hard to come to terms with bereavement.[14] A year after his death Jane Simon recalled her saying 'how hard it was to watch all the Spring loveliness at Babbacombe, – how it all almost seemed disloyal to enjoy it to the full.'[15] She had Juliet for a time, and a large circle of devoted friends and relations whom she kept in contact with, invited to stay at Babbacombe and, whilst she was able, she travelled. Georgina Sumner and Hannah visited.[16] She became involved with Constance Wilde. The two met in London, Constance wrote constantly, and they shared an interest in Dante and the occult. But Constance was the ardent one: eager for a surrogate mother yet uncertain about her Motherling's affections.[17]

FIGURE 18. Lady Mount Temple at Babbacombe, 1889, by Rose K. Durrant and Son, 1889.
By courtesy of the Trustees of the Broadlands Archives.

As ever, some of Georgina's efforts to mitigate suffering were directed at her family, as she attempted to heal the rift between her cousin William Manners Tollemache, ninth Earl of Dysart, and his wife.[18] Logan Pearsall Smith recalled his mother being invited, on occasions when the Tollemaches misbehaved, 'to come and help the erring one back to the righteous path'.[19] Though he gives no specific details, his autobiography, *Unforgotten Years*, refers to Georgina's behaviour in relation to one Tollemache, made to consider her error in running away from her husband, a foreign prince, in Georgina's custody. Hannah, arriving with her Bible and Quakerly wisdom, found that her old friend was concealing a telegram which invited the niece's lover to come, 'since, as she put it, she felt that Matilda was feeling so lonely without him'.[20]

Shelley House, where all had been arranged by William for her, was soon relinquished.[21] Georgina moved to no. 9, Cheyne Walk (her friend Annie Watts had lived at no.19, her niece Edith Leycester also lived in Chelsea[22]). Babbacombe was her refuge, its dining room adorned with Clifford's portrait of her and terraced garden and sea beyond.[23] Babbacombe had been partially rebuilt by Nesfield in 'no particular style' but its interior was Pre-Raphaelite, with Burne-Jones drawings and stained glass in preciously-named rooms with William Morris wallpapers: 'Jessamine', 'Marygold', 'Cornflower' and 'Daisy'. The most important room was 'Wonderland', the drawing room decorated with scenes from *Alice in Wonderland*.[24] Partly built over the carriage drive, it was flooded with light from windows on three sides. In her final years Georgina sat in her wheel-chair in an alcove with views to the setting sun and bay below. The room was in Georgina's apartment which formed virtually a separate house.[25]

There was a garden of woodland flowers and ivy, sloping down sharply from the cliff top. Georgina delighted in the green finches and tom-tits which came to feed by the windows. At the nearby cottage 'The Glen' Georgina had her beloved brother Augustus and Marguerite for company.[26] Babbacombe's romance was evoked in admirers' letters. One American visitor told Georgina that every moment with her was 'like being in heaven, breathing a freer air', and recalled Georgina's voice as she read to her 'Little Lamb who made me'.[27]

FIGURE 19. Babbacombe Cliff. From *Mount Temple Memorials*.
By courtesy of the Trustees of the Broadlands Archives.

Babbacombe was one way of coming to terms with her loss. Another was the creation of memorials. Thus she donated Rossetti's *Beata Beatrix* to the National Gallery, a gesture well received by the public, who crowded to see it. She supported an essay by Hannah Smith on William in the Society of Friends' journal. She had Hannah's assistance as she wrote her memoir (Hannah was now permanently established in Britain). Writing was painful as her back had not improved, though she used a typewriter to aid her.[28] These memoirs, dedicated to Augustus, who had asked her to garner what she could of the life of William whom he had loved so much, appeared privately in 1890.[29] Emelia Gurney begged her not to let 'queenly reserve and intense refinement of perception', make her say too little, 'launch forth blessed Queen on the ocean of your Love – and scatter back to us on the shore, the winged seeds that spring from your blessed memories.' John Llewellyn Davies wanted further memoirs but this was

Georgina's only published work.[30] It revealed talent in constructing a narrative of two truth seekers, carefully weaving in material from William's journals. Hulda Beamish described her letters as charming and regretted that Georgina did not write for the public at large, for her style would have 'few rivals in eloquence of expression and depth, and concentration'.[31] George Russell, who first met Georgina as a young man down from Oxford, begged her not to bowdlerize and recalled: 'My father remembers Lord Mount Temple in a blue jacket with gilt buttons, riding his ponys at Brighton, and a dear little boy he must have been,' and recalled his last visits, 'the gentleman who dined on apples, and old miss Bertie, who hated him for saying he was her cousin!! I think Lord M's speaking should be noted'.[32] He wrote, 'in my "Praeterita" whenever they appear – I shall describe my first sight of you, in St James's Square, in 1876. But I shall not be audacious enough to give you a nick-name.'[33]

Copies went to close family members such as her niece Mabell Airlie,[34] and friends such as Countess Darnley, George MacDonald, and James Farquhar who praised 'its comprehensive earnest simplicity'.[35] Copies went to Gladstone and Archbishop Benson.[36] The work was sacred, reserved for new acquaintances if deemed worthy.[37] There were other memorials to William; Edward Clifford dedicated his account of his visit to Father Damien to Lord Mount Temple in this year.

Inevitably too, spiritualism played a role in her response to bereavement. In 1890 Hulda Beamish had discussed with her '[h]ow far do those who are gone know what we are doing; and how are they able to communicate with us?'[38] She tried to communicate with William but wondered whether the messages were genuine; was it soul speaking to soul?[39] About 1890, her friend Maria Consuelo, with whom she investigated Christian Science, claimed to be channelling William's spirit and wrote of William's loving, gentle presence and efforts to manifest himself, claiming he was leaving white flowers and urging her to write down his thoughts. If Georgina ever felt a soft breeze over her forehead and hands, it was his spirit. Georgina may have believed this: she did at least keep these letters.[40]

Georgina took Juliet to Wiesbaden to consult a doctor and receive electropathy.[41] But Juliet's late returns from socializing made Georgina frightened and cross. She found comfort in a copy of Dante's *Purgatorio* sent by Constance Wilde, and when she returned to England she was in Constance's company reading Dante, going to lectures, viewing Burne-Jones' paintings and watching Greek plays. She attended anti-vivisection meetings. In early April Oscar presented, 'in sincere respect and esteem', a copy of *The Happy Prince*.[42] Later in the year Georgina took Juliet to Geneva for treatment, and also made a public intervention at an Anglophone meeting on international arbitration, asking 'a variety of questions, which assisted in carrying on the proceedings vigorously and pleasantly'.[43] The Wilberforces were there for Georgina's birthday; and she lent money after Basil's secretary stole parish funds.[44]

Georgina became besotted with Georgina Sumner's son Frank, telling Andrew Jukes how loveable he was; Jukes hoped she had 'a dear son, or as he says, a grandson, in him'. Frank had grown up in America, thrown 'into all the whirl of business and competition'.[45] His mother rejoiced that 'you are helping each other', and said she longed for a 'strong young arm too'.[46] Maria Consuelo wrote, 'I hear you have found a son! ... dear Mrs Sumner's son must be wise.'[47] This was ambiguous, and George Russell's joke about 'young sailors and stock-brokers' suggests some thought the relationship unseemly.[48] But as Juliet grew apart from her, such company was important to Georgina. When Juliet travelled to Italy at the end of 1890, she joked 'You only love your love with an F.'[49]

She had another new admirer, the composer Clement Harris, perhaps an acquaintance through Oscar Wilde. Harris, one of Clara Schumann's last pupils, played the piano for Georgina and visited Juliet at Babbacombe. From Port Said in March 1893 he told her he was 'full of new ideas from Egypt – both musically and otherwise'; sadly his promise was unfulfilled for he died fighting in the Greco-Turkish war of 1897.[50] Georgina also had Emily Ford and Constance, though Juliet imagined these two hated each other.[51]

Frank Sumner joined Georgina for Easter at Babbacombe, whilst Juliet enjoyed festivities in Naples with Mrs Sumner.[52] Juliet wrote of a new friend, Marie Corelli (Mary Mackay), the well-known and soon to be best-selling novelist. 'I can't think why she is so *very very* nice to me,' Juliet said. Corelli claimed they met in a previous life, for they seemed to 'have known each other all our lives'.[53] But Juliet thought, as she told Georgina to tell Constance, *Wormwood*, on absinthe addiction, was a 'horrible book but there are beautiful bits in it'. Juliet was chaperoned by Mrs Sumner, Mrs Brewster Macpherson and her daughter Edith. They met the cream of Neapolitan society and attended Christian Science lectures patronized by Harriet Meuricoffre, Josephine Butler's beloved sister.[54]

Juliet got into trouble for suggesting that Neapolitan society was angry with her for visiting a relation by adoption, Teresa, who was in disgrace. A flood of letters deepened the crisis and Georgina offered to come and soothe things.[55] Then Juliet became enamoured with a young aristocrat who spoke no English.[56] Her chaperone wrote about the suitability of the Marquis Luigi Mastelloni, son of the Duca de San Lorenzo, knowing 'how anxious you expressed yourself to me at Babbicomb [sic] that the dear child should be settled & have a protector & I think "Luigi" will prove one'.[57] Mrs Sumner thought Luigi unsuitable, as his reputation was bad, he was poor and 'his caring seems only a fierce sort, which might soon pass'.[58] Georgina wondered if Luigi could accept poverty or English life, and told Juliet that her consent was needed to make the engagement bona fide and that she needed to consult Augustus and her lawyers, though she desired to help all she could, even to her impoverishment.[59] She would 'go into it with Frank' and find out how much the settlement could be. She wished them to have 'Babb', of course, when she died, as 'the place prepared for me by my Beloved'. Shortly after, it was agreed that there would be no marriage.[60] Juliet admitted, 'I don't think I ever cared only rather felt I might be left with the crooked stick, you see I am 25 next year and also I always wonder if it is wise or right to refuse great love.'[61]

Juliet befriended the American poet and actor William Theodore Peters (brother of the artist Clinton Peters). She later asked Georgina to help 'Peterken', when she could, as he was 'so lonely and sad'.[62] With letters of introduction to Georgina and others, he glittered in private theatricals in metropolitan mansions. Peters was immortalized in a poem by his Rhymers' Club associate, Ernest Dowson, whose *Pierrot of the Minute* was performed with Peters as Pierrot wearing a 'superb buckle' from the Palmerston jewels, lent by Georgina.[63] Peters described her to the *Brooklyn Eagle*'s reporter as 'the perfection of a lily, of Dante's Beatrice' and included a poem to her in his 'meagre volume of minor verse', *Posies out of Rings*.[64] Drawn like a moth to the stronger flame of the Parisian *fin de siècle*, he starved to death in penury in 1904.

Frank Sumner married the American Mrs Rachel Thouron in March 1892, with a mortgage secured by him from Georgina's estate. They honeymooned in Babbacombe.[65] 'Well it is *done* Grannie,' Georgina imagined him saying.[66] 'Of course I rather sigh over the Funeral of my boy as the day dawns near but I really now hope the Event is going to be happy for him and one must not be selfish,' she told Juliet.[67] She still had the attentions of Constance Wilde and it was in her company in October that she had a serious fall after attending a lecture on Plato. She invited Constance to holiday with her sons in Babbacombe whilst she was away in late 1892. In fact Oscar stayed, looking after his sons, working on *Salome*, and entertaining Bosie, Lord Alfred Douglas, while Constance was in Italy.[68]

Juliet returned to Italy in the spring of 1893, now intent on marriage to Luigi. She worried about opposition from Augustus and the family, due to the change of religion and the impact on Georgina's finances which would be involved: 'I dare not think of my Uncle I know he will be so angry.'[69] Yet Georgina Sumner now approved of Luigi and Hannah Smith wrote to congratulate Juliet after visiting Georgina.[70] Juliet was received into the Catholic Church. But a problem emerged. Luigi's father would provide little so Juliet asked if Babbacombe could be sold.[71] Her travelling companion pleaded her case, describing Luigi's figure, 'good-looking in the Italian style – short black beard and curled up moustache, and very firm mouth'.[72] Juliet then telegraphed to be rescued, the attachment was over. She had alluded to marriage as an escape, prompting the comment from Georgina, in feeble hieroglyphs: 'escape! From one of the fondest, most loving hearts that ever beat!!! And sweetest little Homes!' But Juliet, nearing twenty six, dreaded remaining a spinster without her own home.[73]

Juliet travelled to Paris in late 1893, staying there into the new year, with her new acquaintance Baroness Faverot de Kerbrech, her husband and their English-born son Maurice, godson of Empress Eugenie. Juliet said her relationship to Maurice was discussed at the Opéra, 'because you see I am not distinctly English in appearance quite the reverse and he was rather too smart with his very carefully tied white Carnation to be my brother'.[74] Séances revealed she would marry a tall, fair Englishman.[75] This was what Georgina hoped. She told one foreign suitor's mother of at least two handsome English youths aspiring to marriage: 'I mean to give her every opportunity of becoming a Mrs Bull! And of keeping my Child by my side!' Our 'stiff English ways and ideas' would make her a poor wife for a Frenchman.[76]

In 1894 Georgina herself teetered on the edge of conversion to Catholicism. Kenelm Vaughan, Cardinal Vaughan's brother, tried to persuade her that the Protestant Church was a cruel stepmother and that she would find a heaven whilst she was still on earth in the true mother church. He visited Torquay and offered to answer any difficulties about the catechism. Georgina had known the Irish poet, essayist and Catholic convert Aubrey de Vere since at least the mid-1880s, when they had memorably 'pleasant conversations' about Saint Catherine of Genoa's work on Purgatory. De Vere sent works by Cardinal Manning (who 'spoke to me about you with great interest the last time I saw him last summer, though I am not sure he spoke of you as one with whom he was personally acquainted') and talked of converts. But Hannah Smith convinced her Catholicism was no 'new medicine' for spiritual troubles.[77] Her son Logan claimed that Georgina also came under the 'almost intolerable domination of a pious cook'.[78]

With the publication by Lord Dufferin (former Viceroy of India) of his mother's *Poems*, Georgina took the opportunity of writing, recalling his mother Helen Blackwood as her 'fairy Queen', reminding him of his place in her youth, his 'beautiful dawning manhood', and Fanny Jocelyn's belief that he and William had been the two men she had known untouched by the world although immersed in it. Georgina said she was 'past recognition, old and ill, I may almost say dying'. Dufferin offered to give

Juliet every attention in Paris, where he was ambassador, on her account and in memory of Harriet d'Orsay.[79]

For Juliet remained with the Kerbrechs, and fell in love with a Monsieur Eugene Deschamps, a stockbroker of humble origin.[80] Georgina gave her blessing to the engagement. Problems ensued as Juliet's *acte de naissance* and certificate of baptism were sought for marriage in Paris: there was uncertainty about her place and date of birth, and her parents' fate. Georgina sent a charming if feebly written letter to her future son-in-law, signed 'Votre Mere de Coeur'.[81] In April 1894 the twenty-seven year old Juliet was married at the Roman Catholic Church at Chelsea. The ex-Viceroy of India, Liberal statesman and Catholic convert, the first Marquess of Ripon (one of the trustees under William's will), who was a de Grey relation of the Cowpers, made a 'capital stage-father', according to George Russell.[82] Cardinal Vaughan gave a blessing.[83] Georgina was told the bride was the most 'delicious' ever, a portrait featured in the *Pictorial News* and announcements appeared.[84]

To begin with the newly-weds stayed with Georgina, and thereafter Juliet wrote frequently to her Lily from Paris where they set up home. Georgina naturally missed her daughter, but she was comforted by the belief that in Eugene Juliet had found not only a husband but a 'mother's love … brooding over you & comforting you & preserving you from draughts & all evil that he can prevent'. Georgina's concern now was that the Deschamps should have a healthy residence. She offered more money and gave furniture to fill their house at Rue Meyerbeer.[85]

Georgina had the companionship of Emily Ford who was 'very nice and dear', and delighted that the Academy had accepted her paintings.[86] Visitors included Waggie, Eveleen Myers, Theodore Watts-Dunton, Eliza Keary, and George Russell.[87] Georgina sat for the Hellenic-looking stepdaughter of Marie Spartali Stillman the Pre-Raphaelite, 'it is a very sad but a beautiful Drawing,' she told Juliet; Augustus thought it dreadful.[88] Georgina had a little assembly, with her old friends the Frederick Maxses, Edward Maitland, Baldwyn Leighton, Hannah, and Constance Wilde.[89] Earl Cowper and Countess Katie came, and said that they should live with her at Bab. An exuberant Alys Pearsall Smith announced her marriage to Bertrand Russell.[90] The writer Stopford Brooke, formerly Anglican chaplain to the Empress Frederick and now a Unitarian, befriended her. Frank Sumner watched her overdraft after letters from Coutts, taking her cheque book and superintending bills. They made a party of two at night when he sang music-hall songs that he made 'refined and touching'.[91]

Mary Fawcett, who had attended the Broadlands conferences and had a 'quaint way of dressing', now helped with correspondence as Georgina's strength ebbed; Juliet's daily letter was 'our grand recreation'.[92] On one occasion a children's party was arranged, with Georgina's chair positioned to see the fun from the dining room.[93] She delighted in her pet dogs and read new works, like Julia Wedgwood's *The Moral Ideal*, 'It does not seem to me very difficult [,] so clearly written – What a beautiful mind she has.'[94]

In 1895 and 1897 Constance sheltered at Babbacombe from the scandal of her husband's arrest, trials and sentencing. Georgina also offered Oscar refuge, despite telling Juliet: 'I do not think there could be a greater trial with such disgusting shame … one cannot bear even to allude to it. Can one touch pitch and not be defiled? You are quite right in keeping aloof – so would I if I did not feel called upon to shelter her.' Juliet had written once, 'Constance can see you without staying. I am sorry for her but pity is not always akin to love. Please burn this.' Though she dreaded meeting Constance, Georgina hoped Babbacombe would be an 'ark of refuge'.[95]

'I am now so poorly and stupid and uninteresting,' she told Juliet in early 1895, but those 'on the edge of my life' were so kind.[96] Despite efforts by others to control her expenditure Georgina thought she was 'not nearly so out at elbows as dear Hannah evidently thinks me'.[97] The next year her extravagant generosity resulted in a rift. Augustus and Evelyn Ashley, alerted by her solicitor's resignation, discovered she had made money over to Frank, whom they saw as a predatory stranger. Sumner had already 'abstracted so much', Augustus told Evelyn, and Georgina hid the fact that she had signed a deed in Frank's favour. Augustus now refused to be executor of her will. Georgina's generosity or failing intelligence encouraged exploitation, for Frank asked a solicitor to obtain her signature to documents making her liable for £2000 and interest if he and a partner could not pay, 'some wretched deception has been at work.' Mary Fawcett feared that if anything was said against Frank, nothing could prevent Georgina from leaving him any amount of money, and felt that she was afraid of Augustus's interference.[98] With a tiny balance at Coutts, Magsie was also alarmed over Eugene's financial embarrassment. Georgina talked as though she was rich, but had to accept that she was unable to meet current household expenses. Augustus and Mary did their best to order affairs, but were disheartened at so many claims of which they had no knowledge.[99]

Fresh sorrow came with Emelia Gurney's death in October. Basil was there to comfort her and Georgina's memorial appeared in the *Guardian*.[100] An illness of Juliet's, feared to be diphtheria, was concealed lest it should weaken her.[101] Though Juliet recovered, her husband's business was, in Augustus's words, very shady. Eugene had received and lost £2000 when Juliet appealed for a further sum. Augustus thought Eugene's idea of a new firm ludicrous: 'You might as well chuck it in the Seine for all the good it will do.' Since the wedding they had asked for £4000 additionally to Juliet's allowance, 'The more my sister gives the more he wants.'[102] A new blow came in late 1896 with Magsie's stroke and death, which caused Georgina to rail against God.[103] After a marriage of fifty years, the bereaved Augustus was utterly crushed. There was talk of joining Georgina, but she was wary of this when she could give little comfort.[104] He stubbornly refused financial aid.[105] She felt increasingly isolated: 'I am indeed as one dead and out of sight unable to walk write think and everything but love and remember my friends gratefully,' she told Frederic Myers in a sad scribble. She was consoled by spiritualistic hopes 'so mercifully confirmed of late years … I am out of the way of all sympathy in this – so pray tell me of any blessed helps you get – and if you have any Message from my friend'.[106] Visitors, such as her cousin Lord Dysart and George MacDonald, still came.[107] George Russell imagined her with 'ladies-in-waiting' reading St Augustine's *Confessions*.[108] But from 1898 she never left Babbacombe and acquaintances detected mental decline.[109]

Her young worshipper Constance Wilde died in April. Hannah had urged sympathy with Constance, 'I cannot help hoping that thee will let her go to thee for a little while when you can,' hoping Georgina would encourage Constance to divorce and return to her maiden name for her boys' sake, which was what had happened.[110] Eugene's difficulties with the Bourse took their toll. Georgina could offer little assistance; Basil tried to safeguard Juliet's settlements and Augustus ensured Babbacombe was not mortgaged.[111] In August Eugene arrived in London ill; he died in September. Basil said Juliet had been 'very calm and self sufficient and wise and the horror of the whole thing has been unspeakable'.[112]

One late glimpse of Georgina in her words comes from Easter Eve 1899, when a maid brought a fish breakfast: 'Oh! Hannah? What have you brought! Those dear fish! I could not eat them, I love them too much. I could not bear them to suffer and die for me.' She was persuaded that they were borne from the sea dead, and that Juliet had left them for her.[113]

Her generation was passing. Her eldest brother died in 1890.[114] At the start of the new century John Ruskin died.[115] Georgina's letter to Joan Severn after her friend's transfiguration was moving: 'Loved from my earliest days and to be mourned till my latest. The world will always be darker without him, and oh how I feel for you.'[116] George Russell kept her informed about the Gladstones, who often thought of the 'old days', Catherine Gladstone told her.[117] He said her condolences after Mrs Gladstone's death brought 'immense pleasure', and reassuringly said *quietus* had been painless.[118] Edward Clifford sent her a postcard at Queen Victoria's funeral and news of Lady Simon's passing.[119]

During the census in March 1901, Georgina had the company of Juliet, Georgina Sumner, Jessie Cowper and seven servants. In early October Jessie died at Frankfurt. She was buried with Catholic rites, beside Spencer in Romsey.[120] Georgina herself became ill in September, and Juliet tended her with advice from Florence Craven, the nurse who had given the controversial lecture at the Cowper-Temples' in 1878. But Juliet's attempts to light candles around her bed and comfort with water annoyed Augustus.[121] The wrath of the 'House of Tollemache' also meant that Frank's attempt to see 'Grannie' was thwarted.[122] Early on 17 October, Georgina died; her last words were Wesley's, 'Gentle Jesus ... pity my simplicity,' which Ernest Fane had uttered in his illness in 1850.[123]

Emily Ford said she simply could not understand the world without her godmother. Letters came from other mourners such as Frances Power Cobbe ('I loved the dear, beautiful being who has left us more than I could ever tell her. Now, she is to be to me – ever more, one of the Hopes of Heaven'), Laura Hope ('so different and infinitely above ordinary mortals') and the biographer Augustus Hare, mourning 'that gentle and that so beloved presence' and remembering her 'still so beautiful – though so much tried by age and illness – so contented on her couch in her lovely room – so willing to accept her present state and see the brightest side of it.'[124] Cyril Holland longed for a last look at her 'beautiful and peaceful face'.[125]

At the funeral in Romsey Abbey there were deputations from the Band of Mercy and Women's Temperance Union. Frank kept away, fearful of 'the Uncle'.[126] Her grave beside William was marked with modest and pious inscriptions and evergreens.[127]

FIGURE 20. The Mount Temple graves, Botley Road Cemetery, Romsey.

Torquay commemorated her contribution to a pier sheltering fishing boats and sea bird protection, with a statue by Arthur Walker unveiled in 1903 in Basil Wilberforce's presence. The Tate received Rossetti's *Sancta Lilias* (derived from *The Blessed Damozel* in 1874) as a memorial from Juliet, in 1909.

Juliet was now alone. Earl Cowper had feared that Georgina would leave little, its having been 'all muddled away. She was so very kind and generous that she never could refuse anybody anything'.[128] Babbacombe Cliff was put up for sale in 1903 and again in 1911 when there were rumours that royalty was investigating a seaside home.[129] Juliet was ill and found little medical help, but devoted herself to good works, supporting a Convent of Mercy and work in the East End.[130] Cyril Holland wrote her a touching letter in 1907, full of youthful wisdom about the 'hidden tragedy of it all, behind the flickering footlights of frivolity'.[131] About 1915 she married the Italian who had so beguiled her: it was a disaster.[132]

CONCLUSION

William once said that he had endured no great affliction or terrible grief: he did not know why as it could not have been that he did not need them, and he wondered if they would be given to him in the new life.[1] Certainly his marriage was not tested by any crisis of confidence. Lady Palmerston noted in 1848 that Georgina 'evidently quite adores him, and he is evidently very proud of her' and that she shared 'all his feelings and notions'.[2] Her friend Emelia Gurney spoke of 'very near a perfect union'. Another recalled a remarkable 'partnership'.[3] In the press one observer wrote that they led 'so entirely sympathetic a life that it is quite pleasant to look at them together'.[4] Little evidence of serious dispute survives; at any rate Georgina recalled no ruffle on William's serenity. Not that Georgina was complaisant; Clifford recalled she 'always had her own way everywhere'.[5] Was marital harmony surprising, given their different temperaments, he often placid, she so often the reverse? Georgina wrote of their different upbringings, and that they had 'met at the same point from opposite ends'.[6] If Shaftesbury's unlikely union with Minny proved successful, in William's case he chose a woman who shared his religiosity.

But there were no children. Reticence and the destruction of diaries and letters means that we can only speculate on the more private aspects of their married life – what fragmentary evidence there is suggests that Georgina's maternal feelings were thwarted by a physical problem. Noting Ruskin's dedication of *Sesame and Lilies* to her, Mark Girouard included her in a group of 'queenly ladies' in *The Road to Camelot* (with Emelia Gurney, Lady Waterford and Lady Canning) who were 'noble by nature and usually noble by name as well, chatelaines of great houses, as good as they were beautiful and as artistic as they were good, sailing serene and splendid through Victorian drawing-rooms in a distinctive atmosphere of love, worship and deference'.[7] Naturally, her friends included 'queenly ladies' and Broadlands conferences attracted earnest aristocrats such as Lady Waterford. Girouard noted that these marriages were often childless, and wondered whether some were unconsummated because of the elevation of spiritual over profane love. Yet the Cowper-Temples had their child in Juliet, 'the bright child of Broadlands'.[8]

George Russell described Georgina as 'one of the most remarkable women of her time'.[9] Yet Bradley found, in editing Ruskin's letters to the Cowper-Temples, that Georgina's personality was difficult to evoke.[10] One is left with the impression of a determined woman, willing to be unconventional in her religious views but anxious for reassuring belief, an intellectual who read widely and had an 'absorbing interest in religious, ethical, and psychological problems'.[11] She was physically striking. A golden-haired beauty in her youth, she remained imposing, a Madonna 'as good as she was beautiful', a 'tall graceful figure ... her lovely face happy with smiles', combining 'faultless beauty' with 'a dignity of presence and bearing, the outward and visible sign of a nature singularly noble and elevated'.[12]

She had critics, of course. Her nephew, Lionel, for instance, thought her sympathy 'too often on the stretch for spontaneous and healthful activity'. If, 'when she heard the sorrows of her private friends, her sympathetic spirit was abundantly willing', her flesh was weak and her nerves exhausted, and attempts to hide this led frequently to 'fatigued artificiality of manner, not easily distinguished from affectation', this was because 'the divine *ichor* which flowed in her veins was hardly suited to a daughter of Eve. She was too saintly to be quite human'. Her protégé Edward Clifford wrote that though never exactly afraid of her, he 'often felt more present with her at a great distance than near – just as one does with a range of verdant and snow-capped mountains'.[13]

Her partner in saintliness, William, had not been raised in a shelter from the world like her. A Whig aristocrat, William attained prominence through connections with Palmerston and Melbourne; as Shaftesbury observed of himself, he was 'near the centre of all action in politics, the fountainhood of all information'.[14] Worldly interests of party politics and social and moral reformation attracted him. Yet he combined, according to Augustus Tollemache, 'the sacred with the social element ... it was possible to live in the world without being worldly'.[15] A sister thought him virtually the only man she knew 'who lived in the world quite unspoiled by it'.[16] Hannah Smith identified other-worldliness as his chief characteristic.[17]

Like Shaftesbury, he reacted against the perceived religious apathy of his parents' generation.[18] His relationship with Shaftesbury was close, indeed Shaftesbury latterly told him that outside his own house, he and Catherine Marsh were the only persons who had the least sympathy with, or believed, what he said.[19] At Shaftesbury's death his candidacy as the new 'leading philanthropist' was rejected by *The Spectator* as he was 'too open to impression', but when he died comparison was made with Shaftesbury.[20] One paper judged him 'almost a model of benevolence as a politician, as a peer, as a landlord, and as an unostentatious social reformer', only reformers knew what he had done for every kind of benevolent movement, for certain privileged persons could go to him for funds for almost any philanthropic work.[21]

As philanthropic aristocrats they were not unique, indeed, one leading hostess remembered them among 'a small but powerful set, who mainly occupied themselves with religious and evangelizing work', including Shaftesbury, Lord Harrowby, Lord Kinnaird and Samuel Morley.[22] Spiritually, they strayed from orthodoxy more than many of the philanthropic elite. Lionel Tollemache considered them holy fools, but it was the foolishness of the open, curious and generous mind; and George Russell thought William had managed to combine saintliness with wisdom and agreeableness. Charitable to all, 'cruelty was the only vice that they judged sternly.'[23] Georgina's philanthropy was a practical mission in a life of doubt. Propelled into a brilliant circle by marriage, she chose a role as patron of moral reform and religious inquiry.

Georgina might have taken a dominant role in Society; she figured among the 'Social Queens under three Reigns' in an article in 1920. She had the quality of dignity and grace which ought to have qualified her as one of E.F. Benson's bygone 'great ladies' when he presented his 'Victorian peep-show'.[24] But she was not content with Social eminence; nor had her upbringing made her merely decorative. Her dominant concerns were the search for God and the lessening of cruelty and pain.[25] Such concerns were not inimical, had she been inclined, to that feminist activity which developed in the nineteenth century. We have seen her friendships and associations with middle-class feminists such as Emelia Gurney, Frances Power Cobbe, Emma Cons and Julia Wedgwood, and her support for the vote for women after earlier considering the question of women's rights 'nonsense'. Whether one chooses to call her a feminist depends on how the term is used in the context of the complex and diverse woman's movement: that she was an *aristocratic* woman complicates the situation.[26] There is no engagement with feminist writing in her surviving papers, and no evidence of an intense concern about the general situation for women. Unfortunately we lack her response to John Ruskin's *Sesame and Lilies*, wherein women were warned away from the 'dangerous science' of theology, advice she patently ignored.[27] William, we have seen, supported the advancement of women, at least in the spheres of education and employment.

The impressions of many significant and earnest people whom she inspired convey her appeal. Louisa MacDonald wrote of her as a 'safe sea of love that will receive all kinds of troubles and ill-humours too and once in that sea they are transformed into blessings and patience'.[28] Julia Wedgwood equated her presence with a 'bath of wondrous revival'.[29] Emelia Gurney called her 'Beatissima', 'My precious beloved one', and 'Ladye of Pity'. Eva Gore-Booth rhapsodized about her 'sculptured splendour' and associated her with 'starry music'.[30] Extravagant praise reflected intimate female friendships – ardent but not erotic – which Georgina sustained through her correspondence and socializing.[31]

Men were equally drawn to her. Dante Gabriel Rossetti wrote of the 'noble beauty of her Christ-like character'. Augustus Hare saw 'a marvelous union of beauty, goodness, and intelligence'.[32] Henry Cowper described her as 'the most wonderful and beautiful personality he had ever met, the personification of Divine Love, more nearly an angel than a human being, yet most human in her relations with the sick and the suffering, the helpless and the sad.'[33] The solicitor and radical politician Joseph Guedalla, father of Palmerston's biographer, carried her photograph in adoration.[34] The vegetarian Dr George Black detected a 'divine light' suffusing her face.[35] The actor Norman Forbes-Robertson thought her 'one on whose doorstep he could ever be ringing at'.[36] Such veneration is reminiscent of the response to Josephine Butler, also seen by her admirers as combining beauty and saintliness.

The Cowper-Temples had privileged lives: born in great wealth and in William's case, at the heart of the political and social establishment. He supported anti-slavery and factory reform, yet defended the Protestant ascendancy in Ireland and opposed Chartism. He accepted aggressive foreign policy in the era of Palmerston but condemned Beaconsfieldism and the 'Bulgarian atrocities'. Their philanthropy, in an age whose myriad social, moral or spiritual needs stimulated a rich philanthropic endeavour, involved little material hardship but could, as with Georgina's district and workhouse visiting, exhaust or depress. The obligation of Christian charity stimulated them, rather than any compensatory motive, as some said, for William's political mediocrity.

Ultimately, although this work's subtitle conveys the high political milieu which for a long time provided such an important preoccupation for William and which required the participation, as hostess and partner, of his wife, they were both concerned with what they would have considered more serious subjects than the party politics which William's mother had found so absorbing. These 'two blesseds' – as one writer called them – made Broadlands a space 'impregnated with religion and with a passionate interest in religious questions', where people of diverse denominations and classes conferred on spiritual matters in the belief that the spiritual did matter.[37]

One might leave it there, but another theme is absent from my subtitle. For their interests *were* eccentric at times: an apparently urbane if romantically-inclined Whig not only exhibited piety worthy of Shaftesbury's brother-in-law, but flirted with the ideas of Thomas Lake Harris – characterized by his most famous follower's biographer as an 'evil charlatan' – and pursued, with his wife, spiritualism and faith-healing while they developed a reputation as 'practical philanthropists'.[38] In the Victorian era belief in spiritualism was not peculiar (at any rate, the Cowper-Temples were in the company of such luminaries as Gladstone, in taking a serious interest in it) and faith healing was not absurd. But the juxtaposition in their lives of mundane domestic or political activities with table-turning and millenarian dramatics, which the narrative of their lives has sought to stress, is striking. The surviving papers do not provide us with a clear answer to the question of how far the Cowper-Temples understood and countenanced the outré sexual ideas propounded by such figures as James Hinton, Thomas Lake Harris, and Laurence Oliphant, or perhaps unwittingly embraced by Robert Pearsall Smith; and which contrasted with the purity campaigns the Cowper-Temples supported. It is a reminder, to end on a Stracheyan note, of the oddities and ironies in the lives of many a great Victorian.[39]

NOTES

A Note on Manuscript Collections

The Cowper-Temples' papers are in the Broadlands Archives in the Hartley Library at the University of Southampton. They are extensive but only partially catalogued in detail and material on such key aspects as the conferences are scattered throughout the archive. The Cowper-Temples kept diaries, and although Georgina directed some to be destroyed, not all were. She drew on William's early journals for her memoirs, and although some are missing – including one lent to George Russell for his biography of Gladstone – they offer an intimate view of William's youth. The young William was given to reflection on his character and beliefs, though there are no long passages of self-justification or extended self-analysis. His diaries evoke his equable personality well. Georgina's diaries convey her active life, self-dramatization, intellectual and religious curiosity, and hint at the temperament behind the surface serenity. The Cowper-Temples' idiosyncratic orthography and the absence of dates from many of William's hurried letters provide challenges. Georgina's friend Julia Tomkinson observed that her handwriting was 'so different as you know from all other handwriting' (letter in BR56/24) and William once rhapsodized her 'flickering wobbling lines' (letter in BR53/3). In transcribing, I make minor changes, such as modernizing spellings, using italics for underlining, and dispensing with characteristic abbreviation (like 'i' for 'the'). Also in the Broadlands Archives are letters from Lord Palmerston and Emily Palmerston, and letters to William's nephew and heir Evelyn Ashley (BR60/3/11-12). I have studied Ashley's own papers in this archive, and studied the letters and diaries of his father Lord Shaftesbury. There is only cursory mention of 'Billy' in the Lamb Family Papers at the British Library (BL, Add. MSS 45554). Cowper family papers are preserved in the Hertfordshire Record Office, but there is little of direct relevance for this study. Some material relating to the Broadlands conference of 1876 was auctioned in 1973; some correspondence by William with family and acquaintances, auctioned by Bloomsbury Book Auctioneers in 1999, has not been traced. A collection of legal and financial papers concerning Mount-Temple property in Dublin is now in the Special Collections at the Paterno Library, Pennsylvania State University.

Papers produced in William's official roles, as a Lord of the Admiralty, as President of the Board of Health and in the Education Department, are in the National Archives (not consulted in this study). Official correspondence also appears in the Melbourne and Palmerston papers in the Broadlands Archives (the former, WCF, MEL/CO/1-53). The Broadlands Archives include papers from his period in the Office of Works, and there are also letters in the Royal Archives at Windsor principally from this period and ministerial position. Correspondence with William Gladstone is in the British Library (BL, Add. MSS 44374-788 *passim*) and Broadlands Archives. His correspondence with the sanitary reformer Sir Edwin Chadwick is at University College London. Correspondence with the geologist and physicist James Forbes is in St Andrews

University Library (not consulted for this study). There are letters to the politician and discoverer of Nineveh, Austen Layard; the mathematician Charles Babbage; and the natural scientist Alfred Russel Wallace (BL, Add. MSS 39104, 38997; Add. MSS 37196, Add. MSS. 464440-46441). Letters to Archbishop Tait on the Gallican church are in the Tait Papers and F.A. White Papers in Lambeth Palace Library, which also holds letters from William on education, in the Papers of Canon David Melville. William's extensive circle of friends included William Cavendish, sixth Duke of Devonshire, and letters from William to him, 1834-1848, and copious references to William in the Duke's journals, survive at Chatsworth House. His friendship with the third Lord Holland and his wife is represented by letters in the British Library (BL, Add. MSS 51559). His friendship with the writer Edward Bulwer Lytton leaves traces in correspondence from 1837 to 1865 (Hertfordshire Archives and Local Studies, D/EK). Bulwer Lytton's brother Sir Henry Bulwer wrote Palmerston's official life, and letters in the Broadlands Archives and Bulwer Papers in Norfolk Records Office document William's involvement.

The Cowper-Temples' friendship with John Ruskin was studied by Van Akin Burd, and documented in John Bradley's edition of letters. Derrick Leon had access, in the 1940s, to a mass of letters from Ruskin, Rose La Touche and Maria La Touche, to Georgina, in relation to this tragic relationship. I have consulted material on this subject in the Broadlands Archives and University of Durham Special Collection, including correspondence between Leon and Mrs Detmar Blow, a niece of Georgina who inherited some of this correspondence.

Their association with Laurence Oliphant is documented in the Broadlands Archive, and the many letters to the Cowper-Temples in the Oliphant-Harris Papers (University of Columbia) used by Anne Taylor in her study, *Laurence Oliphant* (1982) but which I have not consulted. Their friendship with the mystic and writer George MacDonald has been documented in biographies of MacDonald which draw on letters from MacDonald in the National Library of Scotland; (NLS, Manuscripts Division, MS 9745) material on the friendship exists in other archives too. There are references to the Cowpers in uncatalogued family correspondence and catalogued letters from Georgina in the George MacDonald Collection, Beinecke Rare Book and Manuscript Library, Yale University.

Georgina's friends included Emelia Gurney, Constance Wilde, and the Americans Hannah Smith and Olive Seward. Her relationship with these women can be traced through correspondence in the Broadlands Archives and in American collections such as the Lilly Library (Bloomington, Indiana). She also corresponded with Florence Nightingale (BL, Add. MS 45799, ff. 155b, 160). Other letters from the Cowper-Temples, or discussing them in passing, appear in archives in the Women's Library, London Metropolitan University, in the Josephine Butler Papers, Louisa Twining Papers, and the autograph collection of female educational pioneers. There is no material in the small collection of Emily S. Ford's papers in the University of Leeds Special Collection (Ford family papers). There is some correspondence in the Ashburton Papers in the National Library of Scotland (Acc.11388), the National Library also has a number of miscellaneous letters from William (a letter to John McLaren on legislation for female university education, in the F.S. Oliver Collection, MS 24800; concerning the Ventilation Commission, in the Campbell papers; invitation to Thomas Carlyle in MS 1770; naval patronage in the Minto Papers, MS12085).

Manuscript Collections consulted

Beinecke Rare Book and Manuscript Library, Yale University
George MacDonald Collection

British Library, Manuscript Collections
A.R. Wallace Papers, Sir Austen Henry Layard Papers, Charles Kingsley Papers, Papers of G.F. Robinson, first Marquis of Ripon, Florence Nightingale Papers, Holland House Papers, Lamb Family Papers, Papers of the fourth Earl Carnarvon, Mary Gladstone Papers, W.E. Gladstone Papers

Chatsworth House, Derbyshire
Papers of the sixth Duke of Devonshire (Devonshire Mss.)

Durham University Library and Special Collections
John Ruskin Biographical Papers, Add. MS 786

B.L. Fisher Library Archives, Asbury Theological Seminary, Wilmore, Kentucky
Hannah Smith Papers

Hertfordshire Archives and Local Studies
Papers of Edward Bulwer Lytton, first Baron Lytton

Lambeth Palace Library
Archbishop A.C. Tait Papers, F.A. White Papers, Canon David Melville Papers

Lilly Library, Manuscripts Department, Bloomington, Indiana
Hannah Smith MSS

National Library of Scotland, Manuscript Collections
Ashburton Papers, George MacDonald Papers, Thomas Carlyle Papers, John Francis Campbell Papers

Norfolk Records Office
Papers of Sir Henry Bulwer, Baron Dalling

The Royal Archives, Windsor Castle
Queen Victoria's Journals, Correspondence of Lord Melbourne, Office of Works Papers

The Royal College of Surgeons of Edinburgh
James Young Simpson Papers

The Women's Library, London Metropolitan University
Autograph collection of female educational pioneers, Josephine Butler Papers, Louisa Twining Papers

University of Nottingham, Manuscripts and Special Collections
Sir Andrew Buchanan Papers

University of Southampton, Special Collections
Broadlands Archives: Papers of William Cowper-Temple, Georgina Cowper-Temple and Juliet Latour Temple, Papers of the seventh Earl Shaftesbury, Evelyn Ashley Papers, Papers of the third Viscount Palmerston and Lady Palmerston, Papers of the second Viscount Melbourne

Wren Library, Trinity College, Cambridge
Papers of Richard Monckton Milnes, first Baron Houghton, F.W.H. Myers Papers

Other material, e.g., transcriptions from the Edwin Chadwick Papers, University College London, or material accessed via online databases (such as the Talbot papers, now in the British Library but previously in the Lacock Abbey Collection, Fox Talbot Museum, and the subject of a digital project archived at http://foxtalbot.dmu.ac.uk/) and cited in the Notes and *Note on Manuscript Collections*, are not listed above.

Introduction

1   Evelyn Ashley, typed note in BR49/3; L.A. Tollemache, *Old and Odd Memories* (London: E. Arnold, 1908), p.77. Board schools were so-called for being managed by boards elected by the rate-payers.

2   See, for instance, R.H. Gretton, *A Modern History of the English People. 1880–1898* (1912; London: Grant Richards, 1913), vol.1, p.20.

3   BR44/19/6, newspaper clipping (probably *Liverpool Evening Express*) 16 October 1888.

4   *Mount Temple Memorials* (London: privately published, 1890), abbreviated hereafter to *MTM* when referring to the British Library copy inscribed by Georgina to a recipient known to William as 'Psyche Child', the copy of *MTM* in the Broadlands Archives has different pagination (the two versions vary by some three or six pages).

5   BR45/5, notebook, entry *c.* 21 November 1850.

6   W.A. Tollemache, *Some Reminiscences of Georgina, Lady Mount Temple By Her Surviving Brother* (privately printed, n.d.); J. McCarthy, *Portraits of the Sixties* (London: T. Fisher Unwin, 1903), pp.134-136; G.W.E. Russell, *Portraits of the Seventies* (London: T. Fisher Unwin, 1916).

7   The entry by A.F. Pollard, *Dictionary of National Biography* (supplementary vol.22, 1901) ignores William's philanthropic or religious activity. See entries in *Encyclopaedia Britannica* (1911 edition); T. Cooper, ed., *Men of the Time. A Dictionary of Contemporaries* (1879), p.278, and *Men of the Mark. A gallery of contemporary portraits of men distinguished in the senate, church, etc .,* series 1 (London: Sampson, Low, Marston, Searle, 1876), p.33.

8   P.A. Wellington, 'The Honourable William Cowper-Temple. Lord Palmerston's heir', *Pots and Papers* 4 (1989) (Lower Test Valley Archaeological Society), pp.13-34, using the Broadlands archives before the material came to the University of Southampton, to create an insightful essay.

9   B. Harrison, 'State Intervention and Moral Reform in nineteenth-century England', in P. Hollis ed., *Pressure from Without in Early Victorian England* (London: Edward Arnold, 1974), pp.293-294.

10   F.P. Cobbe, *Life of Frances Power Cobbe As Told by Herself* (1894; London: Swan and Sonnenschein, 1904), p.665.

11   D. Roberts, *Paternalism in Early Victorian England* (New Brunswick, New Jersey: Rutgers University Press, 1979), pp.199, 209, 216, 217, 245.

12   J.P. Parry, *Democracy and Religion. Gladstone and the Liberal Party. 1867–1875* (Cambridge: Cambridge University Press, 1986), p.15.

13   B. Hilton, *A Mad, Bad, and Dangerous People? England, 1783–1846* (Oxford: Clarendon Press, 2006), p.521, p.523: Ebrington, a Whig MP, became the second Earl Fortescue.

14   M.J.D. Roberts, *Making English Morals. Voluntary Association and Moral Reform in England, 1787-1886* (Cambridge: Cambridge University Press, 2004), p.227, footnote 115.

15   A comment applied to Emelia Gurney, *The Athenaeum*, 7 March 1901, p.296.

16   W.G. Collingwood, 'Ruskin's Isola', *Good Words*, February 1902, pp.77-82.

17   V.A. Burd, *Ruskin, Lady Mount Temple and the Spiritualists: an Episode in Broadlands History* (London: Brentham Press, 1982); Burd ed., *Christmas Story. John Ruskin's Venetian Letters of 1876–1877* (Newark: University of Delaware Press, 1990), chs.2-3; J.L. Bradley, ed., *Letters of John Ruskin to Lord and Lady Mount Temple* (Columbus, Ohio: Ohio State University Press, 1964); T. Hilton, *John Ruskin. The Later Years* (New Haven and London: Yale University Press, 2000), p.145.

18   P. Hoare, *England's Lost Eden: Adventures in a Victorian Utopia* (London: Fourth Estate: 2005).

19   M. Tromp, *Altered States: Sex, Nation, Drugs, and Self-Transformation in Victorian Spiritualism* (Albany, New York: State University of New York, 2006), ch.2.

20   A. Taylor, *Laurence Oliphant: 1829–1888* (Oxford: Oxford University Press, 1982), pp.132-134.

21   Taylor, *Laurence Oliphant*, p.133.

22   The phrases are from John Morley, *The Life of William Ewart Gladstone* (1903; 2 vols, London: E. Lloyd, 1908), vol.1 (Book V, ch.8), p.566; *Belfast News-Letter*, 19 June 1863, and Beresford Hope, in G.W.E. Russell, *Collections and Recollections* (New York and London: Harper and Brothers, 1898), p.143. There is no record of William's specifically Whiggish accent but his sister Fanny enforced this marker in her own family.

23   G. Fletcher, *Parliamentary Portraits of the Present Period. Third Series* (London: James Ridgway, 1862), p.133.

24   BL, Mary Gladstone Papers, Add. MSS 46229, ff.22-23, 24 November 1887.

25   D. Cannadine, *The Decline and Fall of the British Aristocracy* (New Haven, Connecticut: Yale University Press, 1990), pp.25-32; T.A. Jenkins, *Gladstone, Whiggery, and the Liberal Party. 1874–1886* (Oxford: Clarendon Press, 1988), pp.2-4; Adonis, *Making Aristocracy Work. The Peerage and the Political System in Britain 1884-1914* (Oxford, 1993), ch.9.

26   The mountain metaphor from 'The Political prospect', *Fortnightly Review* 79: 469 (January 1906), p.34. Efforts to prevent the development of a threatening 'low politics' did not entail a hermetic politics disengaged from 'the people'. I intend no historiographic *excursus* on the 'high political' here, but this study accepts a view of the nineteenth-century in which national politicians were not just driven by short-term 'party' calculation in a closed-off world (though William's electoral activities in 1841, examined below, show he could be motivated by short-term considerations) but were influenced by *ideas* – religious or otherwise – and in complex relationships with extra-parliamentary experts or special interest groups (like the Social Science Association or Commons Preservation Society, organizations which William was involved with, as we shall see). The antonym 'low politics' was rarely used in the nineteenth-century, a survey of the Chadwyck-Healey *British Periodicals* collection indicates almost no use of 'low politics' – understood as court intrigue or selfishness – and *increased* use of 'high politics' in journalism in the years 1890-1909.

27   B. Disraeli, *Lord George Bentinck: A Political Biography* (London: Colburn, 1852), p.325.

28   Parry, *Democracy and Religion*, p.31; of course, as B. Harrison notes, *Peaceable Kingdom. Stability and Change in Modern Britain* (Oxford: Clarendon Press, 1982) p.226, the aristocrat 'lived in the glare of publicity…his conduct was closely scrutinised'. A. Taylor, *Lords of Misrule: Hostility to Aristocracy in Late Nineteenth and Early Twentieth Century Britain* (Basingstoke: Palgrave Macmillan, 2004), studies radicals' attack on the aristocracy on moral and economic grounds, by exploiting sexual scandal, blood-sports and land monopoly.

29   *Manchester Guardian*, 20 January 1876, p.6.

30   K.J.D. Reynolds, *Aristocratic Women and Political Society in Victorian Britain* (Oxford: Clarendon Press, 1998), p.4; pp.7-8, p.27.

31   Hannah Smith, obituary of Lord Mount Temple, *Friends' Quarterly Examiner*, January 1889, pp.107-119 [p.111].

32   F.K. Prochaska, *Women and Philanthropy in Nineteenth Century England* (Oxford: Clarendon Press, 1980); F.K. Prochaska, 'Philanthropy', in F.M.L. Thompson, ed., *The Cambridge Social History of Britain 1750–1950*, vol.3, *Social agencies and institutions* (Cambridge: Cambridge University Press, 1990), ch.7, and Reynolds, *Aristocratic Women*, pp.110-128.

33   For Ruskin's description, J.L. Bradley and I. Ousby, *The Correspondence of John Ruskin and Charles Eliot Norton* (Cambridge: Cambridge University Press, 1987), p.461; for Benson's, B. Askwith, *Two Victorian Families* (London: Chatto and Windus, 1973), pp.167-168.

34   BR57/26/3, Georgina to Emelia Gurney [watermark 1864]; and similar contrasts, *MTM*, p.77, p.102. Characteristically, he delighted in the sunrise, see *MTM*, p.85.

35   Reynolds, *Aristocratic Women*, p.155, drawing on social anthropological work by S. Ardener and H. Callan, eds, *The Incorporated Wife* (London: Croom Helm, 1984).

36   H.J. Hanham, 'Political Patronage at the Treasury, 1870–1912', *The Historical Journal* 3:1 (1960), pp.75-84 traces the decline of patronage in the civil service to the Order in Council of 4 June 1870, which brought in open competition.

37   Hilton, *A Mad, Bad, and Dangerous People*, p.38; B. Hilton, *The Age of Atonement. The Influence of Evangelicalism on Social and Economic Thought, 1795–1865* (Oxford: Clarendon Press, 1988).

38   Roberts, *Making English Morals*, p.193; R.T. Shannon, *Gladstone and the Bulgarian Agitation, 1876* (1963; Hassocks: Harvester Press, 1975), p.35.

39   The strength of religious sentiment and the Church of England specifically, in the mid-Victorian period, is stressed by P.T. Marsh, *The Victorian Church in Decline. Archbishop Tait and the Church of England 1868–1882* (London: Routledge and Kegan Paul, 1969), p.3. For the 1870s as a time of significant cultural shift, see J. Stoddart, *Ruskin's Culture Wars. Fors Clavigera and the Crisis of Victorian Liberalism* (Charlottesville and London: University Press of Virginia, 1998).

40   E. Chalus, 'Elite women, social politics, and the political world of late-eighteenth century England', *Historical Journal* 43: 3 (2000), pp.669-697; Reynolds, *Aristocratic Women*, p.27, pp.154-155.

41   Tollemache, *Some Reminiscences*, pp.8-9. An unidentified noble acquaintance commented in 1875 that it 'must be a wonderful help to live so much with the Earnest world', see BR57/54/5, an unidentified peer writing from Birkhall, Ballater, 7 September 1875.

42   In studying the Cowper-Temples' reputations and in understanding their public careers and varied associations, I was greatly aided in moving beyond standard sources such as *Punch* and *The Times* (themselves now accessible in digitised format) by digital collections such as *British Periodicals and Periodicals Archive Online; 19th Century Newspapers; Nineteenth Century Serials Edition.*

Chapter 1. The Childhood and Youth of Billy Cowper

1   But he was christened at Hatfield, the Cavendish mansion, 7 January 1812.

2   J.A.W. Gunn and J. Matthews eds, *The Letters of Benjamin Disraeli: 1835–1837* 2 vols. (Toronto and London: University of Toronto Press, 1982), vol.2, p.501, letter 25 April 1836; A. Kenealy, *Memoirs of Edward Vaughan Kenealy, LL.D.* (London: J. Long, 1908), p.192, diary entry in September 1855; C. de L. Ryals and K.J. Fielding, eds, *The Collected Letters of Thomas and Jane Welsh Carlyle*, vol.21 (Durham, North Carolina, and London: Duke University Press, 1993), reprinting Jane Carlyle's gossip, 17 February 1847.

3   BR47/10, article on Lord Mount Temple in *The Christian* in 1880, corrected by William.

4   Quoted, in the context of a conversation between Melbourne and Edwin Landseer, in F.E. Baily, *The Love Story of Lady Palmerston* (London: Hutchinson, 1938), p.23.

5   See C. Rowell, 'George O'Brien Wyndham, third Earl of Egremont', *ODNB*.

6   K.C. Cowper, *Earl Cowper, K.G., A Memoir, by His Wife* (London, privately printed, 1913), p.238. For a likeness of William which suggests his true paternity, see a *carte de visite* in the National Portrait Gallery (NPG Ax16236), depicting him in the mid-1860s, in ministerial court dress.

7   See 'Melbourne-Cowper-Palmerston Circle' in S. Lasdun, *Victorians at Home* (London: Weidenfeld and Nicolson, 1981) for interiors at Brocket and Panshanger; and I. Crosbie, 'The Work and Life of Viscountess Francis Jocelyn: private lives', *History of Photography* 22: 1 (5 February 1998), pp.40-51.

8   *MTM*, p.11, for the assessment, but see M.F.E. Ogilvy, *Lady Palmerston and Her Times* (2 vols, London: Hodder and Stoughton, 1922) vol.1, p.144 'supposed by his family to be rather a nonentity'; see G. le Strange, ed., *Correspondence of Princess Lieven and Earl Grey* 3 vols (London: R. Bentley, 1890), vol.2, p.478, on the marriage.

9   H.J. Coke, *Tracks of a Rolling Stone* ('second edition', London: Smith, Elder, 1905), pp.60-62; 'Doings in Paris', *The Satirist*, 14 April and 8 September 1844.

10   P. Cunningham, ed., *The Letters of Horace Walpole. Fourth Earl of Orford* 9 vols (Edinburgh: J. Grant, 1906), vol.9, p.10.

11   A. Dyce, *Recollections of the Table-talk of Samuel Rogers. To which is added Porsoniana* (London: E. Moxon, 1856), p.153. The fortune that funded the collection partly derived from his mother, daughter of Henry Earl of Grantham (Count of Nassau-Auverquerque).

12   Ogilvy, *Lady Palmerston and Her Times*, vol.1, p.83.

13   C. Hibbert, *Queen Victoria in her Letters and Journals* (1984; Stroud: Sutton, 2000), p.67.

14   J. Wade, *The Extraordinary Black Book: An exposition of Abuses in Church and State, Courts of Law, Representation, Municipal and Corporate Bodies* (London: Effingham Wilson, 1832), p.522. On the Earl's friendship with Thanet and Creevey, see references in H. Maxwell, ed., *The Creevey Papers. A selection from the Correspondence and Diaries of the Late Thomas Creevey MP* 2 vols (London: J. Murray, 1903), vol.2. A portrait of Earl Cowper by Sir Thomas Lawrence appears in T. Lever, *The Letters of Lady Palmerston. Selected and Edited from the Originals at Broadlands* (London: J. Murray, 1957), opposite p.148.

15   P.H. Stanhope, *Life of the Right Honourable William Pitt* (4 vols, 1862), vol.4, pp.388-189. For Cowper's visit to Queen Caroline, see *The Times*, 3 November 1820, p.3.

16   B. Hilton, *A Mad, Bad, and Dangerous People*, p.273.

17   *The Times*, 5 July 1837, p.6.

18   J. Campbell, *The Lives of the Lord Chancellors and Keepers of the Great Seals*, 7 vols (1849; Philadelphia: Blanchard and Lea, 1851), vol.4, p.338.

19   Obituary in *Gentleman's Magazine*, August 1837, p.205.

20   See 'Member of the Middle Temple', *The assembled Commons; or, Parliamentary biographer, with an abstract of the law of election* (London: Scott, Webster and Geary, 1838), p.64.

21   Ogilvy, *Lady Palmerston and Her Times*, vol.1, p.15.

22   Ogilvy, *Lady Palmerston and Her Times*, vol.1, p.28, but note her quotation from Lord Broughton to the contrary.

23   G.S.H. Fox-Strangways, ed., *The Journal of Henry Edward Fox. Afterwards Fourth and Last Lord Holland. 1818-1830* (London: Thomas Butterworth, 1923), p.175, p.356.

24   Ogilvy, *Lady Palmerston and Her Times*, vol.1, p.109, letter of 1823 to Frederick Lamb. See also K.D. Reynolds, 'Lady Palmerston', *ODNB*, quoting Lady Harriet Cavendish.

25   Lever, *Letters of Lady Palmerston*, p.17.

26   A.P.J.C. Gore [Lord Sudley], ed., *Lieven-Palmerston Correspondence. 1828–1856* (London: J. Murray, 1943), p.92; Lever, *Letters of Lady Palmerston*, p.66. P. Guedalla, 'Emily Palmerston', in *Idylls of the Queen* (London: Hodder and Stoughton, 1937), p.300; Ogilvy, *Lady Palmerston and Her Times*, vol.1, p.xiii, p.193.

27   *MTM*, p.69; BR43/3/3, Emily Palmerston to William, Broadlands, n.d.

28   Wellington, 'The Honourable William Cowper-Temple…', p.14, citing letter from Emily to Frederick Lamb, 1821.

29   BR43/10/6, Frances Jocelyn to Harriet Gurney.

30   BR43/10/7, Minny Ashley to Harriet Gurney.

31   Lever, *Letters of Lady Palmerston*, p.15; *MTM*, p.4.

32   BR43/1, George Lamb to Fordwich, 21 February 1816; Ogilvy, *Lady Palmerston and Her Times*, vol.1, p.20; Lever, *Letters of Lady Palmerston*, p.21, Wellington, p.14.

33   Mrs Arbuthnot, 18 September 1829, cited in G.B.A.M. Finlayson, *The Seventh Earl of Shaftesbury* (London: Eyre Methuen, 1981), p.46.

34   Greville cited in Lasdun, *Victorians at Home*, p.83. On Hawk's care, see M. Ogilvy, *In Whig Society, 1775–1818. Compiled from the hitherto unpublished correspondence of Elizabeth Viscountess Melbourne, and Emily Lamb, Countess Cowper, afterwards Viscountess Palmerston* (London: Hodder and Stoughton, 1921), p.177.

35   Undated recollection in BR51/5, private journal.

36   Lever, *Letters of Lady Palmerston*, p.33.

37   See recollections entitled 'Religion and morality', *c*.1833, in BR51/5, private journal, on Money and his time at Wimbledon. On Ossulton, see BR43/7/2, letter from Fordwich to William, Lever, *Letters of Lady Palmerston*, p.66, p.142, and p.215; and Ogilvy, *Lady Palmerston and Her Times*, vol.1, p.148.

38   Ruddock had a school at Fulham which Bulwer Lytton attended, but he went to Hooker due to ill-treatment. To Hooker's fashionable feeder school for Eton and Harrow, went William Henry Fox Talbot, Cardinal Manning, and nephews of the Duke of Wellington and Napoleon.

39   BR51/5, private journal, recollections entitled 'Religion and morality', *c*.1836.

40   S.M. Moens and H.E. Blyth, *Rottingdean. The Story of a Village* (1952; Brighton: Beal, 1953), p.70; *Gentleman's Magazine*, September 1825, p.279.

41   Lever, *Letters of Lady Palmerston*, p.66; BR43/7/2, Fordwich to William. See *MTM*, p.13, on his fondness for hunting and riding.

42   Lever, *Letters of Lady Palmerston*, pp.81-82.

43   Lever, *Letters of Lady Palmerston*, p.83, p.94.

44   L.G. Mitchell, *Lord Melbourne, 1779–1848* (Oxford: Oxford University Press, 1997), pp.6-7.

45   On Eton then, see J. Morley, *The Life of William Ewart Gladstone* (1903), Book 1, ch.2; and C.A. Wilkinson, *Reminiscences of Eton (Keate's time)* (London: Hurst and Blackett, 1888).

46   BR51/5, private journal, recollections entitled 'Religion and morality', *c*.1836.

47   BL, Holland House Papers, Add. MSS 51559, f.107, 23 August 1837.

48   BR51/5, private journal, recollections entitled 'Religion and morality', *c*.1836.

49   Russell, *Portraits of the Seventies*, p.273.

50   He edited *The private diary of William, first Earl Cowper, Lord Chancellor of England* (1833).

51   *MTM*, p.182 (boy unidentified); *MTM*, p.4, quoting a comment by Gladstone in 1890.

52   H.C.G. Matthew, *Gladstone, 1809–1874* (Oxford: Clarendon Press, 1986), p.10. Gladstone recalled William in recollections of Dr F.C. Hawtrey, see J. Brooke and M. Sorensen, eds, *The Prime Ministers' Papers. I: Autobiographica* (London: HMSO, 1971), p.25, letter dated 26 November 1827, p.199.

53   27 October 1827, published in G.W.E. Russell, *The Right Honourable William Ewart Gladstone* (New York: Harper and Brothers, 1891), p.11.

54   BR43/2/2, Emily Cowper to William, 19 October 1826.

55   BR43/2/1, Fordwich to William, 21 September 1826. See Lever, *Letters of Lady Palmerston*, p.151 for Emily Cowper's letter concerning the new governess.

56   BR43/4/1-2, Fordwich to William, 13 March 1827.

57   BR51/5, private journal, recollections entitled 'Religion and morality', *c*.1836.

58   BR43/20/15, William to Georgina, from Brighton *c*. February 1855.

59   BR51/5, private journal, recollections entitled 'Religion and morality', *c*.1836. See Anderson's memoirs, J.S.M. Anderson, *Memoir of the Chisholm, Late M.P. for Invernesshire* (London: Rivington, 1842), p.44; and *MTM*, p.6.

60   BR51/5, private journal, recollections entitled 'Religion and morality', *c*.1836.

61   Russell, *Portraits of the Seventies*, p.274.

62   Russell, *Portraits of the Seventies*, p.274 says Lord John Russell and friends formed the conclave deciding on this career to divert William from the Church.

63   Lever, *Letters of Lady Palmerston*, p.179.

64   BR51/11, notebook subsequently entitled 'First Journey'; BR43/7/3, Fordwich to William.

65   BR51/11, entry for 2 June 1829.

66   BR56/25, report entitled 'de Ville August 1829'.

67   See William's notebook on his time in Edinburgh, BR51/12, which provides the source for his comments on Scottish acquaintances and activities in the following paragraphs.

68   See J. Morrell's entry on John Leslie in *ODNB*.

69 Chalmers lectured before a fashionable metropolitan audience on church establishments in April–May 1838 but there is no evidence that William was present.

70 BR51/12, 9 and 31 December 1829; on romanticism, see Parry, *Democracy and Religion*, p.71; and D.W. Bebbington, *Evangelicalism in Modern Britain: A History from the 1730s to the 1980s* (1989; London: Routledge, 1993), pp.80-81, who associates this 'revolt' against the rational roots of Evangelicalism with Edward Irving.

71 On Brandling, BR51/12, 21 November 1829. On the Kirk, see BR51/5, private journal, notes for 'End of 1829'.

72 BR51/5, private journal, note under 'Edinburgh 1830'.

73 BR45/1, notebook subsequently entitled in typescript, 'Early Thoughts'.

74 BR43/33/2, Sheepshanks to William, Sidmouth, Friday 1 December [after 1828].

75 See entry in fragment of journal *c*.1833, in BR44/5. Sheepshanks appears in J.A. Symington, *Some Unpublished Letters of Sir Walter Scott* (Oxford: Basil Blackwell, 1932) in 1828, p.433.

76 See BR29/13/1-17 for letters about Emily Cowper's plans, especially BR29/13/2.

77 BR43/6/3, Charles John Canning to William, 1832.

78 *Caledonian Mercury*, 28 December 1829 (from *London Gazette*). Frederick Lamb had been a cornet in the Royal House Guards.

79 BR51/5, private journal, entry under 'London, August 1830'.

80 BR43/35/1, William to Miss Scott, 7 August [1830].

81 BR55/43, letter from Dublin dated 8 June 1831.

82 See entry in fragment of journal *c*.1833, in BR44/5. Villiers was perhaps a younger brother of the fourth Earl of Clarendon.

83 Fragment of journal *c*.1833, in BR44/5. Probably Dr John Allen, librarian of Holland House.

84 BR43/34/4, 'HG' to 'Billy', letter subsequently dated in pencil 1834.

85 Finlayson, *The Seventh Earl of Shaftesbury*, p.19.

86 BR35/1, Emily Cowper to Minny, n.d.

87 *MTM*, p.9, from William's journal. According to the *Belfast News-Letter*, 22 November 1833, Cowper had been serving 'nearly 3 years' as aide de camp to the Marquess. See fragment of a letter from the Marquess, BR55/43, (lacking signature) to his son Lord Alfred, also in the Blues, Dublin, 1 December 1832. On Lord Anglesey, see *ODNB* entry. P. Ziegler describes him, *Melbourne. A Biography of William Lamb Second Viscount Melbourne* (London: Collins, 1976), p.150, as a 'neither a tactful nor a subtle man'. His responsibility was partly to Lord Melbourne as Home Secretary.

88 BR50/45, John Robert Townshend to William, Vice Regal Lodge, 15 October 1832.

89 F. Leveson Gower, ed., *Letters of Harriet, Countess Granville, 1810–1845* (2 vols, London: Longmans, Green, 1894), vol.2, p.120.

90 *MTM*, p.9.

91 *MTM*, p.9; letters from Moritz (in French), Southampton University Library, MS 236; and R. Apponyi, *Vingt-cinq ans à Paris (1826–1850). Journal du comte Rodolphe Apponyi, attaché de l'ambassade d'Autriche-Hongrie à Paris* (Paris: Plon Nourrit et Cie, 1913), vol.2, p.225.

92 W.E.K. Anderson, *The Journal of Sir Walter Scott* (Oxford: Clarendon Press, 1972), p.708.

93 On 'country whiggery', see Parry, *Democracy and Religion*, p.61.

94 See A.W. Clifford, *A Sketch of the Life of the Sixth Duke of Devonshire* (London: privately printed, 1870), p.57 for a letter from Georgina.

95 Devonshire Mss., Chatsworth, diary of the 6th Duke of Devonshire, 767.456 (1832), the earliest reference to Cowper is 29 September 1832.

96 *MTM*, p.10. The journal for this period is missing.

97 See K.D. Reynolds, 'William George Spencer Cavendish', *ODNB*.

98   J. Lees-Milne, *The Bachelor Duke. A Life of William Spencer Cavendish, Sixth Duke of Devonshire 1790-1858* (London: J. Murray, 1991). Beamish, incumbent of Trinity Chapel, Conduit Street, London, 1832-1863, was an anti-Romanist and anti-Tractarian.

99   BR43/17/2, Devonshire to William, Chatsworth, 14 August [1837].

100   Lees-Milne, *The Bachelor Duke*, pp.108-115, 124-128; P. Mandler, *Aristocratic Government in the Age of Reform. Whigs and Liberals 1830–1852* (Oxford: Clarendon Press, 1990), p.48.

101   *MTM*, p.19.

102   BR51/5, private journal, *c*.23 April 1837.

103   *Belfast News-Letter*, 22 November 1833; *MTM*, pp.11-12.

104   Devonshire Mss., Chatsworth, 6ᵗʰ Duke's travel journal, 2B 35, p.1.

105   *Gróf Károlyi György naplófeljegyzései, 1833-1836. szerkesztette, a bevezető tanulmányt és a jegyzeteket írta, a képeket válogatta Fazekas Rózsa* (Nyíregyháza: Szabolcs-Szatmár-Bereg Megyei Levéltár, 2002). Károlyi, BR43/34/2, September 1834, advised William to be a diplomat, though it was 'not very lucrative but rather amusing and not much to do'.

106   See BR45/2, a red morocco notebook, subsequently entitled 'Private Journal' and 'Journey with Duke of Devonshire'.

107   BR45/2, entry for 1 December 1833.

108   BR51/5, in recollections entitled 'Religion and morality', *c*.1836.

109   Fragment of journal *c*.1833-1834, in BR44/5. Maria was presumably the Countess Potocka acquainted with Balzac. Prince Schouwaloff was the Russian ambassador.

110   BR45/2, entry for 15 January 1834.

111   Devonshire Mss., Chatsworth, 6ᵗʰ Duke's travel journal, 2B 35.

112   See J. Premble, *The Mediterranean Passion. Victorians and Edwardians in the South* (Oxford: Clarendon Press, 1987), pp.210-227, on this tendency.

113   BR51/5, in recollections entitled 'Religion and morality', *c*.1836.

114   See BR45/2 for William's descriptions of his acquaintances (17 December 1833) and sightseeing; on Guercino, see his entry for 31 December 1833.

115   BR45/2, entry for 3 January 1834; NLS, Ashburton Papers, Acc.11388/41, 1 January 1834. On Harriet Baring, see J. Pope-Hennessy, *Monckton Milnes, The Years of Promise 1809–1851* (1949), pp.158-161.

116   Devonshire Mss., Chatsworth, diary of the 6ᵗʰ Duke, 767.457 (1833), 31 December 1833; and citing entries in 767.458 (1834), 2, 6 and 11 January 1834.

117   BR45/2, entries for 22 January 1834 on Harriet d'Orsay, 25 January 1834 on Eugenie's comments and 31 January 1834 on the visit to the grotto.

118   BR45/2, 14 February 1834; Devonshire Mss., Chatsworth, diary of the 6ᵗʰ Duke, 767.458 (1834), 12 and 24 February 1834.

119   BR44/5, fragment of journal *c*.1834. Thackeray, as W.E. Houghton notes, *The Victorian Frame of Mind 1830-1870* (New Haven: Yale University Press, 1963), p.364, thought it a 'regular topysturvyification of morality'.

120   Devonshire Mss., Chatsworth, diary of the 6ᵗʰ Duke, 767.458 (1834), 11 April 1834.

121   Devonshire Mss., Chatsworth, diary of the 6ᵗʰ Duke, 767.458 (1834), 16 August–31 August, 27 September 1834. On Lavinia, see O.W. Hewett, *Strawberry Fair: A Biography of Frances, Countess Waldegrave, 1821–1879* (London: J. Murray, 1956), pp.56-58.

122   Devonshire Mss., Chatsworth, 6ᵗʰ Duke's Group, 3136, f.1, 13 October 1834.

123   J. Owen, *Of the Mortification of Sin*, 1668. BR51/5, November 1834.

Chapter 2. The Political and Courtly Life of Fascinating Billy

1   BR33/2, Emily Cowper to William, Panshanger, 15 November [1834].

2   BR51/5, private journal, entry for 1835 in recollections penned *c*.1836.

3   *Weekly Dispatch*, 20 April 1856, stated Earl Cowper 'was distinguished from little but a general suavity of manners and a singular willingness'.

4   *MTM*, p.8, on June 1833, on his unworldly worldliness, see p.11.

5   *MTM*, p.9.

6   BR51/5, 21 April 1837, on lack of genius; BR51/5, 8 December 1836, on conversation.

7   BR44/1/3 'Peel's opinions in 1820'; BR44/1/4: Mem.: historical 1834, Althorp on Reform bill (dated South Street December 1840), Puseyism; BR44/1/6, Political history 1834, 23 June 1842, causes of Stanley's resigning office; BR44/1/8: Duke of Wellington 1831, 1834 and Peel; BR44/1/16, on Palmerston and Syrian campaign; BR44/1/18, *c*.1829, 'the manner in which the Canningite party left the Duke of Wellington's Govt.' Later William would furnish material for Hayward's essay on Melbourne, see H.E. Carlisle, ed., *A Selection from the Correspondence of Abraham Hayward from 1834 to 1884*, 2 vols (London: J. Murray, 1886), vol.2, p.4.

8   Hertfordshire Archives and Local Studies, D/EK/ C19/105/1; D/EK/ C19/106; D/EK/ C19/107; D/EK/ C19/108; D/EK/ C19/109; D/EK/ C19/110, letters dating from 1845–1851. See Bulwer Lytton's reply to Cowper, BR43/59, 21 November 1845 on contesting the county and referring to the Corn Laws. He was elected MP for Hertfordshire in 1852, a stumbling block earlier had been his protectionism.

9   P. Mandler, *Aristocratic Government*, p.48; see also V. Rowe, 'The Hertford Borough 1832 Election', *Parliamentary History* 11:1 (1992), pp.88-107 (p.106), for Quaker support for William. William's mother paid Ashley's electoral expenses.

10 Mandler, *Aristocratic Government*, pp.73-74. The borough's ruling body was dominated in the 1830s by Conservatives.

11 Devonshire Mss., Chatsworth, 6th Duke's Group, 3182, 28 November 1834.

12 Devonshire Mss., Chatsworth, 6th Duke's Group, 3236 (6 January 1835).

13 Devonshire Mss., Chatsworth, 6th Duke's Group, 3239, f.1 (9 January 1835).

14 BR33/2, 15 November 1834.

15 BR33/2, Brighton, 27 [month unknown] 1835.

16 Letter in BR50/43, from E. Lavinia Norreys to William, Bristol Hotel, Brighton, n.d. Ashley had been a Lord of Admiralty in Peel's administration.

17 BL, Holland House Papers, Add. MSS 51559. William contributed to the monument for Lord Holland, see *Manchester Guardian*, 17 February 1841, p.1.

18 Letter from Hyde Park barracks, 'Tuesday night', BR43/35/6.

19 L.G. Mitchell, *Holland House* (London: Duckworth, 1980), p.32, pp.35-36.

20 *MTM*, p.19. When she died, the third Lady Holland bequeathed William a set of Doyle's political cartoons, as the *Gentleman's Magazine* reported. Edward Clifford the artist, recalling meeting William *c*. 1869, wrote of his 'beautiful Vandyke-like hands, light blue eyes, and a delicate skin' (*MTM*, p.140).

21 L. Strachey and R. Fulford, eds, *The Greville Memoirs* (1938), vol.5, *January 1842 to December 1847*, p.87.

22 *PD*, 3rd series, vol.32, 14 April 1835, col.1037. His second wife was relieved when he didn't vote for flogging in the army, see her diary entry in BR58/3, for 15 March 1867.

23 April 1835, according to J.C. Sainty, 'Private Secretaries to First Lord 1743-1870', *Office Holders in Modern Britain*, vol.1, *Treasury Officials, 1660–1870* (London: Athlone, 1972). George Edward Anson joined him in May. See Ziegler, *Melbourne*, p.234, p.306; Mitchell, *Lord Melbourne*, pp.229-230, p.263, p.271. The Broadlands Archives include Cowper's papers as private secretary: some 53 letters from Melbourne, 1833–1848.

24 BR, MEL/CO/1, Melbourne to William, Whitehall, 13 November 1833.

25 BR, MEL/CO/2, Melbourne to William, South Street, 3 November 1834.

26 R.H. Brett, ed., *The Girlhood of Queen Victoria. A selection from Her Majesty's diaries between the years 1832 and 1840* (London: J. Murray, 1912), 2 vols, vol.1, p.256, records Melbourne's verdict (according to the Queen) that William's elder brother had 'sounder understanding' than him.

27   Melbourne thought it a shame that he should be unpaid and sent money to pay off debts,
     see BR, MEL/CO/12, Melbourne to William, South Street, 24 May 1837.
28   BR51/5, private journal, in recollections penned *c.* end of 1836.
29   Ziegler, *Melbourne*, p.306.
30   See Melbourne's complaint about errors in a copy of the King's speech, BR, MEL/CO/4-
     6, in August 1836.
31   BR, MEL/CO/15, 6 November 1838 and, praising William for this work, 7 November
     1838. On Durham, see also, William to Lady Holland, BL, Holland House Papers, Add.
     MSS 51559, f.120, 13 December 1838.
32   See Hilton, *Mad, Bad and Dangerous*, p.500.
33   Devonshire Mss., Chatsworth, 6th Duke's Group, 3261, f.1, 7 February 1835.
34   BL, Holland House Papers, Add. MSS 51559, f.83, 22 June 1836; followed by another
     communication, f.85, a letter to Lady Holland.
35   BL, Holland House Papers, Add. MSS 51559, 22 June 1836.
36   J.O. Hoge, and C. Olney, eds, *The Letters of Caroline Norton to Lord Melbourne* (Columbus:
     Ohio State University Press, 1974), p.101.
37   Mitchell, *Lord Melbourne*, pp.229-230. The quotations are from Caroline Norton's letter *c.*
     March 1839, BR43/40.
38   Mitchell, *Lord Melbourne*, p.229.
39   Mitchell, *Lord Melbourne*, p.229: Norton's Infants' Custody Bill was enacted in 1839, see
     William's role, 11 June 1839, in committee stage of the bill in the Commons, *Caledonian
     Mercury*, 15 June 1839.
40   BR43/34/7, Melbourne to William, n.d. [1837].
41   Devonshire Mss., Chatsworth, 6th Duke's Group, 3676, 4 July 1837.
42   BL, Holland House Papers, Add. MSS 51559, 8 August 1837, ff.96-97.
43   BL, Holland House Papers, Add. MSS 51559, f.98, 12 August 1837.
44   Devonshire Mss., Chatsworth, 6th Duke's Group, 4040, 27 March 1839.
45   BL, Holland House Papers, Add. MSS 51559, 8 August 1837, f.94.
46   *Morning Chronicle*, 25 July 1839.
47   BL, Holland House Papers, Add. MSS 51559, f.123, 11 December 1839.
48   Devonshire Mss., Chatsworth, 6th Duke's Group, 4105, 8 July 1839.
49   BR43/41/3, Melbourne to William, n.d.
50   BR43/41/1, Melbourne to William, *c.*March 1839.
51   Reynolds, *Aristocratic Women*, p.196.
52   Devonshire Mss., Chatsworth, 6th Duke's Group, 4040, 27 March 1839.
53   Devonshire Mss., Chatsworth, 6th Duke's Group, 4047, 13 April 1839.
54   Devonshire Mss., Chatsworth, 6th Duke's Group, 4047, 13 April 1839.
55   See R.H. Brett, *The Girlhood of Queen Victoria*, vol.2, p.161.
56   *The Times*, 22 May 1839, p.5, col.c.
57   BR, MEL/CO/22, Melbourne to William, South Street, 18 May 1839. See A. Aspinall, ed.,
     The Correspondence of Charles Arbuthnot (London: Royal Historical Society, 1941), p.201 on
     contacts with *The Times* about this affair.
58   *The Times*, 17 May 1839, p.4, col.b; 20 May 1839, p.4, col.a, 21 May 1839, p.5, col.f.
59   BR, MEL/CO/23, Melbourne to William, South Street, 18 May 1839; see Royal Archives,
     Windsor Castle, RA/VIC/MAIN/Z/501/80, William's letter of 17 May 1839, in which he
     asks Melbourne for 'a few hints' as he is 'afraid of committing another piece of rashness'.
60   Royal Archives, Windsor Castle, RA/VIC/MAIN/QVJ/1839, 21 May 1839.
61   *Annual Register* (1840), p.130. Duncombe was a former MP for Hertford. Yet witness the
     exchange reported in *The Times*, in debating the Horse Slaughtering bill, 25 July 1844, p.4,
     Duncombe ridiculing the bill as a petty sort of legislation, 'an interference by members
     with what did not concern them', replied to by Cowper thus, he 'desired to know what Mr

DUNCOMBE himself was always doing there, but interfering with what did not concern him?'

62   *The Times*, 21 May 1839, p.4.
63   *The Times*, 24 May 1839, p.4; *John Bull*, 2 June 1839.
64   *Morning Chronicle*, 25 July 1839, from *Hertfordshire Reformer*, for celebrations; P.H. Stanhope, *Notes on Conversations with the Duke of Wellington* (1886; Oxford: Oxford University Press, 1938), pp.141-142.
65   BR51/13, private journal, entry for 13 March 1840.
66   Houghton Papers, MSS6/193, 13 August [1841].
67   See BR44/1/5, 'Puseyism', notes by William (relating to Lord Melbourne); Strachey and Fulford, eds, *The Greville Memoirs 1814–1860*, vol.6 *January 1848 to December 1853* (1938), p.5. Pusey was a cousin of Lord Ashley.
68   *Quarterly Review*, 68:136 (September 1841), pp.515-516.
69   BR, MEL/CO/37, Melbourne to William, June 1841; BR, MEL/CO/52 is the address in William's hand with Melbourne's corrections.
70   Ziegler, *Melbourne*, p.338; BR, MEL/CO/38, Melbourne to William, 14 July 1841; BR, MEL/CO/40, Melbourne to William, 21 July 1841.
71   BL, Holland House Papers, Add. MSS 51559, f.128, 28 August [1841].
72   BR51/5, private journal, entry for 22 April 1837. Further reflections on Peel, in the context of Disraeli's onslaught during the Corn Laws crisis, are in BR44/16/16.
73   BR44/1/8, memorandum on the Duke of Wellington and Peel, 1845.
74   BL, Holland House Papers, Add. MSS 51559, f.141, 21 November 1842. See *Morning Chronicle*, 18 March 1839, *Ipswich Journal*, 25 March 1839.
75   *The British Churchman*, August 1845, p.72.
76   *PD*, 3rd series, vol.79, 14 April 1845, cols. 638-642.
77   See *Queen's Gazette*, January 1839, p.95, 26 November–9 December 1838; *Court and Fashionable Intelligence*, October 1837, p.231.
78   R.B. Brett, ed., *The Girlhood of Queen Victoria*, vol.1: p.218, p.235 (William 'as usual … very amusing'), pp.247-248, p.256, and vol.2, p.296.
79   BR43/34/8, unidentified correspondent writing from Lambton, 2 September [1837]. The Queen thought him 'very nice … and amusing. He puts me in mind of his uncle, Lord Melbourne', see Royal Archives, Windsor Castle, RA/VIC/MAIN/QVJ/1837, 18 August 1837.
80   See BL, Holland House Papers, Add. MSS 51559, 26 October 1837 for his report to Lady Holland on life at Brighton.
81   BL, Holland House Papers, Add. MSS 51559, 23 August 1837.
82   BR, MEL/CO/17, Melbourne to William [27 December 1838], and BR50/48, 30 December 1838, Lady Breadalbane to William, concerning her appointment as Lady of the Bedchamber; BR, MEL/CO/18, Melbourne commissioned William to inquire about mourning for a first cousin; and asked him to inquire, BR, MEL/CO/39, 20 July 1841 about future maids of honour.
83   Strachey and Fulford, eds, *The Greville Memoirs. 1814–1860*, vol.4, *January 1838 to December 1841* (London: Macmillan, 1938), p.225; D. Creston, *The Youthful Queen Victoria. A Discursive Narrative* (London: Macmillan, 1952), p.441; and p.340 for Tory rumours.
84   Mitchell, *Lord Melbourne*, p.236.
85   BL, Holland House Papers, Add. MSS 51559, 8 May 1837. Sir Frederick Watson had been master of the Household during William IV's reign.
86   BR51/5, private journal, entry for 18 August 1837. This was Miss Caroline Cocks.
87   BR51/5, private journal, entry for 18 August 1837.
88   BL, Holland House Papers, Add. MSS 51559, 29 August 1837.

89 BR51/13, private journal, entry for 19 November 1838. When William met Feodore he liked her, and spoke with her about Wilberforce, see BR51/13, 17 August 1840.

90 Devonshire Mss., Chatsworth, 6th Duke's Group, 3999, 15 December 1838.

91 BR51/13, private journal, entry for 18 October 1839.

92 BR51/13, private journal, entry for 23 October 1839.

93 BR43/39/11, Fanny to William, n.d., and BR43/39/12, Fanny to William (on Albert's ankles), see also the letter, in BR43/39, from Fanny to William, 13 November 1839 on the Queen as 'dissipated'. BR48/6/5 is an undated eulogy by William on Albert's 'perfect balance of mental power and moral qualities'.

94 BR51/13, private journal, entry for 3 August 1840.

95 *The Scotsman*, 1 April 1840, p.2; 4 April 1840, p.2; 1 August 1840, p.2.

96 W.B. Pope, ed., *The Diary of Benjamin Robert Haydon* (Cambridge, Massachusetts: Harvard University Press, 1963), vol.4, pp.275, 302, 304, 358, 618, 624, 627; vol.5, p.459.

97 The Bridgeman Art Library database lists the location as the *Forbes Magazine* collection.

98 BR50/43, n.d., but addressed to William at Regents Park Barracks.

99 D. Cecil, *Lord M, or, The Later Life of Lord Melbourne* (London: Constable, 1954), p.316.

100 Devonshire Mss., Chatsworth, 6th Duke's Group, 3529 (7 August 1836).

101 BR51/5, private journal, entry for August 1836.

102 Devonshire Mss., Chatsworth, diary of the 6th Duke, 767.460 (1836), final page of diary.

103 BR51/5, private journal, recollections penned *c.* end of 1836.

104 Devonshire Mss., Chatsworth, 6th Duke's Group, 3569 (6 October 1836). Other quotes in this paragraph from BR51/5, private journal, including entry for 'Monday' May 1837. The Duchess, a friend of Gladstone, was 'the centre of a brilliant and powerful social circle', supporter of humanitarian reforms, the nationalist cause in Italy and Poland, a 'high representative of the virtue, purity, simplicity, and sympathetic spirit of the Tennysonian epoch,' Morley, *Life of William Ewart Gladstone*, vol.1, book v, ch.12. *The Satirist* 26 June 1842 was snide about William's relationship with the Duchess and his zeal in taking care of her reputation.

105 Devonshire Mss., Chatsworth, diary of the 6th Duke, 767.461 (1837), 15 January 1837.

106 BR51/5, private journal, entry for 15 April 1837.

107 Devonshire Mss., Chatsworth, diary of the 6th Duke, 767.461 (1837), 6 May 1837, 7 May 1837.

108 BR43/17/1, Devonshire to William, Chiswick, 1 May 1837; and William's note, BR51/5, private journal, entry for 28 April 1837: 'The fact of this book meeting the eye of another person gave its humiliating records a power which they did not possess when reflected directly back upon my own mind, without the intervention of another reproving intellect.' See Strachey and Fulford, eds, *The Greville Memoirs. 1814-1860*, vol.7, *January 1854 to November 1860*, (1938) p.332, on Devonshire's resort to frivolous society.

109 See D. Cecil, *The Young Melbourne, and the Story of His Marriage with Caroline Lamb* (1939; London: Constable, 1954), p.179.

110 BR43/17/1, Devonshire to William, 1 May 1837. The dancer Pauline Duvernay's attractions as 'Florinda' are captured in a lithograph by T. McLean in February 1837.

111 BR43/17/6, Devonshire to William, n.d., but referring to Coronation ticket for Beamish.

112 Devonshire Mss., Chatsworth, diary of the 6th Duke, 767.461, September 1837; BR51/5, private journal, entry for 21 September 1837.

113 BL, Holland House Papers, Add. MSS 51559, ff.108-110, letters to Lord and Lady Holland, 26 October 1837.

114 BR51/5, private journal, entry for 22 October 1837.

115 BR51/5 private journal, comments following entry for Christmas 1837.

116 BR 51/5, private journal, entry for 21 April 1837.

117 BR51/5, private journal, entries for 6 December 1836 and 11 February 1838. See entry in fragment of journal, in BR44/5, '16 to 26' July, refers to dining with Blessington and Bulwer, though this could be Sir Henry Bulwer. See M. Sadleir, *Blessington and d' Orsay. A Masquerade* (London: Constable, 1933).

118 For William's portrait, see W. Connely, *Count d'Orsay, the Dandy of Dandies* (London: Cassell, 1952), p.327. The National Portrait Gallery has a lithograph based on this. On the Blessington circle, see Strachey and Fulford, *The Greville Memoirs. 1814-1860*, vol.4, pp.128-130. D'Orsay sketched Spencer Cowper, 26 October 1845.

119 BR51/5, private journal, entry for 10 June 1837.

120 Devonshire Mss., Chatsworth, 6th Duke's Group, 3656 (7 June 1837).

121 See William's letter to Lady Holland, BL, Holland House Papers, Add. MSS 51559, f.89.

122 BR51/5, private journal, entry for 20 [sic] June 1837.

123 Devonshire Mss., Chatsworth, 6th Duke's Group, 3656 (7 June 1837).

124 BR51/5, private journal, entry for 29 July 1837.

125 *The Scotsman*, 14 March 1838, p.2; BL, Holland House Papers, Add. MSS 51559, f.112, 11 April 1838; he entreated Bulwer to visit too, see Hertfordshire Archives and Local Studies, D/EK C6/133, 'Monday'.

126 BR51/5, private journal, entry for 6 May 1838.

127 Devonshire Mss., Chatsworth, diary of the 6th Duke, 767.462 (1838), citing 12 March 1838, and quoting 4 May 1838. See *MTM*, p.17, on his 'sweetness and brightness' then.

128 Devonshire Mss., Chatsworth, 6th Duke's Group, 3903, Thursday 5 (July 1838).

129 See BR51/13, private journal, entry for 20 August 1838.

130 BR51/5, private journal, entries for August 1838; BR51/13, private journal, entries for 20–22 August 1838. Perhaps the attraction of the Lakes was also due to romantic literature. His associate Bulwer Lytton 'spent several weeks in the Lake District immersed in a self-conscious philosophical solitude' (A. Brown's *ODNB* entry on Bulwer Lytton).

131 BR51/5, private journal, entry for September 1838; BL, Holland House Papers, Add. MSS 51559, f.118, 6 October 1838.

132 BR43/41/1, Melbourne to William, n.d.

133 BR43/39/12, Fanny to William, n.d.

134 V. Surtees, ed., *A Second Self. The Letters of Harriet Granville* (Wilton, 1990), p.280; K.M. Bourne, *Palmerston. The Early Years. 1784–1841* (London: Allen Lane, 1982), p.226.

135 Finlayson, *The Seventh Earl of Shaftesbury*, p.44; BR37/9, letters to Minny 2 January 1827 from Palmerston, and *c*.1829, when he wrote: 'My dear Minny recollect once for all, and for *Life* that you will always be doing me a *real kindness* whenever you can point out to me the means by which I may be able to gratify any wish of yours.'

136 Lever, *Letters of Lady Palmerston*, p.224, letter of 26 December 1839.

137 Fanny, writing to William, noted Fordwich's disapproval, and Anne Cowper's claim she had humbugged her mother-in-law into marriage, see BR43/39/3 [13 November 1839].

138 BR37/9, Palmerston to Minny, 16 December 1856.

139 Fragment of a letter, n.d., in BR55/42.

140 BR33/2, Emily Palmerston to William, 17 December 1839; see also R.H. Brett, ed., *The Girlhood of Queen Victoria*, vol.2, p.296, for the Queen's perception that William was unhappy about the union.

141 See letter, 8 March 1836, BR, GC/CO/230, asking Palmerston to appoint Mr Gausser diplomatic attaché, as his family has considerable influence on Hertfordshire politics; BR51/5, private journal, entry for 19 April 1837; BL, Holland House Papers, Add. MSS 51559, f.142, 22 November 1842.

142 BL, Holland House Papers, Add. MSS 51559, f.147, 27 November 1842.

143 BR50/24, Palmerston to William, Carlton Terrace, 14 June 1844.

[144] See letter from William to Juliet, in BR59/74, n.d.

[145] BR51/13, private journal, entry for 27 August 1839, on the Duchess.

[146] BR51/5, private journal, entry for 31 August 1839, on the Chine; BR51/13, private journal, entries for 30 October and 2 November 1839 on Castle Howard, 12 November on Coleridge, and 23 November on Lilleshall.

[147] BL, Holland House Papers, Add. MSS 51559, f.124, 20 December 1839.

[148] BR51/13, private journal, entry for 22 June 1840.

[149] BR51/13, private journal, entry for 22 June 1840.

[150] BR51/5, private journal, entry for July 1840, alluding to Tupper's *Proverbial Philosophy*.

[151] BR51/13, private journal, entry for Whitsuntide 1840.

[152] BR51/13, private journal, entry for 21 August 1840.

[153] BR51/13, private journal, entry for 22 August 1840.

[154] BR51/13, private journal, entry for 27 August 1840. William met him again, see BR51/13, private journal, entry for 4 September 1840 and also *c*.1841, apparently, see BR43/42/1, Charles Townshend to William, 20 January 1842.

[155] Hilton, *Mad, Bad and Dangerous*, p.488. William read *The Excursion* (1814) as he toured the Lakes, see *MTM*, pp.29-30.

[156] BR51/5, private journal, entry for August 1840.

[157] BR51/13, private journal, entry for 17 September 1840. Apparently Philip Nairn of Waren House, Belford.

[158] BR51/13, private journal, entry for 18 September 1840.

[159] *MTM*, p.32; BR51/13, private journal, entry for 16 October 1840. William's letters to Culling are in BR44/2/1, 15 September 1840; BR44/2/2, 4 December 1840. He discussed religious matters such as the Covenant and the Sultan's edict of toleration for the Jews.

[160] See the *London Teetotal Magazine*, 1840, pp.283-290, for a festival at Dyrham. A Trotter is mentioned by William as a pupil at Rottingdean, possibly they were acquainted from this period. On Trotter see *MTM*, p.17; A.J.C. Hare, *The Story of My Life* (1896; London: G. Allen, 1900) 6 vols, vol.1, p.315. William attended religious meetings at Dyrham Park, see notes, November 1840, BR44/12/3.

[161] BR51/13, private journal, entry for 21 November 1840.

[162] BL, Holland House Papers, Add. MSS 51559, f.126, *c*.7 December 1840. Jones had visited the palace in 1838.

[163] BR51/13, private journal, entry for 24 December 1840.

[164] BR51/13, private journal, entry for *c*.9 January 1841.

[165] BR51/13, private journal, entry for 10 February 1841.

[166] BR51/13, private journal, entry for 20 February 1841.

[167] BR51/5, private journal, entry for 15 April 1841.

[168] BR51/13, private journal, entry for Easter 1841.

[169] BL, Holland House Papers, Add. MSS 51559, f.130, 22 December 1841.

[170] BR33/2, letter posted to 'Durham [sic] Park, Barnet', postmarked 4 January 1842.

[171] BR51/5, private journal, entry for 6 May 1842, *The Times*, 14 May 1842, p.6.

[172] *Report of the Committee of the African Civilization Society*, 21 June 1842, pp.89-90.

[173] *The Satirist*, 24 July 1842, The reference was to Molière's wife Armande Béjart, alleged to be his daughter by an earlier mistress but actually her much younger sister.

[174] In Germany he may have visited Count von der Recke's institute for destitute orphans – the count's son-in-law believed William published an account of the count's work, see BR56/14, for a letter from William Allen Hanbury to Georgina, 16 May 1892.

[175] BR51/13, private journal, entry for 10 August 1842.

[176] BR44/5/10, an unsigned letter from Harriet d'Orsay to William, n.d.

[177] Sadleir, *Blessington and d' Orsay*, p.186, p.319; BR44/5/13, Harriet d'Orsay (signing as 'Your truly attached friend') to William, 15 February 1843.

178 BR44/5/10, also the source of the reference to German studies.
179 BR44/5/13, d'Orsay to William, 15 February 1843.
180 *The Satirist* reported Spencer's 'd'Orsay' mania, 8 August 1847.

Chapter 3. Husband and Widow, 1846–1867

1   Roberts, *Making English Morals*, pp.121-123. Significant relations included Daniel's brothers-in-law, the banker Samuel Hoare III and the anti-slavery agitator Thomas Fowell Buxton. Daniel's other brother, Joseph, was also a prominent philanthropist.
2   BR55/39, 'Journal of Harriet Alicia Gurney', p.14: 'Mr Cooper'.
3   BR55/39.
4   BR55/39, 4 May 1842.
5   BR51/13, private journal, entry for 13 December 1842. Keble's collection of poems was admired by many Evangelicals, despite the author being a prominent High Churchman.
6   BR51/13, private journal, entry for 31 December 1842.
7   BR51/13, private journal, entry for 16 January 1843.
8   BR43/9/5. I have not been able to identify the writer.
9   BR44/5/8, Harriet d'Orsay to William, docketed by him 'Jan. The World'.
10   BR43/9/3, Daniel Gurney to William, Paris, 23 March 1843; BR43/9/4, William to Daniel Gurney, 5 April 1843, BR43/9/6, Gurney to William, 9 April 1843.
11   BR43/10/9, John Motteux to William, 21 April 1843. Motteux is described by Gore, *Lieven-Palmerston Correspondence*, p.275, as a 'rich, effeminate bachelor friend of Lord Cowper. He moved in exalted social circles'. He says, p.260, that Spencer inherited Sandringham because he was the one child resembling the Earl; Lever, *Letters of Lady Palmerston*, describes Motteux, p.20 as 'something of a toady and snob'.
12   BR, MEL/CO/46, Melbourne to William, 4 April 1843 (on St Paul's epistle), and three subsequent letters from Melbourne to William, in BR, MEL/CO/47-49: 7, 9 and 19 April 1843. Quoted in Cecil, *Lord M*, p.317 (1843).
13   BR43/12/17, Anne Cowper to William, Panshanger.
14   BR51/5, private journal, entry for April 1843; BR43/9/2, 3 April [1843], notes in William's hand about the settlement.
15   BR33/2, Anne Cowper to Emily Palmerston, n.d. [September 1843].
16   BR43/10/2, Emily Palmerston to William, Brocket. When she told her friend, the Princess Lieven, she stressed her mother's nobility and 'sensational' beauty, see Gore, *Lieven-Palmerston Correspondence*, p.246, letter dated 21 April 1843.
17   BR43/10/4, Palmerston to William, Brocket, 19 April 1843.
18   BR43/27/14, Devonshire to William, Chiswick, 18 April 1843.
19   BR43/10/1, Trotter to William, Dyrham, 24 April 1843.
20   BR43/3/4, Emily Palmerston to William, Brocket, 'Friday 21'.
21   BL, Holland House Papers, Add. MSS 51559, ff.161-162, 18 April 1843.
22   BR43/3/4, Emily Palmerston to William, Brocket, 'Friday 21'.
23   BR43/12/9, William to Harriet, 'Reform Club, Friday'.
24   See the letters in BR43/11/1-10; BR43/12/1-17.
25   BR43/12/8, William to Harriet.
26   BR43/12/14, William to Harriet.
27   See William's letters BR43/12/12; BR43/12/15; BR43/12/16.
28   BR43/11/9, Harriet to 'Lola', Runcton. Lola was probably the former Lady Ida Augusta Hay, daughter of the eighteenth Earl of Errol.
29   BR43/11/1, Harriet to William.
30   BR43/11/10, Harriet to William, Earlham.
31   BR43/11/3, Harriet to William, Runcton.
32   BR43/10/5, Jocelyn to William, Panshanger.

33   BR43/3/5, Emily Palmerston to William, n.d. [September 1843].

34   G.S.H. Fox-Strangways, ed., *Elizabeth Lady Holland to Her Son. 1821–1845* (London: J. Murray, 1946), p.205, 9 May 1843.

35   BR43/14/12, Elizabeth Gurney to William, Upton, 1 September 1843.

36   A.J.C. Hare, *The Gurneys of Earlham*, 2 vols (London: G. Allen, 1895), vol.2, p.89; BR43/14/5, Elizabeth Gurney to William, September 1843; Anon., *A Brief Sketch of the Life of Anna Backhouse: By One who Knew Her Well, Loved Her Much* (Burlington, New Jersey: John Rodgers, 1852), p.98.

37   BR, SHA/PD/3, Ashley's diary entry for July 1843, reverse of f.25.

38   *Belfast News-Letter*, 12 May 1843, quoting the *Age*.

39   BR43/14/4, Elizabeth Gurney to William, 2 September [1843]; diary of Lady Palmerston, 5 September 1843 (I am grateful to Michael Roberts for this reference).

40   Devonshire Mss., Chatsworth, 2nd series, 40. 3 (4 July 1843), from Broadlands.

41   BR43/10/3, Harriet Cowper to her cousin Rachel, Broadlands, n.d. It is unclear what the problem was, but Ashley later wrote of circumstances of 'peculiar awfulness and distress', BR, SHA/PD/3, f.56, Ashley's diary entry for 9 December 1843.

42   BR43/14/20, Mrs Gurney to a niece, Cromer, 29 August 1843.

43   BR43/14/13, Elizabeth Gurney to William, Upton, 15 September; BR43/14/19, Samuel Gurney to William, 4 September 1843; BR43/14/5, Elizabeth Gurney; BR43/14/1, Rachel Gurney to William (on his generosity); BR43/14/8, a letter to Rachel Gurney from an aunt, Eartham, 11 November 1843, (on his character).

44   Devonshire Mss., Chatsworth, diary of the 6th Duke, 1. 144 (1843), 31 August 1843, 1 and 2 September 1843.

45   BR43/14/17, Queen Victoria to Emily Palmerston, Chateau d'Eu, 4 September 1843.

46   A.C. Benson and R.B. Brett, eds, *The Letters of Queen Victoria: A Selection from Her Majesty's Correspondence Between the Years 1837 and 1861* (1907; London: J. Murray, 1908), 3 vols, vol.1, *1837-1843*, p.491, 6 September 1843.

47   BR43/3/5, Emily Palmerston to William, n.d. (September 1843).

48   BR33/2, Anne Cowper to Emily Palmerston, n.d. (September 1843): 'We know that we did not wilfully neglect any thing, that she had all our love and attention.'

49   BR33/2, Emily Palmerston to William, postmarked 4 September 1843.

50   See the letters from Palmerston to William, Carlton Terrace, in BR50/24, 30 August 1843, 2 September 1843.

51   BR33/2, Anne Cowper to Emily Palmerston, n.d. (September 1843).

52   BR33/2, Emily Palmerston to William, postmarked 4 September 1843; BR33/2, Anne Cowper to Emily Palmerston, n.d. (September 1843).

53   *MTM*, p.34.

54   BR, SHA/PD/3, Ashley's diary entry for 9 December 1843 (f.56).

55   These included Louisa Troubridge, sister of Harriet, who died in 1867.

56   Hertfordshire Archives and Local Studies, Bulwer Lytton Papers, D/EK C7/164-166.

57   BR51/13, private journal, entry for 21 September 1843.

58   BR51/13, private journal, entry for 15 November 1843, on Fry. I cannot identify Wellesley.

59   A society in which he was, with Smith and the Reverend Thomas Pyne, honorary secretary, see *Wesleyan-Methodist Magazine* 21 (January 1842), pp.61-63; and A.M. Kass, 'The Syrian Medical Aid Association: British Philanthropy in the Near East', *Medical History* 31 (1987), pp.143-159. On allotments, see *PD*, 3rd series, vol.73, 13 March 1844, cols.971-973, during the second reading of the General Inclosure Bill.

60   Devonshire Mss., Chatsworth, 2nd Series, 40.7, 3 December 1844, for the letter in behalf of Beamish, see Devonshire Mss., Chatsworth, 2nd series, 40.5, f.1 (29 January 1844).

61 BR51/13, private journal, entries for 15 November 1843, 6 February 1844, and later, 20 July 1844. William was on the Elizabeth Fry Refuge committee after her death.
62 BR51/13, private journal, entry for 8 March 1844. Lady Elizabeth (born 1824) was Harriet Sutherland's eldest daughter, and later Duchess of Argyll.
63 BR, SHA/PD/3, Ashley's diary entry for 9 June 1844, reverse of f.107; diary entry for 29 August 1844, f.124.
64 Houghton Papers, MSS6/194, 26 September 1844; MSS6/195, 30 September 1844; Ashley's diary, SHA/PD/3; the allusion is to the 'Young England' group of Lord John Manners, George Smythe and Disraeli.
65 BR51/13, private journal, entry for 8 October 1844.
66 L. McDonald, ed., *Florence Nightingale on Society and Politics, Philosophy, Science, Education and Literature* (Waterloo, Ontario: Wilfrid Laurier University Press, 2003), p.513.
67 BR51/5, private journal, entry for 6 July 1845.
68 BR51/13, private journal, entry for 2 August 1845; *MTM*, p.38. It was the *bal poudré* with costumes of 1745 that the press had reported.
69 M.G. Wiebe, ed., *Benjamin Disraeli Letters* vol.4 *1842–1847* (Toronto and London: University of Toronto Press, 1989), p.179, 2 August 1845; BR51/13, private journal entry for 9 August 1845. William supported the bishopric project: *Missionary Register*, August 1847, p.334, BR43/60/1, Christian von Bunsen to William, '4 July' [1846].
70 BR51/14, journal subsequently labelled 'Ireland'. The quotations in this, and the following paragraph, come from this source.
71 *Morning Chronicle*, 26 May 1845.
72 G. Battiscombe, *Shaftesbury. A Biography of the Seventh Earl, 1801–1885* (London: Constable, 1974), p.178, presumably citing Ashley's diary and correspondence from Minny.
73 See letters in BR43/44, with William's annotation 9 July 1846.
74 Letter in BR43/44.
75 BR51/5, private journal, entry for 7 November 1846.
76 BR51/5, private journal, entry for 12 November 1846.
77 BR51/5, private journal, entry for 29 November 1846.
78 Devonshire Mss., Chatsworth, 2nd Series, 40.9, f.1, citing 1 February 1847, and quoting 5 February 1847.
79 Devonshire Mss., Chatsworth, 2nd Series, 40.8, 20 October 1846; Battiscombe, *Shaftesbury*, p.201.
80 Lady Sparrow he met in December 1842, and described as a 'curious, talkative woman, rattles on without regard to her hearers'. Daughter of the Earl of Gosford, friend of William Wilberforce, and follower of Irving, she made Brampton Park available for Irvingites, and was a prominent Evangelical, see T.C.F. Stunt, *From Awakening to Secession. Radical Evangelicals in Switzerland and Britain, 1815–35* (Edinburgh: T&T Clark, 2000), p.138. On Stewart, see D.D. Stewart, *Memoir of the Life of the Rev. James Haldane Stewart M.A., late Rector of Limpsfield, Surrey* (1856; London: Hatchard, 1857), p.83. On Hargrove and Bickersteth, see BR51/13, private journal, entries for 17 April and 4 May 1847. William attended a service of Hargrove's, see BR51/5, private journal, 11 May 1846.
81 BR51/13, private journal, entry for 27 July 1847; Devonshire Mss., Chatsworth, 2nd Series, 40.10, f.1, 2 August 1847.
82 BR51/5, private journal, entry for 2 July 1847.
83 BR51/13, private journal, entry for 13 September 1847.
84 BR51/13, private journal, entry for 1 January 1848.
85 BR51/5, private journal, entry for 25 January 1848.
86 Devonshire Mss., Chatsworth, 2nd Series, 40.11, 9 February [1848].
87 'Emerson the Thinker', *Littell's Living Age*, 30 June 1888, vol.1777: 2296, p.777; BR51/13, private journal, entry for 15 June 1848.

88   *The African Repository* (American Colonization Society) 1848, p.214. Palmerston had officially recognised Liberia.

89   J.A.W. Gunn and M.G. Wiebe, *Benjamin Disraeli's Letters*, vol.5, *1848–51* (1993), p.44.

90   BR51/13, private journal, entry for 20 October 1848.

91   Letter in letter book BR56/25, from unidentified correspondent, 27 October 1848.

92   Letters in BR56/25, Palmerston to William, Carlton Gardens, 1 November 1848; Emily Palmerston to William, Brocket, 'Sunday'.

93   BR56/25, Emily Palmerston to William, Brocket, 'Sunday'.

94   BR56/25, Melbourne to William, Brocket [29] October 1848.

Chapter 4. The Childhood of Georgina and a New Life

1   Her birthday was 8 October. For the Tollemache family, see E.D.H. Tollemache, *The Tollemaches of Helmingham and Ham* (London: W.S. Cowell, 1949).

2   *Gentleman's Magazine*, October 1837, p.425.

3   See W.O. Tristram, *Moated Houses* (1910; New York: Dodd, Mead, 1911), pp.188-189.

4   R.H. Gronow, *Recollections and Anecdotes, being a second series of reminiscences of the Camp, the Court, and the Clubs* (London: Smith, Elder, 1863), pp.182-186.

5   *MTM*, p.101.

6   *MTM*, p.101.

7   BL, Holland House Papers, Add. MSS 51778, f.140, 17 December [1844]; Fox-Strangways, *Elizabeth Lady Holland to Her Son*, p.221.

8   They married 28 November 1817. Georgina's niece Emily married Ralph Gerard Leycester of Toft Hall near Knutsford, Cheshire; her son Rafe married Nina de Burgh (known as Edith), his cousin, in 1861.

9   S. Leslie, ed., *The Letters of Mrs Fitzherbert and connected papers* (2 vols, London: Burns, Oates, 1940), vol.2.

10   Augusta Selina Elizabeth Locke, born in 1833, known as Leila, first married Ernest Fane, Lord Burghersh (died 1851), secondly, Luigi Duca di Santo Teodoro and Sant' Arpino, by whom she had a daughter, Teresa Caracciolo, later Princess Colonna, and thirdly, after divorcing Luigi in 1876, the sixth Baron Walsingham. She died in 1906. According to Marguerite Tollemache, there was a great resemblance between Georgina and her niece, see BR55/4, Marguerite to Georgina, Rio de Janeiro, 13 December 1853.

11   *The Times*, 24 June 1824, p.3. See S. David, *The Homicidal Earl. The Life of Lord Cardigan* (1997; London: Abacus, 1998), pp.41-48.

12   Other sisters were Emily Tollemache 1799-1821 and Charlotte Tollemache, 1813-1837 who married George Hope, and was buried at Mentone.

13   *MTM*, p.71. There are few letters from Marcia in the Broadlands Papers, see BR55/69 for a few undated letters.

14   Tollemache, *Old and Odd Memories*, p.93.

15   *MTM*, p.71. Her children were Francis, Augustus, Selina Constance (who married Baron Ward and died in 1851), Nina (Edith, who married Rafe Leycester in 1867) and Eva.

16   See M. Girouard, *The Victorian Country House* (1971; London and New Haven: Yale University Press, 1979), pp.154-163 on John Tollemache and Peckforton, and Tollemache, *Old and Odd Memories*.

17   Letter in BR56/25, Augustus to Georgina [13 December 1848].

18   BR42/3, study by Andrew D. Scott, 9 January 1845, at Toft Hall, Knutsford, a house which belonged to a relation of the Tollemaches. See BR54/8, for Georgina's examination, 3 January 1845.

19   Phrenological examination, 3 January 1845, BR54/8.

20   Letter in BR56/25, Julia Tomkinson to Georgina, Dorfold, 'Saturday'.

21   See letters copied into 'Diary Belonging to Georgina Elizabeth Tollmache', BR56/8.

22   Letter in BR56/25, John Tollemache to Georgina, 17 November 1848.

23   *MTM*, p.45.

24   Letter in BR56/25, Marguerite to Georgina, 21 November 1848; *MTM*, pp.44-45, M. Leicester-Warren, *Diaries* (2 vols, privately printed, Taunton, 1924), vol.2, p.300, for a description of Marguerite (in the early 1870s).

25   J. Ruskin, *Praeterita* (1885-1889; Oxford, 1989), p.251; the event took place in late 1840; Tollemache, *Some Reminiscences*, p.9.

26   V. Caetani, *The Locks of Norbury: the story of a remarkable family in the XVIIIth and XIXth centuries* (London: J. Murray, 1940), p.366.

27   Tollemache, *Old and Odd Memories*, p.78.

28   Tollemache, *Some Reminiscences*, pp.5-7; BR55/19, Augustus to Georgina, Rio de Janeiro, 10 April [1854] 'this time it was not from *curiosity* that the Queen invited you,' referring to a dinner at Court.

29   *MTM*, p.101; Tollemache, *Old and Odd Memories*, p.49.

30   BR56/6, Leila Murray to Georgina, Bath, 21 September 1847.

31   BR56/25, J.C. Ryle to Georgina, Helmingham, 13 November 1848.

32   Tollemache, *Some Reminiscences*, p.7.

33   Letter in BR56/25, Lucy Whitlam to Georgina, Wiganthorpe, 1 November 1848.

34   *MTM*, p.101. Exton Hall, in Rutland, was the home of the Noels, Earls of Gainsborough after the title was revived in 1841. A lithograph of Exton church is in BR56/25. In BR44/10/11 is preserved an account in William's hand, dated June 1847 and docketed 'She let concealment like a worm in the bud feed on her damask cheeks,' of the anxieties of a girl with a London house and home in the country, finding support in Reverend Harrison, in attempts to avoid the attentions of an unnamed man. Her infatuation with him involved 'months and years of self struggle'. Was this an account of Georgina's love for him?

35   Letter in BR56/25, from Portia Galindo to Georgina, Tryon House, 27 October 1848.

36   The appraisals quoted in this paragraph and the preceding one, are notes attached to pages at the beginning of the letter book BR56/25, and are undated. The final passage begins 'Angela': perhaps his 'code' name for her at this time.

37   BR43/36/37, Harriet Sutherland to William, Trentham, 'Sunday 2nd'.

38   Devonshire Mss., Chatsworth, 2nd Series, 40.12, 28 October 1848.

39   Letter in BR56/25, Lucy Whitlam to Georgina, Wiganthorpe, 1 November 1848.

40   BR56/25, Elizabeth Cardigan to Georgina, Tottenham, 29 October 1848.

41   Letter in BR56/25, Augustus to Georgina, Windsor, 20 November 1848.

42   Letter in BR56/25, Augustus to Lady Elizabeth, Genoch, Glenluce, 23 October 1848.

43   BR56/25, Augustus to Lady Elizabeth, Genoch, Glenluce, 23 October 1848.

44   Letter in BR56/25, Emma J. Leycester to Georgina, 30 October 1848.

45   Letter in BR56/25, Augustus to Georgina, 21 November 1848.

46   Tollemache, *Old and Odd Memories*, p.80. Though an Evangelical, John later disapproved of his children's fervour: thinking Hamilton and Minnie going 'too fast' with Bible readings in the drawing room at Helmingham, see BR53/5, Marguerite to William, 35 Berkeley Square, n.d.

47   Letter in BR56/25, John Tollemache to William, Newstead, 8 November 1848.

48   *MTM*, p.62. But in 1859, William loaned Spencer £8,000, and offered to pay interest on the £12, 000; 'You have little enough even with your official salary,' Spencer rather shamefacedly wrote, see BR43/47/1, Paris, 17 December 1859.

49   Reproduced opposite p.78 of Tollemache, *Old and Odd Memories*.

50   L.P. Smith, ed., *A Religious Rebel. The Letters of 'HWS' (Mrs Pearsall Smith)* (London: Nisbet, 1949), p.90.

51   BR43/23/13, William to Georgina, Home Office, 20 April [1855].

52 See letter in BR56/25, from 'FHC' to William, 3 November 1848.
53 BR43/21/16, William to Georgina, n.d. [1855].
54 BR53/4, William to Georgina, n.d. [watermark 1853]. The 1871 edition of Ruskin's *Sesame and Lilies* was dedicated to Georgina, but was first published in 1865.
55 BR43/23/12, William to Georgina, 27 March [1855]. The reference is to Robert Smith Candlish, Free Church of Scotland minister and clergyman.
56 BR43/23/4, William to Georgina, Cheyne Walk, n.d.; BR43/23/6, 3 March [1855].
57 BR43/22/9, William to Georgina, House of Commons, n.d.; one of Hahn Hahn's works was loaned by Lady Palmerston's friend Abraham Hayward, see BR43/23/3.
58 BR58/2, Georgina's diary, 25 January 1862.
59 Tollemache, *Old and Odd Memories*, p.77.
60 Tollemache, *Old and Odd Memories*, p.84.
61 J. Ruskin, *Praeterita*, reprinted in E.T. Cook and A. Wedderburn, eds, *Works of John Ruskin* (Library Edition) (London: G. Allen, 1905) vol.35, p.503.
62 BR44/3/1, 'Phreonological character of Mr William Cowper by Mr Donovan', 25 May 1848.
63 BR44/9/15, docketed 'G.C.', by William.
64 Letter in BR56/25, from Augustus to Georgina, Windsor, *c*.22 November 1848.
65 BL, Lamb Family Papers, Add. MSS 45553, f.221, f.226; letter in BR56/25 Emily Palmerston to Georgina, from Brocket, 'Sunday'.
66 Letter in BR56/25, Augustus to Georgina, 21 November 1848.
67 Letter in BR56/25, Marguerite to Georgina, 21 November 1848.
68 Letter in BR56/25, Mummy to Georgina, 4 Grosvenor Crescent, 21 November 1848.
69 *MTM*, p.47.
70 Letter in BR50/24, Palmerston to William, Brocket, 24 November 1848.
71 H. Nicholson, *Helen's Tower* (London: Constable, 1937), p.146. Georgina, *MTM*, p.68 notes that she only met Palmerston in company. The rare occasion when she sat at dinner beside him was a daunting experience.
72 BR58/8, Georgina's diary for 1880, note after Fanny Jocelyn's death; *MTM*, p.49.
73 *MTM*, p.92; and BR55/57, Anne Cowper to Georgina after death of Dolly, n.d.
74 Ogilvy, *Lady Palmerston*, vol.2, p.125, December 1848. In a letter in BR33/5, Emily Palmerston told Georgina, Christmas Day (watermark 1861), of her 'warmest motherly affection – and the sincere admiration I have for all your good and charming Qualities'.
75 *MTM*, p.50; William, by his uncle's will, had a life interest if he survived Frederick's widow (who remarried), see BR48/4/14, H. Manisty to William, 19 October 1887.
76 William's entry, BR51/5, private journal, 30 May 1849.
77 BR51/13, private journal, entry for 31 July 1849.
78 *MTM*, p.53; Emily Palmerston, BL, Lamb Papers, Add. MS. 45554, f.29, 4 October 1849; BR56/25, Harriet Sutherland to Georgina, 18 October 1849. The Evangelical philanthropist Arthur Kinnaird's association with William is documented in a *Life of Lady Kinnaird*, quoted in *MTM*, p.102.
79 BR51/13, private journal, entry for 30 September 1849.
80 Devonshire Mss., Chatsworth, diary of the 6th Duke, 767.461 (1850), 1.151, 2 February 1850, 13 February 1850.
81 BR51/13, private journal, entry for Easter 1850.
82 BR45/5, notebook, Georgina's entry for 15 July 1850.
83 BR45/5, notebook, Georgina's entry for 16 July 1850.
84 See *MTM*, p.62. Educated in America, ordained a priest at Worcester in 1856, he became famous for appeals for funds as vicar of St Mark's, Victoria Docks, which led to allegations of financial misappropriation which were proved to be false. See J.W. Walker,

'Saint Helen's Church, Sandal Magna', *Yorkshire Archaeological Journal* 24 (1917), p.42. His daughter was christened Georgina, presumably after Georgina.

85 BR45/5, notebook, Georgina's entry for *c*.17 July 1850.

86 BR45/5, notebook, Georgina's entry for 20 July 1850.

87 BR45/5, notebook, Georgina's entry for *c*.27 July 1850, for her self-examination; 25 July entry on the party involving Baylee, and longing for more than outward expression.

88 The discourse at Albury noted in BR51/13, private journal, 1 August 1849, included mysticism, tyranny and dishonesty of popery, transubstantiation, confession, and Catholicity of the church.

89 BR51/13; BR45/5, notebook entry by Georgina, 22 August 1850.

90 BR45/5, notebook entry by William, 20 August 1850.

91 BR45/5, notebook entry by Georgina, 10 October 1850.

92 BR45/5, notebook entry by Georgina, 29 September 1850 on mass, and *c*.11 November 1850, on tapestry.

93 Quotations from BR45/5, entries by Georgina, late November– December 1850.

94 *MTM*, p.53.

95 BR45/5, notebook entry by Georgina, December 1850.

96 BR45/5, notebook, account by Georgina, 8 February 1851.

97 BR51/13, notebook, entry for 9 January 1851.

98 BR53/3, William to Georgina, Albury, 'Saturday night', 1851 watermark.

99 Letter in BR56/24, Julia Rich to Georgina, Rugby, 'Friday' [1851].

100 Two letters in BR56/24, from Julia Rich to Georgina, one dated 14 February [1851].

101 B. Schultz, *Henry Sidgwick: Eye of the Universe. An Intellectual Biography* (Cambridge: Cambridge University Press, 2004), p.46. T. Christensen, *The Divine Order. A Study in F.D. Maurice's Theology* (Leiden: E.J. Brill, 1973) notes Maurice's theological impact in his lifetime was negligible, p.300 and that interest in his views waned by the 1860s.

102 BR56/25, Herman Douglas to Georgina, Würzburg, Bavaria, 17 June 1851.

103 BR51/13, entry by William for 6 August 1851.

104 BR56/24, Baylee to Georgina, 31 October 1851; BR59/9, Georgina to Juliet, *c*.1886.

105 *MTM*, pp.53-54; letters on [Selina] Constance Ward in letterbook BR56/25. For a nasty vignette, see A. Brudenell-Bruce, *My Recollections* (London: Eveleigh Nash, 1909), pp.44-50; for an alternative, see D. Nevill, *Under Five Reigns* (1910, London: Methuen, 1912), p.135. For Augustus' comment, BR55/19, Augustus to Georgina, Rio, 10 June 1853.

106 BR51/13, entry for 21 September 1851; M. Kaufmann, 'Christian Socialists: III', *Good Words* (December 1882), p.1.

107 BR45/5, notebook entry by Georgina, 19 September 1851.

108 BR45/5, notebook entries by Georgina, 24 November 1851, and William, 31 December 1851.

109 BR45/5, notebook entry by Georgina, 1 January 1852.

110 BR51/13, entry for 27 April 1851.

111 Letter in BR53/4, William to Georgina, Somerset House, 'April 14'.

112 *MTM*, p.47.

113 *MTM*, p.47. The phrase derived from the offer of food in return for Protestant conversion.

114 BR51/14, entry by William for August 1852.

115 See letters from Palmerston to William, in BR50/24, 27 August– *c*.3 September 1852.

116 BR57/24/11, Georgina to Emelia Gurney, Broadlands [1869].

117 BR42/4, Augustus Tollemache to Emily Tyrwhitt, 4 January 1852. Alfred d'Orsay had died 4 August 1852.

118 See A. Byng, ed., *Leaves from the Diary of Henry Greville, first series* (London: Smith, Elder, 1883), p.301.

[119]   BR35/4, Emily Ashley to Adine, n.d.

[120]   BR43/47/4, Harriet Cowper to William, c.1854. On her religiosity, see J. Radcliffe, *Recollections of Reginald Radcliffe* (London: Morgan and Scott, 1896), pp.167-169.

[121]   BR43/47/4, Harriet Cowper to William, c.1854.

[122]   H. Jones, *Sandringham, Past and Present* (London: Jarrold, 1888), p.149. Sadleir, *Blessington-D'Orsay*, p.181.

[123]   See the county sale, Bonhams, 18 January 2005, Leeds, sale 11649, Lot 107, P. Gauci after Marguerite Tollemache, 'Rio de Janeiro'.

[124]   See the letters from Marguerite to Georgina in BR55/3 and BR5/4.

[125]   BR53/1, William to Georgina, Trentham [2 January 1854].

[126]   BR53/1, William to Georgina, Trentham [4 January 1854].

[127]   BR53/3, William to Georgina, House of Commons, 17 July [1854].

[128]   O.R. Anderson, *A Liberal State at War. English Politics and Economics during the Crimean War* (London: Macmillan, 1967), p.68.

[129]   BR54/9, Miney Forester to Georgina, Hyde Hall, n.d.

[130]   BR50/48, a letter from the father of the nurse Mary Erskine, 27 April 1855; BR56/20, Charles Wood at the Admiralty to Georgina about Erskine's charge of the hospital, 17 July 1856; Adine Melbourne to Georgina, 24 October 1854 on female nursing, BR55/66; references in BR43/25/2; and *MTM*, p.59. The Cowper-Temples are ignored in the reference to Therapia in A. Hamilton-Gordon, *Sidney Herbert. Lord Herbert of Lea. A Memoir* (2 vols, London: J. Murray, 1906) vol.1, p.332.

[131]   To judge from Augustus' replies from Rio, in March 1854, in BR55/19.

[132]   BR55/4, Augustus to Georgina, Rio, 30 November 1854.

[133]   BR43/46, Augustus to William, 12 February [1855]; BR55/4, Augustus to Georgina, 30 November [1854].

[134]   BR56/3, Davies to Georgina, 12 September 1854: presumably alluding to Biblical 'higher criticism' generally, as no specific work of that name exists. Davies was a disciple of F.D. Maurice, and the Cowpers met George MacDonald through him. Palmerston was persuaded to give Davies the Crown living of Christ Church, Marylebone (*MTM*, p.107) in 1856. The *DNB* (1912-1921), pp.147-148, notes it was Davies who suggested the 'Cowper-Temple' clause. Davies recollected, BR56/3, 20 February 1898, that in his early days when Georgina was so good to him, 'I gave you – I have often feared – more of my company than was reasonable'.

[135]   *Gentleman's Magazine*, 1854, p.317; BR55/4, Marguerite to Georgina, from Rio de Janeiro, 13 September [1854].

[136]   Recalled in Ruskin, *Praeterita*, pp.467-468; in *MTM*, p.65, Georgina thought this occurred ten years after her Roman holiday. In May 1854 William requested, on behalf of Louisa Lady Waterford, a view of Millais' unfinished portrait of Ruskin, work on which brought Effie Ruskin, fatefully, close to Millais, see F.R. Fogle, 'Unpublished Letters of Ruskin and Millais', *Huntingdon Library Quarterly* 20:1 (November 1956), pp.39-51 [p.46], the verdict on the 'social storm' is Fogle's, p.40.

[137]   *MTM*, p.107, where Georgina wrote 'about 1857'. See *ODNB* for G. Herring's entry.

[138]   BR43/20/15, William to Georgina, Brighton, n.d. See Georgina's diary, BR56/10 for engagements in 1855. On Beveridge, see the entry on massage in the *Encyclopaedia Britannica* (Cambridge: Cambridge University Press, 1911), vol.17, p.863, and W. Johnson, *Anatriptic Art a history of the art termed anatripsis by Hippocrates, tripsis by Galen frictio by Celsus, manipulation by Beveridge and medical rubbing in ordinary language, from the earliest times to the present day, followed by an account of its virtues in the cure of disease and maintenance of health* (London: Simpkin, Marshall, 1866). Beveridge's patients included Sir John Maxwell, see BR53/16, William to Georgina, 1 March 1855.

[139]   BR56/7, Jessy Ryle to Georgina, 7 Onslow Crescent, 25 March [1855].

140 BR55/33, Isabella Laurie to Georgina, 66 Euston Square.

141 BR53/16, William to Georgina, 20 March 1855.

142 See entry for May 1855, in journal BR58/17. William visited the Apostolic Church at Gordon Square when he left Georgina, inspecting windows depicting Bede, Hooker and Jeremy Taylor. See BR43/21/5, William to Georgina, Brocket Hall, 'Saturday 5'.

143 See also BR43/25/18, William to Georgina, 23 March 1855, on Guthrie's sermon on the Fast Day.

144 BR53/16, William to Georgina, 21 April 1855.

145 BR53/16, William to Georgina, 5 March 1855.

146 The allusion is to Dr Mathias Roth, who stimulated Georgina and others to found the Ladies' Sanitary Association.

147 BR43/21/3, William to Georgina, House of Commons notepaper, n.d.

148 BR43/23/12, William to Georgina, 27 March 1855.

149 BR43/21/17, William to Georgina, House of Commons notepaper, n.d.

150 BR43/21/20, William to Georgina, Home Office, 19 March 1855.

151 BR53/16, William to Georgina, 21 March 1855; 17 April 1855.

152 BR43/22/13, William to Georgina, House of Commons, n.d.

153 BR43/21/15, William to Georgina, House of Commons, 15 March 1855.

154 BR43/23/9; BR43/22/15, letter of 3 May 1855. John Tollemache offered assistance, worried about the cost of a lengthy stay in Edinburgh, see BR55/1, 24 March 1855; BR43/20/14.

155 BR58/1, Georgina's diary entry for 21 June 1855.

156 *Daily News*, 15 August 1855; *The Times*, 15 August 1855, p.9.

157 *Daily News*, 15 August 1855.

158 BR50/25, Palmerston to William, Broadlands, 13 October 1855.

159 *The Times*, 27 October 1855, p.10, *Manchester Guardian*, 29 October, 1855, p.1.

160 *The Times*, 23 October 1855, p.9. He gave a similar message later, at Leeds YMCA with Shaftesbury, stressing reading, fine arts and music as recreation, see *Daily News*, 19 October 1859.

161 BR43/25/3, William to Georgina, 14 April [1855]; and BR53/16, 8 March 1855.

162 BR55/4, Augustus to Georgina, Rio, 30 November 1854.

163 BR51/13, journal entry 1 January 1856.

164 He was elevated to the peerage as Baron Ebury in 1857.

165 BR51/13, journal entry 13 April 1856; BR60/4/6, Shaftesbury to Evelyn Ashley, 16 April 1856.

166 Cowper, *Earl Cowper*, pp.70-71.

167 *Daily News*, 26 December 1857; on the appointment, see *MTM*, p.60.

168 Leicester-Warren, *Diaries*, vol.2, p.300.

169 M. Ward, *The tragi-comedy of Pen Browning. 1849–1912* (New York and London: Sheed and Ward, 1972), p.18.

170 L. Huxley, ed., *Elizabeth Barrett Browning* (London: J. Murray, 1929), p.252.

171 James Y. Simpson Papers, Royal College of Surgeons of Edinburgh, J.Y.S. 855: 19 August 1856; BR51/13, 6 October 1856; William hoped to discuss medical reform too (see J.Y.S. 856: 27 August 1856 and J.Y.S. 857: 10 October 1856).

172 See *Autobiography of Thomas Guthrie D.D.* (1874-1875; Detroit: Craig and Taylor, 1878), p.475, for Guthrie's meeting with William and Kinnaird, and visit to a Westminster school, p.409.

173 BR43/22/8, William to Georgina, Swan Inn, Stafford, 'Saturday night'.

174 'Address by the Right Honourable William Cowper MP on Education', in *Transactions of the National Association for the Promotion of Social Science* (1858). See BR43/24/1, William to Georgina, n.d. On the Association, see L. Goldman, *Science, Reform, and Politics in Victorian*

Britain. The Social Science Association 1857–1886 (Cambridge: Cambridge University Press, 2002).

175 BR43/22/2, William to Georgina, St Philip's Rectory, Birmingham, 'Tuesday 13'.

176 *Belfast News-Letter*, 23 February 1858.

177 BR, GC/CO/234/1, William to Palmerston, Calais, 10 August 1858; *MTM*, p.63; C.Y. Lang, ed., *The Letters of Matthew Arnold* (Charlottesville, Virginia: University Press of Virginia, 1996), vol.1, p.401. In taking this holiday, they followed an enthusiasm stimulated by Smith's ascent of Mont Blanc in 1851, see P.H. Hansen, 'Albert Smith, the Alpine Club, and the Invention of Mountaineering in Mid-Victorian Britain', *Journal of British Studies* 34: 3 (July 1995), pp.300-324.

178 See *London Quarterly Review* 13 (1860), p.125, on his 'happy skill in reconciling opposing theorists, and singular judgment in summing up the results of each discussion in turn'.

179 See William's letter, in H.E. Carlisle, ed., *A Selection from the Correspondence of Abraham Hayward*, vol.2, pp.16-17, on this meeting with Napoleon; on the Labourers, see BL, Lamb Papers, Add. MSS 45554, f.160, 18 November 1858; Palmerston's advice, BR50/25, 14 November 1858. A photograph of the Cowpers, Palmerston and others at Broadlands in 1859 is in the National Portrait Gallery (P153).

180 R.H. Lathrop, 'Some Memories of Hawthorne. III', *Atlantic Monthly* 77: 462 (April 1896), p.497.

181 See fragment of diary transcribed by Georgina, BR58/17.

182 See *Belfast News-Letter*, 15 August 1859. See William to Georgina, BR43/25/5, n.d., for Board of Trade duties relating to Chelsea pensioners.

183 Bebbington, *Evangelicalism in Modern Britain*, p.116. Presumably Kinnaird's activity drew on his knowledge of the Scottish revivalism.

184 See R. Carwardine, *Transatlantic Revivalism. Popular Evangelicalism in Britain and America, 1790-1865* (Westport, Connecticut: Greenwood Press, 1978), p.172.

185 W. Benham, ed., *Catharine and Craufurd Tait, wife and son of Archibald Campbell archbishop of Canterbury: a memoir* (London: Macmillan, 1879), see pp.69, 447-449.

186 Prochaska, *Women and Philanthropy*, pp.124-125; Prochaska, *The Voluntary Impulse. Philanthropy in Modern Britain* (London: Faber, 1988), p.47.

187 Benham, *Catharine and Craufurd Tait*, p.425; *Morning Chronicle*, 29 November 1859 (dinner at the Taits). Mutual friends included Twining of the Workhouse Visiting Society.

188 W.C. Dowling, 'The Ladies Sanitary Association and the Origin of the Health Visiting Service', MA thesis, University of London, 1963, p.140.

189 *The Scotsman*, 24 June 1857, p.2. The Langham Place circle established a Society for Promoting the Employment of Women in 1859. Georgina read Felicia Skene on 'Women and Work', see the list of works in her diary for 1855, BR56/10.

190 BR56/11, Georgina's diary for 1859, visiting Bessie Rayner Parkes, editor of the *English Women's Journal*, which reported the Association's work, 4 February; revising Susan Power's tract in April. See the list of 50 tracts, at the back of this diary. See BR58/1, entry in diary for 21 June 1855; 5 July 1855, on lectures.

191 She entertained Farr and Blackwell in April 1859, see diary entry in BR56/11.

192 BR56/11, diary entry for 6 March 1859. She remained interested in Hinton, seen by contemporaries as attempting to reconcile religious faith with science (see C.B. Upton, 'James Hinton and his philosophy', *Theological Review*, October 1878, pp.572-594 [p.572]) but the Broadlands Papers do not document any correspondence or intimacy with Hinton, there is no reference to her in E. Hopkins, *Life and Letters of James Hinton* (London: Kegan Paul, Trench, 1882); or E. Ellis, *James Hinton: a sketch* (London: Stanley Paul, 1918).

193 One may speculate about the cause of their childlessness, but it is worth noting the relatively high infertility of the landed classes which Jessica Gerard found in her sample, *Country House Life. Family and Servants, 1815–1914* (Oxford: Blackwell, 1994), pp.24-25. I

find no explicitly sexual references in the papers of the Cowper-Temples, though I have not decoded their 'pigpen' inscriptions. Georgina's diary marked her menstrual cycle. Sharon Marcus argues, *Between Women. Friendship, Desire, and Marriage in Victorian England* (Princeton: Princeton University Press, 2007), p.43, 'If firsthand testimony about sex is the standard for defining a relationship as sexual, then most Victorians never had sex … one rarely finds even oblique references to sex between husband and wife.'

194 Reynolds, *Aristocratic Women*, p.60 on Lady Palmerston; historians increasingly reject the idea that the 'angel in the house' expressed the reality, see M.J. Peterson's pioneering essay, 'No Angels in the House: The Victorian Myth and the Paget Women', *The American Historical Review* 89: 3 (June 1984), pp.677-708.

Chapter 5. Junior Minister, 1846–1867

1   L.C. Sanders, ed., *Lord Melbourne's Papers* (London: Longmans, Green, 1889), pp.527-528.
2   See J.C. Sainty, *Lord High Admiral and Commissioners of the Admiralty 1660–1870. Office-Holders in Modern Britain* vol.4 (London: Athlone, 1975); *The Satirist*, 31 May 1846; 12 July 1846, p.220.
3   BR44/11/5, March 1855, 'Statement of Business devolving on Civil Lord of Admiralty'.
4   C.J. Bartlett, *Great Britain and Sea Power* (Oxford: Clarendon Press, 1963), p.4, p.18
5   *MTM*, p.50. Devonshire Mss., Chatsworth, 2nd Series, 40.8, 20 October 1846.
6   D. McClean, *Education and Empire: Naval Tradition and England's Elite Schooling* (London: British Academic Press, 1999), p.36.
7   In a notebook, BR45/18/2, William noted Sir Charles Napier's letter in *The Times*, 5 December 1849, on the state of the British fleet after 1815.
8   J.H. Briggs, *Naval Administrations 1827 to 1892* (London: Sampson Low, Marston and Co., 1897).
9   BR50/24, Palmerston to William, Broadlands, 9 September 1846.
10   BR51/13, diary entry for 22 December 1851.
11   BR51/13, diary entry for 26 December 1851.
12   BR43/61/1, Dundas to William; BR43/61/2, William to Russell, 7 February 1852.
13   BR54/9, Emily Palmerston to William, n.d.
14   BR53/3, William to Georgina, 'Monday night' [18 April 1853].
15   BR50/24, Palmerston to William, Carlton Terrace, 14 February 1854.
16   BR53/16, William to Georgina, House of Commons, n.d.
17   BR53/16, William to Georgina, House of Commons, 13 March 1855.
18   BR53/16, William to Georgina, 6 March 1855. Russell threatened resignation in July, see BR50/24, Palmerston to William [14 July 1855].
19   BR53/16, William to Georgina, 8 March 1855. BR43/25/3, William to Georgina, 14 April, shows his preferences: 'Ld P is in force tho' he has the Colonial Office to rearrange as well as his own Depart. He finds it uninteresting & says I was quite right not to take it when J. Russell expressed a wish that I shd. Matters of detail relating to places at the other side of the Globe are far less entertaining than what goes on under one's eyes.'
20   Anon., *Engineers and officials; an historical sketch of the progress of 'health of towns works', between 1838 and 1856 in London and the Provinces* (London: Edward Stanford, 1856), p.xxiv; 'Monthly Retrospect', *The Monthly Christian Spectator*, vol.7, August 1857, p.521.
21   R. Lambert, *Sir John Simon, 1816-1904 and English Social Administration* (London: Macgibbon and Kee, 1963), p.242, p.269.
22   Houghton Papers, MSS6/197 (2), 20 November [1856].
23   Lambert, *Sir John Simon*.
24   Perhaps too, we can detect a shared 'Coleridgean' idealism about the State's oversight of medicine at the expense of the Royal College, behind Simon's 1858 Memorandum which lay behind William's bill of March 1858, see T.N. Stokes, 'A Coleridgean against the

Medical Corporations', *Medical History* 33 (1989), pp.343-359. See J. Simon, *English Sanitary Institutions, reviewed in their course of development, and in some of their political and social relations* (London: Cassell, 1890), p.273 for a tribute to William. For Shaftesbury's view on Simon's appointment, see his diary entry, BR, SHA/PD/7, f.24.

25 Another man associated with William's sanitary reform was the physiologist, chemist and author Frederick Oldfield Ward, see BR50/45, Ward to William, 18 May 1859.

26 T. Cooper, *The Life of Thomas Cooper* (London: Hodder and Stoughton, 1872), pp.368-369.

27 NLS, Papers of J.F. Campbell, Adv MS 51.1.15, letter from William establishing the ventilation commission, June 1856; NLS, Papers of J.F. Campbell, Adv MS 51.2.1, f.85, note by J.F. Campbell on Report to General Board of Health by Commissioners appointed to inquire into warming and ventilating of dwellings, 25 August 1857, dated 29 April 1858.

28 *Punch*, 19 July 1856, p.21. On the Manchester Water Bill and advice from Chadwick, prepared as chairman of the committee on the Bill, see Chadwick Papers, University College London, Item 560, ff.1-6. My thanks to Michael Roberts, for transcriptions.

29 *Punch*, 31 (2 August 1856), p.47.

30 BR51/13, diary entry for 29 July 1856.

31 BR51/13, diary entries for 8–23 September.

32 Lambert, *Sir John Simon*, p.256.

33 *Medical Times and Gazette*, 4 September 1858, p.256.

34 *Punch* 33 (1857), p.86.

35 W.F. Cowper, *The Medical Practioners Bill Explained In a Speech* (London: J. Ridgway, 1858); Stokes, 'A Coleridgean against the Medical Corporations', p.357 outlines the difference between this act and the bill drafted by Simon. See also M.J.D. Roberts, 'The Politics of Professionalization: MPs, Medical men, and the 1858 Medical Act' 53:1 (January 2009), pp.37-56.

36 E. d'Azeglio to Cavour, 3 February 1857 (in French), in C.B. Cavour, *Epistolario. a cura di Carlo Pischedda e Rosanna Roccia* (Firenze: Olschki, 1994), vol.14, part 1, pp.48-49, d'Azeglio told Cavour William was ambitious but had not been successful in the Board of Health.

37 E. Fitzmaurice, *The Life of Granville George Leveson-Gower, second Earl Granville, K.G., 1815-1891* (London: Longmans, Green and Co., 1906), vol.1, p.225.

38 *The Monthly Paper of the National Society [for Promoting the Education of the Poor in the Principles of the Established Church]*, March 1857, p.66.

39 *PD*, 3rd series, vol.144, 18 February 1857, cols.786-788.

40 J.T. Smith, *Local Self-Government Un-mystified: A Vindication of Common Sense, Human Nature and Practical Improvement, against the Manifesto of Centralisation* (London: Edward Stanford, 1857), p.44, p.108.

41 'The Present Crisis – Hayters and Cowpers', *Morning Chronicle*, 13 May 1858.

42 Lord John Russell Papers, PRO, PR30/22/20: Palmerston to Russell, 2 July 1859.

43 BR43/25/5, William to Georgina, refers to his role here, in Chelsea Hospital pensions.

44 BR50/25, Palmerston to William, 17 August 1859. Palmerston discusses the advantage of the title of the office being altered and its being assimilated in the duties of undersecretary.

45 BR50/14, Gladstone to William, Downing Street, 9 November 1859.

46 *Belfast News-Letter*, 12 August 1859. See gossip in the *Court Journal*, reported in *Liverpool Mercury*, 3 January 1860. Wags had gossiped about an appropriate appointment to the Office of Woods and Forests as he had so often been planted and transplanted, see *Belfast News-Letter*, 13 February 1860. An engraving and profile of the new Chief Commissioner appeared in the *Illustrated London News*, 25 February 1860, p.176: my thanks to Tom Gillmor of the Mary Evans Picture Library for this information.

47 *Belfast News-Letter*, 5 August 1864.

48 M.H. Port, 'Government and the Metropolitan Image: ministers, parliament and the concept of a capital city, 1840–1915', *Art History* 22: 4 (November 1999), pp.567-592 (p.574, p.578).

49 *Daily News*, 20 July 1860.

50 *Belfast News-Letter*, 19 June 1863.

51 *MTM*, p.51.

52 See the letters from Herbert in BR, WFC/B/12, 4 February 1863.

53 See the Governor of the Tower, Lord De Ros's letters, BR, WFC/D/1-2, 1862 and 1866. On Salvin's work for the Commissioners of Works, see J. Allibone, *Anthony Salvin. Pioneer of Gothic revival architecture* (Cambridge: Lutterworth Press, 1987).

54 See, for instance, on the Paris embassy, BL, Layard Papers, Add. MSS 39104, f.229, f.248; and from Sir Henry Bulwer in Constantinople, BR, WFC/B/36/1, 16 October 1861 and subsequent letters to 1864.

55 H. Emmerson, *The Ministry of Works* (London: G. Allen and Unwin, 1956), p.16.

56 See letters, BR, WFC/B/32-34, from Sir Richard Bromley about bringing departments of analogous character together in one building, to end the 'dilatory and incomplete routine of correspondence upon every small matter', and economy. Copies of letters and plans by Bromley were printed by order of the Commons in February 1861.

57 See the letters from Herbert in BR, WFC/H/3-8.

58 BR, WFC/B/4, Barry to William, 30 June 1866. For the later comment, see M.H. Port, ed., *The Houses of Parliament* (New Haven: Yale University Press, 1976), pp.177-178. The abilities of his father, Sir Charles Barry, architect of the Houses of Parliament, were known to William through work at Trentham Park and Stafford House.

59 BR, WFC/B/27, William to Sir Thomas Bidulph, 4 July 1863.

60 BR54/11, William to Georgina, 'Friday 14'.

61 *The Times*, 21 October 1864, p.8.

62 BL, Layard Papers, Add. MSS 38997, f.69, 28 October 1869.

63 See J. Devey, *The Life of Joseph Locke, Civil Engineer, M.P., F.R.S.* (London: R. Bentley, 1862) p.325, for the belief that Locke was the leading candidate, until William's appointment.

64 BR, WFC/L/1, Layard to William, 27 October 1869. Layard was Under-secretary for Foreign Affairs at Palmerston's insistence, despite Victoria's aversion to his radical, non-aristocratic background, in 1861.

65 On Peel statue, see BR, WFC/C/23, Edward Cardwell to William, 26 March 1861 and BR, WFC/G/36, General Grey (the Prince's private secretary) to William, 11 April 1861; see BR, WFC/G/33-34 on the agricultural show, March 1861. They discussed provision for Florence Nightingale in Kensington Palace, see BR, WFC/G/37, Grey to William, 22 April 1861.

66 BR, WFC/G/32, Grey to William, 19 March 1861.

67 BR, WFC/G/47, Grey to William, 22 November 1862; see also Royal Archives, Windsor Castle, RA/MAIN/F/31/101, 24 November 1862.

68 BR, WFC/G/50, Grey to William, 24 September 1863.

69 See correspondence between Cambridge and the Office, BR, WFC/C/1-21. See G.R. St. Aubyn, *The Royal George, 1819-1904. The Life of H.R.H. Prince George Duke of Cambridge* (London: Constable, 1963).

70 BR, WFC/C/11, 13 April 1862; BR, WFC/C/13, 12 July 1862; BR, WFC/C/17, 25 January 1866. See also the letters from MacDonald, BR, WFC/M/1-13.

71 BR, WFC/C/16, Cambridge to William, 11 January 1866.

72 *West London Observer*, 28 July 1860, clipping in BR206/2, describing William as a 'Man in Office who would be popular if he had the wit to effect or contrive it'.

73 *The Times*, 15 August 1860, p.6, reporting debate in the Commons the previous day; *The Times*, leader 18 August 1860, p.9. The phrase 'horseback interest' comes from an editorial

in the *Daily News*, 20 July 1860. A project to build a new communication across London through St James's Park had interested Palmerston since the 1850s, see J. Ridley, *Lord Palmerston* (1970; London: Panther, 1972), p.694.

74 *Reynolds's Newspaper*, 19 August 1860.

75 *Reynolds's Newspaper*, 19 August 1860; *Morning Chronicle*, 13 August 1860; *Punch*, 25 August 1860, p.72; A. Austin, *The Season: A Satire* (London: R. Harwicke, 1861), p.19; J.E. Ritchie, *The Life and Times of Viscount Palmerston: Embracing the Diplomatic and Domestic History of the British Empire During the Last Half Century* (London: London Printing and Publishing Company, 1866), p.298; *MTM*, p.54.

76 McCarthy, *Portraits of the Sixties*, pp.134-136.

77 Annotations by Gladstone, BL, Gladstone Papers, Add. MSS 44393, ff.3-4.

78 BL, Gladstone Papers, Add. MSS 44395, f.22, 4 January 1861. See f.25 for the printed handbill by Benjamin Steill, with underlining by Gladstone.

79 BL, Gladstone Papers, Add. MSS 44393, ff.3-6, 2 January 1860.

80 *Caledonian Mercury*, 1 March 1862.

81 *Belfast News-Letter*, 12 April 1862.

82 *Birmingham Daily Post*, 19 May 1862

83 *Birmingham Daily Post*, 19 May 1862.

84 T.A. Jenkins, *The Parliamentary Diaries of Sir John Trelawny. 1858–1865* (London: Royal Historical Society, 1990), pp.203-4; *PD*, 3rd series, vol.166, 16 May 1862, cols.1800-1805.

85 *Punch*, 'Punch's Essence of Parliament', 12 July 1862, p.11; 'The Bauld Buccleuch. – A Border Ballad', 12 July 1862, p.17; 'Punch's Essence of Parliament', 2 August 1862, p.42; 'Evident Per Se', 30 August 1862, p.83.

86 *Fun*, 8 November 1862, p.72.

87 *MTM*, p.37.

88 *Birmingham Daily Post*, 30 June 1862.

89 *Daily News*, 1 July 1862.

90 *Belfast News-Letter*, 1 July 1862.

91 BR58/2, diary entry for 5 July 1862. See the reference to the controversy surrounding the select committee, *Annual Register*, 1862, p.136.

92 H. Hoock, 'Reforming culture: national art institutions in the age of reform', in Burns and Innes, eds, *Rethinking the Age of Reform, Britain 1780–1850* (Cambridge: Cambridge University Press, 2003), pp.254-270.

93 W.R.M. Lamb, *The Royal Academy: A Short History of its Foundation and Development* (London: G. Bell, 1951).

94 BR, WFC/G/55/2, draft of letter from William to General Sir C. Grey. See also Royal Archives, Windsor Castle, RA/VIC/MAIN/F/31/95; RA/VIC/MAIN/F/31/99, letters from William to Grey.

95 BR, WFC/G/2, 31 February 1862.

96 For Grant's letters, see BR, WFC/G/9-19. On the National Gallery, *Punch*, 18 June 1864, p.249; 25 June 1864; 17 June 1865.

97 BR, WFC/G/23, draft letter from William to Grant, n.d.

98 BR58/2, Georgina's diary entry for 12 October 1862; 'The War in Hyde Park', *London Review*, October 1862, p.314; S. Gilley, 'The Garibaldi Riots of 1862', *Historical Journal* 16: 4 (December 1973), pp.697-732.

99 BL, Gladstone Papers, Add. MSS 44405, f.49, 18 January 1865.

100 BL, Gladstone Papers, Add. MSS 44401, f.237, 7 December 1863.

101 'Public Works', *Fraser's Magazine*, 9:410 (February 1864), p.173.

102 See BR, WFC/N/1, W.A. Nesfield to William, 13 August 1866.

103 *Leeds Mercury*, 17 October 1888.

104 *PD*, 3rd series, vol.146, 29 June 1857, col. 566.

105   *PD*, 3rd series, vol.164, 8 July 1861, col. 518.

106   BR206/2, clipping from *Edinburgh Evening Courier*, 2 April 1863.

107   Houghton Papers, EP4/2 (a ballad); EP4/3 (1), letter to Houghton, 2 November 1863, from unidentified writer.

108   Nor does Georgina's fragmentary diary enlighten, see BR58/17.

109   Letter in BR33, Emily Palmerston to William [26 October 1865].

110   Clipping from unidentified newspaper, in BR58/3, Georgina's diary for 1867.

111   Jenkins, *Parliamentary Diaries of Sir John Trelawny*, p.204, p.215 and p.259. See also A. Hawkins and J. Powell, eds, *The Journal of John Wodehouse First Earl of Kimberley for 1862–1902* Camden 5th series ix (Cambridge: Royal Historical Society, 1997) p.131, and pp.69-70: 'Billy Cowper in a scrape as usual'. P. Guedalla, *Gladstone and Palmerston. Being the Correspondence of Lord Palmerston with Mr Gladstone, 1851–1865* (London: Gollancz, 1928) pp.175-176, notes a disagreement between them which may have owed something to William's failure to communicate.

112   See J.S. Meisel, *Public Speech and the Culture of Public Life in the Age of Gladstone* (New York: Columbia University Press, 2001).

113   Letter in BR33, n.d. [*c.*1850-1865].

114   Letter in BR33 [late October 1855].

115   Fletcher, *Parliamentary Portraits*, p.136.

116   *Fun*, 8 November 1862, p.72; *Once a Week*, 5 August 1876, p.279.

117   Tollemache, *Old and Odd Memories*, p.83; Russell, *Portrait of the Seventies*, p.279.

118   *MTM*, p.63.

Chapter 6. The Private Life of the Cowper-Temples, 1860–1867

1   BR56/2, Georgina's diary entry for 16 February 1862.

2   BR57/39/16, Emelia Gurney to Georgina, 27 July [1890s].

3   *MTM*, p.101; E.M. Gurney, ed., *Letters of Emelia Russell Gurney* (London: James Nisbet, 1902), p.143; R. Cholmeley, *Edward Clifford* (London: Church Army Book Room, 1907), p.123 for her 'uncommonplace' nature. The Russell Gurneys were friends of Francis Galton: which perhaps accounts for the presence of the Cowper-Temples in his study of hereditary talents, see F. Galton, *Hereditary Genius an Inquiry into Its Laws and Consequences* (London: Macmillan, 1869), p.117.

4   E. Pick, *On memory and the rational means of improving it* (London: Trübner and Co., 1861); a meeting for the Sanitary Association at the Gurneys' followed one at the Cowpers, in July 1860. The Trevelyans were probably Sir Walter Trevelyan and his wife Pauline (*MTM*, p.75 is vague). For the meeting in 1859, BR59/11, April.

5   *The Philanthropist*, 2 July 1860, p.590. Ranyard had established her Mission in 1857, and sanitary reformers recognized the importance of working-class Bible-women as a conduit for sanitary information, see Dowling, 'The Ladies Sanitary Association', ch.6.

6   BR58/17, fragment of William's 1860 diary.

7   *The Times*, 26 May 1859, p.5; 5 January and 6 January 1860, p.3; 'John Pulsford', *The Speaker*, 29 May 1897, p.597.

8   Fragment of William's diary, BR58/17. There is no diary from Georgina for this year.

9   BR57/24/6, Georgina to Emelia Gurney, 1870.

10   See R. Noakes, 'Spiritualism, science and the supernatural in mid-Victorian Britain,' in N. Bown, C. Burdett and P. Thurschwell, eds, *The Victorian Supernatural* (Cambridge: Cambridge University Press, 2004), pp.23-43; A. Gauld, *The Founders of Psychical Research* (London: Routledge and Kegan Paul, 1968); L. Barrow, *Independent Spirits. Spiritualism and English Plebeians. 1850–1910* (London: Routledge and Kegan Paul, 1986); J. Oppenheim, *The Other World. Spiritualism and Psychical Research in England, 1850–1914* (Cambridge: Cambridge University Press, 1985).

11   See the entry in the notebook on séances, BR51/1, for 10 July 1861, and Mummy's account of the séance with Daniel Home, 'much fuller and more accurate than mine'.

12   *MTM*, p.107. A letter from Mary Howitt to Georgina, dated '17 August', on spiritualism and T.L. Harris is in BR56/14. M. Howitt, *An Autobiography*, 2 vols (London: William Isbister, 1889), vol.2, p.263, letter 25 March 1877. Mary was visited in Rome by 'gentle and refined Edward Clifford' who 'spoke much with us of Broadlands' in March 1873.

13   BR49/14, Mrs Milner Gibson to Georgina, 25 May [1861] and 31 May [1861], referring to séance at Dr Ashburner's; J. Home [Mme Dunglas Home], *D.D. Home, his life and mission* (1888; London: Kegan Paul, Trench, Trübner, 1921), pp.94-95 on Mrs Milner Gibson; and J. Home, *The Gift of D.D. Home* (London: Kegan Paul, Trench, Trübner, 1890), p.24.

14   See BR51/1; including William's note (in 1874) on Home at the end of this notebook; Burd, *Christmas Story*, p.37.

15   BR51/1, Georgina's and Mummy's accounts dated 10 July 1861, for séance involving Chambers, Sinclair, and 'Purity'.

16   BR51/1, Mummy's account dated 10 July 1861; Tromp, *Altered States*, p.51.

17   BR51/1, Georgina's account dated 16 July 1861; Home, *D.D. Home*, p.87.

18   Home, *The Gift of D.D. Home*, p.24.

19   BR51/1, Georgina's account for 12 September 1861.

20   BR51/1, William's notes for 13 December; Georgina's for 21 and 23 December 1861.

21   *Spiritual Magazine* (1862), p.144, see in the same magazine, the account of another séance involving Georgina, by William Howitt, September 1872; E. Sargent, *Planchette, or the Despair of Science. Being a Full Account of Modern Spiritualism its Phenomena, and the Various Theories regarding it. With a survey of French spiritism* (Boston: Roberts Brothers, 1869), p.240.

22   Copy of Queen Victoria's letter to Fanny, in Georgina's hand, in BR55/45.

23   BR58/2, Georgina's diary entry for 8 February 1862; BR43/25/10, William to Georgina, n.d. William's signed the letter of condolence, sent to the Queen by ministers, 1 March 1862, *Morning Chronicle*, 14 February 1862.

24   Sadleir, *Blessington-D'Orsay*, p.181.

25   BR58/2, Georgina's diary entry for 24 January 1862.

26   BR58/2, Georgina's diary entry for 28 January 1862.

27   BR58/2, Georgina's diary entry for 14 January 1862.

28   BR58/2, Georgina's diary entries for 2-11 February 1862.

29   On George, see BR58/6, Georgina's diary for 17 February 1876; BR58/2, 2 January 1862, on Maria Shaw, see the same entry.

30   On Heaphy, BR58/2, Georgina's diary entry for 13 January 1862.

31   BR58/2, Georgina's diary entries for 23 April and 3 May 1862. For a letter from her, see BR49/11, 1864, she was the wife of the Swedish spiritualist investigator Baron Goldenstübbe, see S.E.F. De Morgan, *Memorials of Three Score and Ten Years. Reminiscences of the late Sophia Elizabeth De Morgan* (London: R. Bentley, 1895), p.209.

32   E.g., BR58/2, séances 28–29 July and 3 August (with Mr Home), and visit 26 and 28 August. Home, *D.D. Home, his life and mission*, p.126; J.O. Barrett, *The Spiritual Pilgrim. A Biography of James M. Peebles.* (1871; Boston: W. White, 1872), p.246. Zu Solms (or de Solms) is mentioned in E. Sheppard, *George, Duke of Cambridge. A Memoir of His Private Life Based on the Journals and Correspondence of His Royal Highness* (1906), vol.1, p.37 as a friend; and E.H. Britten, *Nineteenth Century Miracles or, Spirits and their work in every country of the earth. A complete historical compendium of the great movement know as 'modern spiritualism'* (Manchester: William Britten, 1884), p.162. He knew the Howitts, Wattses and Laurence Oliphant, see A.M. Lee, *Laurels and Rosemary. The Life of William and Mary Howitt* (London: Oxford University Press, 1955), p.253.

33   Tromp, *Altered States*, p.51, cites Harriet's detailed appearance via Home. In BR51/1, the initials 'H.A.' and 'Harriet Alicia' are used for a visitation before the medium 'Agape' (see

29 July 1862 entries by both the Cowpers). On the Evangelist, see BR51/1, entries 11–17 November 1862.

34   BR58/2, Georgina's diary entry for 8 May 1862.
35   BR58/2, Georgina's diary entry for 5 June 1862.
36   BR58/2, Georgina's diary entry for 14 July 1862.
37   BR58/2, Georgina's diary entry for 14 July 1862. Charlotte Poulett was the fifth Earl Poulett's wife.
38   BR58/2, Georgina's diary entry for 26 August 1862.
39   BR58/2, Georgina's diary entry for 15 May and 27 August 1862. Drayson's works included adventure stories, books on whist, and 'serious' works such as *The Earth we Inhabit*, classed in the *Eclectic Review*, June 1859, pp.66-67, as absurd pseudoscience for its view of an expanding terrestrial globe; *The Cause of the Supposed Proper Motion of the Fixed Stars and an Explanation of the Apparent Acceleration of the Moon's Mean Motion* (London: Chapman and Hall, 1874) and *Experiences of a Woolwich Professor* (1886).
40   BR58/2, Georgina's diary entry for 23 August 1862.
41   BR58/2, Georgina's diary entry for 12 August: 'She [Julia] thinks prolapse came from weakness over exertion &c &c & that operation has certainly done this good.'
42   See William's notes in a fragment from a journal inserted in BR58/3, Georgina's diary for 1867, headed 'Dr Protheroe Smith', on the reverse, on insertion of dilator and 'algae sound'.
43   BR58/2, Georgina's diary entry for 11 August 1862, and Georgina's comments in a fragment from a journal inserted in BR58/3, Georgina's diary for 1867. Llanover had been Sir Benjamin Hall.
44   BR58/2, Georgina's diary entry for 31 May 1862.
45   BR58/2, Georgina's diary entry for 12 July 1862.
46   NLS, MacDonald Papers, MS 9745, f.1, 9 August 1862. See W. Raeper, *George MacDonald. Novelist and Victorian Visionary* (Tring: Lion Books, 1987).
47   A. Byng, *Leaves from the Diary of Henry Greville, fourth series* (London: Smith, Elder, 1905), pp.90-93; *MTM*, p.108.
48   BR58/2, Georgina's diary entry for 5 August 1862. See also 29 and 31 August 1862.
49   Letters from 'Sophia C', 21 August and 23 August 1862, inserted in Georgina's diary BR58/2, and diary entry, BR58/2, for 20 August 1862.
50   BR58/2, Georgina's diary entry for 28 August 1862.
51   BR58/2, Georgina's diary entry for 29 August 1862.
52   BR58/2, Georgina's diary entry for 15 September 1862: 'It's alarming to hear he is in the hands of 7 Italian surgeons!' Lady Palmerston sent a special bed for his release from prison, see J. Ridley, *Garibaldi* (London: Constable, 1974), p.545.
53   Mary Stanley is presumably the nurse, Catholic convert, and sister of A.P. Stanley. For Georgina's comment on the *Stones*, see BR58/2, entry for 3 October 1862.
54   BR58/2, Georgina's diary entry for 5 October 1862.
55   *Fun*, 8 November 1862, p.72.
56   BR58/2, Georgina's diary entries for 9 October on Esterhazy, 12 October on Hyde Park riots, and 14–15 October, on Harriet and F.D. Maurice.
57   BR58/2, Georgina's diary entry for 2 November 1862, on Froude; see Byng, *Leaves from the Diary of Henry Greville, fourth series* (1905), p.79, on Henry Cowper.
58   BR58/2, Georgina's diary entry for 8 December 1862.
59   See BR51/1, William's notes of séance with Home on 16 January 1863, and on Henry's candidacy, 17 September 1863. On William Cowper's unpopularity, see *Trewman's Exeter Flying-Post*, 16 March 1864.
60   BR51/1, William's notes of séances 4, 23 and 27 February 1864.
61   *Belfast News-Letter*, 19 June 1863 and 5 August 1864.

62   See BR51/1, for séances in August 1864, and séance dated 26 November 1864.

63   See BR51/2 for spiritual notes derived from the Miss Greenfields, *c.*1866, and three letters from Orinna (or Oriana) and Margaret in BR49/13.

64   BR45/6/3, William's diary for 1865.

65   *The Times*, 19 July 1865, p.8, 25 July 1865, p.6.

66   BR51/1, account of séance dated 23 August 1865.

67   BR50/25, Palmerston to William, Brocket, 30 September 1865.

68   BR205/2, memorandum by Palmerston to his wife, 22 November 1864; BR187/12/1, memorandum of Evelyn Ashley.

69   BR50/25, Palmerston to William, Brocket, 30 September 1865.

70   Protheroe Smith sent a letter which alleged the conversion of an infidel apparently on hearing an account of the death of Lord Palmerston, 6 January 1866, BR44/16/5. For a detailed study of the episode, see M.J.D. Roberts, 'The Deathbed of Lord Palmerston. An episode in Victorian Cultural History', *Cultural and Social History* 5:2 (June 2008), pp.183-196. William sent telegrams to Balmoral about Palmerston's demise, see Royal Archives, Windsor Castle, RA/VIC/MAIN/R/43/49 and 54.

71   BR53/7, letters from Georgina to Augustus [1865].

72   *Glasgow Herald*, 6 August 1864.

73   BR58/2, Georgina's diary for 1867, clippings from newspapers.

74   BR48/5/6, Sir Henry Bulwer to William.

75   *MTM*, p.71; BL, Nightingale Papers, Add. MSS 45799, ff.149-155b, letter to Nightingale, 31 October 1865.

76   BR51/6, 'Health Journal', William's entries for November 1865.

77   *MTM*, p.60.

78   See BR51/13, William's journal, for an entry on reform in 1866.

79   Byng, *Leaves from the Diary of Henry Greville, fourth series*, p.276, Battiscombe, *Shaftesbury*, p.269. Seeley's work presented the humanity of Christ.

80   BR50/26, Shaftesbury to William, 7 November 1865 (concerning Gladstone), and 15 January and 20 January 1866.

81   BR58/17, diary entry for 8 February 1866.

82   *Manchester Guardian*, 2 April 1866, p.2.

83   BR58/17, diary for 24 June 1866; BR58/20, commonplace book entry, 23 June 1866.

84   *Manchester Guardian*, 24 July 1866, p.7.

85   BR55/9, A.M. Howitt Watts to Georgina, 28 July 1866.

86   Born *c.*1827, she was married to P.W. Wagstaff, MRCSE, with whom the Cowpers seem to have been acquainted from 1855, see BR53/16, William to Georgina, 20 March 1855. See references in *The Zoist*, vol.9, March 1851-January 1852: she could see and prescribe at a distance according to John Elliotson, who noted her husband was an early supporter of mesmerism; D.G. Jones, *The Autobiography of David Jones with an Exposition of Medical Politics and Sidelights on the Medical Profession* (London: Mitchell, 1907), p.36; J. Chapple and A. Shelston, eds, *Further Letters of Mrs Gaskell* (2000; Manchester: Manchester University Press, 2004), p.96, for the novelist's inquiry about her in 1853; and A. Winter, *Mesmerized: Power of Mind in Victorian Britain* (Chicago: University of Chicago Press, 1998), ch.6, note 3. Her clairvoyancy was known in upper-class circles, see Hare, *Story of My Life*, vol.4, p.392, 18 June 1876; J. Batchelor, *Lady Trevelyan and the Pre-Raphaelite Brotherhood* (London: Chatto and Windus, 2006), p.227.

87   BR58/17; BR45/6/4, William's diary, entries for 30 July and 3–4 August 1866.

88   'Mr Ruskin and Rose', in M. Drew, *Acton, Gladstone and Others* (London: J. Nisbet, 1924), from which the phrase quoted comes, attempts to faithfully recount the story as learned from Georgina, see p.117.

89   Ruskin spoke about Rose to Georgina, 19 February 1866, seeking help, see D. Leon, *Ruskin, the Great Victorian* (1949; London: Routledge and Kegan Paul, 1969), pp.363-369; Burd, *John Ruskin and Rose La Touche* (Oxford: Clarendon Press, 1979), pp.103-104.

90   Hilton, *John Ruskin. The Later Years*, p.146. The letters from Rose to Georgina were not cited by Burd in *John Ruskin and Rose La Touche*, but are partially printed in Burd, 'More Letters from Rose La Touche', in *Bulletin of the John Rylands University Library of Manchester* 65: 2 (spring 1983), pp.61-71. Rose corresponded with William on at least one occasion; see reference in BR55/7, 'You will see that I have written to Mr Cowper. It was so nice of him to write.' An engagement diary belonging to William just notes the visit to Harristown. Letters from Georgina to Ruskin from Harristown no longer exist.

91   BR55/7, letter by Rose to Georgina on the day the Cowper-Temples departed.

92   BR55/7, letter by Rose to Georgina, n.d.

93   BR55/7, Rose to Georgina, 'Saturday night'.

94   BR55/7, Rose to Georgina, 9 November 1866.

95   BR55/7, Rose to Georgina, Harristown, 'October'.

96   BR55/7, Rose to Georgina, 29 October, 'Monday night'.

97   BR55/7, Rose to Georgina, November, 'Sunday afternoon'.

98   BR55/7, Rose to Georgina, 'Thursday night'.

99   Drew, *Acton, Gladstone and Others*, p.117.

100 BR55/7, Rose to Georgina, fragment of letter, n.d. Georgina's nickname for Ruskin was 'St Chrysostom', the Golden-mouthed, and derived from St John Chrysostom, the eloquent fourth-century Archbishop of Constantinople.

101 BR55/7, Rose to Georgina, 'Monday night'; and subsequent letter on mourning notepaper, June 11 [1868].

102 BR51/6, entry in 'Health Journal' for 18 October 1866.

103 A.J.C. Hare, *The Story of Two Noble Lives: Being Memorials of Charlotte, Countess Canning* (London: Allen, 1893), p.383. Edith was one of Marianne de Burgh's daughters.

104 BR58/17, Georgina's diary entry for 4 November 1866.

105 BR51/1, entry in séance notebook, 1 December 1866.

106 BR51/1, entry *c*.November 1866. Stopford A. Brooke's *Life and Letters of Frederick W. Robertson* had recently appeared (2 vols, London: Smith, Elder, 1865).

107 BR58/17, entries in Georgina's diary for 13 and 18 December 1866.

108 *The Times*, 14 October 1870, p.7.

109 S.E.M. Jeune, *Memories of Fifty Years* (London: Edward Arnold, 1909), pp.91-92.

110 G.W. Curtis, ed., *The Correspondence of John L. Motley* (2 vols, London: J. Murray, 1889), vol.1, p.326. See also the presence of the Cowpers in S. Dallas, ed., *Diary of George Mifflin Dallas: While United States Minister to Russia 1837-1839, and to England 1856 to 1861* (Philadelphia: J.B. Lippincott, 1892), p.391, p.420.

111 *MTM*, p.53.

112 Tollemache, *Old and Odd Memories*, p.81.

113 BR58/2, Georgina's diary entry for 2 January 1862.

114 BR58/6, Georgina's diary entry for 8 March 1876.

115 Georgina presented Eva de Burgh, *The Times*, 23 March 1870, p.5.

116 BR59/74, William to Juliet, n.d.

117 BR33/6, Emily Palmerston to William, Brocket, 'Monday night', *c*.1867.

118 See Gerard, *Country House Life* for insightful treatment of the country house community, the house at once 'family seat, theatre of hospitality and community centre' (p.6).

119 E.L. Berthon, *A Retrospect of Eight Decades* (London: G. Bell, 1899), recalled William and his 'lovely and most lovable wife', p.160. See BR48/4/1-3, letters from Berthon, 1875.

120 BR53/3, William to Georgina, 'Sunday 12', *c*.1867.

121   For instance, *The General Stud-book, Containing Pedigrees of Race Horses, &c. &c.* (London: Reynell, 1885), p.471, for 'Thistle', bred in 1875.

Chapter 7. The Private Life of the Cowper-Temples, 1867–1877

1   BR53/3, William to Georgina, n.d., but before death of Lady Palmerston.

2   BR58/3, Georgina's diary entry for 2 January 1867.

3   BR58/3, Georgina's diary entry for 4 March 1867.

4   BR58/3, Georgina's diary entry for 20 January 1867.

5   BR58/3, Georgina's diary entry for 2 January 1867. See *ODNB* entry on Lucas and the bizarre *carte de visite* self-portraits created *c.*1858, in the National Portrait Gallery.

6   For instance, BR58/3, Georgina's diary entry for 16 January, on Dressmaking Company and feeding plans, and entry for 26 February, on another Dressmaking Company visit; entry for 7 March on reading Simon's report on Vaccination and Spencer Hall's lecture.

7   BR58/3, Georgina's diary entry for 25 January 1867.

8   BR58/3, Georgina's diary entry for 16 May 1867.

9   BR58/3, Georgina's diary entry for 11 February 1867.

10   In 1846, William corresponded with Price about recording accidents in coal mines. He effected a meeting with Palmerston, see BR50/43, Price to Cowper, 9 February 1846.

11   BR58/3, Georgina's diary entry for 6 May 1867.

12   On Althaus, see B.A. Simpson, ed., *Electrical Stimulation and the Relief of Pain* (Amsterdam and London: Elsevier, 2003), p.8.

13   BR58/3, Georgina's diary entry for 12 April 1867. Though Georgina spells her surname 'Nichols', the medium was [Agnes] Elizabeth Nicholl, later a famous medium as Mrs Guppy (and subsequently Guppy-Volckman), see Richard Noakes' *ODNB* entry.

14   BR58/3, Georgina's diary entry for 13 April 1867.

15   BR58/3, Georgina's diary entry for 15 April 1867.

16   BR44/5/14, note by William, with associated planchette message, n.d.

17   BR58/3 Georgina's diary entry for 2 February; and BR45/6/5, William's diary entries for 2, 6 and 7 February 1867.

18   BR58/3, Georgina's diary entry for 2 April 1867.

19   BR58/3, Georgina's diary entry for 26 February 1867.

20   BR58/3, Georgina's diary entry for 23 February 1867.

21   BR58/3, Georgina's diary entry for 27 February 1867.

22   BR58/3, Georgina's diary entry for 2 March 1867.

23   BR58/3, Georgina's diary entry for 6 March 1867.

24   BR58/3, Georgina's diary entries for 13 and 14 March 1867.

25   *MTM*, p.108.

26   BR58/3, Georgina's diary entry for 24 March 1867.

27   BR58/3, Georgina's diary entry for 31 March 1867.

28   BR58/3, Georgina's diary entry for 7 April 1867. See A. Cobbing, *The Satsuma Students in Britain: Japan's Early Search for the essence of the West* (Richmond, Surrey: Japan Library, 2000), p.113, p.190, and Cobbing, *The Japanese Discovery of Victorian Britain* (Richmond, Surrey: Japan Library, 1998).

29   BR58/3, Georgina's diary entry for 18 April 1867.

30   BR58/3, Georgina's diary entry for 19 April 1867.

31   BR58/3, Georgina's diary entry for 19 April 1867.

32   On the appeal of Swedenborg for Victorians, see I. Sellers, 'The Swedenborgian Church in England', in L. Woodhead, ed., *Reinventing Christianity. Nineteenth Century Contexts* (Aldershot: Ashgate, 2001), ch.5. For the Cowper-Temples, Swedenborg's spiritualism, arcane knowledge, vision of a humanized yet progressive heaven and the emphasis on good works, 'Uses' were probably attractive.

33 BR58/3, Georgina's diary entries for 30 April and 4 May 1867.
34 BR58/3, Georgina's diary entry for 8 October 1867.
35 BR43/48/51, William to Edward Berridge, 22 April 1881.
36 See B. Russell and P. Russell, eds, *The Amberley Papers: Bertrand Russell's Family Background* (1937; London: Allen and Unwin, 1966), vol.2, p.534, and Burd, *A Christmas Story.*
37 BR58/3, Georgina's diary entries for 28 and 29 June 1867.
38 BR58/3, Georgina's diary entry for 19 March 1867. There were two London chapels in the Office of Work's gift and William gave St James's, Westmorland Street to Haweis. See B. Howe, *Arbiter of Elegance* (London: Harvill Press, 1967), pp.132-133.
39 BR58/3, Georgina's diary entries for 29 March on Cobbe, 31 March on Maurice and 23 March on the Court.
40 BR43/25/16, William to Georgina, 29 December 1867. On Michel, see *Medical Times and Gazette,* 9 September 1876, p.287.
41 BR43/29/1, Georgina to William, Avenue Friedland, n.d. See BR58/3, for Georgina's diary entries 10 August–9 September 1867.
42 Rafe corresponded with Walt Whitman, see W. White, ed., *Daybooks and Notebooks, Volume 1: Daybooks: 1876–November 1881* (New York: New York University Press, 2007), p.19. Edith, in black velvet and Pre-Raphaelite melancholy (Leicester-Warren, *Diaries,* vol.2, p.246), adored Georgina, and shared her earnestness and scorn for 'conventionalities'.
43 BR55/25, Georgina to Marguerite Tollemache, Avenue Friedland, n.d.
44 BR43/29/17, Georgina to William, n.d.
45 On the Zouave, see *The Nation,* 19 September 1867; A.B. Peat, *Gossip from Paris During the Second Empire: Correspondence (1864–1869) of Anthony B. North Peat* (London: Kegan Paul, Trench, Trübner, 1903), pp.256-258; William's diary, BR45/6/5, 24 August 1867; Britten, *Nineteenth Century Miracles,* pp.66-69, and *The Spiritual Magazine,* October 1867, pp.449-452.
46 BR58/3, Georgina's diary entry for 5 September 1867; and BR51/1, entry on August in Paris. Lisett Makdougal Gregory was the part-German widow of William Gregory, professor of chemistry at Edinburgh and a psychic investigator.
47 BR43/29/20, Georgina to William, n.d.
48 On Radstock in Russia, see F.M. Dostoevsky, *A Writer's Diary. Fyodor Dostoyevsky, translated and annotated by Kenneth Lantz:* vol.1, *1873–1876* (Evanston, Illinois: Northwestern University Press, 1994), p.418.
49 BR55/25, Georgina to Marguerite Tollemache, Avenue Friedland, n.d.
50 Bebbington, *Evangelicalism in Modern Britain,* p.159.
51 BR43/29/14, Georgina to William, n.d.
52 BR43/47/5, Spencer to William, '6 September', Geneva, n.d; BR43/29/14, Georgina to William, n.d., on Salemites.
53 BR35/7, Emily Palmerston to Evelyn Ashley, 13 September [1867].
54 BR58/3, Georgina's diary entry for 29 September 1867.
55 BR58/3, Georgina's diary entry for 7 October 1867.
56 BR58/3, Georgina's diary, enclosed letter to Georgina from Blanche and Constance Noel, and funeral service. Adelaide was related to William's first wife, as eldest daughter of the sixteenth Earl of Errol.
57 See Cobbing, *Japanese Discovery,* p.109.
58 BR58/3, Georgina's diary entry for 15 December 1867.
59 See Oliphant's letter, January 1868, cited in Cobbing, *Japanese Discovery,* p.109; Taylor, *Laurence Oliphant,* p.142.
60 *Daily News,* 28 February 1868.
61 BR43/24/13, William to Georgina, Broadlands, 'Sunday 22'.
62 Either Minna or Rosalie Praetorius. There is a reference to 'Praetorius have got her £20' in BR43/24/12, William to Georgina, n.d.

63   BR43/29/10, Georgina to William, 1 January 1868.
64   BR43/25/16, William to Georgina, Broadlands, 29 December [1867].
65   BR53/4, William to Georgina, Broadlands, 13 January [1867].
66   BR53/3, William to Georgina, Brocket, 'Monday 7' [watermark 1868].
67   BR43/29/7, Georgina to William, n.d. See *Spiritual Magazine*, 1868, p.4, p.12, p.13.
68   BR43/29/2, Georgina to William, 'Tuesday 24'.
69   BR45/9, notes on Hardinge's lecture in March 1868 and the Davenports', 16 May 1868.
70   J. Evans and J.H. Whitehouse, eds, *The Diaries of John Ruskin*. vol.2, *1848-1873* (Oxford: Clarendon Press, 1958), through March, pp.644-645.
71   BR58/17, Georgina's diary entry for 8 May 1868.
72   Houghton Papers, MSS6/200, 24 July.
73   *The Times*, 23 July 1868, p.10.
74   BR50/20, William to Woodbine (Oliphant), Kingstown, 9 August 1868.
75   BR58/17, Georgina's diary entry for 24 October 1868.
76   Ruskin had first visited Broadlands, meeting Palmerston, in March 1861.
77   He died 30 April 1883.
78   BR 51/1, William's notes on séance with Mrs Watts and Douglas, 16 January 1869.
79   For meetings with Garth Wilkinson, see BR58/17. BR44/5/12 is a pencil sketch of a ship and flower, docketed (not in William's hand) 'Seen in Vision April 14th/69'.
80   Bugnion was a Swiss naturalized in Russia, who taught at a Vaudois colony in Bessarabia and in Mauritius. He proclaimed himself bishop of the 'Church of the Lord' and sought to establish a Swedenborgian see in India (*John Bull*, 6 January 1866); he visited America in 1869 to establish Swiss colonies. From 1873 he was in Australia. See J-F. Mayer, *L'Évêque Bugnion ou les Voyages extraordinaires d'un aventurier ecclésiastique vaudois* (Lausanne: Editions 24 heures, 1989). There are a handful of letters from Bugnion to William, the first is BR50/21, 23 June 1869; and a letter to Georgina after she wrote in concern about him being led by delusive spirits, BR56/16, 3 January 1870.
81   BR50/ 21, Oliphant to William, Salem on Erie, 9 May [1869].
82   BR58/17, Georgina's diary entry for 28 June 1869.
83   See also L. Stephen, *Life of Henry Fawcett* (London: Smith Elder, 1885), p.64.
84   *Journal of the Society of Arts*, 30 July 1869, p.720.
85   See BR58/17, Georgina's diary entries for 18 August–5 September 1869, on the Irish visit. See BR53/7 for Georgina's letters to Augustus on the death of her mother-in-law.
86   A. Hayward, 'Lady Palmerston', *The Times*, 15 September 1869, p.8, reprinted in Hayward, *Biographical and Critical Essays* (London: Longmans, Green, 1873), n.s., vol.2, pp.293-302 [p.301]. See H.E. Carlisle, ed., *A Selection from the Correspondence of Abraham Hayward*, vol.2, pp.201-202 for William's response to this.
87   BR57/24/10, Georgina to Emelia Gurney [September 1869].
88   BR59/55, Georgina [perhaps to Emelia Gurney], mourning notepaper, 'Friday' [17 September 1869].
89   *The Times*, 22 December 1869, p.4. On the estates, see J. Bateman, *The great landowners of Great Britain and Ireland, a list of all owners of three thousand acres and upwards, worth £3,000 a year, in England, Scotland, Ireland, & Wales* (London: Harrison, 1879), p.430.
90   BR58/17, diary entry for 20 September 1869.
91   BR57/24/2, Georgina to Emelia Gurney, 'Sunday evening'.
92   BR57/24/3, Georgina to Emelia Gurney, Curzon Street, 'Thursday'. Faber had converted to Catholicism.
93   BR58/17, diary entry for 11 October 1869.
94   BR45/9, note of séance, Curzon Street, 20 October 1869.
95   BR45/9, note of séance, Curzon Street, c.October 1869.

96 *MTM*, p.72. Surviving papers do not suggest the management of Broadlands ever became the leading concern for Georgina, who instead, *MTM*, p.74 stressed William's role, but she was involved in domestic affairs, of course. For a useful discussion of the role of women in estate management, see Reynolds, *Aristocratic Women*, ch.1.

97 BR58/17, diary entry for 7 December 1869.

98 *MTM*, p.74.

99 BR55/71, Fanny Jocelyn to Georgina [December 1869].

100 BR57/24/11, Georgina to Emelia Gurney, Broadlands, 'Sunday evening'.

101 BR57/24/12, Georgina to Emelia Gurney, Broadlands, 31 December 1869.

102 BR59/74, William to Juliet, n.d.; *MTM*, p.71.

103 *MTM*, p.73.

104 *MTM*, p.73. Juliet was naturalized as a British citizen in 1899.

105 BR56/16, Adelheid Flemming to Georgina, Hamburg, 3 January 1890.

106 BR61/1/5, Evelyn Ashley papers, undated photograph.

107 *MTM*, p.73.

108 Leicester-Warren, *Diaries*, vol.2, p.316.

109 BR58/5, Georgina's diary entry for 21 August 1874.

110 BR57/24/12, Georgina to Emelia Gurney, Broadlands, 25 December 1869.

111 See Louisa MacDonald's letter, postmarked 18 January 1870, Beinecke Rare Book and Manuscript Library, George MacDonald Collection, folder 259, correspondence 1870-1879; on Harcourt, BR58/17, Georgina's diary entry for 7 January 1870.

112 The former Louisa Stuart-Mackenzie, described by Pope-Hennessy in *Monckton Milnes, The Years of Promise*, p.305, as 'tiresome'. A dispute about The Grange, the Baring mansion, involved William as advisor, see NLS, Ashburton Papers, Acc.11388/96, William to Lady Ashburton, 12 January 1871.

113 BR55/48, Georgina to Emelia, Broadlands, 'Friday'.

114 BR55/48, Georgina to Emelia Gurney, n.d.

115 BR59/55, Georgina to 'My own dearest', 'Friday', n.d.

116 BR43/21/4, William to Georgina, Athenaeum, 'Thursday night', watermark 1870.

117 BR45/6/6, William's diary entries, 7–28 September 1870 (La Touche, on 27 September).

118 BR51/13, note dated 18 August 1870 in a journal otherwise covering *c*.1838-1850s. On Georgina's role, see Burd, *John Ruskin and Rose la Touche*, pp.121-122.

119 BR55/48, Georgina to Emelia, Broadlands, 'Friday'.

120 BR55/48, note, 'The last m[ournin]g of our sweet visit to Broadlands Oct. 1870'.

121 BR58/17, Georgina's diary entry for 30 March 1871, on *Beatrix*.

122 Bradley, *Letters of John Ruskin to Lord and Lady Mount Temple*, p.309; J.S. Dearden, ed., *The Professor. Arthur Severn's Memoir of John Ruskin* (London: Allen and Unwin, 1967), pp.43-44; Burd, *John Ruskin and Rose La Touche*, p.123.

123 BR55/48, Georgina to Emelia, 17 Curzon Street (postmark 22 May 1871). Her 'Conversations of Harris', 16 May–June 1871, are in the notebook BR45/8/2.

124 BR57/24/5, Georgina to Emelia Gurney, Broadlands, 4 June 1871.

125 BR45/8//1, notebook entitled 'Conversations of Thomas Lake Harris', 24 March 1871.

126 *New York Times*, 16 May 1871, p.5. The surname was sometimes spelled McLean.

127 BR58/17, Georgina's diary entry for 18 March 1871.

128 For correspondence with Jessie, see BR55/59. A.P. Arnold, *Historic Side-Lights* (New York and London: Harper and Brothers, 1899), p.291, claims she was sent to an asylum so that the family might gain her inheritance when Spencer died.

129 On Herbert, see S.H. Harris, *Auberon Herbert: Crusader for Liberty* (London: Williams and Norgate, 1943); for Oliphant's marriage, Taylor, *Laurence Oliphant*, p.173.

130 BR58/17, Georgina's diary entry for 4 August 1871.

131 *Pall Mall Gazette*, 27 September 1871; also reported in *Daily News* and *Leeds Mercury*.

132　See diary entries in BR58/17 and BR51/5.

133　*MTM*, p.179; letters from William to Gladstone about Basil, BL, Gladstone Papers, Add. MSS 44482, 31 July 1883; from Georgina to Gladstone about Basil, BL, Gladstone Papers, Add. MSS 44472, f.207, 31 October 1881 and Add. MSS 44518, f.35, 21 February 1894. See also C.E. Woods, *Archdeacon Wilberforce, his ideals and teachings* (London: E. Stock, 1917), p.184: this tendency in late-Victorian theology was influenced by the Cowper-Temples' favoured religious thinkers, John Pulsford and Andrew Jukes.

134　*MTM*, pp.139-140; Cholmeley, *Edward Clifford*; J.W. Mackail and G. Wyndham, eds, *Life and Letters of George Wyndham* (London: Hutchinson, 1925), p.55; see also Angela Thirkell's recollection, quoted in J. Maas, *The Victorian Art World in Photographs* (London: Barrie and Jenkins, 1984), p.99. Clifford, a Royal Academy student, was an imitator and collector of Burne-Jones's works. BR44/11/15/2 (apparently notes by Emelia Gurney) describes him as a 'fine gentlemanly young man in London: and mixing in "high society" and who has *set himself to serve GOD* and who works in high Schools etc 4 nights a week'.

135　See G.M. Williams, *Mary Clifford* (Bristol: Arrowsmith, 1920).

136　By the 1870s, Society was more accepting of Eliot's liaison, see R. Ashton, *George Eliot: A Life* (1996; London: Penguin, 1997), p.139, p.290. F.D. Maurice admired and met her, see p.270.

137　Houghton Papers, MSS18/27 (1), 21 August 1872; *The Times*, 6 August 1872, p.8. See BR56/1, Lady Ashburton's thanks for hospitality and help, Broadlands, 'Thursday'.

138　V. Surtees, *The Ludovisi Goddess. The Life of Louisa Lady Ashburton* (Wilton: Michael Russell, 1984), p.178.

139　NLS, Ashburton Papers, Acc.11388/96, William to Lady Ashburton, 31 December 1872; William to Lady Ashburton Christmas, n.d.; and letter from Georgina, 'Tuesday', n.d., from 27 Princes' Gate.

140　Durham University Library, Special Collections, John Ruskin Biographical Papers, Add. MSS 817/21, Georgina to MacDonald, 20 April 1872.

141　Durham University Library, Special Collections, John Ruskin Biographical Papers, Add. MSS 817/22, Georgina to MacDonald [21 May 1872]; Evans and Whitehouse, *Diaries of John Ruskin. 1848–1873* (Oxford, 1958), p.727.

142　Burd, *John Ruskin and Rose La Touche*, p.125; he then had her company briefly at Toft, see Evans and Whitehouse, *Diaries of John Ruskin. 1848-1873*, p.729.

143　BR63/11, Evelyn Ashley's diary entry for 10 October 1872.

144　NLS, Ashburton Papers, Acc.11388/96, William to Lady Ashburton, 22 October 1872.

145　Gurney, *Letters of Emelia Russell Gurney*, p.111 (April 1872), Emelia commiserating with Georgina's loss.

146　Some locks of her hair, 'cut off Oct 25 1872', are preserved in BR44/9/6.

147　Leicester-Warren, *Diaries*, vol.2, p.245, 27 November 1872.

148　BR58/17, Georgina's diary entry for 21 December 1872.

149　NLS, Ashburton Papers, Acc.11388/96, William to Lady Ashburton, 31 December 1872.

150　BR45/8/2, copy of 'Letter from Faithful to Woodbine', February 1873.

151　See entry in BR51/1, for Stanhope Street, 4 August 1873; and drawing.

152　L.E. O' Rorke, *Life and Friendships of Catherine Marsh* (London: Longmans, Green, 1917), p.259. See Marsh's printed Christmas card with handwritten note to Georgina: 'beloved one', BR57/72/1.

153　BR58/17, Georgina's diary entry for 6 May 1873.

154　BR58/17, Georgina's diary entry for 11 July 1873.

155　Bradley, *Letters of John Ruskin to Lord and Lady Mount Temple*, p.342.

156　Burd, *John Ruskin and Rose La Touche*, p.127.

157   Bradley, *Letters of John Ruskin to Lord and Lady Mount Temple*, 5 August 1873, p.347; BR58/17, Georgina's diary entry for 15 August 1873; and anecdote of a foggy view from the Tarns, Collingwood, 'Ruskin's Isola', p.81.

158   BR58/5, Georgina's diary entries for 9 February and 26 January 1874; Durham University Library, Special Collections, John Ruskin Biographical Papers, Add. MSS. 817/23 [21 January 1874].

159   See BR58/5, Georgina's diary for 30 May 1874, for her illuminated letters with Juliet.

160   Durham University Library, Special Collections, John Ruskin Biographical Papers, Add. MSS 817/26-27, letters from Munro to Louisa MacDonald, 3 and 16 November 1874.

161   E. Burman, ed., *Logan Pearsall Smith. An Anthology* (London: Constable, 1989), p.42; Smith, *Religious Rebel*, note I, pp.27-28. See K. Allen's useful essay, 'Representation and Self-representation: Hannah Whitall Smith as family woman and religious guide', *Women's History Review* 7: 2 (1998), pp.227-238.

162   Hannah Smith to Georgina, Yellowstone Park, 17 August 1881.

163   BR58/5, Georgina's diary entry for 23 February 1874. *MTM*, p.116 has a description of the golden haired, distinctively-dressed 'Angel of the Churches' as they called her.

164   *MTM*, p.117; Gurney, *Letters of Emelia Russell Gurney*, p.175; H.W. Smith mss, Lilly Library, Jukes to Hannah, 19 September 1873.

165   A. Jukes, *The Second Death and the Restitution of All Things with some preliminary remarks on the nature and inspiration of holy scripture* (London: Longmans, Green, 1867), the work first appearing anonymously; see G. Rowell, *Hell and the Victorians. A study of the nineteenth century theological controversies concerning eternal punishment and the future life* (Oxford: Clarendon Press, 1974), p.129.

166   BR57/4/1, Hannah Smith to Georgina, 7 April 1874.

167   BR58/5, Georgina's diary for 22 February 1874.

168   See the entry in William's hand in BR58/5, Georgina's diary for 8–9 May 1874: a copy of a letter from Myers to Emelia Gurney referring to 'the beauty & dignity of our hostess, the aristocracy and suavity of our Host'; F.W.H. Myers, *Human Personality and its Survival of Bodily Death* vol.2 (London: Longmans, Green and Co., 1903), p.223. Gauld, *Founders of Psychical Research*, confuses Georgina with Emelia, p.104. On Gurney's personality, see Schultz, *Henry Sidgwick*, p.290.

169   Leicester-Warren, *Diaries*, vol.2, p.313.

170   BR58/5, Georgina's diary entries for 22–26 May 1874.

171   BR58/5, entries for 28 May–4 June and 18 September 1874, and *MTM*, p.79, for view.

172   BR57/4/4, Hannah Smith to Georgina, Philadelphia, 12 July 1874.

173   *The Times*, 8 September 1874, p.8; BR57/4/5, Hannah Smith to Georgina, Philadelphia, 31 October 1874.

174   *Manchester Guardian*, 31 December 1874, p.5; BR58/5, Georgina's diary entries for 25 August; 26–27 December 1874.

175   Smith, *Religious Rebel*, 20 May 1875, p.26.

176   Cowper, *Earl Cowper*, pp.285-286.

177   BR56/20, F.J. Wedgwood to Georgina, 29 November 1875; see *MTM*, p.128, for her response to the conference.

178   Hare, *Story of My Life*, vol.4, pp.340-341.

179   BR57/4/9, Hannah Smith to Georgina, 9 July 1875; BR57/4/13, Hannah Smith to Georgina, 21 August 1875. For the description of the conference, see BR57/4/11, Hannah Smith to Georgina, 4 July 1875.

180   BR57/4/13, Hannah Smith to Georgina, 21 August 1875.

181   BR57/4/6, Hannah Smith to Georgina, Philadelphia, 12 December 1874.

182   10 August 1875, in Bradley, *Letters of John Ruskin to Lord and Lady Mount Temple*, p.360.

183   Bradley and Ousby, *Correspondence of John Ruskin and Charles Eliot Norton*, p.367.

[184] G. MacDonald, *George MacDonald and His Wife* (London: G. Allen and Unwin, 1924), p.472.

[185] Burd, *Christmas Story*, p.123. See *MTM*, p.75 for Georgina's recollections of the 'treat' of Ruskin's delightful and instructive company then.

[186] Burd, *Christmas Story*, p.123. She married Dr Acworth of Hayward's Heath, a homeopathist.

[187] *New York Times*, 13 July 1875.

[188] *The Times*, 18 June 1875, p.12; *The Times* 9 June 1875, p.7; *Dietetic Reformer*, October 1875, p.271. *Punch* associated the activity with the Peculiar People, see 'Faith and Physic', 19 June 1875. On Andreas, see *The Early Life and Conversion of Karl Andreas: with a True Account of Healing by Simple Scriptural Means. Written by Himself* (London: Bemrose and Sons, 1874); see BR57/70/1-2 for Andreas' thanks to the Cowper-Temples.

[189] Cowper, *Earl Cowper*, p.300; BR49/13, J. Manners to Georgina, 1 December 1875.

[190] Burd, *Christmas Story*, p.130; Myers Papers, 24/22, 26 January.

[191] Letters from Mrs Acworth – 'Agape' – to Georgina, December 1881, BR49/13, concern her claim to bring Mummy's message about the risk of cancer for her daughter.

[192] BR58/6, Georgina's diary entry for 29 January 1876.

[193] BR58/6, Georgina's diary entry for 30 January 1876.

[194] BR58/6, Georgina's diary entry for 31 January 1876.

[195] BR58/6, Georgina's diary entry for 2 February 1876.

[196] BR58/6, Georgina's diary entry for 17 February 1876, with newspaper clipping of lecture and drawing of gems. See Bradley, *Letters of John Ruskin to Lord and Lady Mount Temple*, p.367, for Ruskin's letters 13 February and St Valentine's Day, pp.367-369.

[197] BR58/6, Georgina's diary 1876, inserted letter; BR57/39/1, Emelia Gurney to Georgina, 13 September 1876. The MacDonalds visited 1 May 1876; and he gave an 'unwritten sermon', 28 May 1876.

[198] BR58/6, Georgina's diary entry for 29 February 1876.

[199] BR58/6, Georgina's diary entry for 7 March 1876.

[200] BR58/6, Georgina's diary entries for 13–14 March 1876.

[201] BR58/6, Georgina's diary entry for 1 April 1876; Myers Papers, 4/7-17, Ruskin to Myers, 15 March 1876; Myers Papers, 4/10 (1) records his happiness 'in the thought of my time at Cambridge'. See A. Gauld, 'Henry Sidgwick, Theism, and Psychical Research', *Proceedings of the World Congress on Henry Sidgwick. Happiness and Religion* (Catania: Universita degli Studi di Catania, Dipartimento di Scienze Umane, 2007), pp.160-257; Schultz, *Henry Sidgwick: Eye of the Universe*, ch.5.

[202] Cowper, *Earl Cowper*, p.300. *MTM*, p.47 describes William as young in spirit 'and even in countenance and movement, to the end'.

[203] BR58/6, Georgina's diary entry for 30 April 1876.

[204] BR58/6, Georgina's diary for 13 May 1876. For the neo-Gallican and ultramontane context in French Catholicism, see review of J-O. Boudon, *Paris: Capitale religieuse sous le Second Empire* (Paris, 2001), by T. Kselman, *Catholic Historical Review* (2003), pp.559-560.

[205] Lambeth Palace Library, Tait Papers 283, ff. 377-379; Evelyn Ashley and his wife attended the lectures, see BR63/14, Ashley's diary entry for 21 June 1876.

[206] BR58/6, Georgina's diary entry for 23 June 1876.

[207] An exclusive meeting at St George's Hall, Langham Place, where Hyacinthe had lectured in French to an audience including the Bishop of Winchester, the Duke of Argyll, Lord Ebury and William, was reported in *The Times*, 15 June 1876, p.12.

[208] BR53/2, Père Hyacinthe to William, Geneva, 5 September 1876.

[209] BR53/2, Père Hyacinthe to William, Geneva, 5 September 1876.

[210] Myers Papers, 24/20; *The Academy*, 24 February 1877, p.170.

[211] BR58/6, Georgina's diary entry for 10 June 1876.

212 Cowper, *Earl Cowper*, p.303.

213 BR58/6, Georgina's diary entry for 19 July 1876.

214 BR55/9, A.M. Howitt Watts to Georgina, 19 December 1877 ('seeress'); BR58/6, Georgina's diary for 15 October 1876; L. Brewster Macpherson, *Omnipotence belongs only to the beloved* (Edinburgh: Edmonston and Douglas, 1876), p.xxiv. My thanks to Mr Macpherson-Fletcher of Balavil for information on this daughter-in-law of the scientist Sir David Brewster. According to M.M. Gordon, *Home Life of Sir David Brewster* (Edinburgh: Edmonston and Douglas, 1869), she possessed 'peculiar affinities with her father-in-law's mind' (p.267), and seems latterly to have influenced his religious beliefs, see p.315. She was the subject of a sonnet by Sydney Dobell, 'On Receiving a Book from 'X.H.' as she told William, 28 September 1876, see BR44/13/2.

215 See W.E. Fredeman, ed., *The Correspondence of Dante Gabriel Rossetti. The Last Decade. 1873–1882. vol.7. 1875–1877* (Cambridge, 2008), pp.290-304. An album of autographs, photographs, verse by Monod and by Rossetti, was put up for auction in 1973, see lot 424, *Valuable, Printed Books, Autograph Letters and Historical Documents* (Sotheby's Catalogue, 4-5 June 1973), p.91.

216 BR58/6, Georgina's diary for 8 August 1876. See J.Y. Lebourgeois, 'D.G. Rossetti in the Private Books of Frederick Locker-Lampson and Lady Mount Temple', *Notes and Queries* n.s. 18:7 (July 1971), pp.254-255. His arrival followed a 'long talk' with Annie Munro about him.

217 BR58/6, Georgina's diary entry for 6 August 1876. The sketch is now lost.

218 Georgina was the daughter of Thomas Henry Kingscote and with her husband Arthur Holme Sumner belonged to the Prince of Wales's set. In 1872 she gave birth to a son, Berkeley, after an affair with Wilfird Scawen Blunt, see E. Longford, *A Pilgrimage of Passion: The Life of Wilfrid Scawen Blunt* (1979; London, Tauris Parke: 2007), pp.207-208, who describes her as an 'intellectual society woman': it was possibly through Georgina Sumner that Georgina Cowper-Temple became acquainted with Madeline Wyndham. Walburga Paget's *Embassies of Other Days and further Recollections* (London: Hutchinson, 1923) describes her as 'built in the heroic style, tall and well-made, with aquiline features', p.108.

219 *MTM*, p.65.

220 Fredeman, ed., *The Correspondence of Dante Gabriel Rossetti. The Last Decade. 1873–1882. vol.7. 1875–1877*, to Walter Theodore Watts-Dunton, 13 August 1876, p.298; to Henry Treffry Dunn, 13 August 1876, p.300; and Frances Rossetti, 24 August 1876, p.302.

221 A.H. Harrison, ed., *The Letters of Christina Rossetti*, vol.2, 1874–1881 (Charlottesville and London: University Press of Virginia, 1999), p.94, 27 September 1876.

222 BR58/6, Georgina's diary entry for 18 October 1876.

223 BR58/6, Georgina's diary entry for 9 August 1876 on vivisection bill; and entry for 27 August 1876 on Mody, and K. Clement, *Faith on the Frontier: The Life of J.H. Oldham* (Edinburgh: T&T Clark, 1999), pp.9-10.

224 BR58/6, Georgina's diary for 27 August on her intensity; 5 September 1876 on her tantrums.

225 BR58/6, Georgina's diary entry for 12 September 1876. Evelyn Ashley is laconic on this holiday, see BR63/14.

226 BR60, William to Evelyn Ashley, 30 September [1876]; 'London Gossip', *Manchester Times*, 15 January 1881.

227 BR58/6, Georgina's diary 1876, inserted clippings; A. Horstman, *Victorian Divorce* (London: Croom Helm, 1985), p.108. Their daughters were Teresa and Amalia, William was one of her trustees on her second marriage, to the Italian noble, in 1854.

228 BR58/6, Georgina's diary entries for 18–19 November 1876.

229 Frederick Arnold, 'Torquay and its neighbourhood', *London Society* 13: 75 (March 1868), pp.256-266.

230   BR58/6, Georgina's diary entries for 30 November, 1 December 1876.

231   BR50/28, Hannah Smith to Georgina, 25 April 1876.

232   BR58/6, Georgina's diary entry for 10 February 1876.

233   BR58/6, Georgina's diary entry for 16 February 1876.

234   BR58/6, Georgina's diary entry for 23 February 1876.

235   BR58/6, Georgina's diary for 20 April 1876. Presumably, *The Lord: The Two-in-One.*

236   BR58/6, Georgina's diary entry for 6 May 1876.

237   BR58/6, Georgina's diary entry for 10 December 1876.

238   BR58/6, Georgina's diary entry for 13 October 1876. Clifford worked with him in a Tower Hamlets mission.

239   *The Evangelical Magazine and Missionary Chronicle,* May 1877, p.286; Myers Papers, 3/68, 8 January 1877.

240   BR58/7, Georgina's diary entries for 23–24 March 1877. Varley's letter inviting William to a Farewell Meeting in April 1877 is in BR50/45. See H. Varley, *Henry Varley's Life Story* (London: Holness, 1916). He became editor of *Christian Commonwealth* and lectured on social purity.

241   BR58/7, Georgina's diary entry for 9 March 1877. BR50/28, Hannah Smith to Georgina, 21 April 1877, the faith healer was a Dr Cullis.

242   Mrs Leaf and her daughter, of Albion Street, Hyde Park, were invalids, nursed by Mary Gove Nichols.

243   On Farquhar, see A.E. Ridley, *A Backward Glance. The Story of John Ridley. A Pioneer* (London: J. Clarke, 1904), pp.294-295; on Eglinton, *The Spiritualist,* 23 February 1877, p.96.

244   BR57/67/12, J.W. Farquhar to Georgina, 18 October 1884.

245   J. Godwin, 'Lady Caithness and her Connection with Theosophy', *Theosophical History* 8: 4 (October 2000), pp.127-147; R. Guénon, *Theosophy. The History of a Pseudo-Religion* (1965 [in French]; Hillsdale, New York: Sophia Perennis, 2003), ch.19; and K.P. Johnson, *The Masters Revealed. Madame Blavatsky and the Myth of the Great White Lodge* (Albany, New York: State University of New York Press, 1994), pp.63-64. Her circle in Paris included a future guest of the Cowper-Temples, Charles Richet.

246   BR50/41, Roden Noel to William, 21 July 1877; for the conversation on the train, see BR43/25/12, William to Georgina, Broadlands, 'Thursday'.

247   Georgiana Houghton the spiritualist became an acquaintance whilst Rogers was in England, see her *Evenings at Home in Spiritual Séance* (London: E.W. Allen, 1882), p.265.

248   BR58/7, Georgina's diary entries for 17–18, 22–24 August 1877; BR50/23, A.J. Rogers to William, 22 August 1877.

249   M.W. Perry, ed., *Lady Eugenist. Victoria Woodhull, 1838-1927* (Seattle: Inkling Books, 2005), p.17.

250   BR50/23, A.J. Rogers to the Cowper-Temples, 26 August and 30 August 1877.

251   BR58/7, Georgina's diary entries for 12–13 September 1877.

252   BR50/23, A.J. Rogers to William, 14 September 1877.

253   BR48/4/6, A.J. Rogers to William, June 1878.

254   On coffee taverns, see Radstock's letter to William, BR50/43, 27 July 1877; BR58/7, Georgina's diary, e.g., 6 July 1877; *Hull Packet,* 31 August 1877, 'Mr Cowper-Temple on Coffee Taverns'. On the 'blessed Cobbe', see BR58/7, 27 April 1877.

255   BR58/7, Georgina's diary entry for 14 July 1877 (Isaiah 14: 12-15). See her comment on 'poor no.16', BR59/24.

256   BR50/28, Hannah Smith to Georgina, 21 April 1877; *Daily News,* 3 April 1874; BR49/4, G.H. Wilkinson, 28 November 1881, typed copy. Van Deerlin had left Romsey for a parish near Sandringham, *Hampshire Telegraph,* 1 May 1875. He became an Anglican canon at St Michael's by the Sea in California.

257 NLS, MacDonald Papers, MS 9745, 1 April 1877; BR58/7, Georgina's diary entries for 6–9 April 1877.

258 NLS, MacDonald Papers, MS 9745, 14 October 1877, f.17; and 5, 7, 11 and October 1877.

259 MacDonald, *George MacDonald and His Wife*, p.479.

260 NLS, MacDonald Papers, MS 9745, [December 1877], ff.24-25.

261 BR58/7, Georgina's diary entry for 18 September 1877.

262 On Hoare, BR58/7, Georgina's diary entries for 26 and 29 December 1877; BR49/5, Douglas to Mrs Leycester, 12 December 1877, typed copy.

263 Parry, *Democracy and Religion*, p.48.

264 BR44/19/6, newspaper clipping (probably *Liverpool Evening Express*) 16 October 1888.

265 H.W. Smith mss, Lilly Library, letter from William, 14 November 1876; *'Broadlands' By a Tourist. Given with the Romsey and South Hampshire Chronicle* (n.d.), in BR207/2/5; for temperance gathering, H.B. Macartney, *England, Home and Beauty. Sketches of Christian Life and Work in England in 1878* (London: Shaw, 1880), p.74.

266 BR58/17, Georgina's diary entry for 9 April 1868. See M.B. Adams, ed., *Modern Cottage Architecture* (London: Batsford, 1904) for the design, the book also contains Nesfield's design for an estate cottage. See C. Aslet, 'The Country Houses of W.E. Nesfield', *Country Life*, part I, 16 March 1978, and part II, 23 March 1978, which, p.768 suggests the school (and Cowper-Temple's reputation in education) proved influential in that the 'Queen Anne style' came to dominate the London School Board.

267 'A Sketch at Broadlands', *Illustrated Times*, 12 November 1864; Leicester-Warren, *Diaries*, vol.2, p.311.

268 BR59/14, Jukes to Juliet, 24 March 1894; Hare, *Story of My Life*, vol.4, p.71; vol.5, p.295.

269 From 'Fragments of Inner Life' by F.W.H. Myers, in *Fragments of Prose and Poetry*, ed. E. Myers (London: Longmans, Green and Co., 1904), p.39. Other quotes come from Myers' obituary of Ruskin, in the same work, p.90. The key reference to the Cowper-Temples' adventurous hospitality, ranging from east-end workers and plebeian socialists, to Afro-American missionaries, is 'E.C.' [Edward Clifford], *Broadlands as it was* (London: Lindsay and Co., 1890), p.14.

270 Clifford, 'A Talk about Art', in *Father Damien and Others* (London: Church Army, 1905), p.110, pp.130-131.

271 BR58/6, Georgina's diary entry for 15 January 1876; *MTM*, p.119. On the chatelaine's 'overwork', see Gerard, *Country House Life*, pp.133-136. Burd, *Christmas Story*, p.194, n.82, notes that during the Census of 1881 there were nine domestic servants, a comparatively small number (but the total staff on the estate were fourteen, see RG11/1224/85-86); William's notes in BR207/3/2 list the various staff required in even a small country house: fifteen garden staff in 1868 for instance. Georgina's consideration for Juliet's German governess – encouraging artistic interests – was noted by Adelheid Flemming in a letter in BR56/16.

Chapter 8. Lord Mount Temple: the Liberal Statesman

1 *Reynolds's Newspaper*, 25 April 1869; *London Review* 16: 404 (March 1868), p.300.

2 J.R.T.E. Gregory, 'Protecting the legacy of Lord Palmerston: writing and reviewing the official life of Lord Palmerston, *c*.1865-1901', Conference on Modern British History, University of Strathclyde, 20 June 2007.

3 BR33/1, Emily Palmerston to William, n.d.

4 BL, Gladstone Papers, Add. MSS 44412, f.183.

5 BR58/3, Georgina's diary entry for 30 March 1867; to Gladstone, BL, Gladstone Papers, Add. MSS 44412, 28 March 1867.

6 *The Times*, 23 July 1868, p.10; *MTM*, p.40, rejecting the infallibility of the people, 1846.

7 See BR58/3.

8   BR206/3, *Southampton Times*, 25 February 1871.
9   M. Drew, *Catherine Gladstone. By Her Daughter Mary Drew* (1919; London: J. Nisbet, 1928), p.153.
10   For his weak voice in the Commons, see *The Scotsman*, 15 June 1874, p.2.
11   *MTM*, p.71.
12   *The Times*, 23 July 1868, p.10.
13   BR43/25/20, William to Georgina, n.d.
14   Report from the Select Committee on Inclosure Act: together with the proceedings of the Committee, minutes of evidence and appendix. Inclosure Act 8 and 9 Vict. c.118 (whether provisions for the labouring poor have been carried out).
15   *Hampshire Telegraph*, 15 December 1869.
16   *Hampshire Telegraph*, 21 April 1869.
17   Melville Papers, Lambeth Palace Library (MS 1995), ff.74-75 (William to Melville, 27 December 1869; with later annotation by Melville); f.78 (William to Melville, June 1870; obituaries of Melville in this volume, and f.126, recollection of R.W. Forest, 13 May 1904; see also J. Murphy, *The Education Act 1870. Text and Commentary* (Newton Abbot: David and Charles, 1972); D.K. Jones, *The Making of the Education System, 1851-81* (London: Routledge and Kegan Paul, 1977).
18   The Elementary Education Act, 1870 (33 & 34 Vict.c.75), clause 14 (2). T.W. Reid, *Life of the Right Honourable William Edward Forster* (1888; London: Chapman and Hall, 1889), p.277 (as Georgina records in a notebook, BR45/18/1) notes Forster's belief that Cowper-Temple's clause was virtually identical to his proposals in letters to Lord Ripon, the former Christian Socialist, who was closely involved with the bill.
19   E.R. Norman, *Church and Society in England 1770–1970* (Oxford: Clarendon Press, 1976), p.112.
20   J.P. Parry, 'Religion and the collapse of Gladstone's first Government, 1870-1874', *Historical Journal* 25:1 (March 1982), pp.71-101. For assessments of the clause, see K.T. Hoppen, *The mid-Victorian generation, 1846–1886* (Oxford: Clarendon Press, 1998), p.599; Sir John Gorst's bill of 1896 sought to repeal the clause, see E.G. Taylor, 'The Educational Crisis', *Westminster Review*, June 1896.
21   BR45/18/1, pencil note by William after Georgina's note re Forster's *Life* on the clause.
22   *Authorized Report of the Church Congress held at Southampton October 11, 12, 13 and 14 1870* (Southampton: Gutch and Co., 1870), p.115.
23   Liberal Association of Southampton and South Hampshire, dinner, reported in *Southampton Times*, 25 February 1871, clipping in BR206/3.
24   *Manchester Guardian*, 13 April 1871, p.5.
25   PD, 3rd series, vol.199, 14 February 1870, cols.256-257; 28 April 1871, cols.1852-1858.
26   'Sketches in Parliament (By an Independent Member)', in *Birmingham Daily Post*, 6 May 1871. A. Ramm, 'The Parliamentary Context of Cabinet Government, 1868-1874', *English Historical Review* 99: 393 (October 1984), pp.739-769. William suggested getting the involvement of the City of London, see Stephen, *Life of Henry Fawcett*, p.319.
27   BR43/25/6, William to Georgina, House of Commons [1871].
28   BR43/24/11, William to Georgina, Brookes, 1.45 am; and (with thanks to Michael Roberts for the reference), Houghton Papers, CB88/5, 8 January 1871.
29   *Hampshire Telegraph*, 22 May 1872.
30   *The Times*, 28 September 1872, p.12 (26 September 1872); 30 September 1872, p.9; *Hampshire Telegraph*, 2 October 1872.
31   See BR58/5, Georgina's diary for 3 February 1874, for her criticism of the Liberals.
32   *The Scotsman*, 19 January 1876, p.8.
33   *Manchester Guardian*, 13 October 1876, p.5.

34 BL, Gladstone Papers, Add. MSS 44452, ff.212-213. Gladstone wanted him to be a member of the Conference. William visited Beaconsfield's London residence when he was dying, see *The Times*, 30 May 1881, p.7.

35 *Trewman's Exeter*, 1 October 1879; BR206/3, *Weekly Hampshire Independent*, clipping, 1879.

36 *Daily News*, 4 September 1878.

37 *Leeds Mercury*, 8 October 1878. *The Times*, 9 October 1878, p.10.

38 BR206/3, *Weekly Hampshire Independent*, clipping (1879). On attacks on the landed, see D. Southgate, *The Passing of the Whigs* (London: Macmillan, 1962), pp.364-366.

39 *Manchester Guardian*, 4 March 1875, p.5; *The Scotsman*, 4 March 1875, pp.4-5. See also *The Scotsman*, 25 February 1875, p.4.

40 *Manchester Guardian*, 17 May 1871, p.7.

41 *Southampton Times*, 25 February 1871, clipping in BR206/3.

42 Parry, *Democracy and Religion*, p.116; Jenkins, *Gladstone, Whiggery and Liberalism*, p.47, quoting a letter from William to Harcourt 28 January 1875.

43 BL, Gladstone Papers, Add. MSS 44461, f.25, 11 September 1879.

44 BR60/3/11, William to Evelyn Ashley [9 December 1879].

45 *Manchester Guardian*, 21 June 1878, p.5.

46 BR44/11/1, fragmentary draft of letter by William to the electors of South Hants; *The Times*, 16 March 1880, p.10.

47 See Bradley, *Letters of John Ruskin to Lord and Lady Mount Temple*, p.376.

48 BR56/6, Annie Munro to Georgina, Alister Cottage, Inverness, 16 March [1880].

49 BR43/30/2, Georgina to William, Hotel Californie, Cannes, Tuesday, '10 am'.

50 BR50/47, W.P. Snell to William, 23 June 1881; for William's role after 1881, see material in BR44/18.

51 *The Times*, 26 May 1880, p.5.

52 BL, Gladstone Papers, Add. MSS 44463, f.228, 27 April 1880.

53 *Manchester Guardian*, 29 June 1876, p.5; indeed he introduced the Père at the St James's Hall lecture in late June 1876.

54 BL, Gladstone Papers, Add. MSS, 44464, f.253, 14 June 1880.

55 BL, Gladstone Papers, Add. MSS, 44466, f.248, 2 November 1880.

56 'Our London Correspondent', *Liverpool Mercury*, 14 July 1881.

57 See, for instance, *The Standard*, 28 April 1882.

58 *Reynolds's Weekly Newspaper*, 11 March 1883; H.W. Wack, *The Story of the Congo Free State* (1905), p.530: in relation to Portugal's territorial aspirations, and slavery and free trade.

59 W.F. Cowper-Temple, *Organisation the result of Opinions, A reply by Lord Mount Temple, (President of the South Hants Liberal Association) to 'Organisation without Opinions', A letter addressed to him by Mr Auberon Herbert respecting the opinions of the Association* (Lymington: H. Doman, 1882), copy in BR44/18/6. Although he thought Herbert's proposal would turn away 'men of independent character and self respect as candidates', he wrote, 'I recognise a danger that menaces the country in the increasing habit amongst members of Parliament to enrol themselves in a party, as soldiers enter a regiment, abandoning their individual responsibility, and undertaking to obey orders, and to follow their leaders wherever they may be led'.

60 *Leeds Mercury*, 6 March 1883; *Aberdeen Weekly Journal*, 1 June 1883.

61 *Select Committee of House of Lords on Smoke Nuisance Abatement (Metropolis) Bill House of Lords Report, Proceedings, Minutes of Evidence*, session 1887, House of Commons Papers, Reports of Committees, 321, vol.XII.

62 N.E. Johnson, *The Diary of Gathorne Hardy, later Lord Cranbrook, 1866–1892: Political Selections* (Oxford: Clarendon Press, 1981), pp.665, 667, 674. 1887 (322) *Select Committee of House of Lords on Rabies in Dogs. Report, Proceedings, Minutes of Evidence, Appendix, Index*.

63 *Aberdeen Weekly Journal*, 18 May 1888.

64   *Select Committee of House of Lords to inquire into State of Law Relating to Protection of Young Girls from Artifices to induce them to lead Corrupt Life. Report, Proceedings, Minutes of Evidence, Appendix* (1881).

65   In private, they visited Rebecca Jarrett, involved in Stead's stunt to procure a girl, when she managed Resume cottage, and prayed with the inmates, see J.E. Butler, 'Some Personal Recollections of Lord Mount Temple', *The Dawn*, 1 November 1888, p.24.

66   *The Sentinel*, 51, July 1883, p.217.

67   *The Sentinel*, 52 (August 1833), p.221.

68   *Leeds Mercury*, 13 June 1883; *Reynolds's Weekly Newspaper*, 8 July 1883.

69   *The Sentinel*, 61 (May 1884), p.297; for the Act, passed in August 1885, see 48 & 49 Victoria, Chapter 69 'An Act to make further provision for the Protection of Women and Girls, the suppression of brothels, and other purposes.' See also Roberts, *Making English Morals*, pp.263-265.

70   BR60/3/11, William to Evelyn Ashley, 2 February 1883.

71   Draft letter, BR50/14, William to Gladstone, 1 December 1884.

72   Cannadine, *Decline and Fall of the British Aristocracy*, pp.42-43.

73   Add.44491, ff.219-220, 27 January 1885.

74   BR60/3/11, William to Evelyn Ashley, Babbacombe, 17 December 1885.

75   BR58/10, Georgina's diary entry for 6 May 1882.

76   BR60/3/12, William to Evelyn Ashley, 2 May 1886.

77   BR50/1, Evelyn Ashley to William, Cannes, 6 May 1886.

78   Jenkins, *Gladstone, Whiggery and the Liberal Party*, p.223, quoting *Leeds Mercury*, 28 November 1885.

79   Letter of 1 February 1886, in MacDonald, *George MacDonald and His Wife*, p.533.

80   BR60/3/11, William to Evelyn Ashley, 'Saturday 28'.

81   Adonis, *Making Aristocracy Work*, pp.241-244.

82   *English Illustrated Magazine*, quoted in *Brooklyn Eagle*, 20 December 1885, p.14.

83   On Reid's collection, see Jenkins, *Gladstone, Whiggery and the Liberal Party*, pp.15-16.

84   Tollemache, *Old and Odd Memories*, p.77.

85   BR43/22/5, William to Georgina, Admiralty, 'April 11'.

86   Notes on Bright, in notebook of political anecdotes, BR51/9.

87   H. Lucy, *Sixty Years in the Wilderness. More Passages by the Way. A second series* (London: Smith, Elder, 1912), p.149.

Chapter 9. The Final Decade of Marriage, 1878–1888

1   H.P. Smith, May 1887, quoted in K. Fitzpatrick, *Lady Henry Somerset* (London: J. Cape, 1923), p.140; Shannon, *Gladstone and the Bulgarian Agitation*, p.29.

2   Hilton, *John Ruskin. The Later Years*, pp.354-355.

3   NLS, MacDonald Papers, MS 9745, 17 February 1878, f.29.

4   Durham University Library, John Ruskin Biographical Papers, Add. MSS 817/24, letter to Louisa MacDonald, 12 March 1878.

5   Drew, *Acton, Gladstone and Others*, pp.104-105.

6   *Hampshire Telegraph*, 29 June 1878, from *Truth*, 27 June 1878.

7   *Hampshire Telegraph*, 13 July 1878. A garbled account in the Melbourne *Argus*, 1 December 1888, p.5, claimed London society was 'in a state of explosion' as a result.

8   See BR49/15, notes, apparently by Georgina, of the conference from 5–9 August 1878.

9   See Macartney, *England, Home, and Beauty*, p.172 on Monod. Admired by Mrs Brewster-Macpherson, Pulsford's publications included *The Supremacy of Man* (1876) and *Morgenröthe, a book of the age for the children of the age* (1881). Formerly chairman of the Congregational Union of Scotland, he went with the Reverend Newman Hall to the Holy Land with American and British Cook tourists in 1870, and supported aid to Christians in Turkey in

1876. Praising Edward Maitland and Anna Kingsford's *Clothed with the Sun* in a letter to Maitland, he supported the Esoteric Christian Union.

10   *The Times*, 22 April 1878, p.10, 9 May 1878, p.5; *Evangelical Christendom: Christian Work and the News of the Churches* (1878), p.346.

11   BR59/54, Georgina to Juliet, 15 Great Stanhope Street.

12   NLS, MacDonald Papers, MS 9745, 7 July 1878, f.34.

13   BR56/15, Furnivall to Georgina, 25 September 1878; BR53/6, Marguerite to Georgina, Treport, '8 August'.

14   BR59/53, Georgina to Juliet, Broadlands, 'Wednesday'.

15   *Morning Post* clipping, in BR34/283.

16   *Annual Register* (1880), p.185; *Dublin University Magazine*, May 1879, p.638.

17   See E. Lawton Smith, *Evelyn Pickering De Morgan and the Allegorical Body* (Madison, New Jersey: Fairleigh Dickinson University Press, 2002), p.27.

18   See letters from Emily Ford to Georgina, *c*.1879, BR57/68/11-13; the nickname remained, see BR55/42, Emily Ford to Georgina, 23 November 1893.

19   Letter in BR49/5, Emelia Gurney to William, Hereford, 1 August 1883.

20   Entry in health journal, BR51/6, for 11 June 1879.

21   Entry in health journal, BR51/6, for 1 July 1879.

22   Letter in BR49/7, Roden Noel to Georgina, 14 August 1879. Georgina sent Jukes a perplexing letter from Macpherson, see BR57/64/11, Jukes to Georgina, 29 November 1879. A fragment, BR43/21/12, from William to Georgina, refers to her *Omnipotence belongs only to the Beloved* (1876) and *Perfection* (not identified) which he had read.

23   See Stockmayer's letter, in BR49/7, 15 October 1879.

24   BR57/68/3, R.W. Corbet to Georgina, 18 October 1879. Corbet wrote *Letters from a Mystic of the Present Day* (1883). Emelia Gurney and Dorothea Beale came to his conferences, see E. Raikes, *Dorothea Beale of Cheltenham* (London: A. Constable, 1908), pp.196-197 and Gurney, *Letters of Emelia Russell Gurney*, p.143.

25   BR50/41, Mountain to William, 25 August and 2 September 1879. See Bebbington, *Evangelicalism in Modern Britain*, p.225, on the British Israelites.

26   Myers Papers, 3/71, 27 October 1879.

27   BR51/17, William's diary for 1880, note on 24 December 1879. *MTM*, p.80.

28   BR57/64/12, Jane Ely to Georgina, Osborne, 26 January 1880; see also Royal Archives, Windsor Castle, RA/VIC/MAIN/S/12/29, Georgina's letter of 13 January 1880.

29   Myers Papers, 3/75, 19 January 1880.

30   BR60/3/11, William to Evelyn Ashley, Hotel Californie, Cannes, 22 March 1880.

31   BR60/3/11, William to Evelyn Ashley, Hotel Californie, Cannes, 15 February 1880.

32   BR58/8, Georgina's diary entry for 10 March 1880.

33   BR43/30/5, Georgina to William, Hotel Californie, Cannes, 'Thursday'; BR58/8, Georgina's diary entry for 12 March 1880.

34   BR43/30/4, Georgina to William, Cannes, 'Sunday evening'.

35   BR55/14; BR59/25, n.d., letter from Hotel Californie, Cannes; BR43/30/5, n.d.

36   BR53/4, William to Georgina, House of Commons, 'Monday evening'. See Cholmeley, *Edward Clifford*, p.102 for Clifford's studio talks for 'educated people', on religious and other questions of the day.

37   BR53/4, William to Georgina, 25 February [1880].

38   *MTM*, p.80. She died 26 March 1880.

39   BR55/14, letters to and from Evelyn Ashley.

40   BR51/17, William's diary entry for 26 March 1880.

41   BR53/4, William to Georgina, Broadlands, Monday 11, n.d. William also spoke to Lord Acton about the 'world of the spirits', see M. Drew, *Letters of Lord Acton to Mary, daughter of the Right Hon. W.E. Gladstone* (1904; London: Macmillan, 1913), p.3.

42   BR51/17, William's diary entry for 13 April 1880.

43   NLS, MacDonald Papers, MS 9745, 13 June 1879.

44   NLS, MacDonald Papers, MS 9745, 7 March [1880], ff.47-50, Louisa MacDonald to Georgina.

45   BR58/8, Georgina's diary entry for 28 April 1880.

46   G.W.E. Russell, *Collections and Recollections*, p.56.

47   BR58/8, Georgina's diary entry for 27 May 1880; William asked Houghton, as 'so old and valued a friend', Houghton Papers, MSS 18/28, 29 May 1880.

48   BR50/43, 11 June 1880.

49   BR59/3, Georgina to Juliet, 15 Great Stanhope Street [1880]. This letter is typical of the affectionate and humorous letters – rarely dated – that Georgina wrote to Juliet.

50   Myers Papers, 24/11.

51   *Daily News*, 19 August 1880.

52   H.E.W. Slade, *A Work Begun: The Story of the Cowley Fathers in India, 1874–1967* (London: SPCK, 1970), p.52, p.59.

53   Myers Papers, 3/77, 24 September 1880. Mallock's work was serialized 1876–1877, before publication as a novel. This gathering is a reminder that the Cowper-Temples held religious meetings distinct from the conferences: R.M. Theobald, *Passages from the Autobiography of a Shakespeare Student* (London: R. Banks, 1912), p.70, recalled meetings at Great Stanhope Street, where Farquhar read papers that became *The Gospel of Divine Humanity*. My thanks to Barbara Amell for this reference.

54   BR43/30/1, Georgina to William, Hotel Californie, Cannes, 1 March 1880.

55   She was nursed by 'the Martlet', Fanny Martin, a 'wise and most devoted woman', see *MTM*, p.82. Martin's death as she prepared to be the head of a deaconess house, in 1885, shocked the Cowper-Temples, and they published obituaries in *Romsey Chronicle* (see BR58/12) and *The Guardian*, 23 September 1885 (BR50/38).

56   BR58/9, Georgina's diary entries for 20, 24, 26, 27 January 1881. The possibility that the world would end in this year was entertained by the spiritualist journal *Light*, Lady Caithness, and Kingsford and Maitland.

57   BR58/9, Georgina's diary notes opposite pages for 22 January and 30 January 1881.

58   See C. Head, ed., *Charlotte Hanbury* (London: Marshall Brothers, 1901), p.140: she came to a Broadlands conference in 1879, and knew Theodore Monod and William Pennefather.

59   BR50/6, R.W. Corbet to the Cowper-Temples, 9 March 1881.

60   On Welby, BR50/6, R.W. Corbet to Cowper-Temples, 9 March 1881; E. Cust, ed., *Echoes of a Larger Life. A Selection from the Early Correspondence of Victoria Lady Welby* (London: J. Cape, 1929), pp.76-77, p.126. W.N. Massey, MP and barrister, was appointed in William's office in the Board of Health, see *Legal Observer*, 12 August 1855, p.311. C.C. Massey accepted an invitation to the Cowper-Temples, 5 July 1880, see BR50/45.

61   BR58/9, Georgina's diary entry for 4 April 1881.

62   Taylor, *Laurence Oliphant*, p.205.

63   BR53/11, Jukes to William, 27 August 1881.

64   BR57/68/1, Jukes to the Cowper-Temples, 20 June 1877.

65   BR58/10, Georgina's diary entry for 1 January 1882. See *MTM*, p.109, on Alice.

66   BR58/10, Georgina's diary entry for 30 January 1882.

67   *Daily News*, 6 November 1882.

68   BR58/10, Georgina's diary entries for 10, 19, 27 November 1881. I am grateful to the present owners of 'Cloudlands', for sharing their research. The address 'Mrs Annie Borel Northlew, Cloudlands, Torquay', is in William's diary for 1884, BR51/18.

69   Smith, *Religious Rebel*, p.102. BR59/29, Juliet to Georgina, 1893]; Juliet declined to see Countess Borel, 23 June 1897, see Juliet to Georgina, 44 Glebe Place, Chelsea, BR59/29.

70   Joseph Leycester Lyne, established a monastery at Llanthony, Capel-y-Ffin, in Wales. BR58/8, Georgina's diary entry for 20 September 1880 noted the miracles at Llanthony for 1883; In BR56/12, Georgina's diary entry for January 1883, is a note: 'Llanthony test, drawn for me, "Labour not for the meat wh. perisheth".' See A. Calder-Marshall, *The Enthusiast, an enquiry into the life and character of the Rev. Joseph Leycester Lyne alias Fr. Ignatius, O.S.B., Abbot of Elm Hill, Norwich and Llanthony, Wales* (London: Faber and Faber, 1962). He apparently attended the Broadlands conference.

71   *Liverpool Mercury*, 11 October 1882.

72   BL, A.R. Wallace Papers, Add. MSS 46441, f.63, 24 July 1881. Wallace declined the invitation. Myers Papers, 24/14, 14 August. On Barrett and the Cowper-Temples, see W.F. Barrett, *On the Threshold of the Unseen: an examination of the phenomenon of spiritualism of the evidence for survival after death* (London: Kegan Paul, 1917), p.63.

73   BR57/5/6, Hannah Smith to Georgina, San Francisco, 12 October 1882.

74   BR59/3, Georgina to Juliet, 15 Great Stanhope Street, n.d; BR48/5/13, Oliphant to William, Constantinople, 18 May [1882]. On Oliphant's project in Palestine, pursued since 1878, see N.C. Moruzzi, 'Strange Bedfellows: The Question of Lawrence Oliphant's Christian Zionism', *Modern Judaism* 20: 1 (2006), pp.55-73.

75   Watts came to lunch 12 May 1882, see diary entry BR58/10. F.J. Mather, 'The Rossettis', *The Bookman* 49 (New York, 1919), pp.139-147 [p.143] (to Christina).

76   BR58/10, Georgina's diary entry for 3 April 1882.

77   BR58/10, Georgina's diary entry for 12 May 1882.

78   BR58/10, Georgina's diary entries for 14 February 1882; 20 March 1882.

79   E. Blackwell, *Booth. Or the Factory Boy who became a Gospel Temperance Evangelist* (London: Passmore and Alabaster, 1883), pp.238-239.

80   *Daily News*, 13 April 1882, *Belfast News-Letter*, 14 April 1882, *Reynolds's Newspaper*, 16 April 1882.

81   BR58/10, Georgina's diary entry for 18 February 1882.

82   BR58/10, Georgina's diary for 12 March 1882. Kingsford and her husband visited the next day.

83   L. Masterman, ed., *Mary Gladstone. Diaries and Letters* (London: Methuen, 1930), p.257.

84   Masterman, *Mary Gladstone*, 1 August, p.258.

85   *Daily News*, 28 August 1882, *Belfast News-Letter*, 30 August 1882.

86   BL, A.R. Wallace Papers, Add. MSS 46440, f.46, 14 August 1882; A.R. Wallace, *My Life. A Record of Events and Opinions* (London: Chapman and Hall, 1905), vol.2, p.102.

87   BR94/2, poster for the show.

88   BR57/5/5, Hannah Smith to Georgina, San Francisco, 25 August 1882.

89   BR49/11, Violet Cuthbert to the Cowper-Temples, Vine Cliff, 29 June 1882.

90   BR50/21, Laurence Oliphant to Georgina, Paris, 21 April [1882]. Cuthbert published *The Life and World Work of Thomas Lake Harris* (Glasgow: C.W. Pierce, 1908).

91   BR50/20, Alice Oliphant to Georgina, Pine Cliff, Prinkipo, 17 September 1882.

92   BR53/10, Jukes to Georgina, 24 September 1882 (typed copy).

93   BR50/28, Hannah Smith to William, Philadelphia, 10 April 1882.

94   BR53/10, Jukes to William, 26 December 1882; BR53/10, Jukes to Georgina, 8 January 1883 (typed copies).

95   BR53/10, Jukes to Georgina, 4 January 1884 (typed copy).

96   BR60/3/11, William to Evelyn Ashley, 2 February 1883; BR53/10, 2 January 1883, Jukes to Georgina (typed copy); BR51/6, William's entry in health journal, 17 December 1882.

97   BR56/12, Georgina's diary entries for 26–27 January 1883; BR57/6/1, Hannah Smith to Georgina, Newport, 7 January 1883.

98   BR56/12, Georgina's diary entry for 1 April 1883 on Myers, on indexing Welby's work, entries for 15–16 April 1883.

99   BR56/12, Georgina's diary entries for 26 March 1883 on Shaftesbury and Lymington; and 31 March and 2 April on letter campaign.

100   BR50/45, Hunt to William, 18 June 1883; Dalhousie to William, 5 June 1883. A letter of thanks from the artist (1888), for a quotation useful to the repeal effort, is in the miscellaneous Letter File, Special Collections, Bryn Mawr College.

101   G.A. Sala, *Echoes of the Year Eighteen Hundred and Eighty Three* (London: Remington, 1884), p.160. A 'real Cross for the Duchess to take up,' Georgina said; William chaired the meeting, see BR59/54, Georgina to Juliet, 15 Great Stanhope Street; BR56/12, Georgina's diary entry for 21 April 1883.

102   BR53/9, Jukes to William, 17 September 1883 (typed copy).

103   BR56/12, Georgina's diary entry for 6 May 1883. Alice Oliphant concluded Georgina should more carefully husband 'out-going vital force', see William's note dated January 1884, in BR45/18/3.

104   BR56/12, Georgina's diary entries for 5 June–7 October 1883.

105   BR53/10, Jukes to William, 30 November 1883 (typed copy).

106   BR53/10, Jukes, 1 October and 6 November 1883 (typed copies).

107   BR57/39/3, Emelia Gurney to Georgina, Cheltenham, 16 November 1883.

108   *The Literary World* 19 (New York; January-December 1888), p.473, describes Lord Mount Temple as 'a devoted friend' and she was always a welcome visitor to Broadlands.

109   Newspaper clipping in BR58/11, Georgina's diary for 1884; *MTM*, p.84.

110   BR58/11, Georgina's diary entry for 1 January 1884.

111   BR57/38/7, Emelia Gurney to Georgina, n.d., notes on Gordon from 'Operative Jewish Converts Institution', BR57/38/15-16; copy by William of Gordon's letter to Emelia Gurney from Khartoum, 18 February 1884, BR44/16/4. Georgina heard of Emelia's contacts with Gordon via Emelia's efforts to deal with the spiritual doubts of Herbert Drake, who attended Corbet's religious meetings at Stoke Rectory, and became fixated on Gordon.

112   BR58/11, Georgina's diary entries for 5–6, 15 May 1884.

113   E.F. Benson, *As We Were. A Victorian Peep-Show* (London: Longmans, Green and Co., 1930), who identified the moving figure as Lady Tavistock, sister of Lady Henry Somerset, p.101.

114   The society was established by Kingsford and Maitland in May 1884. The audience included a young W.B. Yeats.

115   *Reynolds's Newspaper*, 22 June 1884; *The Graphic*, 28 June 1884. On Bishop, see R. Luckhurst, 'Passages in the invention of the psyche: mind-reading in London, 1881-84', ch.6 in Luckhurst and J. McDonagh, eds, *Transactions and Encounters: Science and Culture in the Nineteenth Century* (Manchester: Manchester University Press, 2002), p.144; and S. During, *Modern Enchantments: The Cultural Power of Secular Magic* (2002; Cambridge, Massachusetts: Harvard University Press, 2004), pp.161-167.

116   H.S. Olcott, *Old Diary Leaves. The Only Authentic History of the Theosophical History* (London: Theosophical Publishing Society), 3rd series, p.98. On Chatterji, see BR51/8, William's diary entry for 12 July 1884.

117   Cannadine, *Decline and Fall of the British Aristocracy*, p.351.

118   See M. Asquith, *The Autobiography of Margot Asquith* (1920; London: Penguin Books, 1936), 2 vols, i, p.122, on the 'period of "spooks"', under the influence of Percy Wyndham, Myers and Gurney. See BR44/10/14, letter from Laura, after presentation to the Queen, praying to be kept from the world and senseless life, 8 May 1881.

119   BR59/23, Georgina to Juliet, Wildbad, 15 August 1884.

120   See BR57/68, 8-9, Janet Catherine Symonds to Georgina from Davos Hof, 1 February. On Mrs Symonds' admiration for her, see Margaret Symonds' memoirs, *Out of the Past* (London: J. Murray, 1925), p.308.

121 BR43/36/52, Sutherland to Georgina, Stafford House.

122 BR57/6/2, Hannah Smith to William, Main Street, Germantown, 17 December 1884.

123 BR55/49, Edward Clifford to Georgina, 28 December 1884.

124 BR55/12, Georgina's diary entries for 17–18 March 1885; *The Times*, 18 March 1885, p.10.

125 BR58/12, Georgina's diary entry for 17 March 1885.

126 Georgina Sumner to Georgina, Geneva, 12 November, letter fragment in BR58/12. Beatrice married C.B. Fry the cricketer, see R. Morris, *The Captain's Lady* (London: Chatto and Windus, 1985)

127 *The Sentinel*, 77 (September 1885), pp.484-485; and F. Whyte, *The Life of W.T. Stead*, 2 vols (London: J. Cape, 1925) vol.1, p.173, where William is listed with Shaftesbury, Canon Wilberforce, Auberon Herbert and others.

128 On Hopkins, follower of James Hinton, and called by Bristow a 'sublimated and suffering evangelical spinster', see E.J. Bristow, *Vice and Vigilance. Purity movements in Britain since 1700* (Dublin: Gill and Macmillan, 1977), p.96; and S. Morgan, 'Faith, Sex and Purity: The Religio-Feminist Theory of Ellice Hopkins', *Women's History Review* 9: 1 (2000), pp.13-34.

129 BR50/47, letter from Aberdeen, 15 January 1885; Arthur Kinnaird, 13 January 1885; Furze, 23 January 1885; Lord Ebury, 17 January 1885; and Archbishop Benson of Canterbury, 24 January 1884 [sic].

130 NLS, Ashburton Papers, Acc.11388/96, [5 June]. See *MTM*, pp.85-86.

131 The Women's Library, London Metropolitan University, Josephine Butler Papers, 3JBL/07/02, early 1873 (on William as lisping fool); 3JBL/03/28, 4 April 1871, William was on the Royal Commission on Contagious Diseases Act, Butler replied to his question about whether she had been nervous about appearing before the Commission with a condemnation of 'so base and low a moral standard as you [the Commission] seem to have, and such utter scepticism about God and human nature', (William voted for the Bill to repeal the Acts). See The Women's Library, London Metropolitan University, 3JBL/25/46, Josephine Butler to Emily Ford, 15 November 1886; 3JBL/25/47, 5 December 1886, Georgina Sumner to Emily Ford (on their 'real, great humility'). Bryn Mawr possesses a letter, August 1888, from Josephine Butler to William. See BR56/1, Josephine Butler to Georgina, Cannes, 2 January, n.d., recalling visits to her in Winchester; and J. Butler, *Recollections of George Butler* (Bristol: J.W. Arrowsmith, 1892), p.422.

132 A.V.G. Allen, *Life and Letters of Philip Brooks* (New York: E.P. Dutton, 1901), vol.3, p.157; Taylor, *Laurence Oliphant*, p.224.

133 NLS, Ashburton Papers, Acc.11388/96, [5 June]; 'International Faith Healing Conference', *Daily News*, 6 June 1885; W.E. Boardman, *Record of the International Conference on divine healing and True Holiness* (London: Snow and Bethshan, 1885); and account in *Annual Register*. Catherine Marsh had edited an edition of Boardman's *Higher Christian Life*.

134 Emelia Gurney to William, BR57/39/5, 9 August 1885. Her companion was her goddaughter Emily Gore (1848-1912) unmarried daughter of Charles Alexander Gore.

135 Gurney, *Letters of Emelia Russell Gurney*, p.209. Georgina's diary is full of accounts of Shaftesbury's last days.

136 *Leeds Mercury*, 21 March 1885.

137 BR36/6, letter from Shaftesbury, 16 and 28 March 1885, replying to a letter from Mount Temple, 27 March 1885, with several drafts from Mount Temple, two dated 25 and 26 March 1885. See E. Hodder, *The Life and Work of the Seventh Earl Shaftesbury* (London: Cassell, 1886), vol.3, p.508, on Lord Thurlow's motion on Sunday opening.

138 BR60/3/11, William to Evelyn Ashley, Broadlands, 4 October 1885.

139 BR60/3/12, William to Evelyn Ashley, Eastbourne, 17 September and 3 October 1886.

140 BR36/3, Shaftesbury to William, 27 and 30 December 1878.

141 BR60/3/12, William to Evelyn Ashley, Eastbourne, 3 October 1886.

142 Lady Welby's letter in March 1885 classes them as friends of Gordon, see BR50/45.

143   BR50/21, Alice Oliphant to Georgina, Haifa, 2 March 1885.
144   *Sympneumata. Evolutionary Forces now Active in Man* (1884). See Taylor, *Laurence Oliphant*, pp.220-221; and Oliphant on Gordon's response, BR50/21, Haifa, 31 March 1885.
145   NLS, MacDonald Papers, MS 9745, 30 September 1885, f.55; on the ruling, see BR205/5/1-2, and William to George MacDonald, 1 February 1886, in MacDonald, *George MacDonald and His Wife*, pp.532-533.
146   *MTM*, p.90; BR55/14, Georgina to Evelyn Ashley, Shelley House, Chelsea Embankment.
147   BR43/53/4, Henry Cowper to William, 2 September.
148   BR58/13, Georgina's diary entries opposite page for week beginning 24 February 1886.
149   *Daily News*, 11 February 1886, 24 March 1886.
150   BR50/21, writings on divinity's dual nature, n.d.
151   BR49/5, Emelia Gurney to Georgina, Hotel Paoli, Florence, 'Easter Day'.
152   BR58/13, diary entry for *c.* May 1886. See BR57/52/12, Dolly to Georgina, 8 April 1886.
153   BR60/3/12, William to Evelyn Ashley, 2 May 1886.
154   BR51/19, entry in William's diary opposite 21 November 1886. Lady Sandhurst, wife of the first Baron, supported massage and magnetism, and established a home for crippled poor children in Kilburn, see R.C. Windscheffel, 'Politics, Religion and Text: W.E. Gladstone and Spiritualism', *Victorian Studies* 11:1 (winter 2006), pp.1-29 [p.8]. The medium Gladstone encountered was Mrs Duncan, whom the Cowper-Temples knew.
155   BR50/28, Hannah Smith to Georgina, 40 Grosvenor Road, SW, 16 May 1886.
156   Taylor, *Laurence Oliphant*, p.233. Taylor describes it as the 'transmission of spiritual love through physical contact'.
157   BR57/6/11, Hannah Smith to Georgina, 26 August 1886; see R. Strachey, *Group Movements of the Past* (London: Faber and Faber, 1934; reprinting papers first published as *Religious Fanaticism* in 1928), p.225; and Smith, *Religious Rebel*, p.85. The house may have been Milton Court, owned by the Cowper-Temples' friends the Rates.
158   BR58/13, Georgina's diary entry for 23 July 1886.
159   BR57/6/10, Hannah Smith to Georgina, 28 May 1886.
160   BR49/3, Anna Kingsford to Miss Walker, Broadlands, 27 August 1886 (copy).
161   About this time, Georgina lent Oliphant a copy of Kingsford's *The Mother Clothed with the Sun* (2 parts, 1885-1887), 'is not strange book', Oliphant told his motherling [7 May, n.d., Athenaeum], BR50/21.
162   BR60/3/12, William to Evelyn Ashley, 17 September 1886.
163   BR55/16, Edith Ashley to Georgina, 6 October 1886.
164   BR60/3/12, William to Evelyn Ashley, *c.* October 1886.
165   BR60/3/12, William to Evelyn Ashley, Broadlands, 15 October 1886.
166   My thanks to Michael Roberts, for a transcription of letters from the *LSA* to Chadwick, from the Chadwick Papers, University College London, item 153, ff.4-8, 13-15.
167   Chadwick Papers, item 559, ff. 1-2, 3-4, transcription of letters from Georgina to Chadwick, n.d; and item 560, ff.20-21, 22-29, kindly supplied by Michael Roberts.
168   E. Wordsworth, *Glimpses of the Past* (1912; London: A.R. Mowbray, 1913), 23 June 1887, pp.215-216.
169   Chadwick Papers, item 560, ff.17-19, transcription of letters from William to Chadwick, 15 July 1884, my thanks to Michael Roberts.
170   BR190/18 is the dedication poem by George MacDonald, reprinted *MTM*, p.91.
171   BR58/14, Georgina's diary entry for 20 April 1887, *MTM*, p.90.
172   See BR56/7, George Russell, 21 November [1887], on Henry's comment: 'I think I would rather have Lord M.T. by me at such a time than most of the clergymen I know.'
173   BR58/14, Georgina's diary, opposite page for 9–15 October 1887 (letter from Henry to Lady Wallop); Cowper, *Earl Cowper*, pp.650-651. It was reported, e.g., *Pall Mall Gazette*, 23 November 1887, that his death left William as heir presumptive to Earl Cowper.

174 BR60/3/12, William to Evelyn Ashley, Eastbourne, 27 October 1887.
175 BL, Mary Gladstone Papers, Add. MSS 46229, ff.22-23, William to Mary Gladstone, 24 November 1887: 'He did not appear to be at home in this world, but went through it more as a pilgrim looking beyond it than as a denizen busy with its avocations. He did not care to take part in Politics that his intellect and judgement would have enabled him to fulfil successfully.'
176 BR55/40, William to Emelia Gurney, Grand Hotel, Cimiez, Nice, 18 December 1887.
177 BR50/47, Sir Andrew Clark to William.
178 BR55/40, William to Emelia Gurney, Grand Hotel, Cimiez, Nice, 18 December 1887.
179 BR51/20, entry in William's diary for 20 December 1887.
180 BR58/15, Georgina's diary entry for 23 February 1888.
181 *MTM*, p.86. On Canrobert, see Taylor, *Laurence Oliphant*, p.234.
182 BR60/3/12, William to Evelyn Ashley, Broadlands, 1 February 1888.
183 BR59/74, William to Juliet, Hotel de Cimiez, Nice, 2 February 1888.
184 BR59/33, Floyer to Georgina, 27 May 1888.
185 BR59/1, Georgina to Juliet 'Tuesday' [June 1888].
186 BR58/15, Georgina's diary entry for 1888, entry before diary proper.
187 E.C. Stanton, *Eighty Years and More Reminiscences 1815 to 1897* (1898; Montana: Kessinger, 2004), p.238, said Lord was a 'woman of rare culture and research' who turned to psychical studies. See E. Crawford, *The Women's Suffrage Movement. A Reference Guide, 1866-1928* (New York: Routledge, 2001), pp.357-358. On Whitman, see BR59/65, n.d.; H. Traubel, *With Walt Whitman in Camden*, vol.1 (Boston: Small, Maynard, 1906), pp.93-94.
188 Theosophist, spiritualist and lecturer; von Bergen founded the Swedish Society for Psychical Research.
189 BR59/1, Georgina to Juliet, 'Tuesday' [July 1888]; BR59/4, Georgina to Juliet, Addiscombe, 'Tuesday'.
190 Huldine Beamish, memorialized by von Bergen, was a grandmother of Hermann Göring's first wife. She established the Edelweiss religious sisterhood.
191 BR59/74, William to Juliet, Shelley House, 23 July [1888].
192 *Reynolds's Weekly Newspaper*, 29 July 1883.
193 *MTM*, p.93.
194 BR57/6/14, Hannah Smith to Georgina, 19 August 1888.
195 *MTM*, p.186; H. Smith, 'Lord Mount Temple', *Friends' Quarterly Examiner*, January 1889, pp.107-119 [p.108].
196 *Belfast News-Letter*, 17 October 1888.
197 Whitall Smith Papers, B.L. Fisher Library, Wilmore, Kentucky, letter from Emelia Gurney to Hannah Smith, Broadlands, 15 October.
198 See *MTM*, p.95.
199 *The Times*, 22 October 1888, p.10. A memorial pamphlet appeared in the *Hampshire Independent*, 20 October 1888.
200 *The Times*, 13 February 1886, p.9. His death and funeral were reported 17 October, p.7; 18 October, p.7; 22 October, p.10; and 23 October, p.13. Will and bequests were reported 9 January 1889, p.6. An obituary and portrait appear in *Illustrated London News*, 27 October 1888, pp.481-482 and *The Graphic*, 27 October, see BR44/19/4.
201 BR 44/19/9, *The Hampshire Independent*, 20 October 1888.
202 *MTM*, p.169. Copies of the poem are in BR56/25. See BR50/28 for Hannah Smith on the poem, 16 May 1886.
203 Smith, 'Lord Mount Temple', p.108.

Chapter 10. William and Georgina as Reformers

1   For the meaning of 'reform' in this period, which after the 1830s and its association with the Whig ministry, lost some of its particular political bias, see J. Innes, '"Reform" in English Public life. The fortunes of a word', in Innes and Burns, *Rethinking the Age of Reform*, pp.94-97.

2   BR51/5, William's journal entry for 19 January 1839.

3   BR48/6/2, William's undated memorandum on the object of his life.

4   BR51/5, William's journal entry for 6 July 1845.

5   BR44/16/1, an undated note by William.

6   BR44/16/12, an undated note by William.

7   BR206/3, newspaper cutting, probably from *Hampshire Chronicle* 16 November 1867.

8   Russell, *Portraits of the Seventies*, p.276. An entry in Dod's *Parliamentary Companion* of 1880, reprinted in *Who's Who of British Members of Parliament* ed. M. Stenton (Hassocks: Harvester Press, 1976) vol.1, p.93, describes him as Liberal, 'in favour of local taxation being "relieved of its heavy burdens" also of tenant farmers being secured the value of their improvements'.

9   Tennyson, quoted by Hannah Smith to Georgina, BR57/5/6, 12 October 1882.

10   BR59/33, H.R. Haweis to Juliet, notes of sermon delivered at death of Lord Mount Temple, 23 October 1888.

11   Russell, *Portrait of the Seventies*, p.284.

12   L. Bending, *The Representation of Bodily Pain in Late Nineteenth-Century English Culture* (Oxford: Clarendon Press, 2000).

13   See Hilton, *The Age of Atonement*, and Rowell, *Hell and the Victorians*.

14   L.P. Smith, 'Boyhood and Youth', *Atlantic Monthly* (1932), p.422; reprinted in Burman, *Logan Pearsall Smith. An Anthology*.

15   Gurney, *Letters*, p.128 (to Julia Wedgwood, 13 October 1873).

16   Helmingham Hall Papers, T/Hel/1/610, William Cowper to Lady Elizabeth Tollemache, n.d. Her acquaintance with Octavia Hill reflected mutual friends such as the Maurices, Llewellyn Davies, Ruskin, Emelia Gurney and the MacDonalds, and a shared interest in preserving open spaces. She visited Octavia Hill's district of Ruskin's Houses in Marylebone in 1869; see BR58/17, 3 May 1869. Annie Munro, writing of Octavia's sister Florence, told Georgina, 'all her family esteem yourself and Mr Temple most highly for your never ending good deeds,' 16 March [no year given], BR56/6.

17   BR56/11, Georgina's diary entry for 3 March 1859.

18   BR56/11, Georgina's diary entries for 22 March and 17 April 1859.

19   BR56/11, Georgina's diary entry for 12 February 1859.

20   *MTM*, p.106, on the works' reception, see Dowling, 'The Ladies Sanitary Association', p.97. See BR56/14, Tom Hughes' letter inviting Georgina and William to tea, 15 November 1860; and his memorial to William, *MTM*, p.151.

21   William and Sir Thomas Dyke Acland had agreed to be trustees, 'it being distinctly understood that it that office they accept no responsibility for the conduct of the scheme, and refrain from expressing any opinion of its principles'. Collingwood, 'Ruskin's Isola', p.80, admitted the difficulty in tracing Ruskin's direct influence on William's circle. *Fors Clavigera* exhorted the Cowper-Temples to cultivate land. Ruskin had associated with the Christian Socialists, see E. Norman, *The Victorian Christian Socialists* (Cambridge: Cambridge University Press, 1987), ch.7.

22   This paragraph draws on J. Burchardt, *The Allotment Movement in England, 1793-1873* (Woodbridge: Boydell, 2002), ch.3.

23   Burchardt, p.167, citing *Labourer's Friend Magazine* lxxxvi (1851), p.113; *Salisbury and Winchester Journal*, 13 January 1877.

24   *The Times*, 12 April 1843, p.2.

25 Burchardt, *The Allotment Movement*, p.126.

26 Burchardt, *The Allotment Movement*, p.96.

27 Burchardt, *The Allotment Movement*, p.85.

28 *PD*, 3rd series, vol.76, 10 July 1844 (during the second reading of the Field Gardens Bill), col.563; G.J. Holyoake, *History of Co-operation in England. Its Literature and Its Advocates* vol.2, *The constructive period – 1845–1878* (London: Trübner, 1879), p.205.

29 BR53/2, *Hampshire Independent*, 7 December 1881.

30 BR206/3, newspaper cutting, probably from *Hampshire Chronicle*, 16 November 1867.

31 BR206/3, *Salisbury and Winchester Journal*, 13 January 1877.

32 BR206/3, cutting, probably from *Hampshire Chronicle*, 16 November 1867; *Southampton Times c.*1878, 24th annual meeting of the Romsey Association; *Salisbury and Winchester Journal*, 13 January 1877.

33 BR44/19/9, newspaper clipping, *Hampshire Independent*, 20 October 1888.

34 *MTM*, p.74; and BR206/3, cutting, probably from *Hampshire Chronicle*, 16 November 1867. See Reynolds, *Aristocratic Women*, Gerard, *Country House Life*, ch.5; C. Howse, 'From Lady Bountiful to Lady Administrator: women and the administration of rural district nursing in England, 1880-1925', *Women's History Review* 15: 3 (July 2006), pp.423-441. See also A. Summers, 'A Home from Home – Women's Philanthropic Work in the Nineteenth Century', in S. Burman, ed., *Fit Work for Women* (London: Croom Helm, 1970), pp.33-63.

35 BR58/6, Georgina's diary entry for 14 January 1876.

36 BR58/6, Georgina's diary entry for 18 April 1876.

37 *Belfast News-Letter*, 28 July 1877.

38 *MTM*, p.79.

39 On William's involvement in the scheme, in which cultivation of waste land addressed the problem of unemployment, see the prospectus, *The Church of England Self-Supporting Village* (London: J.W. Parker, 1850), printing the petition William presented to the Commons, 22 March 1844; J.M. Morgan, *Letters to a Clergyman: on institutions for ameliorating the condition of the people, chiefly from Paris in the autumn of 1845* (London: Chapman and Hall, 1846), p.153, p.191, on the meeting in Exeter Hall which William chaired, 27 May 1846, when he endorsed 'associated assistance' based on religion; W.H.G. Armytage, 'John Minter Morgan's Schemes, 1841–1855', *International Review of Social History* 3:1 (April 1958), pp.26-42; and J.F.C. Harrison, *Robert Owen and the Owenites in Britain and America. The Quest for the New Moral World* (London: Routledge and Kegan Paul, 1969), p.35, which characterises the scheme as 'gentlemanly philanthropy' on the pattern of agricultural society and opposed to industrialism and Malthus. Minter Morgan became influenced by Maurice's theology. Support for this utopian scheme anticipated William's involvement in Christian Socialism.

40 BR, SHA/PD/3, Ashley's diary for 15 April 1845, f.177; *PD*, 3rd series, vol.86, 13 May 1846, cols.466-493. J.T. Ward, *The Factory Movement. 1830–1855* (London: Macmillan, 1962).

41 *Manchester Guardian*, 10 June 1848.

42 *Hampshire Telegraph*, 19 January 1861, p.7; *The Times*, 5 August 1873, p.10.

43 *The Times*, 17 June 1873, p.8.

44 BR58/6, Georgina's diary entry for 21 February 1876, see also 24 and 25 February.

45 BR 206/3, unidentified Hampshire newspaper, 12 December 1874.

46 Prochaska, *Women and Philanthropy*, pp.175-179, these included Mrs Tait, Anna Jameson, Lady Shaftesbury, and F.D. Maurice. See L. Twining, *Recollections of Workhouse Visiting and Management During Twenty- Five Years* (London: Kegan Paul, 1880); L. Twining, *Recollections of Life and Work. Being the Autobiography of Louisa Twining* (London: Arnold, 1893), p.156; Ritchie, *Life and Times of Lord Palmerston*, p.583; Roberts, *Making English Morals*, p.205.

47 BR58/2, Georgina's diary entry for 9 January 1862; 7LOT/081, Georgina to Louisa Twining, n.d., The Women's Library, London Metropolitan University, Louisa Twining

Papers. She became a Lady Visitor of St Luke's, alongside Mrs Tait, Mrs Gladstone and Lady Frederick Cavendish, see 7LOT/104b, The Women's Library, London Metropolitan University. For William's role, see 7LOT/022b and 7LOT/022c.

48   On district visiting, see typical reference in BR58/1, Georgina's diary entry for 23 June 1855. On the Dressmaking Company, see *Punch*, 18 February 1865; *The Times*, 28 March 1870, p.13, and BR58/17, Georgina's diary entry for 2 September 1863.

49   BR58/17, Georgina's diary entry for 29 April 1870.

50   The select committee 'inquire[d] into the circumstances affecting the Health of the Inhabitants of large Towns and Populous Districts, with a view to improved Sanatory Regulations for their benefits'.

51   *PD*, 3rd series, vol.163 (6 June 1861), col.630; vol.164 (12 July 1861) col.800.

52   *MTM*, p.63. Flower cultivation was initiated by Benjamin Hall, as Georgina acknowledged. For a wider history, see H. Conway, *People's parks. The design and development of Victorian parks in Britain* (Cambridge, 1991). William later joined the Metropolitan Public Gardens Association (founded 1882).

53   Clipping pasted into BR58/3, Georgina's diary for 1867.

54   BR58/2, Georgina's diary entry for 6 September 1862. The Tuileries gardens provided one model.

55   Russell, *Portraits of the Seventies*, p.280.

56   *PD*, 3rd series, vol.201, 11 May 1870, col.561. J. Ranlett, '"Checking Nature's Desecration": Late Victorian Environmental Organisation', *Victorian Studies* 26 (winter 1983), pp.197-222; B. Cowell, 'The Commons Preservation Society and the Campaign for Berkhamsted Common, 1866-70', *Rural History* 13: 2 (2002), pp.145-161 [p.147].

57   Parry, *Democracy and Religion*, p.116; J.P. Parry, *The Rise and Fall of Liberal Government in Victorian Britain* (London and New Haven: Yale University Press, 1993) p.265; pp.271-272. The Epping Forest campaign by the CPS began in 1865, running parallel with other campaigns against enclosure of spaces such as Hampstead Heath and Wimbledon.

58   Cutting, probably from *Hampshire Chronicle*, 15 December 1877; *The Times*, 29 May 1877, p.7. Robert Hunter, *The Times*, 18 October 1888, p.7, summarizes his role in open spaces campaigns.

59   'Mr Clifford, Lord Henry Scott and Mr Cowper-Temple on the New Forest', *Hampshire Telegraph*, 24 June 1871.

60   Helena Comtesse de Noailles (née Baring), who supported the Langham Place circle and became an anti-vaccinator, said she and Georgina started the Association; see W. White, *The Story of a Great Delusion in a Series of Matter of Fact Chapters* (London: E.W. Allen, 1885), p.547; *British Homoeopathic Review* 32 (1888), p.439; *MTM*, p.61 mentions Lady Ebury and Mrs Sutherland. See Dowling, 'The Ladies' Sanitary Association'; *Transactions of the National Association for the Promotion of Social Science, 1860* (1860); *LSA* tracts in the British Library; *The Philanthropist*, 1 August 1859, pp.433-434; Octavia Hill, *Homes of the London Poor* (London: Macmillan, 1875), ch.7. The *English Woman's Journal* was the *LSA*'s organ.

61   *MTM*, p.61.

62   See for instance, the lectures arranged through her application, at University College London in 1861, see H.H. Bellot, *University College, London, 1826–1926* (London: University of London Press, 1929), p.369.

63   Reynolds, *Aristocratic Women*, p.111.

64   BR57/8, Anna Jameson to Georgina, 16 Chatham Place, Brighton, '30 November'; G.H. Needler, ed., *Letters of Anna Jameson to Ottilie von Goethe* (London: Oxford University Press, 1939), pp.228-229, on encountering Cowpers at the SSA congress at Bradford in 1859, and at the Monkton Milnes'; and C.E.M. Thomas, *Love and Work Enough. The Life of Anna Jameson* (London: Macdonald, 1967), pp.206-207; letter by Garth Wilkinson:

http://www.historicalautographs.co.uk/catalogue.asp?content=Medicine%20and%20Surgery (accessed 9 May 2007).

65 BR58/2, Georgina's diary entry for 8 February 1862.
66 *The Times*, 1 February 1862, p.12.
67 BR58/2, Georgina's diary entry for 31 January 1862.
68 See BR56/23, Simon to Georgina [1 February 1862]. See *The Medical Times and Gazette*, 8 February 1862, p.139. Georgina's role is not noted in P.W.J. Bartrip, 'How Green was my Valance? Environmental Arsenic Poisoning and the Victorian Domestic Ideal', *English Historical Review* 109 (1994), pp.891-913. See 'Englishman', *The Green of the Period; or, The unsuspected foe in the Englishman's home* (London: Routledge, 1869), dedicated to William.
69 See Bodleian Library, MS Acland, d.80, ff.186-189, n.d., W.C. Temple to Dr Acland, my thanks to Michael Roberts for a transcription. The lectures were advertised in *Englishwomen's Review* and *Journal of Women's Educational Union*. See Dowling, 'The Ladies Sanitary Association', p.92, on the *Lancet*'s early support.
70 BR57/41/6, Shaftesbury to Georgina, 29 June 1878; BR36/3, Shaftesbury to William, 19 October 1878.
71 She apparently gave a paper on 'Women's Work in Sanitation', at the Health Congress at Hastings, see *Women's Penny Paper*, 25 May 1889.
72 My thanks to Michael Roberts, for a transcription of letters from Georgina to Chadwick, Chadwick Papers, University College London, 559, ff.5-6, n.d.
73 Russell, *Portraits of the Seventies*, p.277; *Alliance News*, 20 October 1888, p.835.
74 'The Temperance Movement in the Metropolis', *Daily News*, 2 June 1868; though Georgina in *MTM* thought it was 'about 1862', p.88.
75 The English branch of the Blue Ribbon movement was founded in 1877, and peaked before the late 1880s, see L.L. Shiman, *Crusade against Drink in Victorian England* (New York: St Martin's Press, 1988), pp.109-121.
76 BR 44/19/1, *Western Morning News*, 20 October 1888.
77 B. Harrison, *Drink and the Victorians. The temperance question in England, 1815-1872* (1971; Keele, 1994), p.176.
78 A coffee tavern company organization was established in 1876 under Cowper-Temple's presidency: and a 'Temple Arms' tavern established (see BR53/6, Marguerite Tollemache to Georgina, referring to this). See M. Girouard, *Victorian Pubs* (London: Studio Vista, 1975), p.175. See BL, Gladstone Papers Add. MSS 44460, f.292, printed advertisement for 'Coffee Music Halls for the People'; William hoped to get Gladstone on the Provisional Council, see BL, Gladstone Papers, Add. MSS 44460, f.289, 28 July 1879. 'Music Halls for the Million', *Punch*, 13 September 1879, p.110.
79 *The Times*, 18 August 1923, p.9.
80 *Ragged School Union Magazine*, 15 November 1888, p.119. On Charrington, see G. Thorne, *The Great Acceptance. The Life Story of F. Charrington* (1912; London: Hodder and Stoughton, 1913), p.62; Harrison, *Drink and the Victorians*, p.328; Shiman, *Crusade against Drink*, pp.125-127.
81 See B.T. Hall, *Our Fifty Years: The Story of the Working Men's Club and Institute Union, Together with Brief Impressions of the Men of the Movement* (London: Working Men's Club and Institute Union, 1912).
82 Bristow, *Vice and Vigilance*, p.49; J.E. Butler, 'Some Personal Recollections of Lord Mount Temple', *The Dawn*, 1 November 1888, p.24.
83 *The Times*, 28 August 1888, p.11. See advice about anti-vice efforts of Anthony Comstock in New York, in BR50/47, Blantyre to William, 15 July 1888.
84 BR53/3 includes fragmentary letters by William about the Contagious Diseases Acts.
85 See P. McHugh, *Prostitution and Victorian Social Reform* (1980); and Roberts, *Making English Morals*, pp.255-257, on Vigilance Association and Church of England Purity Society.

86   Haweis, in *MTM*, p.152.
87   'One we all Love', in M. de Burgh, *Chimes* (London: Smith, Elder, 1858), pp.17-22 [p.21].
88   Russell, *Portraits of the Seventies*, p.281.
89   *Seeking and Saving* vol.3 (1883), the journal of the society for reclamation of prostitutes, listing for Torquay supporters, p.18.
90   BR57/6/9, Hannah Smith to Georgina, n.d., concerning welcome meeting for the released W.T. Stead.
91   Benson, *As We Were*, pp.98-103 [p.101].
92   BR43/22/3, William to Georgina [1855]; Houghton Papers, EG5/14/10, 7 June [1883].
93   BR 56/14, Holman Hunt to Georgina, 17 June 1888.
94   In the Commons in early March, William was praised by Sir Robert Inglis and others for condemning duelling as anti-Christian. He supported courts of honour instead of the 'spurious satisfaction' of duelling, see *The Times*, 12 March 1844, p.2; 15 March 1844, p.2.
95   BR44/11/14, 'Heads of Proposals for establishing a system of arbitration for the amicable adjustment of differences on pints of honour.'
96   Evangelicals opposed duelling in their campaign to improve aristocratic manners and behaviour, see D.T. Andrew, 'The code of honour and its critics: the opposition to duelling in England, 1700-1850', *Social History* 5: 3 (1980), pp.409-434.
97   BR43/35/5, William to Anson, Runcton, 9 April 1843.
98   *Eclectic Museum of Foreign Literature, Science and Art*, 1843, from the *Examiner*.
99   His correspondence with the Duke of Wellington on the 'unchristian and barbarous custom' is well-known. See H. Bolitho, *Albert, Prince Consort* (Indianapolis: Bobbs-Merrill, 1964), p.77.
100   *Addresses of the Earl of Shaftesbury and the Honourable W.F. Cowper on Tuesday October 12th 1858 on the health, physical condition, moral habits, and education of the people* (Liverpool: Benson and Mallett, 1858), p.15.
101   Lofft's *Self-formation* was published 1837. Reading it 14 February 1847, William was again stirred, 'I resolve to cultivate energy of will in all my proceedings small and great' (journal, BR51/5).
102   See William's journal, BR51/13, for visits to ragged schools with Kay Shuttleworth and others in March and April 1846; *MTM*, p.27, p.39.
103   *MTM*, p.106; G. Perkins, *Scenes of Village Labour, and Lower Life in London: A Missionary Sketch* (London: Partridge and Oakey, 1854), p.iiii (book dedication, referring to the Well Street District and William's support for the Glasshouse Street Free School). BR45/17/1, a notebook *c*.1850s, entitled 'ragged schools', has William's thoughts on ragged schools, education, and cooperative associations. See the obituary in *The Ragged School Union Magazine*, 15 November 1888, p.119.
104   *Ragged School Union Magazine*, March 1869, p.58. In this year William became a vice-president of the C.O.S., which planned co-ordination and disciplining of charity, see M.J.D. Roberts, 'Charity Distesablished? The Origins of the Charity Organisation Society Revisited, 1868-1871', *Journal of Ecclesiastical History* 54:1 (January 2003), pp.40-61.
105   *Ragged School Union Magazine*, March 1869, p.60.
106   *The Times*, 1 November 1870, p.6.
107   BR45/17/2, notebook entitled 'Education', n.d. BR45/17/3 has William's notes on Board schools. He made notes on nonconformity and education, requirements of different classes, education in social sciences, and Lancastrian natural history clubs.
108   *MTM*, p.39, 7 April 1846 (from William's journal).
109   He later supported technical education, contrasting provision in Britain with France and Germany, see *The Times*, 21 October 1870, p.3.

110　Roberts, *Making English Morals*, p.144, classes Kay-Shuttleworth as one of the Whigs' 'favourite policy advisers'. See *PD*, 3rd series, vol.67, 24 March 1843, cols.1464-1465, for William on the Graham's Factory Bill.

111　BR206/3, *Hampshire [Chronicle?]* 16 November 1867.

112　*Daily News*, 1 October 1875.

113　NLS, MS 24800, ff. 32-35.

114　*Daily News*, 1 October 1875; *PD*, 3rd series, vol.222, 3 March 1875, col.1129.

115　*PD*, 3rd series, vol.230, 5 July 1876, col.996; *The Times*, 26 June 1877, p.10; A. Burton, 'Contesting the Zenana: The Mission to Make "Lady Doctors for India" 1874-1885' *Journal of British Studies* 35: 3 (July 1996), pp.368-397 [p.372]

116　BR58/5, Georgina's diary entry for 9 June 1874; see 9/04/17, William Cowper-Temple to Emily Davies, 3 June 1874, The Women's Library, London Metropolitan University, Autograph Letter Collection: Female Education Ref 9/04.

117　See BR205/7/1 for shares certificate; *The Times*, 10 January 1883, p.11. Other projects which the Cowper-Temples supported included Dr William Moon's establishment for the production of Braille Bibles and an attempted revival of the Useful Knowledge Society, see *The Times*, 4 May 1872, p.13.

118　'Women's Suffrage. A Reply', *Fortnightly Review* 46: 271 (July 1889), p.132.

119　*The Times*, 26 June 1872, p.11.

120　*Chamber's Journal*, 4: 182, June 1887, p.413. See Johnson, *Diary of Gathorne Hardy*, p.665, p.667, p.674 for references.

121　*The Zoophilist*, 1 November 1888, p.118, clipping in BR58/15, Georgina's diary for 1888. Georgina was described as 'sharer of his thoughts and labours especially for wrongs of women and children'.

122　BR59/73, J. Frewen Moor to Juliet, 19 October 1901. His *Thoughts Regarding the Future State of Animals* Winchester: Warren, 1893) had a dedication to Georgina.

123　See Suckling's letters to Georgina, BR56/18; and *The Quiver* 30: 421 (January 1895), pp.777-778.

124　BL, Carnarvon Papers, Add. MSS 60855, f.14, 1 November 1882.

125　See the dedication to Cowper-Temple, in M. Hooper, *Ways and tricks of animals, with stories about Aunt Mary's pets* (London: Griffith and Farran, 1880).

126　BL, Carnarvon Papers, Add. MSS 60855, f.17, proof of prospectus, November 1882.

127　*Ragged School Union Quarterly Record*, October 1879, p.150. See *MTM*, p.81.

128　See *Leeds Mercury*, 19, 21 and 22 December 1885. For the Reverend F.O. Morris' initiatory letter, M.C.F. Morris, *Frances Orpen Morris: A Memoir* (London: J.C. Nimmo, 1897), p.296; on nascent wildlife conservation, see J. Turner, *Reckoning with the Beast. Animals, Pain, and Humanity in the Victorian Mind* (Baltimore: Johns Hopkins University Press, 1980), ch.7. Wild birds became 'second only to domestic pets' for bourgeois zoophilists, see D. Weinbren, 'Against *All* Cruelty: the Humanitarian League, 1891-1919', *History Workshop Journal* 38 (1994) pp.86-105 [p.97]. See also M.A. Elston, 'Women and Anti-vivisection in Victorian England. 1870-1900', in N.A. Rupke, ed., *Vivisection in Historical Perspective* (London: Routledge, 1987), pp.259-294, an examination of links between anti-vivisection, philanthropy and the women's movement (it refers to William in relation to links between moral reform and zoophilia).

129　Turner, *Reckoning with the Beast*, pp.99-103.

130　*The Times*, 21 March 1876, p.8; BR58/6, Georgina's diary entries for 3 and 4 April 1876, see also 22 May 1876. It is not clear what she meant by the 'Animal Friends' Society'.

131　William was a vice-president; Georgina bequeathed £50 to the society, see *The Times*, 28 January 1902, p.1. See reference to her letters, *Daily News*, 29 April 1886, p.5. See Cobbe, *Life of Frances Power Cobbe*, pp.561-562, pp.678-679, p.690.

132   BR56/2, two letters from Cobbe to Georgina, Hengwrt, Dolgelly; one after William's death.

133   BR55/26, Anna Kingsford to Georgina, '19 August' [1886]; E. Maitland, *Anna Kingsford. Her Life, Letters, Diary and Work* (2 vols, London: G. Redway, 1896), vol.2, pp.263-264.

134   *MTM*, p.89.

135   On blood sports, however, Russell, *Portraits of the Seventies*, p.278 suggests it was due to William's 'keen sympathies'. Taylor examines, *Lords of Misrule*, ch.3, hunting as symbolic of aristocratic viciousness for radicals, perhaps consciousness of this played a   part in the Cowper-Temples' response. On the trough, see BR59/23, Georgina to Juliet, 15 Great Stanhope Street, 'Wednesday evening'.

136   BR58/5, Georgina's diary entry for 17 October 1874.

137   BR58/6, Georgina's diary entry for 9 March 1876; 20 March 1876 she recorded 'A Vegetarian Feast!' A friend was cured through the advice of the American naturopath Mrs T.L. Nichols and vegetarianism, see 6 March.

138   She contributed to a 'Special Mission Fund' of 1890 (£2), and attended a vegetarian meeting at the People's Palace, see *Vegetarian Messenger*, August 1887, p.262.

139   *Reynolds's Daily Newspaper*, 16 April 1882; *Dietetic Reformer*, May 1882, p.95, pp.98-99.

140   *Vegetarian*, 2 September 1893, p.415, with photograph.

141   BR45/9, William's spiritualist notebook entitled 'Mission', after *c*.1 September 1876, entry on 'Food'. He tried 'vegetable diet with great success', in October 1837 (see *MTM*, p.21); on Wallace's alleged role, *Herald of Health*, March 1911, p.63.

142   BR45/12/1, notes at the back of William's notebook (*c*.1876-1882) labelled 'Mystic'. The Swedenborg Society preserves a letter to the prominent Swedenborgian Garth Wilkinson, from William (K/425). The Cowper-Temples were interested in Swedenborgianism via spiritualism (*MTM*, p.108).

143   Clifford, *Broadlands as it was*, p.6, suggests Georgina was the more committed vegetarian, as he refers to her refusal to eat anything that had been killed and does not mention William's opinion. See BR48/6/8 for William's undated notes for a lecture on the value of non-meat foods, beginning, 'My lady and I wish you to know about a variety of nice, very nice foods that are as nourishing as meat and cost much less money…'

144   *The Times*, 19 November 1873, p.7; *The Times*, 22 May 1874, p.12.

145   *Vegetarian Messenger*, July 1887, p.207.

146   *Homeopathic World*, 1 November 1888; typescript in BR 44/19/7.

147   White, *Story of a Great Delusion*, pp.496-500; *PD*, 3rd series, vol.141, 31 March 1856, cols. 271-273.

148   BR58/5, Georgina's diary entry for 22 February 1874.

149   BR49/14, John Ashburner to Georgina, 7 Hyde Park Place, 'Monday 21' [*c*.1861-1869].

150   See H.D. Curtis, '"Acting Faith": Practices of Religious Healing in Late-Nineteenth Century Protestantism', in L.F. Maffly-Kipp, L.E. Schmidt, M.R. Valeri, eds, *Practicing Protestants. Histories of Christian Life in America, 1630-1965* (Baltimore: Johns Hopkins University Press, 2006), pp.137-158 [p.139].

151   BR58/13, Georgina's diary entry for 3 January 1886.

152   BR57/65/9, Frances Lord to Georgina, 8 November 1887; Frances Lord, *Light*, 16 June 1888, p.295; the *British Medical Journal* was scornful. William also dined with the Australian politician and magnetic healer George Milner Stephen, see *Pall Mall Gazette*, 21 February 1887; *Australian Dictionary of Biography* (Carlton, Victoria: Melbourne University Press, 1967), vol.2, pp.472-474.

153   BR43/58/1-2, de Saint Anthoine to William, 6 August 1840, representing Institut d'Afrique.

154   BR56/11, notebook, April 1859; *The Observer*, 16 July 1860 (advertisement). Shaftesbury championed the *Risorgimento*. William's notes on Italy in 1849 appear in *MTM*, p.51.

155 Byng, *Leaves from the Diary of Henry Greville, first series*, pp.198-200.
156 *Manchester Guardian*, 14 April 1864, p.3.
157 *The Times*, 6 October 1870, p.6. She was treasurer along with Florence Nightingale, Mrs Russell Gurney, Mrs Salis Schwabe and Lady Lyell.
158 *The Times*, 5 May 1877, p.1; G.S.R. Kitson Clark, 'Introduction', in Shannon, *Gladstone and the Bulgarian Agitation*, p.xii.
159 Shannon, *Gladstone and the Bulgarian Agitation*, p.56.
160 BR58/9, Georgina's diary for 1881, 'Lord Mount Temple's Sayings and Doings in Parliament'.
161 *Liverpool Mercury*, 18 October 1888.
162 G.W.E. Russell, *Basil Wilberforce. A Memoir* (London: J. Murray, 1917), p.66.
163 *MTM*, p.60.
164 Cook and Wedderburn, eds, *Library Edition of the Works of John Ruskin*, vol.36, *Letters*. I, 1827-1869, p.xcix.
165 Clifford, *Broadlands as it was*, pp.14-15.
166 See Roberts, *Making English Morals*, p.257, on the 'opportunity for national elites to use social purity as a symbolic assertion of their continuing fitness to lead'; see Harrison, *Peaceable Kingdom*, p.229, on the aim of philanthropy 'to erode aristocratic values' by integrating women, nonconformists and the middle-class. On the charitable activities organized by working people themselves, and the charitable impulse of poor for poor, see Prochaska, *The Voluntary Impulse*, pp.27-31.
167 On middle-class competition with aristocrats in philanthropy, see Reynolds, *Aristocratic Women*, ch.3, especially pp.110-112. Perhaps the Cowper-Temples, like Shaftesbury, felt press coverage impelled them to sustain a reputation for virtue. Georgina, like her acquaintances Catherine Gladstone and Victoria Buxton, was unable to relax in the face of charitable demands, see Prochaska, *Women and Philanthropy*, pp.161-162.
168 BR57/40/4, Shaftesbury to Georgina, 4 June 1860, and BR57/40/6, 13 June 1860.

Chapter 11. The Cowper-Temples and Religion

1 Smith, 'Lord Mount Temple', p.114.
2 *MTM*, p.102.
3 As applied to William by Lionel Tollemache, *Old and Odd Memories*, p.85.
4 Shannon, *Gladstone and the Bulgarian Agitation*, p.28; G.M. Young, *Victorian England. Portrait of an Age* (1936; London: Oxford University Press, 1960), p.117.
5 Parry, *Democracy and Religion*, p.6.
6 Parry, *Democracy and Religion*, p.27.
7 Parry, *Democracy and Religion*, p.5, and quotation from p.53.
8 *Romsey Register*, 26 July 1888, p.1; Smith, 'Lord Mount Temple', p.115.
9 Parry, *Democracy and Religion*, p.59.
10 *Official Report of the Church Congress held at Nottingham* (London: Bemrose, 1897), p.137.
11 As told to Basil Wilberforce, see his *In Memoriam. William Francis Baron Mount Temple. A Brief Sketch* (Southampton, April 1889, supplement to *St Mary's Parish Magazine*). For Wilberforce's response to Broadlands, see Russell, *Basil Wilberforce*, ch.4.
12 *MTM*, p.183.
13 *MTM*, p.20, 19 January 1839.
14 A. Reid, ed., *Why I am a Liberal Being Definitions and Personal Confessions of Faith by the Best Minds of the Liberal Party* (London: Cassell, 1885), p.78.
15 Parry, *Democracy and Religion*, p.62.
16 Russell, *Portrait of the Seventies*, p.274.
17 BR51/5, William's journal entries for 5 April and 29 July 1829.
18 BR51/5, William's journal entry for 9 November 1829.

19   BR49/11, William's note, 'The Xian's Post is in [the] world', paper watermarked 1829.

20   BR49/11, note by William, *c*.1840s. William believed the devil hated mirth and *MTM*, p.46, stresses his 'brightest temperament'.

21   Mandler, *Aristocratic Government*, p.277.

22   BR43/3/6, Emily Palmerston to William, Broadlands, Sunday, n.d.

23   BR43/16/1-2, William's drafts of letter, 1 November 1845. See Bebbington, *Evangelicalism in Modern Britain*, p.130, for Shaftesbury on Lady Palmerston's scorn for the serious.

24   Burd, *Ruskin, Lady Mount Temple and the Spiritualists* attributes this to Lady Palmerston, but it is the widow of the sixth Earl. On William's Evangelicalism, see also B. Hilton, 'Whiggery, Religion and Social Reform: the case of Lord Morpeth', *Historical Journal* 37: 4 (1994) pp.829-859 [pp.838-839].

25   BR51/13, William's journal for 4 January 1840 on *Deerbrook*; BR51/5, his journal entry for 22 August 1840 on attending a Unitarian chapel in Liverpool, and the same journal, after entry on 'City Missions', on visits to other denominations (printed in *MTM*, p.17).

26   BR51/5, William's journal entry for 1836. BR43/55, Beamish's letter to William, 1 November 1837, sets out his anti-Romanism, ideas on church reform, and refers to a preferment mentioned by William. William summarized Beamish's sermons among 'stray leaves of sermons' in a notebook.

27   BR51/5; see also BR51/13, 6 August 1840 for discussion involving Trotter, and Caleb Morris, covering socialists in Regent's Park, deficiencies of missionaries, teetotalism.

28   On the *LCM*, see Finlayson, *The Seventh Earl of Shaftesbury*, p.111; and Perkins, *Scenes of village labour*, p.iii.

29   G.W.E. Russell, *A Short History of the Evangelical Movement* (London: A.R. Mowbray, 1915).

30   *MTM*, p.102; Russell, *A Short History of the Evangelical Movement*, p.121.

31   Parry, *Democracy and Religion*, p.62; see Bebbington, *Evangelicalism in Modern Britain*, p.99.

32   *MTM*, p.103.

33   See BR54/9, Rachel Gurney's response to Drummond's eccentricity, in a letter to William, October 1848.

34   *MTM*, p.104.

35   BR55/44, Drummond inviting the Cowpers to Albury, 25 July 1849.

36   *MTM*, p.104.

37   BR56/3, Drummond to Georgina, 15 November 1852; in *MTM*, p.105 she recalled being 'carried away…though scepticism always shadowed and bound me'.

38   BR56/1, Baylee to Georgina, 1 January 1853. William made critical notes on Irving and Mormons in his notebook, BR45/18/2.

39   *MTM*, p.105.

40   See BR56/14, Edward Huntingford to William, 8 March 1881.

41   William supported with Shaftesbury the Palestine Exploration Fund established to uncover Biblical illustration (identifying Israelite settlements, and researching the area's zoology and botany) and hosted a meeting at Broadlands, *Quarterly Statement, Palestine Exploration Fund* (1877), p.87.

42   *Caledonian Mercury*, 30 September 1864. The Broadlands papers preserve no detailed engagement with the 'neological' works which worried Shaftesbury, thus, though Georgina read J.R. Seeley's *Ecce Homo* (1865), one finds no sustained discussion of Colenso's *Critical Examination of the Pentateuch* (1862), or *Essays and Reviews* (1860) comprising controversial essays by Frederick Temple, Benjamin Jowett and others. The evidence of a link with Dean Stanley, one of the leading 'neologists', are letters from William to the Dean in 1878, about Père Hyacinthe, see Papers of F.A. White (treasurer of the French Committee of the Anglo-Continental Society), Lambeth Palace Library (MS 1480, ff.365-367), and R.E. Prothero, *The Life and Correspondence of Arthur Penrhyn Stanley: Late Dean of Westminster*

(London: J. Murray, 1894), p.311. Tollemache, *Old and Odd Memories*, p.81, refers to Stanley and Cowper-Temple as leaders of the 'Hell-Abolition Company'.

43 *PD*, 3rd series, vol.96, 11 February 1848, col.476. See Ashley's comment on his brother-in-law's speech in BR, SHA/PD/5, f.29, diary entry for 12 February 1848; reports in *The Jewish Herald and Record of Christian Efforts for the Spiritual Good of God's Ancient People*, 1848; *Missionary Register*, August 1847, p.334; and allusion by W.F. Campbell, *A Short statement of the grounds which justify the House of Lords in repeating their decision of last year upon the Jewish question* (London: F. and J. Rivington, 1849), p.23.

44 BR44/2/2, William to Sir Culling Eardley Smith, 4 December 1840. Ashley was trying to influence Palmerston about Jewish colonization, and although there were geopolitical reasons why this could be entertained by the latter, E. Bar-Yosef, 'Christian Zionism and Victorian Culture', *Israel Studies* 8: 2 (summer 2003), pp.18-44, argues that Ashley's espousal of restoration of the Jews put him 'beyond the cultural consensus', associated as this cause was with eccentricity and religious enthusiasm.

45 BR, Palmerston Papers, GC/CO/232, William to Palmerston, 14 December 1849.

46 BR58/3, Georgina's diary entry for 28 February 1867.

47 Lambeth Palace Library, Tait Papers 162, ff.231-236, Douglas to Tait, 5 April 1869, which *inter alia* shows Georgina interceded with Tait when Douglas had an accident; Manuscripts and Special Collections, University of Nottingham, Bu 22/65, William to Sir A. Buchanan, 17 May 1867: William did not 'in the least agree with the notions that are filling his mind as to the diplomacy of Europe', which were better suited to the ambitions 'of the 3 Emperors than to the progress of liberty & justice & to the National Conscience of England'. William had helped Douglas obtain his living in Northamptonshire.

48 *MTM*, p.105; C.E. Raven, *Christian Socialism. 1848-1854* (London: Macmillan, 1920), p.280, mentions William's support for cooperative distribution. A useful entrée is C. Walsh, 'The Incarnation and the Christian Socialist Conscience in the Victorian Church of England', *Journal of British Studies* 34: 3 (July 1995), pp.351-374.

49 Parry, *Democracy and Religion*, p.60.

50 BR58/2, Georgina's diary entry for 12 January 1862; see E.C. Mack and W.H.G. Armytage, *Thomas Hughes. The Life of the Author of Tom Brown's Schooldays* (London: Benn, 1952), p.53.

51 BR50/45, F.D. Maurice to William, 31 July [1860].

52 BR58/2, Georgina's diary entry for 15 October 1862.

53 BR58/2, Georgina's diary entry for 21 October 1862.

54 Houghton Papers, MSS 6/207. Other Maurice-related correspondence on patronage includes a letter from Charles Kingsley, BR50/26, 14 June 1869; and Gladstone, BR50/14, 13 October 1869.

55 See O. J. Brose, *Frederick Denison Maurice. Rebellious Conformist* (Athens, Ohio: Ohio University Press, 1961).

56 BR58/2, Georgina's diary entry for December 1862. H.R. Haweis, 'Frederick Denison Maurice', *Contemporary Review*, June 1894, pp.873-886 [p.876] recalls meeting Maurice in the company of John Morley, Evelyn Ashley and Shaftesbury at Broadlands or Curzon Street.

57 BR43/21/3, William to Georgina [1855].

58 BR58/7, Georgina's diary entry for 10 March 1877; BR55/29, Georgina F. Maurice to Georgina, *c.*1862. Marguerite Tollemache was an old friend of Mrs Maurice, see dedication to *French Jansenists, by the author of 'Many Voices' and 'Spanish Mystics'* (London: Kegan Paul, Trench and Trübner, 1893). William joined a 'Maurice Club', see BR58/10, Georgina's diary entry for 25 April 1882.

59 Kingsley turned to William for preferment; and became a friend, see *MTM*, p.106. He supported the Ladies' Sanitary Association. His *David: Four Sermons Preached Before the University of Cambridge* (1865) in the Parrish Collection, Princeton University, is inscribed

'Mrs Wm Cowper with the very kind regards of the Author.' William gave information on Palmerston's response to cholera in 1853, to Mrs Kingsley, writing her husband's life, see BL, Kingsley Papers, Add. MSS 41299, f.250. Thomas Hughes in *MTM*, p.151, recalled first meeting William *c*.1848 at Lincoln's Inn Chapel. William's attempt to advance his career with Gladstone is documented in BR50/14, Gladstone to William, 30 September 1872. On Robertson, a 'great and helpful delight', see *MTM*, p.65.

60   *MTM*, p.151.
61   Parry, *Democracy and Religion*, p.71.
62   R.A.J. Walling, ed., *The Diaries of John Bright* (London: Cassell, 1930) p.341, 31 May 1869.
63   *PD*, 3rd series, vol.205, 29 March 1871, col.844. On Church rates, a grievance for Dissenters which he hoped to address by allowing contributions for non-Anglican places of worship to be considered, see H.E. Carlisle, ed., *A Selection from the Correspondence of Abraham Hayward*, vol.2, p.17. William had supported Ashley and others in the repeal of the Conventicle Act, see *MTM*, p.40 (12 October 1846).
64   'Mr Cowper-Temple and the Act of Uniformity', *Hampshire Telegraph*, 8 July 1871.
65   *PD*, 3rd series, vol.215, 14 May 1873, cols.1962-1966; see his Arnoldian treatment of comprehensive Anglicanism, *PD*, 3rd series, vol.209, 20 February 1872, col.791; 'Mr Cowper-Temple and occasional sermons', *Gentleman's Magazine*, 1873, p.334.
66   'Mr Cowper-Temple and the Occasional Preachers', *Hampshire Telegraph*, 29 June 1872.
67   *Vanity Fair*, 7 September 1872.
68   'Dissenters in Church Pulpits', BR206/2, from unidentified newspaper.
69   'The Chesterfield Letters of 1873', *London Society*, 24: 142, October 1873, p.312.
70   Copies of these bills are in BR44/17/1-2.
71   *PD*, 3rd series, vol.205, 29 March 1871, cols. 843-845. Shaftesbury wished to promote the 'priesthood of all the laity' too, see Battiscombe, *Shaftesbury*, p.104.
72   Parry, *Democracy and Religion*, p.100.
73   Roberts, *Making English Morals*, p.257.
74   Parry, *Democracy and Religion*, p.45, pp.99-100; Marsh, *The Victorian Church in Decline*, pp.40-51.
75   *MTM*, p.76; *Report of the Church Congress* (1870) p.11. See *Addresses of the Earl of Shaftesbury and the Honourable W.F. Cowper*, p.15, for earlier thoughts on a state system of rate-maintained schools necessitating 'the sword of secularism'.
76   Asserted in a published letter, 7 August 1876, see C. Wordsworth, *Diocesan Addresses delivered at his Third triennial Visitation in the year 1876* (Lincoln: Williamson, 1876), pp.54-56.
77   Parry, *Democracy and Religion*, p.434. See the joint letter to *The Times*, 4 November, pp.9-10; and his letter, 25 November 1885, p.15 on the Church as defence against atheism and its duty to aid all parishioners especially the poor, suffering and ignorant. The context, Whig aristocrats' attempt to counter the Liberation Society, is referenced in Jenkins, *Gladstone, Whiggery and the Liberal Party*, p.223; Parry, *Rise and Fall of Liberal Government*, p.265. See BR43/28/2, for William to Georgina, 5 April 1871, concerning the Church Reform Union, on which, see G.I.T. Machin, *Politics and the Churches in Great Britain. 1869 to 1921* (Oxford: Clarendon Press, 1987) p.49.
78   BR, SHA/PD/7, f.43, Shaftesbury's diary entry for 14 February 1856; see also entry in late May, f.56 and 8 June, f.57, see J. Wolffe, 'Lord Palmerston and Religion: A Reappraisal', *English Historical Review* 120: 488 (2005), pp.907-936; and Finlayson, *Shaftesbury*, pp.378-379, fn. 43 and fn. 44; p.381. N.A.D. Scotland, *'Good and Proper Men'. Lord Palmerston and the Bench of Bishops* (Cambridge: J. Clarke, 2000), draws on Shaftesbury's diaries and correspondence with Palmerston but neglects his anxiety about William's role.
79   BR, SHA/PD/7, f.57, Shaftesbury's diary entry for 8 June 1856; J.L. and B. Hammond, *Lord Shaftesbury* (1923, Harmondsworth: Pelican, 1939), p.222.
80   BR50/25, Palmerston to William, 11 August 1856.

81 My thanks to Michael Roberts for the reference to this, in a letter to Milnes, 25 August 1856, Houghton Papers, CB88/3 (1), 25 August [1856]; see also Houghton Papers, MSS6/197 (3).

82 *MTM*, p.107; BR50/36, Wilberforce to William, 21 June 1856: 'I thank you on behalf of religion' (William was cautious in reply, see Wilberforce's reply, BR50/36, 23 June 1856); BR, WFC/T/4-5, letters from Richard C. Trench, 19 February and 4 July 1856; M. Trench, ed., *Richard Chenevix Trench, archbishop. Letters and memorials* (London: Kegan Paul, Trench and Co., 1888), vol.1, p.309. Cowper discussed with Milnes the retirement of Trench, who 'might advantageously be installed in the tranquil post of Dean where he might devote his energies to study and exercise his taste in his Cathedral', see Houghton Papers, CB88/3 (1), 25 August [1856]. BR43/24/9, William to Georgina [1855], seems to discuss Trench as lacking the abilities to manage a large London parish, 'more Literary than Parochial'.

83 *MTM*, p.106. Maurice resigned this in 1869 for health reasons. See also BR50/26, Tait of London asking William to press the claims of a former Fellow of Balliol, after the death of Bishop Villiers, 19 August 1861.

84 BR43/21/19, William to Georgina, 16 March [1855], BR43/22/1, William to Georgina [1855]; BR/43/25/2, William to Georgina [1855]. For the view of Ryle's wife, a close friend of Georgina, see BR56/7, Jessy Ryle to Georgina, 25 March [1855].

85 BR43/24/4, William to Georgina, 25 April [1855].

86 BR45/17/3, William's notes from C.M. Sawell, on Sunday openings of Galleries, April 1883; *MTM*, p.19 records earlier (1837) qualms about Sunday dining.

87 Tollemache, *Old and Odd Memories*, p.149.

88 See *Moody and Sankey, the new evangelists, their lives and labours* (1876), p.68, for a meeting at the Islington Agricultural Hall, involving Cowper-Temple on the platform.

89 BR45/19, William's notebook entry on Moody; 'Rt Hon. W. Cowper-Temple MP on Religion', *Hampshire Telegraph*, 10 April 1875. W.D. Maclagan, Bishop of Lichfield, invited to Broadlands for the conference, discussed Moody and Sankey with William in December 1874, believing the Church should cooperate with them.

90 BR47/11, clipping of *The Christian*, 1 April 1886, no. 844.

91 H.W. Smith mss, Lilly Library, letter from William, 4 January 1875.

92 BR45/19, William's notebook entry headed 'Salvation Army'.

93 BR45/19, William's notes on Prayer Book and further notes on Salvation Army.

94 BR45/19; see also note in BR45/18/3, 31 May 1888, on Eva Booth, 'the sympathy of the lower classes is with her'.

95 K. Hylson-Smith, *Evangelicals in the Church of England* (Edinburgh: T&T. Clark, 1988), p.179. Shaftesbury feared threats to his missions, see Hodder, *Shaftesbury*, vol.3, pp.433-440.

96 *Hampshire Telegraph*, 20 May 1882; *Belfast News Letter*, 17 May 1882.

97 *The Official Year-book of the Church of England* (1883), p.420; *Romsey Advertiser*, 18 October 1901.

98 BR45/19, William's note dated 'J 84': the Church Army's founder, Wilson Carlisle, dined with them, see BR58/11, Georgina's diary entry for 21 June 1884. On Clifford's Church Army activity, see BR44/16/15; and Clifford, *Broadlands as it was*, pp.138-152.

99 E.V. Jackson, *The Life that is Life Indeed: Reminiscences of Broadlands Conferences* (London: J. Nisbet, 1910) p.42.

100 S.P. Day, *Life in a Convent* (London: A. Hall, 1847), p.22. Day became a reporter.

101 See BR50/44, Johann Czerski to William, 29 August 1846.

102 BR50/44, Bunsen to Cowper, 31 August 1849.

103 BR50/43, a letter by Antonio Panizzi, 25 August [1844], criticises the attempt.

104 BR, SHA/PD/7, f.43, Shaftesbury's diary entry for 14 February 1856.

105 Parry, *Democracy and Religion*, p.427.

[106]   BL, Gladstone Papers, Add. MSS 44464, f.253, 14 June 1880, for arranging a breakfast meeting. See notes on Old Catholics in Georgina's diary, BR58/6, 25 May 1876.

[107]   BL, Gladstone Papers, Add. MSS 44460, f.132, 6 June 1879. See also Gladstone's letter to William, 7 August 1879, in BR50/14, which refers to the 'arduous nature' and 'excellent object in view' of Cowper-Temple's undertaking. Another letter, BR50/14, of 25 June 1879, discusses French, Swiss and eastern religion connections, in order to strengthen the hand of a reforming or moderate party in the Catholic Church.

[108]   Shannon, *Gladstone and the Bulgarian Agitation*, p.9.

[109]   BL, Gladstone Papers, Add. MSS 44466, f.248, 2 November 1880; Papers of F.A. White, Lambeth Palace Library (MS 1480), ff.352-356, especially f.356, 5 July 1880 concerning Gladstone.

[110]   Count Enrico di Campello, BR48/4/13, C.R. Conybeare to William, 8 August 1883.

[111]   BL, Ripon Papers, Add. MSS 43625, f.190, 14 September 1874. See also L. Wolf, *Life of the first Marquis of Ripon* (London: J. Murray, 1921), p.350.

[112]   Parry, *Democracy and Religion*, pp.43-45.

[113]   See *PD*, 3rd series, vol.221, 28 July 1874, for William's interventions in the committee stage of the bill, to ensure 'common sense' prevailed by giving bishops discretionary powers. For his support for the bill's anti-ritualism, see *PD*, 3rd series, vol.221, 17 July 1874, col.263. See Marsh, *The Victorian Church in Decline*, p.198; Lambeth Palace Library, Tait Papers 237 ff.148-149.

[114]   Clifford, *Broadlands as it was*, p.9.

[115]   *MTM*, p.48 (Shaftesbury); *MTM*, p.68 (Palmerston); BR55/48, Georgina to Emelia Gurney, Broadlands, postmarked 23 [January or June] 1871, on Newman.

[116]   Reynolds, *Aristocratic Women*, pp.73-80 (p71); see *MTM*, p.48

[117]   Gurney, *Letters of Emelia Russell Gurney*, p.159 (Gurney to Andrew Jukes, 5 March 1877). On the gendered experience of death and disease in this period, and the insight that 'Christianity ...fed on the dying', see Prochaska, *Women and Philanthropy*, p.123, p.160.

[118]   Bradley, *Letters of John Ruskin to Lord and Lady Mount Temple*, p.11. Bradley admitted the 'hint of the sanctimonious' is based on a reading that is fragmentary (p.8).

[119]   Tollemache, *Some Reminiscences*, p.10.

[120]   *MTM*, p.117.

[121]   See the letters from Julia Tomkinson to Georgina in BR56/24.

[122]   S. Oldfield, *Jeanie, an 'Army of One'. Mrs Nassau Senior. 1828–1877. The First Woman in Whitehall* (Brighton: Sussex Academic Press, 2008); J. Lewis, *Women and Social Action in Victorian England* (Aldershot: Edward Elgar, 1991), p.28.

[123]   Bebbington, *Evangelicalism in Modern Britain*, p.92. See Erskine's *The Unconditional Freeness of the Gospel* (1828).

[124]   BR58/2, Georgina's diary entry for 26 June 1862. William had notes from Erskine, 1860, see BR44/16/9. Erskine's letter to Emelia Gurney in May 1862 includes good wishes for Mrs Cowper, see W. Hanna, ed., *Letters of Thomas Erskine of Linlathen, from 1840 till 1870* (1877; Edinburgh: David Douglas, 1884), p.592.

[125]   BR56/24, Baylee to Georgina, 13 April 1850. On Baylee, see *MTM*, p.62. His zealotry stimulated violence between Irish Catholics and Protestants in Birkenhead in 1862.

[126]   BR56/24, Baylee and Georgina, 22 July 1850. On relationships between aristocratic women and clergymen, see Reynolds, *Aristocratic Women*, pp.80-91.

[127]   It will be recalled that *MTM* states she was perplexed by the incompatibility of a loving God with fears of the perilous world beyond her home, fostered by her Evangelical sisters, a variation of the ethical or moral doubts which scholars of the Victorian crisis of faith identify as operating *prior* to the impact of Biblical criticism and evolutionism, see S. Budd, *Varieties of Unbelief. Atheists and Agnostics in English Society 1850–1960* (London: Heinemann,

1977); H.R. Murphy, 'The ethical revolt against Christian orthodoxy in early Victorian England', *American Historical Review* 60: 4 (1955), pp.800-817.

128 BR56/24, Julia Tomkinson to Georgina. J. Godwin, *The Theosophical Enlightenment* (Albany: State University of New York Press, 1994), examines Boehme's appeal among Christian esoterics in this period, p.228.

129 BR56/15, E.J. Gibbs (of Bellfield Road, Brixton) to Georgina, 25 September 1877.

130 See BR49/13, Penny to Georgina, '23 July'. Anne Judith Penny was the widow of Edward Burton Penny, another scholar of mysticism; see her *Studies in Jacob Böhme* (London: J. Watkins, 1912), and C.C. Massey, *Light*, 30 December 1893. A.M.H. Watts' letters allow this episode to be pieced together, see BR55, e.g., BR58/8, 11 July 1880.

131 Myers Papers, 3/73. See *Glasgow Herald*, 28 February 1871, and *Ipswich Journal*, 18 July 1871 for reviews of her pseudonymous *Gifts for Men* (by 'X.H.', Edinburgh: Edmonston and Douglas, 1870).

132 Quoted in Gurney, *Letters of Emelia Russell Gurney*, p.147. See BR56/16, Farquhar to Georgina, 7 October 1886. Farquhar had been Presbyterian, Swedenborgian, spiritualist and atheist. See BR55 for his intended involvement with the Greaves text, and E. Keary, *Memoir of Annie Keary, by her Sister* (London: Macmillan, 1882), p.207, for reference to him, and obituary, *Aberdeen Weekly Journal*, 2 November 1898.

133 See preface to *Hamartia: an enquiry into the Nature and origin of Evil* (London, Elliot Stock, 1878), on the Broadlands conference's role in encouraging him to publish this work; R. Noel, 'Gospel of Divine Humanity', *Academy*, June 1884, pp.449-450; *Things to Come. Being Essays towards a fuller apprehension of the Christian Idea* (1892): see *Liverpool Mercury*, 11 November 1891, for a pre-publication review. After earlier associations with the Ladies' Sanitary Association, William supported Blackwell's work to aid little girl paupers, 'Such a horror!!!' Georgina noted, BR58/10, diary entry for 23 May 1882.

134 BR48/4/8, Pulsford to the Cowper-Temples, 28 July 1879. Pulsford supported the Esoteric Christian Union. Pulsford's mystical influence is recalled in J.E. Hine, *Days Gone By: Being some Account of Past Years Chiefly in Central Africa* (London: J. Murray, 1924), p.3. Pulsford died in 1897.

135 BR57/69/12, Pulsford to William, Edinburgh, 13 March 1882.

136 W. Garret Horder, 'Character Sketch: George MacDonald: a Nineteenth Century Seer', *Review of Reviews*, 32: 190 (October 1905), p.360; 'John Pulsford', *The Speaker*, 29 March 1897, p.596.

137 BR56/20, J. Garth Wilkinson to Georgina, 13 December 1879; see BR56/1, a short note from Blavatsky's successor, Annie Besant, to Georgina, 29 May 1894.

138 BR56/14, Kingsford to Georgina, 27 Montpelier Square, Rutland Gate, 1 May; BR53/42, continued in BR57/62/16, Kingsford, 3 July [1884] 21 Henrietta Street, Cavendish Square.

139 BR59/1, undated letter to Juliet requesting the copy of Kingsford and Maitland's *The Perfect Way; or, the Finding of Christ* (1882); letter from Oliphant, n.d., in BR50/21 in which he asked 'is it not a strange book?'

140 BR44/10/17. Maitland kept in touch, see BR57/65/10, after he received *MTM*.

141 See her comments, BR58/5, diary entry for 6 June 1874.

142 *MTM*, p.107; H. Tuttle and J.M. Peebles, *The Yearbook of Spiritualism for 1871* (Boston: W. White, 1871); Smith, *Religious Rebel*, p.67.

143 BR58/2, entries in Georgina's diary for 1862, conversation with Fanny, 9 January, and response to Maurice, 12 January 1862.

144 See BR49/13, several letters from Marguerite Tollemache, n.d. For the 'enabling' role that spiritualism offered women, see A. Owen, *The Darkened Room. Women, Power, and Spiritualism in Late Victorian England* (London: Virago, 1989).

145 BR49/14, Newman Hall to Georgina, 1 January, n.d.

146   See BR49/13, Home to Georgina, attempting to renew the association, 18 April 1870; and BR51/1, for a note on Home in 1874, by William.

147   *MTM*, p.107; BR58/2, Georgina's diary entry for 1 January 1862.

148   BR58/5, Georgina's diary entry for 24 February 1874.

149   BR58/5, Georgina's diary entry for 1 November 1874.

150   BR58/2, Georgina's diary entry for 6 January 1862.

151   BR45/9, note on séance *c.* October 1869.

152   *MTM*, p.108.

153   On Leaf, see 'M.A., Oxon' [W. Stainton Moses], *Spirit-Identity* (London: W.H. Harrison, 1879), 'Child-Spirits communicating'. Moses had been introduced to her at the Cowper-Temples. Several letters from Moses on spiritual healing and automatic writing are in BR50/43, *c.*1883. For séances with Leaf, see entries in notebook BR45/9, e.g., for 1 September 1876; BR55 has letters from A.M.H. Watts seeking to contact the healer Mary Gove Nichols to attend to Leaf's health.

154   BR45/9, note on séance with Julia Leaf, 23 February 1877.

155   See *Light*, 20 October 1888, p.519.

156   BR56/6, John Morley to Georgina, 28 April 1874.

157   BR57/65/1. Dated 9 September 1883.

158   Tollemache, *Old and Odd Memories*, p.85; probably on the basis of the pivotal meeting between Myers and Stainton Moses, 9 May 1874. For letters from Edmund Gurney, see BR55/68. Gurney's brother Alfred attended the Broadlands conference in 1876. They were nephews of Emelia Gurney.

159   BR50/46, T.L. Harris to William, 1875.

160   BR45/8/1-2, notebooks covering conversations and quoting from letters from Harris and followers, from 1867 to 1878.

161   BR56/9, Mary Eliza Ruxton to Georgina, Staten Island, 17 November 1868.

162   Oliphant asked if Harris could recuperate by fishing at Broadlands, see letter from Oliphant to Georgina, in BR50/21, n.d.

163   BR50/46, T.L. Harris to William, 22 February 1875, on William's health and the cottage; see the notebook BR45/8/1, on the fairies and Georgina's name.

164   BR50/46, T.L. Harris to Georgina, 12 March 1875 (fragment).

165   *MTM*, p.108.

166   BR43/20/11, William to Georgina, n.d. [references to Russians, Roth and Beveridge suggest a date of 1855, yet Harris was not in England until 1859]. See *MTM*, p.61.

167   See the notebook BR45/8/1: 'Pray for more conjugial love, it is an element of Regeneration', BR45/8/2. Conjugial celestial relations were a Swedenborgian theme. See B. Strachey, *Remarkable Relations. The Story of the Pearsall Smith Family* (London: Gollancz, 1980) p.104, for Hannah Smith's comment that Georgina had been led to think that the 'objectionable part of their practices' was abandoned.

168   Gurney, *Letters of Emelia Russell Gurney*, p.112, p.119, pp.121-22. BR57/68/4, is a fragment of A.J. Penny's letter to Georgina on Hannah's 'admirable' précis, 23 September 1880.

169   BR43/48, William to Berridge, 22 April 1881.

170   BR58/6, references in Georgina's diary for 1876, e.g., 23 February. BR55/45, Georgina, writing to 'dear Friend of the Past and Future', Broadlands, Thursday 28 September [1882], a fragment, perhaps to Harris.

171   *MTM*, p.108. Letters from Oliphant to them appear in H.W. Schneider and G. Lawton, *A Prophet and a Pilgrim* (New York: Columbia University Press, 1942). The Cowper-Temples sent a painting of St Anthony to him, *c.*1870, see Clifford, *Broadlands as it was*, p.4.

172   BR50/46, Reverend H.B. Browning of Stamford, 6 March 1877, told William that the Bible if subjected to the same study as Jukes' on Harris, might be rendered doubtful.

173   *MTM*, p.108, my emphasis.

174 BR58/5, Georgina's diary entries for 26–27 December 1874.
175 See *The Times*, 4 January 1875, p.8, William's appeal for money – he sought legal redress for their eviction; H.W. Smith mss, Lilly Library, Georgina to Hannah, 3 January 1875. On the sect, see P. Hoare, *England's Lost Eden*, and D. Hardy, *Alternative Communities in Nineteenth Century England* (London: Longman, 1979) pp.145-150.
176 BR58/13, Georgina's diary entry for 20 September 1886.
177 Tollemache, *Old and Odd Memories*, p.80.
178 Tollemache, *Old and Odd Memories*, p.84.
179 BR56/24, R.J. Morrison to William, 11 October 1850; BR49/14, fragment of letter, n.d., 'a vast number of Educated people congregate we believe daily – Fashionable men, Ladies of high rank who bring Children to hear questions put…'
180 BR58/6, Georgina's diary entries for 7 and 11 October 1876. In response to Bacon's *Essay on Truth*, she told the Baconian Robert Theobald 'I don't agree with Bacon: No one loves a lie for its own sake', see Theobald's *Shakespeare Studies in Baconian Light* (London: Sampson, Marston, Low, 1901), p.54.
181 Fletcher, *Parliamentary Portraits*, p.133.
182 See Gurney, *Letters of Emelia Russell Gurney*, pp.142-150; Jackson, *The Life that is Life Indeed*; Clifford, *Broadlands as it was* (1890; in abbreviated form in *MTM*, pp.139-142) and *Fragments from a Broadlands Conference. Love, Faith, Life* (Hereford, 1887); Smith, 'Lord Mount Temple'. See *Hampshire Independent*, 21 July 1888, on the final conference.
183 Hare, *Story of My Life*, vol.4, 20 July 1875, p.340.
184 BR49/3, anon., *Private and Confidential. Letters relating to the Conference on the Higher Life Held at Broadlands 1875* (London: Carter, 1875), an eighteen page account.
185 Suggestions for the Meeting, a printed card dated 17 July 1875, in BR58/6, Georgina's diary for 1876.
186 BR190/17, 'On Leaving Broadlands', Theodore Monod, Broadlands, 20 July 1885.
187 BR50/28, R.P. Smith to William, 22 September 1874.
188 Bebbington, *Evangelicalism in Modern Britain*, pp.151-180. Bebbington shows that before the Smiths, there was a renewal of interest in holiness in British Methodism. Bebbington (dating the first conference as 1873) emphasizes the affinity (though not identity) of Keswick and Broadlands (p.171). See M.E. Dieter, *The Holiness Revival of the Nineteenth Century* (1980; Lanham, Maryland: Scarecrow Press, 1996); L.E. Elliott-Binns, *Religion in the Victorian Era* (1936; London: Lutterworth Press, 1964) p.225; and D. Hilborn and D. Horrocks, 'Universalistic trends in the Evangelical tradition: A Historical perspective', ch.11 in R.A. Parry and C.H. Partridge, eds, *Universal Salvation?: The Current Debate* (Grand Rapids, Michigan: W.B. Eerdmans, 2003), pp.229-230.
189 *The Evangelical Magazine and Missionary Chronicle*, May 1877, p.286; and the detailed review of critical pamphlets, in 'The Brighton Convention and its doctrinal Teaching', *Quarterly Review*, 44: 89 (October 1875), pp.84-128.
190 Clifford, *Broadlands as it was*, p.16. Clifford was present and said it was Georgina, but in *MTM*, pp.117-118, she said William offered, when another estate became unavailable.
191 *The Christian*, 21 August 1879. A letter to William listing students from Cambridge is in BR50/45, from Charles Lea Wilson of Trinity College, 11 June 1874.
192 'Prospectus', *Christian's Pathway of Power*, 1:1, February 1874.
193 *Christian's Pathway of Power*, 1 August 1874, p.124; *Sunday at Home*, November 1874, p.767.
194 A letter from Lilias Trotter to Georgina is preserved at BR57/72/13.
195 BR50/41, Robert Westlake to William, 17 September 1875. Jukes 'unveiled' Jewish history with Douglas at the conference, *MTM*, p.123.
196 A.J. Mason, *Memoir of George Howard Wilkinson* (1909; 2 vols, London: Longmans, 1910), vol.1, p.321. The phrase is Maud Warrender's, *My First Sixty Years* (London: Cassell, 1933),

p.16. For Clifford's concern that Wilkinson might be wary, BR55/43. In BR48/4/4, 12 July 1877, Wilkinson suggested guests.

[197] BR50/45, G.R. Thornton to William, 4 and 19 November 1874; BR50/48, Stevenson Blackwood to William, n.d.

[198] H.S.M. Blackwood, *Some Record of the Life of Sir Arthur Stevenson Blackwood, K.C.B. Compiled by a friend and edited by his widow* (London: Hodder and Stoughton, 1896), p.328.

[199] *MTM*, pp.126-127 (Monod and St Hilaire, who spoke of the curse of Babel being lifted); the Smiths brought the Higher Life to France and Germany before the conference. On Franco-German amity at the conference, see Jukes, *MTM*, p.148.

[200] BR44/14, recollections by Clifford (1875). The pastiche of participants was bequeathed to the Church Army in 1907 (information kindly supplied by Mrs Pat Lee) and passed to Keswick Conference; subsequently sold, the image reproduced in this study derives from Cholmeley, *Edward Clifford*, p.86.

[201] NLS, MS 11388/96, letter from William, 15 Great Stanhope Street, 26 July [1874].

[202] NLS, Ashburton Papers, Acc.11388/116, William to Lady Ashburton, 18 September 1874.

[203] Bebbington, *Evangelicalism in Modern Britain*, p.161. On the conference at Brighton, see *Record of the Convention for the Promotion of Scriptural Holiness, May 29th to June 7th 1875* (Brighton: W.J. Smith, 1875), which refers to Broadlands and Georgina's role, p.19.

[204] *Christian's Pathway of Power*, 1 September 1874, p.165.

[205] *Christian's Pathway of Power*, 1 January 1875.

[206] *Christian's Pathway of Power*, 1 September 1874, p.165; BR50/45, 16 December 1874.

[207] BR50/28, R.P. Smith to William, 22 September 1874; BR50/42, Fishbourne, 24 December 1874. Fishbourne was a friend of Shaftesbury and Pennefather.

[208] BR50/42, Paul Gobat to William, Bâle, 20 October and 31 October 1874.

[209] The journal ran from 1875-1878, and was continued as *Der Glaubensbote*. See S. Fuchser, *Auf der Suche nach Erneuerung und Erweckung. Carl Heinrich Rappard und die Oxford Bewegung* (Riehen/Basel, 2005).

[210] H.W. Smith mss, Lilly Library, note by Hannah on envelope of letter dated 4 January 1875, from William; BR50/28, R.P. Smith to William, 25 December 1874. Fishbourne's anti-spiritualism is noted in *Spiritual Magazine*, 1874, p.161.

[211] H.W. Smith mss, Lilly Library, Georgina to Hannah, January 1875.

[212] BL, Gladstone Papers, Add. MSS 44447, f.32, letter to Gladstone, 10 April 1875. Moody stayed with Stevenson Blackwood: critics of the Holiness movement were more favourable to Moody, see *Quarterly Review*, 44: 89 (October 1875), p.87.

[213] BL, Gladstone Papers, Add. MSS 44447, ff.147-8, 17 May 1875.

[214] Blackwood, *Life of Sir Arthur Stevenson Blackwood*, p.335.

[215] BL, Gladstone Papers, Add. MSS 44447, ff.195-6, 4 June 1875. BL, Gladstone Papers, Add. MSS 44447, f.205, 8 June 1875, Gladstone declined.

[216] *Evangelical Christendom*, 2 August 1875.

[217] BR50/28, Hannah Smith to Georgina, March 1876. Taylor, *Laurence Oliphant*, p.237, notes, in the posthumously published *Religious Fanaticism* (1928) that Hannah identified the source as the American spiritualist Dr Foster.

[218] 'London and Paris Gossip', *Trewman's Exeter Flying Post*, 5 January 1876; also *Freeman's Journal*, 15 October 1875; *Liverpool Mercury*, 21 December 1875; *North Wales Chronicle*, 25 December 1875; *Newcastle Courant*, 7 January 1876, quoting *North British Review*; *The Record*, 14 January 1876; and N.A.D. Scotland, *Evangelical Anglicans in a Revolutionary Age, 1789-1901* (Carlisle: Paternoster Press, 2004), p.276.

[219] BR44/15/9, note by William, 'March '76'.

[220] BR50/28, Hannah Smith to Georgina, 25 April 1876.

[221] BR50/28, R.P. Smith to William, 4 July [c.1876–1877]; R.P. Smith to William, 6 January 1877.

222 BR50/28, Hannah Smith to Georgina, 25 January 1875; 'London Gossip', *Freeman's Journal*, 15 October, 1875.

223 Anon., *Letters relating to the Conference on the Higher Life Held at Broadlands 1875*; Gurney, *Letters of Emelia Russell Gurney*, p.146.

224 BR44/14, notes by Edward Clifford, Isel Hall, Cockermouth [August 1875].

225 BR58/6, 16 August 1876; H.W. Smith mss, Lilly Library, letter from William, 14 November 1876.

226 BR50/43, Radstock to William, 27 July 1877.

227 Trotter dates this to the 'early 80s', see E. Trotter, *Lord Radstock. An Interpretation and Record* (London: Hodder and Stoughton, 1914), p.30, p.86.

228 BR50/45, Radstock to William, 'Tuesday 25th'.

229 BR50/46, Eli Johnson to William, 14 August 1878; Mary Johnson, to Cowper-Temples, 18 August 1878. See the Dean of Melbourne's reports from this conference, H.B. Macartney, *England, Home and Beauty. Sketches of Christian Life and Work in England* (1880).

230 BR49/1, letter from J.W. Farquhar, 30 July 1878; BR49/3, Niebuhr, 19 August 1878.

231 See BR49/3, Keith-Falconer to William, 18 August 1878; R. Sinker, *Memorials of the Honourable Ion Keith-Falconer* (Cambridge: Deighton, Bell and Co., 1888), p.51, pp.66-67. Guy Thorne entitled the relevant chapter, 'David and Jonathan' and spoke of their friendship 'passing the love of women', see Thorne, *The Great Acceptance*, p.84.

232 A. Smith, *An Autobiography. The Story of the Lord's Dealings with Mrs Amanda Smith the Coloured Evangelist* (Chicago, Illinois: Meyer, 1893), pp.260-261, p.274; 'The Experience of Mrs Amanda Smith', *The Christian*, 21 August 1879, p.9; BR49/3, Hopkins to William, 29 July 1878; the verdict on Amanda is George J. Monteith, in a letter in BR50/41, 15 August 1879. On Hopkins and Broadlands, see A. Smellie, *Evan Henry Hopkins. A Memoir* (London: Marshall, 1920), pp.62-64.

233 BR50/43, Francis McDougall (former bishop of Sarawak) to William, 4 August 1879.

234 *Hampshire Observer*, 13 August 1887, p.7; BR49/5, 1 August 1883.

235 Maitland, *Anna Kingsford*, vol.2, pp.236-237, letter dated 27 August 1886.

236 *Hampshire Observer*, 13 August 1887, p.7, *Hampshire Chronicle*, 6 August 1887, p.5; BR56/15, Forbes-Robertson to Georgina, 8 August 1887; BR53/9, Jukes to Georgina, quoting Clifford, 6 August 1887.

237 The Catholic Stanton's response is recorded in *MTM*, p.131. Hulda Beamish, memorialized by Karl von Bergen, was grandmother of Hermann Goring's first wife.

238 Smith, 'Lord Mount Temple'; BR49/3, Edward Clifford to Emelia Gurney, 18.7.88 [sic].

239 Additional testimony includes W.S. Rainsford, *The Story of a Varied Life* (1923; Ayer, 1970), p.145, by the son of Lord Roden's vicar and friend of Frederick Charrington.

240 Russell, *Portraits of the Seventies*, p.286; G.W.E. Russell, *The Household of Faith. Portraits and Essays* (London: Hodder and Stoughton, 1902), pp.208-210.

241 BR50/42, Edward Clifford, n.d; T.E. Varley to William, 30 July 1886.

242 Russell, *The Household of Faith*, pp.208-210.

243 BR190/17, Monod, 'On Leaving Broadlands', 20 July 1885; Macartney, *England, Home and Beauty*, p.73. Emelia Gurney, in *MTM*, p.123, wrote of her 'swift imagination ... at the service of charity', ready to encourage timid participants or prevent a jar between speakers.

244 *Christian's Pathway of Power*, 1 July 1874. The journal had contributions from Hannah Smith and Mrs Rundle Charles. On female public roles in the holiness movement, see Bebbington, *Evangelicalism in Modern Britain*, p.175. Emelia Gurney's comments on Hannah's 'sun-illumined' intervention in 1874 are in *MTM*, p.122.

245 Macartney, *England, Home and Beauty*, p.89.

246 BL, Gladstone Papers, Add. MSS 44461, f.25, 11 September 1879. Baxter had spoken at Keswick.

247 E. Jordan, 'Charlotte M. Yonge, Woman of Letters', *The Princeton University Library Chronicle* 65 (2003), pp.451-478 [p.456]; BR56/7, letter dated 24 July 1888 (Quinton).

248 BR55/43, unidentified correspondent to Jukes, mourning paper, n.d.

249 Jackson, *The Life that is Life Indeed*, p.29; *MTM*, p.115 also calls it an 'adventure'.

250 *The Christian*, 21 August 1879, pp.8-9.

251 Russell, *Portraits of the Seventies*, p.279.

252 Clifford, *Broadlands as it was*; Gurney, *Letters of Emelia Russell Gurney*, p.145; Gurney, *Letters of Emelia Russell Gurney*, p.148 (on William as 'mainspring').

253 On the epithet, *MTM*, p.134; on his view, 14 November 1837, of the *LCM* restoring 'unity of spirit', *London City Mission*, 1837, p.188; on the conferences, BR50/42, draft letter by William to unknown recipient, c.1875.

254 BR50/42, draft letter by William to unknown recipient, c.1875. William informed Canon Westcott: 'We have had high, low and Broad Church, Baptists, independents [sic], Methodists, Quakers – French Protestants – and though Romanists are forbidden by the law of their Church to join in prayer with Protestants two Romish ladies got a novena offered up in a Romish Church on behalf of our first conference,' BR50/41, '2 June', n.d. Westcott founded the Christian Social Union.

255 'The Rt. Hon. William Cowper-Temple, MP, on Religion', *Hampshire Telegraph*, 10 April 1875.

256 H.W. Smith mss, Lilly Library, letter from William, 14 November 1876. Perhaps, like Shaftesbury, who believed (Battiscombe, *Shaftesbury*, pp.272-273) that religion and science would be harmonized, he was unperturbed by Darwinian evolution and modern science in themselves. MacDonald also accepted modern science; see Raeper, *George MacDonald*, p.247. As Marsh notes, *The Victorian Church in Decline*, p.9, this period saw the Church 'defensive and hesitant' in intellectual controversy; William's concerns about scientific arrogance were shared, Gladstone lecturing on the subject at Liverpool College, December 1872, and Archbishop Tait organizing a conference.

257 'Rt Hon. W. Cowper-Temple MP on Religion', *Hampshire Telegraph*, 10 April 1875; on the Camberwell lectures of the London Free Art Gallery, see BR50/38, report for 1888.

258 Maitland, *Anna Kingsford*, vol.2, pp.236-237.

259 Russell, *Household of Faith*, p.210.

260 H.H. Jeaffreson, ed., *The Letters of Andrew Jukes* (London: Longmans, Green, 1903) citing *The Pilot*, 26 October 1901.

261 Letter in BR56/9, Robert C.S. Reade to William, 26 August 1876.

262 *The Christian*, 21 August 1879, pp.8-9.

263 Review of Mrs Augustus Craven, *Reminiscences, Souvenirs d'Angleterre et D'Italie* in *The Nation* 29: 745, 9 October 1879; and *Lippincott's Magazine of Popular Literature and Science* 25, February 1880, pp.258-260. Georgina thought her description of the alteration to Broadlands 'Very pretty & very kind', see BR58/6, diary entry for 21 April 1876; *MTM*, p.93. See M.C. Bishop, *Mrs Augustus Craven* (2 vols, London: Bentley, 1894), vol.1, p.376.

264 A governess from Romsey, Edna Jackson, for instance, published ecstatic memories in 1910. See her verse, BR190/18; and praise for the conference in 1887, BR57/65/7.

265 See Hare, *Story of My Life*, vol.5, 29 October 1880, p.295. This echoed comments by the philanthropist Louisa, Lady Waterford, whose estate at Highcliffe was nearby, Hare, *Story of My Life*, vol.4, 20 July 1875, p.340.

Chapter 12. The Cultural Patronage of the Cowper Temples

1 *MTM*, p.47.

2 *MTM*, p.63 and p.46 (and references to his delight in nature, p.12, p.14).

3 *Glasgow Herald*, 18 October 1888. In opening up their collection, the Cowper-Temples followed a trend developing since the 1800s, see Hoock, 'Reforming culture', p.257.

4   W. Bagehot, 'Wordsworth, Tennyson and Browning, Or, Pure, Ornate, and Grotesque Art
     in English Poetry', *National Review*, n.s., no.1 (November 1864), pp.27-67 [p.54].
5   Lasdun, *Victorians at Home*, p.88, citing the Queen's journal for 29 October 1837.
6   Devonshire to Mitford, 18 May 1837, A.G. L'Estrange, ed., *The Friendships of M.R. Mitford.
     As Recorded in Letters from Her Literary Correspondents* (New York: Harper, 1882), p.245.
7   BR44/5/14, a fragment of William's diary for *c*.21 July [1836], *Aspasia and Pericles* was a
     novel by W.S. Landor, published 1836; BR51/5, entry for 3 December 1836.
8   BR43/12/6, William to Harriet Gurney, Brocket, 1843.
9   Hertfordshire Archives and Local Studies, Bulwer Lytton Papers, D/EK C7/164-166.
     Bulwer's response to critics of his crime fiction was a 'Word to the Public' in 1847.
10   BR59/4, Georgina to Juliet, n.d., writing about a dinner involving Millais, Browning, the
     Austrian ambassador, and Lord Lansdowne.
11   F.W. Haydon, ed., *Benjamin Robert Haydon. Correspondence and Table Talk* (London: Chatto
     and Windus, 1876), p.395, prints a letter to William. Georgina refers to Haydon's
     'wandering ray of genius' after an exhibition, diary BR58/3, 19 January 1867.
12   BR43/24/16, William to Georgina, 30 December [1867].
13   *The Times*, 18 January 1871, p.4.
14   *Glasgow Herald*, 18 October 1888.
15   BR58/5, Georgina's diary entry for 18 February 1874.
16   BR58/2, entry by William in Georgina's diary, 9 October 1862.
17   BR58/2, Georgina's diary entry for 10 October 1862.
18   BR58/6, Georgina's diary entries for 30 March and 28 April 1876.
19   Letter from Lady Elisabeth Theresa Fielding to William Henry Fox Talbot, 12 January
     1846, Fox Talbot Collection, British Library, quoted from the transcription in the William
     Henry Fox Talbot Correspondence project, document no.05526.
20   *MTM*, p.63.
21   *The Athenaeum*, 'Fine Art Gossip', 14 October 1865.
22   On Nesfield's Regent's Park lodge, apart from the essays by Aslet in *Country Life*, 1978,
     cited above, see R.P. Spiers, 'Development of Modern Architecture', *Magazine of Art*
     (January 1898), p.86. On Barry, see *PD*, 3rd series, vol.210, 13 May 1870, cols.670-681
     [col.675]. *The Times*, 6 April 1878, p.10.
23   BR43/25/7, William to Georgina, Ramsgate, some time after Pugin's death (1875).
24   See BR58/20, entry in commonplace book for 25 April 1866 for Georgina's record of a
     disagreement over these.
25   See the list of books (not made by the Cowper-Temples) in BR45/21. The titles in this
     paragraph derive from this document.
26   BR58/13, Georgina's diary for 17 September 1886 on *Washington Square*; BR57/31/17,
     Emelia Gurney to Georgina, 12 February 1886.
27   BR58/13, Georgina's diary entry for 21 September 1886.
28   See BR58/13, Georgina's diary entry for 2 September 1886, on R.L. Stevenson.
29   G.S. Haight, *George Eliot: A Biography* (New York: Oxford University Press, 1968), p.453.
30   G.S. Haight, ed., *The George Eliot Letters* (New York: Oxford University Press, 1956) vol.5,
     p.276. F. Locker-Lampson met Eliot and Lewes at the Mount Temples, see *My Confidences:
     An Autobiographical Sketch Addressed to My Descendants* (London: Smith, Elder, 1896), p.309.
31   BR56/11, Georgina's entry in diary for 1 May 1859; BR58/20, entry in commonplace
     book for *c*.8 July 1866.
32   Gurney, *Letters of Emelia Russell Gurney*, p.261. See BR58/4, Georgina's diary for 1872, for
     passages from, and notes on, Dante. Dante's Victorian revival is discussed in A. Isba,
     Gladstone and Dante: Victorian Statesman, Medieval Poet (London: Boydell Press, 2006).
33   D.J. DeLaura, 'The Poetry of Thought', in J.L. Altholz, *The Mind and Art of Victorian
     England* (Minneapolis: University of Minnesota Press, 1976), pp.35-57; D. Thomas, *Robert*

Browning: A Life within Life (London: Weidenfeld and Nicolson, 1982), pp.129-135; though as Thomas points out, p.167, the poet rejected 'honest doubt' as a fallacy.

34   P. Kelley and R. Hudson, *The Brownings' Correspondence. A Check List* (Winfield, Kansas: Browning Institute, 1978): letters from 1856 in the Armstrong Browning Library, Baylor University, Texas; and database at http://www.browningguide.org/

35   W.S. Peterson, *Interrogating the Oracle* (Athens, Ohio: Ohio University Press, 1969), p.12.

36   E.C. McAleer, *Learned Lady. Letters from Robert Browning to Mrs Thomas FitzGerald* (Cambridge, Massachusetts: Harvard University Press, 1966), letter 51, 17 March 1883; letter 70, 2 April 1887, p.195.

37   BR58/8, Georgina's diary entry for 22 February 1880.

38   See BR50/26, 29 August 1864 on an 'Orgue Expressif' from a Mr Bunsen. On Wagnerism as *avant garde*, see M. Killigrew, *Your Mirror to my Times. The Selected Autobiographies and Impressions of Ford Madox Ford* (New York: Holt, Rinehart and Winston, 1971), p.37; and *The Musical Times*, 1 April 1877, p.162; *Musical World*, September 1876, p.623; and J.F. Rowbotham, 'The Wagner Bubble', *Nineteenth Century* (October 1888), pp.501-512.

39   BR57/72/9, Rockstro to Georgina, n.d. For his life, see *ODNB* entry by J.A.F. Maitland (rev., D.J. Golby), and *Musical Herald*, 1 August 1895, p.246.

40   BR58/5, Georgina's diary entry for 20 November 1874.

41   BR58/6, Georgina's diary entry for 29 February 1876.

42   BR58/6, Georgina's diary entry for 29 April 1876; though she said, *MTM*, p.106, writing of *c*.1850, that 'above all, we learnt from our great poet' to trust that good should fall (*In Memoriam*, canto 54).

43   W.G. Collingwood, 'Ruskin's Isola', pp.79-82.

44   *Praeterita*, reprinted in E.T. Cook and A. Wedderburn, eds, *Works of John Ruskin* (Library Edition) (1905), vol.35, p.349.

45   C.W. Morley, *John Ruskin: Late Work 1870-1890. The Museum and Guild of St George: An Educational Experiment* (1984), pp.214-215, suggests the name echoed 'Georgina', and, p.19, that as a 'religious solution' the Guild was inspired by the Cowper-Temples and that Georgina was the focus of his initial plans. See also J.M. Lloyd, 'Raising Lilies: Ruskin and Women', *The Journal of British Studies* 34: 3 (July 1995), pp.325-350 [pp.339-340] on Ruskin's appeal to women of virtue.

46   Collingwood, 'Ruskin's Isola', p.80.

47   *MTM*, p.65.

48   Preface to 1871 edition of *Sesame and Lilies*, reprinted in E.T. Cook and A. Wedderburn, eds., *Works of John Ruskin* (Library Edition) (London: G. Allen, 1905), vol.18, p.47.

49   BR56/1, Burne-Jones to Georgina, The Grange, West Kensington, n.d. (after 1880).

50   Preface to 1871 edition of *Sesame and Lilies*, in Cook and Wedderburn, eds., *Works of John Ruskin* (1905), vol.18, p.46; BR58/13, diary entries for 19, 22, 27 September 1886.

51   BR58/2, Georgina's diary for 21 February 1862.

52   MacDonald, *George MacDonald and His Wife*, p.366.

53   G.E. Sadler, ed., *An Expression of Character. The Letters of George MacDonald* (Grand Rapids, Michigan: W.B. Eerdmans, 1994), p.138; *George MacDonald and his Wife*, pp.472, 544-545.

54   MacDonald, *George MacDonald and His Wife*, p.436: MacDonald paid back £100 in 1873.

55   NLS, MacDonald Papers, MS 9745, ff.24-25, December 1877.

56   NLS, Ashburton Papers, Acc.11388/96, letter from Georgina, 15 Great Stanhope Street to 'Beloved', n.d.; printed programme for lectures, 21 and 25 June 1884 in the Beinecke Rare Book and Manuscript Library, George MacDonald Collection (my thanks to Barbara Amell for this reference).

57   See *Two Hundred Extraordinarily Important Books, Autographs and Manuscripts* (London: Michelmore, 1923), p.75.

58 W.E. Fredeman, ed., *The Correspondence of Dante Gabriel Rossetti. The Chelsea years 1863–1872: prelude to crisis* vol.3 *1863–1867* (Woodbridge: D.S. Brewer, 2003), 24 August 1866, p.463.

59 *Glasgow Herald*, 18 October 1888 (reporting Rossetti's conversation with the London correspondent).

60 BR58/3, Georgina's diary entries for 9 April 1867 and 7 June 1867.

61 BR59/4, Georgina to Juliet, n.d.

62 *Glasgow Herald*, 18 October 1888. *MTM*, p.65, states the 'Blessed Damozel' was painted at Broadlands. See letter from Rossetti to W.T. Watts on a portrait of Georgina, in O. Doughty and J.R. Wahl, eds, *Letters of Dante Gabriel Rossetti*, vol.3 (Oxford: Oxford University Press, 1967), pp.1452-1453.

63 BR58/5, Georgina's diary entry for 10 September 1874.

64 W.M. Hardinge, 'A Reminiscence of Rossetti', *Universal Review* 6: 23 (March 1890), p.405.

65 Durham University Library, Special Collections, Add. MS 786, letter from D.G. Rossetti, 3 March 1878; H.R. Angeli, *D.G. Rossetti: His Friends and Enemies* (London: Hamish Hamilton, 1949), p.173.

66 Harrison, *Letters of Christina Rossetti*, vol.2, pp.92-93, pp.293-294.

67 BR58/19, entry in copy of G. MacDonald's *Diary of an Old Soul*, for 1886. She noted in this book, that when Rossetti died he was 'full of kind thoughts for us all'.

68 J. Douglas, *Theodore Watts-Dunton. Poet, Novelist, Critic* (London: Hodder and Stoughton, 1904), p.149, p.270; BR58/13, Georgina's diary, for visits by Watts-Dunton, 2 and 4 October 1886.

69 BR57/72/7, 'Margaret L' to [Aunt] Georgina, 18 Chester Street, S.W.

70 P.J. and A.E. Dobell [of Bruton Street, London], *Catalogue of Autographs, Letters, Manuscripts, Etc.,* (London: Dobell, 1927), p.53.

71 W.E. Fredeman, ed., *The Correspondence of Dante Gabriel Rossetti. The Last Decade. 1873–1882. vol.7. 1875–1877* (Cambridge: D.S. Brewer, 2008), pp.319-320; *Manchester Guardian*, 28 June 1906, p.12.

72 J. Rothenstein, *Summer's Lease. Autobiography 1901–1938* (London: Hamish Hamilton, 1965), p.11, p.30.

73 BR56/16, F.S. Ellis to Georgina, Sidmouth, 15 March 1899; BR57/68/17.

74 Georgina admired 'Dorothy' in his studio, see BR58/3, diary entry for 9 April 1867. She visited his studio with Clifford in 1873. See Bradley, *Letters of John Ruskin to Lord and Lady Mount Temple*, p.53 for Ruskin's role in the acquaintance.

75 V. Woolf, *Freshwater* (London: Hogarth Press, 1976), p.27, p.29; BR58/2, Georgina's diary entries for 22 and 26 December 1862.

76 Watts produced a painting and bronze sculpture of Clytie, an unfinished marble version was exhibited at the Royal Academy. BR56/5, Georgina's diary for 8 August 1874 records seeing Watts about Clytie and viewing his portraits. The bust cost £900, see BR55/14, Georgina to Evelyn Ashley, *c*.1888.

77 H. Macmillan, *The Life-work of George Frederick Watts, R.A.* (London: J.M. Dent, 1903), p.89. The work was reproduced in *Magazine of Art*, and *Good Words*, 43 December 1902, p.12. Apart from portraits exhibited by Clifford and Watts, there was M.D. Langée's, 'a good piece of draughtsmanship' according to *The Athenaeum*, 25 May 1872, p.661. See M.S. Watts, *George Frederic Watts* 3 vols (London: Macmillan, 1912), vol.2, p.189, on Georgina's type of a beauty.

78 See Hare, *Story of My Life*, vol.4, p.72 for the painting *The Maimed and the Halt* [called into the feast], in William's room in Broadlands, depicting the Cowper-Temples, Augustus, Lord Roden, Lady Palmerston and 'Clifford's favourite drummer', with 'our Saviour looking in at the window'. *Looking for the Prodigal's Return* (see p.165) adorned the Cadet's study of the Church Army headquarters.

79   B.R. Belloc, *In A Walled Garden* (London: Ward and Downey, 1895). References to Clifford as artist, and saintly individual, appear in memoirs, see E. Cadogan, *Before the Deluge. Memories and Reflections, 1880–1914* (London: J. Murray, 1961), p.106; W.E. Paget, *In My Tower. Memoirs* (London: Hutchinson, 1924), p.375.

80   BR53/11, Andrew Jukes to Hannah Smith, 24 December 1881 (typed copy). Thorne, *The Great Acceptance* has a frontispiece portrait from Edward Clifford's sketch. A friend who lived with him for many years, recalled, Cholmeley, *Edward Clifford* (1909 edition), that he liked to wrestle with an ex-soldier he met in a gymnasium, and took 'great, and I thought, curious, pleasure in the society of men like young guardsmen'.

81   BR57/43/1, Shields to Georgina, 23 October 1896. On Shields, see Gurney, *Letters of Emelia Russell Gurney*, pp.270-284. The Cowper-Temples presented Jukes with one drawing by Shields, 'Love Stealing ... Time', in 1882, see BR57/42/14, Jukes to Georgina, 31 December 1894.

82   BR56/17, Shields to Georgina, Merryfields, Melton, Surrey.

83   See letters from Furnivall in BR56/15, from 1866 onwards.

84   BR58/3, Georgina's diary entry for 14 March 1867.

85   BR55/9, A.M. Howitt Watts to Georgina, 2 April 1879.

86   M. Belloc Lowndes, *I, Too, Have Lived in Arcadia: A record of love and of childhood* (London: Macmillan, 1941), p.347; E.R. Charles, *Our Seven Homes. Autobiographical Reminiscences of Mrs. Rundle Charles* (London: J. Murray, 1896), pp.205-206; and letters in BR56/2, e.g., Charles to Georgina, 23 December 1892.

87   NLS, Letters to Thomas Carlyle, 1871-1873, MS 1770, f.249, 22 May 1873.

88   *MTM*, p.74.

89   Whitman presented Georgina with a copy of *Specimen Days and Collect* in 1886, she sent him a waistcoat, although the poet complained about the postal expense incurred, see E.H. Miller, ed., *The Collected Writings of Walt Whitman*, vol.4 *1886–1889* (New York: New York University Press, 1969), p.170. Her diary for 1887 (BR58/14) has a newspaper clipping on Whitman's birthday. Rafe Leycester received a copy of verse from the poet.

90   Madox Ford recalled seeing Wilde with a walking stick from Georgina, one of his few remaining treasured possessions, in Paris, see Killigrew, ed., *Your Mirror to My Times*.

91   F.M. Ford, *Henry James* (1913; New York, 1980), p.76; *Society Pictures Selected from Punch, Drawn by George du Maurier* (London: Bradbury, Agnew, 1890-1891). Georgina met Du Maurier, see BR59/26, Georgina to Juliet, n.d.

92   BR59/26, Georgina to Juliet, 'Sunday evening', n.d; C. Denney, 'Acts of worship at the Temple of Art: the Grosvenor Gallery and the second generation Pre-Raphaelites', ch.6 in M.F. Watson, *Collecting the Pre-Raphaelites: the Anglo-American enchantment* (Aldershot: Ashgate, 1997). Georgina had attended the Gallery's opening, see BR58/7, 30 April 1877.

93   *MTM*, p.65.

94   *MTM*, p.65.

95   *Morning Chronicle*, 21 January 1861.

96   Stanhope Street: This must have been the room Georgina called 'Greenery'.

97   Leicester-Warren, *Diaries*, vol.2, p.245.

98   Drew, *Acton, Gladstone and Others*, pp.104-105.

99   On Nesfield, who moved in Pre-Raphaelite circles, see M. Girouard, *The Victorian Country House*, p.67, pp.70-72.

100 BR 57/61/16, Robert Pearsall Smith to Georgina, Babbacombe, [March] 1890.

101 Clifford, *Broadlands as it was*, p.9; photograph in Russell, *Portraits of the Seventies*, p.274; Leicester-Warren, *Diaries*, vol.2, p.308. Interestingly, Père Hyacinthe's wife wore a black habit and large silver cross on a chain, see *Brooklyn Eagle*, 29 May 1887, p.12.

102 BR57/37/6, Emelia Gurney to Georgina, 3 Orme Square, '5 November'.

Chapter 13. After William, 1888–1901

1   BR57/37/11, Emelia Gurney to Georgina, 26 September [1890s].
2   V. Holland, *Son of Oscar Wilde* (1954; Harmondsworth: Penguin Books, 1957), p.48.
3   Warrender, *My First Sixty Years*, pp.10-11.
4   *The Times*, 9 January 1889, p.6. William's personal estate thus ran into many millions (one modern equivalent might be over £6,000, 000).
5   BR55/59, Jessie to Georgina, Hotel Continental, 3 Rue Castiglione, Paris, 'le 18th'. Informing Georgina that he was to be offered a peerage and asking permission to use the title 'Mount Temple', BR55/53, he explained that the name had not been assumed because the oldest portion of the Temple property was *permanently and for ever* alienated from the Temple estate' (30 November 1895).
6   Unidentified newspaper article in BR58/15, Georgina's 1888 diary; *Northern Echo*, 13 November 1888.
7   BR55/14.
8   BR55/53, Evelyn Ashley to Georgina, 20 December 1888.
9   *The Times*, 9 January 1889, p.6; 3 November 1894, p.7; 15 November 1894, p.14, 8 February 1895, p.14; BR58/59, n.d. William gave financial support when Spencer died.
10   BR56/3 (MacDonald to Georgina, Hillfield, Hampstead; see the letter 26 October 1888 in the Beinecke Rare Book and Manuscript Library, George MacDonald Collection).
11   BR55/58, Earl Cowper to Georgina, Torquay, 'Thursday', *c.* February 1894.
12   BR190/24, quoting his verse, 'To My Aging Friends.'
13   NLS, MacDonald Papers, MS 9745, 9 December [1888], f.66.
14   Russell, *Portraits of the Seventies*, p.282.
15   BR56/17, Lady Simon to Georgina, 12 October 1889.
16   Gurney, *Letters of Emelia Russell Gurney*.
17   See J.R.T.E. Gregory, 'Lady Mount Temple and Her Friendship with Constance Wilde', *The Oscholars* 3: 31 (November-December 2006); A.C. Amor, *Mrs Oscar Wilde. A Woman of Some Importance* (London: Sidgwick and Jackson, 1983), p.114. Jane Simon wrote that she was glad Georgina liked Constance, in October 1889. The earliest letter in the Broadlands Records from Constance is BR57/8, to Juliet, 19 June 1889.
18   BR56/3, Dysart to Georgina, Ham House, Petersham, '14 August' and '16 August'.
19   Burman, ed., *Logan Pearsall Smith. An Anthology*, p.44.
20   Burman, ed., *Logan Pearsall Smith. An Anthology*, p.44.
21   BR53/9, Jukes to Georgina, 5 March 1889.
22   BR59/15/50, Marguerite Tollemache to Georgina (typed copy), n.d.
23   See BR56/17, Frederic Shields to Georgina, Merton, Surrey.
24   BR59/23, Georgina to Juliet, 'Saturday', *c.*1876.
25   A description of Babbacombe is based on Holland, *Son of Oscar Wilde*, p.47. It was the first West Country house centrally heated, but the system was dangerous and erratic.
26   Augustus wanted to rent the Glen but Miss Keyse wanted to sell it, and he 'greatly pained' Georgina, see BR53/5, '23 November'. The property was acquired before they left Nutfield, see BR55/19. He lived there into the first decade of the new century.
27   BR56/18, Sara Carr Upton (writer, and friend of Olive Seward), Washington, 26 July 1890.
28   On Rossetti's painting, see newspaper clipping, BR58/16 (diary for 1890). When the Tate Gallery was established in 1897 it formed part of the collection. On Hannah's essay, BR56/19, Richard Westlake to Georgina, 18 February 1889; H.W. Smith, 'Lord Mount Temple'; and BR50/38, Richard Westlake to Georgina, 13 February 1889. On the memoir, see BR50/28, Hannah Smith to Georgina, 24 June 1890: 'How delightfully this "Quest" reads! The book is going to be *lovely*.' On typing, see BR53/5, Marguerite Tollemache to Georgina, 12 July 1889; and BR55/50, 'October 26', Maria Consuelo to Georgina.

29   The cipher on the cover of Marguerite Tollemache's posthumous work, *Sayings and Sketches* (Bury St Edmunds: Bury Post Co., 1898), echoed Georgina's in her *Memoirs*.

30   BR57/37/6, Emelia Gurney to Georgina, 3 Orme Square, '5 November'; BR57/43/3, Davies to Georgina, 8 November 1896.

31   BR55/40, Hulda Beamish to Georgina, 29 March 1892.

32   BR55/20, G.W.E. Russell to Georgina, 26 November 1890. The lady referred to is the spinster Elizabeth Bertie-Mathew, an old friend of Georgina.

33   BR55/20, G.W.E. Russell to Georgina, '1 February'. He recalled the Cowper-Temples in his published recollections. Indeed, Georgina would have been prepared for this as a fragment of a letter, '29 January' [1891], BR55/20 has Russell say 'you will be a chapter'.

34   BR56/2, Mabell Airlie to Georgina [9 June 1891]. See M. Ogilvy, *Thatched with Gold* (London: Hutchinson, 1962).

35   BR56/16, Farquhar to Georgina, 3 October 1890; BR56/7, MacDonald to Georgina, 31 July 1891; BR56/3, Darnley to Georgina [December 1890].

36   BR56/1, Mary Benson to Georgina, 5 August 1891.

37   BR59/52, Juliet to Georgina, New Year's Day [1891], Naples, concerning Canon Carter.

38   BR49/14, 28 June 1890 [typed note, by Georgina presumably]. Hulda Beamish wrote of her vision of Lord Mount Temple and his interest in her moral reform society called 'Edelweis', see BR55/40, Hulda Beamish to Georgina, 29 March 1892.

39   BR49/13, an undated typed note, corrected by hand by Georgina, 9 Cheyne Walk.

40   After Christian Science lectures by Charles Bowles (possibly the American Charles S. Bowles, former banker and friend of the Red Cross's founder) Consuelo wrote to Georgina on Bowles, 'he is *not*, most emphatically *not* to be trusted.' But William's spirit told her that Christian Science and faith healing were good: BR55/50, Maria Consuelo to Georgina, 'Friday night'. Consuelo, a friend of Antoinette Stirling, was into theosophy.

41   BR56/16, Adelheid Flemming to Georgina, Hamburg, 3 April 1890.

42   A.W.S. Rosenbach, *Catalogue of English Literature comprising early plays, ballads, poetry from Chaucer to Swinburne etc. etc.* (Philadelphia: Rosenbach, 1913), p.152.

43   BR56/6, Annie Munro to Georgina, 6 October 1890; *The Herald of Peace and International Arbitration*, 1 October 1890, p.143, reporting a meeting on 4 September.

44   BR57/39/8, Emelia Gurney to Georgina, 8 October 1890; BR57/2/5, Basil Wilberforce to Georgina, 18 December [1890] and subsequent letters in BR57/2.

45   BR53/9, Jukes to Georgina, 20 April 1892 (typed copy). Frank Sumner was a stockbroker.

46   BR55/6, Georgina Sumner to Georgina, 7 August 1891; BR59/52, Georgina Sumner to Georgina, Naples.

47   BR55/51, Maria Consuelo to Georgina, n.d., *c.*1890-1891.

48   BR55/20, G.W.E. Russell to Georgina, 29 January [1891].

49   BR59/17/16, Juliet to Georgina, n.d.

50   On Clement Harris, see BR59/18/17; BR59/52; BR59/58.

51   BR59/17/9, Juliet to Georgina, Naples, 'Tuesday', 'Please burn this at once', she added.

52   BR59/15/43, Juliet and Georgina Sumner, Naples, 'Tuesday' 7 April [1891].

53   BR59/17/17, Juliet to Georgina, Naples, n.d.; BR59/52, Juliet to Georgina, Naples, n.d.

54   On *Wormwood*, BR59/52, Juliet to Georgina, Naples, n.d.; on Christian Science, BR59/42, Juliet to Georgina, Naples, n.d.

55   BR55/42, Leila to Aunt Georgina, Palazzo Sto Teodoro, 6 March [1892]; BR59/20, 14 March [1892].

56   BR59/22, Juliet to Georgina, Naples, 22 February [1892].

57   BR56/14, Baroness Faverot de Kerbrech to Georgina, Rome, 'Monday'.

58   BR55/6, Georgina Sumner to Georgina, 26 February 1892.

59   BR59/37, Georgina to Juliet, 9 Cheyne Walk, Chelsea; BR59/4, 31 April.

60   BR59/21, Georgina Sumner to Georgina, 4 March 1892; BR59/21, Juliet to Georgina, n.d.

61 BR59/22, Juliet to Georgina, Naples, 23 February [1892].

62 BR59/15/13, Juliet to Georgina, Geneva, 7 May [1892]; BR59/18/28, Juliet to Georgina, 5 March, Naples, on Peters sending her *St James's Gazette* on *Lady Windermere's Fan*.

63 D. Flower and H. Maas, eds, *The Letters of Ernest Dowson* (Rutherford, New Jersey: Farleigh Dickinson University Press, 1968), p.254; BR57/44/3 and *Hearth and Home*, 4 May 1893. Georgina later sent a ring for Christmas. Juliet visited him in Paris.

64 *Brooklyn Eagle*, 31 December 1893, p.5; W.T. Peters, *Posies out of Rings and Other Conceits* (London: J. Lane, 1896), p.9. The judgement is B. Muddiman, 'The Tragedy of Theodore Peters', *Academy and Literature* 84: 2122 (4 January 1913), p.19.

65 See the letters from Juliet to Georgina, BR59/20, 14 March [1892], BR59/16/4 and BR59/16/7; BR59/17/28. Rachel Thouron of Philadelphia had two teenage sons.

66 BR59/54, Georgina to Juliet, 9 Cheyne Walk, Chelsea, [March 1892].

67 BR59/37, Georgina to Juliet, 9 Cheyne Walk, Chelsea [March 1892].

68 On the fall, BR57/48/8, Constance Wilde to Georgina, 17 October 1893; on Wilde's stay, P.H.W. Almy, 'New Views of Mr Oscar Wilde', *The Theatre*, March 1894, pp.119-127.

69 BR59/18/6, Juliet to Georgina, 21 April; BR59/17/29, Juliet to Georgina, 24 April [1893].

70 BR55/38, Georgina Sumner to Georgina, 29 April 1893; BR59/48, Hannah Smith to Juliet, 28 April 1893.

71 BR54/10, Juliet to Georgina, 27 April [1893].

72 BR59/61, Ethel M. Trower to Georgina, Naples, 20 April 1893.

73 BR59/26, n.d., Georgina to Juliet, 9 Cheyne Walk; BR59/41, Juliet to Georgina.

74 BR59/21, Juliet to Georgina, Paris, 63 Avenue Kléber, Paris, 18 January [1894].

75 BR59/21, Juliet to Georgina, 63 Avenue Kléber, Paris, 3 February [1894].

76 BR59/15/27, copy of letter from Georgina to Madame de Labarde, n.d.

77 See Vaughan to Georgina, BR56/21, 8 May 1894 and 6 January 1895; BR59/17/30, Juliet to Georgina. On De Vere, BR50/38, 13 August 1885; BR56/19, De Vere to Georgina, 19 June 1892. On Hannah, see Smith, *Religious Rebel*, pp.126-127 (16 March 1894).

78 L.P. Smith, *Unforgotten Years* (Boston: Little, Brown, 1939), p.49.

79 BR55/62, Georgina to Dufferin, 'Tuesday'; BR54/8, Dufferin to Juliet, 7 December 1894; A. Lyall, *The Life of the Marquis of Dufferin and Ava* (1905; London: Nelson, 1908), p.537. A Whig peer and protégé of Lady Palmerston, his 'chivalrous devotion' to Lady Jocelyn when a Lord in Waiting caused gossip, see Nicholson, *Helen's Tower*, p.93.

80 BR59/14, Georgina Sumner to Georgina, 12 February 1894.

81 BR59/26, Georgina to Eugene Deschamps, 9 Cheyne Walk, 22 March 1894.

82 *The Times*, 5 April 1894, p.10.

83 BR59/33, letters from Vaughan; BR55/20, G.W. E. Russell to Georgina, 5 April 1894.

84 BR59/36, Georgina to Juliet, 9 Cheyne Walk, 6 April; BR59/39, n.d., Georgina to Juliet.

85 BR54/13, Juliet to Georgina, n.d.; BR59/59, n.d.

86 BR59/5, Georgina to Juliet, 9 May 1894; BR59/39, n.d; BR59/56, Georgina to Juliet, 4 May.

87 BR59/39, Georgina to Juliet, n.d., including reference to Watts.

88 BR59/5, Georgina to Juliet, 24 April 1894; BR59/39, Georgina to Juliet, 9 Cheyne Walk [May 1894].

89 BR59/36, n.d.

90 BR59/57, Georgina to Juliet, 28 May 1894 on Cowpers; BR59/56, Georgina to Juliet, on Alys Smith's marriage.

91 BR56/1, Stopford Brooke to Georgina, 1 April and 17 July 1894; for Frank Sumner, BR59/5, 25 April 1894 and BR59/39, Juliet to Georgina, 9 Cheyne Walk, 'Friday'.

92 BR54/13, Mary Fawcett to Juliet, 'Fraiday evening'; on her dressing, BR57/65/11, Teresa to Georgina, 17 July [perhaps 1896].

93 BR54/13, Mary Fawcett to Juliet.

94   BR59/38, Georgina to Juliet, n.d.
95   BR59/41, Juliet to Georgina; BR54/13, Georgina to Juliet [Easter time].
96   BR59/57, Georgina to Juliet [January 1895].
97   BR59/36, Georgina to Juliet, Babbacombe, n.d.
98   BR60/4/11, Augustus to Evelyn Ashley, 17 March 1895; BR59/49, Mary Fawcett to Juliet. Augustus' suspicions were correct. Frank was charged with conspiring 'by false pretences to obtain and with obtaining large sums of money from persons who had been mortgagees of certain estates of which Sumner was tenant for life, with intent to defraud'. Juliet advanced money, see *The Times*, 26 March 1909, p.3. He left the Stock Exchange; see *The Times*, 12 July 1906, p.13. See BR59/17/34, Frank to Juliet, 20 December 1911.
99   BR59/15/52, Augustus to Juliet, Babbicombe Glen, Torquay, Festival of All Saints, Festival of All Saints, 1895.
100   See BR57/6/22, Hannah Smith, 20 November 1896; BR57/52/1, Myers to Georgina, 19 January 1897, would 'try and hear for her'; and John L. Davies, 8 November 1896, in BR57/43/3.
101   See letters from the Tollemaches, contained in BR59/32.
102   BR59/15/53, Augustus to Juliet, 2 Cheyne Walk, 14 September; BR59/61, 12 October [1896]; 24 December [1896].
103   Smith, *Religious Rebel*, p.132.
104   BR57/43/6, G.W.E. Russell to Georgina, Advent Sunday 1896.
105   BR57/44/12, Leila to Georgina, 14 January; BR57/44/15, Leila to Georgina, n.d.
106   Myers Papers, 3/74, Tuesday 26 January [1897].
107   *Pall Mall Gazette*, 16 March 1897; *The Times*, 24 December 1924, p.6.
108   BR55/20, G.W.E. Russell to Georgina, 'St Grouses' Day', 1897.
109   BR57/66/3, unidentified correspondent to Georgina, Abbey Lodge, Regent's Park, 29 May 1899; *Romsey Advertiser*, 18 October 1901. See BR59/70, Florence S. Craven to Juliet, on her mental state (late October 1901).
110   BR57/6/16, Hannah Smith to Georgina, Paris, 11 April 1895.
111   BR54/13, Georgina to Juliet, n.d.; BR55/19, Augustus to Juliet, Selsey, 17 September.
112   BR57/3/3, Basil Wilberforce to Georgina, Croydon, 13 September [1895].
113   BR59/56, Georgina to Juliet, Babbacombe, Easter Eve [envelope, 1 April 1899].
114   See *Ipswich Journal*, 13 December 1890.
115   Ruskin received cream from Georgina on his birthday, 'as I know little boys (& you will remember he is mine!) like nice things to eat better than sentimental cards and flowers wh I generally send him', BR54/13. Juliet as a newlywed visited Ruskin, see BR59/56.
116   *Manchester Guardian*, 25 January 1900.
117   BR56/15, Catherine Gladstone to Georgina, 24 May 1890.
118   BR56/7, G.W.E. Russell to Georgina, Hawarden; and G.W.E. Russell to Georgina, Easter Eve 1901. He sent her a sermon from Gladstone's requiem.
119   BR57/66/8 Edward Clifford to Georgina, 2 February 1901; BR55/49, Edward Clifford to Georgina, 20 August 1901.
120   *The Times*, 16 October 1901, p.7.
121   Smith, *Religious Rebel*, p.147, letter of Hannah Smith, 26 October 1901.
122   BR59/63, Frank Sumner to Juliet, 8 October 1901.
123   E. Clifford, *A Green Pasture. Letters to Comrades, with Stories and Essays, second series* (London: Church Army, 1901), p.426.
124   BR59/35, Emily Ford to Juliet, 3 October 1901; BR59/71, Cobbe to Juliet, 19 October 1901; BR59/69, Laura Hope to Juliet, 12 October 1901; BR59/34, Augustus Hare to Juliet, 22 October 1901.
125   BR59/33, Cyril Holland to Juliet, Radley College, Oxford.

126   See BR59/71, letters (by G.H. Sumner and another) on Frank; for deputations, *The Times*, 18 October 1901, p.4; 22 October 1901, p.7; 28 January 1902, p.10. *Romsey Advertiser*, 18 October 1901, dwelt on her perfect marriage and called her a 'ministering angel to be worshipped, loved and admired'.

127   See *The Observer*, 18 August 1889, p.7, on the grave, which she had ordered for William, a 'very chaste but unpretending memorial', the kerb of Sicilian marble and the Latin crosses 'of the purest marble'. Rose trees were originally planted in each corner.

128   BR60/1, Earl Cowper to Evelyn Ashley, 28 October 1901.

129   *The Times*, 30 April 1903, p.16; BR59/60, Herbert Ellis, 21 November 1911. It became a hotel and eventually was divided into flats.

130   BR59/60, letter to Juliet from Convent of Mercy, 83 Harding Street, Commercial Road, London, 24 August 1906.

131   BR59/62, Cyril Holland to Juliet, The Camp, Woolwich, 1 February 1907.

132   BR54/13, Teresa to Juliet, Marchesa Mastelloni, '24 January'.

Conclusion

1   G. MacDonald, *George MacDonald and His Wife*, pp.544-545. Tollemache, *Old and Odd Memories*, p.82 noted, as one similarity between him and Lord Palmerston, William's 'indifference' to pain.

2   Ogilvy, *Lady Palmerston and Her Times*, vol.2, p.125: Lady Palmerston to Fanny Jocelyn, December 1848 (*not* Lord Palmerston as Burd states, *Ruskin, Lady Mount Temple and the Spiritualists*, p.9).

3   Gurney, *Letters of Emelia Russell Gurney*, p.139 (to Julia Wedgwood, 1 December 1875), Russell, *Portraits of the Seventies*, p.280.

4   'Penelope', in 'Our Ladies' Column', *Bristol Mercury and Daily Post*, 30 January 1886.

5   *MTM*, p.46; Clifford, *Broadlands as it was*, p.9.

6   *MTM*, p.101.

7   M. Girouard, *The Return to Camelot. Chivalry and the English Gentleman* (New Haven and London: Yale University Press, 1981), p.199.

8   *MTM*, p.73; Clifford, *Broadlands as it was*, p.22; Bradley, *Letters of John Ruskin to Lord and Lady Mount Temple*, p.360.

9   *The Manchester Guardian*, 1901, reprinted in Russell, *Portraits of the Seventies*, p.280.

10   Bradley, *Letters of John Ruskin to Lord and Lady Mount Temple*, p.11.

11   Russell, *Portraits of the Seventies*, p.281.

12   Jackson, *The Life that is Life Indeed*, pp.25, 27, 45; and G.W.E. Russell, 'Great Ladies', *Manchester Guardian*, 16 March 1907.

13   Tollemache, *Old and Odd Memories*, p.78; Clifford, *A Green Pasture*, p.408.

14   Hodder, *Shaftesbury*, vol.3, p.191.

15   Tollemache, *Some Reminiscences*, p.8.

16   Jackson, *The Life that is Life Indeed*, p.43.

17   Smith, 'Lord Mount Temple', p.114.

18   *MTM*, p.48 recalls Shaftesbury's kindness and her worship of his character; yet he disapproved of her heretical influence on her husband.

19   BR56/24, Shaftesbury to William, St Giles House, 29 October 1884.

20   'The Old and the New Philanthropist', *The Spectator*, reprinted in *Littell's Living Age* 167: 2159 (7 November 1885), pp.321-384 (p.382).

21   *Liverpool Mercury*, 16 October 1888.

22   Jeune, *Memories of Fifty Years*, p.227. See also O.C. Niessen, *Aristocracy, Temperance and Social Reform. The Life of Lady Henry Somerset* (London: I.B.Tauris, 2008).

23   Russell, *Portraits of the Seventies*, p.280; Edward Clifford, in *MTM*, p.141.

24   'Social Queens under three Reigns', *Fortnightly Review* 107:640 (April 1920), p.590; Benson, *As We Were*, ch.9.

25   Russell, *Portraits of the Seventies*, p.283. On cruelty and pain, see Tollemache, *Some Reminiscences*, p.10; and BR56/7, Robert Reade to Georgina, 31 December 1899: 'your love & compassion has made it almost unbearable to you to see or think of other people suffering & thro' this problem of suffering your joy & hope has been often dimmed.'

26   See B. Caine, *Victorian Feminists* (Oxford: Oxford University Press, 1992), pp.4-7, on the problem of using the term 'feminist' in relation to individuals and groups in the 'women's movement'. The relationship to the women's movement and feminist historiography is explored in Reynolds, *Aristocratic Women*; see also Gerard, *Country House Life*, p.140. The Cowper-Temples associated with several leaders in women's movements, among these were Millicent Fawcett; her letter in the Broadlands Archives concerns a National Political Union, not feminist activity, see BR57/65/4, Mary Fawcett to Georgina, 20 March 1886.

27   *Sesame and Lilies*, in Cook and Wedderburn, eds., *Works of John Ruskin*, vol.18, p.127. Ruskin did not argue that women should be wholly in a private sphere, seeing a public role in ordering, comforting and beautifying, see p.136. 'Feminists' at the time appreciated the work, see K. Millett, 'The Debate over Women: Ruskin versus Mill', *Victorian Studies* 14 (1970), pp.63-82; and L.H. Peterson, 'The Feminist Origins of "Of Queens' Gardens"', in D. Birch and F. O'Gorman, eds, *Ruskin and Gender* (Houndsmill: Palgrave, 2002), pp.86-106. As noted above, Georgina was perhaps the lady alluded to in the 1872 edition, denying Ruskin knew about 'Lilies,' i.e. women.

28   NLS, MacDonald Papers, MS 9745, 7 March [1888], ff.47-48.

29   Gurney, *Letters of Emelia Russell Gurney*, p.128 (9 April 1876).

30   'To a Lady – now dead', E. Gore-Booth, *Poems of Eva Gore-Booth* (London: Longmans, Green, 1929), p.578.

31   Not that *homoerotic* friendships need be lesbian, see Marcus, *Between Women*. The Cowper-Temples knew of women in 'female marriage' such as Frances Cobbe and perhaps knew of Harriet Hosmer's relationship with Louisa Ashburton.

32   Fredeman, ed., *The Correspondence of Dante Gabriel Rossetti. The Last Decade. 1873–1882. vol.7. 1875-1877*, p.302. A.J.C. Hare, *Story of My Life*, vol.5, 29 October 1880, p.295.

33   Drew, *Acton, Gladstone and Others*, pp.104-105.

34   Juliet to Georgina, n.d., in BR59/52.

35   BR59/72, George Black to Juliet, 28 October 1901.

36   BR57/72/10, Teresa Caracciolo to Georgina, London, n.d.

37   For the epithet 'blesseds', see Whitall Smith Papers, B.L. Fisher Library, Wilmore, Kentucky, Emelia Gurney to Hannah Smith, 8 September [*c*.1886]. The verdict on Broadlands is Pauline Craven's, quoted in Jackson, *The Life that is Life Indeed*, p.26.

38   Taylor, *Laurence Oliphant*, p.258.

39   L. Strachey, *Eminent Victorians* (1918; London: Chatto and Windus, 1924), p.210, the 'mingling contradictions' of the English, 'their eccentricity and their conventionality ... matter of factness and their romance'. It reflects post-Victorian attitudes, thus the 'conspiracy of silence' surrounding Shaftesbury's premillenialism, see Battiscombe, *Shaftesbury*, pp.102-103; by 'oddities' I mean activities which might disturb contemporaries e.g., Gladstone's nocturnal work among prostitutes or Melbourne's taste for flagellation. With the Cowper-Temples, the oddities were credal. I also refer to 'contradictions' and 'perturbations' which Strachey identified in his eminent Victorians, see W.C. Lubenow, 'Lytton Strachey's Eminent Victorians: the rise and fall of the intellectual aristocracy', in M. Taylor and M. Wolff, eds, *The Victorians since 1901. Histories, Representations and Revisions* (Manchester: Manchester University Press, 2004), pp.17-28.

INDEX

References to illustrations appear in italics, peers are listed by surnames rather than titles.